# ESSENTIALS OF RETAILING

**Dale M. Lewison**
University of Akron

# ESSENTIALS OF RETAILING

MERRILL PUBLISHING COMPANY
A Bell & Howell Information Company
Columbus  Toronto  London  Melbourne

Cover Photo: © PhotoEdit, Mary Kate Denny

Title page photo: Larry Hamill
Interior photos: Part opening background, Jake Raj/The Image Bank; inset photos, Larry Hamill.
Page 120, *top right, bottom left, bottom right,* pp. 220, 235, 508, Tim Cairns—Cobalt
Productions/Merrill; page 120, *top left,* pp. 222, 522, Michael Pogony—Photographic
Communication/Merrill. All other photos, Larry Hamill.

Published by Merrill Publishing Company
A Bell & Howell Information Company
Columbus, Ohio 43216

This book was set in Italia.

Administrative Editor: Pamela B. Kusma
Developmental Editor: Jim Kilgore
Production Coordinator: Molly Kyle
Art Coordinator: James Hubbard
Cover Designer: Cathy Watterson
Text Designer: Cynthia Brunk

Library of Congress Catalog Card Number: 88-63983
International Standard Book Number: 0-675-20651-0
Printed in the United States of America
1 2 3 4 5 6 7 8 9—93 92 91 90 89

# PREFACE

The emergence of retailing as a dominant marketing institution has created great demand for trained retail decision makers and problem solvers at all managerial levels. The number and variety of employment opportunities in the retailing industry have grown enormously over the last several decades. This expansion of retail career opportunities has created a corresponding growth in the need for pragmatic college retailing courses that will help students secure entry-level management positions as well as provide the necessary background for subsequent advancement.

*Essentials of Retailing* is a comprehensive presentation of the basic concepts and practices of retailing. It introduces all the various theoretical and practical aspects of operating and managing a retailing business. The text presents the subject of retailing from both an academic and pragmatic viewpoint. A theoretical framework and an extensive assortment of practical applications and trade examples illustrate and clarify the subject.

To provide the student with both theory and a practical perspective, the text incorporates many special features and learning aids supported by a complete package of supplements. The text features and supplements together enable students to develop their decision-making and problem-solving talents.

## Special Features

- ☐ Comprehensive yet concise coverage of all major marketing/merchandising topics (consumer behavior, product assortments, pricing tactics, promotional strategies) and financial/operational subject matter (retail accounting, store location, personnel management, store layout and design).
- ☐ Timely and realistic examples and applications from the real world of retailing (for example, Sears, The Limited, Toys 'R' Us, May Department Stores, Safeway, Hypermarket USA, Avon, McDonald's, and a host of other known and hypothetical retail operations).
- ☐ A decision-making and problem-solving approach to contemporary retail situations (including planning, executing, and controlling store organization; personnel decisions; trade-area evaluation and site selection; product mixes; inventory systems; buying and handling procedures; pricing strategies; and advertising campaigns).

☐ Exhibits (graphs, tables, photos) from authoritative works, as well as original exhibits.
☐ Extensive documentation from academic sources (*Journal of Marketing, Journal of Retailing, Journal of Academy of Marketing Sciences*) and trade sources (*Stores, Progressive Grocer, Business Week, Forbes*).
☐ Author and subject indexes.

## Learning Aids

Student learning and involvement is promoted through the use of such learning aids as chapter outlines, chapter objectives, chapter summaries, student study guides, and student applications manuals.

☐ Chapter outlines tell students what topics will be discussed and how the subject matter is organized.
☐ Chapter objectives focus and direct the learning process by defining learning outcomes.
☐ Chapter summaries allow quick review of key concepts.
☐ A Student Study Guide at the end of each chapter contains three aids to enhance learning through repetition: (1) a list of key terms and concepts; (2) a set of review questions; and (3) a series of true or false questions that serve as a review exam.
☐ A Student Applications Manual concludes each chapter, offering opportunities for the student to become involved in retail decision making and problem solving through two participative activities: (1) projects for investigation and application and (2) cases to examine and resolve.

## Ancillaries and Supplements

Several ancillaries and supplements support the effectiveness of *Essentials of Retailing*:

☐ An *Instructor's Manual* contains detailed lecture outlines for each chapter, answers to review questions, answers to the review exams, suggestions for student projects, and solutions for cases.
☐ *Transparency Masters* of key illustrations and supplementary text material is offered.
☐ A *Test Bank* (written and computerized) contains both multiple choice and true/false questions.
☐ A casebook, *Cases in Retail Management* by Dale Lewison and Jon Hawes, contains 30 cases for expanding students' analytical and decision-making capabilities. *Cases in Retail Management* can be obtained from Merrill Publishing Company.

## Acknowledgments

I would like to thank these reviewers for their valuable suggestions: Eric Pratt, New Mexico State University; Paul Mackay, East Central College; Ray Tewell, American River College; Dennis Schneider, Fresno City College; Karen Zwissler, Milwaukee Area

Technical College; Dr. Beth Mariotz, Philadelphia College; Ethel Fishman, Fashion Institute of Technology; Leonard J. Konopa, Kent State University; Dr. Holly Bastow-Shoop, North Dakota State University; Joan Weiss, Bucks County Community College; Charlene Jaeb, Cleveland State University; Terry Paul, University of Houston—Clear Lake; Rebecca Kaminski Shidel, Bauder Fahion College; Dr. Jean Darian, Rider College; David Sullivan, Indian River Community College; Myrna Glenny, Fashion Institute of Design and Merchandising; Dennis Pappas, Columbus State Community College; John Konarski, Syracuse University; and Hub Worrell, Rose State College. I also thank Pam Kusma, my editor at Merrill Publishing, for her support, and the many students whose questions and comments help guide the teaching of retailing.

# CONTENTS

# 13
# Inventory Planning and Control  404

# PART FIVE
# RETAIL PRICES AND PROMOTIONS

# 17
## Visual Merchandising, Sales Incentives, and Publicity

## PART SIX
## RETAIL OPPORTUNITIES

# 18
## Careers in Retailing  546

# PART ONE
# Retail Environments

# 1

## Outline

## Objectives

- [ ] Appreciate the complexities of operating a retail business.
- [ ] Distinguish retailers and their activities from other marketing institutions.
- [ ] Discuss the retailer's problem of striking a balance between the customer's merchandising needs and the retailer's financial and operating needs.
- [ ] Explain what merchandising factors are involved with offering the right product . . . in the right quantities . . . in the right place . . . at the right time . . . at the right price . . . by the right appeal.

# Retailing: Its Nature and Dimensions

Successful retailing is a complex undertaking. In many respects, retailing requires greater skill for survival than most other business enterprises do. Successful retailers combine the creative aspects of art with the rigid requirements of science. Retailing activities such as advertising, personal selling, merchandising, and interior store design are as much an art as a science. Other activities such as inventory control, market research, and financial accounting demand the discipline of a science.

The real challenge of retailing is knowing how to *stay* in business. The failure rate among retailers is extremely high; approximately two out of every four retailers fail within the first year. To avoid such fate, the would-be J. C. Penney or Bill Walton needs formal training in the art and science of retailing.

## The Retailer

The many definitions of retailing all share the same basic thought: **Retailing** is the business activity of selling goods or services to the final consumer. A **retailer** is any business establishment that directs its marketing efforts toward the final consumer for the purpose of selling goods or services. The key words in this definition are "the final consumer." A business selling the same product to two different buyers may in one instance perform a retailing activity but in the other instance *not* perform a retailing activity. As an example, assume that you buy a chandelier to hang in your living room. In this case, the lighting company has made a retail sale. On the other hand, assume that a home builder walks into the *same* store, purchases the *same* chandelier, and installs it in a home he or she is building. In this case, the lighting company did *not* make a retail sale because the chandelier was not sold to the final consumer (user) of the product. Thus, a sale is a retail sale when the ultimate consumer purchases the product. What distinguishes a retail sale from other types of sales is the buyer's *reason* for buying. If the buyer purchases the product for personal use, the sale is considered a retail sale. If the buyer purchases the product for resale at a profit or to use in a business, the sale is *not* a retail sale. Instead, it is a business sale.

In the preceding example, is the lighting company a retailer? The answer depends on the amount of business the company does with *final* consumers. According to the U.S. Bureau of the Census in its *Census of Retailing*, a retailer is any business

Retailing is the art and science of selling goods and services to the final consumer.

establishment whose retail store can make both retail and business (nonretail) sales but is classified as a retailer when its retail sales exceed 50 percent of its total sales.

## The Retail Level

Retailers are referred to as "middlemen" or "intermediaries." Both references suggest that retailers occupy a position "in the middle of" or "between" two other levels. In fact, retailers do occupy a middle position. They purchase, receive, and store products from producers and wholesalers to provide consumers with convenient locations for buying products.

As shown in Figure 1–1, retailers are part of a chain, or channel, that enables the movement of products from producer markets to local customers. This chain of business is called a marketing channel. A **marketing channel** is a team of marketing institutions that directs a flow of goods or services from the producer to the final consumer. Generally, the team consists of a producer, one or more wholesalers, and many retailers.

Operating characteristics distinguishing retailers from other members of the channel team (producers and wholesalers) are as follows:

1. Retailers sell in smaller quantities (individual units) on a more frequent basis, whereas the less frequent typical order quantity sold by wholesalers and producers is much larger (cases and truck load lots).
2. Retailers' places of business are open to the general consuming public, but producers and wholesalers do not normally make over-the-counter sales to the general public (factory and wholesaler outlets are exceptions).
3. Retailers charge higher per-unit prices than those commonly associated with producers and wholesalers (loss leaders are a notable exception).
4. Retailers tend to use a one-price policy, whereas producers and wholesalers make more extensive use of variable prices based on some form of discounting structure.

4

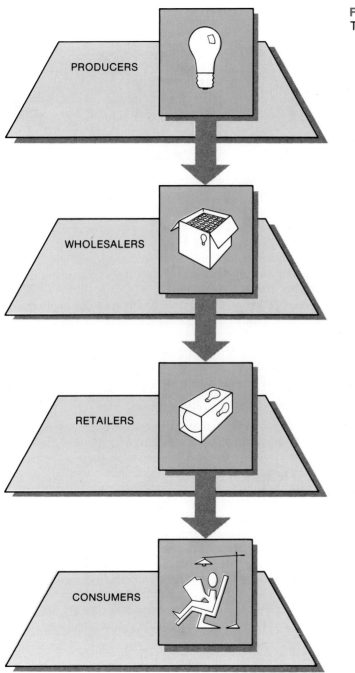

FIGURE 1–1
The marketing channel

Retailers place greater emphasis on internal atmospherics than do wholesalers.

5. Retailers rely on consumers to make the initial contact by visiting the store or placing mail or telephone orders, whereas producers and wholesalers employ outside sales representatives to make initial sales contacts (at-home retailing is a notable exception).
6. Retailers place greater emphasis on the external and internal atmospherics of their physical facilities and fixtures as major merchandising tools.

## THE PROBLEM OF RETAILING

The retailer's problem is how to maintain a proper balance between the ability of the firm's merchandising programs to satisfy consumer needs and the ability of the firm's management to achieve stated operational and financial objectives. This problem statement is in keeping with the broader idea of the marketing concept.

The **marketing concept** is the philosophy that the overall goal of every business organization is to satisfy consumer needs at a profit. A firm adopting the marketing concept, strives to sell what the customer wants. "It is the willingness to recognize and understand the consumer's needs and wants and a willingness to adjust any of the marketing mix elements, including product, to satisfy those needs and wants."[1] The marketing concept, stresses keying supply to demand rather than keying demand to supply. As Stanley Marcus, chairman emeritus, Nieman-Marcus Co, Dallas, describes it, "satisfaction means that customers come back."[2] The equally important objective in addition to customer satisfaction, of course, is profit. Without profit, the firm cannot stay in business to satisfy anyone's needs. Successful retailers are neither customer driven nor profit driven; rather, they seek a workable balance between these two important goals.

Satisfying the customer at a profit is not a simple task, however. By definition, the solution to the marketing concept—and to the problem of retailing—is developing the right merchandising blend.

## THE IMPORTANCE OF RETAILING

Retailing has a profound effect on our society and the people it comprises. The large number of establishments engaging in retail activities, the number of people those establishments employ, and the tremendous sales volume they generate indicate the importance of retailing within our society.

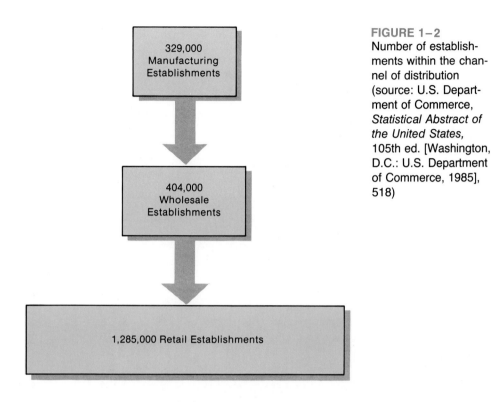

FIGURE 1–2
Number of establishments within the channel of distribution (source: U.S. Department of Commerce, *Statistical Abstract of the United States,* 105th ed. [Washington, D.C.: U.S. Department of Commerce, 1985], 518)

Retail establishments (individual operating units) outnumber the combined total of the other two major members of the distribution channel, manufacturers and wholesalers. As Figure 1–2 shows, 1.285 million retail establishments operate within the U.S. economy, compared with 329,000 manufacturers and 404,000 wholesalers. In relative terms, there are approximately 3.9 retail establishments for each manufacturing establishment and 3.1 retailers for every wholesaler.

Retailing's significance for the nation's economic welfare is reflected by the status of the retail industry as an employer of U.S. workers. Figure 1–3 portrays 1985 employment figures by industry. Retailing is the third largest employer, exceeded only by the manufacturing and service sectors. Retailers provide employment for approximately one of every six workers. If past trends continue, retail employment is expected to exceed twenty million persons by the end of the decade.

Total retail sales, as well as per capita retail sales, have netted steady gains over the last nineteen years (see Figure 1–4). Total retail sales in 1985 were about $1,374 billion, compared to total retail sales of $293 billion in 1967. Per capita retail sales increased from $1,484 to $5,755 during the same time period. These figures increase in significance when one considers that retail sales account for approximately 45 percent of personal income.

Retail store sales by type of business are shown in Figure 1–5. The dominance of our stomachs and our love of the automobile are readily apparent in our spending. Combined food and drink sales account for 30.1 percent of total retail sales, and automotive-related expenditures exceed 29 percent.

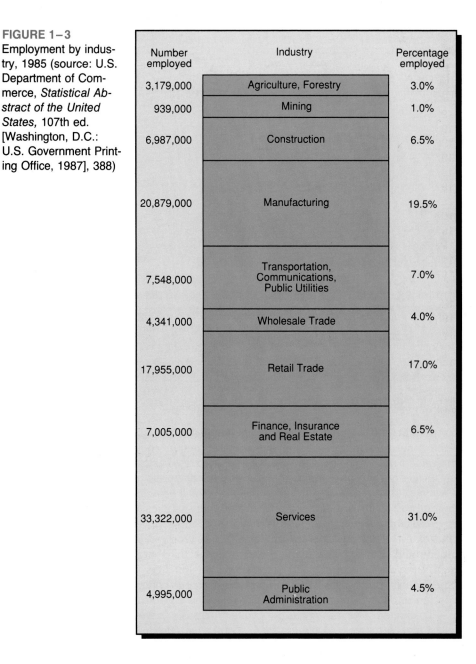

**FIGURE 1–3**
Employment by industry, 1985 (source: U.S. Department of Commerce, *Statistical Abstract of the United States,* 107th ed. [Washington, D.C.: U.S. Government Printing Office, 1987], 388)

| Number employed | Industry | Percentage employed |
|---|---|---|
| 3,179,000 | Agriculture, Forestry | 3.0% |
| 939,000 | Mining | 1.0% |
| 6,987,000 | Construction | 6.5% |
| 20,879,000 | Manufacturing | 19.5% |
| 7,548,000 | Transportation, Communications, Public Utilities | 7.0% |
| 4,341,000 | Wholesale Trade | 4.0% |
| 17,955,000 | Retail Trade | 17.0% |
| 7,005,000 | Finance, Insurance and Real Estate | 6.5% |
| 33,322,000 | Services | 31.0% |
| 4,995,000 | Public Administration | 4.5% |

**THE RIGHT MERCHANDISING BLEND**

The right **merchandising blend** matches the ingredients of the retailer's merchandising program with the decisions the consumer faces in making the right choice. Figure 1–6 illustrates this problem. The right blend includes the following six ingredients:

☐ Offering the right product
   ☐ In the right quantities
   ☐ In the right place

| Year | Total Retail Sales ($ Billions) | Annual Percentage Change (%) | Per Capita Retail Sales ($) |
|------|------|------|------|
| 1967 | 293.0 | — | 1,484 |
| 1968 | 324.4 | 10.7 | 1,627 |
| 1969 | 346.7 | 6.9 | 1,722 |
| 1970 | 368.4 | 6.3 | 1,806 |
| 1971 | 406.2 | 10.3 | 1,964 |
| 1972 | 449.1 | 10.6 | 2,146 |
| 1973 | 509.5 | 13.4 | 2,411 |
| 1974 | 541.0 | 6.2 | 2,536 |
| 1975 | 588.1 | 8.7 | 2,729 |
| 1976 | 677.4 | 11.8 | 3,022 |
| 1977 | 725.2 | 10.3 | 3,300 |
| 1978 | 806.9 | 11.3 | 3,633 |
| 1979 | 899.4 | 11.5 | 4,005 |
| 1980 | 960.8 | 6.8 | 4,228 |
| 1981 | 1,043.5 | 8.6 | 4,546 |
| 1982 | 1,074.6 | 3.0 | 4,636 |
| 1983 | 1,174.0 | 9.3 | 5,018 |
| 1984 | 1,293.1 | 10.1 | 5,468 |
| 1985 | 1,373.9 | 6.3 | 5,755 |

**FIGURE 1–4**
Total and per capita retail sales, 1967 to 1985 (in current dollars)

Source: U.S. Department of Commerce, *Statistical Abstract of the United States,* 107th ed. (Washington, D.C.: U.S. Government Printing Office, 1987), 756.

☐ At the right time
☐ At the right price
☐ By the right appeal

The right blend is thus the one that satisfies both customer and retailer. The right choice is the set of decisions that best satisfies the consumer's needs before, during, and after the purchase decision. Consumer shopping choice decisions include what, where, when, how much, and from whom should I buy and how much should I pay. The remainder of this chapter is devoted to a discussion of the retailer's problem of developing the right merchandise blend.

## The Right Product

A "**right**" product is a unique composite of three product elements—merchandising utilities, intrinsic qualities, and augmenting extras.

*Merchandising Utilities.* The merchandising utilities associated with each product provide the foundation for building the right product offering. A product's **merchandising utilities** are benefits the consumer seeks in buying, using, and possessing the product. Stated differently, a product's merchandising utilities are satisfactions that either are *perceived* (a woman feels her new suit makes her look more distin-

FIGURE 1–5
Estimated sales of all
retail stores, by kind of
business, as a percent-
age of total retail sales,
1985 (source: U.S. De-
partment of Commerce,
*Current Business Re-
ports, 1985 Retail
Trade,* [Washington,
D.C.: U.S. Government
Printing Office], 3)

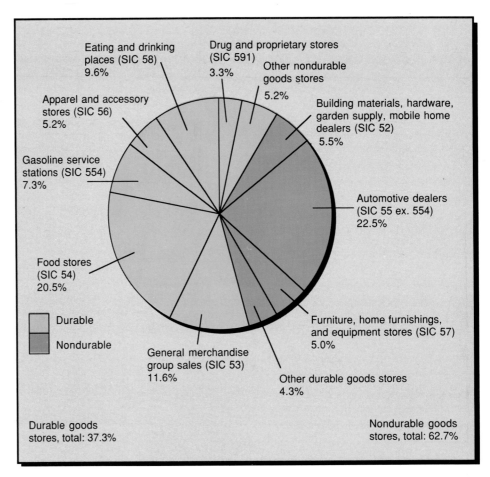

guished), *real* (other people think she looks more distinguished in her new suit),
*functional* (a woman's new suit is a comfortable fit), or *psychological* (she believes
the new suit makes her look thinner). We must then ask what the retailer is really
selling. Is it deodorant or security, cosmetics or hope, club membership or acceptance? From the merchandising utilities perspective, the retailer is selling the expected
benefits of security, hope, and acceptance.

*Intrinsic Qualities.* The tangible aspects of a product are also important in the consumer's evaluation of what makes a product right. **Intrinsic qualities** are the inherent
physical attributes such as product form, features, materials, and workmanship that
satisfy consumer needs. The intrinsic qualities of a product are important because
they determine whether the product is capable of doing what it is supposed to do,
looking the way it is supposed to look. Intrinsic qualities strongly influence the consumer's perception of a product's quality, suitability, and durability. Some aspects
that determine a product's intrinsic qualities are style, design, shape, weight, color,
and material.

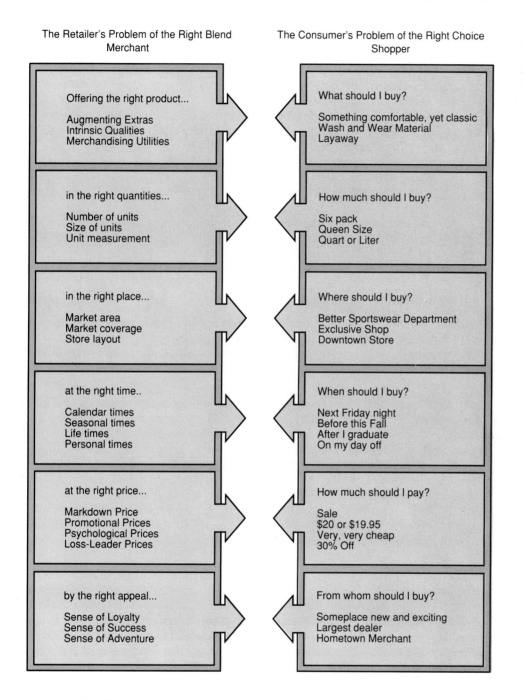

**FIGURE 1-6**
The problem of retailing—finding the right match

The Retailer's Problem of the Right Blend
Merchant

The Consumer's Problem of the Right Choice
Shopper

Offering the right product...

Augmenting Extras
Intrinsic Qualities
Merchandising Utilities

What should I buy?

Something comfortable, yet classic
Wash and Wear Material
Layaway

in the right quantities...

Number of units
Size of units
Unit measurement

How much should I buy?

Six pack
Queen Size
Quart or Liter

in the right place...

Market area
Market coverage
Store layout

Where should I buy?

Better Sportswear Department
Exclusive Shop
Downtown Store

at the right time..

Calendar times
Seasonal times
Life times
Personal times

When should I buy?

Next Friday night
Before this Fall
After I graduate
On my day off

at the right price...

Markdown Price
Promotional Prices
Psychological Prices
Loss-Leader Prices

How much should I pay?

Sale
$20 or $19.95
Very, very cheap
30% Off

by the right appeal...

Sense of Loyalty
Sense of Success
Sense of Adventure

From whom should I buy?

Someplace new and exciting
Largest dealer
Hometown Merchant

*Augmenting Extras.* **Augmenting extras** are auxiliary product dimensions that provide supplementary benefits to the customer. Warranties, delivery, installation, packaging, instructions, and alterations are some of the major extras that can greatly enhance the customer's satisfaction with the product. The type and extent of the benefits such extras provide depend on the customer's buying and usage behavior. For example, the additional benefit of convenience can be provided by offering home delivery and packages with handles. A customer's need for additional security and reassurance when making a purchase decision can be augmented by warranties, maintenance contracts, and liberal return policies.

Quicksilver's, a children's clothing store, understands both the need of the buyer (the parent) and the role of the user and influencer (the child). To keep both parties happy, each store features entertainment for children (e.g., computer games and tables with coloring/comic books) and conveniences for the parents (e.g., a comfort station featuring a rocking chair, bottle warmer, and diaper kit). These service extras help to (1) attract customers, (2) keep them in the store longer, and (3) build return trade.[3]

All three elements—merchandising utilities, intrinsic qualities, and augmenting extras—are needed to ensure buyer acceptance of a product. Therefore, each element is a necessary component of the "right product."

### The Right Quantity

The **right quantity** is the exact match between the consumer's buying and using needs and the retailer's buying and selling needs. Factors the retailer must consider in determining the right quantity are (1) the number of units, (2) the size of units, and (3) the unit measurements.

*Number of Units.* For some consumers, a single unit is the right quantity: one tube of toothpaste, one pack of cigarettes, one can of Coke, or one box of bandages. For other consumers, multiple-unit quantities are the right quantity: two tubes of toothpaste, a carton of cigarettes, a six-pack of Coke, or a home first-aid kit.

A single tube of toothpaste might be the right quantity if the retailer knows that consumers either are not concerned about price, are unmarried, have only one bathroom, or shop frequently. However, a retailer whose customers are price sensitive, married, have more than one bathroom, or shop infrequently should offer larger quantities at a price savings per unit. For example, the retailer could offer two tubes of toothpaste for $1.39 instead of one tube for $.75.

*Sizes of Units.* Products come in many sizes: small, medium, large, and extra large; short, regular, and long; king, queen, and regular; super, jumbo, and superjumbo; individual and family. Retailers know that the "size" labels they carry affect the kind of clientele they attract and the sales they make. A shrewd clothing retailer, for example, knows that the right size for Bill is "extra large," but the right size for Mary is one for the "full-figured woman." The right size, then, is the size that fits the customer's needs, both physically and psychologically. On the basis of its success with its "For You" catalog featuring upscaled apparel (e.g., Bill Blass and Carol Bird) for large women, Spiegel, Inc., the 122-year-old mail-order retail firm, is opening retail "For You" stores to appeal to this "right size" market.[4] With 33 to 47 percent of American women wearing plus sizes (size 14 and above), full-figure fashions are one of the hottest new markets. K mart's new line of Jordache clothing for bigger women is still another example of targeted retailing based on the right size dimension. And even though the sizes consumers desire are usually predictable, without proper inventory control, retailers can lose many sales by stocking the wrong sizes.

*Unit Measurement.* Quantities are expressed in various units of measurement: inches, feet, yards, and miles; centimeters, decimeters, meters, and kilometers; ounces, pounds, and English tons; grams, kilograms, and metric tons; pints, quarts, and gallons; liters and dekaliters. Retailers realize, at least for the present, that most Americans think the inch, pound, and quart are the right quantities and the centimeter, kilogram, and liter are the wrong quantities. Recent government efforts at metric education, however, could soon make metric measurements acceptable quantity expressions.

## The Right Place

A retailer trying to determine the **right place** should consider the following place factors in making the decision: (1) market area, (2) market coverage, and (3) store layout and design.

*Market Areas.* A **market** is a geographic area where buyers and sellers meet to exchange money for products and services. The "right" marketplace for retailers is the area containing enough people to allow retailers to satisfy consumer needs at a profit. The retailer's marketplace can range from one block to several hundred miles, and it can range from thousands of miles, even countries, to a corner in a small rural crossroads town. To find the "right" market area, the retailer must consider (1) **regional markets**, (2) **local markets**, (3) **trading areas**, and (4) **site**.

For the retailer, the *regional market* is the right part of the country. Chain retailers, often must evaluate different parts of the country to determine where to locate new stores.

At the *local market* level, retailers must determine the right town and the right part of town. For some retailers the right town is one with a minimum population of 100,000. Large general merchandise and variety discount stores such as K mart need a large population base to develop the sales volume they need to operate their stores profitably. On the other hand, smaller retailers are less concerned with a town's total population but rather with the size and demographic composition of a *segment* of the town's population. In some cases, a smaller town might be the preferred local market if it represents a better competitive environment. For example, Best Buy Co., a Minneapolis/St. Paul operator of consumer electronics superstores, is expanding into smaller cities, such as Sioux Falls, S.D., which are not as tempting to other superstore competitors.[5] The right part of town for some retailers is the central city; for others, the suburbs.

Finding the right *trading area* is synonymous with the problem of determining the right shopping area or the right shopping center. Some retailers (i.e., convenience food stores) go it alone, relying on their own abilities to draw customers. Other retailers (i.e., specialty stores) rely on the drawing power of a cluster of stores. They believe that by grouping together in shopping centers or associating with anchor stores (such as department stores), they can create the "right" place. For Bob Evans, a family restaurant chain in eleven eastern and midwestern states, the right trading area is incorporated into its "I-75 strategy." This plan calls for restaurants to be located on a major interstate highway or thoroughfare and within the immediate vicinity of a major shopping center or mall with a minimum of 50,000 residents living within a five-mile radius of the proposed location.[6]

The final market area concern is selecting the right *site*. For the freestanding retailer, the right site allows the store to intercept customers on their way to work or on their way home; is readily accessible to consumers from the standpoints of approaching, entering, and exiting; and is visible to passing consumer traffic. Within a shopping mall, the right site may be on the ground floor, at one end of the mall, or, next to a retailer who sells complementary goods.

*Market Coverage.* The right place may be every place, a few places, or a single place. *Market coverage* is the number of retail outlets operated by the retailer within a given market area. As part of the "right place" decision, retailers must decide whether they want **intensive market coverage, selective market coverage,** or **exclusive market coverage** (Figure 1–7).

With an *intensive market* strategy, the retailer selects and uses as many retail outlets as are justified to obtain "blanket" coverage of an entire market area. Generally, convenience-goods retailers use an intensive market strategy. (Convenience goods are products and services consumers want to purchase with a minimum of effort; examples are snack foods and soft drinks.) The ultimate intensive market coverage is to offer home delivery. Domino's pizza has become the second largest chain in the pizza industry by offering home delivery convenience under the theme "one call does it all." Its success has forced number-one Pizza Hut to adopt a similar strategy in many of its markets.[7]

When a retailer sells shopping goods, the logical strategy is to cover *selective markets*. (Shopping goods are products that consumers want to compare for style, price, or quality before making a purchase decision; examples are clothing, furniture, and appliances.) For these products a retailer should choose enough locations to ensure adequate coverage of selected target markets. The number of outlets the retailer establishes in the selective coverage strategy should equal the number of market segments served. Generally speaking, chain retailers such as apparel stores, department stores, hardware stores, discount-department stores, auto repair shops, and drugstores follow a selective market coverage strategy. In this case, the right place is the *select* place.

**FIGURE 1–7**
Market coverage strategies

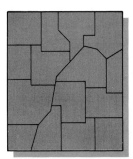

Intensive Coverage:
"Everyplace"

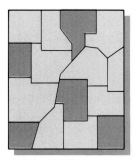

Selective Coverage:
"A Few Places"

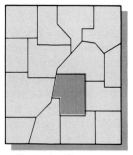

Exclusive Coverage:
"A Place"

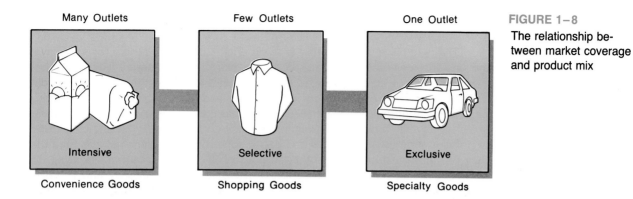

Many Outlets          Few Outlets          One Outlet

Intensive          Selective          Exclusive

Convenience Goods          Shopping Goods          Specialty Goods

FIGURE 1-8

The relationship between market coverage and product mix

In an *exclusive market* coverage strategy, the retailer elects to use one location to serve either an entire market area or some major segment of that market. An exclusive strategy is ideal for retailers who sell specialty goods. (Specialty goods are those that consumers are willing to put forth considerable effort to obtain.) Many specialty stores dealing in well-known, prestigious products such as Mercedes-Benz, Jaguar, and Steuben Glass use this form of market coverage. An ethnic restaurant in an ethnic neighborhood provides another example of an exclusive market strategy.

In sum, market coverage is related to the nature of the retailer's product mix. As shown in Figure 1-8, retailers attempt to achieve intensive coverage when their product mix is convenience oriented. At the other end of the continuum, using one outlet (exclusive coverage) is most appropriate when merchandising specialty goods. An intermediate strategy (selective coverage) is used when shopping goods predominate the product mix.

*Store Layout and Design.* Store layout and design are two essential elements to consider in creating the right shopping atmosphere for the chosen target market. In some department stores the right place in a store for a product, department, display, event, or activity may be the basement, the first floor, or the top floor. Customers often think of the basement as the "bargain basement," the first floor as the "main floor," and the top floor as the "exclusive floor." Chicago-based Marshall Field Department Stores' renovation of its downtown store involves an eight-story glass atrium with (1) the first floor being devoted to high-margin specialty shops, (2) the second floor containing the junior department, contemporary young men's clothing, and the World of Liz Claiborne, supported by a youth-oriented theme environment set to rock music, and (3) the third floor featuring coats, designer fashions, shoes, and a fur department in a more elegant, refined setting.[8] The right floor is the one that is most consistent with where customers think things should be and where the retailer can provide the level of service consumers expect.

Retail merchandisers and marketers generally agree that the best place to shelve merchandise is at **eye level**. Placing merchandise at eye level is especially important when the retailer wants to attract new or additional sales. For example, in a supermarket, Campbell often will place several popular varieties of its soups such as tomato, chicken noodle, and vegetable beef at *non—eye-level* positions. These soups are in great demand and customers will seek them out. New varieties and slower-selling varieties, however, often are positioned at eye level to generate additional sales.

The right place within a store for a product, a customer service, or a display is the one that best conforms to customer in-store traffic patterns. The right place therefore might be either in front, in back, along the sides, or in the center of the store. The in-store layout of most supermarkets, for example, is based on the "ring of perishables" principle. Food retailers know that consumers purchase their perishables (eggs, milk, butter, meat, vegetables, etc.) every week. By placing perishables in a ring around the store (sides and back), supermarket retailers have learned that they can draw customers into other sections of the store. Supermarkets using this technique greatly increase the chances that customers will pass by and purchase other products in the store's total merchandise offering. Supermarket managers believe that the result of their strategy is additional impulse sales—purchases the consumer did not plan to make.

Another strategy some retailers use is the attractors and interceptors strategy. Many department stores place merchandise such as men's suits, better women's wear, furniture, appliances, and other big-ticket items in the back of the store to act as attractors, drawing customers through the entire length of the store. In the process, customers are intercepted by departments carrying complementary product lines, such as shirts, scarves, jewelry, and other possible impulse products. Because the interceptor items normally produce a higher percentage of profit per unit for the store, this layout strategy contributes to the store's overall profit rate.

Retailers use visual presentations to draw attention to their product offerings. The right place must be found for them. Whether at end-of-aisle, at the checkout stand, or in a freestanding location near high-traffic areas, the right place is the "visible" place for these special displays. For example, supermarkets often place their weekly features of cakes, cookies, and pies at highly visible, end-of-the-aisle sites where frequently purchased items such as breads, buns, and rolls are located.

Within the display itself, "right is also right": the best position within a display is the right side. The right-side bias is based on the belief that most consumers view a display from right to left. So right is "right" because it is the first place consumers look.

## The Right Time

The "right" timing is critical in athletics, war, politics, business, and other human endeavors. In business, retailers realize that there are good times and bad times to sell certain merchandise and services. The **right time** to sell is when consumers are willing to buy. Because time affects consumers in different ways, retailers must develop retailing strategies that coincide with consumer buying times. As the proportion of two-income families approaches the 50 percent mark, time is becoming increasingly scarce for these families. Therefore, people are willing to buy time in order to make life a little simpler. The importance of time and convenience to the consumer is not an issue that can be ignored by retailers in developing their merchandising programs.[9] Some particular times that retailers consider in developing time strategies are (1) calendar times, (2) seasonal times, (3) life times, and (4) personal times.

The right place for special displays is where they are most visible.

*Calendar Times.* In the category of calendar times, consider times of the day, times of the week, times of the month, and times of the year. Because consumers' behavior is largely geared to these times, any one of these times can be an opportune time for the retailer.

Whether morning, noon, afternoon, or evening, many retailers have businesses with daily peak periods. Restaurants, for example, have definite "right times" of the day: breakfast, lunch, and dinner times. For most restaurants these are the only times for sales and profits. "Bennigan's, a unit of Pillsbury Co., puts stopwatches on its restaurants' tables and promises to serve in 15 minutes or [the meal is] free. Pizza Hut offers a second pizza free if the first takes more than five minutes."[10] In essence, the lunch hour has become the third rush hour. Evenings are "most times" for motion picture theaters. By reducing prices for the afternoon matinee, however, the theater manager can make afternoons a "sometimes" for some moviegoers. Morning and afternoon rush hours are the right times for some retailers who want to intercept consumers going to and from work.

Certain days of the week are better times to sell some products than other days. Sunday is the right time of the week for some consumers because they have free time to shop. On the other hand, Sunday might not be the right time for other consumers, because for them it is "God's time" or in their area it is an illegal time (where Sunday closing laws are in effect). Blue Monday is often a poor time for a retailer because the consumer's mood usually is bad at the start of a new work week.

Payday and bill-paying day are two examples of times of the month of which every retailer should be aware. Paydays are usually once, twice, or four times a month, and they could very well be the most important times for the retailer regardless of when they occur. With money in their pockets, consumers are most susceptible to advertising, new merchandise, and old merchandise clearance sales. Many homeowners have to make house payments, for example, at the beginning of the month, so unless they are paid monthly, they are likely to have hard times until the next payday.

Holiday seasons often represent the "best times" of the year for retailers. Christmas, Easter, Thanksgiving, Memorial Day, Labor Day, and New Year's Eve are "special times" for consumers and provide special opportunities to retailers. For many retailers, back-to-school time is second only to Christmas in its potential to generate sales.

*Seasonal Times.* Consumers' buying patterns change with the seasons of the year. These are not only spring, summer, fall, and winter but perhaps football, basketball, and baseball seasons; or planting, growing, and harvesting seasons; or even opera, social, and theater seasons. Depending upon geographic and cultural regions of the country, most retailers know which times are best for selling seasonal goods. Retailers also know that the best part of the season is the beginning of the season, when they can sell goods at full markup.

*Life Times.* In everyone's life there are special times—births, weddings, graduations, and many more—that are rare times for the retailer to make a special effort to sell merchandise. They are also the right time for the retailer because consumers are in one of their most susceptible buying moods. At these times the retailer can generate additional sales by "trading up" the consumer, that is, inducing the customer to buy a higher-quality, higher-price, or markup product or to add features and extras to the selection.

*Personal Times.* Every consumer experiences working times, leisure times, and maintenance times. Every retailer should be sensitive to the merchandising times of the weekday, the weekend, the workday, and the day off. A building materials firm that caters to the home handyman, for example, makes most sales on Friday and Saturday.

For the retailer, all of the times just discussed can be either good or bad times, fast or slow times, profitable or unprofitable times. In summary, a right time is any time that helps the retailer either avoid losing sales or create new sales that ordinarily would not have been made.

## The Right Price

The **right price** is the amount consumers are willing to pay and retailers are willing to accept in exchange for merchandise and services. Consumers experience various

Back to school is the right time of year for many retailers. (Courtesy of Gold Circle Stores)

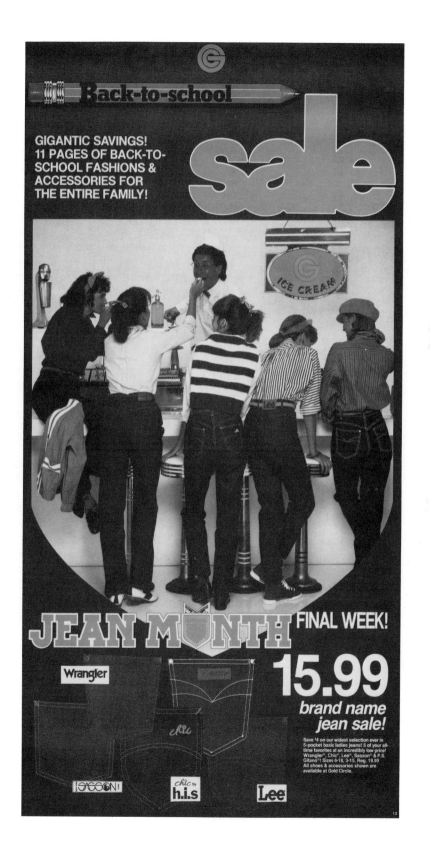

forms of prices in the marketplace. They encounter odd prices, even prices, prices with coupons, sticker prices, bid prices, bargain prices, status prices, sales prices, manufacturers' suggested list prices, and retailers' prices, among many other price forms. Like consumers, retailers also face different forms of prices. There are markup prices, markdown prices, price lines, base prices, unit prices, package prices, promotional prices, regular prices, loss-leader prices, illegal prices, and prices that include accessories. These are only a few of the price forms that retailers deal with every day.

In developing a pricing strategy, the retailer must price merchandise low enough to generate sales but high enough to cover costs and make a fair profit. At the same time the retailer must consider pricing products in a manner consistent with consumers' expectations. F.A.O. Schwartz, a purveyor of pricey playthings, operates under the assumption that there is a large market for fashion toys. Buyers of expensive toys are not motivated as much by price as by the product.[11] Unique products, special services, and exciting store atmospherics equal successful prestige pricing.

*Customer Expectations.* The right price is one that is satisfactory to the customer not only before the sale but after the sale as well. A consumer who is willing to pay a "premium" price for a product generally expects premium performance and service. If the product does not display this expected level of performance, the customer might not ever buy products from the same retailer again. Even worse, the dissatisfied customer is very likely to communicate that bad experience to friends and others and discourage their patronage at the store.

*Competitive Conditions.* Finally, the right price must be competitive—if not with all competitors, then at least with those in the same trading area or with those who have similar operations. In a large city, for example, one record store might price albums 50 cents higher than another record store across town. Although competitors in the sense that both stores sell records, these two retailers are not in *direct* competition because they are in *different trading areas* within the same city. Additionally, two stores that sell the same basic product such as men's clothing and are located three doors apart in a shopping mall may not be in *direct* competition. One might be a "high fashion" men's store, whereas the other is a men's "value clothing" store. Thus, competitive pricing means setting a price that is about the same as that found in similar stores catering to the same targeted consumers within the same trading area.

### The Right Appeal

The **right appeal** represents the **right message** to the **right audience** through the **right media**. Though the product, place, and price are right, the retailer will not be successful unless it can communicate its offering effectively to its target market. The retailer must inform and persuade consumers that its product mix precisely meets their particular needs. In making the right appeals, the retailer's problem is how to identify the target audience, create the appropriate message, and select the best medium of communication.

Product appeals emphasize the "rightness" of a retailer's product

*The Right Message.* The right message is the right thing to say (the right message *content*) presented in the right *manner*. The right message content emphasizes what consumers are most concerned about and explains how the retailer's offerings can satisfy those concerns. For example, homemakers deciding among supermarkets may be more concerned with what they buy and how much they pay (e.g., selection and value) than from whom, where, and when they buy. In this case the best message emphasizes the *what* and *how much*. When deciding among furriers, however, the same individuals may be more concerned with what and from whom they buy (e.g., quality and status) and less concerned with where and when they buy and how much they pay. In this situation the retailer should emphasize the *what* and *from whom*.

The retailer must determine which purchase factors are most important to the consumer's buying decision and emphasize those appeals in the message. After gathering consumer information, a retailer may decide to make a **product appeal,** emphasizing the rightness of its products for consumers; a **patronage appeal,** emphasizing the rightness of the store, location, and hours; or a **price appeal,** emphasizing the economy, value, or prestige nature of the retail price. Or, the retailer may make a combined appeal if it thinks several "right choice" elements are important to the consumer.

In structuring the message content, the retailer must also choose between direct action and indirect action. **Direct-action messages** urge the consumer to come to the store now either to take advantage of a sale or to redeem a coupon. **Indirect-action messages,** on the other hand, have long-run goals. They attempt to change consumers' attitudes toward the retailer by cultivating its image as the "right" place for the consumer to buy (e.g., "When you think of fine furniture, think of us"). Both types of messages have advantages and disadvantages. Direct-action messages usually result in immediate sales but normally do not encourage regular patronage. Indirect-action messages encourage regular patronage, but the retailer must invest considerable time and money to develop it.

The retailer must not only present the right message content but also present it in the right manner. Method presentation involves choosing either a logical or an emotional approach to the problem of getting the retailer's message across. Using the **logical approach,** a retailer makes a factual presentation about its offering and then shows consumers why buying from that source is the "right" choice. For example, a retailer might say, "Compare prices, and you'll see why you should shop with us." A retailer that uses an **emotional approach** speaks not to what consumers think, but to what they feel (pride, fear, etc.). Retailers that create emotional appeals in their messages try to incite the following among consumers:

- ☐ Sense of loyalty ("Shop your local hometown merchants")
- ☐ Sense of security ("We'll sell only brand-name merchandise")
- ☐ Sense of fair play ("Please, before you buy, check our. . .")
- ☐ Sense of tradition and stability ("Serving you from the same location for 25 years")
- ☐ Sense of adventure ("A new shopping experience. . .")

A logical price appeal supported by an emotional message that appeals to the customer's sense of tradition and stability

# tradition
quality and value for 30 years

### Famous maker sport shirts
### comparable in quality at $25

A stock-up price on long sleeve, patterned sport shirts from two prestigious names. Polyester/cotton, sizes S-M-L-XL. First quality.

marshalls price
**9⁹⁹**

### Famous maker twill pants
### comparable in quality at $40

From a leading sportswear name, belted slacks for dress or casual. Assorted colors, in polyester/cotton twill. Sizes 32 to 40. First quality.

marshalls price
**16⁹⁹**

### Famous maker dress shirts
### comparable in quality at $20

Terrific value on these long sleeve, machine wash-and-dry polyester/cotton dress shirts. Assorted patterns. Sizes 14½ to 17. First quality.

marshalls price
**9⁹⁹**

### Famous maker dress pants
### comparable in quality at $35

A collection of famous maker gabardines in polyester/wool. Plain or pleated fronts. Assorted colors. Sizes 30 to 40. First quality.

marshalls price
**16⁹⁹**

**Designer and famous maker ties.** First quality. Pre-ticketed by the famous makers at 8.50 to $20 . . . . . . . **marshalls price 4.99 to 8.99**

☐ Sense of success (". . .the largest dealer in the state")
☐ Sense of belonging ("Shop with us, where only the discriminating shop"), among other target emotions

*The Right Audience.* The right message must be directed to the right audience. In seeking to determine the right audience, the retailer can make one of two choices—either pursue the mass-market audience or pursue one or more target-market audiences. In reaching the mass-market audience, a retailer appeals to all of the consumers within a market area using a broad appeal. By using a broad appeal the retailer hopes to attract a few customers from all segments of the market. The message must be general enough to appeal to a wide range of consumers and their needs but specific enough to stimulate consumers to action.

In a *target-market audience* strategy, the retailer appeals to a select group of customers within a market area. The process of dividing a market into smaller sub-sets is called *market segmentation,* and the market segment to which the retailer directs its appeal is the *target market.* Any market can be segmented along the lines of various characteristics. The three most common of these are demographic char-acteristics, patronage motives, and psychographic profiles.

*Demographic characteristics* include age, sex, income, race, occupation, family structure, and social class. *Patronage motives* describe consumers' shopping and buying habits. How much they buy, when, where, what, and why they buy are all patronage market dimensions. *Psychographic profiles* are composite "pictures" of different consumer life-styles—living patterns that are the result of a consumer's activities, interests, and opinions. Most experts agree the marketplace is becoming more and more fragmented. As described by one author, the number of market segments is almost limitless:

> We're all familiar with the YUPPIES—the 25- to 39-year old singles—but we also have the BUPPIES—black urban professionals. And the VUMMIES—very upwardly mobile mothers, 18 to 34; plus the YUMMIES, the young urban mothers, 18 to 34.
>
> What about the Star Network—the 6- to 12-year-old kid with a mom, grand-mother, aunt, and others around the star? Or the FLYERS—fun-loving youth, 18 to 24?[12]

Regardless of which target market the retailer selects, the right message appeals to the needs and desires of its chosen market segment. However, the best appeal cannot be effective without the right media.

*The Right Media.* The means by which a retailer communicates its product offering to consumers is just as important as the content. Typically, a retailer has several choices in reaching an audience: newspapers, television, radio, magazines, tele-phone, direct mail, window displays, outdoor signs, in-store demonstrations, and personal sales representatives. The right medium for the retailer effectively and eco-nomically reaches the largest portion of the mass or target audience.

## THE RETAILING PLAN

The **retailing plan** is an organized framework of activities directed at achieving a profitable retail operation. It addresses the operational questions of why, what, when, where, and how specific retail business activities are to be accomplished. The com-ponents of the retailing plan are illustrated in Figure 1–9.

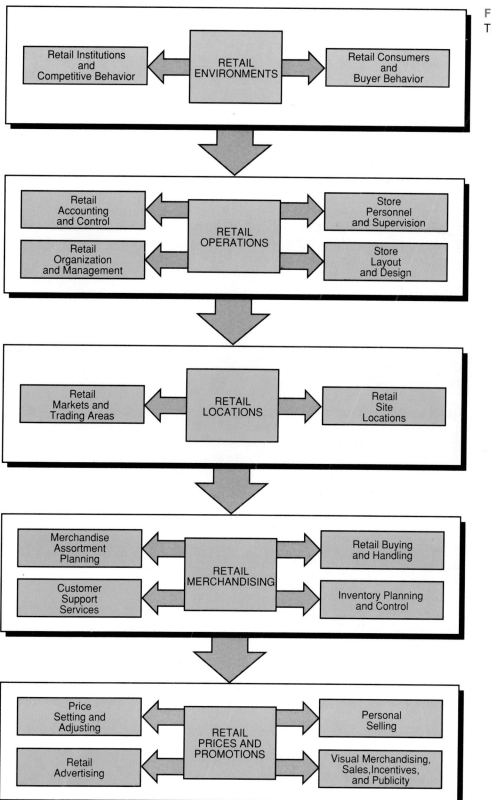

FIGURE 1–9
The retailing plan

**RETAIL ENVIRONMENTS**

Retail Institutions and Competitive Behavior ⟷ Retail Consumers and Buyer Behavior

**RETAIL OPERATIONS**

Retail Accounting and Control ⟷ Store Personnel and Supervision

Retail Organization and Management ⟷ Store Layout and Design

**RETAIL LOCATIONS**

Retail Markets and Trading Areas ⟷ Retail Site Locations

**RETAIL MERCHANDISING**

Merchandise Assortment Planning ⟷ Retail Buying and Handling

Customer Support Services ⟷ Inventory Planning and Control

**RETAIL PRICES AND PROMOTIONS**

Price Setting and Adjusting ⟷ Personal Selling

Retail Advertising ⟷ Visual Merchandising, Sales, Incentives, and Publicity

25

The process of retail planning is a cyclical activity involving five stages: (1) analyzing, defining, and describing the retailing environments, (2) planning, executing, and controlling financial, organizational, human, and physical resources, (3) identifying, evaluating, and selecting retail markets, trading areas, and sites, (4) developing, securing, and managing product/service offerings, and (5) creating and implementing promotion strategies.

In the remainder of Part One, Retail Environments, the uncontrollable environments of retailing are examined with respect to the competitive strategies of retail institutions (Chapter 2) and the structure of retail consumer markets and buying behavior of consumers (Chapter 3).

Part Two—Retail Operations—focuses on managing the retailer's resources. Effective and efficient use of the store's financial (Chapter 4), organizational (Chapter 5), human (Chapter 6), and physical (Chapter 7) resources are highlighted in this topical coverage on resource assessment.

Identification, evaluation, and selection of retail markets are covered in Part Three—Retail Locations. Chapter 8 is concerned with assessing the potential of local and regional markets and trading areas. Appraising retail site locations is the focal point of the discussion presented in Chapter 9.

Part Four—Retail Merchandising—discusses the management of the product/service mix. Planning merchandise assortments (Chapter 10) and customer services (Chapter 11) is supported by an examination and discussion of merchandise buying and procuring (Chapter 12) and inventory planning and control (Chapter 13).

Value and communications concerns are the topics examined in Part Five—Retail Prices and Promotions. Chapter 14 addresses the issues of setting and adjusting retail prices. The center of discussion in Chapter 15 is retail advertising. Chapter 16 explores the personal selling process, and Chapter 17 reviews concerns with the effective use of visual merchandising, sales incentives and publicity.

Part Six—Chapter 18—deals with the issues of finding and securing a career in retailing.

## SUMMARY

The successful operation of a retail store is a very complex and difficult undertaking—a truth vividly illustrated by the number of retail enterprises that fail each year.

A retailer is a business organization within a marketing channel of distribution that makes most of its sales to final consumers. Retailers differ from other marketing institutions in that they (1) sell in small quantities on a more frequent basis, (2) open their place of business to the general public, (3) charge higher per-unit prices, (4) use a one-price policy, (5) rely on consumers to make the initial contact, and (6) use store atmospherics as a major merchandising tool.

The basic task of retailing is to balance the product and service needs of the consuming public with the operational and financial needs of the retail organization. Elements of the retailer's right merchandising blend are offering the right products in the right quantities, in the right place, at the right time, at the right price, by the right appeal.

The right products decision involves an understanding of the three product dimensions of merchandising utilities, intrinsic qualities, and augmenting extras. The number and size of units together with the type of unit measurement used are all important considerations for the retailer when determining the right quantity. An assessment of market areas and coverage are basic elements in the right place decision. Store layout and design are additional right place problems that must be solved. Calendar, season, life, and personal times are all part of the challenge of finding the right time. The right price is one that meets both customer expectations and competitive realities. Finally, making the right appeal requires the retailer to develop the right message for the right audience using the right media.

The operational questions of why, what, when, where, and how specific retail business activities are to be accomplished is addressed by the retailing plan.

## STUDENT STUDY GUIDE

### KEY TERMS AND CONCEPTS

| | |
|---|---|
| augmenting extras | product appeal |
| direct-action message | regional market |
| emotional approach | retailer |
| exclusive market coverage | retailing |
| eye-level merchandising | retailing plan |
| indirect-action message | right appeal |
| intensive market coverage | right audience |
| intrinsic qualities | right media |
| local market | right message |
| logical approach | right place |
| market | right price |
| marketing channel | right product |
| marketing concept | right quantity |
| merchandising blend | right time |
| merchandising utilities | selective market coverage |
| patronage appeal | site |
| price appeal | trading area |

### REVIEW QUESTIONS

1. What is retailing? How do retailers differ from other members of the marketing channel of distribution (wholesalers and producers)?
2. Why is retailing important? Explain the role of retailing in our national economy.
3. Define the marketing concept. How does it relate to the problem of retailing?
4. Describe the match between the retailers' decisions of the right merchandising blend and the consumers' decision of the right shopping choices.
5. Profile the three elements that comprise the retailer's right product decision.
6. What quantity is the right quantity? Provide an original example for each of the factors considered by the retailer in determining the right quantity.

7. Outline the geographic dimensions of regional and local markets, trading areas, and site locations.
8. Compare and contrast intensive, selective, and exclusive market coverage.
9. Identify the four types of time categories. Provide two examples of merchandising strategies for each category that retailers use to meet the needs associated with different consumer buying times.
10. When is a retail price right for both the consumer and the retailer?
11. The right appeal equals the right message plus the right audience plus the right media. Briefly characterize each element of this equation.
12. Describe the five stages of the retailing plan.

---

## REVIEW EXAM

True or False

_____ 1. If a buyer purchases a product from a retailer for purposes of reselling the product at a profit or to use it in a business, the sale is still considered to be a retail sale.
_____ 2. Retailers differ from wholesalers in that retailers tend to use variable prices, whereas wholesalers tend to use a one-price pricing policy based on some form of discounting structure.
_____ 3. The marketing concept stresses matching supply to demand rather than matching demand to supply.
_____ 4. A product's merchandising utilities are benefits the customer seeks in buying, using, and possessing the product.
_____ 5. Exclusive market coverage is most appropriate when merchandising specialty goods.
_____ 6. Customer satisfaction is the most important factor in determining the right price.
_____ 7. The retailer's problem in making the right appeal consists of how to identify the target audience, how to create the appropriate message, and how to select the best medium of communication.

# STUDENT APPLICATIONS MANUAL

## PROJECTS: INVESTIGATIONS AND APPLICATIONS

1. "McDonald's Sears Introduce Clothes for Small Fries." In 1987, Sears unveiled its McKids sportswear line of popular-priced clothes. The line incorporates subtle and overt use of the fast-food company's logo and special line identifiers and bears McKids labels and hang tags. In addition to sportswear, nightwear, shoes, and accessory lines are also included in the total McKids product mix. Is this a case of *offering the right product in the right place*? Investigate this issue by (1) surveying children and parents for their perception of the idea, (2) reviewing trade literature to discover the opinions of the industry, and (3) visiting your local Sears store to ascertain how well Sears is merchandising the product line. Explain and support your answer to the above question.
2. Benetton Sportswear Shops have expanded rapidly throughout the world and the United States. The number of U.S. stores jumped from 250 in 1983 to 758 in 1988, an impressive growth rate for the Italian manufacturer of colorful knitwear and cotton apparel. One of the "right place" strategies employed by this prestigious specialty retailer is to cluster several retail shops in one upscaled trading area on the theory that the more there are, the larger the total market they create. Do you agree with this strategy? Identify and explain some of the pros and cons that might be associated with such a strategy.

**3.** Burger King, the nation's No. 3 burger chain, has introduced a new mini-burger product called Burger Bundles. The product line consists of 1-oz. burgers in $1.19 three-pack and $2.38 six-pack cartons, with or without cheese, and a pickle. Is this the *right product*, in the *right quantity* (size and number of units), at the *right price?* Justify your answer.

## CASE 1–1
### The Case Assignment—Creating the Right Match*

It was time to face reality; it was do or die time for Ralph Reed, Lindsay Barta, and Bob Prentice. The case analysis assigned ten weeks ago by Dr. Rebecca Palmer was due in three weeks. Class policy in Retail Management-705 was that all late papers were discounted two percentage points per day regardless of the reason. "Old Palmer" was a hardnose.

The procrastinating trio sat around the large rear table in "The Pit," the now-famous eatery in the old student center. Having spent the last two hours reviewing the information in the case, it was time to get down to business.

*Bob:* Look, all we have to do is to find the right match between a camera store and its customers.

*Lindsay:* Your problem statement is a bit generalized. According to the text, the right match is finding an acceptable balance between the retailer's right merchandise blend of products, quantities, places, times, prices, and appeals and the consumer's right choice.

*Ralph:* How do we know what the right choice is?

*Lindsay:* By analyzing and interpreting the psychographic customer types shown in Exhibits 1, 2, and 3. Keep in mind that most of our grade is based on analysis and interpretation of the case situation.

*Bob:* OK, let me see if I got this straight; for each of the three customer types we are to develop a merchandising blend or plan. Does it have to include each one of the six "rights" for the three "customers"?

*Lindsay:* That's right. Better safe than sorry.

*Ralph:* I have ideas for the right product, price, or appeal; but what do you do for the right quantity or time?

*Bob:* Be creative, I guess.

*Lindsay:* OK, I have a test tomorrow, so let's decide who's going to do what.

*Ralph:* Each one of us can take a customer type and develop the merchandising blend for it. We can meet in two weeks and edit each other's work.

*Lindsay:* That's OK with me, but remember each of us had better do a good job because we will be out of time in two more weeks.

*Bob:* OK, but let's make a specific list of things to do for each customer type and merchandising ingredient.

*Ralph:* Just follow the text, be creative, and develop specific recommendations.

*Lindsay:* Bob, you take the professional customer (Exhibit 1), Ralph, the striver (Exhibit 2), and I will cover the underachiever (Exhibit 3).

*Bob:* One last time, we are to develop an appropriate merchandising blend for our customer type.

*This case was prepared by Dale Lewison and Jon Hawes, The University of Akron.

*Ralph:*     Keep in mind that we are to develop a blend that would be used by a specialty camera store.

*Bob:*     I think we should get as creative as possible; for example, I am going to develop a newspaper advertisement, the layout—the whole thing.

*Ralph:*     Good idea. Do whatever you think it will take to get an A.

*Lindsay:*     Boy, look who is getting ambitous, but if you are willing to shoot for an A, so am I.

*Bob:*     Two weeks from today. We've been slow out of the gate, let's finish strong.

## ASSIGNMENT

Assume the responsibilities of Ralph, Lindsay, and Bob.

**EXHIBIT 1**
Customer profile: The professional

1. Market share equals 15.1 percent of active owners.
2. Professional occupations.
3. Male "baby boomers."
4. Not people-oriented, low in emotionalism and social interaction.
5. Do not view photography as important in social and family situations.
6. Photography interest stems from high involvement with camera.
7. Prefer manually controllable camera.
8. Uninfluenced by where others buy their cameras.
9. Least motivated by low price.
10. Most likely to notice print photo advertising and least likely to notice electronic advertising.
11. Strong ego involvement with camera.
12. Interested in objects rather than people.
13. Interested in high-performance equipment.
14. Newest camera is 35 mm SLR programmable.
15. Camera store is most likely outlet for new camera purchases.
16. Most likely to photograph scenery, flowers, and nature.
17. Most likely to have entered a photo contest, earned money in some way related to photography, and taken photo lessons.
18. Responsible for 25.4 percent of all film exposures.
19. Most likely to choose drug stores and mail order for their processing.
20. Above-average users of 1-hour processing.
21. Below-average users of minilabs.
22. Picture quality major factor in choosing a processing outlet.
23. Above-average users of different finishing services.
24. A high outlet-return rate in purchasing accessories after initial camera purchase.
25. Overall, the highest rate of accessory purchases.

Source: Glenn S. Omura, *Photo Consumer Life-styles* (Jackson, Michigan: Photo Marketing Association International, 1986): 4–13.

1. Market share equals 8.6 percent of active owners.
2. Extremely high achievement orientation.
3. Very materialistic and creative.
4. Love high-tech consumer products.
5. Very people-oriented; emotional and compassionate toward children.
6. Have fewest children per household.
7. Like to take pictures that are different and difficult to shoot.
8. Believe picture taking is an important way to demonstrate affection.
9. Willing to pay a premium for a camera that allows them to be more creative.
10. Tend to be loyal to store and store personnel.
11. Prefer shops that cater to photo experts.
12. Relish personal attention at stores.
13. Patronize stores that show them how to be more professional and creative.
14. Prefer finishers that automatically correct for bad exposures.
15. Would take more pictures if finishers would provide further assistance, such as creating special effects.
16. Most likely to incorporate photography into their lifestyles.
17. True photography enthusiasts, not just camera hobbyists.
18. Recall print media better than electronic advertising.
19. Most likely to shop department stores and drugstores for any type of merchandise.
20. Not as price-sensitive and are value-conscious; enjoy negotiating lower prices but want the best they can get.
21. 35-mm programmable most popular camera.
22. Interested in picture quality, ease of operation, versatility, and technological sophistication.
23. Camera stores favorite outlet for camera purchases.
24. Expect greater quality reputation, service, knowledgeable staff, product selection from their outlet.
25. Most likely to take photos at large gatherings.
26. Most likely to take pictures to give as gifts.
27. Greatest finishing profit potential on a per household basis.
28. Most likely to choose drugstores as their finishing outlet, but camera stores are also popular finishing outlets.
29. Expect more of their finishing outlet than any other group—picture quality, added services, knowledgeable staff, personalized attention, convenient location, turnaround time, and selection of photo and nonphoto merchandise.
30. Most likely to use ancillary finishing services of all types.
31. Good 1-hour processing potential customers.
32. Most likely to use nonminilab outlets.
33. Heavy buyers of camera accessories.

**EXHIBIT 2**
Customer profile: The striver

Source: Glenn S. Omura, *Photo Consumer Life-styles* (Jackson, Michigan: Photo Marketing Association International, 1986): 4–13.

**EXHIBIT 3**
Customer profile: The underachiever

1. Market share equals 13.6 percent of active owners.
2. High self-confidence, yet least likely to engage in do-it-yourself projects; hence name of market segment.
3. Economic rationality ranks high in their value hierarchy; enjoy seeking the best possible deal.
4. Greater proportion of women.
5. High need for control.
6. Prefer simple equipment; do not believe that expensive and sophisticated cameras are needed to capture important emotions in photographs.
7. Prefer professional photos of loved ones because they do not trust their own photographic abilities.
8. Like finishers to automatically correct their pictures for poor exposures.
9. Want finishers to help record children's development by offering such aid as printed dates on photos.
10. Little involvement with cameras as long as they get good pictures.
11. Respond to appeals that emphasize simplicity and "you can do it."
12. Most sensitive to price.
13. Least able to recall photo advertising.
14. Better recall on TV ads.
15. Word of mouth important.
16. Outlet does not need a strong photo image.
17. Lowest in profit potential for cameras because of price sensitivity.
18. Prefer cameras for ease of operation, low price, low film cost, and picture quality.
19. Favorite camera is 110, but can be traded up to a range finder; also interested in disc and instant camera.
20. Most likely to buy from discount store, but some chance at buying at camera store to upgrade camera.
21. Low finishing profit potential.
22. Drugstores primary outlet for finishing but also other low-cost outlets.
23. Modest ancillary finishing potential.
24. Below average in purchase of camera accessories.
25. Above average in use of frames and albums.

Source: Glenn S. Omura, *Photo Consumer Life-styles* (Jackson, MI: Photo Marketing Association International, 1986): 4–13.

### CASE 1–2
## What Happened to the Department Store—Creating the Right Match*

January 10, 1989

"What's Happening to Department Stores?"

At the turn of the century, department stores had positioned themselves for absolute dominance of the retail market. Through mergers and integration, these retail organizations became large conglomerate corporations capable of dominating many supply markets. As a dominant retail force, department stores established the competitive position by which all other retailers were judged. There, dominance continued into the post-World War II period and through the 1960s.

*This case was prepared by Dale Lewison and Jon Hawes, The University of Akron.

However, by the early 1970s, department stores were being outflanked by savvy competitors whose specialty and/or value-discount business formats were delivering more and better goods for the money. While total retail sales continue to increase, the conventional department store market share is decreasing. In addition, specialty stores have passed department stores in profitability, and discounters have drawn about even with department store operations.

Many conventional department stores have become so aggressive in price promotions, that it is almost impossible to distinguish them from discounters. By employing this suicidal pricing practice, department stores can expect the continuing loss of consumer confidence, the steady declining of operating profits, and ever-stiffening of competitive actions. So, What's happening to department stores? One answer is that they have forgotten the other five "rights" of merchandising (product, quantity, place, time, and appeal) in their never-ending quest for cheaper prices.

by Jeb Brown, Senior Staff Writer, *Retail Weekly*, New York

One more trade article lamenting the downturn in department store fortunes: To Stan Morris, it seemed he had read basically the same article five times in the last couple of months. As an associate in the firm Retail Associates International, a consulting organization specializing in strategic retail planning, Stan had a vested interest in department store futures; he was one of the firm's principal resident experts in department store strategies and tactics. What troubled Stan was that everyone was an expert on the fact that department stores seem to have entered the late-maturity stage of the retail life cycle; however, these armchair experts seem to have very few concrete suggestions for reviving the industry. Perhaps that is why Stan has been so busy lately; if everyone had a workable answer for the revival of the department store business, Stan might be out of work.

It was time for Stan to prepare the firm's annual report on the state of the department store industry. Given the fact that each of Retail Associates International's twenty-four department store clients pays an annual fee of $20,000 for this report and the right to access the firm's extensive research files on all aspects of retailing, Stan had better be able to identify the specific causes for the woes of department store retailing. More importantly, some constructive strategies and tactics for overcoming past problems and promoting the growth and revitalization of the industry was absolutely essential to the report's credibility. One comment in Mr. Brown's article rang true: department stores need to place less emphasis on price promotions and pay greater attention to the other five merchandising "rights."

## ASSIGNMENT

Assume the role of a student who has a summer internship with Retail Associates International. Stan Morris has asked you to conduct a library search to find trade and other articles that

1. Identify specific merchandising and operational problems within the department store industry.
2. Identify specific merchandising and/or operating strategies and tactics that might aid in overcoming the problems of department store retailing.

Prepare a well-organized written report to Mr. Morris on your findings. You might want to think of future employment opportunities and make your own recommendations, fully supported by a complete rationale.

---

**ENDNOTES**

1. Franklin S. Houston, "The Marketing Concept: What It Is and What It Is Not." *Journal of Marketing* 50 (April 1986): 86.
2. Joe Agnew, "Marcus on Marketing: Profits Are By-products of Rendering Satisfactory Customer Service." *Marketing News*, 10 April 1987, 16.

3. Sallie Hook, "All the Retail World's a Stage." *Marketing News,* 31 July 1987, 16.

4. See Charlotte Ahern, "Spiegel Rolls with Punches." *Advertising Age,* 14 Dec. 1987, 85; "Large-Size Market Shows Hefty Growth." *Chain Store Age Executive* (June 1987): 42; and Patricia Strand, "Big Idea Links K Mart, Jordache." *Advertising Age,* 2 March 1987, 58.

5. Mary J. Pitzer, "Electronics 'Superstores' May Have Blown a Fuse." *Business Week,* 8 June 1987, 90, 94.

6. Joe Agnew, "Breakfast Only Image Shed as Bob Evans Flees the Farm." *Marketing News,* 5 June 1987, 13.

7. See Raymond Serafin, "Escalating Pizza Wars Move to the Streets." *Advertising Age,* 14 April 1986, 26. Also, see Kevin T. Higgins, "Home Delivery is Helping Pizza to Battle Burgers." *Marketing News,* 1 Aug. 1986, 1.

8. See Sara E. Stern, "Planting New Fields." *Advertising Age,* 21 Sept. 1987, 62MW.

9. Susan Benway, "Presto! The Convenience Industry: Making Life a Little Simpler." *Business Week,* 27 April 1987, 86.

10. Robert Johnson and Dae Tononarive, "Eatery Chains Pour on Speed at Lunchtime." *The Wall Street Journal,* 1 Feb. 1988.

11. Amy Dunkin, "F.A.O. Schwartz: A Short Move—and Big Plans." *Business Week,* 27 April 1986, 32–33.

12. Bob Marbut "Retailing and Newspapers—A New Ballgame." Lecture series (College Station TX: Center for Retailing Studies, Texas A&M University, 1986): 2–3.

# 2

**Objectives**

☐ Identify and discuss the four major types of retail competition.

☐ Describe and measure the three factors that determine the levels of competition faced by a retailer.

☐ Recognize the different types of retailing institutions that the retailing community comprises.

☐ Identify the organizational and operational traits that characterize each type of retailer.

☐ Discuss the principal product, price, place, and promotional strategies each type of retailer employs.

☐ Discern the relative advantages and disadvantages that accrue to each type of retailer.

☐ Identify and discuss the theories of retail institutional change that are used to explain past evolution and predict future developments in retailing.

# Retail Institutions and their Competitive Behavior

Retailing is an intensely competitive industry, a "24-hour-a-day-war." To survive and prosper, retailers must compete aggressively, create a differential advantage over competitors, and give consumers a reason to shop at their stores.[1]

Successful retailers historically have used multidimensional market strategies in developing a differential advantage in the marketplace. Merchandise quality, selection, assortment, and services typically have been used in conjunction with prices to build store traffic and loyalty.[2]

One of the most dramatic developments in today's world of retailing is the number of alternative types of stores available to consumers. "By and large, people have a wide repertoire of stores that they patronize. And they are open to all kinds of retail alternatives. So a store is not simply competing with other stores in its own retail category. It's competing with retailers across the board."[3]

As consumers, all of us have shopped at specialty and department stores, discount and chain stores, stores that use the supermarket method of operations, and stores that operate by the warehouse method. Also, many of us have made retail purchases over the telephone, by mail, and through catalogs. In this chapter, we extend understanding beyond personal experiences with retailing institutions. Understanding the competitive behavior of retail institutions first requires a basic knowledge of types and levels of retail competition, the competitive strategies of current retail institutions, the processes by which retailers change, and finally, a grasp of the environmental and institutional forces that bring about institution change.

**THE NATURE OF RETAIL COMPETITION**

Retailers compete with one another on the basis of their product, place, price, and promotion strategies. These strategies are directed at securing the attention and patronage of ultimate consumers and serve as the focus for retail competitive actions. As described by *Business Week* magazine, "power retailers" are highly competitive organizations who succeed by sharply defining their customer base and fully understanding what their target customer wants. What the customer wants is the feeling that the retailer is on the cutting edge and that there is good reason to visit them frequently.[4] In assessing the competitive structure faced by a particular retailer, two dimensions of competition must be examined: the type of competition and the levels of competition.

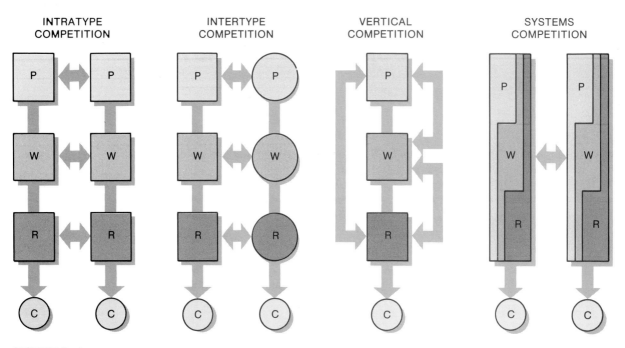

**FIGURE 2-1**
Types of competition

### Types of Competition

Retail competition is more complex than just two similar stores competing against each other. Figure 2–1 shows the four different types of retail competition: intratype, intertype, vertical, and systems competition. **Intratype competition** involves the competition between two or more retailers using the same type of business format. For example, in a regional shopping mall we often see several small independent women's apparel shops competing with one another. Competition between two or more retailers using different types of business formats to sell the same type of merchandise is referred to as **intertype competition**. A supermarket (Safeway) and a discount store (Wal-Mart) attempting to sell Crest toothpaste to the same customer are engaging in intertype competition. **Vertical competition** is the competition between a retailer and a wholesaler or producer that is attempting to make retail sales to the retailer's customers. For example, if a retailer were to stock and sell a product line that the manufacturer was also offering through a catalog operation, the retailer and manufacturer would be engaged in vertical competition. Many manufacturers sell their goods directly to consumers through their own outlets located in factory outlet malls. Bass Shoes, Calvin Klein Sportswear, and Palm Beach, Inc., makers of Evan Picone and Giant sportswear, are just a few examples of producers who are in vertical competition with their retail outlets.[5] The final type of competition occurs between entire marketing channel systems. **Systems competition** is the competition between two or more vertical marketing systems. The competition between McDonald's,

Burger King, and Wendy's is between three highly integrated marketing systems at all levels of the distribution channel.

## Levels of Competition

The level of competition a retailer faces in any market area is a function of the number, size, and quality of competitors within that area. Ideally, the retailer who faces a few small competitors is better off than the retailer who must compete against either a large number of small competitors or a few large competitors. The number and size of competitors can be determined with reasonable accuracy; Figure 2–2 shows the number (existing units) and size (sales volume) of the top fifty retail chains. The quality of each competitor is difficult to measure and analyze. The aggressiveness and effectiveness of competitors are important determinants of the level of competition for a market area. In the following pages, the competitiveness and effectiveness of various types of retailers are examined in detail.

Retailers can be classified on the basis of their ownership, merchandise, size, affiliation, contractual, location, service, organizational, and operational characteristics. The diversity and complexity of business formats found within the retailing industry preclude developing a mutually exclusive classification that clearly differentiates each type of retailer. For example, specialty and department stores can be distinguished on the basis of their respective merchandise mix; however, each might also be classified as a chain, affiliated, or integrated operation. Figure 2–3 outlines the multiplicity of characteristics that classify retail institutions.

**THE COMPETITIVE STRATEGIES OF RETAILERS**

This section discusses the competitive strategies of various retail institutions from the perspective of twelve general types of retail operations. In reading this chapter, you should keep in mind the variety and complexity of retail characteristics as shown in Figure 2–3.

## Specialty Store Retailing

**Specialty store** retailers "specialize" in the merchandise or service they offer a consumer. Specialty stores vary significantly in their degree of merchandise specialization. *Single-line specialty stores* offer only one or a very few closely related product lines. For example, retailers that specialize in either jewelry, shoes, hardware, furniture, or apparel are single-line specialty retailers. *Limited-line specialty stores* specialize in more than single-line specialty stores—within a single line of merchandise. For example, the retailer that specializes in either men's, women's, or children's shoes is a limited-line specialty store. Some retailers even limit their merchandise line to one manufacturer's brand, such as The Levi's Place and the Lazy Boy Shop. Within any given merchandise line, retailers can specialize on the basis of price (e.g., discount or off-price), size (e.g., tall or big men's), quality (e.g., exclusive), style (e.g., early American), or fashion (e.g., new wave).

Figure 2–4 identifies the top specialty store chains in terms of sales volume. Of the top fifty specialty stores, twenty-one are apparel outlets; eight specialize in con-

FIGURE 2–2
The top 50 retail chains

| Chains | 1986 Sales ($ Millions) | 1986 Earnings as Percentage of Sales (%) | Existing Units (1985) |
|---|---|---|---|
| 1. Sears, Roebuck[a] | 27,074 | 2.7 | 1,047 |
| 2. K mart[b] | 23,812 | 2.4 | 3,782 |
| 3. Safeway[c] | 20,311 | NA | 1,909 |
| 4. Kroger | 17,123 | 0.3 | 735 |
| 5. American Stores | 14,021 | 1.0 | 1,498 |
| 6. J. C. Penney | 13,390 | 3.4 | 1,793 |
| 7. Wal-Mart | 11,909 | 3.8 | 1,029 |
| 8. Federated Dept. Stores | 10,512 | 2.7 | 631 |
| 9. May Dept. Stores | 10,328 | 3.7 | 2,766 |
| 10. Dayton Hudson | 9,259 | 3.4 | 475 |
| 11. Winn-Dixie[d] | 8,225 | 1.4 | 1,262 |
| 12. Southland | 8,039 | 3.3 | 8,137 |
| 13. A&P | 7,835 | 1.2 | 1,200 |
| 14. F. W. Woolworth | 6,501 | 3.3 | 6,309 |
| 15. Lucky | 6,441 | 34.5 | 579 |
| 16. Supermarkets General[c] | 5,508 | 1.1 | 310 |
| 17. Albertson's | 5,380 | 1.9 | 452 |
| 18. Zayre | 5,351 | 1.7 | 1,092 |
| 19. Melville | 5,262 | 4.5 | 5,833 |
| 20. Army/Air Force Exchange | 5,187 | 4.4 | 5,441 |
| 21. R. H. Macy[c,d] | 4,653 | 4.4 | 87 |
| 22. Allied Stores[e] | 4,435 | NA | 697 |
| 23. Montgomery Ward | 4,383 | 2.4 | 295 |
| 24. Carter Hawley Hale | 4,090 | 0.0 | 302 |
| 25. Stop & Shop | 3,872 | 1.0 | 275 |
| 26. Publix | 3,797 | 2.2 | 307 |
| 27. Walgreen[f] | 3,661 | 2.8 | 1,273 |
| 28. The Limited | 3,143 | 7.2 | 2,682 |
| 29. Von's | 3,000 | NA | NA |
| 30. Grand Union | 2,746 | 1.2 | 369 |
| 31. Revco[c,d] | 2,743 | 2.1 | 2,031 |
| 32. Jack Eckerd[c] | 2,700 | NA | 1,596 |
| 33. Radio Shack | 2,687 | NA | 4,863 |
| 34. Price[d] | 2,667 | 2.2 | 25 |
| 35. Wickes[a] | 2,656 | NA | 565 |
| 36. Giant Food | 2,528 | 1.8 | 142 |
| 37. Service Merchandise | 2,527 | NA | 313 |
| 38. Batus | 2,500 | NA | 197 |
| 39. Toys 'R' Us | 2,445 | 6.2 | 338 |
| 40. Food Lion | 2,407 | 2.6 | 388 |
| 41. Circle K | 2,289 | 2.2 | NA |
| 42. Lowe's | 2,283 | 2.3 | 300 |
| 43. Super Valu[a] | 2,269 | 2.5 | 170 |
| 44. Best Products | 2,142 | NA | 205 |
| 45. Mercantile Stores | 2,028 | 5.5 | 82 |
| 46. Ames | 1,888 | 1.4 | 463 |
| 47. Dillard | 1,851 | 4.0 | 115 |
| 48. Rite Aid | 1,757 | 4.4 | 1,586 |
| 49. Fred Meyer | 1,688 | 1.3 | 93 |
| 50. Long's | 1,635 | 2.4 | 222 |

NA, not available

Profit/earnings ratios are based on primary per share earnings as reported by the companies for the most recent four quarters. Extraordinary items generally are excluded.

[a]Retail only. [b]Operating earnings, retail. [c]Company has gone private during last twelve months. [d]Fiscal year ended in summer of 1986. [e]Acquired in last twelve months. [f]Formerly American Can.

Source: Reprinted by permission from *Chain Store Age Executive*, August 1987, pp. 11–12. Copyright © Lebhar-Friedman, Inc., 425 Park Avenue, New York, New York 10022.

A. By ownership of establishment
  1. Single-unit independent stores
  2. Multiunit retail organizations
    a) chain stores
    b) branch stores
  3. Manufacturer-owned retail outlets
  4. Consumers' cooperative stores
  5. Farmer-owned establishments
  6. Company-owned stores (industrial stores) or commissaries
  7. Government operated stores (post exchanges, state liquor stores)
  8. Public utility company stores (for sale of major appliances)
B. By kind of business (merchandise handled)
  1. General merchandise group
    a) department stores
    b) dry goods, general merchandise stores
    c) general stores
    d) variety stores
  2. Single-line stores (e.g., grocery, apparel, furniture)
  3. Specialty stores (e.g., meat markets, lingerie shops, floor coverings stores)
C. By size of establishment
  1. By number of employees
  2. By annual sales volume
D. By degree of vertical integration
  1. Nonintegrated (retailing functions only)
  2. Integrated with wholesaling functions
  3. Integrated with manufacturing or other form-utility creation
E. By type of relationship with other business organizations
  1. Unaffiliated
  2. Voluntarily affiliated with other retailers
    a) through wholesaler-sponsored voluntary chains
    b) through retailer cooperation
  3. Affiliated with manufacturers by dealers franchises

F. By method of consumer contact
  1. Regular store
    a) leased department
  2. Mail order
    a) by catalog selling
    b) by advertising in regular media
    c) by membership club plans
  3. Household contacts
    a) by house-to-house canvassing
    b) by regular delivery route service
    c) by party plan selling
G. By type of location
  1. Urban
    a) central business district
    b) secondary business district
    c) string street location
    d) neighborhood location
    e) controlled (planned) shopping center
    f) public market calls
  2. Small city
    a) downtown
    b) neighborhood
  3. Rural stores
  4. Roadside stands
H. By type of service rendered
  1. Full service
  2. Limited service (cash-and-carry)
  3. Self-service
I. By legal form of organization
  1. Proprietorship
  2. Partnership
  3. Corporation
  4. Special types
J. By management organization or operational technique
  1. Undifferentiated
  2. Departmentalized

Source: T. N. Beckman, W. R. Davidson, and W. W. Talarzyk, *Marketing,* 9th ed. (New York: Ronald Press Co., 1973), 239.

**FIGURE 2–3**
Classifying retail institutions

The diverse and complex world of retailing precludes a mutually exclusive classification of retailers

sumer electronics; six are shoe stores; four merchandise toys; two sell either books, textiles, or sporting goods; and the remaining five members of the Top 50 Club are a jewelry, furniture, giftware, record, and hard goods specialty chain.

A key tactic in the specialty retailer's product strategy is merchandise assortment. Although specialty stores carry only a limited variety of products, they offer consumers the opportunity to choose from a deep assortment within each line. The large number of brands, models, styles, sizes, and colors within each product line is the principal means by which specialty retailers attract customers. In general, the more specialized the retailer, the greater the depth of the product assortment. A specialty store might stock national brands, designer labels, private labels, or some combination of these products. Most specialty stores also stress the quality of their customer support services as part of their customer offering.

Specialty retailers can be either high-margin operations (The Limited), or low-margin (T. J. Maxx) operations. Specialty retailers normally operate in various-size facilities with decor and layouts that complement the nature of their merchandise and support their mode of operation. Specialty retailers are found in a variety of locations including large shopping centers, downtown malls, specialty malls, and string/strip developments along major traffic arteries.

Specialty stores' promotions stress the uniqueness and distinctiveness of their product offerings and the depth of selection they offer the consumer. In final analysis, the product, price, place, and promotional strategies of the specialist are directed at serving the needs of a more targeted and homogeneous market segment. The specialty retailer attempts to serve all consumers in one or a limited number of market segments.

## Department Store Retailing

**Department stores** are large retailing institutions that carry a wide variety of merchandise lines with a reasonably good selection within each line. What distinguishes the department store is its organizational structure, specifically the high degree of "departmentalization." From an operational standpoint, most of the basic functions of buying, selling, promoting, and servicing are conducted entirely or at least in part at the department level. Also, accounting and control procedures are organized on a departmental basis. The advantages of this type of organization are that it allows both *functional* (buying, selling, etc.) and *merchandise* (apparel, shoes, etc.) specialization, while at the same time gaining the economies of scale associated with a large retailing operation.

Some department stores are local independents (see Figure 2–5, p. 46); others are part of a national chain (e.g., Sears and J. C. Penney) or an ownership group (e.g., see Figure 2–6, pp. 48–49).

Some department stores limit their departmentalization to a few (less than 30) broad merchandise lines, whereas others departmentalize into many (more than 100) very limited merchandise groups. Whatever the degree of departmentalization, department stores commonly divide merchandise into "hard" and "soft" line departments. Home furnishings is an example of a broad, hard-line department that could be further departmentalized into consumer electronics, floor coverings, furniture, major appliances, and decorative furnishings. The women's department is a soft line

FIGURE 2-4

The top 50 specialty store chains

| Rank | Company/Chain (Headquarters) | Type | Sales ($000,000s) | Units |
|------|------------------------------|------|-------------------|-------|
| 1. | The Limited | Apparel | 3,143 | 2,682 |
| 2. | Mervyn's | Apparel | 2,862 | 175 |
| 3. | Radio Shack[a] | Consumer Electronics | 2,700 | 4,795 |
| 4. | Toys 'R' Us | Toys | 2,445 | 295 |
| 5. | Marshall's | Apparel | 1,410 | 261 |
| 6. | Petrie Stores | Apparel | 1,198 | 1,478 |
| 7. | Circuit City | Consumer Electronics | 1,011 | 87 |
| 8. | T. J. Maxx | Apparel | 1,010 | 226 |
| 9. | Zale[b] | Jewelry | 939 | 1,216 |
| 10. | Volume Shoe | Shoe | 934 | 2,210 |
| 11. | Gap Inc.[c] | Apparel | 848 | 724 |
| 12. | Levitz | Furniture | 831 | 101 |
| 13. | Kinney Shoe | Shoe | 700 | 1,535 |
| 14. | Highland Superstores | Consumer Electronics | 656 | 53 |
| 15. | Waldenbooks | Books | 650 | 944 |
| 16. | Brown Shoe | Shoe | 630 | 1,324 |
| 17. | Herman's[d] | Sporting Goods | 630 | 205 |
| 18. | Child World | Toys | 629 | 134 |
| 19. | Businessland[a] | Consumer Electronics | 600 | 95 |
| 20. | B. Dalton[e] | Books | 585 | 820 |
| 21. | Foot Locker | Shoe | 572 | 765 |
| 22. | Edison Bros. Shoe | Shoe | 570 | 1,403 |
| 23. | Ross Stores | Apparel | 534 | 121 |
| 24. | Casual Corner | Apparel | 530 | 702 |
| 25. | Charming Shoppes[f] | Apparel | 521 | 678 |

[a]Estimates for fiscal year ended June 30, 1987, for US company-owned stores.
[b]Continuing operations only, for fiscal year ended March 31, 1987.
[c]Includes 65 Banana Republic and 10 GapKids stores.
[d]Estimate for fiscal year ended April 30, 1987.
[e]Acquired by Barnes & Noble in November 1986.
[f]For fiscal year ended July 16, 1986.
[g]Cyclops Corp. now 83% owned by Dixon PLC.

that can be further departmentalized by creating separate departments for dresses, footwear, hosiery, lingerie, jewelry, and ladies' accessories. Department stores offer a wide selection of brand-name and designer-label merchandise. Because of the competition from off-price retailers, however, "many department stores have developed private-label programs that enable them to offer exclusive merchandise and receive higher profits than for brand name merchandise."[6]

Several inherent advantages to departmental organization aid the retailer in developing and implementing a product strategy. First, department managers are in a good position to supervise and control each individual product line closely. Second, sales personnel operating at the departmental level are directly in touch with consumers' needs, buying problems, and special concerns. Third, a departmental organization allows the retailer to segment the consumer market. Figure 2-7 illustrates

FIGURE 2-4

*continued*

| Rank | Company/Chain (Headquarters) | Type | Sales ($000,000s) | Units |
|------|------------------------------|------|-------------------|-------|
| 26. | Alexanders' | Apparel | 520 | 14 |
| 27. | Silo Electronics[g] | Consumer Electronics | 494 | 119 |
| 28. | Kay Bee | Toys | 487 | 639 |
| 29. | Thom McAn | Shoe | 484 | 1,033 |
| 30. | Lechmere | Hard Goods | 476 | 17 |
| 31. | Federated Group | Consumer Electronics | 430 | 65 |
| 32. | Hartmarx Specialty[h] | Apparel | 415 | 230 |
| 33. | C. R. Anthony | Apparel | 412 | 268 |
| 34. | Brooks Fashion | Apparel | 412 | 777 |
| 35. | Musicland[i] | Records | 412 | 525 |
| 36. | Burlington Coat[j] | Apparel | 392 | 87 |
| 37. | Crazy Eddie | Consumer Electronics | 353 | 34 |
| 38. | Loehmann's | Apparel | 351 | 90 |
| 39. | Edison Apparel | Apparel | 334 | 1,072 |
| 40. | Bealls | Apparel | 325 | 150 |
| 41. | County Seat | Apparel | 325 | 301 |
| 42. | Oshman's[k] | Sporting Goods | 323 | 315 |
| 43. | Hit or Miss | Apparel | 320 | 461 |
| 44. | House of Fabrics | Textiles | 316 | 707 |
| 45. | Pic 'n Save | Apparel | 305 | 101 |
| 46. | Spencer Gifts[l] | Giftware | 302 | 439 |
| 47. | McDuff-Scott[a] | Consumer Electronics | 300 | 294 |
| 48. | Ups 'N' Downs[m] | Apparel | 300 | 667 |
| 49. | Hancock[n] | Textiles | 290 | 325 |
| 50. | Lionel | Toys | 288 | 65 |

[h]For year ended Nov. 30, 1986.
[i]Includes Sam Goody, Licorice Pizza, and Discount Records stores.
[j]For fiscal year ended Nov. 1, 1986.
[k]Includes 27 Abercrombie & Fitch stores.
[l]Includes mail-order sales as well as results of Intrigue jewelry and A2Z—The Best of Everything stores.
[m]Includes sales of Caren Charles, Petite Sophisticate, and August Max.
[n]Prior to spinoff by Lucky Stores in May 1987.
Source: David P. Schulz, "The Top 100 Specialty Stores," *Stores* (August 1987): 26–27.

how retailers can use store departmentalization to satisfy a particular market segment's needs. Chicago's Carson Pirie Scott & Co. has made a major statement of its targeting strategy by creating Corporate Level, a separate department tailored to the needs and wants of executive and professional women. Not just any working woman will be targeted, only those with individual incomes of at least $25,000.[7] To attract the professional woman, Corporate Level offers a mix of goods and services; "a customer can buy a wardrobe, get a haircut, and drop off the dry cleaning."[8]

Department stores usually are high-margin operations. Because of the high operating expenses (30 to 403 percent of sales) stemming from the store's organizational structure, service offering, physical facilities, and high-risk merchandise, margins between merchandise costs and retail selling prices must be substantial to ensure a fair profit. Department stores normally appeal to middle- and upper-income

FIGURE 2–5
The top 10 indepen-
dent department stores

| Organization (Location) | Sales Volume ($ Millions) | Number of Units |
|---|---|---|
| Dillard's (Little Rock, AR) | 1,851 | 115 |
| Nordstrom (Seattle) | 1,630 | 53 |
| Woodward & Lothrop (Washington, D.C.) | 497 | 16 |
| Carson Pirie Scott (Chicago) | 435 | 20 |
| Strawbridge & Clothier (Philadelphia) | 410 | 12 |
| P. A. Bergner (Milwaukee) | 391 | 34 |
| McRae's (Jackson, MS) | 331 | 29 |
| Jacobson's (Jackson, MI) | 308 | 20 |
| Elder-Beerman (Dayton, OH) | 287 | 26 |
| Boscou's (Reading, PA) | 270 | 11 |

Source: David P. Schulz, "The Top 100 Department Stores," *Stores* (July 1987): 13–16.

consumers. To appeal to such a diverse group of consumers, some department stores have at least three pricing points. "Low or economy" prices are directed at the lower- to middle-income consumer; "midline" prices appeal to those who want neither the lowest- nor the highest-priced merchandise; "prestige" prices are aimed at the upper-income consumer who desires the best. These good, better, and best price lines not only allow the department store to project a broad price appeal, but also help consumers to make price and quality comparisons. Some upscaled department stores, like Bloomingdale's and Nieman-Marcus, focus their attention on the middle and upper pricing points.

Department stores typically occupy high-rent locations within major commercial centers. The place strategy of most department stores has been to locate in an "anchor" (end) position at one or more major suburban shopping centers. The exterior and interior motifs of the average department store are designed to create a prestige image. Externally, the architectural form might communicate either bigness, success, uniqueness, strength, security, elegance, or any number of store images. Internally, the store's layout, fixtures, and decor create consumer buying moods by appealing to all the customers' sensory modes of sight, sound, smell, taste, and touch.

The department store's principal promotional appeals are product selection and quality, service offerings, and shopping atmosphere. Nordstrom's of Seattle has become the model for good service, and as a result, it enjoys the highest sales per square foot of any department store: $310 versus the industry average of $150. Nordstrom's service is based on having highly motivated sales associates—"an attitude, a kind of caring on the part of everybody in the store."[9] Each of these appeals is directed toward enhancing the prestige image of the department store. "A well-honed identity helps persuade customers that they are getting their money's worth even if the department store is higher priced than some of its rivals. Bloomingdale's is renowned as a yuppie emporium where trendiness makes up for higher prices. Macy's aims for the shopper on a budget who is interested in wide assortment and name brands. A reputation for quality merchandise, hassle-free returns, and a more personal service may still draw a value-conscious crowd."[10] Both product and institutional advertising are an integral part of the department store's strategy to favorably influence potential consumers. Although advertisements feature several carefully selected products, every department store advertising campaign subtly communicates the message that "this is the place to shop." Department stores like to create the "big event" by developing shopping themes consistent with the customer's moods and needs, the seasons or current events, the merchandise, and the store's environment. For example, Bloomingdale's likes to stage multimillion-dollar extravaganzas honoring individual countries' crafts.

## Chain Store Retailing

In retailing, the term *chain* is used in a variety of ways. As commonly used, a **chain store** is any retail organization that operates multiple outlets. To be properly classified as a chain, however, a retail organization must meet several additional criteria. What distinguishes chain operations from similar types of operations are the number of units (stores), the merchandise mix, and the form of ownership and control.

Technically, any retail organization that operates more than one unit can be classified as a chain. However, the *Census of Business* considers chains as retail organizations that operate 11 or more units. A workable compromise is to discuss chain organizations as *small chains* (two to ten units) and *large chains* (eleven or more units). Another criterion for classifying a conglomeration of stores as a chain is that each unit in the chain must *sell similar lines of merchandise.* So long as the product is basically the same, a chain store organization could be a multiunit operation of specialty stores, discount stores, department stores, or food stores. The third criterion used to determine if a group of stores is a chain is whether there is a *central form of ownership and control.* With central ownership, the parent organization has control over all operating and merchandising aspects of the entire chain of stores.

Traditionally, chain stores offer highly standardized merchandise. Frequently, the home office establishes a basic stock list in which the standard items on the list are typically staple merchandise items that have a relatively high market demand and turnover rate. The merchandise items are the most popular brands, styles, models, sizes, and colors as perceived by the store's targeted consumers. Store-to-store variation in product mix is receiving considerable attention. Montgomery Ward has launched its specialty store strategy in which seven specialty shops (e.g., apparel, appliance, automotive, home care, home electronics, home store, and recreation and leisure) have been developed. A given Ward's store may get two, three, or up to all seven shops, depending on the marketplace characteristics. Store to store merchandise variations are allowed but tightly controlled.[11]

In recent years, many of the larger chain organizations have engaged in "private-label" branding (the retailer's brand) as part of their overall product strategy. In some cases, a few of the private brands of very large chains have become, in effect, national brands. For example, most consumers think of Sears' "Craftsman" and "Kenmore" brands as high-quality, national brands. In the apparel lines, Sears is aggressively merchandising its Stefanie Powers career collection, its Cheryl Tiegs sportswear line, and its Arnie (Palmer) menswear.[12] By virtue of the fact that Sears' operations are national in scope, many more of their private labels are viewed in the same perspective.

**FIGURE 2–6**
Major department store
"ownership groups"

| Chain and Division(s) | Sales Volume ($ Millions) | Number of Units |
|---|---|---|
| **Federated Department Stores** | | |
| Bloomingdales (New York) | 1,050 | 16 |
| Abraham and Straus (Brooklyn) | 779 | 15 |
| Foley's (Houston) | 1,107 | 37 |
| Burdine's (Miami) | 810 | 29 |
| Bullock's (California) | 752 | 28 |
| Rich's (Atlanta) | 691 | 20 |
| Lazarus (Cincinnati) | 905 | 32 |
| Filene's (Boston) | 391 | 16 |
| Goldsmith's (Memphis) | 174 | 6 |
| Boston Stores (Milwaukee) | 131 | 8 |
| I. Magnin (San Francisco) | 317 | 26 |
| **Dayton Hudson** | | |
| Dayton Hudson (Minneapolis) | 1,566 | 37 |
| **May Department Stores** | | |
| May Co. (California) | 814 | 34 |
| Hecht Co. (Washington, D.C.) | 624 | 22 |
| Famous-Barr (St. Louis) | 495 | 17 |
| Kaufman's (Pittsburgh) | 455 | 14 |
| May Co. (Cleveland) | 248 | 10 |
| Meier & Frank (Portland) | 226 | 8 |
| G. Fox & Co. (Hartford) | 264 | 9 |
| M. O'Neil Co. (Akron) | 182 | 9 |
| May D&F (Denver) | 175 | 10 |
| Strouss (Youngstown) | 104 | 8 |
| May-Cohens (Jacksonville) | 80 | 6 |
| Lord & Taylor (New York) | 865 | 45 |
| J. W. Robinson (California) | 586 | 24 |
| L. S. Ayres (Indianapolis) | 440 | 25 |
| Sibley, Lindsay & Curr (Rochester) | 192 | 14 |
| Denver Dry Goods (Denver) | 151 | 12 |
| Hahne (Newark) | 153 | 8 |
| Goldwaters (Phoenix) | 157 | 9 |
| Robinson's (St. Petersburg) | 136 | 10 |
| **Mercantile Stores** | | |
| Gayfer's (Mobile) | 350 | 12 |
| McAlpin (Cincinnati) | 325 | 9 |
| Castner-Knott (Nashville) | 225 | 11 |
| Jones Store (Kansas City) | 220 | 8 |
| Joslin's (Denver) | 215 | 11 |
| Gayfer's (Montgomery) | 175 | 6 |
| Bacons/Roots (Louisville) | 160 | 7 |

FIGURE 2–6
*continued*

| Chain and Division | Sales Volume ($ Millions) | Number of Units |
|---|---|---|
| **Mercantile Stores** *(continued)* | | |
| J. B. White (Augusta) | 145 | 7 |
| Lion (Toledo) | 120 | 3 |
| Hennesey's (Billings) | 75 | 5 |
| **Allied Stores** | | |
| Jordon Marsh (New England) | 537 | 19 |
| The Bon (Seattle) | 490 | 39 |
| Joske's (Texas) | 349 | 27 |
| Sterns (New Jersey) | 484 | 24 |
| Maas Bros. (Tampa) | 332 | 21 |
| Jordon Marsh (Florida) | 251 | 17 |
| Pomeroy's (Pennsylvania) | 149 | 16 |
| Bonwit Teller (New York) | 157 | 13 |
| Miller & Rhoads (Richmond) | 138 | 17 |
| Donaldson's (Minneapolis) | 181 | 15 |
| Garfinckel's (Washington) | 112 | 10 |
| Miller's (Knoxville) | 107 | 12 |
| Read's (Bridgeport) | 111 | 6 |
| Block's (Indianapolis) | 86 | 10 |
| Cain Sloan (Nashville) | 64 | 4 |
| **Carter Hawley Hale** | | |
| The Broadway (California) | 1,045 | 43 |
| Emporium Capwell (San Francisco) | 710 | 22 |
| Neiman-Marcus (Dallas) | 850 | 22 |
| John Wanamaker (Philadelphia) | 433 | 16 |
| Weinstock's (Sacramento) | 236 | 12 |
| Thalheimer's (Richmond) | 360 | 24 |
| Broadway-Southwest (Phoenix) | 210 | 13 |
| Bergdorf Goodman (New York) | 120 | 1 |
| **R. H. Macy & Co.** | | |
| Macy's (New Jersey) | 1,440 | 24 |
| Macy's (New York) | 1,575 | 22 |
| Macy's (California) | 1,335 | 25 |
| Macy's (Atlanta) | 605 | 16 |
| **Batus** (retail group) | | |
| Saks Fifth Avenue (New York) | 1,005 | 44 |
| Marshall Field's (Chicago) | 925 | 25 |
| Ivey's (Charlotte, FL) | 275 | 25 |

Source: Adapted from David P. Schulz, "Stores' Annual Ranking," *Stores* (July 1987): 13–18.

FIGURE 2–7
Market segmentation through store departmentalization

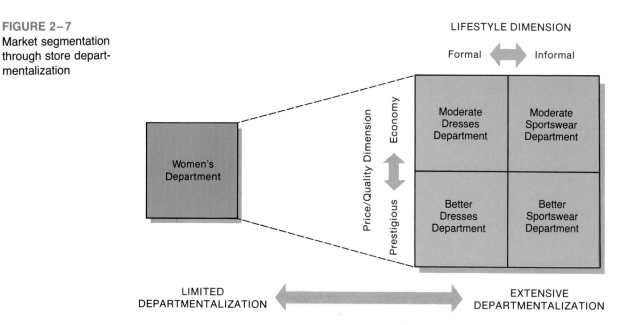

Economies of scale are an important part of the chain's central buying policies. By buying in large quantities, often directly from the manufacturer, chain stores receive substantial quantity discounts. Large-quantity purchases also reduce the cost of merchandise because the chains can take advantage of lower transportation rates on carload and truckload shipments. An additional benefit associated with large-scale purchases are *promotional allowances* (payments that chains receive from suppliers to help defray the cost of advertising the suppliers' products). The net result of the chain's centralized buying policies is that it can acquire merchandise at the lowest costs in the retailing industry.

Several advantages accrue to chain store operations. First, by operating a large number of stores within a particular market, chains can exert substantial control over their stores and achieve economies of scale through a centralized distribution system. The result is high turnover rates and few stockouts and overstocks. Second, chains can spread risk over many different stores in many different markets. Third, chain organizations obtain benefits from vertically integrating their channels of distribution. Sears, for example, obtains approximately 50 percent of its merchandise from manufacturers in which it has equity interest (partial ownership). Finally, chain operations enjoy the advantage of a high level of consumer recognition. The use of a standardized sign and architectural motif reinforces consumers' awareness of the chain and what it has to offer.

Chain stores usually promote both their store image and their individual products. Generally, chains promote the standardized nature of their operations and therefore the consistency (product quality, customer service, etc.) of their product offerings from store to store. Chains also commonly promote their convenience and large number of locations available to their customers. Many chains stress the reliability of buying from a large national or regional firm. Finally, with multiple locations within a given market, chain stores can effectively use the most expensive media (television) and exposure time (prime time).

## Discount Store Retailing

The **discount store** is a retailing institution that sells a wide variety of merchandise at less than traditional retail prices. Targeted to meet the needs of the economy-minded consumer, the discount store uses mass-merchandising techniques that enable it to offer discount prices as its major consumer appeal. The discount store sells name-brand (national or manufacturers' brands) and private-label merchandise at prices that consumers easily recognize as below traditional prices. The discount store carries a fairly complete variety of hard and/or soft goods. In its drive for high turnover, the typical discounter stocks only the most popular brands, styles, models, sizes, and colors, along with its own private labels. In general, the product strategy of the discount store is to carry many different product lines but limit the amount of selection within each line.

A few nationally well-known brands in key product line areas are an integral part of the discounter's product strategy. In selling national brands, the discounter takes advantage of the fact that consumers know the going price for various products. Thus, it sells most of its merchandise to the price-conscious shopper. Also, selling national brands below suggested manufacturer's retail price greatly enhances the store's discount image. This image helps the discounter convince the general public that its large selection of private labels are also a good value. To capitalize on its value image, K mart is installing five distinctive private label lines of women's clothing; they range from the classically styled Hunter's Glen label to the dressier Jaclyn Smith line; K mart wants to sell customers something more than pantyhose, hair spray, and school supplies.[13]

The discounter's service offering is limited to services necessary to run the operation. Traditionally cash-and-carry businesses, most major discount chains now offer credit services. Sales personnel are used in departments (jewelry, camera, etc.) that absolutely need them. Store personnel also include those who staff information booths, return and credit approval counters, and checkouts.

The pricing strategy of the conventional discount store promotes the highest possible turnover rate. A high rate of stock turns is the key to success and profitability for the discount retailer. Although the amount of the discount varies greatly from one product line to another, it is large enough for the majority of the consuming public to recognize it as a discount.

Conventional discounters select suburban locations convenient to the large, middle-class consumer market; discount houses frequently serve as anchors for community shopping centers and, in some rare cases, as the major anchors of a regional shopping center. An exception to this strategy is Wal-Mart, which became the seventh largest retailer to follow a location strategy of "selling name-brand merchandise at a discount in small-town America."[14] The typical discounter operates out of a modern one-story building ranging in area from 20,000 to 150,000 square feet. The store size depends on the local market size. Many discount stores create a carnival-like environment through their store decor and special sales events. Tile floors, plain pipe racks, bargain tables and bins, and rows of shelving are the primary ways for these discounters to display their merchandise.Centralized checkout areas are a prominent part of all discount operations. Some leased departments and high-ticket item departments have localized checkouts.

Most discount stores are aggressive advertisers. Discounters use a broad message appeal highlighting variety, selection, and especially price. Newspapers are the discounter's principal medium, but television and radio advertising are increasing. Another key promotional strategy discounters use to inform and persuade the consumer is the point-of-purchase display. Bargain tables, bins, and stacks greet consumers as they enter, check out, and exit. End-of-aisle and main-aisle displays intercept shoppers as they travel through the store. In-store loudspeaker announcements of unadvertised specials are used to draw customers throughout the store.

### Off-Price Retailing

**Off-price retailers** are specialty retailers that sell both soft goods and/or hard goods at price levels (20 to 60 percent) below regular retail prices. There are two general types of off-price operations: (1) **factory outlet** stores or direct manufacturers' outlets (e.g., Levi Strauss, Manhattan's Brand Name Fashion Outlet, Burlington Coat Factory Warehouse, and Bass Shoes), which sell their own seconds, overruns, and pack-aways from last season, and (2) *independents* (e.g., Loehmann's, T. J. Maxx, Marshall's, and Clothestime), who buy seconds, irregulars, canceled orders, overages, or leftover goods from manufacturers or other retailers.[15] A key concept in the off-price retailer's strategy is selling designer labels and branded merchandise; consumers know if the price is an "off-price" if they can make price comparisons on like goods.

The off-price retailer's mode of operation can be described as follows:

☐ Low buying prices, often lower than for conventional discounters and lower than could be expected on the basis of quantity discounts

☐ A high proportion of established, often designer, brands from manufacturers that seek the highest prices they can get for distressed and leftover merchandise, overruns, and irregulars

☐ Merchandise often of higher quality than usually found in "discount stores"

☐ A changing and unstable assortment in that the customer can't confidently predict exactly what the retailer will have on a given day—a major factor distinguishing off-pricing from simple discounting

☐ Customer services varying from minimal to extensive, sometimes including wrapping, exchange, refunds, and credit card acceptance

☐ Variety ranging from very narrow (for example, men's suits) to very broad (for example, family apparel)[16]

One explanation for the ability of off-price retailers to secure favorable terms is that they tend to pay promptly and do not ask for such extras as advertising allowances, return privileges, and markdown adjustments.

On the selling side, off-price retailers strive to keep their overhead low to maintain lower margins. Operating expenses are reduced by operating out of modest facilities located in strip malls, where rent is half that charged by large shopping centers.

A variation of the off-price retailer is the **close-out store**—an outlet that specializes in the retailing of a wide variety of merchandise obtained through close-outs, retail liquidations, and bankruptcy proceeds. "The merchandise mix varies, depending on wholesale buying opportunities that arise, but fall into certain broad categories, including household products, small appliances, toys, snack foods, and health and beauty aids."[17] An 80/20 product mix (hardgoods to softgoods) is common for close-out operations.[18] Like other off-pricers, close-out stores strive to keep operating expenses at a minimum. Consolidated Stores of Columbus, Ohio, operators of Odd Lots and Big Lots stores, Job Lot Trading of New York, and Pick 'n' Save of Los Angeles, are the major players in this form of off-price retailing.

## Supermarket Retailing

**Supermarket** retailing as we know it began in the early 1900s, when Piggly Wiggly experimented with the self-service method of food retailing. Today, food store sales (over $300 billion) account for one-fifth of all retail sales in the United States. No commonly accepted definition of a supermarket exists because of the wide range of business formulas used in this industry. One common definitional classification of supermarkets follows:

- ☐ *Conventional supermarket:* a self-service grocery store that offers a full line of groceries, meat, and produce with at least $2 million in annual sales
- ☐ *Superstore:* a modern, upgraded version of the conventional supermarket with at least 30,000 square feet in total area and more than $8 million in annual sales; offers an expanded selection of nonfoods and service departments (e.g., deli, bakery, seafood)
- ☐ *Food and drug combo:* combination of superstore and drugstore under a single roof and common checkout; drugstore merchandise represents at least one-third of the selling area and a minimum of 15 percent of store sales
- ☐ *Warehouse store:* a low-margin grocery store that combines reduced variety, lower service levels, simpler decor, streamlined merchandising presentation, and aggressive prices
- ☐ *Superwarehouse store:* a high-volume hybrid of the superstore and the warehouse store offering full variety, quality perishables, and low prices
- ☐ *Limited-assortment store:* a very "bare bones," low-price grocery store that eliminates services and carries fewer than 1,000 items with few, if any, perishables[19]

The market share of each of these formats is shown in Figure 2–8. The growth of the economy (price-oriented) and extended (selection-oriented) formats are at the expense of the more traditional supermarket operation.

The products offered by a supermarket include a relatively broad variety and complete assortment of dry groceries, fresh meats, produce, and dairy products. In recent years, the basic food lines have been supplemented by a variety of prepared food lines (the deli department) and nonfood lines. By adding prepared foods, the

FIGURE 2–8
U.S. supermarkets' for-
mat share (source:
Cynthia Valentino, "In a
fragmented market."
Reprinted with permis-
sion of *Advertising
Age,* 4 May 1987.
Copyright © Crain Com-
munications, Inc.)

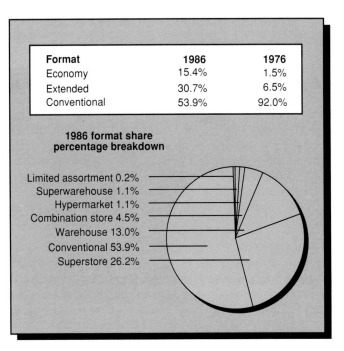

| Format | 1986 | 1976 |
|---|---|---|
| Economy | 15.4% | 1.5% |
| Extended | 30.7% | 6.5% |
| Conventional | 53.9% | 92.0% |

**1986 format share
percentage breakdown**

Limited assortment 0.2%
Superwarehouse 1.1%
Hypermarket 1.1%
Combination store 4.5%
Warehouse 13.0%
Conventional 53.9%
Superstore 26.2%

supermarkets hoped to negate the threat posed by the fast-food restaurants. The addition of "carry-out services" and "eating-in areas" for such foods as deli products, fresh bakery products, and fast-food restaurant lines (e.g., hamburgers, hot dogs, chicken, tacos, and fish) represents a direct effort to obtain a large share of this eating-out business.

By broadening their merchandise lines to include nonfood products, supermarkets have successfully increased sales and profits. With large numbers of customers moving through their stores each week, this product strategy has resulted in numerous sales of convenience and shopping goods. Today, supermarkets' upgraded and upscaled operations include such nonfood lines as prescription drugs, small appliances, linens, auto accessories, books, magazines, clothing, flowers, and housewares. Recently, many supermarkets have added numerous services—including dry cleaning, post-office, banking, tailoring, medical, dental, insurance, and legal services. If the "scrambling" process continues, the supermarket of the future could well become the modern version of the "general store."

Supermarkets are low-margin operations that depend on very high stock turnover rates to sustain profits. Operating out of clean, modern facilities (an extremely important patronage motive for most food shoppers), the supermarket is basically a self-service operation offering few free services with the exception of parking and bagging. Although some supermarkets accept credit cards and offer tote services to automobiles, cash and carry is the preferred method of doing business. The most distinguishing promotional characteristic of supermarkets is the weekly advertising of loss or low-price leaders (products sold below or at cost). Leader pricing is aimed at attracting consumers into the store, where it is hoped they will purchase the rest of their weekly shopping list at full markup prices.

## Convenience Store Retailing

The modern-day version of the corner "mom and pop" grocery store is the **convenience store**. As its name suggests, the convenience store offers customers a convenient place to shop. In particular, it offers time convenience by being open longer and during the inconvenient early morning and late night hours, and place convenience by being a small, compact, fast-service operation that is close to consumers' homes and places of business. Their time and place convenience appeals are suggested in their trade names—7-Eleven, Stop-N-Go, Majik Markets, Quik-Pik, Minit Markets, and Jiffy.

The basic premise of the convenience store is capturing fill-in or emergency trade—after the consumer has forgotten to purchase a needed product during the planned weekly trips to the supermarket or has unexpectedly run out of a needed product before the next planned supermarket trip. Because these stores are frequently located between the consumer's home and the nearest supermarket, they serve as effective "interceptors" of fill-in and emergency trade.

Convenience stores carry both food and nonfood merchandise lines. Like supermarkets, convenience stores have broadened their basic product mix to include items such as motor oil, toys, prepared foods (7-Eleven's Hot-To-Go), firewood, iced drinks, and self-service gasoline. Product assortment within each line is very limited. Major national brands dominate the product line, although some of the major chain organizations offer private labels in beverages and some canned goods.

Because they provide time and place utilities, convenience stores charge appreciably higher prices than other stores. From a promotional viewpoint, the store's sign and location are the most important weapons in the war to attract consumers. The convenience store's facilities include buildings that range from 1,000 to 3,200 square feet and parking areas that accommodate five to fifteen cars. Store layouts are designed to draw customers through the store to increase impulse purchasing. To accomplish this, convenience store managers place high-volume items (e.g., beer and soft drinks) at or near the back of the store.

## Contractual Retailing

Independent retailers often attempt to achieve economies of operations and an increased market presence by integrating their operations with those of other retailers and wholesalers. By entering contractual arrangements, retailers can formalize the rights and obligations of each party in the contract. The terms of the contract can, and often do, cover all aspects of the retailer's product, place, price, and promotional activities. **Contractual retailing** exists in several forms, but the four most common forms are retailer-sponsored cooperative groups, wholesaler-sponsored voluntary chains, franchised retailers, and leased departments.

The **retailer-sponsored cooperative group** is a contractual organization formed by many small independent retailers and usually involves the common ownership of a wholesaler. Originally formed to combat competition from large chain organizations, this type of contractual system allows the small independent to realize economies of scale by making large-quantity group purchases. The contractual agreement usually requires individual members to concentrate their purchases of products from the cooperative wholesaler and, in turn, receive some form of patronage refund.

Associated Grocers and Certified Grocers are two large food wholesalers having cooperative contractual arrangements with independent food retailers.

The **wholesaler-sponsored voluntary chain** is a contractual arrangement in which a wholesaler develops a merchandising program that independent retailers voluntarily join. By agreeing to purchase a certain amount of merchandise from the wholesaler, the retailer is assured of lower prices. These lower prices are possible because the wholesaling organization can buy in larger quantities with the knowledge that it has an established market. The Independent Grocers Alliance (IGA) and Super Valu Stores, Inc., are both food wholesalers that sponsor voluntary chains. Other examples include Western Auto in the automotive and household-accessories market and Ben Franklin in the variety store market.

A large and growing percentage of retail marketing is conducted today through a franchise system, a form of retailing in which a parent company (franchisor) obtains distribution of its products, services, or methods through a network of contractually affiliated dealers (franchisees). The International Franchise Association defines **franchising** as "a continuing relationship in which the franchisor provides a licensed privilege to do business, plus assistance in organizing, training, merchandising, and management in return for a consideration from the franchisee."[20] In other words, what the franchisor offers the franchisee is a patterned way of doing business that includes product, price, place, and promotional strategies.

In practice, this means that the franchisee is the owner of his or her own business, distributing the goods or services of the franchisor and paying for that privilege through an initial fee and/or a percentage of future sales or profits. Though the franchisee owns the business, the franchisor usually exercises control over some aspects of its operation to ensure conformity to the franchisor's proven methods and standards for products, services, quality, and methods.

In return for the fees and royalties paid by the franchisee, the franchisor may provide some or all of the following services: (1) location analysis and counseling; (2) store development, including lease negotiations; (3) store design and equipment purchasing; (4) initial employee and management training, and continuing management counseling; (5) advertising and merchandising counsel and assistance; (6) standardized procedures and operations; (7) centralized purchasing with consequent savings; (8) financial assistance in the establishment of the business; (9) an exclusive territory in which to operate; and (10) the goodwill and recognition of a widely known brand or trade name.

Franchisors expect franchisees to conform to the business pattern and also to provide them with some form of compensation for their right to use the franchise. Franchisor compensation usually involves either one or a combination of the following:

1. *Initial franchise fee*—a fee that the franchisor charges up front for the franchisee's right to own the business and to receive initial services
2. *Royalties*—an operating fee imposed on the franchisee's gross sales
3. *Sales of products*—profits the franchisors make from sales to franchisees of raw and finished products, operating supplies, furnishings, and equipment
4. *Rental and lease fees*—fees that franchisors charge for the use of their facilities and equipment
5. *Management fee*—a fee that franchisors charge for some of the continuous services they provide the franchisee[21]

Business in the franchise system is thriving, both in terms of retail sales of goods and services through franchise outlets and in the growth of the number of franchises themselves. Retail sales of franchising companies in 1987 were estimated at $515.2 billion, or about 33 percent of total U.S. retail sales.[22] The Naisbitt Group, a national forecasting firm, predicts that by the year 2005 franchising will become a $1 trillion industry and account for 50 percent of all retail sales.[23]

Among the primary advantages of owning a franchise unit are that it usually requires less capital to set up a franchise than it would to start up independently; it is often unnecessary to possess knowledge about a particular type of business because of franchisor training programs; and business risk is frequently reduced because of the recognition and goodwill of the franchisor's name and product and through the initial and continued help the franchisor provides in running the business. Franchising, however, should not be considered an easy and failure-proof way to financial success. The franchisee faces a number of disadvantages. First, the relationship between the franchisor and franchisee usually involves control over many aspects of the franchisee's business operations, and some owners find that this overly inhibits their creativity and independence. Second, to acquire a blue-chip franchise such as a McDonald's or Pizza Hut requires considerable financial resources and high royalty payments. Someone wishing to purchase a McDonald's in 1986, for instance, was required to have $140,000 in unborrowed funds plus the ability to obtain outside financing for an additional $160,000 to $200,000, on top of which were added royalty and advertising fees of 15 percent of sales.[24] Third, the success of each individual franchise unit depends on the workings of the parent company, and even the best managers can find their business—and investment—jeopardized if trouble develops in the franchisor's operations. For example, more than 50 Arthur Treacher's Fish and Chips franchises went bankrupt in the mid-1980s after the parent company sold out to a new owner, who promptly changed practices and policies. Finally, experts urge those thinking of purchasing a franchise to remember that it is usually much more a full-time job than an investment, with most new owners finding themselves putting in well above an average work week. Said the president of the International Franchise Association: "Franchising brings opportunities, not miracles."[25]

Today, there are over 2,000 franchise companies involved in almost every type of retail business area, from molars to mufflers, as evidenced by The American Dental Centers joining Midas shops on the scene. In the 1980s, firms starting franchise operations for the first time were adding to this total at a rate of over 200 per year.

Franchise companies can be divided into two main types. The first are called *product or trade-name franchises* and are characterized by franchised dealers that carry one company's product line and identify their business with that company and product. Examples of this type include automobile dealers, gasoline stations, and soft drink bottlers. Together, product franchises accounted for an estimated 71 percent of franchise sales in 1987, though this percentage has been slowly decreasing. These types of operations are often referred to as manufacturer-sponsored and wholesaler-sponsored retailers (see Figure 2-9).

The second type is called *business format franchising,* or service firm-sponsored retailer, a system in which the franchisee not only carries the franchisor's products and trade name but the entire business format itself, from merchandising to store design (see Figure 2-9). Most aspects of the franchisee's operations are coordinated to ensure a certain and consistent image that is designed to appeal to particular market segments. This category includes restaurants (McDonald's), auto repair

FIGURE 2–9
Types of franchising
systems

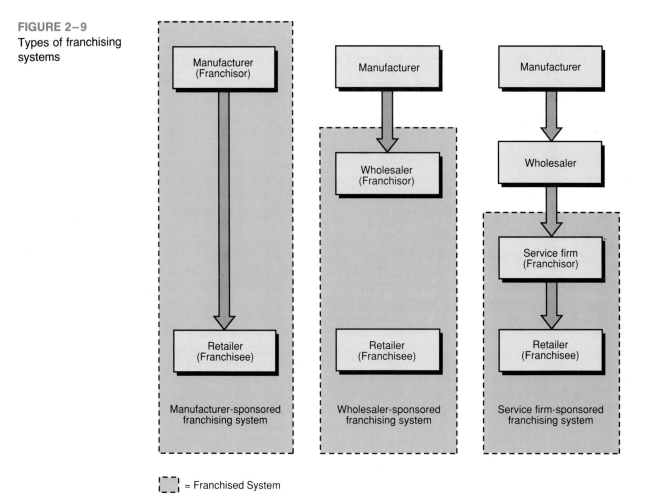

= Franchised System

shops (MAACO), personal and business services (H&R Block), and many others and is increasing at a much greater rate than product franchises. Sales in 1987 were an estimated $171 billion, compared with $141 billion in 1985, a 21-percent increase. Estimated sales for 1987 for various kinds of franchised businesses are shown in Figure 2–10.

The rapid rate of franchise sales growth experienced in the past three decades is expected to continue. This trend will be fueled by the entrance of many new and small companies into the franchise system, attracted by both the ability to expand rapidly despite limited company capital and the competitive advantages that franchising often can provide. Growing customer preference for convenience and consistent quality—two of franchising's principal strengths—should also accelerate franchise growth. Another important factor will be increasing activity by U.S. franchisors in foreign markets, a pattern that has developed significantly in the 1980s.

Much of the increase in domestic franchise sales is expected to come from the service sector. With the average age of the U.S. population rising and the increasing

**FIGURE 2–10**
Franchising in the economy: 1987[a]

| Kinds of Franchised Business | Establishments (No.) | | Sales ($000s) | |
|---|---|---|---|---|
| | Company Owned | Franchise Owned | Company Owned | Franchise Owned |
| Total, all franchising | 90,952 | 407,543 | 76,292,106 | 515,049,824 |
| Automobile and truck dealers | 0 | 27,750 | 0 | 305,617,000 |
| Automotive products and services | 5,214 | 35,157 | 4,503,595 | 8,406,869 |
| Business aids and services | 6,495 | 54,822 | 2,390,135 | 13,154,421 |
| Accounting, credit, collection agencies, and general business systems | 23 | 2,572 | 4,283 | 207,502 |
| Employment services | 1,865 | 4,107 | 1,455,125 | 2,109,520 |
| Printing and copying services | 142 | 5,831 | 35,656 | 1,188,017 |
| Tax preparation | 3,392 | 4,868 | 257,520 | 227,281 |
| Real estate | 335 | 15,822 | 89,700 | 5,832,465 |
| Miscellaneous business services | 738 | 21,622 | 547,851 | 3,589,636 |
| Construction, home improvements, maintenance and cleaning services | 776 | 21,389 | 1,443,857 | 3,493,430 |
| Convenience stores | 9,654 | 6,922 | 7,720,141 | 5,082,990 |
| Educational products and services | 537 | 8,567 | 140,560 | 710,637 |
| Restaurants (all types) | 26,293 | 60,106 | 10,376,297 | 37,574,835 |
| Gasoline service stations | 21,060 | 95,940 | 17,083,000 | 77,824,000 |
| Hotels, motels, and campgrounds | 1,206 | 7,372 | 4,945,493 | 11,783,961 |
| Laundry and drycleaning services | 269 | 2,888 | 52,931 | 372,115 |
| Recreation, entertainment, and travel | 484 | 8,460 | 881,605 | 2,309,470 |
| Rental services (auto–truck) | 2,479 | 9,041 | 3,737,836 | 2,800,299 |
| Rental services (equipment) | 511 | 2,392 | 292,385 | 524,000 |
| Retailing (nonfood) | 11,617 | 39,108 | 7,838,512 | 17,340,000 |
| Retailing (food other than convenience stores) | 3,742 | 19,795 | 3,134,185 | 8,508,334 |
| Soft drink bottlers | 122 | 1,128 | 1,603,000 | 18,429,000 |
| Miscellaneous | 493 | 6,706 | 138,574 | 1,118,463 |

[a]1987 data estimated by respondents.

Source: U.S. Department of Commerce, *Franchising in the Economy 1985–1987* (January 1987): 27.

number of two-earner families, forecasters see further creation of franchise opportunities in such areas as maid services, repair and home remodeling, carpet and other cleaning services, and various maintenance functions.

Franchises specializing in business services are expected to grow at an even faster rate, a product of the so-called "age of information" and the increasing preference of many firms to contract out functions they once performed internally. Growth is expected to come in franchises supplying services for businesses such as accounting, advertising, packaging and shipping, consulting, security, personnel, and copying and printing. Though there are currently many independent firms supplying these services to local businesses, some see them giving way to national or regional franchise operations in the coming years. Projected growth in various retail franchising categories is illustrated in Figure 2–11.

| Business Category | Sales ($ millions) | | Annual Growth (%) |
|---|---|---|---|
| | 1985 | 1990 | |
| Restaurants (all types) | 48,926 | 86,109 | 12.0 |
| Retailing (nonfood) | 18,790 | 33,560 | 12.3 |
| Hotels/motels/campgrounds | 14,631 | 22,511 | 9.0 |
| Convenience stores | 12,309 | 19,377 | 9.5 |
| Business services | 12,076 | 21,282 | 12.0 |
| Automotive products and services | 10,604 | 15,944 | 8.5 |
| Food retailing (other than convenience stores) | 10,370 | 14,544 | 7.0 |
| Rental services (auto–truck) | 5,282 | 8,900 | 11.0 |
| Construction and home services | 3,720 | 9,255 | 20.0 |
| Recreation/entertainment/travel | 1,840 | 6,573 | 29.0 |
| Total | 138,548 | 238,055 | 11.5 |

Source: The Nesbitt group, *Nation's Business* (February 1986): 44.

Other specific types of franchises targeted by the Commerce Department for above-average growth throughout the 1980s include weight control centers, hair salons, temporary help services, printing and copying services, medical centers, and clothing stores.[26]

**Leased departments** are retailers that operate departments (usually in specialized lines of merchandise) under contractual arrangements with conventional retail stores. Many supermarkets and department stores, for example, lease space to outside organizations to sell magazines (as in supermarkets) and auto supplies and shoes (as in many department and discount stores). The most frequently leased-out departments are beauty salon, books, cameras, candy, costume jewelry, electronics, family shoes, fine jewelry, furs, and photo.[27] The lessor usually furnishes space, utilities, and basic in-store services necessary to the lessee's operation. In turn, the lessee agrees to provide the personnel, management, and capital necessary to stock and operate a department with carefully defined merchandise. Generally, the contract calls for the lessee to pay the lessor either a flat monthly fee, a percentage of gross sales, or some combination of the two.

### Warehouse Retailing

The typical **warehouse** retailing operation involves some combination of warehouse and showroom facilities. In some cases, these facilities are located in separate but adjacent areas; in others, the warehouse and showroom are combined into one large physical structure. Generally, the warehouse retailer uses warehouse principles to reduce operating expenses and thereby offer discount prices as a primary customer appeal. Five types of warehouse retailers can be identified: warehouse showroom, catalog showroom, home center, hypermarkets, and warehouse clubs.

The **warehouse showroom** is generally a single-line hard-goods retailer that stocks merchandise such as furniture, appliances, or carpeting. To help the consumer make price comparisons with conventional home-furnishing retailers, the warehouse showroom typically stocks only well-known, nationally advertised brands. These retailers set up sample merchandise displays in showrooms so potential consumers can get an idea of what the products will look like in their homes. After making a selection, consumers immediately receive the merchandise in shipping cartons from the completely stocked adjacent warehouse. Although they prefer the "cash-and-carry" mode of operation, most warehouse retailers offer credit, delivery, and installation services. Warehouse retailers provide these services at an additional fee over the selling price. Because of space and delivery requirements, plus the need to attract consumers from a large market area, warehouse showroom locations usually are freestanding sites near major traffic intersections such as interstate highway systems.

The **catalog showroom** is a warehouse retailer featuring hard goods such as housewares, small appliances, jewelry, watches, toys, sporting goods, lawn and garden equipment, luggage, stereos, televisions, and other electronic equipment at a discount. The distinguishing feature of the catalog showroom is that a merchandise catalog is combined with the showroom and an adjacent warehouse as part of the retailer's operation. By adding a catalog of products to showroom products, the retailer provides consumers with both an in-store and at-home method of buying merchandise.

Catalogs, which are generally issued biannually, sometimes incorporate a unique method of illustrating the discounted price. List prices appear in plain bold numerals while the actual discounted prices are the last several digits of a code. This method often accentuates the discount nature of the price by forcing the customer to calculate the difference. The price tags on the sample merchandise on display in the showroom incorporate the same pricing method. As with the warehouse showroom, the catalog showroom features nationally branded merchandise that facilitates consumer price comparisons with conventional hard-goods retailers.

For consumers, the typical shopping trip to a catalog showroom involves (1) filling out an order form using the merchandise/price code found on either the showroom price tag or in the catalog, (2) ordering and paying for merchandise at a cashier's desk, and (3) picking up the merchandise at a pick-up desk. The pick-up desk is directly connected to an adjacent warehouse containing a complete stock of merchandise. Best Products, Consumers' Distributing, and Service Merchandise are the three companies that account for the bulk of catalog showroom sales.[28]

The modern **home center** combines the traditional hardware store and lumberyard with a self-service home-improvement center. The typical merchandise mix includes a wide variety and deep assortment of building materials, hardware, paints, plumbing and heating equipment, electrical supplies, power tools, garden and yard equipment, and other home-maintenance supplies. Some home centers have also expanded their merchandise offerings to include household appliances and home furnishings. Home centers usually have large showrooms that display sample merchandise (large, bulky items) and complete stock (small, standardized items). Consumers purchase showroom sample merchandise by placing an order at the order desk, and clerks pull the order from adjacent warehouse stocks. Customers simply serve themselves with showroom stock. While appealing to all home owners, the home center has been particularly successful in appealing to the "do it yourselfer." By providing customers with information on materials and equipment and by offering "how-to" services, home centers have developed a strong customer following. Major home center operators include Mr. How, Home Depot Inc., K mart's Builders' Square, Payless Cashways, and Handy Dan.

The **hypermarket** is a general-merchandise warehouse retailer that stocks and sells food products and a wide variety of both hard and soft goods. Operating out of a warehouse, the hypermarket displays offerings in wire baskets, metal racks, wooden bins, and simple stacks of merchandise that often reach heights of 12 to 15 feet. A self-service retailer with central checkouts and a sophisticated system of materials handling, the hypermarket attempts to underprice traditional retailers by as much as 15 to 20 percent. A European innovation, the hypermarket is making inroads into U.S. retailing. One example is the 245,000-square-foot hypermarket that Meijer, Inc., built near Detroit. Recent entries into the hypermarket field include Bigg's in Cincinnati (joint venture between French-based Euromarche and American-based SuperValue) and Wal-Mart's new Hypermart USA in Texas.[29]

**Warehouse clubs** are "huge outlets open to members only and typically sell merchandise at 20 to 40 percent below prices at supermarkets and discount stores."[30] As a special type of discount house, warehouse clubs are also referred to as wholesale clubs, membership clubs, and wholesale centers.[31] The principal players in the warehouse club market are identified in Figure 2–12. Most warehouse

**FIGURE 2–12**
The warehouse club merchandisers

| Company | Number of Outlets | Membership Policy | |
|---|---|---|---|
| | | Wholesale | Retail |
| B. J.'s Wholesale Club (Zayre) | 8 | $30 annual fee; up to two additional memberships $10 each | 5% markup |
| Buyers Club | 2 | [not available] | |
| Club Mart of America | 1 | [not available] | |
| Club Wholesale (Elixir) | 2 | $25 annual fee | 5% markup |
| Costco Wholesale Club | 21 | $25 annual fee | 5% markup |
| Metro Cash & Carry of Illinois | 3 | No fee | 5% markup |
| Money's Worth | 1 | $25 annual fee | 5% markup |
| Pace Membership Warehouse | 15 | $25 annual fee | 5% markup |
| Price Club | 24 | $25 annual fee | Either $15 annual fee and 5% markup or $25 annual fee without 5% markup |
| Price Savers (Kroger) | 5 | $25 annual fee | 5% markup |
| Sam's Wholesale Club | 23 | $25 annual fee | 5% markup |
| Super Saver | 9 | [not available] | |
| The Warehouse Club (joint partnership with W. R. Grace) | 7 | $25 annual fee | 5% markup |
| The Wholesale Club | 5 | $25 annual fee | 5% markup |
| Wholesale Plus | 1 | $25 annual fee | 5% markup |
| Value Club | 5 | $25 annual fee | $5 fee and 5% markup |

Source: Jack G. Kaikati, "The Boom in Warehouse Clubs," *Business Horizons* (March–April 1987): 72.

clubs have a two-tiered membership plan: (1) wholesale members who pay an annual fee and must be operators of small businesses and (2) group members who usually pay about 5 percent above the ticket price of the merchandise. The principal retail mix strategies are as follows:

- ☐ Product mix—a vast array of product categories but a limited selection of the best selling brands, sizes, and models in each category
- ☐ Service mix—cash and carry business with limited hours and no amenities (e.g., bathrooms)
- ☐ Place mix—large (100,000 square feet) bare-bones facilities (warehouse) located in out-of-the-way low-rent locations
- ☐ Price mix—rock-bottom wholesale prices that produce paper-thin gross margin profits (10 to 11 percent)
- ☐ Promotional mix—minimal advertising (less than 1/2 percent of sales) supported by minimal sales support, visual merchandising, and sales incentives

## Nonstore Retailing

**Nonstore retailing** involves retailers that do not use conventional store facilities as part of their standard mode operation. Nonstore, direct marketing methods are used to target a select group of consumers.[32] A major strategy of the nonstore retailer is to take the "store" (i.e., party, catalog, videodisc) to the customer rather than wait for the customer to come to the retailer (i.e., store). Nonstore retailers include a wide variety of retailing formats; Figure 2–13 identifies those formats.

**At-home retailing** is the market approach of making personal contacts and sales in the consumers' homes. This form of retailing offers the consumer the ultimate in *place convenience* and, with some planning on the part of the salesperson (such as making an appointment), can provide an equal amount of *time convenience*. At-home retailing provides several other advantages to the consumer. First, it is a highly personalized service because of the one-on-one relationship between the customer and salesperson. Second, at-home retailing aids consumers in making a product evaluation before the purchase by letting them try the product in a home setting. Next, it saves the consumer the time and effort of going to the store, searching for needed merchandise, and waiting in checkout lines. Finally, this type of retailing usually includes home delivery, which appeals to most customers, especially the elderly.

At-home retailing also offers the seller certain advantages, including (1) no direct competition because the seller presents its products in "isolation" in the home, where consumers cannot make direct comparisons with similar products; (2) avoidance of uncontrollable intermediaries; and (3) elimination of investments in stores and other facilities because sales representatives are compensated on a commission basis and pay their own expenses.

The at-home method of retailing, also referred to as "door-to-door" and "house-to-house" selling, exists in several forms. The three principal forms are the cold-canvass, the established territory or route, and the party plan. The *cold-canvass method* involves soliciting sales door-to-door without either advance selection of homes or prior notice to potential consumers of an intended sales call. Vacuum cleaners, magazines, and books are some of the more common products sold by the cold-canvass method. The *established territory method* assigns salespeople to prescribed geographical areas, in which they must make their door-to-door sales and delivery calls at regular, predetermined time intervals. Some of the best-known users of the established territory method are Avon (cosmetics), Fuller Brush (household products), Stanley Home Products (household products), and Sarah Coventry (jew-

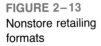

**FIGURE 2–13**
Nonstore retailing formats

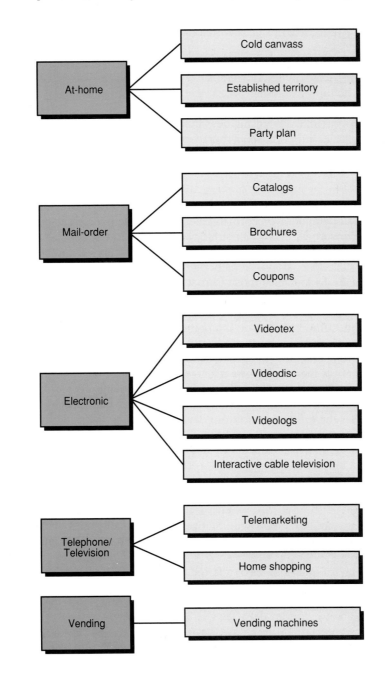

elry). The *party plan method* of at-home retailing requires a salesperson to make sales presentations in the home of a host or hostess who has invited potential customers to a "party." Usually, the party plan includes various games and other entertainment activities in which participants receive small, inexpensive gifts. Closing the sale occurs when the salesperson takes orders from the people attending the party. As a reward for holding the party, the host or hostess receives either cash or gifts from the salesperson. Tupperware and Wearever Aluminum Products make extensive use of the party method. Toys, books, home-decorating products, household goods, jewelry, health and beauty aids, and apparel are just a few of the products sold in this manner.

Mail-order sales to the final consumer was a $33.6 billion business in 1987.[33] **Mail-order retailers** use business formats that contact prospective customers by mail, receive orders by mail, and/or make deliveries by mail. Mail-order operations vary significantly in terms of their merchandise lines and operations (i.e., methods of customer contact, order placement, and delivery arrangements). As we shall see, "mail-order" probably is a misnomer for the modern mail-order retailer.

Mail-order operations differ tremendously in the variety and assortment of merchandise lines they offer the mail-order customer. Three important types of mail-order operations have been identified. The *general merchandise mail-order house* is a mail-order retailer offering a wide variety of merchandise lines. The depth of the assortment within each merchandise line varies among houses and among lines. Sears, J. C. Penney, and Spiegel of Chicago all operate general merchandise mail-order operations. The second type of mail-order operation is the *novelty mail-order retailer* whose lines are often limited to unusual products not normally carried by conventional retailers. Frequently, the novelty operator directs merchandise appeals to a small market segment. For example, intimate wearing apparel, unusual reading materials, specialized sporting equipment, exotic foods, unusual hobby equipment, and novel gifts are the kind of merchandise that novelty mail-order retailers sell. The Sharper Image is an excellent example of this type of cataloger. The third type of mail-order retailing is the *supplementary mail-order operations of department and specialty stores*. Many conventional department and specialty stores offer mail-order service for the convenience of their customers. The Neiman-Marcus Christmas catalog and the "Hot Properties" life-style catalog by Marshall Field exemplify this type of mail-order retailing.[34]

Because of different operating characteristics, three forms of mail-order retailing have emerged. They are catalogs, brochures, and coupons. Any given mail-order retailer can use one or any combination of these three forms.

*Catalog operations* involve the use of specially prepared catalogs that present the retailer's merchandise both visually and verbally. Basic product assortment (sizes, colors, materials, styles, models, etc.) and pricing information are included along with directions stating how to order on the order blanks provided. Modern catalog operations allow the customer to place orders by mail, telephone, or in person at a catalog desk. In addition, catalog operations offer a variety of delivery arrangements such as mail, parcel post, express service, customer pickup, and store delivery.

Some retailers use a brochure form of mail-order retailing by preparing a small booklet or leaflet that they mail to potential consumers. The distinguishing feature of this type of brochure is that it usually displays only a limited number of product items that can attract consumer attention and interest. These interesting and attention-getting brochures usually emphasize either the innovative nature or the good value of the product.

The coupon form of mail-order retailing involves using magazine and newspaper advertisements. Advertisements featuring special merchandise and mail-order coupons are placed in magazines and newspapers that appeal to specific market segments. To some extent, most magazines and newspapers segment their markets either geographically (regional or local editions) or psychographically (subscribers to specialty publications usually have certain common activities, interests, and opinions).

**Electronic retailing** via electronic and video systems is in the innovation stage of the retail life cycle. Although a large number of potential electronic retailing options exist and the number of options is expected to expand as new technologies are brought on line, retailers are currently focusing their attention on videotex, videodisc, videologs, and interactive cable television.

*Videotex* is "an interactive electronic system in which data and graphics are transmitted from a computer network over telephone or cable lines and displayed on a subscriber's TV or computer-terminal screen."[35] The basic components and interactions of a videotex system appear in Figure 2–14.

Shopping with a videotex system consists of selecting from a series of choices, called menus, that are displayed on the screen. For example, a shopper narrows down the choice by selecting from a menu of product lines and product items (brands, styles, sizes, colors, prices, and so on). In addition to at-home shopping, videotex systems can provide subscribers a wide selection of services including news, weather, sports, financial, and consumer information; at-home banking, reservations, and travel information; electronic encyclopedias and magazines, videocoupons and educational/instructional games; directories; real-estate and employment listings; home energy management; security, medical, and fire monitoring; and electronic mail/messaging.

*Videodisc* "is an interactive electronic system that uses flat optical discs capable of storing vast amounts of information in the form of moving pictures, still pictures, printed pages, and sound—for display on a TV screen."[36] One such system is the "Electronic Bed and Bath Fashion Center" developed by the J. P. Stevens Co., an in-store videodisc, text, and printer information system that allows consumers to see and purchase virtually the entire product line. "A printout from the Stevens unit gives a record of the entire order for the customer . . . the customer is helped at the console by a store salesperson specially trained by Stevens. After she punches all her keypad buttons, she is given the order printout, which must be taken to a cashier for completion of the sale."[37]

*Videologs* are shop-at-home videotapes. In essence, it is the next wave of catalog shopping. "Customers either receive the video for free by mail or pay a fee that is credited toward any purchase."[38] A third distribution alternative is to make the videologs available free-of-charge to customers through video stores; however, the video must be returned to the video store. Videologs can be produced to reflect product usage, consumers' life-styles, or any other merchandising theme that might prove successful. The two-fold sight and sound appeal provides a competitive edge over the sight-oriented printed catalog.

*Interactive cable television* provides the ultimate in shopping convenience; it "permits viewers to purchase merchandise displayed on their television screens and

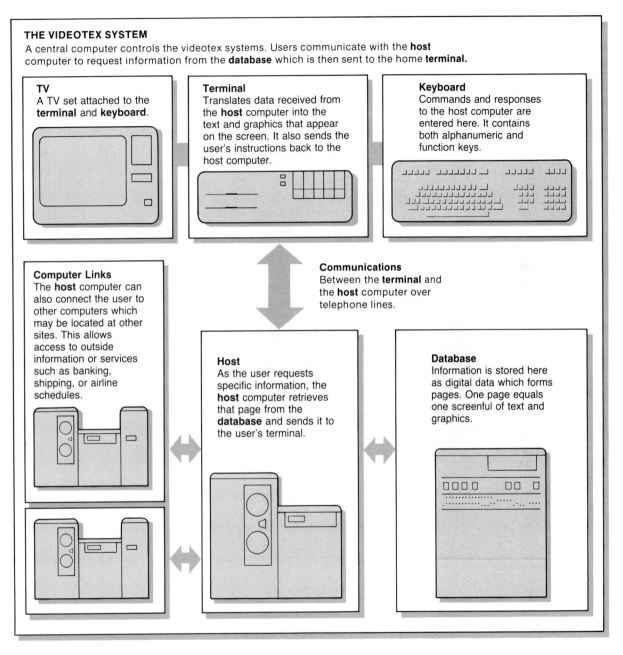

**THE VIDEOTEX SYSTEM**
A central computer controls the videotex systems. Users communicate with the **host** computer to request information from the **database** which is then sent to the home **terminal.**

**TV**
A TV set attached to the **terminal** and **keyboard**.

**Terminal**
Translates data received from the **host** computer into the text and graphics that appear on the screen. It also sends the user's instructions back to the host computer.

**Keyboard**
Commands and responses to the host computer are entered here. It contains both alphanumeric and function keys.

**Computer Links**
The **host** computer can also connect the user to other computers which may be located at other sites. This allows access to outside information or services such as banking, shipping, or airline schedules.

**Communications**
Between the **terminal** and the **host** computer over telephone lines.

**Host**
As the user requests specific information, the **host** computer retrieves that page from the **database** and sends it to the user's terminal.

**Database**
Information is stored here as digital data which forms pages. One page equals one screenful of text and graphics.

**FIGURE 2–14**
Basic components and interactions of a videotex system (source: Tom Mach, "High-Tech Opportunities Getting Closer to Home," *Advertising Age,* 16 [April 1984]. Copyright Crain Communications Inc. Reprinted by permission.)

charge the cost to a credit card or bank account by punching a keypad."[39] Warner-Amex Cable Communications QUBE service in Columbus, Ohio, is one example of this type of electronic retailer.

Telephone (telemarketing) and the telephone/television (home shopping) business formats are two more methods of nonstore retailing that are experiencing impressive growth rates. In recent years, **telemarketing**—the selling of goods and services through telephone contact—has helped some retailers increase service satisfaction by providing greater customer convenience. For customers who want to avoid traffic congestion and parking problems, telephone shopping is a desirable alternative. This form of retailing also can be of service to shut-ins, the elderly, parents with babysitting problems, working people who do not have time to shop, and consumers who do not like to shop.

Retailers' major reasons for using telephone retailing are that it (1) provides customers with information on new merchandise and upcoming sales events, (2) allows customers to order merchandise that retailers are willing to deliver to the customers' homes, and (3) gives consumers a convenient way to hold merchandise that they can pick up at a later date.

Home shopping combines two of America's favorite pastimes—watching television and going shopping. A price-value–oriented retailing operation, *home shopping* is a business format whereby (1) merchandise items are displayed, described, and demonstrated on television; (2) customers order the merchandise by calling a toll-free number; (3) customers pay for the order by credit cards, C.O.D., or check; (4) the retailer (home-shopping network) delivers the merchandise by United Parcel Service (UPS) or some other parcel post company; and (5) the retailer typically offers money-back guarantees if the merchandise is returned within 30 days.[40] The principal players in the shop-by-television game are (1) Home Shopping Network, Inc., Clearwater, Florida; (2) Television Auction Shopping Program, Inc., of San Jose, California; and (3) Cable Value Network of Minneapolis, Minnesota. An analysis of the largest system, Home Shopping Network (HSN), found that:

1. Seventy-five percent of the merchandise offered by HSN consisted of manufacturers' overruns and closeouts, and the overstock inventory of wholesalers and retailers.
2. Twenty-five percent of the goods sold is special-order merchandise, much of it from foreign sources of supply.
3. The product mix is 25 percent jewelry, 15 to 20 percent electronics and phones, 15 percent soft goods, and the miscellaneous items contributes the remainder of the mix.
4. Fifty to seventy-five percent gross margins on jewelry and soft goods with price points of $30 to $70.[41]

Consumer demand for greater time and place convenience and concurrent technological developments spurred the successful introduction and market expansion of the self-contained, automatic vending machine in the late 1940s. Rather than competing with store retailing, **vending machine retailing** became a complement of the store's operations by vending products that are usually a nuisance to handle within conventional store operations. On a much smaller scale, vending machines are similar to convenience store retailing in that they usually serve to meet the "fill-in," "emergency," and "after- or off-hour" needs of consumers.

Products that vending machines dispense have several characteristics in common. They typically are small, branded, and standardized products of low-unit value. Candies, soft drinks, hot beverages, and cigarettes are the most popular vending machine items. Among other food products commonly sold in vending machines are milk, snack foods, bakery products, and sandwiches. Nonfood products frequently sold by vending machines include life insurance policies for air travel, postage stamps, newspapers, ice, health and beauty aids, and some novelty items. One of the most significant developments in the use of vending machines is in the field of entertainment. Jukeboxes, pinball machines, and electronic games have greatly expanded the sales potential of vending operations.

Retailing and the institutions of retailing are still undergoing numerous changes in response to numerous environmental trends. Innovative merchandising strategies and operational methods are constantly being developed to meet these competitive challenges. What the future will bring to the everchanging retailing world is a matter of speculation. Given that "the past is the key to the future," however, some retailing experts have identified patterns of competitive change that they express as theories of retail institutional change. Four of the more commonly accepted theories are the wheel of retailing, the dialectic process, the retail accordion, and the theory of natural selection.

**THE CHANGING CHARACTER OF RETAIL INSTITUTIONS**

### Wheel of Retailing

One of the most widely recognized theories of retail institutional change is the **wheel of retailing**. First hypothesized by Malcolm P. McNair, the wheel of retailing states that the dynamics of institutional change are a "more or less definite cycle"; the cycle "begins with the bold new concept, the innovation" and ends with "eventual vulnerability . . . to the next fellow who has a bright idea."[42] A careful examination of the wheel theory reveals three distinct phases to each cycle and that a pattern of cycles will develop over a period of time. Figures 2–15 and 2–16 illustrate the three phases

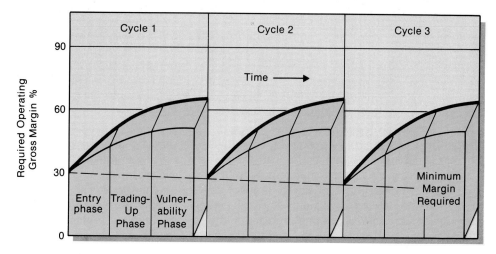

**FIGURE 2–15**
The wheel of retailing

FIGURE 2–16
The retailer and the
wheel of retailing

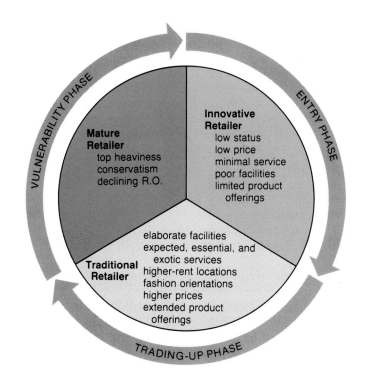

of entry, trading up, and vulnerability and how each cycle might be repeated to form a wavelike pattern.

*Entry Phase.* In the first phase of the cycle, an innovative retailing institution enters the market as a low-status, low-price competitor. By reducing operating expenses to a minimum, the new institution can operate at a gross margin substantially below (e.g., 30 percent as opposed to 50 percent) the required gross margins of the more established retailers in the market. Operating expenses usually are maintained at low levels by (1) offering minimal customer services, (2) providing a modest shopping atmosphere in terms of exterior and interior facilities, (3) occupying low-rent locations, and (4) offering limited product mixes. Generally, market entry is easier for retailers selling low-margin, high-turnover products. Although consumers and competitors consider the innovative institution low-status, it does gain market penetration primarily on the basis of price appeals. Once the new form of retailing has become an established competitor, it enters the second phase of the cycle.

*Trading-Up Phase.* Emulators quickly copy the successful innovation because of its success and market acceptance. The competitive actions of these emulators force the original innovative business to differentiate itself by engaging in the process of trading up. The trading-up phase of the cycle involves various changes to upgrade and distinguish the innovative institution.[43] Trading up usually takes the form of acquiring more elaborate facilities, offering expected and exotic as well as essential services, and locating in high-rent neighborhoods. Also, product lines frequently are traded up to include high-markup items, often with a fashion orientation. The end result of the trading-up phase is that the original innovative institution matures into a higher-status, higher-price operation with a required operating gross margin comparable to that of many established competitors. In other words, the innovative institution matures into a traditional retail institution.

*Vulnerability Phase.* With maturity, the now-established innovative institution enters a phase "characterized by top-heaviness, conservatism, and a decline in the rate of return on investments."[44] Eventually, the original innovator becomes vulnerable "to the next fellow who has a bright idea and who starts his business on a low-cost basis, slipping in under the (price) umbrella that the old-line institutions have hoisted."[45] The entry of a new low-price innovator into the retail market signals the end of one cycle and the beginning of a new competitive cycle.

In practice, the theory of the wheel of retailing has been used to explain numerous changes in the institutional structure of U.S. retailing. In the food industry, the independent corner grocery store was replaced to a large extent by the chain grocery store, which in turn, became vulnerable to the competition of the supermarket operation. A second commonly cited example of the "wheel" concept is the emergence of the department store innovation as an alternative to the small specialty retailer, and its subsequent vulnerability to discount retailers. Recently, some discount retailers have progressed far enough into the trading-up phase that they, in turn, are becoming vulnerable to discount warehouses, showroom operations, and off-price retailers.

## Dialectic Process

The **dialectic process** is a "melting pot" theory of retail institutional change in which two substantially different competitive forms of retailing merge together into a new retailing institution, a composite of the original two forms. Figure 2–17 illustrates the dialectic process, involving a thesis (the established institutional form), an antithesis (the innovative institutional form), and a synthesis (the new form drawn from the other two). The dynamics of the dialectic process, as outlined by Maronick and Walker, are as follows:

> In terms of retail institutions, the dialectic model implies that retailers mutually adapt in the face of competition from "opposites." Thus, when challenged by a competitor with a differential advantage, an established institution will adopt strategies and tactics in the direction of that advantage, thereby negating some of the innovator's attraction. The innovator, meanwhile, does not remain unchanged. Rather, as McNair noted, the innovator over time tends to upgrade or otherwise modify products and institutions. In doing so, he moves toward the "negated" institution. As a result of the mutual adaptions, the two retailers gradually move together in terms of offerings, facilities, supplementary services, and prices. They thus become indistinguishable or at least quite similar and constitute a new retail institution, termed the synthesis. This new institution is then vulnerable to "negation" by new competitors as the dialectic process begins anew.[46]

## Retail Accordion

The **retail accordion** theory (also known as the general-specific-general process) is based on the premise that the changing character of retail competition stems from strategies that alter the width (selection) of the merchandise mix.[47] Historically, retail

FIGURE 2–17
The dialectic process

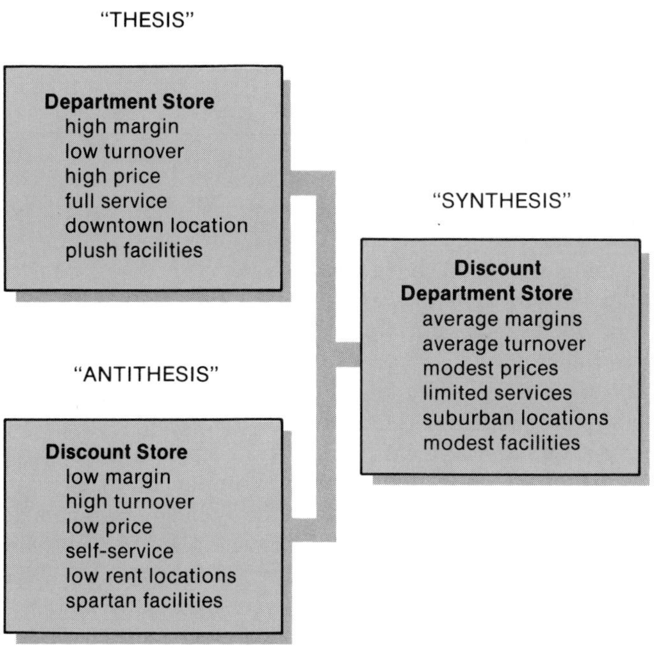

"THESIS"

**Department Store**
high margin
low turnover
high price
full service
downtown location
plush facilities

"SYNTHESIS"

**Discount
Department Store**
average margins
average turnover
modest prices
limited services
suburban locations
modest facilities

"ANTITHESIS"

**Discount Store**
low margin
high turnover
low price
self-service
low rent locations
spartan facilities

institutions have evolved from general store (offering a wide variety of merchandise) to the specialty store (offering a limited variety of merchandise) back to general-line stores and so on. The term accordion is used to suggest the alternating expansion and contraction of the retailer's merchandise mix. As described by Ralph Hower in his book, *The History of Macy's of New York:*

> Throughout the history of retail trade (as, indeed in all business evolution) there appears to be an alternating movement in the dominant method of conducting operations. One swing is toward the specialization of the function performed on the merchandise handled by the individual firm. The other is away from such specialization toward the integration of related activities under one management or the diversification of products handled by a single firm.[48]

Figure 2–18 provides one author's interpretation of the retail accordion.

### Natural Selection

The concept of the "survival of the fittest" is the central theme in Darwin's theory of **natural selection**. Environmental suitability and adaptive behavior are necessary traits for the long-term survival of a species. The species most willing and able to adapt to changing environmental conditions is the one most likely to prosper and grow. An unwillingness or inability to change could result in a species stagnation or possible extinction. As an economic species, competitive retailers are both willing and able to change and adapt to the environmental conditions under which they operate. The potential list of environmental conditions that might require adaptive behavior on the part of the retailer is almost endless. In general terms, the dynamic environments of

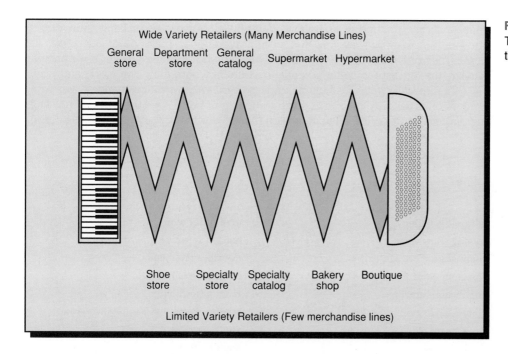

FIGURE 2-18
The retail accordion
theory

retailing include changes in the social, cultural, political, legal, technological, economical, and competitive structure of the marketplace. Required adaptions by retailers might include alterations in the product, price, place, and/or promotional mix offered to the retailer's targeted consumers.

**SUMMARY**

The retailer must operate in a very complex competitive environment. Retail competition can take one of several forms: intratype, intertype, vertical, and systems. Retailers also face different levels of competition as defined by the number, size, and quality of competitors.

The various types of retailing institutions are distinguishable on the basis of product-line variety, organizational structure, price appeals, customer convenience, and many other criteria. Based on the variety of product lines offered and their organizational structure, retailers are classified as either specialty or department stores. Chain stores are multiunit retailers that use a high degree of centralization in their operations. The discounter and off-price retailer emphasize price by offering nationally branded and designer merchandise at below market prices. A major development in food retailing has been the supermarket with its emphasis on a complete, self-serve product offering. Time and place convenience distinguish the convenience store in its efforts to provide the "fill-in" and "emergency" needs of consumers. Some retailers try to formalize their relationships with suppliers and other retailers by entering a contractual arrangement. The retailer-sponsored cooperative group, the wholesaler-sponsored voluntary chain, the franchising organization, and the leased department are all examples of contractual retailing. Other retailers tend to stress a certain method of operation. Warehouse showrooms, catalog showrooms, and home centers are retailers that employ warehouse methods of operation. At-home, mail-order, telephone, electronic, and vending machine retailing are nonstore retailers that attempt to serve potential customers where they live, work, and play.

Theoretically, retail institutions undergo certain competitive changes over time. Four theories that help to explain these competitive changes are the wheel of retailing, the dialectic process, the retail accordion theory, and the theory of natural selection.

## STUDENT STUDY GUIDE

**KEY TERMS AND CONCEPTS**

at-home retailing

catalog showroom

chain store

close-out store

contractual retailing

convenience store

department store

dialectic process

discount store

electronic retailing

factory outlet

franchising

home center

hypermarket

intertype competition

intratype competition

leased department

mail-order retailers

natural selection

nonstore retailing

off-price retailer

retail accordion

retailer-sponsored cooperative group

specialty store

supermarket

systems competition

telemarketing

vending machine retailing

vertical competition

warehouse

warehouse club

warehouse showroom

wheel of retailing

wholesaler-sponsored voluntary chain

**REVIEW QUESTIONS**

1. Identify the four types of retail competition. Illustrate and describe each type of competition and provide two nontext examples of each type.
2. How are retailers classified? Identify the classification criteria and the types of retailers within each classification group. Provide trade examples (e.g., Sears, Ace Hardware, etc.) of each type of retailer.
3. What distinguishes specialty store retailing from other forms of retailing? Describe the key merchandising strategies employed by the specialty retailer.
4. Develop a profile of the operational and merchandising strategies of department stores.
5. Compare and contrast the merchandising tactics of the conventional discounter and the off-price retailer. How are they alike and how do they differ?
6. How are supermarkets attempting to negate the competitive threat posed by the fast-food industry? What other competitive merchandising trends are currently being employed by the supermarket industry to be more competitive?

7. What is contractual retailing? Describe the four types of contractual retailers.
8. Describe the similarities and differences of the various types of warehouse retailers.
9. What are the customer and retailer advantages and disadvantages of at-home shopping. Do the advantages and disadvantages vary with the form of at-home retailing?
10. Why do retailers use telephone retailing?
11. Outline the differences between videotex, videodisc, and videolog methods of electronic retailing.
12. What is the basic premise of the wheel of retailing theory of institutional change? Characterize the three phases of the wheel.
13. What does the dialectic model of retail institutional change imply?
14. How does the concept of "survival of the fittest" describe the competitive conditions faced by retailers?

---

True or False

**REVIEW EXAM**

_____ 1. Intertype competition exists between two or more retailers using different types of business formats to sell the same type of merchandise.
_____ 2. Specialty store retailers typically stock a limited variety of product lines with a limited assortment or selection within each line.
_____ 3. To appeal to both middle- and upper-income consumers, many department stores use two or three pricing points for most merchandise lines.
_____ 4. A local retail firm operates a hardware store, a drugstore, a sporting goods shop, and a supermarket; it is by definition a retailing chain.
_____ 5. A major reason why conventional discount stores sell name-brand merchandise at below-market prices is to enhance their discount image.
_____ 6. The hypermarket is a general merchandise warehouse retailer that stocks and sells food products, as well as a wide variety of hard and soft goods.
_____ 7. Videotex is an interactive electronic system in which data and graphics are transmitted from a computer network over telephone or cable lines and displayed on a subscriber's TV or computer-terminal screen.
_____ 8. The basic premise of the retail accordion theory is that a retail institution facing competition will adopt strategies and tactics of the competitor and will eventually become just like the competitor.

**STUDENT APPLICATIONS MANUAL**

---

1. Retail competition intensifies each year. With increased competition more and more retailers are relying on price reductions to sustain sales volume. Having no unique differential advantage, me-too retailers are competing with each other to become the lowest-cost supplier of goods to the ultimate consumer. Conduct a search of the trade literature and find the answer to these questions: (1) Why is retail competition increasing? Identify the major reasons or causes for this increase. (2) What methods are being used by retailers to avoid or lessen the effects of greater competition? (3) How are retailers differentiating themselves from their competitors?

2. Review the list of the top fifty chain store operations (see Figure 2–2). Classify the organizations on the list as to the type of retail operation each represents (e.g., specialty, de-

**PROJECTS: INVESTIGATIONS AND APPLICATIONS**

partment, off-price, warehouse showroom, etc.). Which type of retail organization is the largest in terms of sales volume and number of units? Which type of retailer is the most productive in terms of earnings? Can you explain why one type of retailer must be more productive than the others?

3. Many upscaled department stores are turning to private brands and labels as a competitive measure to offset the inroads made by off-price retailers. Sears, on the other hand, is pursuing the opposite strategy. As a major private label merchandiser of hard goods (e.g., Kenmore and Craftsman), Sears is now adding national brands of hard goods to their product mix to expand their market appeal. Evaluate this product strategy. Do you think it is a good merchandising tactic? Explain and justify your answer.

4. Who's winning the "burger wars?" Analyze the data cited below. Describe the various ways in which the winner is outperforming the loser. Explain the "whys" of winning and losing by conducting your own field investigation of a Burger King and a McDonald's restaurant. Determine and describe the pros and cons of each operation relative to the problems of (1) offering the right product, (2) in the right quantities, (3) in the right place, (4) at the right time, (5) at the right price, and (6) by the right appeal.

|  | McDonald's | Burger King |
|---|---|---|
| Annual Sales | $12.4 billion | $5.03 billion |
| Advertising Spending | $329 million | $248 million |
| Sales per Store | $1.37 million | $1.00 million |
| Number of Stores Worldwide | 9,410 outlets | 5,179 outlets |
| Market Share Percentage | 46.4 percent | 18.8 percent |

5. Referring to the hypermarket format, the respected New York retail consultant, Arthur B. Britten, made the following statement: "I question whether people want to do their food shopping on the same trip that they do their clothes shopping." Do you agree with this statement? Why or why not? What merchandising tactics might the hypermarket employ to overcome the objection raised by Mr. Britten?

## CASES: PROBLEMS AND DECISIONS

### CASE 2–1
### Ray's Super—Responding to Competitive Threats*

#### BACKGROUND

"We can't make money on groceries," Ray Henry said, reacting to the recent price war that had turned the grocery business upside down. Henry is a manager of a moderate-size (20,000 square feet) supermarket operation located in a middle- to upper-income suburban area of the community. Until recently, the operation had managed to generate a reasonable return. New competition had begun to squeeze profits, however.

The area's economy was recovering from a recession that had reduced the population by seven percent because of job layoffs. Decreased volume placed greater importance on price competition. "Almost every trick of the trade was employed," Henry said, "including double and triple coupon redemptions." As a result, increases in area food prices were substantially below the national norm.

In the face of high labor costs, grocery chains attempted to negotiate wage concessions to improve profitability. Unsuccessful in this endeavor, National Groceries pulled out of the market, closing eight stores—including three large-scale superstores that had opened during the past two years.

*This case was prepared by Jeffrey Dilts, The University of Akron.

Sav-More, a regional grocery wholesale operation, responded by opening three of the former National superstores and converting five of its existing area stores to a super-discount warehouse format. An "Every Day Low Prices" policy on all items replaced weekly specials and double- and triple-coupon promotions. Sav-More advertising claimed price cuts on approximately 8,000 items, with the biggest cuts in packaged foods and paper goods.

Competitors, for the most part, responded in kind by cutting prices across the board. Overnight, the cost of a basket of 30 commonly purchased items had been reduced by an average of $7.89 in a majority of area stores.

## CURRENT SITUATION

Very concerned with the turn of events, Henry noted, "If this continues, I won't be able to stay in business." He suspected that the average purchase made in his store had declined, largely because of a reduction in volume for packaged goods. Revenues generated by perimeter departments, such as the deli and produce, appeared to be maintaining their previous levels.

Henry was not at a loss for alternatives; his personnel had recommended various solutions. He had to determine which action would help maintain customer patronage and build sales.

Mike Walle, assistant manager and part owner, had suggested an immediate price cut across the board to regain volume. Alf Dunlap, produce manager, disagreed because he thought such action would adversely affect profitability. On the basis of his previous management experience with a national chain, Dunlap argued that the size of the present store was not sufficient to generate the volumes necessary to be profitable at the lower margins suggested. Alternatively, he recommended that the operation build upon its strengths in perishables and personal service.

Ray Nader, head butcher, agreed that the operation could differentiate itself from competitors by employing service departments. "The main attraction of warehouse operations is price, not service," he commented. Accordingly, he recommended expanding the service areas to include a specialty fish department, based on customer suggestions. "The margin on specialty items and perishables can make up for the volume lost on low-margin packaged groceries," Nader pointed out.

## ASSIGNMENT

1. Evaluate the alternatives described in this situation. Under what conditions would one alternative be more appropriate than another?
2. What action would you recommend that Ray Henry take? Explain.

## CASE 2–2
## Quinn's Department Store—Using Leased Departments*

In his five years as president of Quinn's Department Stores, John Spalding had continued the local chain's successful strategy of catering to the upper-end consumer market with high-quality, distinctive merchandise, excellent service, and innovative product and marketing techniques. Sales growth at the flagship store downtown and the six branch stores in area shopping malls had been impressive under Spalding's leadership, attributable in part to his ability to identify and support profitable changes and innovations that maintain the stores' fashionable image and develop better ways to meet customer needs.

In this tradition, Spalding and other company executives had recently decided to add a new food department and accompanying "cafe" in the downtown store. Though many of

*This case was prepared by Dan Gilmore, The University of Akron.

the details had yet to be finalized, the plan called for the department to offer a variety of fancy, gourmet, and hard-to-find food and wine items, including many imported goods. Complementing this shop would be a delicatessen serving specialty salads and light meals for take-home or on-premise dining inside an open store "sidewalk cafe." The atmosphere of both the minigrocery and cafe was planned to exude fashionable elegance and feature expensive fixtures, lighting, and displays.

Spalding was convinced the concept would work. A few department stores in other areas of the country had been successful with similar ventures, and Spalding felt that Quinn's customer base would be especially receptive to the new offering, particularly because no grocery retailers in the downtown area offered the types of foods Quinn's planned to carry. "This department will have great appeal to the upscale shoppers whom we serve, provide them with an extra service not currently available in our market area, and make Quinn's a more enjoyable and distinctive place to shop," Spalding had told upper management at a recent meeting.

But while there was general agreement among store executives that the new department was right for Quinn's, there was considerable difference of opinion as to whether the grocery and deli should be run entirely by company personnel or be created and managed by an outside operator on a lease basis. "Leased departments" have been used by retailers for many years, particularly by department stores in such product areas as shoes, jewelry, millinery, books, and photography. After a period of decline in the early 1980s, these leased departments have enjoyed a resurgence in popularity in recent years.

Under most lease agreements, customers are unable to distinguish leased departments from store-owned ones. These departments are, however, operated by the lessee, who is responsible for buying and pricing its merchandise, hiring its employees, and managing daily operations. In return for a monthly rental and/or a pecentage of department sales, the leasing store typically provides services such as delivery, credit, payroll, accounting, utilities, and space lighting to the lessees. Many of these lessees are national companies that have departments in hundreds of different stores, though some operate on a much smaller regional or local basis.

Alex Archwell, Quinn's vice-president of marketing, favored leasing the new department, and had already conducted some preliminary discussions with a food retailer in a nearby city who operated several specialty food stores that were very similar in style and merchandise to that considered by Quinn's. Though this company had never before operated a leased department, its owner was enthusiastic about the prospect.

"John, these guys are just what we need to make a success of this thing," Archwell told his boss. "While I think the idea is great, what do we know about food retailing? For instance, I could see significant problems developing in inventory management. I think that leasing will enable us to provide the service we want as well as make a profit—with considerably less risk."

Jane Roberts, manager of the downtown store, disagreed. "Who knows and can serve our customers better than we can?" she asked. "Isn't that one of the reasons that we have avoided any lease agreements in the past, such as in shoes or jewelry? Besides, I think the quality of our in-store management is one of the chief factors in Quinn's success, and putting outsiders in control of even one of our departments is asking for trouble."

John Spalding had always had great faith in the judgment of both Archwell and Roberts and recognized that each of them raised important points with regard to the decision to lease or not lease the new department. He also realized that the new department's eventual success might well be dependent on the right choice being made about leasing. Earlier, he had been so confident that the fancy foods and sidewalk cafe idea would work in the main store that he had already thought about how long it would take before he could introduce similar departments in Quinn's branch stores. Now he realized that he would have to take a closer look at the practice of leasing and its desirability for Quinn's fancy foods department and cafe.

## ASSIGNMENT

1. Assume Mr. Spalding has asked you, a new Quinn's employee with college coursework in retailing, to help him analyze this situation. What do you see as the pros and cons of leased departments?
2. What decision would you recommend to Mr. Spalding for Quinn's fancy foods department and sidewalk cafe? Justify your decision.
3. If Quinn's decides to lease the new department, what can management do in terms of its relationship with the lessee to help ensure the project's long-term success?

**ENDNOTES**

1. Avijit Ghost, "Customer Service: The Key to Successful Retailing," *The Channel of Communication* 3 (Winter 1988): 1.
2. Joseph Barry Mason, "Redefining Excellence in Retailing," *Journal of Retailing* 62 (Summer 1986): 115.
3. Belinda Hulin-Sakin, "Value Heads Up the New Shopper List," *Advertising Age,* July 1983, 16.
4. Amy Dunkin and Michael Oneal, "Power Retailers," *Business Week,* 21 Dec. 1987, 86–89, 92.
5. Lois Therrien and Amy Dunkin, "The Wholesale Success of Factory Outlet Malls," *Business Week,* 3 Feb. 1986, 92, 94.
6. Gail Hutchinson Kirby and Rachel Dardis, "Research Note: A Pricing Study of Women's Apparel in Off-Price and Department Stores," *Journal of Retailing* 62 (Fall 1986): 329.
7. Joanne Cleaver, "New Leader Directs Carson's Rebuilding," *Advertising Age,* 9 Aug. 1984, 16.
8. Amy Dunkin, "How Department Stores Plan to Get the Registers Ringing Again," *Business Week,* 18 Nov. 1985, 66–67.
9. Joan O'C. Hamilton, "Why Rivals Are Quaking as Nordstrom Heads East," *Business Week,* 15 June 1987, 99–100.
10. Anthony Ramirez, "Department Stores Shape Up," *Fortune,* 1 Sept. 1986, 51–52.
11. "Specialty Store Strategy," *Stores* (October 1985): 58.
12. Michael Oneal, "Can Sears Get Sexier But Keep the Common Touch?" *Business Week,* 6 July 1987, 93–95.
13. Russell Mitchell, "How They're Knocking the Rust Off Two Old Chains," *Business Week,* 8 Sept. 1986, 45.
14. Todd Mason, "Sam Walton of Wal-Mart: Just Your Basic Homespun Billionaire," *Business Week,* 14 Oct. 1985, 143.
15. "Off-Pricers Grab Growing Retail Market Share," *Marketing News,* 3 March 1987, 9, 14.
16. Ibid.
17. Jules Abend, "Closing in on Closeouts," *Stores* (March 1986): 21.
18. "Consolidated Ups Share of Close-Out Market," *Chain Store Age Executive* (April 1987): 98.
19. "There's One for All," *Advertising Age,* Oct. 1983, M11; *Competitive Edge* (Barrington, IL: Willard Bishop Consulting Economists, June 1983).
20. U.S. Department of Commerce, *Franchise Opportunities Handbook* (Washington, D.C.: U.S. Government Printing Office, November 1986): XXIX.
21. Louis W. Stern and Adell I. El-Ansary, *Marketing Channels* (Englewood Cliffs, N.J.: Prentice-Hall, 1988), 341.
22. U.S. Department of Commerce, *Franchising in the Economy 1985–1987* (Washington, D.C.: U.S. Government Printing Office, January 1987): 15.
23. Thomas Petzinger, Jr., "So You Want to Get Rich?" *The Wall Street Journal,* 15 May 1987.

24. U.S. Dept. of Commerce, *Franchise Opportunities Handbook:* 141.
25. Ellen Paris, "Franchising—Hope or Hype?" *Forbes* 138 (Dec. 15, 1987): 43.
26. U.S. Department of Commerce, *Franchising in the Economy:* 6.
27. Lewis A. Spalding, "On Leased Departments," *Stores* (September 1987): 42.
28. Kimberly Carpenter, "Catalog Showrooms Revamp to Keep Their Identity," *Business Week,* 10 June 1985, 117.
29. Iris S. Rosenberg, "Hypermarkets Now!" *Stores* (March, 1988): 54–61.
30. Frank E. James, "Big Warehouse Outlet Breaks Traditional Rules of Retailing," *Wall Street Journal,* 22 Dec. 1983, 21.
31. This description of warehouse clubs is based on the excellent article by Jack G. Kaikati, "The Boom in Warehouse Clubs," *Business Horizons* (March/April 1987): 68–73.
32. Jean C. Darian, "In-Home Shopping: Are There Consumer Segments?" *Journal of Retailing* 63 (Summer 1987): 163–186.
33. Janice Steinberg, "Cacophony of Catalogs Fills All Niches," *Advertising Age,* 26 Oct. 1987, S-1.
34. Cara S. Trayer, "Retailers, Catalogers Cross Channels," *Advertising Age,* 26 Oct. 1987, S-8.
35. "Videotex: What It's All About," *Marketing News* (November 1983): 16.
36. Louis W. Stern and Adel I. El-Ansary, *Marketing Channels,* 3d ed. (Englewood Cliffs, N.J.: Prentice-Hall, 1988), 81.
37. JoAn Paganetti, "High-Tech Ads Gleam to Service with a Smile," *Advertising Age,* 25 July 1983, M24.
38. Wayne Walley, "Home Shopping Moves Onto Tape," *Advertising Age,* 16 Nov. 1987, 76.
39. Stern and El-Ansary, *Marketing Channels,* 81.
40. Betsy Lammerding, "Shopping by TV a Big Turn-On for Many Buyers," *Akron Beacon Journal,* 25 Jan. 1987, A-1, A-15.
41. Jules Abend, "Electronic Selling," *Stores* (November 1986): 23.
42. Malcolm P. McNair, "Significant Trends and Developments in Post War Period," in *Competitive Distribution in a Free, High-Level Economy, and Its Implications for the Universities,* ed. A.B. Smith (Pittsburgh: University of Pittsburgh Press, 1958): 18.
43. Arieh Goldman, "The Role of Trading-Up in the Development of the Retailing System," *Journal of Marketing* 39 (January 1975): 54–62.
44. Arieh Goldman, "Institutional Changes in Retailing: An Updated 'Wheel of Retailing' Theory," in *Foundations of Marketing Channels,* ed. A.G. Woodside, J.T. Sims, D.M. Lewison, and I.F. Wilkinson (Austin, TX: Lone Star, 1978), 193.
45. McNair, "Significant Trends and Developments," 18.
46. Thomas J. Maronick and Bruce J. Walker, "The Dialectic Evolution of Retailing," in *Proceedings: Southern Marketing Association,* ed. Burnett Greenburg (1974), 147.
47. See Stanley C. Hollander, "Notes On the Retail Accordion," *Journal of Retailing* 42 (Summer 1966), 20–40, 54.
48. Ralph Hower, *The History of Macy's of New York 1858–1919* (Cambridge, MA: Harvard University Press, 1943), 73.

# 3

## Outline

## Objectives

☐ Delineate the structure of buying populations and nature of buying behavior.

☐ Identify and explain U.S. population trends.

☐ Describe the major demographic population trends and their impact on retailing practices.

☐ Discuss the major geographic population patterns and their effect on retailing strategies.

☐ Understand the concept of product tangibility, durability, availability, and its impact on consumer buying behavior.

☐ Explain the concept of market potential and discuss the elements of the market potential equation.

☐ Describe the psychological, personal, and social factors that influence consumer buyer behavior.

☐ Outline and discuss the five stages of the consumer buying process.

# Retail Consumers and Their Buying Behavior

T he marketplace is the battleground for the recognition, acceptance, and adoption of various merchandising programs offered by competing retailers. An understanding of the marketplace and its behavior is essential to any successful marketing effort. After you have completed studying this chapter, you will have a deeper appreciation of the terrain in which the battle for profitable sales must be fought. More importantly, you will possess more of the information needed to develop a viable retailing plan and wage a successful merchandising campaign.

Fundamental to an understanding of the marketplace and its behavior is a definition of a market. The term *market* can be used in conjunction with a variety of places (i.e., going to the farmers' market or a trade show), products (i.e., the bond or housing market), levels (i.e., the wholesale or retail market), and activities (i.e., an individual who markets a good or a service). In this text, however, the term *market* has a precise meaning and usage. As shown in Figure 3–1, a **market** is a group of actual and potential buyers at a given time and place whose actions lead to an exchange of goods and services or create the potential for an exchange process. In essence, a market is a buying population and its corresponding buying behavior. An appreciation of the concept of a market dictates an understanding of both the structure of buying populations and the nature of their buying behavior.

## Structure of Buying Populations

Buying populations can be classified into one of two groups—consumer markets or organizational markets. **Consumer markets** are composed of individuals and/or households who are the ultimate consumers of goods and services. **Organizational markets** are composed of industrial firms, resellers, and governments who represent intermediate consumers of goods and services. This market accounts for the nonretail sales made by retailers. The discussion in this chapter, however, is limited to consumer markets and their impact on retail decisions. Regardless of consumer type, the structure of buying populations needs to be examined in terms of "how many are they" (population analysis), "who are they" (demographic analysis), and "where are they" (geographic analysis). (See Figure 3–2.)

FIGURE 3–1
A market definition

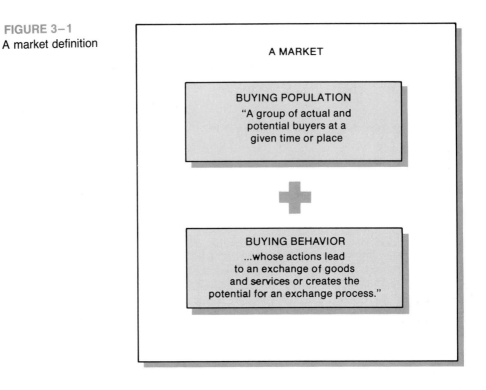

FIGURE 3–1
A market definition

## Nature of Buying Behavior

The second part of the market equation (see Figure 3–1) is buying behavior. Buyers act in a variety of ways when faced with a market situation that requires a purchase decision. The nature of buying behavior comprises a number of issues. An analysis of buying behavior is directed at answering the questions of "what buyers buy," "how much buyers buy," "who does the buying," "why buyers buy," "how buyers buy," and "where buyers buy" (see Figure 3–3).

The remainder of this chapter is devoted to an examination and discussion of the structure of consumer markets (e.g., population, demographic, and geographic analysis) and the nature of consumer buying behavior (e.g., what, how much, who, why, how, and where buyers buy).

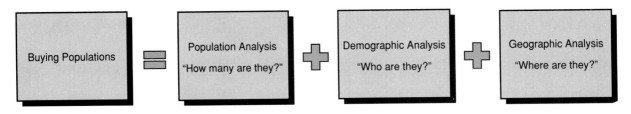

FIGURE 3–2
The structure of buying populations

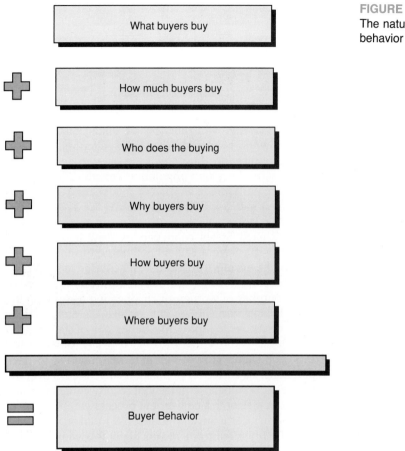

FIGURE 3–3
The nature of buying behavior

**CONSUMER MARKETS**

The consumer market is made up of ultimate consumers. Who are they? **Ultimate consumers** are individuals who purchase goods and services for their own personal use or for use by members of their household. The purchase intent of an ultimate consumer is to consume the utility of a product. As discussed in Chapter 1, sales to the ultimate consumer represent retail sales transacted by retailers, service firms, and to a lesser extent, wholesalers and other organizations.

**POPULATION ANALYSIS**

In this discussion of population analysis, we will examine the question of "how many ultimate consumers are there?" The actual and potential market for any particular product is determined in part by **total population**—the total number of persons residing within an area at a given time. An area's total population is determined by relationships between birthrates and deathrates and immigration and emigration rates. As illustrated in Figure 3–4, births and immigration are net contributors to an area's population whereas deaths and emigration reduce total population.

**FIGURE 3–4**

Determinants of total population

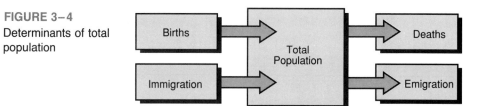

The past and projected population growth rates of the United States exhibit some noteworthy differences from world population growth experiences. Although the United States did experience a population "boom" for almost two decades, the nation celebrated its bicentennial by reaching **zero population growth** (ZPG); that is, the fertility rate fell below 2.0 children per average woman of childbearing age (fifteen to forty-four years). Fertility rates have increased somewhat during the 1980s but are projected to decline again during the 1990s.

The total population of the United States continued to grow in spite of its declining fertility rates (see Figure 3–6). Several factors contributed to this growth. First, the average life expectancy of the average American has increased as a result of improvements in diet and medical care. Second, the baby boom during the post-World War II years increased the number of women of childbearing age during the ZPG years. Finally, both legal and illegal immigration has swelled the nation's population figure as the United States continues to represent a better way of life for many peoples of the world.

The ebb and tide of U.S. population growth has and will continue to have profound merchandising implications. As each new population wave breaks over the retailing system, new target market opportunities emerge that require continuous and innovative adjustments. Classic examples of this adjustment process can be found in the baby products industry. The Gerber Company and Johnson & Johnson were both left with volatile markets as the birthrate fell from record highs following WWII to record lows during the ZPG years of the mid-1970s. Gerber answered the challenge by altering the exclusivity of its business. In contrast to its former slogan, today "babies are *not* Gerber's only business"; Gerber now markets insurance programs to "golden agers." In addition, Gerber diversified out of baby foods by "buying a maker of nursery lamps and other novelty items; a producer of cribs, dressers, and youth beds; and Biltrite Juvenile Products Co., which makes strollers, high chairs and carriages. . . . Gerber has also snapped up . . . the leading maker of car seats" for children.[1] Johnson & Johnson responded to the unsettling nature of their markets by repositioning their baby products for usage by adults. Their success in persuading adults to use baby shampoo and baby powder is evidenced by the large number of "me-too" products that competitors have introduced into the market.

Other companies have also adjusted to the changing baby business. In response to few children per family and the resulting desire for and the ability to buy additional and more upscaled products, the Health-Tex division of Chesebrough-Ponds stresses fashion for kids at moderate prices. Along the same theme, such fashionable items as Christian Dior Pajamas, Izod shirts, Norma Kamali jumpsuits, and Pierre Cardin diaper covers are being marketed for children. Retailers reacted to these population changes by (1) altering the width and depth of their product lines, (2) adjusting the amount and location of display space devoted to a particular product item, (3) changing the type and amount of promotional support used to enhance sales of certain products, and (4) adapting product-line pricing points to current market expectations.

Who is the "average American" or the "typical American family"? In past years reasonably descriptive profiles were possible. Today under novel family, marriage, living, and working arrangements, the average or typical profile is considerably less representative of the population as a whole. This section addresses the question of who the ultimate consumers are in terms of their demographic makeup. **Demography** is the study of statistics that are used to describe a population. Each person can be characterized in terms of age, sex, education, income, occupation, race, nationality, family size, and family structure. These individual characteristics can be aggregated into relatively homogeneous profiles of population groupings that represent consumer market segments and the opportunity to tailor a firm's marketing efforts to one or more of these segments (see Figure 3–5).

In the following discussion, we shall examine some of the more pronounced shifts in the demographic makeup of the U.S. population and the changes in marketing strategies and tactics that will be required to accommodate those shifts. Although demographic shifts are treated individually, you should be aware that all or most of these changes are interrelated.

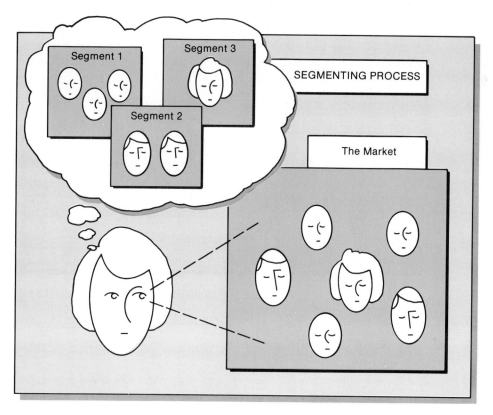

**FIGURE 3–5**

The market segmentation view of the total market

Segment 1

Segment 3

Segment 2

SEGMENTING PROCESS

The Market

## The Aging Population

The American population is aging as a result of a declining fertility rate and an increasing life expectancy. Consumer markets in the 1980s have been reshaped by the same baby boom generation that has had such a profound effect on marketing strategies for the last 30 years. It is the age group that created the 1950s infant market, the 1960s teenage market, the 1970s young adult market, and the 1980s middle-aged market. The realignment of the nation's population by age group is pictured in Figure 3–6.

As Figure 3–6 shows, the **youth market** (17 and under) is in the process of registering a notable 7.63 percent decrease; from 34.11 to 26.48 percent of the total U.S. population. Although this decline has signaled a de-emphasis in the youth-oriented marketing that has held center-stage since WWII, the absolute size of this age group (approximately one-fourth of the population) still makes it a formidable retail market. The importance of the youth market to most retailers is twofold. First, older youths have billions of dollars for discretionary spending on both nondurable and durable goods.[2] Important teen-oriented expenditures include fast foods, sporting equipment, casual clothing, audio and visual entertainment products, soft drinks, and personal accessories. Second, youths of all ages are major influencers on the buying behavior of their parents. They play an important role in deciding what products and brands are purchased, as well as when and where purchases are made. From the

**FIGURE 3–6**
Percentage change in total population by age group, 1970 to 1990 (source: U.S. Census Bureau, *Projections of the Population of the U.S., 1977 to 2050* [Washington, D.C.: U.S. Government Printing Office])

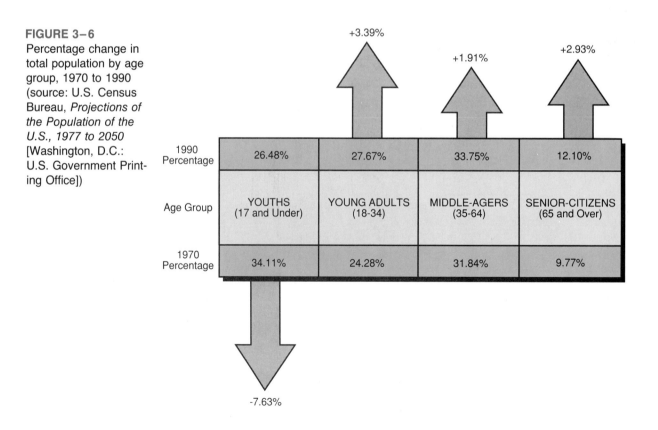

retailer's viewpoint, perhaps the most difficult aspect of merchandising this age group is the multiplicity of consumer life-styles and the dynamics of change that are associated with each life-style segment. It can be a very faddish world.

The coming of age of the baby boom generation is reflected in the significant growth (see Figure 3–6) of the **young-adults market** (ages eighteen to thirty-four). Within this age group, it is the older half (ages twenty-five to thirty-four) that accounts for the vast majority of this group's growth. Some demographers have painted a somewhat bleak picture for these tail-end members of the baby boom. With entry- and lower-level employment positions bulging with earlier baby boomers, these later cohorts are experiencing difficulties in satisfying career aspirations. Nevertheless, this age group will still seek to satisfy the needs associated with early adulthood. The demand for housing will continue to increase for both the single-family homes and apartments that cater to the growing number of single-adult, one-child, and childless households. Smaller domiciles and limited incomes suggest that successful merchandising to this group in the future will require smaller multipurpose appliances, do-it-yourself products, and durable household furnishings.

As seen in Figure 3–6, a modest increase (from 31.28 to 33.75 percent of the total U.S. population) is projected through 1990 for the **middle-aged market** (ages thirty-five to sixty-four). Beyond 1990, the relative size of this age group will continue to expand as late baby boomers enter middle age. Early middle-agers (thirty-five to forty-four), the fastest-growing market throughout the 1980s, can typically be characterized as a higher-income, free-spending group whose purchase motives are directed more at quality, durability, and variety. Today's late middle-agers (forty-five to sixty-four) contain a large number of empty-nest families wherein the parents feel free to spend on themselves and seem less intent on leaving an estate for their offspring. This attitudinal change reveals a big market for new retirement products, a trend that has not gone unnoticed by the financial community. In the 1980s, these affluent families will stimulate retail sales of top-of-the-line big-ticket items in a wide variety of product lines, such as autos and home furnishings. In general, consumers in their middle years will heighten demand for entertainment, travel, recreation, adult education, and other convenience- and experience-oriented goods and services. A major plus in retailing to this group is that they tend to have more established careers and community roots; therefore, they are less likely to move and represent a stationary market segment that is conducive to target marketing efforts.

A significant increase in the **senior-citizens market** will occur over the next several decades. According to the Census Bureau estimates, the percentage of the population aged sixty-five and over is expected to increase from 11.4 percent in 1981 to 13.1 percent in 2000 and 21.7 percent in 2050. Marketers should also take note that the market potential of the upper end of the senior-citizens market will be notably greater in the future. For example, the percentage of the population aged eighty-five and over is projected to grow from 1.0 percent in 1981 to 1.9 percent in 2000 and 5.2 percent in 2050. The senior-citizen market has changed drastically in recent years. Because of the fact that people are living longer, a life span of 20 to 25 years following retirement, they are faced with a wide variety of buying concerns. Age-based merchandising strategies are often inappropriate because it is usually a mistake to sell products to older people by telling them it's a product designed for the elderly. A more effective strategy is to sell product benefits that fit the interests and aspirations of this age group. "Marketers should avoid age typing products in their messages."[3] In product and service lines such as food, housing, clothing, transportation, health care, personal care, and recreation, the senior-citizen's share of the market is greater than that suggested by their numbers. Sears is wooing customers over fifty with their Mature Outlook Club. It provides special services and discounts on everything from eyeglasses to lawnmowers.[4]

### The Shrinking Household

While the total number of households is expected to increase dramatically (from approximately 63 million in 1970 to 96 million in 1990), the size of each individual household is expected to shrink. The shrinking household is well illustrated by the changing mix of household types. As depicted in Figure 3–7, the number of traditional family-type households will decrease by 11.1 percent between 1970 and 1990, while the individual nonfamily household will increase by the same percentage. Further evidence of the shrinking household is the increased number of "male–no wife" (+0.3 percent) and "female–no husband" (+3.5 percent) family-type households. It is also worth noting that the number of single-male households will more than double (from 6.4 to 13.6 percent). Government projections are that the average family size will slip from 3.3 persons in 1978 to 3.0 in 1990; the average household size has decreased from 3.14 in 1970 to 2.66 persons in 1987.[5] When one considers that a major portion of this changing household makeup is associated with the middle-age groups of thirty-five to forty-four and forty-five to fifty-four year olds, there is a strong underpinning for booming retail sales in household goods and services. Typically, these middle agers are the most lavish spenders in that they spend 27 percent more on goods and services than the average domicile. Some of the more direct merchandising impacts of the shrinking household lie with product design and packaging. The old adage that "bigger is better" is simply an inappropriate strategy for accommodating this demographic trend.

### The Working Woman

Merchandising strategies that cater to working women will become increasingly more important during the next several decades. The participation rate of women in the nation's work force has increased dramatically since the post-WWII period. In 1950,

FIGURE 3–7
Changing mix of household types, 1970 to 1990

| Household Type | Year (%) | |
|---|---|---|
| | 1970 | 1990 |
| Family type | 81.2 | 70.1 |
|   Husband and Wife | 70.6 | 55.7 |
|   Male, no wife | 1.9 | 2.2 |
|   Female, no husband | 8.7 | 12.2 |
| Nonfamily type | 18.8 | 29.9 |
|   Male | 6.4 | 13.6 |
|   Female | 12.4 | 16.3 |

Source: U.S. Census Bureau, *Projections of the Number of Households and Families, 1979 to 1995,* Series P-25, No. 805 (Washington, D.C.: U.S. Government Printing Office).

women accounted for 29.6 percent of the total labor force. By 1990, their participation is expected to account for about one-half of the U.S. work force. The changing needs and roles of working women have had a major impact on their buying behavior. Let's examine these alterations in buying behavior by viewing working women in their role as a working partner, a head of household, and a working person.

As an equal working partner within a marriage, the "work wife" has shed the stereotypical role of the chief purchasing agent for most of the family's household needs. Today, a teamwork trend is emerging, where the wife and husband share the responsibilities for the decisions on and procurement of household requirements. For the retailer, this shared purchasing behavior requires targeting the products, prices, promotions, and distribution channels toward the team rather than the individual wife or husband. Joint satisfaction of both partners will become an increasingly important factor in future successful merchandising tactics.

Being the head of a single, separated, widowed, or divorced household, the working woman has become the decision maker and procurer of both traditional household purchases and nontraditional purchases of goods and services. For example, in her role as head of a household, the working woman is becoming an increasingly important consideration in the marketing of homes (apartments, condominiums, and houses); financial services (banking, investment, and retirement programs); and professional services (law, tax, and insurance). In this role, she is solely responsible for purchase decisions that formerly were either made by or shared with her partner. With more female household heads in the workplace, the traditional distinction between women-dominated purchases (i.e., food and clothing) and men-dominated purchases (i.e., investment and insurance) is fading rapidly.

Employee responsibilities and employer expectations are an integral part of any job. In an attempt to meet these responsibilities and expectations, the product—service needs and the buying behavior of working women have undergone dynamic changes. As an illustration, the professional woman requires a professional wardrobe that is sufficient in size and consistent in character with her profession. In contrast with the housewife who is a "special occasion" buyer of "better dresses and suits," the professional woman is required to make such purchases on a regular and frequent basis. As such, the working woman tends to be a "wardrobe builder" in that each new clothing purchase is often viewed in terms of how well it can be integrated into her current wardrobe. Durability of each new clothing purchase tends to be a very important purchase motive for the professional, whose usage rate of the item is notably greater than a purchase made for occasional use. Nordstrom's, the Seattle-based department store, has developed an executive shopping club called "Personal Touch," which provides a full range of services from fashion consultants to hair care.[6] The professional working woman also has a specialized need for "tools of her trade"; these tools may consist of briefcases, appointment books, tape recorders, record-keeping ledgers, or a home personal computer.

## The Diversified Minorities

The concept that the United States is one large "melting pot" where all ethnic groups are assimilated into the American culture simply is an inappropriate and inoperative assumption for the retailer. Not only are there nonassimilated geographic concentra-

# "McDonald's is music to my ears."

"I started out as a freelance arranger-composer and one of the first national spots I ever produced was for McDonald's. Then I formed my own company and they gave me enough work to get me over the hump and establish myself in the business. At the time, McDonald's was one of the first advertisers to produce commercials directed to the Black consumer on such a large scale. As a result, I was able to open the door for a lot of talented Black musicians and singers who had never worked professionally before. So McDonald's really opened up the business for many people in this town. And we're all still working for McDonald's. And that's great."

McDonald's continues to support Black-owned businesses and individuals in communications. Morris "Butch" Stewart and his Joy-Art Productions is one of them. And his work is music to our ears.

Morris "Butch" Stewart
Joy Art Music Production
Chicago, Il.

## WE'RE INVOLVED.

McDonald's

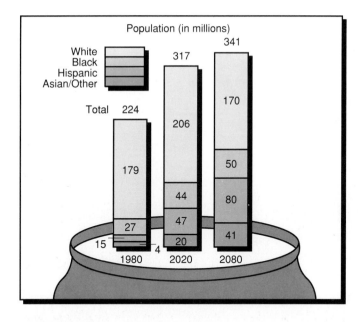

Population (in millions)

White
Black
Hispanic
Asian/Other

Total 224

FIGURE 3–8
A changing population:
Sometime in the next
century, blacks, Asians,
and Hispanics will out-
number whites (source:
"Selling to the New
America." Reprinted
with permission, *INC.*
Magazine [July 1987],
p. 45. Copyright © 1987
by INC. Publishing
Company, 38 Commer-
cial Walk, Boston MA
02110)

tions of ethnic minorities (e.g., Hispanics in Miami and Los Angeles), within each of the major minority markets (Hispanic and black Americans) there are numerous market segments. As with so many other American markets, success in reaching minority markets requires market segmentation and the tailoring of the firm's retailing mix. Mass-marketing strategies will find limited application in appealing to most minority markets. "What 'minority' consumers respond to most eagerly is a level of respect—targeted advertising, bilingual salespeople, and special events all help to break down barriers. But their long-term value is to confirm for minorities that they are welcome and valued not just as consumers, but as people—and as Americans."[7]

The major trend that characterizes minority markets is their growth both in number and income. Ethnic minority groups are increasing faster than the population as a whole. The number of blacks in the nation could almost double between now and 2080; during this time their share of the total population would increase from 12 to 18 percent.[8] Hispanics are the fastest growing ethnic group in the U.S.; by 2080 the number of Hispanics is expected to exceed the number of blacks (see Figure 3–8). By 1990, blacks are expected to comprise 12.6 percent of the total population, and Hispanics are projected to account for 10.7 percent of the nation's people.

Few markets are growing as fast as the Hispanic and Asian markets. Annual income for these market segments will almost double between 1980 and 1990, and that trend is expected to continue into the year 2000 (see Figure 3–9). The total minority market in 2000 is expected to be close to $800 billion. In addition to a demographic diversity, minority groups show considerable variance in their life-styles as defined by the activities they engage in, what interests them, and the opinions they hold.

Targeting the black consumer. (Courtesy of McDonald's Corporation)

**FIGURE 3–9**

A changing market-place: If it's growing markets you seek, few are growing faster than the Hispanic and Asian markets (source: "Selling to the New America." Reprinted with permission, *INC*. Magazine [July 1987], p. 45. Copyright © 1987 by INC. Publishing Company, 38 Commercial Walk, Boston MA 02110)

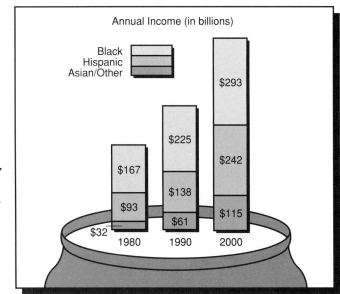

Annual Income (in billions)

Black
Hispanic
Asian/Other

$293

$225

$242

$167

$138

$93

$61

$115

$32    1980    1990    2000

## GEOGRAPHIC ANALYSIS

Americans tend to be a very mobile society. It is estimated that approximately one American in five moves every year. Therefore, a necessary part of any successful marketing program is the identification of current geographic population patterns and future shifts in those patterns. This discussion concerns the issue of where consumers are today and where consumers will be tomorrow.

### Regional Markets

The dimensions of a market area are defined by several factors, one of the more important is *population density*—the number of persons living within a delineated geographic area. By knowing how many people occupy an area, the retailer has one major element in the equation for determining the consumption potential of that area. Our examination of regional patterns and shifts of U.S. population can be delineated in terms of the nine census regions and the fifty states. According to the Census Bureau, one third of the nation's population now lives in the South. The second largest concentration of population is in the North Central region; it contains 26 percent of the nation's population. Following in order of size of population are the Northeast region (21.6 percent) and the West (19 percent). Of the ten largest states, three are in the Northeast (New York, Pennsylvania, and New Jersey), three are in the North Central (Illinois, Ohio, and Michigan), three are in the South (Texas, Florida, and North Carolina), and one is in the West (California). The South is the only region that is not represented in the ten least-populated states. One-half of the least populated states are in the West (Idaho, Nevada, Montana, Wyoming, and Alaska), three states are in the Northeast (New Hampshire, Delaware, and Vermont), and two sparsely populated states are in the North Central region (North and South Dakota). Judging from these patterns, it appears that the previous population dominance of the Northeastern/Great Lakes manufacturing belt has been replaced by a somewhat more even regional distribution of population.

If the old adage is true that "retailers follow markets," then retailers are shifting their attention toward the West and South. The ten fastest growing states (percentage change) during the seventies and eighties were all in the West (Nevada, Arizona, Wyoming, Utah, Alaska, Idaho, Colorado, and New Mexico) and the South (Florida and Texas). A similar trend emerges when we view population change in terms of absolute numbers of people. California, Texas, and Florida are the most powerful population magnets. Other major absolute population gainers include Arizona, Georgia, North Carolina, Washington, Virginia, Colorado, and Tennessee.

What do these population shifts mean to the retailer? Regional differences stimulate new expenditure patterns. Different climates, life-styles, and customs necessitate modification of existing merchandising programs and development of new retailing strategies. From the more formal life-styles of the northeast to the informality of western living, from the more rigorous climates of the north to the moderate environs of the south, from southern fried chicken to New England boiled lobster, the retailer is faced with different customer expectations requiring different marketing tactics.

## Metro Geography

America is an urbanized society; 75 percent of the nation's population lives within one of the 318 metropolitan areas. This is almost a complete reversal from 1880, when three out of four Americans lived in largely rural areas. Metro-area residents are of two types: urbanites who dwell in the central cities and suburbanites who live in the suburbs that surround the core city. The suburbs continued to dominate the population growth pattern of the metro areas. While the percentage increase for all metropolitan areas registered approximately 10 percent, suburbanites increased 18 percent while gains in central city populace were almost stagnant at 0.1 percent.

## Nonmetro Geography

Nonmetro markets consist of the many small hamlets, villages, and towns that dot the nation's countryside together with the rural farm areas. Since 1800, the population of nonmetro areas has been declining, largely as a result of migration to the metropolitan areas. However, during the 1970s, the migration process reversed itself as nonmetro markets experienced both a population growth and a net in-migration.

In the migrational interchange of population between metro and nonmetro markets, the nonmetro areas experienced a net gain. A number of reasons have been cited as explanations for this turnabout. Nonmetro areas appear to be attracting population because of (1) more casual life-styles, (2) greater opportunity for outdoor experiences, (3) slower pace of living, (4) lower cost of living, (5) less competitive environment, and (6) changing preferences from cultural amenities to physical environmental amenities.

---

Consumer **buying behavior** is the manner in which consumers act, function, and react to various situations involving the purchase of a good or service or the acceptance of an idea. Effective retailing requires both an understanding and an appreciation of the buying behavior of consumers. "Real consumer insight means understanding more about your target (market) than your competitor does."[9] Retailers

**CONSUMER
BUYING
BEHAVIOR**

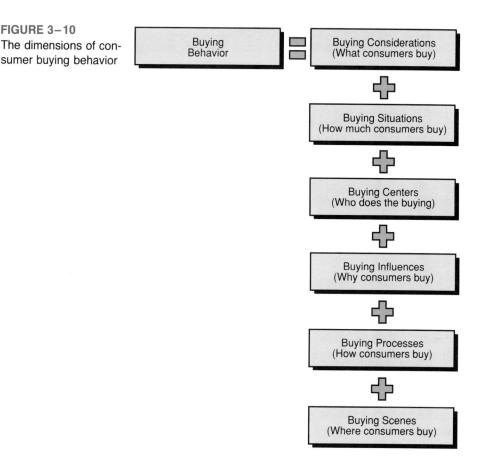

**FIGURE 3–10**
The dimensions of consumer buying behavior

Buying Behavior = Buying Considerations (What consumers buy)
+ Buying Situations (How much consumers buy)
+ Buying Centers (Who does the buying)
+ Buying Influences (Why consumers buy)
+ Buying Processes (How consumers buy)
+ Buying Scenes (Where consumers buy)

require such buying behavior information as what and how much consumers buy, who does the buying, and how, and where consumers buy (see Figure 3–10). This section examines the ultimate consumer's actual act of buying and the situations and influences that impact on the consumer's choice of retailers and their products and services.

**BUYING CONSIDERATIONS**

"What do consumers buy?" is the first question that needs to be answered if we are to gain an understanding of consumer buying behavior. Consumers buy products. **Products** are bundles of benefits capable of satisfying consumer wants and needs. A product can be "anything" that can be offered to a market as a need and want satisfier. Consumers have "benefit expectations" that need to be realized in buying, using, and possessing products. Successful products are those that provide the tangible and/or intangible features necessary for the realization of the consumer's expectations of benefits. Viewed in this broad perspective, the retailer has great latitude in planning and implementing the "basic offering" that is to be presented to the consuming public. To enhance our conception of what is a product, marketers have developed several classifications based on various product and/or buyer behavior dimensions. Let's look at the dimensions of tangibility, durability, and availability (see Figure 3–11).[10]

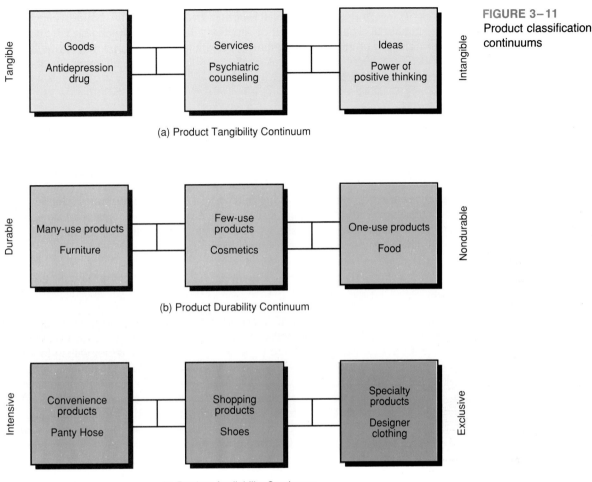

(a) Product Tangibility Continuum

(b) Product Durability Continuum

(c) Product Availability Continuum

FIGURE 3-11
Product classification
continuums

## Product Tangibility

Tangibility is the degree to which an item has physical and material properties that are capable of being perceived. The sense of touch is generally considered to be the deciding factor in determining tangibility. Tangible products can be held, hefted, and felt; intangible products cannot be touched.

Product tangibility ranges from goods to services to ideas (see Figure 3-11a). **Goods** are tangible items defined by their size, shape, and weight together with their chemical and/or biological makeup. This book is a good example of a tangible item, as is the chair you are sitting in and the desk where you are sitting. **Services** are largely intangible activities that typically involve the application of human skills within a consumer problem-solving context. A service may or may not be associated with the sale of a good. Services range from personal services like hair styling and massages to professional services such as medical attention and legal advice, from household services of housekeeping and gardening to automotive services of maintenance and repair, from recreational services of amusement parks and campgrounds to cultural services of plays and concerts; the list is almost endless. **Ideas** are concepts and ways of thinking about a particular event or situation. These highly intangible products are often extensions of the opinions, attitudes, and interests of the person marketing the idea. Ideas are often categorized as business, religious, political, social, or personal expressions of conceptual thinking.

### Product Durability

Durability is the ability of something to endure or to last. **Durables** are products that are capable of surviving many uses. An automobile is a durable good that can provide the transportation function for 100,000 miles or more assuming proper maintenance. Appliances and home furnishings are additional examples of durables. **Nondurables** are perishable products that are used up in one or a few uses. Faddish goods, services, and ideas last for a short period of time with a limited useful life. Figure 3–11b illustrates the continuum of product durability.

### Product Availability

Product availability is a means of classifying products on the amount of effort the consumer is willing to exert to secure a particular good, service, or idea (see Figure 3–11c). **Convenience products** are those that the consumer is not willing to spend time, money, and effort in locating, evaluating, and procuring. Consumers expect convenience products to be readily available. If a particular brand of a convenience product is not available, the consumer will select another brand. Bread, cigarettes, and soft drinks are all examples of convenience goods, while dry cleaning and automotive maintenance are typical convenience services. "By the early 1990s more than half of all families will wield two paychecks—with more money to spend and less time to spend it." The convenience goods and services industry can expect to continue its past steady growth rate.[11]

**Shopping products** are products for which consumers want to make price, quality, suitability, and/or style comparisons. Consumers are willing to spend a considerable amount of time, money, and effort in securing shopping goods; therefore, these goods can be distributed selectively. What constitutes shopping products varies from one consumer to another; however, we usually think of clothing, furniture, and linens as shopping goods. In a similar vein, people shop around for ideas by attending different lectures, churches, and other events.

**Specialty products** are those in which the consumer's buying behavior is directed at securing a particular good, service, or idea without regard to time, effort, or expense. The consumer will not accept a substitute; therefore, they will expend whatever effort is required to procure the product. For example, a specialty good may be a specific branded good such as Lagerfeld cologne or a company product line such as Royal Copenhagen figurines. For the individual who insists on a particular hair stylist and is willing to travel to, wait for, and pay whatever the price, that service is a specialty service to that consumer. Given the insistent character of the consumer, specialty products tend to be exclusively distributed in a very limited number of outlets.

## Consumer Population

This discussion of buying situations focuses on how much consumers buy. Viewed from the perspective of the individual consumer, the question of how much he or she buys is a function of his or her needs and desires plus the ability, willingness, and authority to buy. Taking a broader market perspective, how much consumers will buy in total is the problem of determining **market potential**—a market's total capacity to consume a given good, service, or idea. As seen in Figure 3–12, market potential equals the consuming population within a market plus the consumption requirements and potential of that population. Let's examine each of these elements of the market potential equation.

A market's total capacity to consume is, in part, a function of the total number of consumption units that make up that market. Therefore, the first step in determining market potential is to obtain an accurate count of the number of consumption units. However, before consumption units can be counted, they must be defined. The definition of a consumption unit will depend on the type of product that is the focus of the market potential determination. The "number of persons" is the most appropriate population count when market potential is being determined for such personal goods and services as clothing and accessories, health and beauty aids, or medical and legal services. On the other hand, a count of the "number of households" or "the number of residential units" probably is more indicative of a market's consumption capacity for hardware and household goods, furniture, and appliances, lawn and garden equipment, or plumbing and heating services. Although these population

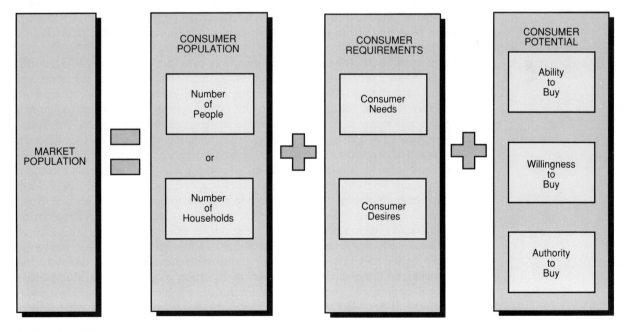

FIGURE 3–12
Market potential as the capacity to consume

figures are important, they must be qualified in terms of their likelihood of a purchase either now or in the near future.

## Consumer Requirements

Prerequisites to the consumer buying process are needs and desires; they motivate and direct the buying activities of consumers. Although the distinction between needs and desires is open to debate, the main difference is in their essentiality. **Needs** are essential physiological or psychological requirements necessary to the general physical and mental welfare of the consumer. **Desires** are more akin to wishes, in that they are conscious impulses toward objects or experiences that hold promise of enjoyment in their attainment. However, the attainment of desires is less essential to the consumer's well-being than is the satisfaction of needs.

## Consumer Potential

Consumers must distinguish between having a need or desire for a product and buying it. Many consumers have product needs (i.e., a new toaster) that go unsatisfied and desires (i.e., a new Porsche) that go unfulfilled. The essential difference between needing or desiring a product and buying it is the consumer's ability, willingness, and authority to purchase the needed or desired good, service, or idea. With respect to product purchases, the list of what each of us would *like* to buy is far more extensive than the list of what we are *willing* and *able* to buy.

*Ability to Buy.* A consumer's ability to buy is his or her **buying power**—the financial resources that are available to the consumer for making purchases. The determining elements of buying power are the consumer's spendable income, asset position, and available credit.

There are many different expressions of income. **Total income** refers to the total amount of money received from salaries, wages, interest investments, pensions, and profit-making activities. Average family income in 1987 was about $33,000, up from $17,125 in 1950, in today's dollars.[12] Unfortunately, not all of an individual's or family's total income is available for spending as the individual or family pleases—taxes have to be paid, savings accounts need to be enhanced, and basic living expenses need to be covered. To accommodate for these unavoidable expenditures, additional income expressions are in common usage. **Disposable income** is the income that remains after taxes and other required payments (e.g., Social Security) have been deducted from total income. It is the total amount of money that is available for spending and saving. Although disposable income is an appropriate and useful expression of available income for the retailer of essential goods and services, it is not a useful tool in examining the capacity of a market to consume nonessential or luxury goods and services. The expression *discretionary income* therefore has been developed. **Discretionary income** is that portion of an individual's or family's disposable income that remains after purchasing the basic necessities of life—food, clothing, and shelter. Consumers are free to purchase whatever they want to with their discretionary income. Marketers of many recreation, entertainment, household, automotive, and personal products depend on the amount of discretionary income for satisfactory sales volumes.

The relationships between type of income and consumer expenditure patterns are stated in terms of laws developed from the work of Ernest Engel, a nineteenth-century German statistician. Briefly, these laws state that as a family's income increases, the following result:

1. The percentage of that income spent on food decreases.
2. The percentage of that income spent on clothing is roughly constant.
3. The percentage of that income spent on housing and household operations remains roughly constant.
4. The percentage of that income spent on luxury and other goods increases.

Credit and assets are the second and third buying power determinants. **Credit** is (1) the borrowing power of a consumer, (2) an amount of money that is placed at a consumer's disposal by a financial or other institution, and (3) a time allowed for payment for goods and services sold on trust. **Assets** are anything of value that is owned by an individual. The role of assets in determining buying power is twofold: (1) they can be converted to cash and (2) they are a major factor in determining the amount of credit that borrowers are willing to extend.

*Willingness to Buy.* A consumer may have a need and the ability to satisfy that need, yet, for a number of reasons, may be unwilling to make a purchase decision. As consumers, our willingness to buy or not to buy a product is related to the many influences acting on us and the way in which we make purchase decisions. Psychologically, we may or may not be motivated to make a purchase, or our perception of a product is such that we do not feel it is capable of meeting our needs. From a personal standpoint, a product may not be congruent with our self-image or our life-style. On the other hand, our willingness to buy may be based on whether a product meets our "belongingness" need to be accepted by our family, peer groups, or social class. Finally, our willingness to buy or not to buy may slow our actual buying process. We may postpone a purchase because we need more information about the product or more time to evaluate the information we already have.

*Authority to Buy.* Even with the ability and willingness to buy, a certain degree of authorization must be present before a consumer will finalize the purchase decision. Authority to buy can be of either a formal or an informal type. Formal authorization consists of the consumer meeting various eligibility requirements such as age, residency, and occupation constraints. Minors cannot legally purchase alcoholic beverages. Nonresidents of a state are ineligible for many services provided by state and local governments. Many social and professional organizations make available their products only to members of certain occupations (e.g., American Medical Association or Wisconsin Bar Association).

Informal authorization for making purchases is an expected courtesy when more than one individual is involved and when the purchase can be classified as being of major importance (special occasion or expensive). For example, when either a husband or wife is considering the purchase of a new automobile, the other partner would expect to be consulted before the purchase is made. The family vacation decision as to what, where, and when is one in which informal approval and/or input is expected by all family members.

**BUYING CENTERS**

A pertinent question in any study of buying behavior is "Who does the buying?" To answer this question, marketers have developed the concept of a buying center. A **buying center** is a basic unit of consumption that engages in the buying process. In consumer products marketing, the basic consumption units tend to be either individuals or households. In certain situations, individuals buy products for their own consumption with no or little regard for the needs or opinions of others. In other situations, purchases are made for a household by one of its members. In a household that is buying, purchase decisions are based on collective needs and influenced by most or all of the members of the household.

The distinction between individual and household buying centers is important in studying buyer behavior and developing merchandising programs that are appropriate to that behavior. In the following sections, we look at the influences on the individual and household buying behavior and the processes that are employed in making purchases by these two types of buying centers.

**BUYING INFLUENCES**

Why do consumers buy what, when, where, and how they buy? Marketers, like psychologists, do not fully understand the "whys" of human behavior. Although we have a fair understanding of what factors influence behavior, our knowledge of how those factors interact to influence behavior is limited. The human mind is often compared to a "black box"; we know the inputs (stimuli) and the outputs (responses) but not the inner workings of the mind (processes) with respect to the transformation of inputs and outputs. Nevertheless, by detecting patterned buying responses that emerge from planned marketing stimuli, retailers can draw inferences about the processing system of the human mind. One viewpoint on the nature of retailing is that it is the art and science of creating and delivering a package of stimuli (products, prices, promotions, and places) that is capable of producing consistent patterns of buying behavior. Fortunately or unfortunately, depending on your perspective, retailing is still more art than science.

In this section we explore the many interacting factors that influence buying behavior and serve as a basis for formulating marketing strategies and tactics. Figure 3–13 is an overview of the major determinants of the buying behavior of the ultimate consumer.

### Psychological Factors

The field of psychology has contributed greatly to the marketer's quest for explanations to the "whys" of consumer behavior. Motivation, perception, learning, and attitude are four major psychological factors that influence consumers in the determination of their buying choices.

*Motivation.* Preceding any action is the mental process of motivation. The act of buying starts with a motive. **Motivation** refers to the process by which consumers are moved or incited to action. Motivation starts with stimulated needs that lead to aroused tensions and result in goal-directed actions. A basic tenet of psychology is "look behind the behavior." What retailers have found when they have examined the buying choices of consumers are unsatisfied needs. A **need** is the lack of something

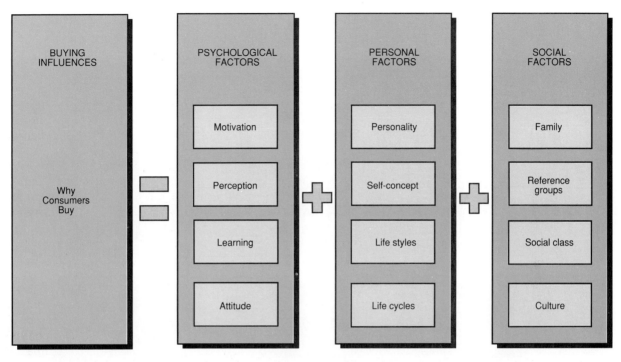

**FIGURE 3–13**
Determinants of consumer buying behavior

that is necessary to the well-being of the individual. Needs are the basic source of buyer behavior, but they must be stimulated before the consumer is driven to action. Activation of a need is the result of some internal or external stimulus that arouses tensions. A headache is an internal stimulus that creates an uncomfortable feeling (an aroused tension) that activates the goal-directed action of taking aspirin for relief from the headache (the need). An external stimulus might be a department store advertisement announcing the arrival of the latest fall fashions; this cue may stimulate our need to be noticed as a contemporary dresser, thereby promoting the action of purchasing something distinctive to wear.

Having portrayed motivation as a needs-based process, a further explanation of the nature and intensity of human needs is required. Needs have been categorized in a variety of ways; one of the more widely accepted need classification schemes is that of the psychologist Abraham H. Maslow. According to Maslow, human needs are hierarchical and can be rank-ordered on the basis of their motivational power. Lower-order needs, those that are related to our physiological well-being, are basic innate needs that must be satisfied before higher-order needs can emerge as strong motivators of our behavior. Higher-order needs are learned needs that are largely psychological in nature. Although higher-order needs are secondary to physiological needs, once these basic needs are satisfied, psychological needs will emerge as extremely important motivators of consumer behavior. Let's explore Maslow's hierarchy of needs.

**Physiological needs** are life-sustaining and creature comforts that need to be reasonably satisfied before the search for fulfillment of higher-order needs. Food, fluids, shelter, rest, waste elimination, and clothing are all basic to the physiological

well-being of the individual. In reading this text, for example, your thirst for knowledge and an "A" on the next exam may be secondary to your need for sleep if you were out partying half the night. On the other hand, if you are well rested, your concern (aroused tension) over improving your grade point (need) may encourage you to review this chapter several times in order to earn a grade of "B" or better on the next exam (goal-directed action). However, one thing you can be sure of—once you have satisfied either or both of these needs, other needs will arise (e.g., getting a date for the weekend).

**Safety needs** are satisfied by feelings of security and stability. To be secure, a person must feel free from physical harm or danger. Product and service retailers that focus on the need for protection include those that sell smoke- or burglar-alarm systems, insurance and retirement plans, exercise and health programs, warranties and guarantees, and caffeine-free, sugar-free, and salt-free foods and beverages. Stability is an equally important factor in meeting the need for safety. Generally, people feel more secure when there is a reasonable amount of order and structure in their lives. The often heard expressions "I need to simplify my life" or "I need to get organized" are directed at obtaining relief from the tensions that are aroused by an unstructured, unorganized, and chaotic life-style. Simplification and organization are both excellent concepts to be used by retailers in developing product lines, designing store and display layouts, creating advertising appeals, and establishing pricing points.

As social creatures, we all have **social needs**—the desire for love, belongingness, affection, and friendship. Because of our relatively affluent society, social needs have become powerful motivators of our behavior and influential organizers of our perceptions. Capitalizing on this need to "be accepted" or to "fit in," retailers structure many merchandising strategies around the need for satisfying relationships with family, friends, peers, and reference groups. Social need gratification influences where we live, what we wear, what organizations we belong to, what stores we patronize, and how much we are willing to pay.

**Esteem needs** involve consumer aspirations regarding prestige, recognition, admiration, self-respect, success, and achievement. An individual who seeks to fulfill esteem needs wants to "stand out" as contrasted to the social need to "fit in." In satisfying esteem needs, a consumer is more likely to (1) purchase "limited edition" merchandise (e.g., collectable figurines); (2) patronize distinctive outlets (e.g., specialty shops); (3) respond to individualist retail promotions (e.g., image-building advertisements); and (4) react in a less price-sensitive manner (e.g., prestige price preference). The retailer's task in meeting esteem needs is to make the consumer feel special and appreciated.

"Doing what you are capable of doing" is a phrase that summarizes an individual's need for **self-actualization**. The desire for self-fulfillment is the highest-order need; it reflects the desire to reach one's full potential as an individual—"what you can be, you must be." A good example of an industry directed toward helping consumers realize their potential are the numerous motivational books, tapes, seminars, and programs designed to provide the means for realizing self-actualization. By

This ad attempts to influence store patronage through an appeal to social needs of love and belongingness. (Courtesy of Chess King; Jan Schoenbrun, art director)

combining the self-actualization need of self-fulfillment with the social need of recognition, the retailer has target-market opportunities for a wide range of goods and services of a conspicuous nature.

*Perception.* How motivated consumers act out the buying process is determined, in part, by their perceptions of the buying situation. **Perception** is the process by which consumers attach meaning to incoming stimuli by forming mental pictures of persons, places, and objects. An individual's perception is how he or she views the world. The basic perceptual process consists of receiving, organizing, and interpreting stimuli. *Stimulus reception* is accomplished through the five senses of sight, sound, taste, touch, and smell. For most people, the sense of sight is the most used and developed sense mode, a fact that retailers should keep in mind when planning all aspects of their retailing mix. Exposure is the key to receiving stimuli; perception follows exposure. A major tactic in any retailing program is the inclusion of plans for gaining buyer exposure for the firm's product offering.

*Stimulus organization* is a mental data processing system whereby incoming stimuli (data) are organized into descriptive categories. Received stimuli must be simplified through organization if they are to be mentally converted into meaningful information that can be useful in problem solving, that is, making purchase decisions. Individuals vary greatly in their ability to mentally receive, store, and organize stimuli; hence, their interpretations of stimuli exhibit equal variance.

*Stimulus interpretation* is the process of assigning meaning to stimuli. When the consumer attaches meaning to something he or she has sensed, the perceptual process is completed. Interpretation of stimuli is accomplished by the mental comparison of what is sensed to what the individual knows or feels from previous experience. Having reviewed how we perceive, let's examine how we tend to be selective about what we perceive.

Selectivity is a nature phenomenon occurring within the perceptual process of receiving (selective exposure), organizing (selective retention), and interpreting (selective distortion) stimuli. "What you see [hear, feel, taste, and smell] is what you get. But what consumers actually perceive is always vastly different from the actual stimuli presented—not sometimes, not usually, but ALWAYS!"[13] The selectivity of perception is a key factor in explaining why different people have different perceptions of the same stimuli. **Selective exposure** is the act of limiting the type and amount of stimuli that are received and admitted to awareness. It is a screening process that allows us to select only the stimuli that interest us. For example, most consumers watch only certain types of television programming or read selected sections of their local newspaper. **Selective retention** is the act of remembering only the information that individual wants to remember. Individuals tend to retain information that is consistent with their feelings, beliefs, and attitudes. Information that is conflicting is likely to be forgotten. **Selective distortion** is the act of misinterpreting incoming stimuli to make them consistent with the individual's beliefs and attitudes. By changing incoming information, people can create a harmonious relationship between that information and their mind-set and avoid the tension that results from not having one's beliefs supported by new inputs. For example, if we like a particular retail store because of its friendly sales personnel, we might distort the fact that their higher prices are not competitive. The selectivity of perception places a considerable strain on the retailer, who must get messages admitted to awareness without being misinterpreted or forgotten.

*Learning.* The logical extension of the motivational and perceptual process is learning. A considerable amount of human behavior is learned. **Learning** is the process of acquiring knowledge through past experiences. Behavioral psychologists view learning as a stimulus-response mechanism wherein drives, cues, and responses interact to produce a learned pattern of behavior. A **drive** is whatever impels behavior; it arises from a strongly felt inner need that requires action. A fear of failure, for example, may drive an insecure individual to work longer and more efficiently. **Cues** are external stimuli that direct consumers toward specific objects that can satisfy basic needs and reduce drives. To illustrate, an advertisement promoting a new book on time management is likely to catch the attention of an unsure individual who is looking for ways to improve his or her work efficiency. **Responses** are the actions taken to reduce a cue stimulated drive. In a buying situation, these actions typically include identifying, trying, evaluating, and selecting purchase alternatives. To continue the example, our fearful individual may respond by visiting the bookstore and after previewing the book may or may not decide to buy it.

The extent to which an individual learns from this stimulus-response mechanism is influenced by three factors: reinforcement, repetition, and participation. *Reinforcement* is the comparing of anticipated results with the actual results experienced from a chosen response. If actual results compare favorably with anticipated results, response reinforcement occurs and learning takes place. *Repetition* is the act of repeating a past experience. Learning is enhanced by performing the same action several times. *Participation* is the active involvement in the learning process. An active role in any activity generally results in the acquisition of more knowledge about that activity.

The retailer's efforts regarding the learning process should be directed at enhancing reinforcement, repetition, and participation. Reinforcement may take the form of return and allowance policies that confirm the retailer's intent to correct product deficiencies. Frequent advertisements that expose the consumer to the retailer's products and services is a commonly employed tactic used in supporting the learning process through repetition. Free samples, trial sizes, and demonstrations are participation devices used in marketing to guide the consumer's learning process toward the retailer's products.

*Attitudes.* An **attitude** is an evaluative mental orientation that provides a predisposition to respond in a certain fashion. People use their attitudes as evaluative mechanisms to pass judgment (i.e., good or bad, right or wrong) and as orientation mechanisms to focus that judgment on particular persons, places, things, or events. Attitudes can perform an important simplification function of the buying process by providing the consumer with a preset way to respond to the object of the attitude. For example, if Bob thinks that department stores are overpriced, he can avoid shopping there.

What is the makeup of an attitude? Figure 3–14 portrays the three basic components of an attitude—cognitive, affective, and behavior. The **cognitive component** consists of what the consumer believes about an object based on available information and knowledge. Essentially, a cognition is what is known about the object and its attributes. Feelings, not beliefs, are the focal point of the **affective component**—the emotions a consumer feels about an object. The third element of an attitude is the **behavior component**—the predisposition to respond in a certain way to the object based on one's beliefs and feelings.

FIGURE 3–14
Components of an atti-
tude (mind set)

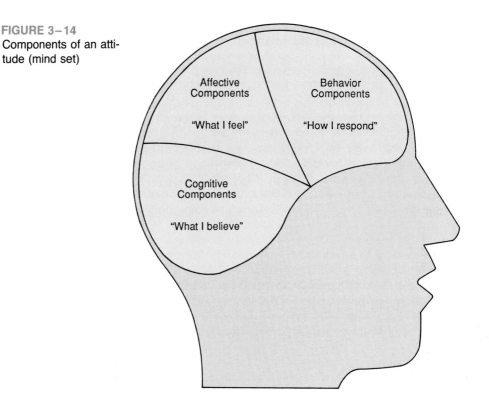

Attitude formation is the result of past experiences. Attitudes are learned through interactions with family members and a wide range of peer and reference groups. People often adopt the prevailing attitudes of their associates. The learning of an attitude takes one of several forms: (1) trial and error (purchasing and using a product), (2) visual observation (watching a product demonstration), and (3) verbal communications (listening to the product opinions of others). Through involvement in trial and error, visual observation, and verbal communication experiences of consumers, retailers can influence attitude formation.

### Personal Factors

An individual's personality, self-concept, life-style, and position in the life cycle are all personal factors that impact on that individual's buying behavior (see Figure 3–13). We continue our exploration of the "whys" of consumer behavior by discussing each of the four personal factors.

*Personality.* Everyone has a personality; unfortunately, there is considerable disagreement as to what it is and to what extent it influences buying behavior. Because of its complex nature, personality is perhaps best defined in general terms; therefore, **personality** is a general response pattern used by individuals in coping with their environment. For example, an individual may be positive or negative, pessimistic or optimistic, aggressive or passive, independent or dependent, sociable or unsociable, and friendly or withdrawn. Logically, the existence of a particular personality trait will affect an individual's buying behavior. For example, a person with a pessimistic personality will approach buying situations with a considerable amount of doubt whereas an optimistic individual should be more impulsive and confident about buying choices. Market researchers, however, have been largely unsuccessful in their efforts to find significant statistical relationships between personalities and buying behavior.

*Self-Concept.* Who are we? One answer to that question is that we are what we perceive ourselves to be; that is, our **self-concept**—the set of perceptions that people have of themselves within a social context. Each individual has a general awareness of his or her capabilities and attributes and how they are perceived within a social setting. The self-concept consists of four parts:

1. Real self—the way you actually are
2. Ideal self—how you would like to be
3. Looking-glass self—how you think others see you
4. Self-image—how you see yourself

As illustrated in Figure 3–15, our self-image is to some extent a composite of the real, ideal, and looking-glass selves. The importance of the self-concept to retailers in understanding consumer behavior is twofold; first, consumers often purchase products and/or brands that they feel support and reinforce their self-concept, and second, consumers never consciously purchase products that are incompatible with their

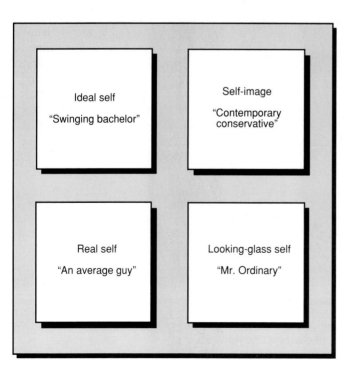

**FIGURE 3–15**
The four parts of the self-concept

Ideal self

"Swinging bachelor"

Self-image

"Contemporary conservative"

Real self

"An average guy"

Looking-glass self

"Mr. Ordinary"

self-concept. For example, the "contemporary conservative" may purchase a blue blazer with gray slacks because it is consistent with each of his "selfs"; such an apparel selection would allow this individual to fantasize about being a swinging bachelor (what he would like to be) while preserving his image as an average (what he really is) and ordinary (what others see him as) guy. One major use of the self-concept by retailers is in the creation of advertising appeals. By directing an advertising message to such self-images as the "homebody," the "good provider," the "budding scholar," and the "professional," the retailer has an additional tool for targeting selected consumer markets, developing product lines, planning price tactics, and designing store layouts.

*Life-Styles.* Some people lead an active life, others have **life-styles** that are more sedentary. Some people's are centered around their home and family; others center their lives around jobs, organizations, hobbies, or events. A consumer's life-style affects what, when, where, how, and why they buy. Life-style can be defined as *the way consumers live.* It is a patterned style of living that stems from the individual's needs, perceptions, and attitudes; as such, it represents a behavioral profile of the individual's psychological makeup. How consumers choose to live is also a reflection of the influences exerted by family members, peers, and other groups. Both conforming and nonconforming life-styles are behavioral reactions to what are expected and accepted modes of living.

Life-style analysis (psychographics) is an attempt by marketing researchers to develop consumer profiles based on consumers' ways of living. Life-style profiles are composite pictures of the consumer's **activities, interests, and opinions (AIO),** together with their demographic makeup. Figure 3–16 identifies a commonly used enumeration of AIO variables. To develop life-style profiles, consumers are asked to respond to a multitude of AIO statements by indicating their degree of agreement or disagreement with those statements (see Figure 3–17). By finding patterned responses to AIO statements (e.g., strong agreement with all statements that reflect favorably on work-oriented activities, job-related interests, and probusiness opin-

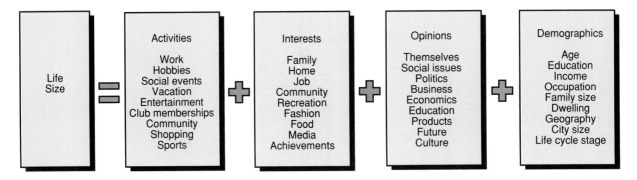

FIGURE 3–16
Dimensions of life-style (source: Joseph T. Plummer, "The Concept and Application of Life-Style Segmentation," *Journal of Marketing* 38 [January 1974]: 34)

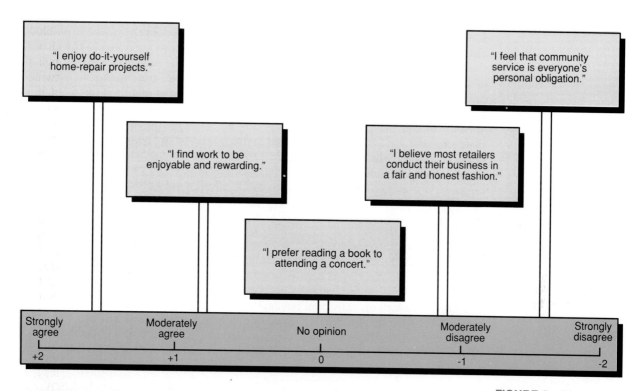

FIGURE 3–17

AIO statements (activities, interests, and opinions)

ions), the retailer is better able to identify market segments and to target marketing programs).

Life-style analysis tends to be special-purpose research; that is, it is directed at determining life-style profiles relative to a particular market, product, or retailing program. As an illustration, let's assume that a retailer wants to develop a fashion merchandising program based on life-style dimensions. After having administered a series of AIO statements to a represented sample, the following life-style profiles emerge:

1. The "perfectionist"—a career-oriented, free-spirited, active fashion leader who is concerned with uniqueness and individuality to support her avant-garde image; an individual who can be nonconforming and impractical when in an adventurous mood
2. The "traditionalist"—a job-oriented, conforming fashion follower who is extremely label-conscious and interested in being accepted as well as presenting a dignified and practical image

Having identified two distinct market segments based on life-style dimensions, the retailer can choose to (1) appeal to the perfectionist by offering the most advanced fashion apparel, stocking only one of each type of garment and timing new arrivals every week or (2) appeal to the traditionalist by offering stylish yet accepted fashions, stocking well-established labels and displays in practical combinations (outfits) of apparel. "Lifestyle analysis is not a panacea. . .but used well, psychographics can give us that critical bit of insight we need for added leverage in the marketplace."[14]

*Life Cycle.* Are you single, married, widowed, or divorced; are you with or without children; and are you young, middle-aged, or elderly? These are some of the factors that determine which stage of the life cycle you are in. The **life cycle** is a description of the changes that occur in an individual's demographic, psychographic, and behavioristic profile while progressing through a series of stages during his or her life time. The life cycle starts with the singles stage and ends with the retired solitary survivor of a family. The nine stages of the life cycle and their key demographic, psychographic, and behavioristic elements are portrayed in Figure 3–18. The differences in buyer behavior can often be explained by very practical considerations. Families with children buy toys, large families buy large-sized packages, and empty-nest families are in a position to more readily afford luxury products and services.

## Social Factors

Conformity to group expectations is a basic element of human behavior. Much of what we do is directed at gaining acceptance from other people; so it is with our buying behavior. We buy certain products, select particular brands, and patronize certain stores because we want the approval and support of others. The importance of group influences on individual buying behavior is great. Human interactions affect our motivation, perception, and learning processes and help shape our attitudes, personality, self-concept, and life-style. The following discussion examines the impact of the family, reference groups, social class, and culture on our individual buying behavior (see Figure 3–13).

*The Family.* A family can be described in terms of the *nuclear family,* consisting of a father, mother, and their children, or as the *extended family,* which includes the nuclear family plus grandparents, aunts, uncles, and cousins. Regardless of how the family unit is defined, it represents one of the most important social factors impacting on our buying behavior. The importance of the family to planning merchandising strategies lies in the fact that (1) every family member's behavior is strongly influenced by the interactions that occur within the family; (2) every family represents both a buying and consuming unit within our economy; and (3) as more and more children boost buying power by returning to the family nest, that consuming unit has increased purchasing capabilities.[15]

*Family influences* on individual buyer behavior stem from childhood. Consciously or unconsciously, we adopt many of our parents' attitudes, values, morals, and ways of doing things. These basic orientations remain with us long after we have left our family of origin. As we establish a new family by getting married and having children, the influences of our spouse and children assume a primary role of importance in the acquisition of new orientations and the development of new behavioral patterns.

**Family buying roles** are a key issue in understanding consumer behavior. From a merchandising perspective, a consumer is often not an individual but a family represented by an individual. Therefore, retailers must recognize and understand the various roles played by various family members within a given purchase situation. Five specific roles have been identified as follows:

1. Initiator—the family member who first recognizes the problem
2. User—the family member who will actually use or consume the product or service

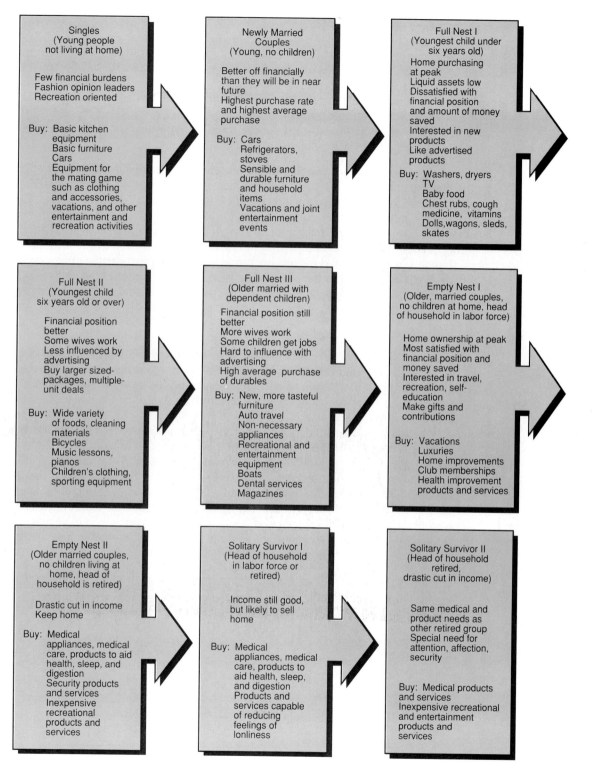

**FIGURE 3-18**

The life-cycle progression (source: William D. Wells and George Gubar, "Life Cycle Concept In Marketing Research," *Journal of Marketing Research* 3 [November 1966]: 362)

3. Decision maker—the family member who decides what will be bought and at what time, place, and source
4. Decision influencer—the family member who has input to affect the choice of the decision maker
5. Purchasing agent—the family member who actually visits the store and makes the purchase

To be effective, a merchandising program must take into account each family member and their respective roles. For example, the retailer's persuasive and informational advertising might be directed at (1) the initiator to create awareness, (2) the decision influencer and decision maker to develop comprehension and conviction, (3) the user to provide reinforcement, and (4) the purchasing agent to guide shopping trip behavior. Role specialization in family buying is common in most families. Although some purchase decisions are made jointly or independently, other purchases are dominated by either the husband or wife. With the increase of working mothers, many teens are taking on adult buying roles of decision maker and purchasing agent. "While both parents may be the breadwinners, teenagers now are the bread buyers."[16]

*Reference Groups.* Reference groups provide individuals with a "frame of reference" in making such purchase decisions as what and where to buy. A **reference group** is a group that serves as a model or standard for an individual's behavior and attitudes. An individual may develop associations with such reference groups as friends, colleagues, co-workers, clubs, and associations.

Reference group influences on purchase behavior vary by product and brand. Purchases of highly conspicuous and visible products such as clothing, furniture, and automobiles are strongly influenced by reference groups. The importance of peer group influence in the purchase of fashion is shown in Figure 3–19. If the brand name is also conspicuous (e.g., the Izod alligator), reference group influences become an important decision factor. The retailer's image as the "right or in place" for a particular reference group can also be an important consideration in deciding what retailer to patronize. The distinctive package of a distinctive retailer may be as important as the product in a group gift-giving situation.

**FIGURE 3–19**
Setting the style on campus: When it comes to fashion, most college students are influenced by their friends (source: Elys McLean-Ibrahim, "What Makes Workers succeed." *USA Today* [September 1987], pB-1. Copyright © 1987 USA TODAY. Reprinted with permission)

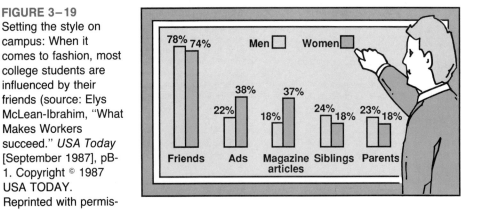

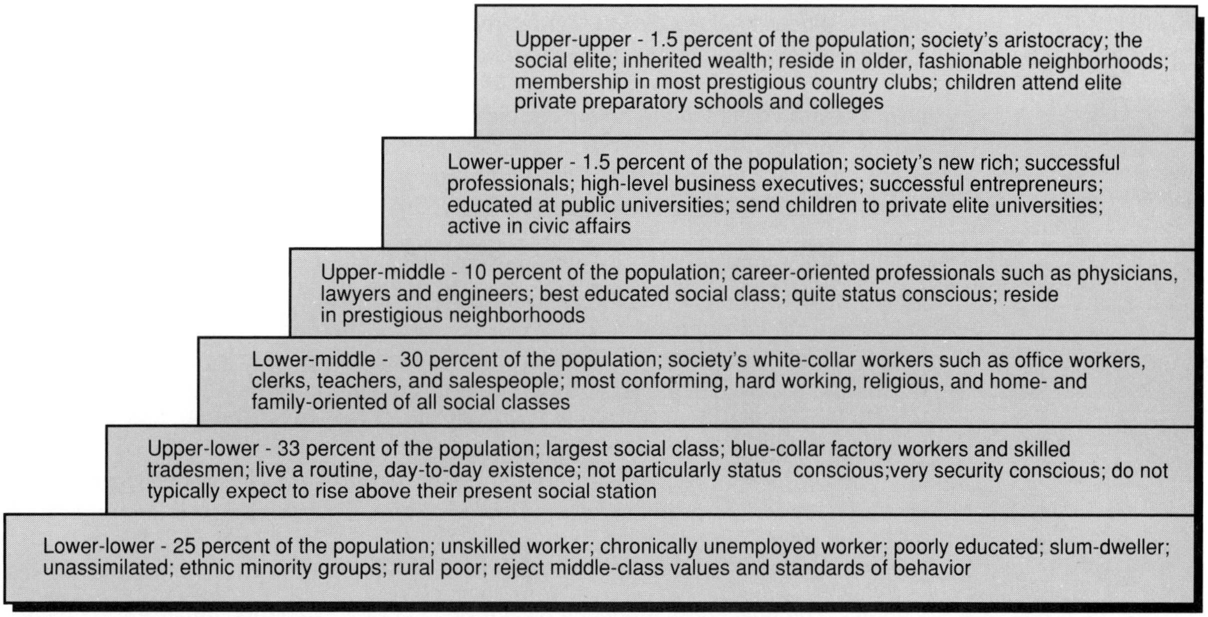

Upper-upper - 1.5 percent of the population; society's aristocracy; the social elite; inherited wealth; reside in older, fashionable neighborhoods; membership in most prestigious country clubs; children attend elite private preparatory schools and colleges

Lower-upper - 1.5 percent of the population; society's new rich; successful professionals; high-level business executives; successful entrepreneurs; educated at public universities; send children to private elite universities; active in civic affairs

Upper-middle - 10 percent of the population; career-oriented professionals such as physicians, lawyers and engineers; best educated social class; quite status conscious; reside in prestigious neighborhoods

Lower-middle - 30 percent of the population; society's white-collar workers such as office workers, clerks, teachers, and salespeople; most conforming, hard working, religious, and home- and family-oriented of all social classes

Upper-lower - 33 percent of the population; largest social class; blue-collar factory workers and skilled tradesmen; live a routine, day-to-day existence; not particularly status conscious; very security conscious; do not typically expect to rise above their present social station

Lower-lower - 25 percent of the population; unskilled worker; chronically unemployed worker; poorly educated; slum-dweller; unassimilated; ethnic minority groups; rural poor; reject middle-class values and standards of behavior

**FIGURE 3–20**
The staircase of social classes (source: Adapted from W. Lloyd Warner, *American Life, Dream and Reality* [Chicago: University of Chicago Press, 1953])

*Social Class.* Based on occupation, education, place of residence (i.e., prestige of neighborhood), income, and wealth, social scientists have developed societal, rank-ordered groupings of individuals and families known as **social classes**. The higher the class rank, the higher the status (greater prestige) of the class. A widely used classification scheme of American social classes is that developed by W. Lloyd Warner. His scheme consists of six levels ranging from upper-upper class to lower-lower class. The Warner classification is reported in Figure 3–20. A number of generalizations can be made concerning the marketing implications stemming from our social class groupings.

Upper-upper class consumers typically do not engage in conspicuous consumption; rather, they tend to be governed by conservative tastes and a selective buying process. They represent potential markets for unique and expensive products (e.g., "originals" in fashion apparel). Patronage motives tend toward personalized services and individualistic merchandising at exclusive retailers. The buying patterns of this class often serve as a reference point for the consumption activities of lower classes.

Lower-upper class consumers engage in conspicuous consumption of a wide range of highly visible personal, recreational, and household products and services. This buying behavior is often directed at impressing lower social classes. A primary consideration of lower-upper class purchase behavior is social acceptability of their peer class and the acceptance of the upper-upper class; in other words, much of this class's buying behavior is directed at achieving status.

Upper-middle class consumers are quality-conscious purchasers of products that are acceptable to the upper class; hence, they tend to be cautious consumers of prestigious products that communicate "who they are" to others. On the other hand, they also tend to be venturesome in their willingness to try new products and seek out new places to shop. For the upper-middle class, their home is the center of their personal and social life and therefore is a focus for their buyer behavior.

Lower-middle class consumers focus a considerable amount of buying behavior around maintaining a respectable home within a do-it-yourself context. They tend to be quite value conscious in that they seek an acceptable relationship between lower prices and good quality. Standardization is a key factor in their buying behavior; they therefore purchase products of standard design from traditional retail operations.

Upper-lower class consumers are less concerned with purchasing products that enhance status and are more concerned with buying goods and services for personal enjoyment. In comparison to other classes above them, this class spends a lower portion of their incomes on housing and a higher proportion of their incomes on household goods. They tend to be impulsive buyers yet remain loyal to previously bought brands that they believe to be a reflection of good quality. As heavy users of credit, this class is hesitant to try new retail outlets.

Lower-lower class consumers use credit extensively and impulsively to purchase highly visible products of a personal nature. They prefer well-known brands and local stores with easy credit terms.

*Culture.* The final social influence on our behavior is the cultural environment within which the consumer lives. **Culture** is the sum total of knowledge, attitudes, symbols, and patterns of behavior that are shared by a group of people and transmitted from one generation to the next. Cultural traits include (1) profound beliefs (e.g., religious); (2) fundamental values (e.g., achievements); and (3) customs (e.g., ladies first). Because cultural environmental influences are a major determinant of human behavior, it is essential for the retailer to adapt and conform merchandising programs to the cultural heritage of his or her chosen markets.

The American culture is undergoing dynamic changes that have a profound effect on consumption patterns and buying behavior. For some products and firms, ongoing cultural trends spell new opportunities and merchandising success; for others, it equates to new threats and possible market failure. In developing and implementing merchandising programs, the retailer must ascertain the type and extent of influence exerted by the cultural traits of their local market area.

**BUYING PROCESS**

Being loved and accepted, overcoming loneliness and insecurity, or gaining status and prestige are all problems that consumers attempt to solve in part by engaging in buying activities. Individuals make purchase decisions by passing through the five stages of what we can call consumer buying process. The **consumer buying process** is the sum total of the sequential parts of problem recognition, information search, alternative evaluation, purchase decision, and postpurchase evaluation. The duration and extent to which an individual gets involved in any one stage of the buying process varies greatly, depending on such factors as urgency of need, frequency of purchase, importance of purchase, and so on. A preview of each stage is presented in the following discussion; see if you can recognize these stages in your own buying behavior.

## Stage 1: Problem Recognition

A felt discrepancy between an ideal state of affairs and the actual state of affairs starts the consumer's buying process by creating an awareness that a problem exists. Problem recognition is, then, a feeling that things are not what they should be. Internally felt physiological and psychological needs are tension-producing stimuli that create an awareness that something is lacking. In addition, external cues attract and direct the consumer's attention toward the recognition that he or she is unsatisfied with his or her state of affairs. Exposure to the retailer's stores, products, advertisements, merchandising incentives, personal selling efforts, and price structures are all potential reminders to consumers of unfulfilled needs and wants.

Based on importance, cost, knowledge, and/or experience factors, there are three types of problem-solving situations—extensive, limited, and routinized problem solving. **Extensive problem solving** involves a buying situation in which the consumer is considering the purchase of an important and costly product under the favorable circumstances of having no knowledge of an experience with the product. First-time purchases, once-in-a-lifetime purchases, and highly infrequent purchases are all buying situations that require extensive consumer effort in achieving a satisfactory solution. Providing useful and readily available information and reducing risk and uncertainty of the purchase are key variables to be considered by the retailer when developing merchandising tactics to assist the consumer faced with an extensive problem-solving situation.

**Limited problem solving** occurs when the consumer has some knowledge and experience with purchasing and using the product under consideration. The problem may or may not involve an important purchase and/or costly product. In either case, the buyer is able to limit the range of considerations (e.g., brands, sizes, colors, materials, and so on) because of existing knowledge and previous experience. The retailer's task is to discover which limited decision factors are being used in making product selections, then use these selective factors as local points in developing appropriate product, price, distribution, and promotion strategies.

**Routinized problem solving** involves making the same purchase decision time after time. Consumers purchase many products frequently and regularly. Typically, these purchases tend to involve products of lower importance and cost that arise as repurchase needs. The typical weekly grocery list represents this type of purchase. Consumers simply repeat a previous purchase decision with little thought or deliberation because they feel there is no reason to change.

## Stage 2: Information Search

Gathering information and gaining experience make up the second stage of the consumer buying process. A *low-level information search* involves an increased awareness of readily available information. The consumer pays closer attention to advertisements, store displays, sales pitches, and comments of others in an effort to gather additional information to supplement existing product knowledge. A *high-level information search* consists of a conscientious effort to seek out and gather new and supplementary information from new and existing sources. It involves actively talking with, reading from, and observing information sources that will be useful to an extensive problem-solving situation involving re-evaluation and reinforcement purchases.

### Stage 3: Alternative Evaluation

Product, brand, and store information needs to be processed before it is useful in the evaluation of purchase alternatives. Consumers use a variety of criteria in making different purchase decisions. What evaluation criteria would you use in purchasing a tube of toothpaste, a desk lamp, a winter coat, a color television, and a new automobile? A comprehensive list of evaluative criteria consumers use in purchasing these products is far too complex and extensive to fully enumerate here; however, a general list of potential evaluation criteria is presented in Figure 3–21.

Criteria do not carry the same weight or have the same importance in deciding on a purchase. In some cases we are simply interested in having the product do what it was designed to do (e.g., clean and polish, cool or heat); therefore, we place greater weight on the functional features of the product. In other cases, our needs may be more social in character; hence, we emphasize the psychological features of the product or brand and the personal considerations of the product's or brand's appro-

**FIGURE 3–21**
Product, brand, and store evaluation criteria

I. Product Evaluation Criteria
   A. Functional Features
     1. Size
     2. Shape
     3. Weight
     4. Material
     5. Workmanship
   B. Aesthetic Features
     1. Color
     2. Texture
     3. Odor
     4. Taste
     5. Sound
     6. Style
   C. Service Features
     1. Delivery
     2. Alteration
     3. Installation
     4. Warranty
     5. Maintenance
   D. Psychological Features
     1. Prestige
     2. Image
     3. Acceptability
     4. Safety
     5. Security
     6. Uniqueness

II. Merchandising Evaluation Criteria
   A. Price Features
     1. Selling Price
     2. Perceived Value
     3. Credit Terms
   B. Place Features
     1. Convenience
     2. Availability
     3. Prestige
   C. Promotional Features
     1. Labels
     2. Logos
     3. Packages

III. Personal Evaluation Criteria
   A. Compatability Considerations
     1. Substitutive
     2. Complement
     3. Different
   B. Appropriateness Considerations
     1. Life-Style
     2. Life Cycle
   C. Other Considerations
     1. Durability
     2. Suitability
     3. Quality

priateness to our life-style and circle of friends. In essence, for a given purchase, criteria may be weighted along an importance scale as illustrated in Figure 3–22.

### Stage 4: Purchase Decision

The purchase decision is actually two decisions—*if* and *when*. The "if decision" deals with the issue of whether or not to make a purchase. Based on the previous evaluation stage, the consumer may decide that there are several products, brands, or stores that are capable of resolving the problem identified in the first stage of the buying process—*the buy decision*. On the other hand, the consumer may conclude that of the known alternatives evaluated, none meet minimum expectations for need satisfaction—*the no-buy decision*. A no-buy decision terminates the current cycle of the buying process; the consumer can either dismiss the problem or start the buying process anew with hopes of gaining a different perspective on the problem.

The "when decision" is concerned with deciding whether to make an immediate purchase or to wait until some future date. A *decision to proceed* with the purchase may stem from urgently felt needs, currently available opportunities, and other circumstances that mediate against delaying the decision. A *decision to postpone* a purchase is frequently associated with a high level of perceived risk. The consumer becomes anxious because of the importance, cost, and/or uncertainty of the decision.

### Stage 5: Postpurchase Evaluation

The purchasing of a product does not end the consumer buying process. Once a purchase has been made, the consumer proceeds to re-evaluate the decision in an attempt to judge whether or not he or she made the right (e.g., best or acceptable) decision. Essentially, the postpurchase evaluation stage consists of comparing the actual performance of the product/service or the actual experience with the store with the expected or hoped for performance or experience. The basic question to be answered by the consumer in the postpurchase evaluation stage is "Did the product or store relieve aroused tensions stemming from felt needs?" In other words, "Did the

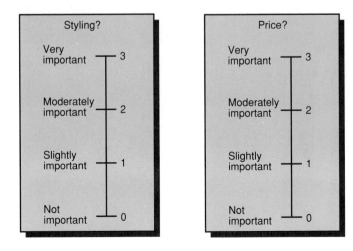

**FIGURE 3–22**
Criteria-weighting scale

product or store solve the problem?" An affirmative answer promotes *postpurchase satisfaction* and encourages the consumer to repeat the purchase behavior at the same outlet when the same or a similar problem arises. A negative answer results in *postpurchase dissonance*—being dissatisfied with the purchase and the process that led to it. To relieve the feelings of uneasiness that are associated with an unsatisfactory product, the consumer may engage in a variety of actions: (1) discard the product and write it off as a bad experience; (2) obtain some type of an allowance from the retailer, thereby increasing the product's perceived value; (3) return the product to the retailer and attempt to improve on the purchase decision process; and (4) write the retailer off as a poor place to shop.

Often consumers have mixed feelings concerning their purchases—a mild case of postpurchase dissonance. In such cases they attempt to confirm a right decision or at least an acceptable decision by (1) seeking positive comments from others, (2) distorting information so that it fits the purchase decision, and (3) emphasizing positive information and de-emphasizing negative data.

## BUYING SCENES

The final buyer behavior issues to be considered are buying scenes—where consumers buy. A **buying scene** is the actual place where consumers complete a purchase transaction. There are four possible buying scenes: (1) a retail store, (2) a

The four buying scenes

consumer's home, (3) a consumer's workplace, and (4) a parasite point of consumption. Americans make a majority of their purchases by visiting a retail store or responding to in-the-home marketing efforts. While a consumer's place of work is a place of production, not consumption, some retailers (e.g., hair stylists and food vendors) have had success by providing the consumer with a high level of time and place convenience. Snap-on-Tool Corp. uses step vans to take its products to the customer.[17] Convenience is also the key for successfully marketing a limited number of products at "parasite" scenes (e.g., newspaper stand at a restaurant, hot dog vendor at a football game, and magazine rack at an airport). A rapidly growing example of this retail format is the pushcart market, or temporary, seasonal tenants found in various malls, marketplaces, and airports. Hickory Farms of Ohio has more than 1,000 such operations in addition to its 500 stores. The temporary nature of such activities is illustrated by the fact that the Jubilee Market at Jackson Brewery in New Orleans offers one-week leases.[18]

**SUMMARY**

A market is a buying population and its corresponding buying behavior. Buying populations can be classified into one of two groups—consumer markets (ultimate consumers of goods and services) and organizational markets (intermediate consumers of goods and services). The structure of buying populations was examined from the perspective of population analysis, demographic analysis, and geographical analysis. Population analysis answers the question "How many are they?" The total population of a consumer market determined in part the actual and potential market for a particular market. Demographic analysis answers the question "Who are they?" Demography is the study of statistics that are used to describe a population. People can be described in terms of age, sex, education, income, occupation, race, nationality, family size, and structure. Major demographic trends are (1) an aging population, (2) a shrinking household, (3) a changing role for women, and (4) an increasing role of many diversified minorities. Geographic analysis answers the question "Where are they?" People move, therefore markets change. Some important geographic trends and patterns are (1) population is shifting from the north and eastern U.S. to the south and western sectors of the country, (2) America is an urbanized society (e.g., 75 percent urbanized), (3) there are more suburbanites than urbanites, and (4) nonmetro areas are making a comeback.

Buying behavior is the manner in which consumers act, function, and react to various situations involving the purchase of a good or service or the acceptance of an idea. The dimensions of consumer buying behavior include understanding buying considerations, situations, centers, influences, processes, and scenes. Buying consideration is concerned with the question "What do consumers buy?" Consumers buy products—bundles of benefits capable of satisfying consumer wants and needs. Products are viewed in terms of their tangibility (goods, services, or ideas); durability (durables and nondurables); and availability (convenience, shopping, and specialty products).

Buying situations are concerned with the question "How much do consumers buy?" The answer is a function of the individual's needs and desires together with the individual's ability to buy (the financial resources—income, credit, assets—that are available to the consumer); willingness to buy (psychological, personal, and social reasons for buying); and authority to buy (formal and informal authorization). Buying centers deal with the issue "Who does the buying?" A buying center is a basic unit of consumption that engages in the buying center. Basic consumption units tend to be either individual or household.

"Why consumers buy" is the question of concern in the discussion of buying influences. The major influences of consumer buying behavior include psychological, personal, and social factors. Motivation, perception, learning, and attitudes are the four major psychological factors that influence consumers in the determination of the buying choices. An individual's personality, self-concept, life-style, and position in the life cycle are all personal factors that have an impact on his or her buying behavior. Conformity to group expectations (family, reference groups, social class, and culture) is the basic premise behind the impact of social factors on consumer buying behavior.

The buying process is the sum total of the sequential arts of problem recognition, information search, alternative evaluation, purchase decision, and postpurchase evaluation. In other words, the buying process answers the question "How do consumers buy?" "Where consumers buy" is described by the four buying scenes. A buying scene is the actual place where consumers complete a purchase transaction; it can be at a retail store, a consumer's home, a consumer's workplace, or a parasite point of consumption.

## STUDENT STUDY GUIDE

**KEY TERMS AND CONCEPTS**

| | |
|---|---|
| activities, interests, and opinions (AIO) statement | durable |
| affective component | esteem need |
| attitude | extensive problem solving |
| asset | family buying role |
| behavior component | goods |
| buying behavior | idea |
| buying center | learning |
| buying power | life cycle |
| buying scene | life-style |
| cognitive component | limited problem solving |
| consumer buying process | market |
| consumer market | market potential |
| convenience product | middle-aged market |
| credit | motivation |
| cues | need |
| culture | nondurable |
| demography | organizational market |
| desire | perception |
| discretionary income | personality |
| disposable income | physiological need |
| drive | products |
| | reference group |

response
routinized problem solving
safety need
selective distortion
selective exposure
selective retention
self-actualization
self-concept
senior-citizens market
service

shopping product
social class
social need
specialty product
total income
total population
ultimate consumer
young-adults market
youth market
zero population growth

1. A market is comprised of two major components. What are they? Provide a brief description.
2. Who are ultimate consumers? What are their purchase intentions?
3. What is demography? A demographic description is based on what variables?
4. Profile the changing age structure of the U.S. population. Discuss the impact of these changes on the retailing of goods.
5. How is the U.S. household mix changing? Is it good or bad news for American retailers? Explain.
6. What are the three working women roles? Describe the impact of these roles on the merchandising of goods and services.
7. Illustrate the basic geographic shifts in the distribution of the nation's population.
8. Define product. Develop a graphic presentation of the various product classifications. Provide a description of each product class.
9. Describe the determinants of consumer buying power.
10. Identify the elements of the motivational process. Distinguish between the various types of needs that direct individual consumer behavior.
11. How is perception accomplished? Delineate between the various forms of selectivity that are portrayed in the perception process.
12. Discuss the stimulus-response mechanisms inherent in the learning process.
13. What are attitudes used for? Describe the components that make up an attitude.
14. Who are we? Identify and define the four parts of the self-concept.
15. Life-style profiles are composite pictures of what factors? How do life-styles affect buying behavior?
16. Portray the various roles that various family members might play relative to a given purchase situation.
17. Outline the various stages of the consumer buying process.

True or False

_____ 1. A market consists of a buying population and its corresponding buying behavior.
_____ 2. One of the major retailing implications of the trend of increasing numbers of working women is the need to develop strategies that are not aimed solely at the woman as the family's major purchasing agent.
_____ 3. Durables are perishable products that are used up in one or a few uses.
_____ 4. Selective retention is the act of remembering only that information the individual wants to remember.

_____ 5. The AIO variables in life-style profiles are attitudes, influences, and opportunities.

_____ 6. Upper-upper social class consumers often engage in conspicuous consumption to meet their need or recognition.

_____ 7. Realization of a discrepancy between an ideal state of affairs and the actual state of affairs is the initial stage of the buying process called problem recognition.

## STUDENT APPLICATIONS MANUAL

**PROJECTS: INVESTIGATIONS AND APPLICATIONS**

1. Population and demographic profiles are essential in determining the market potential of a given area. Develop complete population and demographic profiles of your town, city, or county. Consult several different sources (e.g., Census Bureau reports, Survey of Buying Power) and prepare a list of the ten most important population or demographic trends in your area. For each identified trend, provide two or more merchandising implications that retailers should consider in the future.

2. Classify each item on the following list of products as to its (1) product tangibility, (2) product durability, and (3) product availability.

   1. meat
   2. pet food
   3. furniture
   4. electricity
   5. church service
   6. auto insurance
   7. legal advice
   8. movie
   9. Datsun 300 ZX
   10. air conditioner
   11. Big Mac
   12. bag of apples
   13. telephone service
   14. tennis shoes
   15. pencil
   16. film
   17. business suit
   18. prescription drug
   19. haircut
   20. music concert
   21. college course
   22. candy bar
   23. wedding ring
   24. gasoline
   25. lawn mower
   26. open-heart surgery
   27. birthday dinner
   28. textbook

3. Determine your ability to buy by estimating your buying power.

4. Consult the list of products in project 2. Which products do you purchase to meet (1) physiological needs, (2) safety needs, (3) social needs, (4) esteem needs, and (5) self-actualization needs?

5. Describe specific examples of your selective perception in terms of your selective exposure, retention, and distortion.

6. Life-style is the way people live. One interesting life-style segmentation scheme for high school students was uncovered by Bickley Townsend, associate editor of *American Demographics*. Review the six high school life-styles described below. Assume the role of a small specialty clothing store and develop some merchandising strategies that you believe would be appealing to each of the six life-style segments.

   Greaseballs:    At one end of the high school life-style spectrum are the Greaseballs, including Farmers and Farmers' Daughters. The boys wear brown jackets from Agway and tractor caps that say "Brooktondale Volunteer Firemen." The girls sport heavy makeup and tight sweaters.

   Also in the Greaseball segment are Wrestlers (other jocks have status, but wrestlers do not), and Headbangers. Headbangers wear chains and black concert shirts that say "Twisted Sister"; advanced cases are called Burnouts.

Rah-Rahs:     This psychographic segment includes jocks, their girlfriends, and the guys who wish they were jocks. Rah-Rahs are popular conformists, with few intellectual or political interests. They used to include Preppies, but this is a disappearing segment, reflecting the elusiveness of teen-age fashion.

New Wavers:   Also popular, but more involved in current events, New Wavers are fashion-conscious in an attention-getting way. They are distinguished by melon and light-green clothing, including color-coordinated socks, all carrying an Esprit label. New Wavers are emulated by Pseudo-Wavers, who want to be Wavers but don't quite make it.

Apes:         These are the smart kids, the ones who take the advanced placement (A.P.) courses. They are arrogantly articulate and fiercely competitive for 4.0 averages. They are the driving force behind the student newspaper. Although they think of themselves as Achievers, they are known to outsiders as Encyclopedias.

Zobos:        Mostly female, Zobos are distinguished by their high political consciousness and studied bag-lady fashion look. Zobos shop in used-clothing stores and eschew high heels. A typical Zobo outfit is a long skirt made from an Indian bedspread, accompanied by high, laced-up hiking boots. Zobos spend a lot of time on worthwhile causes like sponsoring Laotian refugees, and they carry hand-woven purses from Guatemala to demonstrate their solidarity with the Third World.

Resistors:    This category represents the pinnacle of psychological development. Resistors defy psychographic classification or fashion identification, evident in their uniform of T-shirts, sweatshirts, and chinos. Their message is that they are totally unaware of image, being above such trivia.

7. A consumer's "values" play an important role in his or her buying behavior. Develop a list of five or six values that you believe are basic to most consumers. Describe each key value and provide an example of how each type of value might have an impact on the consumer's buying behavior.

---

**CASE 3–1**
### Doug's Video—Developing Competitive Positioning Strategies Based on Consumer Patronage Behavior*

CASES:
PROBLEMS AND
DECISIONS

Doug Deitz' story was not unlike those of many other New Englanders who successfully survived the migration to the sunbelt of many types of manufacturing. Doug had graduated from high school in the late 1940s, taken a job in a textile mill, enlisted in the Army Reserve, spent two years on active duty during the Korean conflict, and then returned to the mill. When the mill headed south in the sixties, Doug took advantage of his G.I. bill and completed an associate degree in business.

He started his retailing career with a family-owned department store. Failure of the department store management to follow the movement into shopping centers led to the sale of the store to a chain. It became apparent to Doug that the new management favored persons with baccalaureate degrees. When Doug realized how long it was going to take him

*This case was prepared by Ken Mast and Dale Lewison, The University of Akron.

to complete his degree on a part-time basis, he regretted his decision not to continue his education at the time he completed the associate degree. As others with less experience received promotions to buying responsibility, Doug sought a change of scenery and obtained more managerial responsibility in the employ of a discount store chain. He worked for two different discount chains until two years ago when, with the benefit of an inheritance from the passing of his parents, he acquired a video store.

Doug benefited from the increasing popularity of video rentals and the sale of video equipment, but the success of his business seemed to indicate that he had more managerial talent than former employers had perceived. Proof of self-perception is the additional success Doug achieved in providing unique and profitable video services. His first video service was the videotaping of houses for sale. The tapes were sold to more progressive area realtors who used them to screen home buyers' interests. Because the tapes benefited both the realtors and the prospective home buyers, they had been very successful. Recently, Doug had expanded the video service to include videotaping of homes and contents for insurance purposes. Although the insurance service didn't generate the volume or the regularity of revenues the realtor service did, it did not require any additional investment in equipment and staff. The only added cost was for promotion; hence it represented the addition of a complementary line of service.

Doug's Video was located in a community shopping center complex that had been built as part of a relatively new housing development. The introduction and expansion of local high-tech industries had created a miniboom for the local economy. New people were being attracted by these high-tech firms because job salaries in the $50–100,000 range were common. These high-income families constituted the majority of the buyers of the homes in the housing development that surrounded the shopping center. Additional retailers in the complex were a junior department store, a large super-food store, a dry cleaner, a bakery, a hardware store, a small pharmacy, three apparel stores, a pizza/sub shop, and a delicatessen.

The video rental business generated a fairly lively traffic volume for the store. Doug's prior expansion of services had taken advantage of existing products and staff capabilities, but only indirectly of the high-volume in-store traffic. Because all systems seemed to be "go" in terms of the local economy, Doug was giving serious consideration to some type of expansion.

One expansion idea was to add a complementary line of merchandise that would fit into the current business format and capitalize on the high in-store traffic generated by the video rental business. The addition of a complete line of cameras and accessories was a product extension strategy that Doug felt that he and his staff could handle within current operating abilities. The buying and merchandising aspects of adding new camera and accessory lines did not create any major obstacles. What concerned Doug was developing a business format that would be competitive with other retailers and consistent with consumer patronage behavior. Recently, Doug had obtained from a vendor an excellent trade survey on what factors influenced consumer choice of outlet for camera purchases. As revealed in the survey, the importance of patronage factors varies for different types of retailers (see Exhibits 1–7). The discount store camera customer is different from the department store customer. Through experience, Doug has learned that "competitive positioning" is often a key variable in introducing a new product or service. A quick mental survey of local retailers who sell cameras reveals that Doug will be facing each of the six types of competitors identified in the trade report.

### ASSIGNMENT

1. On the basis of consumer patronage behavior for camera purchases, develop three competitive positioning strategies Doug might pursue in establishing his camera department. Provide an analysis for each strategy and make a recommendation.

**2.** On the basis of your competitive positioning recommendation, identify key merchandising tactics that Doug should use to successfully introduce this new line of products.

| Rank | Influencing Factor | Average Rating 1985 |
|------|--------------------|---------------------|
| 1 | Low price | 5.36 |
| 2 | Services offered | 5.08 |
| 3 | Knowledgeable sales staff | 5.03 |
| 4 | Quality reputation | 5.00 |
| 5 | Selection of photo goods | 4.44 |
| 6 | Close to home or work | 3.90 |
| 7 | Attractive atmosphere | 3.07 |
| 8 | Selection of other goods | 2.83 |

**EXHIBIT 1**
Overall average

Source for Exhibits 1 through 7: 1985 *Consumer Photographic Survey* (Jackson, MI: Photo Marketing Association International): 21.

| Rank | Influencing Factor | Outlet Rating | Overall Average |
|------|--------------------|---------------|-----------------|
| 1 | Low price | 5.77 | 5.36 |
| 2 | Services offered | 4.92 | 5.08 |
| 3 | Quality reputation | 4.59 | 5.00 |
| 4 | Knowledgeable sales staff | 4.40 | 5.03 |
| 5 | Selection of photo goods | 4.12 | 4.44 |
| 6 | Close to home or work | 4.07 | 3.90 |
| 7 | Selection of other goods | 3.60 | 2.83 |
| 8 | Attractive atmosphere | 3.25 | 3.07 |

**EXHIBIT 2**
Discount store

| Rank | Influencing Factor | Outlet Rating | Overall Average |
|------|--------------------|---------------|-----------------|
| 1 | Knowledgeable sales staff | 5.84 | 5.03 |
| 2 | Services offered | 5.73 | 5.08 |
| 3 | Quality reputation | 5.64 | 6.00 |
| 4 | Selection of photo goods | 4.91 | 4.44 |
| 5 | Low price | 4.80 | 5.36 |
| 6 | Close to home or work | 4.00 | 3.90 |
| 7 | Attractive atmosphere | 3.15 | 3.07 |
| 8 | Selection of other goods | 2.19 | 2.83 |

**EXHIBIT 3**
Camera store

**EXHIBIT 4**
Mail order

| Rank | Influencing Factor | Outlet Rating | Overall Average |
|------|--------------------|---------------|-----------------|
| 1 | Low price | 5.81 | 5.36 |
| 2 | Quality reputation | 5.40 | 5.00 |
| 3 | Selection of photo goods | 5.00 | 4.44 |
| 4 | Services offered | 4.68 | 5.08 |
| 5 | Knowledgeable sales staff | 4.44 | 5.03 |
| 6 | Close to home or work | 2.75 | 3.90 |
| 7 | Selection of other goods | 2.16 | 2.83 |
| 8 | Attractive atmosphere | 2.00 | 3.07 |

**EXHIBIT 5**
Department store

| Rank | Influencing Factor | Outlet Rating | Overall Average |
|------|--------------------|---------------|-----------------|
| 1 | Low price | 5.35 | 5.36 |
| 2 | Services offered | 5.18 | 5.08 |
| 3 | Knowledgeable sales staff | 4.98 | 5.03 |
| 4 | Quality reputation | 4.97 | 5.00 |
| 5 | Selection of photo goods | 4.25 | 4.44 |
| 6 | Close to home or work | 4.15 | 3.90 |
| 7 | Attractive atmosphere | 3.46 | 3.07 |
| 8 | Selection of other goods | 3.19 | 2.83 |

**EXHIBIT 6**
Catalog showroom

| Rank | Influencing Factor | Outlet Rating | Overall Average |
|------|--------------------|---------------|-----------------|
| 1 | Low price | 5.73 | 5.36 |
| 2 | Services offered | 4.90 | 5.08 |
| 3 | Quality reputation | 4.80 | 5.00 |
| 4 | Knowledgeable sales staff | 4.63 | 5.03 |
| 5 | Selection of photo goods | 4.60 | 4.44 |
| 6 | Close to home or work | 3.81 | 3.90 |
| 7 | Attractive atmosphere | 3.41 | 3.07 |
| 8 | Selection of other goods | 3.34 | 2.83 |

**EXHIBIT 7**
Discount camera store

| Rank | Influencing Factor | Outlet Rating | Overall Average |
|------|--------------------|---------------|-----------------|
| 1 | Low price | 5.56 | 5.36 |
| 2 | Knowledgeable sales staff | 5.26 | 5.03 |
| 3 | Quality reputation | 4.79 | 5.00 |
| 4 | Services offered | 4.69 | 5.08 |
| 5 | Selection of photo goods | 4.64 | 4.44 |
| 6 | Close to home or work | 3.36 | 3.90 |
| 7 | Attractive atmosphere | 2.39 | 3.07 |
| 8 | Selection of other goods | 1.87 | 2.83 |

CASE 3-2
## DINKs, DINKdom, and No DINKerbells—Targeting Consumer Life Cycles and Life-Styles*

Who are the DINKs? They are *double income, no-kids* couples who work a combined 100-hour-plus workweek and earn a combined salary that is notably higher than either their "dual-income, with kids" or "single-income, no kids" counterparts. Nevertheless, there is a class system even within this limited consumer segment. "Philip Kotler, professor of marketing at Northwestern, divides DINKs into upper and lower classes: U-DINKs and L-DINKs. No doubt, while the L-DINKs are rushing to graduate from K mart to Marshall Field, the U-DINKs will be deserting the Banana Republic for Abercrombie & Fitch."

What is DINKdom? Is it a place or a state of mind or is it both? DINKdom for the U-DINKs is often an architect-designed house in a pricier suburb or a refurbished gentrified flat in a trendy urban neighborhood. For the L-DINK, home is the best residential area within reach of a stretched pocketbook. DINKdom is also a state of mind; it is a desire for security, privacy, a nest, the finer things, and Persian duck in pomegranate sauce. But beware, it could also be a transitory state—"the moment before tradition sets in."

No DINKerbells are desired in the near future. DINKs are not ready "to give up the quality time that is necessary to devote to their careers and transfer that to children." However, if the recent mini-baby boom among the thirtyish crowd is any indication, DINKs may find that "children may be the next pleasure source after they have tried everything else."

Never fear, if DINKs disappear, there are several snappy target market acronyms to take their place (e.g., TIPS—*tiny income, parents supporting,* and NINKs—*no income, no kids*).

## ASSIGNMENT

Prepare a report titled "Merchandising Strategies for *Double-Income, No Kids Couples*." The report should profile the key psychological, personal, and social factors that influence the buying behavior of this consumer segment. The report should make specific recommendations as to the most appropriate product, price, place, and promotional strategies that retailers should follow in targeting this unique market segment.

**ENDNOTES**

1. John A. Byrne and Paul B. Brown, "Those Unpredictable Babies," *Forbes* (November 1982): 206.
2. Selina S. Guber, "The Teenage Mind," *American Demographics* (August 1987): 44.
3. David B. Wolfe, "The Ageless Market," *American Demographics* (July 1987): 28.
4. Paul B. Brown, "Last Year It Was Yuppies—This Year It's Their Parents," *Business Week,* 10 March 1986, 68.
5. Heidi E. Capousis, "Household Size Shrinks," *USA Today,* 15 Oct. 1987, A-1.
6. Janet Wallach, "Career Dressing," *Stores* (January 1987): 51.
7. Joel Kotkin, "Selling to the New America," *INC* (July 1987): 47.
8. Dwight Johnson, "Black Population: Present and Future," *Black Enterprise* (July 1987): 39.
9. "2000," *Chain Store Age Executive* (May 1987): 22.
10. Martin L. Bell, "Some Strategy Implications of a Matrix Approach to the Classification of Marketing Goods and Services," *Journal of the Academy of Marketing Sciences* 14 (Spring 1986): 13–20.

*This case was prepared by Dale Lewison and Doug Hausknecht and is based on Christine Gorman and Bill Johnson, "Here Comes the DINKs," *Time* (April 20, 1987): 75–76.

11. Susan Benway, "Presto! The Convenience Industry: Making Life a Little Simpler," *Business Week,* 27 April 1987, 86.

12. "Standard of Living Rate Increasing 20% Per Decade," *Marketing News,* 13 Feb. 1987, 3.

13. Robert B. Settle and Pamela L. Alreck, "Knowing Your Consumer Inside and Out," *Marketing Communications* (March 1987): 50.

14. Bickley Townsend, "Psychographic Glitter and Gold," *American Demographics* (November 1985): 79.

15. Nancy Giges, "Prodigal Offspring Boost Buying Power by Returning to Roost," *Advertising Age,* 2 March 1987, 36.

16. "If Both Parents Are Bread Winners, Teenagers Often Are the Bread Buyers," *Marketing News,* 13 Feb. 1987, 5.

17. "Step Vans Serve as Store on Wheels," *Marketing News* (June 1987): 6.

18. Eric C. Peterson, "Temporary Tenants," *Stores* (January 1987): 144; Barbara Bryan, "Airport Retailing," *Stores* (July 1987): 37; "Airport Retailers Expected to Reach New Sales Heights," *Marketing News,* 15 Feb. 1988, 23.

# PART TWO
# Retail Operations

# 4

**Objectives**

☐ Defend the need for fiscal control as an essential ingredient in any successful retail operation.

☐ Identify and define the basic financial records required to accomplish fiscal control.

☐ Discuss the concept of profit and its impact on retailing activities.

☐ Prepare a basic income statement for a retailing enterprise.

☐ Prepare a basic balance sheet for a retailing enterprise.

☐ Analyze and evaluate the operational and financial performance of a retail firm.

☐ Explain how to generate and maintain sufficient capital to conduct a retail business.

☐ Describe the procedures for managing the retailer's operating expenses.

# Retail Accounting and Control

Fiscal control is an essential ingredient to the success of any retail operation. To develop and maintain a viable retail enterprise, the retailer must control the financial health of the firm. Many retailers encounter financial trouble in spite of respectable sales volumes. A common cause of such trouble is insufficient planning and control of the firm's financial affairs. Before the retailer can improve operations, it must be fully aware of the present state of operations. This chapter examines the retailer's financial system. As Figure 4–1 illustrates, the retailer's financial system consists of (1) developing and maintaining good financial records, (2) preparing and analyzing financial statements, (3) constructing and evaluating financial performance ratios, (4) obtaining and managing capital funds, and (5) planning and controlling operating expenses. Each of these tasks is examined in this chapter.

## THE RETAILER'S FINANCIAL RECORDS

Size and operational complexities of the retail firm determine the type and level of sophistication of the financial record-keeping system the retailer uses. Most retailers, however, maintain a number of ledger accounts. "An **account** is a record of the increases and decreases in one type of asset, liability, capital, income, or expense. A book or file in which a number of accounts are kept together is a **ledger** [emphasis added]."[1] The following basic ledger accounts or records are fairly standard:

- Cash receipts—record the cash received
- Cash disbursements—record the firm's expenditures
- Sales—record and summarize monthly income
- Purchases—record the purchases of merchandise bought for processing or resale
- Payroll—records the wages of employees and their deductions, such as income tax and social security
- Equipment—records the firm's capital assets, such as equipment, office furniture, and motor vehicles
- Inventory—records the firm's investment in stock, needed to arrive at a true profit on financial statements and for income tax purposes
- Accounts receivable—record the balances that customers owe to the firm
- Accounts payable—record what the firm owes its creditors and suppliers[2]

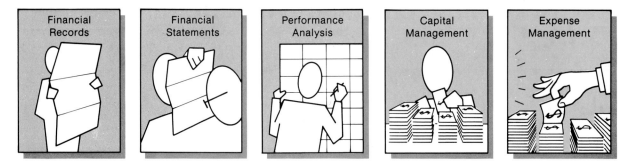

FIGURE 4–1
The retailer's financial system

As one accountant found, "A set of books is like a roll of exposed film. The latter must be developed before you can see the picture. Similarly, your books contain facts and figures which make up a picture of your business. They have to be arranged into an order before you see the picture."[3]

## THE RETAILER'S FINANCIAL STATEMENTS

To gain a clear picture of the firm's financial position, the retailer must prepare two standard financial statements: the income statement and the balance sheet. The **income statement** (also referred to as the profit and loss statement, operating statement, or earnings statement) is a picture of the retailer's profits or losses over a period of time; it summarizes the firm's income and expenses. The **balance sheet** is a picture of the firm's assets, liabilities, and net worth on a given date; it summarizes the basic accounting equation of assets equal liabilities plus net worth.

### The Income Statement

To understand fully the many dimensions of profit, the retailer must have some procedure for organizing these dimensions. The retail accounting procedure known as the income statement is an excellent means for organizing and understanding the many facets of profit. The income statement summarizes the retailer's financial activity for a given period. The principal objective of the income statement is to show whether the retailer had a profit or a loss.

*Preparation of the Income Statement.* Time, unit, and usage are three important variables retailers must consider in preparing the income statement. *Time* considerations concern when income statements are prepared. Federal and state income tax regulations require that the retailer prepare at least an annual income statement. By preparing the income statement more frequently, however, the retailer can maintain closer control over operations.

   *Unit* considerations influence how many income statements are prepared and at what organizational level. For the small, independent retailer, a single income statement should suffice for the entire store. For a departmentalized chain store operation, income statements are prepared for the department and store unit as well as for the entire chain organization. As with more frequent preparation, greater control of operations is the primary advantage of preparing income statements for each of the retailer's operating units.

*Usage* considerations involve the type of format to use in preparing income statements. Because retailing organizations differ in size, type, and organizational structure, no single or standardized income statement format is appropriate for all firms.

*Elements of the Income Statement.* Each retailer should understand the basic elements of the income statement and the relationships among them. Every income statement has at least nine basic elements, regardless of the size, type, or organizational structure of the retail enterprise. Figure 4−2 illustrates the nine elements and the relationships among them, and it shows that the elements of an income statement can be divided into two major groups: income measurements and income modifications.

**Income measurements** are different expressions of the monetary gain the retailer realizes from retailing activities. The exact nature of each income measurement depends on where it appears in the income statement and the income modifications that have been applied in calculating it. Figure 4−2 shows five income measurements—gross sales, net sales, gross margin, operating profit, and net profit. In essence, each income expression represents the monetary gain the retailer realizes before making certain adjustments.

**Income modifications** are monetary additions or reductions applied to one income measurement to calculate another measurement of income. These income modifications simply reflect normal adjustments required by the operating charac-

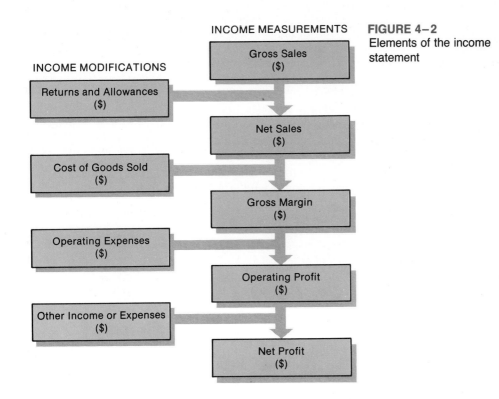

INCOME MEASUREMENTS

INCOME MODIFICATIONS

**FIGURE 4−2**
Elements of the income statement

teristics of the retailer. Most income modifications are reductions; they represent the various costs the retailer incurs in conducting the business, and they are necessary to arrive at the retailer's true income—the bottom line of the income statement or net profit before taxes. In one case, an income modification represents an addition to a measurement of income. This "other income" usually represents income the retailer generates outside normal retailing activities. As illustrated in Figure 4–2, there are four general income modifications—returns and allowances, cost of goods sold, operating expenses, and other income or expenses.

The basic format for the income statement is shown in Figure 4–3. The retailer must carefully follow the format to maintain the correct relationships between the basic statement elements.

*Gross Sales.* **Gross sales** can be defined as the total dollar revenues the retailer receives from the sale of merchandise and services. The gross sales figure, which includes both cash and credit sales, is obtained by first posting in a sales ledger all cash and credit sales at the price actually charged customers, then totaling those sales for the appropriate accounting period. The gross sales figure is the starting point from which all other income measurements are calculated. This figure is important because it reflects the total dollar amount that not only must cover all of the retailer's costs of doing business but also must provide a reward (profit) for conducting that business.

*Returns and Allowances.* Not all customer purchases are finalized with the initial sale. Some customers will become dissatisfied with their purchases and will expect the retailer to make some sort of adjustment. **Returns from customers** and **allowances to customers,** two means by which retailers adjust for customer dissatisfaction, represent cancellation of sales; therefore, the gross sales figure must be adjusted to reflect the cancellations.

*Net Sales.* **Net sales,** the income measurement that results when returns and allowances are subtracted from gross sales, represent the amount of merchandise the retailer actually sold during the accounting period.

*Cost of Goods Sold.* The value of the merchandise the retailer sells during any given accounting period is the **cost of goods sold**. This value represents the total dollars

**FIGURE 4–3**
Format of the income statement

```
Gross sales .................................. $_____
  — Returns and allowances .... $_____
Net sales .................................... $_____
  — Cost of goods sold ......... $_____
Gross margin ............................... $_____
  — Operating expenses ........ $_____
Operating profit ........................... $_____
  ± Other income or expenses .. $_____
Net profit before taxes .................... $_____
```

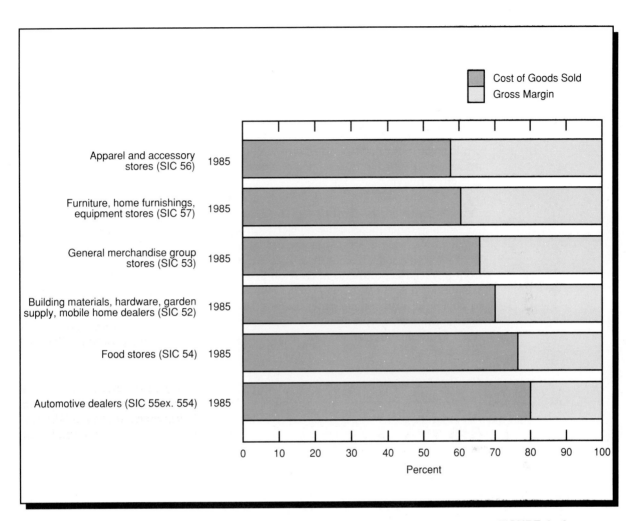

FIGURE 4–4

Estimated gross margin
and cost of goods sold
as a percentage of
sales, by selected
kinds of business: 1985
SIC—standard indus-
trial classification.
(source: U.S. Depart-
ment of Commerce,
Current Business Re-
ports, 1985 Retail
Trade, 12)

paid out by the retailer for the merchandise, its transportation to the store, and its
preparation for sale.

*Gross Margin.* **Gross margin** is defined as the dollar difference between the retailer's
net sales and the total cost of goods sold (see Figure 4–3). It represents the funds
available for covering operating expenses and generating a profit. The relationship
between gross margin and cost of goods sold for various kinds of business is shown
in Figure 4–4. Gross margins for department stores averaged about 40 percent of net
sales in 1986; specialty stores' gross margins were slightly better at about 41
percent.[4]

*Operating Expenses.* Every retailer incurs certain expenses (payroll, rent, utilities,
supplies, etc.) in operating a business. To realize a profit, the retailer's **operating
expenses** must be less than the gross margin figure identified in the previous discus-

sion. In 1986, department stores' operating expenses were about 34 percent of total store sales; specialty stores tend to have operating expenses that are 2 to 3 percent higher.[5]

*Operating Profit.* The difference between gross margin and operating expenses is the retailer's **operating profit** (see Figure 4–3). It is what remains after the retailer has covered the cost of goods sold and its cost of doing business. Operating profit defines productivity of the capital and labor invested in the retail store; it is derived from retail management's skill in maintaining a reasonable spread between operating expenses and gross margin.[6]

*Other Income and/or Expenses.* The final modification to the income statement is considering other income the retailer receives and other expenses incurred in conducting the business. **Other income** can be defined as additional revenues that result from retailing activities other than the buying and selling of goods and services. Rent from a leased department, interest on installment credit, and interest on deposited bank funds are all examples of other income that must be added to operating profit to obtain the retailer's net profit. Before the retailer can compute the final net sales figure, however, some additional expenses must be deducted from the operating profit figure. Interest paid by the retailer on borrowed funds is an example of **other expenses**.

*Net Profit.* **Net profit** is operating profit plus other income and minus other expenses (see Figure 4–3). Net profit is the figure on which the retailer pays income tax, and it is usually referred to either in terms of "net profit before taxes" or "net profit after taxes."

## The Balance Sheet

The second accounting statement used in reporting financial information is the balance sheet—a statement of the retailer's financial condition as of a given date. In its most basic form, the balance sheet summarizes the relationship among the retailer's assets, liabilities, and net worth. The following equation shows this basic balance sheet relationship:

$$assets = liabilities + net\ worth$$

The balance sheet is prepared to show what the retailer owns (the amount and distribution of assets), what the retailer owes (the amount and distribution of liabilities), and what the retailer is worth (the difference between assets and liabilities). By comparing the current year's balance sheet with those of previous years, the retailer can identify any changes in the firm's financial position and determine whether any operational improvements are possible.

A typical balance sheet format, illustrated in Figure 4–5, consists of two major parts. The first part lists assets; the second part lists the retailer's liabilities and states the equity position (the net worth of the owners). As Figure 4–5 shows, the total assets figure always equals the sum of total liabilities plus net worth.

*The Retailer's Assets.* The first part of the balance sheet reports the retailer's asset position. An **asset** is anything of value owned by the retail firm. Assets are categorized into two groups: current assets and fixed assets.

**Current assets** include all items of value that the retailer can easily convert into cash within a relatively short time, usually within one year or less. In addition to cash on hand, current assets include accounts receivable, merchandise inventory, and supply inventory. Accounts receivable are amounts that customers *owe* the retailer for goods and services. The value of the merchandise on hand at the time of preparing the balance sheet is a part of the retailer's current assets. Supply inventory reflects operating supplies on hand that have been paid for but not used; in effect, they represent prepaid expenses. The retailer arrives at the total current asset figure by totaling cash on hand, accounts receivable, merchandise inventory, and supply inventory (see Figure 4–5).

**FIGURE 4–5**
Balance sheet format

| Assets | | |
|---|---|---|
| **Current assets** | | |
| Cash | $10,000 | |
| Accounts | 15,000 | |
| Merchandise inventory | 90,000 | |
| Supply inventory | 5,000 | |
|   Total current assets | | $120,000 |
| **Fixed assets** | | |
| Building (less depreciation) | 75,000 | |
| Fixtures and equipment | 25,000 | |
|   (less depreciation) | | |
|   Total fixed assets | | 100,000 |
| **Total assets** | | 220,000 |
| | | |
| Liabilities and net worth | | |
| **Current liabilities** | | |
| Accounts payable | $25,000 | |
| Payroll payable | 10,000 | |
| Taxes payable | 5,000 | |
| Notes payable | 15,000 | |
|   Total current liabilities | | $55,000 |
| **Fixed liabilities** | | |
| Mortgage payable | 50,000 | |
| Notes payable | 20,000 | |
|   Total fixed liabilities | | 70,000 |
| **Net worth** | | |
| Capital surplus | 85,000 | |
| Retained earnings | 10,000 | |
|   Total net worth | | 95,000 |
| **Total liabilities and net worth** | | $220,000 |

**Fixed assets** are those that require a significant length of time to convert into cash (more than one year). These long-term assets include buildings, fixtures (e.g., display racks), and equipment (e.g., delivery trucks). The value of fixed assets is expressed in terms of their cost to the retailer minus an assigned depreciation. This depreciation is necessary because fixed assets have a limited useful life; therefore, depreciation better reflects their true value. The depreciation also helps to avoid overstating the retailer's total assets.

**Total assets** equal current assets plus fixed assets (see Figure 4–5). Now let's look at the other half of the balance sheet.

*The Retailer's Liabilities.* Part two of the balance sheet reflects the retailer's liabilities and net worth. A **liability** is a debt owed to someone. On the balance sheet, liabilities represent a legitimate claim against the retailer's assets. Liabilities are classified as either current or long-term.

**Current liabilities** are short-term debts that must be paid during the current fiscal year. Included in the current liabilities column are accounts payable, payroll payable, and notes payable that are due within one year. Accounts payable represent money owed to suppliers for goods and services they have provided. Payroll payable is money owed to store employees for labor performed. Principal and interest the retailer owes on a bank loan (notes payable) and taxes the retailer owes local, state, and federal governments (taxes payable) are classified as current liabilities.

**Long-term liabilities** are long-term indebtedness. Mortgages and long-term notes and bonds not due during the current fiscal year are the most common long-term liabilities. Another category sometimes treated as a long-term liability is a reserve account to provide the retailer with funds for emergencies. The total liability figure is computed by combining the current and long-term liabilities.

*The Retailer's Net Worth.* **Net worth** represents the owner's equity in the retail business and is defined by the following equation:

$$\text{net worth} = \text{total assets} - \text{total liabilities}$$

Another way to look at net worth is to view it as the owner's share of the firm's total assets.

---

**PERFORMANCE ANALYSIS**

The income statement and the balance sheet provide the retailer with a wealth of data. To convert these data into meaningful information, retailers rely on **ratio analysis**—an examination of the relationship between elements in the income statement and/or the balance sheet. A number of different ratios and relationships can assist retailers in appraising the firm's past and present performances and can provide some insight into the firm's future performances. By making comparisons among the firm's past ratios and the ratios of similar national and local firms, the retailer can constructively evaluate the firm's performance. Ratios can be grouped into two general categories: operating ratios and financial ratios.

## Operating Ratios

**Operating ratios** express relationships between elements of the income statement. They are used to judge how efficiently the retailer generates sales and manages expenses. To obtain operating ratios, one element of the retailer's income statement must be divided by another element and multiplied by 100. To illustrate the use of operating ratios, we use Figure 4−6. This figure uses information from an income statement (see Figure 4−6a) to calculate several operating ratios (see Figure 4−6b)

FIGURE 4−6
The use of operating ratios

**(a) 1986 Income Statement:**
**The Smart Shop**

| | |
|---|---|
| Gross sales............................. | $220,000 |
| − Returns and allowances ...... $ 4,000 | |
| Net sales ............................... | $216,000 |
| − Cost of goods sold ........... $104,000 | |
| Gross margin.......................... | $112,000 |
| − Operating expenses ......... $ 80,000 | |
| Operating profit ...................... | $ 32,000 |
| + Other income ............... $ 1,000 | |
| − Other expenses ............. $ 3,000 | |
| Net profit.............................. | $ 30,000 |

**(b) 1986 Operating Ratios**
**The Smart Shop**

| Ratio | Calculation | Interpretation |
|---|---|---|
| $\dfrac{\text{Gross sales}}{\text{Net sales}}$ | $\dfrac{\$220,000}{\$216,000} \times 100$ | Gross sales equal 102 percent of net sales. |
| $\dfrac{\text{Cost of goods sold}}{\text{Net sales}}$ | $\dfrac{\$104,000}{\$216,000} \times 100$ | Cost of goods sold equals 48.1 percent of net sales. |
| $\dfrac{\text{Gross margin}}{\text{Net sales}}$ | $\dfrac{\$112,000}{\$216,000} \times 100$ | Gross margin equals 51.9 percent of net sales. |
| $\dfrac{\text{Operating expenses}}{\text{Net sales}}$ | $\dfrac{\$80,000}{\$216,000} \times 100$ | Operating expenses equal 37 percent of net sales. |
| $\dfrac{\text{Operating profit}}{\text{Net sales}}$ | $\dfrac{\$32,000}{\$216,000} \times 100$ | Operating profit equals 14.8 percent of net sales. |
| $\dfrac{\text{Net profit}}{\text{Net sales}}$ | $\dfrac{\$30,000}{\$216,000} \times 100$ | Net profit equals 13.9 percent of net sales. |

that show the basic relationship between net sales and (1) gross sales, (2) cost of goods sold, (3) gross margin, (4) operating expenses, (5) operating profit, and (6) net profit.

### Financial Ratios

**Financial ratios** express relationships between the elements of a balance sheet or between a balance sheet element and an element in the income statement. These ratios are used to identify relative strengths and weaknesses in the retailer's financial status and to discover trends that will affect future performance capabilities. Liquidity and leverage ratios are two key financial areas of concern.

Liquidity determines whether the retailer can meet payment obligations as they mature. It is the state of possessing sufficient liquid assets that can be quickly and easily converted to cash to meet scheduled payments or to take advantage of special merchandising opportunities. **Liquidity ratios** answer the question of "how solvent is the retailer?"

The **current ratio** is a liquidity ratio that represents the retailer's ability to meet current debts with current assets; it is computed by dividing current assets by current liabilities (see previous definitions of current assets and liabilities). A current ratio of 2:1, $2 of current assets to $1 of current liabilities, is the most common benchmark used in retailing. Low current ratios suggest liquidity problems; high ratios indicate good long-term solvency.

Owner financing versus creditor financing is addressed by leverage ratios. A **leverage ratio** measures the relative contributions of owners and creditors in the financing of the firm's operations. One type of leverage ratio is the **debt ratio**—total debt (current plus long-term liabilities) divided by total assets (current plus fixed assets). The higher the ratio, the greater the role of creditors in the firm's total financing. Within reason, owners like to limit their own financial investment; hence they prefer high debt ratios while creditors prefer the lower risks associated with more moderate debt ratios.

## CAPITAL MANAGEMENT

A major concern of every retailer is how to create and maintain sufficient capital to conduct business. Careful financial planning and control are means to alleviate this concern. Few retailers, if any, have enough money available at all times to finance daily business operations and meet long-term investment requirements. Hence, the retailer's ability to *obtain* money and to secure *credit* is essential to sustaining a healthy financial situation.

Capital management involves planning and controlling the retailer's **equity capital** (what the retailer owns) and **borrowed capital** (money the retailer has obtained from outside sources). The following discussion examines the retailer's capital requirements, types of retail financing, and various sources of funds.

### Capital Requirements

A retailer needs money for a variety of purposes. **Fixed capital** is money needed to purchase such physical facilities as buildings, fixtures, and equipment. This type of capital requirement represents long-term investments that tie up capital for extended periods. **Working capital** is money needed to meet day-to-day operating costs. It is used to pay the rent and utility bills, to purchase inventories, and to cover payroll expenses. **Liquid capital** is money held in reserve for emergency situations, usually in the form of cash or disposable securities (e.g., stocks, bonds, certificates of deposit).

The amount of fixed, working, and liquid capital required by a particular retail operation is a function of the size and nature of that operation. Capital requirements for larger retailers are greater than those for smaller retailers, other things being equal. Upscale retail operations featuring complete product assortments, plush facilities, personal selling, and many services have a greater need for capital than retailers offering limited product assortments, spartan facilities, and limited services.

## Types of Financing

The first step a retailer takes in securing capital funds is determining what kind of money is needed. The retailer's purpose for the money (e.g., for use as fixed, working, or liquid capital) determines the type of financing. There are three types of financing: short-, intermediate-, and long-term credit. **Short-term credit** is money the retailer can borrow for less than one year. Lending institutions provide retailers with short-term loans primarily for working capital. For example, banks extend short-term credit to retailers to purchase next season's inventory. In such cases, the loans are self-liquidating because they generate sales dollars. **Intermediate-term credit** usually is offered for periods longer than one year but less than five years. Retailers secure such loans to finance smaller, fixed capital expenditures (e.g., fixtures and equipment). **Long-term credit** takes the form of loans that retailers secure for periods greater than five years. Typically, retailers use long-term financing to purchase major fixed capital investments such as buildings and land. For both intermediate- and long-term credit, the retailer must make periodic installment payments (monthly, quarterly, or annually) from earnings.

## Sources of Funding

To obtain funds, retailers can turn to a number of sources, including equity, vendors, lending institutions, and the government. Determining which source to use depends on the type of financing the retailer needs, the nature and size of the business, and the retailer's particular financial condition.

*Equity sources* of funds are obtained by selling part ownership in the business. Equity sales allow the retailer to raise funds without borrowing money or having to pay interest and repay a loan. Investors in a retail business are individuals willing to accept a certain amount of risk (i.e., the amount of their investment) for potential long-term gains. Before selling equity shares, however, the retailer should determine how much control over the business would be relinquished by making the sale.

*Vendors,* who supply retailers with merchandise, are frequently used as sources for short-term credit. This form of "trade credit" is made available by vendors when they extend dating terms—the amount of time the retailer has to pay the net invoice price for a shipment of merchandise. By extending dating terms to 60, 90, and even 120 days, the vendor is effectively financing the retailer's inventory for that period.

Favorable dating terms often give the retailer time to sell the merchandise before having to pay for it.

*Lending institutions* are sources of short- and long-term retail financing. Commercial banks, credit associations, and insurance companies are the most common lending institutions willing to make loans to credit-worthy retailers. When lending institutions make short-term working capital loans, they expect repayment immediately after they have served the purpose for which the loan was made. For example, a seasonal inventory loan must be repaid at the end of the season. The lender carefully specifies repayment and other terms associated with fixed capital loans in written contractual agreements.

To obtain outside institutional financing, the retailer must demonstrate good knowledge of business trends, possess reliable sales forecasts, have a keen appreciation of the marketplace, and produce superb merchandising plans.[7] Figure 4–7 identifies the various methods by which a loan can be secured.

*Government sources* of funds are usually the only viable alternative for the small retailer whose credit rating is either uncertain or not established. The Small Business Administration (SBA) was established to provide consulting services for small business enterprises on a number of business activities. The SBA also is entrusted with the responsibility of making available financial resources for small businesses, including retailers, that have exhausted all other avenues (e.g., traditional sources such as banks) for financing. The SBA provides financing by acting as a (1) "guarantor," guaranteeing a loan made by a bank to a retailer, or (2) "lender," directly lending money to retailers when local banks will not.

## EXPENSE MANAGEMENT

Expense management is the planning and control of operating expenses. To ensure an operating profit, operating expenses must be less than the retailer's gross margin. The retailer that fails to plan and control operating expenses risks losing financial control over an important segment of the business. Expense management entails three basic planning and control activities: classifying expenses, allocating expenses, and budgeting expenses.[8]

### Expense Classification

All planning and control activities require careful identification and classification of every relevant factor. Hence, the first step in expense management is to recognize the various costs of doing business and to classify these costs into logical groupings based on some common feature. In retailing, four fundamental perspectives on operating expenses will lead to different classifications. They are sales, control, allocation, and accounting perspectives.

*Sales Perspective.* One way to look at operating expenses is to see how such expenses are affected by sales. From a sales perspective, operating expenses are classified as fixed and variable. **Fixed expenses** are usually fixed for a given period of time (e.g., the life of a contract, or a planning or operating period). Expenses are classified as fixed when they remain the same regardless of the sales volume. As sales increase or decrease, fixed expenses remain constant.

| | |
|---|---|
| **Endorser** ........ | A third party signs a note to bolster the retailer's credit. If the retailer fails to pay the note, the bank expects the endorser to make the payments. |
| **Comaker** ........ | A third party creates an obligation jointly with the retailer. The bank can collect directly from either the retailer or the comaker. |
| **Guarantor** ....... | A third party guarantees the payment of a note by signing a guaranty commitment. |
| **Assignment of leases** ........ | An arrangement in which the bank automatically receives the rent payments from a leasing agreement made between a retailer and a third party. Used in franchising to finance buildings. |
| **Warehouse receipts** ........ | An arrangement in which the bank accepts commodities as security by lending money on a warehouse receipt. Such loans are generally made on staple merchandise that can be readily marketed. |
| **Floor-planning** ........ | An arrangement in which banks accept a trust receipt for display merchandise as collateral. Used for securing loans on serial-numbered merchandise (automobiles, appliances, boats). When the retailer signs a trust receipt, it (1) acknowledges receipt of the merchandise, (2) agrees to keep the merchandise in trust for the bank, and (3) promises to pay the bank as soon as the merchandise is sold. |
| **Chattel mortgage** ....... | An arrangement in which the bank accepts a lien on a piece of new equipment as security for the loan needed to buy the equipment. |
| **Real estate** ...... | An arrangement in which the bank accepts a mortgage on real estate as collateral for a loan. |
| **Accounts receivable** ....... | An arrangement in which the bank accepts accounts receivable (money owed the retailer) as collateral for a loan. Under the *notification plan* the retailer's customers are informed by the bank that their accounts have been assigned to the bank and all payments are made to the bank. Under the *nonnotification plan,* the retailer's customers are not informed of the assignment to the bank. The customer continues to pay the retailer who, in turn, pays the bank. |
| **Savings accounts or life insurance** ....... | An arrangement in which the bank extends a loan to a retailer that assigns to the bank a savings account or the cash value of a life insurance policy as collateral. |
| **Stocks and bonds** ...... | An arrangement in which the bank accepts as collateral marketable stocks and bonds. Usually the bank will accept as collateral only a certain percentage of the current market value of the stock or bond. |

Source: Adapted from *ABCs of Borrowing,* Management Aids No. 170 (Washington, D.C.: Small Business Administration, April, 1977) 2–3.

**FIGURE 4–7**
Methods for securing a retail loan

Expenses that vary with the volume of sales are called **variable expenses**. As sales increase or decrease, variable expenses also increase or decrease. Although the relationship between sales and expenses is not always directly proportional, they are sufficiently related that the retailer can reasonably predict changes in operating expenses. By being attentive to specific relationships between a variable expense and sales, the retailer can identify opportunities for increasing profits. For example, initial increases in advertising expenditures could increase sales to such a degree that profit increases are greater than the advertising expense.

*Control Perspective.* The second way to look at operating expenses is to see whether a particular expense is controllable. As the name implies, **controllable expenses** are those over which the retailer has direct control. Retailers can adjust these expenses as warranted by operating conditions. For example, part-time help can be reduced during slack sales periods.

    **Uncontrollable expenses** are outlays over which retailers have no control and that, in the short run, they cannot adjust to current operating needs. Expenses incurred as a result of long-term contractual arrangements are uncontrollable over the short run.

*Allocation Perspective.* In using the allocation perspective, the retailer looks at operating expenses to see if they can be directly attributed to some operating unit. Many retailers find it useful for purposes of analysis and control to allocate operating expenses to various operating units, such as store units or departmental units.

    Under this approach, retailers classify operating expenses as either direct or indirect expenses. **Direct expenses** are those directly attributable to the operations of a department or some other defined operating unit. If the retailer eliminated a department or unit, then the direct expenses associated with that department would also be eliminated. Salaries and commissions of departmental sales personnel are examples of direct expenses. Expenses not directly attributable to the operations of a department are classified as **indirect expenses**. These costs cannot be eliminated if a particular department is dropped. Indirect expenses are general business expenses a retailer incurs in running the entire operation.

*Accounting Perspective.* A final way to look at operating expenses is to classify them into well-defined groups that the retailer can use to identify year-to-year trends for each expense class and to make comparisons with trade averages of similar retailers. This expense classification system helps the retailer to identify, analyze, and initiate controls for expenses that are out of line with either last year's figures or those of similar retailers. Using the accounting approach, the retailer can classify operating expenses using either a natural division of expenses or expense-center accounting.

    Using the **natural division of expenses,** the retailer classifies expenses on the basis of the kind of expense each is, without regard for (1) which store functions (e.g., selling, buying, or receiving) incurred the expense, or (2) where (e.g., store or department) the expense was incurred. The natural division method of expense classification is used primarily by small- and medium-sized retailers looking for simple yet acceptable means of classifying expenses. The natural classification of expenses as recommended by the National Retail Merchants Association appears in Figure 4–8.

**Natural Division 01—*Payroll***

Includes all items of compensation for services actually rendered by employees of a company—wages, salaries, commissions, promotion money, bonuses, prizes, and vacation, sick, and holiday payments.

**Natural Division 02—*Allocated Fringe Benefits***

Includes a transfer account to allocate fringe benefits out of their appropriate expense centers to all other expense centers with a payroll natural division.

**Natural Division 03—*Media Costs***

Includes all cost of media—the cost of newspaper, periodical, program, streetcar and billboard space, the cost of radio and television time, and the cost of direct mail advertising.

**Natural Division 04—*Taxes***

Includes all state and local taxes (excluding taxes based on income), unemployment, social security and disability taxes, and government license fees.

**Natural Division 06—*Supplies***

Includes the cost of items consumed in the operation of the business—stationery and related items, wrapping, packaging, cleaning, and repairing materials, and heating, cooling, lighting, and other power expenses.

**Natural Division 07—*Services Purchased***

Includes charges for all nonprofessional services rendered by outsiders that aid, supplement, or substitute for the normal routine activity of the store—cleaning, delivery, shopping, detective, alarm, armored car, statistical, typing, and collection services.

**Natural Division 08—*Unclassified***

Includes all expenses not otherwise classified as chargeable to another natural division.

**Natural Division 09—*Travel***

Includes all expenses resulting from domestic (local or out of town) and foreign travel of all employees of the company for business purposes—transportation, hotel bills, meals, tips, and incidentals.

**Natural Division 10—*Communications***

Includes all expenses relative to the cost of store and central organization communications—local and long distance telephone services and postage.

**Natural Division 11—*Pensions***

Includes all expenses relating to pensions, retirement allowances, pension funds, insured and trusteed plans, and direct payments to retired employees.

**Natural Division 12—*Insurance***

Includes the cost of all insurance.

**Natural Division 13—*Depreciation***

Includes depreciation of the original cost of the capital assets employed in the operation of the business—building, leasehold improvements, equipment, furniture, and fixtures.

**Natural Division 14—*Professional Services***

Includes the cost of any service of a highly specialized and professional character furnished by outside organizations—legal, accounting, appraisal, management service, architectural, and survey fees.

**Natural Division 16—*Bad Debts***

Includes actual bad debts written off or the provision relating to an allowance for doubtful accounts; it also includes losses due to bad checks and fraudulent purchases, less recoveries.

**Natural Division 17—*Equipment Rentals***

Includes the costs of all equipment rented or leased and is restricted to expense centers where equipment represents a significant investment in the center's operations.

**Natural Division 18—*Outside Maintenance and Equipment Service Contracts***

Includes the costs of outside contractual arrangements for servicing and maintaining equipment.

**Natural Division 20—*Real Property Rentals***

Includes expenses incurred or rent paid for real estate used in the operation of the business.

**Natural Division 90—*Expense Transfers In***
**Natural Division 91—*Expense Transfers Out***
**Natural Division 92—*Credits and Outside Revenues***

Source: Adapted from *Retail Accounting Manual, Revised* (New York: Financial Executives Division, National Retail Merchants Association, 1978), III-3.

**FIGURE 4–8**
Natural division of expenses

**FIGURE 4–9**

Major expense centers

010   Property and equipment
020   Real estate, buildings, and building equipment
030   Furniture, fixtures, and nonbuilding equipment
100   Company management
110   Executive office
130   Branch management
140   Internal audit
150   Legal and consumer activities
200   Accounting and management information
210   Control management, general accounting, and statistical
220   Sales audit
230   Accounts payable
240   Payroll and time-keeping department
280   Data processing
300   Credit and accounts receivable
310   Credit management
330   Collection
340   Accounts receivable and bill adjustment
350   Cash office
360   Branch/store selling location offices
400   Sales promotion
410   Sales promotion management
420   Advertising
430   Shows, special events, and exhibits
440   Display
500   Service and operations
510   Service and operations management
530   Security

The second accounting method for classifying operating expenses is **expense-center accounting**. An expense center is a functional center within the store's operation or a center of a certain store activity. The center incurs expenses in the process of providing its assigned functions or performing its required activities. Expense-center accounting is a system of classifying operating expenses into such functional or activity classes as management, direct selling, customer services, and so on. The National Retail Merchants Association has identified 44 major expense centers, shown in Figure 4–9. Expense-center accounting is used most frequently by large, departmentalized retailers.

In using the expense-center accounting system, the retailer follows a two-step procedure. The first step is to classify operating expenses according to natural divisions. The second step is to cross-classify each of the natural expenses with each of the 23 expense centers. As illustrated in Figure 4–10, the retailer can use expense-center accounting to identify, analyze, and control operating expenses either by the kind or type of expense (i.e., natural divisions) or by the function or activity that incurred the expense (i.e., expense center). Typically, the expense-center accounting system provides greater detail in classifying operating expenses than do other methods. After operating expenses have been classified, the retailer's second task is to

FIGURE 4–9
*continued*

```
550  Telephones and communications
560  Utilities
570  Housekeeping
580  Maintenance and repairs
600  Personnel
   610  Personnel management
   620  Employment
   640  Training
   660  Medical and other employee services
   670  Supplementary benefits
700  Merchandise receiving, storage, and distribution
   710  Management of merchandise receiving, stor-
        age, and distribution
   720  Receiving and marking
   730  Reserve stock storage
   750  Shuttle services
800  Selling and supporting services
   810  Selling supervision
   820  Direct selling
   830  Customer services
   840  Selling support services
   860  Central wrapping and packing
   880  Delivery
900  Merchandising
   910  Merchandising management
   920  Buying
   930  Merchandise control
```

Source: *Retail Accounting Manual, Revised* (New York: Financial Executives
Division, National Retail Merchants Association, 1978), III-3.

allocate expenses to each of the operating units, such as departments within a store
or stores within a chain organization.

A comparative expense distribution between department stores and specialty
retailers is shown in Figure 4–11. While several similarities exist, several differences
are noteworthy: (1) department store expenses are higher for services/operations,
sales promotions, and merchandise receiving/storage, and (2) specialty stores spent
a greater percentage on property/equipment, company management, and
accounting/management information systems.[9]

## Expense Allocation

The small retailer views operating expenses from the standpoint of the entire store
and therefore gives little thought to the problem of allocating operating expenses to
various operating units. On the other hand, large retailers that are either departmentalized or multiunit (chain) operations have a great need for examining the operating
expenses of individual operating units.

Three methods by which retailers allocate operating expenses to operating units
are (1) the net profit plan, (2) the contribution plan, and (3) the net profit contribution

**FIGURE 4–10**

Expense-center accounting system

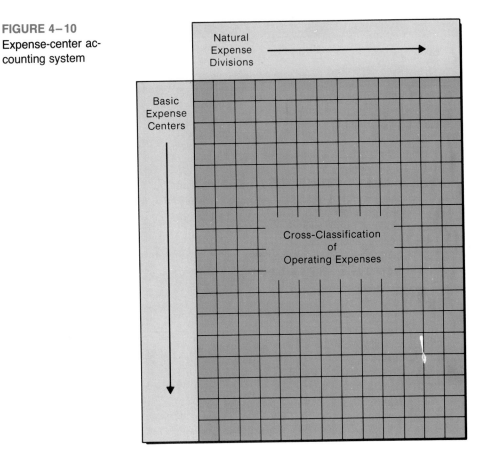

plan. Figure 4–12 illustrates each of these expense allocation plans. Several points are notable. First, the bottom line for a departmental income statement is its operating profit. However, this profit expression is often referred to as the department net profit. Second, the allocation methods are quite similar; the principal differences are in treatment of indirect expenses and calculation criteria for the operating unit.

*Net Profit Plan.* When employing the **net profit plan,** the retailer allocates all direct and indirect expenses. Direct expenses are directly attributed to the particular department that incurred them. Indirect expenses are not *directly* attributed to a particular department, but instead are allocated to departments on the basis of a prejudged set of criteria. Figure 4–13 lists common criteria for retailers. To illustrate, the salary of a department manager would be considered a direct expense that could be allocated to the department. The salary of the store manager would be an indirect expense to any given department, however, and the store manager's salary could be allocated to various departments on the basis of each department's percentage of total net sales.

As shown in Figure 4–12, the department's gross margin minus both the department's direct and indirect expenses equals the department's net profit. The treatment of each department as a profit-producing center has the advantage of

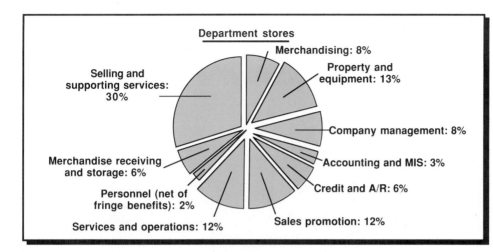

FIGURE 4–11
Expense distribution for
department and spe-
cialty stores
(percentage of total
expenses) (source:
David P. Schulz, "86:
Better for Some,"
*Stores* [November
1987]: 94. Reprinted by
permission of *Stores*.
Copyright National Re-
tail Merchants Associa-
tion)

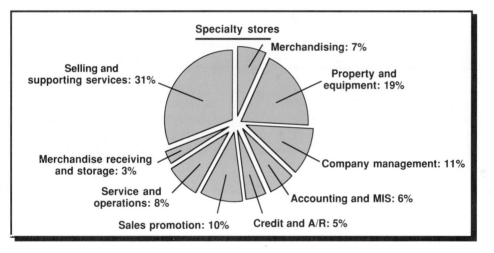

providing a "hard-figure" (net profit) evaluation of departmental operations and encourages each department to be expense-control conscious.

*Contribution Plan.* The **contribution plan** can be characterized as follows: (1) direct expenses are allocated to the departments that incurred them, and (2) indirect expenses are not allocated to departments, but instead to a general expense account. The department's *contribution* is defined as the department's gross margin minus its direct expenses. Again referring to Figure 4–12, we see that each department is judged on the basis of its contribution to the store. The sum of the contributions from each department is treated as a "reservoir" to cover the indirect expenses in the general expense account and to provide an operating profit for the store.

*Net Profit Contribution Plan.* Using the **net profit contribution plan,** the retailer calculates both the department's net profit and its contribution (see Figure 4–12). This plan involves a two-step procedure. First, the department's contribution is cal-

**FIGURE 4–12**
Allocating operating
expenses

```
Net profit plan
   Department gross margin ...................................... ($)
      – Direct expenses of the department .......................... ($)
      – Indirect expenses charged to department .................... ($)
   Department net profit ........................................ ($)*

Contribution plan
   Department gross margin ...................................... ($)
      – Direct expenses of the department .......................... ($)
   Contribution of the department ............................... ($)*

Net profit contribution plan
   Department gross margin ...................................... ($)
      – Direct expenses of the department .......................... ($)
   Contribution of the department ............................... ($)*
      – Indirect expenses charged to department .................... ($)
   Department net profit ........................................ ($)*
*Measurement used to evaluate departmental performance.
```

culated by subtracting the department's direct expenses from its gross margin. Second, the department's net profit is calculated by subtracting the department's indirect expenses from its contribution. The combination net profit contribution plan allows examination of departmental performance from both the contribution and net profit perspectives.

## Expense Budgeting

An **expense budget** is a plan or a set of guidelines that a retailer uses to control operating expenses. It is an estimate or a forecast of the amount of money needed during a given accounting period to operate the business. Essentially, the expense budget is a continuation of the retailer's total budgetary process. Just as merchandise budgets are developed to plan and control expenditures for merchandise items, the

**FIGURE 4–13**
Selected expense-
center allocation
criteria

| Type of Expense | Allocation Criteria |
| --- | --- |
| Property and equipment | Weighted floor space |
| Company management | Net sales |
| Accounting and management information | Gross sales |
| Credit and accounts receivable | Number of transactions |
| Sales promotion | Number of displays |
| Personnel | Number of employees |
| Merchandise receiving storage and distribution | Number of invoices |
| Selling and supporting services | Number of units |
| Merchandising | Net sales |

major purpose of expense budgets is to plan and control the amount of money the retailer spends in merchandising those items.

An annual expense budget for the entire store is the normal starting point in expense control. The annual budget is then broken down into monthly and weekly expense plans. While small retailers typically operate on a storewide expense budget, larger departmentalized retailers usually find it necessary to prepare departmental expense budgets separately from the store budget.

In practice, expense budgets should act as a general game plan, not as a straitjacket of unbreakable rules. As a plan of action, budgets must be flexible enough for management to adjust as conditions warrant, but rigid enough to provide meaningful guidance.

One of the first steps in preparing an expense budget is to determine an overall expense figure for the prescribed operating period. This figure is a general estimate of the amount of money the retailer will have available to cover operating expenses. The estimate can be figured simply with these two steps: (1) secure a net sales estimate for the forthcoming period (obtained from the merchandising budget) and (2) make a gross margin estimate by subtracting a cost of goods sold estimate from the net sales estimate. This estimated gross margin represents the amount of money available to cover operating expenses plus achieve an operating profit. By subtracting the desired level of operating profit from gross margin, the retailer has an estimate of money that should be available to cover both fixed and variable expenses. In some cases, retailers take the process one step further. Because fixed expenses are generally known and fairly constant, they are deducted to determine the amount of money that can be allocated to variable expenses.

Several specific budgetary procedures have been developed for expense planning and control. The retailer can elect to use any one of three approaches to expense budgeting: zero-based budgeting, fixed-based budgeting, and productivity-based budgeting.

*Zero-Based Budgeting.* As the name implies, under **zero-based budgeting**, each operating department or unit starts with no allocated operating expenses. To secure operating funds, each operating department must justify its need for each expense item on the budget. While past expenditures may be considered supporting evidence, management does not accept past expenditures as total justification for future expense allocations. To obtain operating funds, department personnel must use justifications based on current merchandising plans, market conditions, competitive atmospheres, and operating requirements. Although zero-based budgeting is generally time-consuming and costly, it does force each operating department to reevaluate its expenses and to define the needs and benefits that should be derived from each expenditure. Zero-based budgeting is the most appropriate way to establish an expense budget for a new retailer or a new department.

*Fixed-Based Budgeting.* In the **fixed-based budgeting** process, each expense (e.g., payroll, supplies) is budgeted at a specific dollar amount. The predetermined amount is based on past experience as well as on evaluating the need for incurring the expense in the forthcoming budgeting period. A fixed-based budgeting form is illustrated in Figure 4–14. To facilitate control, the retailer should fill in the form for both

| Period: Third Quarter | | | Store: 12 | | | Expense Center: | 721-Receiving | |
|---|---|---|---|---|---|---|---|---|
| Natural Division | | Current Period | | | | Year-to-Date | | | |
| | | Amount | | Variance | | Amount | | Variance | |
| No. | Expense | Actual | Budget | Dollar | Percent | Actual | Budget | Dollar | Percent |
| 01 | Payroll | 4,000 | 4,000 | 00 | 00 | 12,000 | 12,000 | 00 | 0.0 |
| 06 | Supplies | 1,000 | 800 | (200) | (25) | 2,600 | 2,400 | (200) | (8.3) |
| 07 | Services Purchased | 500 | 600 | 100 | 16.7 | 1,400 | 1,800 | 400 | 22.2 |
| 10 | Communications | 100 | 100 | 00 | 00 | 270 | 300 | 30 | 10.0 |
| | Total | 5,600 | 5,500 | (100) | 1.8 | 16,270 | 16,500 | 230 | 1.4 |

**FIGURE 4–14**
Fixed-based budgeting form

the budgeted and the actual expenditure in the current budget period, as well as complete a year-to-date summary.

The form also provides space for the retailer to report variances between actual and budgeted amounts in both dollars and percentages. Management carefully scrutinizes these variances; when they exceed either a predetermined dollar or percentage amount, the manager of the operating department should examine and correct the situation and submit either a written or oral report to the supervisor. The example in Figure 4–14 shows that the manager of the receiving department appears to be controlling the department's expenses quite adequately. Although the current period shows the department slightly over budget, the year-to-date expenses are slightly below the budgeted amount.

| Natural Division | | Period: April | | Store: 12 | | Expense Center: 410— | | Sales Promotion | |
|---|---|---|---|---|---|---|---|---|---|
| | | Unit Sales | | | | | | | |
| No. | Expense | 500 | 1000 | 1500 | 2000 | 2500 | 3000 | 3500 | 4000 |
| 01 | Payroll | $2,000 | $2,000 | $2,500 | $2,500 | $3,000 | $3,500 | $4,000 | $4,500 |
| 03 | Advertising | 500 | 1,000 | 1,500 | 2,000 | 2,500 | 3,000 | 3,500 | 4,000 |
| 06 | Supplies | 500 | 550 | 600 | 700 | 800 | 1,000 | 1,200 | 1,400 |
| | Total | $3,000 | $3,550 | $4,600 | $5,200 | $6,300 | $7,500 | $8,700 | $9,900 |

**FIGURE 4–15**
Productivity-based budgeting form

*Productivity-Based Budgeting.* Expense budgets based on levels of productivity provide a high degree of flexibility in the budgetary process. Under a **productivity-based budget,** the retailer prepares a series of expense budgets to correspond to various sales levels (or some other productivity measure). As illustrated in Figure 4–15, an increase in unit sales automatically increases the amount budgeted for each item in the department's expense budget. Given that numerous operating expenses are either directly or indirectly related to sales, a budget based on sales productivity should help the retailer make operational adjustments to meet changing market conditions. Some retailers think that a productivity-based budget is the most appropriate approach to expense budgeting, especially when reliable sales estimates are difficult to make or when there is a high likelihood for extreme sales variations. Essentially, this budget approach allows the retailer to allocate limited financial resources based on actual need, as opposed to anticipated requirements.

A key means of gaining retailing success is fiscal control. To ensure an adequate degree of control over financial affairs, the retailer must develop and maintain a set of financial records that provide a broad picture of the firm's financial condition. A typical set of records includes a separate record for each of the following: sales, cash receipts, cash disbursements, purchases, payroll, equipment, inventory, accounts receivable, and accounts payable. The retailer then uses these records to prepare two essential financial statements: the income statement and the balance sheet.

The income statement summarizes the retailer's financial activity for a stated accounting period. It is prepared to show the profit (or loss) a retailer has made during an accounting period. The income statement is a systematic set of procedures that helps the retailer identify five income measurements: gross sales, net sales, gross margin, operating profit, and net profit.

The balance sheet is a statement of the retailer's financial condition on a given date. It summarizes the basic relationship between the retailer's assets, liabilities, and net worth. The balance sheet gets its name from its principal objective of showing how the sides of the accounting equation (assets = liabilities + net worth) are balanced.

In performance analysis, the retailer must make judgments on the firm's operating and financial performance. By using several standardized operating and financial ratios, the retailer can compare performance, on either a historical basis or a trade basis, to national norms.

Capital management involves planning of and controlling the retailer's equity capital (what the retailer owns) and borrowed capital (what the retailer owes). A retailer needs money for a variety of reasons, including funds for fixed, working, and liquid capital requirements. The type of financing a retailer needs depends on its capital requirements. Short-term credit is used when the retailer needs working capital, whereas intermediate- and long-term credit are used to meet fixed capital requirements. Equity sales, vendor credit, and loans from lending institutions and government agencies are the major sources of funds for the retailer.

Expense management entails three basic planning and control activities: classifying, allocating, and budgeting expenses. Expenses can be classified on the basis of sales (variable or fixed), control (controllable or uncontrollable), or allocation (direct or indirect) characteristics, and according to accounting procedures (natural division of expenses or expense-center accounting). In departmentalized or chain store organizations, operating expenses must be allocated to various operating units. Expense allocation is accomplished by using the net profit plan, the contribution plan, and the net profit contribution plan. An expense budget is used to plan and control operating expenditures. The retailer can elect to use one of several budgeting procedures: zero-based, fixed-based, or productivity-based.

## STUDENT STUDY GUIDE

**KEY TERMS AND CONCEPTS**

account
allowances to customers
asset
balance sheet
borrowed capital
contribution plan
controllable expenses
cost of goods sold
current asset
current liability
current ratio
debt ratio
direct expenses
equity capital
expense budget
expense-center accounting
financial ratios
fixed asset
fixed-based budgeting
fixed capital
fixed expenses
gross margin
gross sales
income measurements
income modifications
income statement
indirect expenses
intermediate-term credit

ledger
leverage ratios
liability
liquid capital
liquidity ratios
long-term credit
long-term liability
natural division of expenses
net profit
net profit contribution plan
net profit plan
net sales
net worth
operating expenses
operating profit
operating ratios
other expenses
other income
productivity-based budgeting
ratio analysis
returns from customers
short-term credit
total assets
uncontrollable expenses
variable expenses
working capital
zero-based budgeting

**REVIEW QUESTIONS**

1. What is the purpose of an income statement? Identify and define the role of the nine elements of an income statement.
2. Why is a balance sheet prepared? Describe the basic balance sheet equation.

3. Distinguish between current and fixed assets and current and long-term liabilities. Provide specific examples of each.
4. How should the retailer view the concept of net worth?
5. What is ratio analysis?
6. Describe the relationships expressed by operating ratios. Cite examples of these relationships.
7. Compare and contrast the current and the leverage ratios. What does each ratio measure?
8. What are fixed, working, and liquid capital needed for?
9. What types of financing are available to the retailer? Where would the retailer find this financing?
10. How can expenses be classified? Describe the various expense classification systems.
11. Expense allocation is accomplished through the use of three allocation methods. Describe each method.
12. Expense budgeting can be accomplished in several different ways. Describe the three expense budgeting approaches.

---

**REVIEW EXAM**

True or False

_____ 1. The income statement is a picture of the retailer's assets, liabilities, and net worth on a given date; the balance sheet is a picture of the retailer's profits or losses over a period of time.

_____ 2. Operating profit is the difference between gross margin and other income and expenses; it is the figure that determines the retailer's tax liability.

_____ 3. Fixed assets are those assets that require a significant length of time to convert to cash.

_____ 4. A high current ratio suggests liquidity problems; a low current ratio indicates good long-term solvency.

_____ 5. If a retailer eliminated a department, the indirect expenses allocated to that department would not be eliminated and would need to be allocated elsewhere.

_____ 6. The contribution plan of expense allocation will almost always show a positive contribution. This means the department is contributing its fair share to the store's profit.

_____ 7. Productivity-based budgeting is characterized by a high degree of flexibility.

**STUDENT APPLICATIONS MANUAL**

---

**PROJECT: INVESTIGATIONS AND APPLICATIONS**

1. Excessive customer returns and allowances can be a major problem for the retailer. Control procedures should be initiated to identify and analyze the causes of returns and allowances. Review the causes of returns and allowances in Chapter 11. Then develop a customer-survey instrument that could be used by a department store retailer for identifying and analyzing customer returns and allowances.
2. The value of fixed assets equals their cost to the retailer minus an assigned depreciation. Identify and describe some of the methods retailers might use to depreciate their fixed assets.
3. Interview several vendors (e.g., wholesalers) and determine the terms and conditions under which they are willing to extend short-term (less than 1 year) and intermediate-term (1 to 5 years) credit to retailers. Evaluate these terms and conditions from the viewpoint of the retailer. Are they acceptable? Why or why not?

4. Contact your local Small Business Administration (SBA) office and determine the procedures and requirements for obtaining a small business loan.

5. Classify the following list of expenses as either fixed or variable, controllable or uncontrollable: (1) sales commissions, (2) store manager's salary, (3) a weekly newspaper advertisement, (4) a business license, (5) employees' health insurance payments, (6) the services of an accounting firm, (7) a donation to the United Way, (8) cost of new fixtures, (9) store rent, and (10) monthly telephone bill. Explain your classification.

## CASES: PROBLEMS AND DECISIONS

## CASE 4–1
## The Family Shoe Shop*

### BACKGROUND

The Family Shoe Shop is an independently owned and operated shoe store located in a large regional shopping center. R. P. Evans, the proprietor, has organized the store around three departments: 1,800 square feet of selling space are devoted to men's shoes, 1,600 square feet for women's shoes, and 1,200 square feet for the children's department.

### CURRENT SITUATION

Each year Evans faces the task of completing the store's annual income statement. With this year's gross sales totaling $250,000, Evans hopes that he will end the year with a greater operating profit than last year's $39,800. An examination of the current year's sales records shows that it took 8,450 sales transactions and an average investment in inventory of $88,000 to generate the $250,000 figure. Further examination of various records provides Evans with the following information: (1) the store opened the year with $48,000 of inventory; (2) the beginning inventory was supplemented throughout the year by net purchases of $112,000; (3) the year ended with an inventory on hand conservatively valued at $36,000; (4) workroom costs of $1,000 were incurred in getting the products ready for sale, and $4,000 was spent on transportation charges in getting the products to the store; and (5) the store earned a $2,000 cash discount by paying for the goods as soon as the invoice was received.

One figure that greatly disturbed Evans was the $1,100 in goods returned by customers. In addition, he had to make allowances totaling $250 for damaged merchandise.

Another one of Evans' major concerns is operating expenses. After a concerted effort to control this year's operating expenses, he hopes that a lower expense figure will substantially improve his profit picture. Records kept by natural divisions reveal the following expenses:

| | |
|---|---:|
| Payroll | $26,000 |
| Advertising | 3,000 |
| Taxes | 1,700 |
| Supplies | 900 |
| Services purchased | 500 |
| Unclassified | 100 |
| Travel | 350 |

*This case was prepared by Dale M. Lewison, University of Akron.

| | |
|---|---|
| Communications ................................................ | 550 |
| Insurance ......................................................... | 2,600 |
| Pensions........................................................... | 1,100 |
| Depreciation ..................................................... | 1,450 |
| Professional services ......................................... | 3,500 |
| Donations.......................................................... | 250 |
| Bad debts......................................................... | 400 |
| Equipment......................................................... | 600 |
| Real property rentals ......................................... | 36,000 |

In addition to these operating expenses, Evans is very concerned about the $2,500 interest payments to the First Republic Bank. Something will have to be done to reduce the principal on that business loan. If nothing else works out, at least the income from the candy machine increased 100 percent from $75 last year to $150 this year.

## ASSIGNMENT

Given the information in the case, lend Evans a hand by developing a complete income statement.

## CASE 4–2
## The Island Shops Franchise—Making A Financial Investment Decision*

### CURRENT SITUATION

Penny Shaheen and her husband were listening intently to the presentation being given to them in their home by a representative of The Island Shops, a chain of franchised clothing outfits in the Midwest that featured casual Hawaiian and safari-style clothing and accessories. The franchise was of the busines format type, which meant that it provided not only the right to do business under The Island Shops name but also a standardization of store design and operations as well as assistance at some specified level in such areas as management training, accounting, merchandising, site location, and many others. The representative, Mr. Long, was here because Penny had called the company after seeing a franchise opportunity ad in a well-known national business publication, after which the company had set up this initial meeting. Though she had called the firm on little more than a whim, Penny had been considering for some time the idea of leaving her present job and starting her own business. She had read that franchising might be a good choice for achieving this goal, and The Island Shops advertisement had made the opportunity it offered sound quite appealing.

"The fact that you have no retail management experience, Mrs. Shaheen, should not be of concern," said Mr. Long shortly after he began his presentation. "Believe me, our complete training and assistance program will enable you to learn successful procedures with little difficulty. That's one of the great advantages of franchising."

He went on to explain that becoming an Island Shops store owner, or franchisee, required the payment of an initial franchise fee of $60,000, plus the ability to secure an additional $40,000 of capital. On top of that, continuing royalty fees of 3 percent of gross sales were required.

*This case was prepared by Dan Gilmore of the University of Akron.

"Our franchise fee is somewhat high for this type of store," Long conceded. "But that is more than balanced by the low royalty fees we collect." He noted that McDonald's, for instance, charges franchisees an 11.5 percent royalty fee plus another 4 percent for advertising.

As required by Federal Trade Commission law, Mr. Long gave Penny a franchise disclosure statement, or prospectus. This document must contain detailed information concerning 20 subjects of interest to potential franchise investors, such as the terms of sale, any continuing fees, operating restrictions, and a variety of financial and business figures, including a company balance sheet, income statement, and a statement of changes in financial position. A copy of a sample franchise contract must also be attached. A selected sample of the information in the disclosure statement for The Island Shops is provided in Exhibits 1 and 2.

"I know it's a lot to think over," said Mr. Long, "but you'll need to make a decision rather quickly. You are just one of many people we're interviewing, and only one franchise is available in this area. I can give you a week, but after that I'm afraid someone else will snap this opportunity up."

Long continued, "I've been impressed by our meeting here, however. If you can meet our capital requirements, I can say with near certainty you will be selected as this area's Island Shops franchisee."

Penny had never been to an Island Shops store, but the concept did sound appealing. She had purchased a Hawaiian outfit herself recently and knew this type of clothing was currently quite popular.

"Let me tell you, these stores are hot," said Mr. Long. "The merchandise really moves. Everybody is interested in this type of clothing now, as some of our other franchi-

**EXHIBIT 1**

---

Disclosure Statement
as of February 1, 1988

*Name of Company:*    The Island Shops, Inc.
310 Riverside Drive
Rock Island, IL 50432
(242) 555-6812

The Island Shops is a wholly owned subsidiary of Omega, Inc., San Jose, California.

*Description of Operations:* Franchised and company-owned retail clothing stores. The Island Shops, typically located in shopping malls and plazas, carry an exciting line of Hawaiian and safari-style clothing and accessories for men and women.

*Number of Stores:* 20 franchise stores and five company-owned stores in five states.

*Number of Franchises Sold in 1987:* 14

*In Business Since:* 1985

*Managerial Assistance Provided:* Initial and continuing management assistance in the areas of general retail management, accounting merchandising, site selection, lease negotiations, and advertising is provided franchisees at company expense.

---

EXHIBIT 2

Income Statement
for Year Ending 12/31/87

| | |
|---|---|
| Total Revenue (stores, royalties, franchise sales) | $ 2,912,000 |
| Cost of Goods Sold | (1,450,000) |
| Income from Operations | 1,462,000 |
| Administrative and Other Expenses | (720,000) |
| Net Income before Taxes | $    742,000 |

*List of Franchises:*    1543 Boucher Blvd.
Indianapolis, IN 49202
(315) 555-9123
Owner: Jim Plezak

[The remaining franchisees were listed]

sees could tell you. I would suggest if you want to find out more about the stores that you call Jim Huscroft in Toledo or Alice Schaub in Ft. Wayne. They're both fairly typical of our owners and very easy to talk to."

The presentation lasted nearly two hours in total, after which Penny and her husband felt they knew a great deal about both the chain and the opportunity. Mr. Long had been very informative and thorough. Having read a little bit about franchise deals, they were pleased about several aspects of the opportunity, including the low royalty payments and Mr. Long's promise that the outlet would have an exclusive territory; that is, no other company stores would be opened in their defined territory during the first five-year contract.

As he was leaving, Mr. Long said, "You know, not many franchisors can advertise in the type of prestigious publication like the one in which you saw our ad. I think that tells you something about our company's commitment to quality." Then he added, "And one more thing—please review our standard contract. I think you'll find it is written quite favorably for franchisees."

After he had left, Penny and her husband talked things over. The opportunity sounded great, but it was an awfully big decision to make in a short time. Penny was unhappy with her insurance job, though as a district manager for claims adjustment she was earning nearly $40,000 per year. But her current job dissatisfaction, combined with the desire she had always had to own her own retail clothing business, made the offer seem very attractive. The Shaheens decided they could raise the capital required without too much strain and that if the store was successful their return on this investment would be substantial. Both agreed, nevertheless, that they had a lot to think over and do in the next week before making a decision.

## ASSIGNMENT

1. If you were Penny Shaheen, what steps would you take in helping you in making your decision? Outline a plan, including what you would do and why, for making a franchise investigation and investment decision.
2. Critique the proposal and presentation given by Mr. Long and The Island Shops from an investor's perspective. Are there any actions, evidence, or statements that you feel are misleading or a cause for concern?

**ENDNOTES**

1. Robert C. Ragan, *Financial Recordkeeping for Small Stores,* Small Business Management Series No. 32 (Washington, D.C.: Small Business Administration, 1976): 5.
2. Irving M. Cooper, *Accounting Services for Small Service Firms,* Small Marketers Aids No. 126 (Washington, D.C.: Small Business Administration, March 1977): 3.
3. Ibid.
4. David P. Schulz, "86: Better for Some," *Stores* (November 1987): 92.
5. Ibid.
6. Ernest H. Risch, "Operating Profit in the Conventional Department Store: A Statistical Prognosis," *Retail Control* (January 1986): 40.
7. Gordon E. Pillsbury, "Management of Financing," *Retail Control* (February 1986): 54.
8. Nathan Katz, "12 Keys to Effective Expense Control," *Retail Control* (February 1987): 11–21.
9. David P. Schulz, "86: Better for Some," 94.

# 5

## Outline

## Objectives

☐ Understand those factors that determine the best organizational structure for meeting the retailer's operational needs.

☐ Develop organizational objectives that can provide focus for the structure and activities of the retail firm.

☐ Identify the organizational tasks necessary to realize the firm's organizational objectives.

☐ Explain the basic principles of organization that are an inherent part of any effective retail structure.

☐ Pepare an organizational chart capable of expressing the formal relationships among various parts of the retail organization.

☐ Distinguish among the organizational patterns of various types of retailers.

# Retail Organization and Management

O rganization is essential to any group of people having a common purpose or goal. Whether the group is an army, a church, a football team, or a retail business, organization is the binding force that coordinates, channels, and propels the group toward its stated mission.

As with any organized group of people, retailers can use a vast number of different structures to organize their people. All retailing organizations, however, incorporate certain common organizational elements and principles structured around one of several basic organizational forms. This chapter examines these organizational elements, principles, and forms, and presents the general organizational patterns that small independent retailers, department store retailers, and chain store retailers use in organizing groups of people.

The particular organizational foundation a retail firm adopts depends on several factors. Some of these factors are (1) the type of merchandise to be offered, (2) the variety and assortment of the merchandise stocked, (3) the type and number of customer services performed, (4) the type and number of locations used, (5) the type and degree of promotional activities, (6) the nature of pricing levels and margin requirements obtained, and (7) the legal requirements and/or restrictions. Given this vast array of influential factors, the firm's organization must center around specific organizational objectives and tasks.

**ELEMENTS OF RETAIL ORGANIZATION**

## Organizational Objectives

In retailing, the firm's organizational foundation focuses on achieving the firm's objectives. Establishing well-defined organizational objectives is an important step because it forces the retailer to think through what the firm is trying to accomplish, where the firm is going, and how the firm intends to get there. In addition, organizational objectives provide a realistic orientation to the retailer's planning process as well as a means of evaluating the firm's past performance and its current status.

Three levels of organizational objectives correspond to the three general levels of retail management (see Figure 5–1). They are (1) strategic objectives developed by top managers at the strategic level of management, (2) operational objectives identified by middle managers within the administrative level of management, and

FIGURE 5–1
Managerial levels
and organizational
objectives

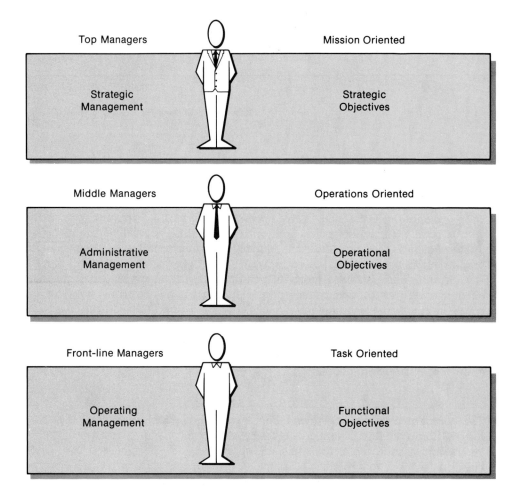

Top Managers                                    Mission Oriented

Strategic                                         Strategic
Management                                        Objectives


Middle Managers                                 Operations Oriented

Administrative                                    Operational
Management                                        Objectives


Front-line Managers                             Task Oriented

Operating                                         Functional
Management                                        Objectives

(3) functional objectives that direct front-line managers at the operational management level.

**Strategic objectives** are general, long-term goals that the retail firm intends to pursue. Essentially, a strategic objective identifies an overall mission that the firm's management wishes to realize. **Operational objectives** are general, long-term operational requirements necessary to achieve a strategic objective. Operational objectives establish the general framework within which a particular merchandising or operating function can be identified. **Functional objectives** are specific task objectives that identify a specific function and how it is to be accomplished. The unique value of functional objectives is their quantifiability, which makes them especially useful in planning, executing, and controlling a particular retailing activity. Figure 5–2 provides examples of strategic, operational, and functional objectives for an upscale specialty retailer of women's apparel. The objectives in Figure 5–2 identify not only the target markets, but also how to serve them in terms of product offering and assortment.

| Strategic Objectives | Operational Objectives | Functional Objectives |
|---|---|---|
| To appeal to the "perfectionist," the "updated," the "traditionalist," and the "establishment" consumer | To offer the "perfectionist" consumer the most advanced fashion apparel | To ensure the "perfectionist" consumer a new and fresh selection of fashionables by stocking only one garment in each size category (e.g., Misses 4–14) and by timing new arrivals every week |
| | To offer the "updated" consumer new styles that have gained wide acceptance | To ensure the "updated" consumer stylish yet not extreme fashion apparel by stocking a limited selection of last season's perfectionist styles in Misses sizes 4–16 |
| | To offer the "traditionalist" and the "establishment" consumer well-established yet fashionable apparel | To ensure the "traditionalist" and "establishment" consumer a complete selection of stylish yet dignified fashion apparel by stocking a representative offering of well-established designer labels in Misses sizes 8–20 |

**FIGURE 5–2**
Examples of organizational objectives

## Organizational Tasks

In developing the retail organization, the retailer must identify and assign the various tasks necessary to realize the firm's stated organizational objectives. The number of organizational tasks that can be identified is large. Figure 5–3 lists the basic organizational tasks inherent to any retail organization. Although the list of tasks in Figure 5–3 can help a retailer develop a general organizational structure, a more detailed description of tasks must be made in assigning responsibilities and authority to each position in the organization. Additionally, the retailer should develop written job descriptions for each job classification.

**PRINCIPLES OF RETAIL ORGANIZATION**

There are several basic principles of organization that every retailer should consider in establishing a retail organization. Organizational principles that are particularly appropriate to the retail firm are the principles of specialization and departmentalization, of lines of authority and responsibility, of unity of command, and of span of control. By applying these principles, retailers can avoid managerial confusion and employee discontent.

FIGURE 5–3
Basic organizational
tasks

1. **Operating the store**
   a. Recruiting store personnel
   b. Training store personnel
   c. Supervising store personnel
   d. Planning information systems
   e. Meeting legal obligations
   f. Designing store facilities
   g. Maintaining store facilities
   h. Ensuring store security

2. **Finding the best location**
   a. Analyzing regional markets
   b. Assessing trading areas
   c. Appraising site locations

3. **Developing the merchandise mix**
   a. Determining consumer product needs
   b. Evaluating product alternatives
   c. Planning product-mix strategies
   d. Determining consumer-service requirements
   e. Evaluating service alternatives
   f. Planning service-mix levels

4. **Buying the merchandise**
   a. Identifying sources of supply
   b. Contacting sources of supply
   c. Evaluating sources of supply
   d. Negotiating with sources of supply

5. **Procuring the merchandise**
   a. Ordering merchandise
   b. Receiving merchandise
   c. Checking merchandise
   d. Marking merchandise
   e. Stocking merchandise

6. **Controlling the merchandise**
   a. Planning sales
   b. Planning stocks
   c. Planning reductions
   d. Planning purchases
   e. Planning markups
   f. Planning margins
   g. Controlling inventories
   h. Taking inventory
   i. Valuating inventory
   j. Evaluating inventory

7. **Pricing the merchandise**
   a. Setting prices
   b. Adjusting prices

8. **Promoting the merchandise**
   a. Planning advertising strategies
   b. Selecting advertising media
   c. Preparing advertisements
   d. Designing promotional displays
   e. Planning promotional events
   f. Gaining favorable publicity
   g. Managing the personal-selling effort

## Specialization and Departmentalization

Specialization and departmentalization are inherent parts of any efficient retail organizational structure. With job **specialization**, employees concentrate their efforts on a limited number of tasks. Retailers have learned that specialization improves the speed and quality of employee performance.

**Departmentalization,** an extension of the specialization principle, occurs when tasks and employees are grouped together into departments to achieve the operating efficiencies of specialization for a group performing similar tasks. Specialization and departmentalization can be based on *product type* (such as apparel, home furnishings, and appliances), *activity* (such as buying, selling, and stocking), *activity location* (such as main store, branch store, and warehouse) and *consumer type* (such as household consumer and business customers). In choosing which of these bases to

| Department Sales Manager's Responsibilities | Equals | Department Sales Manager's Authority |
|---|---|---|
| 1. to ensure that the store's customer service standards and policies are maintained | | 1. to direct customer service standards and procedures; make customer adjustments |
| 2. to provide (ensure) adequate floor coverage while controlling personnel budgets | | 2. to assign personnel within area; prepare weekly personnel schedule; request additional personnel |
| 3. to ensure that the physical appearance of the area is visually appealing and orderly | | 3. to determine the merchandising set-up of area; request the removal or addition of fixtures; request and followup maintenance services |
| 4. to communicate selling trends and other merchandise information to merchants and associates | | 4. to request sales and merchandising information; analyze current reports and information |
| 5. to supervise the receipt, movement, maintenace, and display of merchandise on the selling floor and in the stockroom area | | 5. to determine merchandising set-up of selling-floor area; coordinate merchandising set-up of stockroom area; maintain a merchandise-movement information file |
| 6. to ensure that advertised merchandise is available and properly priced, ticketed, and displayed | | 6. to communicate information about advertised merchandise to Central Stock, Receiving, and/or the merchandising staff; make necessary price and/or ticket changes |
| 7. to shop the competition | | 7. to visit the competition to determine competitive pricing; communicate and/or adjust price changes for competition |
| 8. to lead, delegate, control, discipline, and train associate employees | | 8. to establish, monitor, and appraise selling personnel on standards of performance; enforce store policies and procedures; communicate all information pertinent to the department operation |
| 9. to maintain inventory control | | 9. to inspect and approve all paperwork within area; ensure that adjustments are properly recorded |

**FIGURE 5–4**
Authority should equal responsibility

use in departmentalizing the store, a retailer should select the one providing management with the best level of control and producing the highest employee efficiency.

## Authority and Responsibility

**Lines of authority and responsibility** is the organizational principle that each store employee (managerial and nonmanagerial) should be given the authority to accomplish whatever responsibilities have been assigned to that individual. Figure 5–4 demonstrates the relationship between the responsibilities and the authority of a sales manager whose general charge is to direct the customer service, personnel, sales, merchandising, and operations activities of a department to achieve sales goals and to maximize profit. To assume certain responsibilities and accomplish them most efficiently, an employee must be given the necessary authority to call on whatever resources are necessary to complete the task.

An equally important aspect of this principle is that all members of the organization know and respect the established lines of authority and responsibility. A retailer's "chain of command" comprises lines of authority that link together the various managerial levels of the organization. Line and staff relationships are the linkages that join management levels and create organizational hierarchies. **Line relationships** are affiliations among managers at different organizational levels or between a manager and a subordinate within the same level who are directly responsible for achieving the firm's strategic, operational, and/or functional objectives. In a line relationship, the manager has direct authority over the subordinate. On an organizational chart, line relationships typically are shown as solid lines. **Staff relationships** are advisory or supportive and appear on organizational charts as broken lines. Staff employees are typically specialists with expertise in a particular area of concern (e.g., legal affairs, taxation, or market analysis), and their primary function is to assist line managers to realize their objectives.

### Unity of Command

The principle of **unity of command** states that the organizational structure of the retail firm should ensure that each store employee should be directly accountable to only one immediate supervisor at any one time for any given task. Most employees find it difficult if not impossible to satisfy several superiors at the same time. It is not unusual for different supervisors to want subordinates to accomplish a particular task in a different way at a different time. The store employee who must serve several masters at one time is often confused, inefficient, and frustrated.

### Span of Control

Every organization must determine how many subordinates one person can manage. One rule of thumb suggested by authorities on management is that the ideal number of subordinates ranges from four at the highest levels to twelve at the lowest levels of organization.[1] The principle of **span of control** sets guidelines for the number of subordinates a superior should control, depending on the level within the organization and the nature of the tasks being performed. Three of the guidelines follow:

1. As employees' tasks become more complex and unstandardized, their supervisor's span of control should narrow.
2. Where supervisors and employees are highly competent and well trained, the supervisor's span of control can be broader.
3. Where tasks are highly centralized in one location, a person can supervise more subordinates than if the tasks are scattered throughout a location.

These guidelines suggest the latitudes within which organizers vary the "4–12" rule for supervisors. In retailing, these guidelines can help determine the size of the various merchandising and operating departments and divisions.

The organizational structure of the retail firm can assume many different forms. To help employees understand the organizational structure, the retailer prepares organizational charts that show the formal relationships existing between various parts of the organization. In planning an organizational structure, the retailer must ask two critical questions. The first is how many organizational *levels* are needed for effective and efficient operation of the firm; the second, how the various tasks should be organized into *areas of responsibility* (jobs) and how many of these areas should be designated. Some answers to these questions are given in the following sections.

**FORMS OF RETAIL ORGANIZATION**

## Number of Organizational Levels

The number of levels separating the firm's top manager from its lowest-level employee can be viewed as a hierarchy of organizational levels. Firms that limit the number of organizational levels to one or two levels are using a **flat organizational structure**. Small, independent retailers and low-margin retailers attempting to keep their operating expenses at the lowest possible level typically use a flat organizational structure. In addition to lower operating expenses, the flat organizational structure allows direct communications with employees, higher employee morale, and quicker reaction time to problems that may arise. A flat organizational structure is often a wide organizational structure, however, which means the supervisor might have too many people to manage at one time.

**Vertical, or tall, organizational structures** have many layers of supervisor–subordinate relationships. Large retailers (e.g., department stores) and multiunit retailers (e.g., chain stores) typically use a taller organizational structure. The impersonal nature, lack of direct communications, and rigidity associated with a large number of organizational levels are the primary limitations of such organizations. These limitations may be offset by the benefits of having well-defined areas of responsibility and gaining increased supervision over employees and their assigned tasks.

## Job and Task Organization

The exact form of organizational structure of any retailer depends on how the retailer classifies jobs that employees must perform. A retailer can classify jobs on the basis of their functional nature, geographic location, product involvement, or some combination of the three. Using the **functional approach** to retail organizational structure, the retailer groups tasks and classifies jobs according to such functional areas as store operations, buying and selling merchandise, promotional activities, or recruiting and training store personnel. In essence, the functional approach is one of task and job specialization in one or more general functions.

Small, independent retailers usually have a two-function organizational structure, thereby limiting specialization. Merchandising and store operations are the first two functional divisions that retailers usually create. As their firms become larger and more complex, retailers will create additional functional divisions. In the three-function organizational structure, retailers add a third division to the basic merchandising and operating divisions, typically one of the following: a financial controls division, a sales promotion division, or a personnel division. It is not unusual for the

**FIGURE 5-5**
Geographic organiza-
tion structure

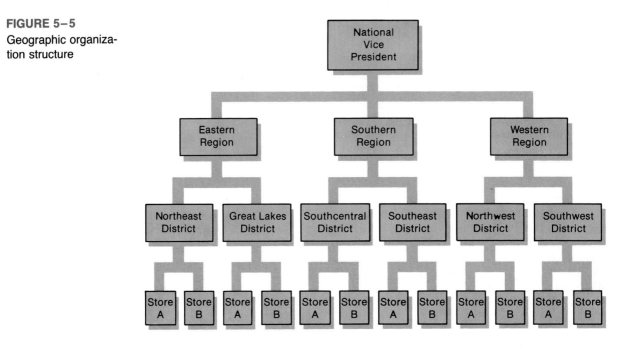

retailer to create four, five, or more functional divisions. (Four- and five-function organizations are illustrated and discussed under department store organizational patterns.)

The **geographic approach** to organizational structure is one in which the retailer organizes tasks and assigns jobs on the basis of where those tasks and jobs are performed. Multiunit retailers (such as chain stores) frequently use the geographic approach. The geographic size of the retailer's market influences both the number of organizational levels and the degree of market specialization at each level. A multiunit retailer with a limited number of stores within a concentrated geographic market usually has only two levels (the main store with several branch stores) and a local market specialization (neighborhood or community). On the other hand, large chain organizations with many stores operating all over the country typically form organizational structures with several levels and various degrees of market specialization. Figure 5-5 illustrates a national retail firm that uses the geographic approach of organization.

**FIGURE 5-6**
Product organization
structure

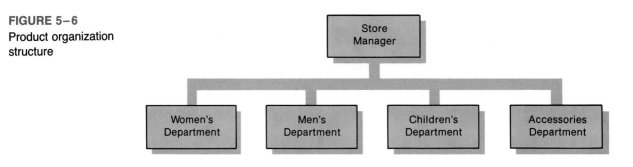

In the **product approach** to retail organizational structure, the retailer organizes the store by product line. This organizational form centers around task and job specialization to meet the consumers' buying needs for certain products. For many shopping and specialty goods, for example, consumers think, shop, and buy in terms of product groupings. Figure 5–6 illustrates a family apparel store organized around the general product lines of women's, men's, and children's apparel and accessories.

Over the years various retail organizational patterns have emerged as the result of the diverse sizes and natures of firms. To characterize these patterns, we shall look at the organizational structures of small, independent retailers, department store retailers, and chain store retailers.

**PATTERNS OF RETAIL ORGANIZATION**

## Small Store Organization

Many retailers began business as a one-person, owner-operator shop. In these cases, the owner-operator was the organization. As such, the individual had the responsibility and authority for all organizational tasks. As the firm grew, the owner-operator hired additional store personnel to handle the increasing number of complex tasks that accompany a larger, more formal organizational structure.

The typical organizational structure of the small, independent retailer has previously been characterized as flat, typically with two levels and a general organization and a limited amount of specialization. As illustrated in Figure 5–7, the owner-manager develops store and personnel policies; administers expense, sales, and merchandising budgets; and oversees accounting and other control procedures. In most small retail firms, however, it is common for the owner-manager to become directly involved with many of the routine merchandising tasks and day-to-day operations.

Also illustrated in Figure 5–7 are the two most common functional divisions that small retailers use: the merchandising and operations divisions. The merchan-

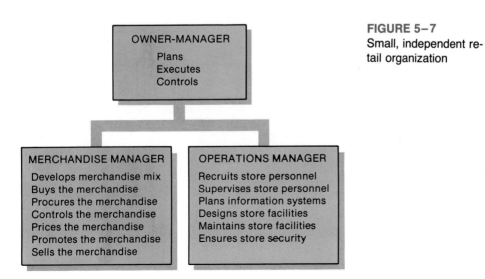

**FIGURE 5–7**
Small, independent retail organization

dise manager usually is a salesperson with considerable experience in merchandising and has been an employee for a long time. Typically, this person is assigned the responsibilities of buying and selling the firm's merchandise. The operations manager is an employee who assumes the responsibilities for recruiting and supervising store personnel; for planning, securing, and maintaining store facilities, equipment, and supplies; and for many of the back-room activities of receiving and stocking merchandise and overseeing the activities of the office staff.

## Department Store Organization

Department store organizations are more formal and complex than small retailers'. As mentioned earlier, the organizational structure of department stores is taller and more specialized than it is for small retail stores. To understand department store organization, we shall examine the Mazur Plan of retail organization and its functional and geographic modifications.

Most retailing experts date modern retail organizational structures from 1927, when an investment banker named Paul Mazur introduced his ideas on how to structure a retail store.[2] The **Mazur Plan** divides the retail organization into four functional divisions: finance, merchandising, promotion, and operations. Each division manager has specific responsibilities (see Figure 5–8).

The *finance manager's* chief responsibilities are to control the firm's assets and to ensure that sufficient working capital is available for each of the firm's functional divisions. In particular, the finance manager is responsible for (1) developing and maintaining accounting and other record-keeping systems; (2) planning and controlling physical inventory, merchandise budgets, and expense budgets; and (3) prepar-

**FIGURE 5–8**
The Mazur Plan for department store organization

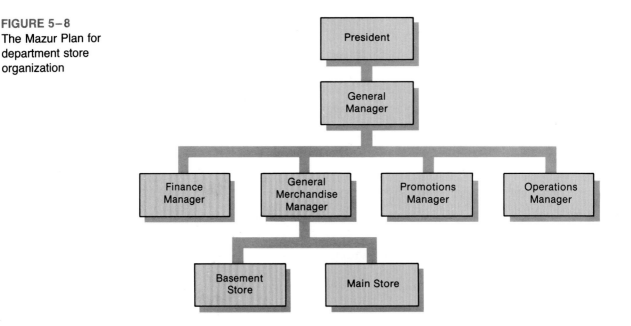

ing financial reports for the firm's general management, government agencies, and trade organizations.

The *general merchandising manager* is responsible primarily for supervising the firm's buying and selling activities. An equally important responsibility is to coordinate these activities with those of the finance, promotions, and operations managers. Given the consumer orientation of retailing, the general merchandise division is usually one of the most important functional areas within the organization.

The *promotions manager* is responsible for directing the firm's persuasive communications to consumers. Specifically, the promotions manager oversees all advertising, sales promotional activities (e.g., fashion shows, demonstrations), interior and window displays, public relations, and publicity. In addition, the promotions manager handles consumer feedback and directs advertising research in companies that conduct these activities.

The *operations manager* is generally responsible for all the physical operations of the store that are not directly assigned to one of the other divisions. Major tasks assigned to the store operations division are facilities development and maintenance; customer services and assistance; credit and collections; receiving, checking, marking, and stocking incoming merchandise; store security; and general store housekeeping. Recruiting, training, and evaluating store personnel also are responsibilities assigned to the operations manager in a four-function organization.

*Functional Modifications of the Mazur Plan.* The two most common functional modifications in the Mazur Plan are (1) changing the number of functional divisions and (2) separating the buying and selling functions. In changing the Mazur Plan, department stores most often create a five-function organization by establishing a personnel division, equal in status to the other four divisions. Other functional activities that retailers might consider for separate divisional status are distribution, real estate and construction, and catalog operations.

According to the Mazur Plan, the buying and selling functions both fall under the direct supervision of the general merchandise manager. Some retailing experts argue, however, that these functions should be separated. Proponents of separation believe that (1) buying and selling require different skills, talents, and training; (2) selling activities suffer because buying takes up a considerable amount of the buyer's time spent away from the store; (3) feedback on consumer needs can be handled better by a well-developed and maintained merchandise-control system; (4) greater flexibility in the use of sales and buying personnel is possible when these individuals specialize in either selling or buying activities; and (5) in-store grouping of merchandise should be based on selling, not buying, activities. Those who argue against separation of buying and selling activities, however, hold that (1) the buyer must have direct contact with customers to determine their needs; (2) if the individuals who buy the merchandise are responsible for selling it, they will therefore exercise greater care in buying activities; and (3) it is easier to assign responsibility for the department's profit performance if buying and selling are conducted by the same person because the buyer cannot blame the seller for not putting out the necessary selling effort and the seller cannot blame the lack of a good profit performance on buying mistakes. Both sides of the issue offer valid arguments. (The combination and separation of buying and selling activities in department stores are discussed later in conjunction with branch store organizations.)

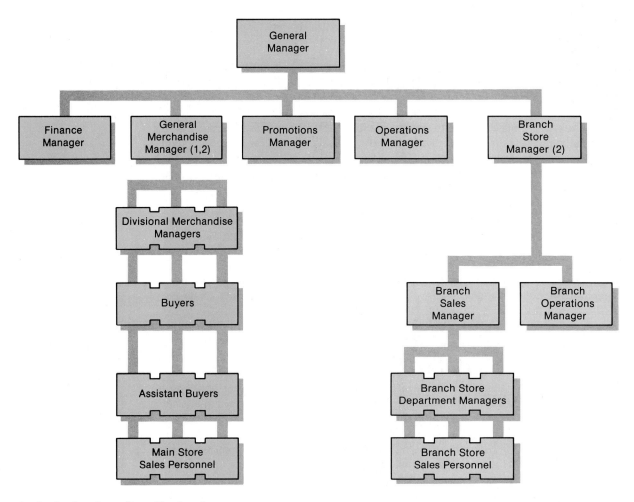

1 = buying function     2 = selling function

**FIGURE 5–9**

The main-store approach to branch department-store organization

*Geographic Modifications of the Mazur Plan.* When department stores began to "branch out" into other geographic areas, they necessitated several additional changes in the basic Mazur Plan. These new organizational arrangements, based on geographical modifications, were the main-store approach, the separate-store approach, and the equal-store approach.

With the **main-store approach** to branch organization, the parent organization (the main store) exercises control over branch stores. As illustrated in Figure 5–9, main-store managers of finance, general merchandise, promotion, and operations are responsible for supervising the same functions in the branch stores as at the main store. Under this organizational plan, main-store buyers and their assistants are responsible for securing merchandise for the main store and all branches. Sales activities in the main store are under the direct supervision of buyers, whereas sales activities in all branch stores are the responsibility of branch sales managers. In essence, those who use the main-store approach treat branch stores as sales organizations, performing merchandise and operation functions from within the main store.

Used by department stores in the initial stages of expansion, the main-store approach is most appropriate when (1) there are only a few branches; (2) customer preferences and the merchandise mix are fairly similar for the main and branch stores; (3) branch stores are located near the main store; and (4) main-store management and supporting staff can comfortably supervise branches without overextending themselves.

The **separate-store approach** to branch department-store organization treats each branch as an independent operation with its own organizational structure of managers, buyers, and sales personnel. Under this plan, branch-store management assumes both the merchandising responsibilities of buying and selling and the routine responsibilities of operating the branch store. As shown in Figure 5–10, each branch has its own store manager as well as personnel, merchandise, and operations managers, who operate separately from the parent organization.

The separate-store approach generally is used by department stores that have four to seven branches approximately the size of the main store. The major advantage of this approach is that each branch has great flexibility in tailoring its merchandise and operations to meet the needs of its local clientele. The principal disadvantages are (1) a loss in economies of scale in buying; (2) an increase in operating costs because of additional management and staff needs; (3) increased difficulties in maintaining a consistent image from store to store; and (4) increased problems of coordination (e.g., stock transfers, promotion activities, etc.).

In response to the increasing number of branch stores, retailers have developed an alternative strategy to the separate-store approach. Instead of the decentralized authority and responsibility of the separate-store approach, the **equal-store approach** emphasizes centralization of authority and responsibility. Under the equal-store plan, all major managerial functions are controlled from a central headquarters. The finance, merchandise, promotions, and operations functions are under the direct supervision of headquarters managers. This approach has two unique features. First, the buying and selling functions are separated; the buying function remains a centralized activity under the general merchandise manager, and the selling function becomes a decentralized activity under the manager of stores. This centralized buying and decentralized selling concept has considerable support within the ranks of department store managers.[3] Second, all stores (main and branches) are treated equally as basic sales units (see Figure 5–11). The equal-store plan attempts to combine the advantages of centralized buying (economies of scale) with the advantages of localized selling (target market selling).

## Chain Store Organization

Chain store organizations vary considerably in size, geographic spread, local markets, product mix, and number of operating units. Although all of these factors influence how a chain store will organize, three distinctive elements characterize all chain store organizations: centralization, specialization, and standardization.

**Centralization** is the concentration of policy and decision making in one location, called either *central headquarters* or the *home office*. Within the chain-store

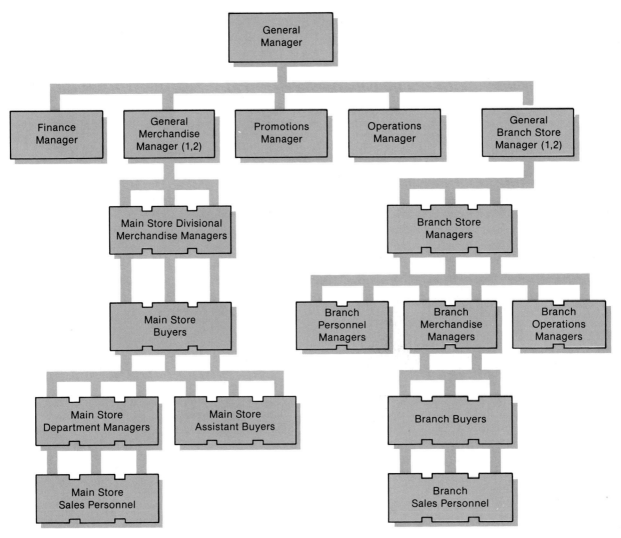

1 = buying function    2 = selling function

**FIGURE 5–10**

Separate-store
approach to branch
department-store
organization

organizational structure, the authority and responsibilities for most operating and merchandising functions are assigned to home office management personnel. Greater effectiveness and cost reductions are two important reasons why chains like F. W. Woolworth pursue a centralization policy.[4] The primary exception is sales, which are under the decentralized control of local management. In recent years chain store organizations have tended to adopt limited decentralization. Thus, more and more functional authority and responsibility are being given to regional and divisional levels of the organization. The main reason behind this change is the gigantic size of many chain store retailers (see Figure 5–12).

A high degree of specialization is another distinguishing feature of chain store organizations. Typically, the chain store incorporates a greater number of functional

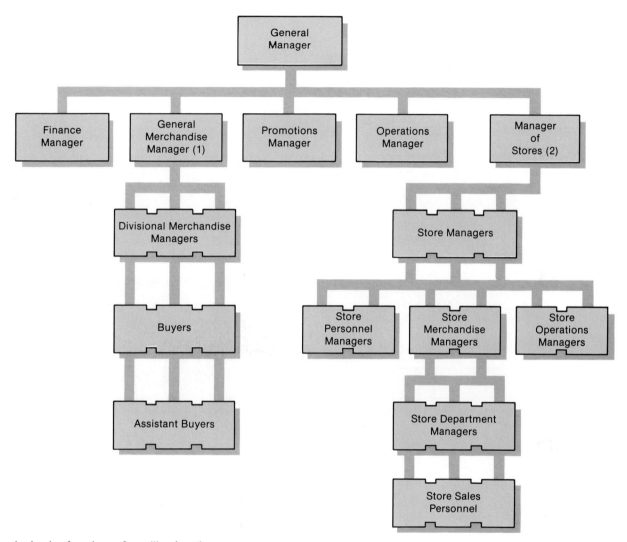

1 = buying function     2 = selling function

FIGURE 5–11

Equal-store approach
to branch department-
store organization

divisions in its organizational structure. In addition to the four basic functional divisions of finance, merchandising, operations, and promotions, many chain stores include one or more of the following functional divisions: distribution (traffic and warehousing), marketing, real estate and construction, personnel, and industrial relations. Some large chains also specialize geographically.

The third distinguishing feature of chain organizations is a high degree of **standardization,** or similarities between the operating and merchandising operations of the business. To support standardization, chain store management establishes an elaborate system of supervision and control mechanisms to keep fully informed. Through standardization, the chain projects a consistent company image and minimizes total costs of doing business.

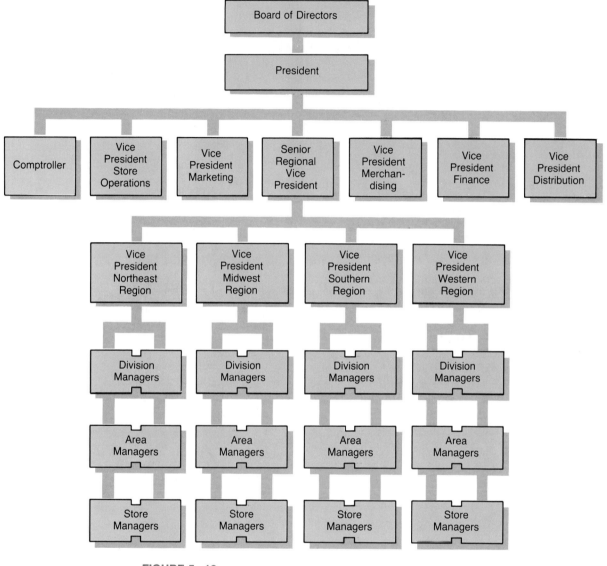

**FIGURE 5–12**
Chain store organization

## LEGAL FORMS OF RETAIL ORGANIZATION

Three basic forms of business organization are recognized by law: the sole proprietorship, the partnership, and the corporation. The **sole proprietorship** is a business owned and managed by a single individual. It is the simplest and most flexible legal form of organization. When two or more persons form a business without incorporating, the business is a *partnership*. Partnerships can consist of any number of partners, whose share and control of the business is determined at the time the organization is formed. In a **general partnership**, all partners take part in the control and operation of the partnership. In a **limited partnership,** one or more members of the partnership contribute capital to the formation and running of the partnership, but limited partners do not take part in managing the firm's retail operations. A **corporation** is a legal business entity authorized by state law to operate as a single person even though it may consist of many persons. The type of legal organization a retailer chooses will depend on the degree of operational flexibility desired, the willingness to assume liability and risk, the preferred tax status, the need for capital, and the need for managerial and operational skills.

**SUMMARY**

Retailers use numerous different structures to organize their people, tasks, and operations. In retailing, the firm's organization is directed at accomplishing certain strategy objectives (general, long-term goals); operational objectives (long-term operational requirements to obtain strategy objectives); and functional objectives (specific task-oriented objectives). Also, retailers must organize in such a manner that the basic operational tasks of planning and controlling the product, price, promotion, and place can be facilitated readily.

The retailer should consider several basic principles of organization in developing the structure of the firm. Of particular interest are the organizational principles of specialization and departmentalization, lines of authority and areas of responsibility, unity of command, and span of control.

Many retailers prepare charts to illustrate their form of retail organization. Some retail organizational structures are characterized by a limited number of levels (flat organizations), while others incorporate many levels of organization (vertical structures). Organizational forms are strongly influenced by how retailers classify jobs and tasks. Depending on the firm, jobs and tasks can be classified on the basis of their functional, geographic, or product relationships; also, a combination of these three factors can be used in job and task classification.

Patterns of retail organization vary considerably between the simple structures of the small, independent retailer and the often complex organization of the department and chain store retailer. Centralization, specialization, and standardization are the key characteristics of chain store organizational structures, while the Mazur Plan and its variations characterize department store organizations.

Legal forms of retail organization include sole proprietorship, general partnership, limited partnership, and corporation.

**STUDENT STUDY GUIDE**

**KEY TERMS AND CONCEPTS**

centralization

corporation

departmentalization

equal-store organization

flat organizational structure

functional approach to organizational structure

functional objectives

general partnership

geographic approach to organizational structure

limited proprietorship

line relationships

lines of authority and responsibility

main-store organization

Mazur Plan

operational objectives

product approach to organizational
structure

separate-store organization

sole proprietorship

span of control

specialization

staff relationships

standardization

strategic objectives

unity of command

vertical organizational structure

---

**REVIEW
QUESTIONS**

1. What are the three levels of organizational objectives? Define each and describe its relationship to the general levels of retail management.
2. Describe the organizational principles of specialization and departmentalization. How can specialization and departmentalization be accomplished?
3. Distinguish between line and staff relationships. How do these relationships impact the organizational chart?
4. What is the principle of unity of command? Why is the principle important?
5. What is span of control? Is there an ideal span of control? Describe the guidelines for determining span of control.
6. Compare and contrast the pros and cons of vertical and flat organization structures.
7. Job classification is based on three criteria. Describe each.
8. What are the four functional divisions in the Mazur Plan of retail organization? How is this plan usually modified?
9. Outline the advantages and disadvantages of separation of buying and selling activities.
10. Compare and contrast the main-store, separate-store, and equal-store approaches to branch department-store organization.
11. What distinguishes chain store organizations? Discuss each distinctive element.

---

**REVIEW EXAM**

True or False

_____ 1. Operational objectives are general statements of long-term operational requirements that are necessary to achieve a strategy objective.

_____ 2. Line managers are typically specialists whose primary function is to assist staff managers in realizing their objectives.

_____ 3. Where tasks are highly centralized in one location, the supervisor's span of control can be broadened.

_____ 4. The organizational structure of department stores is flatter and more generalized than small, independent retail organizations.

_____ 5. Small, independent retailers usually have a two-functional organizational structure, thereby limiting specialization.

_____ 6. A major argument for combining the buying and selling functions is that it is easier to assign responsibility for the department's profit performance.

_____ 7. Under the equal-store approach to branch department store organization, each branch has its own store manager as well as personnel, merchandise, and operations managers, who operate separately from the parent store.

1. Obtain an organizational chart from a department store chain and a specialty store chain. Compare and contrast the two organizational charts. What are the strengths and weaknesses of each organization form? On the basis of organizational structure, which organization would you most prefer as a career path? Why?
2. Outline two specific examples each of strategy, operational, and functional objectives for a stereo/hi-fi department.
3. Explain how specialization, departmentalization, lines of authority and responsibility, unit of command, and span of control help the retailer avoid managerial confusion and employee discontent.
4. What are the advantages and disadvantages of working for a retail organization characterized by a flat organizational structure and for one having a vertical organizational structure?
5. Describe the conditions under which the retailer should consider a functional approach to retail organization structure and the classification of jobs and tasks. Tell why he or she might consider adopting a geographic approach.

**PROJECTS:
INVESTIGATIONS
AND
APPLICATIONS**

## CASE 5–1
### The Case of the Organic Gardener—Investigating Various Forms of Business Ownership*

**CASES:
PROBLEMS AND
DECISIONS**

Gareth Reed was known for his melons. Actually, Gareth was known and respected by those folks who practiced organic gardening. Organic gardeners use only natural fertilizers and forms of insect control. Compost, natural or dehydrated manures, and dehydrated seaweed are some of the fertilizers used. Bug traps using pheromones, powders or sprays using rotenone or pyrethrins, and side-by-side planting or combinations of vegetables or flowers and vegetables are means of insect control.

Gareth had graduated with a bachelor's degree in biology and after a couple of false starts had become a medical laboratory technician. He had enjoyed doing the individual tests in serology, hematology, and blood chemistry. However, a blood specimen could now be run through an automatic "hemoanalyzer," which performs several diagnostic tests. The loss of opportunity for individual investigation had diminished his enthusiasm for that line of work.

Gareth had found out that a lawn and garden store he occasionally patronized was for sale because of illness of the owner. He knew of no lawn and garden store within a 30-mile radius of the location of this store that carried a full line of organic gardening products and seeds that were not treated with chemicals or poisons to repel birds and other unwanted scavengers. At present, he had to drive 40 miles to patronize his preferred source of organic garden supplies, but figured that not all organic gardeners were as persnickety as himself. Thus, he figured he could enhance the business of the store that was for sale by carrying a full line of organic gardening supplies. He was known and respected throughout the county among an informal network of organic gardeners.

Gareth felt pretty comfortable with the prospect of the operations aspect of a lawn and garden store because he had worked in a hardware store part-time for many years. Of

*This case was prepared by Ken Mast and Jon Hawes, The University of Akron.

some concern was the fact that he had not taken any business courses in college and had never been involved in the financial aspects of running a business. There was also the issue of raising the necessary capital if he were to try to buy the business from the present owner.

Gareth stopped in the store one day on his way home from work. He talked with the owner and his wife, who had living quarters in the back of the store. It was around closing time, and when the owners became convinced that Gareth's interest was more than a casual inquiry, they closed for the day and invited Gareth to ask any questions he wished. While Mrs. Mofit prepared supper, Mr. Mofit showed Gareth the financial records and even quoted his asking price. When Gareth expressed concern, Mr. Mofit even indicated that he and Mrs. Mofit would consider staying on as partners with the "right" person.

As a result of his visit with the Mofits, Gareth decided to do some further investigation. A high school classmate, Kim Falanga, was a managing partner in a highly successful certified public accounting firm. An appointment was arranged and he was pleased to find her to be cordial, professional, and very well prepared to discuss all financial aspects of retail ventures similar to and including lawn and garden stores. She asked some questions he hadn't really thought about and he felt embarrassed by some of his attempts at answers. He was suprised that she encouraged him to formally develop a proposal for funding along guidelines that she provided. His surprise turned to amazement when she hinted that she might personally be interested in investing in such a venture.

Another surprise developed when he contacted a number of fellow organic gardeners. His purpose was merely to ascertain their interest in a more accessible source of full-line organic gardening supplies. He discovered not only interest, but also inquiries about investing and in one instance, an inquiry regarding part-time employment. One thing led to another and eventually to a meeting at his house of organic gardeners who had expressed unexpected interest beyond just a closer source of supplies. Among this group united by a common interest in organic gardening was a lawyer who was very knowledgeable and helpful in explaining the advantages and disadvantages of general and limited partnerships as well as corporations. No consensus was established as to the form of ownership, but only a couple of those present appeared to have any reservations about some type of financial interest in the venture. Although no one indicated dollar amounts, there were adequate indications that all were reasonably well established financially.

After everyone left, Gareth pondered his situation. He wasn't sure he could raise enough money to buy the lawn and garden store by liquidating his own resources. Even if he could, the risk would be high because everything he had would be invested in the store. Furthermore, selling his house would leave him without a place to garden. He could rent a plot of ground, but he dearly hated to part with all that compost-rich dirt that he had carfully nurtured over the years.

His discussion with the Mofits had revealed little interest on their part in carrying a full line of organic supplies. Mr. Mofit claimed that even the limited organic supplies that he carried didn't "move very fast." As for Kim Falanga, he wistfully wondered if the heart of an organic gardener could somehow beat beneath the lapels of her tailored business suits. Her polished nails had probably never turned the handle of a compost maker. The "organic group" was long on enthusiasm, but other than the lawyer, appeared to have relatively little business experience that would compensate for Gareth's relative inexperience with the financial management of the business.

### ASSIGNMENT

1. Outline the advantages and disadvantages of the alternative forms of business ownership available to Gareth.
2. Rank the form of business you perceive to be best for Gareth on the basis of the information provided. Justify your ranking.

3. What additional information, if any, do you believe would be particularly helpful if you were the person in Gareth's garden shoes?

1. Lyndall Vrwicke, "Axioms of Organization," *Public Administration* (October 1955): 348–349.
2. Paul M. Mazur, *Principles of Organization Applied to Modern Retailing* (New York: Harper & Row, 1927).
3. Clarence E. Vincent and John S. Berens, "Changes in Department Store Organization: Implications for Curriculum Requirements for Management Trainees," *Journal of Marketing Education* 3 (Spring 1981): 21.
4. "Centralization Pays for Woolworths," *Stores* (June 1985): 26.

# 6

## Outline

## Objectives

☐ Conduct a job analysis to determine the specific tasks and skills required of the employee.

☐ Write a job description and develop specifications for each position.

☐ Identify potential sources of store employees and describe the criteria and methods for screening job applicants.

☐ Understand and use the basic techniques for matching job requirements with employee attributes.

☐ Specify the different procedures used in training and supervising store personnel.

☐ Discuss when to evaluate, what to evaluate, and how to evaluate employees and their performances.

☐ Evaluate the various methods used in compensating store personnel.

# Store Personnel and Supervision

P eople make a successful business! Regardless of the number and quality of machines, product lines carried, floor and shelf space, and other material aspects of a business, people make the difference. Therefore, staffing the retail store may be one of the most difficult and certainly most important tasks facing the retailer. Some retailers experience annual employee turnover rates in excess of 50 percent. Generally, employee turnover rates are highest in lower-level positions and among part-time employees. With high employee turnover rates, the retailer incurs large recruiting and training expenses, lower labor productivity, and disruptions in store operations. Given these problems, the retailer must develop and maintain an effective employee staffing process, particularly because employee compensation generally accounts for more than 50 percent of the retailer's expenses.

The retailer's staffing process involves not only finding capable store personnel, but also developing working environments that will enable the retailer to keep productive employees. Specifically, the staffing process consists of the eight steps shown in Figure 6–1.

The first step in the staffing process is to develop a well-defined and clearly expressed **job description**. Not only does this step force the retailer to carefully determine its personnel needs, but it also provides the potential employee with a means of evaluating the job. Before writing a job description, the retailer should conduct a job analysis to determine (1) specific job-performance objectives and standards; (2) the tasks, duties, and responsibilities of the job; and (3) the skills, aptitudes, experience, education, and physical abilities that potential employees must possess to meet the minimum job requirements.[1]

After the job analysis is completed, the retailer can write a job description containing the following items: (1) the job title (e.g., sales representative, assistant store manager); (2) the job location (e.g., store, department); (3) the job position and relationships with the firm's organizational structure (e.g., identify superiors and subordinates, if any); and (4) job description (i.e., duties and responsibilities). Figure 6–2 presents a typical job description for a sales manager position. Note that it is better to write job descriptions in the form of job "objectives" because it gives the employee a greater latitude in job interpretation and performance.

**DESCRIBING THE JOB**

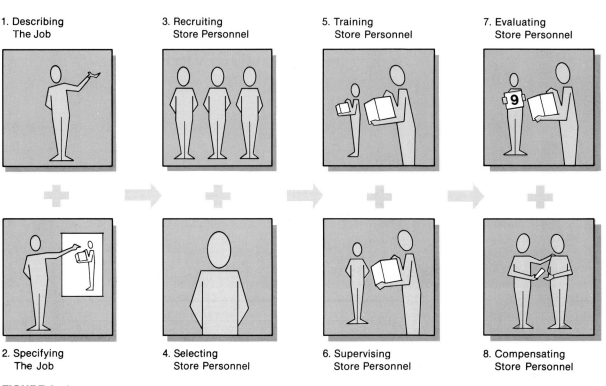

1. Describing
   The Job

2. Specifying
   The Job

3. Recruiting
   Store Personnel

4. Selecting
   Store Personnel

5. Training
   Store Personnel

6. Supervising
   Store Personnel

7. Evaluating
   Store Personnel

8. Compensating
   Store Personnel

**FIGURE 6–1**
The retail staffing process

## SPECIFYING THE JOB

To meet federal, state, and local regulations on hiring practices, many retailers provide potential employees with a written job specification. A **job specification** clearly states the minimum qualifications a person must have to obtain the job applied for. Qualification criteria include education and training requirements and/or basic knowledge and skill requirements. Retailing is still a business where a college degree is not necessary to succeed; however, because of increased complexities of store merchandising and operations, coming up the hard way is becoming more difficult.[2] Because of recent legislation, retailers need to recognize that they might be asked to prove that their qualifying criteria are directly related to successful performance in the positions outlined in their job descriptions. To avoid costly lawsuits, they must establish the validity of the relationship between job success and the stated job qualifications. Before filling any position, the retailer should protect itself by gathering evidence that the job qualifications actually enable an employee to meet job expectations. The retailer must avoid certain illegal conditions for employment in writing job qualifications, such as any requirement related either directly or indirectly to the applicant's race, age, creed, color, sex, religion, or national origin.

## RECRUITING STORE PERSONNEL

Recruiting is the active search for qualified employees. The astute manager recruits personnel by aggressively *seeking* lists of qualified prospects, *screening* large numbers of applicants, and *maintaining* a pool of prospective employees. Successful

| | |
|---|---|
| **Job title:** | Sales manager |
| **Job location:** | Men's shoe department<br>Walnut Valley Branch<br>Selmer's Department Stores |
| **Job position:** | Reports to assistant store manager |
| **Job description:** | To achieve sales goals by setting and maintaining customer service standards, training and motivating a professional sales staff, and maintaining merchandise presentation standards. |

**Job objectives:**

1. To work as a partner with the merchandise analyst to develop sales plans and to reach sales goals within the area of responsibility.
2. To ensure that the store's customer service standards and policies are maintained.
3. To train, develop, motivate, and appraise the sales associates working within the area of responsibility.
4. To work as a partner with the merchandise analyst and assistant store manager in developing stock assortments and quantities.
5. To verify that the appearance and presentation of merchandise on the selling floor adhere to the visual merchandising guidelines.
6. To ensure that selling services provide appropriate floor coverage to meet or exceed productivity goals.
7. To communicate with the branch store coordinator, assistant store manager, and merchandise analyst concerning floor presentation.
8. To ensure that advertised merchandise is properly priced, ticketed, and displayed and to ensure that sales associates are aware of this merchandise.
9. To control merchandise inventories, including but not limited to receiving, pricing, transfers, price changes, security, and damages.
10. To conduct all stock counts.
11. To supervise the control of sales register media and cash register shortage.
12. To shop the competition.
13. To input information into major sale resumes.
14. To disseminate all pertinent information to all sales associates including night contingents.
15. To ensure the correct documentation of time sheets within the area.
16. To implement credit promotions and other programs in the area.

**FIGURE 6–2**
A typical job description

recruiting is the process of knowing where to look, what to look for, and how to find qualified people.

## Finding Employees

Several internal and external sources can provide the names and general backgrounds of prospective employees. Internal sources include lists of current and past employees as well as employee recommendations. *Current employees* should not be overlooked if they possess the necessary qualifications for the job. Promotions and transfers are not only a means of finding qualified persons, but also a way to improve employee morale by demonstrating that advancement is possible within the firm. *Past employees* with satisfactory service records are an internal source of employees that retailers often overlook. The third internal source comprises *employee recommendations*. Frequently, the firm's employees know of friends, relatives, and acquaintances who are in the job market and have the necessary skills and training to fill a position. Neiman-Marcus has a hiring bonus program for employees who recommend qualified persons who are hired and stay for a prescribed period of time.[3]

External sources of prospective employees come from advertisements, employment agencies, educational institutions, and unsolicited applications. *Advertisements* in newspapers, trade publications, and professional papers and journals are common methods of attracting applicants. These printed media frequently devote sections to employment opportunities at certain times or in particular issues. Private and public *employment agencies* are also sources of prospective employees. Two advantages of using employment agencies are that they provide initial screening for a large number of prospects and that they maintain the retailer's anonymity during the initial stages of the recruiting process. Before using the services of a private or government employment agency, the retailer should determine the agency's fee structure and which party is responsible for paying the fee—the employer or the employee.

The third external source of prospective employees is *educational institutions*. Career counselors at most high schools often can provide a list of suitable prospects for part-time and entry-level positions. Placement offices at two-year colleges and four-year colleges and universities are always eager to supply retailers and other businesses with the names and qualifications of prospective employees for low- and middle-management positions. Walk-ins and mail-ins represent *unsolicited applications* that retailers should keep on file and periodically review when a job becomes available. One additional external source of employees is *pirating*—hiring an employee who works for a noncompeting retailer. The major advantage of pirating is the retailing experience the prospective employee undoubtedly has. However, the retailer should proceed cautiously when hiring another retailer's employee.

### Screening Applicants

In the screening process, personnel managers examine the applicant's qualifications to determine whether the person has the requisite background and capabilities to perform the job. The most common criteria retailers use in the initial screening process are educational background, ability to communicate in oral and written form, experience in working with people, and knowledge, experience, or skills to perform a particular activity (e.g., typing). Other screening criteria retailers use indirectly and subjectively are personal appearance, general attitude, motivation, and personality.

| **SELECTING STORE PERSONNEL** | From the list of qualified applicants, the retailer must select the individual best suited to the job. Matching job requirements to employee attributes is the point of the selection step of the staffing process. In finding the best match, the retailer has available several methods of generating additional information on the prospective |

employee before deciding to make an offer. These methods include application forms, personal interviews, reference checks, testing instruments, and physical examinations.

## Application Forms

All retailers should require each prospective employee to complete an application form as a prerequisite for further processing. Application forms provide the retailer with preliminary information on each applicant and (1) serve as a means of checking minimum qualifications during initial screening; (2) provide basic information to guide the interviewer during the personal interview process; (3) allow a preliminary check on the applicant's ability to follow instructions; and (4) provide background information for a permanent record if the applicant is hired.[4] A typical application form provides space for the applicant's name, address, telephone number, employment history (when and where the applicant has previously worked, levels of compensation, and reasons for leaving previous jobs), formal education and training, personal health history, and demographic information allowed by state and federal regulations. The application form also usually includes space for a list of personal references. Although the retailer should carefully review all the information on the application form, special attention should be given to *omissions* and *job changes*. What is *not* on the application form can be as important as what *is* on it. The retailer should seek clarification of all omissions on application forms. Frequent job changes without good cause can also reveal something about the applicant's character.

## Reference Checks

After the retailer has initially screened prospective employees' application forms and eliminated those who are unqualified, the references of the remaining prospects should be contacted. Although most references the applicants list are favorably biased, they do give the retailer a way to verify the accuracy and completeness of the applicant's form. Telephone calls to references normally provide more complete and honest evaluations than do letters. Telephone contact gives the retailer a chance to ask questions about issues of particular concern. To reinforce reference checks, many retailers contact former employers, teachers, and other individuals who might have specific knowledge of the applicant's character and abilities. Some retailers even check applicants' credit by calling local credit bureaus.

## Personal Interviews

Retailers use personal interviews to question and observe applicants in a face-to-face situation. Formal, highly structured interviews have the advantage of establishing the relative roles of each party in the interview, permitting a controlled interviewing environment and facilitating complete, effective information gathering. Informal and unstructured interviews help the applicant to relax, to talk freely, and to act naturally— thereby allowing the interviewer to view the applicant in an unguarded state. Most retailers prefer to compromise by injecting enough formality and structure into the interview to promote efficiency but not enough to create undue tension in the applicant. The number of interviews usually depends on the level of the position to be filled. When retailers are trying to fill upper-level managerial positions, they normally interview each applicant several times; for entry-level positions, one interview generally suffices.

The location of any interview should be private and in pleasant surroundings. Both factors help to relax the prospective employee and give the retailer a chance to see the applicant in a natural setting. The length of an interview may be from a few minutes for low-echelon, part-time employees to several days for the applicant who is interviewing for a high-level management position. Many retailers find it advantageous to have the applicant interview with several of the firm's managers so they can elicit several opinions of the applicant's qualifications.

The personal interviewing process should fully comply with state and federal equal employment opportunity regulations. Questions asked in the interview must be job-related and necessary to judging the applicant's qualifications and abilities. To avoid charges of discrimination, the retailer should construct a list of questions to use in the interviewing process and have the store's legal department review it for any possible discriminatory inquiries.

## Testing Instruments

In the hiring process, some retailers use testing instruments to evaluate prospective employees. These instruments are pencil-and-paper tests that applicants take to demonstrate their abilities to handle a job.

Retailers use two general types of instruments to evaluate their applicants: psychological tests and achievement tests. **Psychological tests** are designed to measure an applicant's personality, intelligence, aptitudes, interests, and supervisory skills. **Achievement tests** are designed to measure a person's basic knowledge and skills. Tests that measure an applicant's ability to do basic arithmetic computations or to operate mechanical devices, such as cash registers, typewriters, and calculators, are examples.

Generally, retailers prefer achievement tests to psychological tests because they are easier to administer and interpret.[5] Also, most retailers believe that achievement tests are more valid than psychological tests because the statistical relationship between the skills they measure and job success is stronger. Target discount stores, a division of Dayton Hudson, uses an assessment center (AC) concept in which a series of simulated experiences provides the potential employee with "an opportunity to demonstrate competencies in certain areas. What distinguishes it from testing per se is testing looks at intellectual capability, past background, and tries to forecast the future . . . the AC puts the candidate in an actual experience—one that will be encountered at retail—then measures performance."[6]

## Physical Examinations

Some retailers require applicants to undergo a physical examination. Usually this examination is requested only after the applicant has been judged the most qualified person for the job. Some states have laws requiring a physical examination for employees who handle food and drug products. In addition, some firms' health, life, and disability insurance programs require exams. Testing for drug usage and acquired immune deficiency syndrome (AIDS) is also an issue being addressed by some retailers.

## Final Selection

Ultimately, the retailer must make a final selection among the qualified applicants. No absolute, totally objective method can determine the most qualified person; rather, the final selection is largely a subjective choice based on all available information. An experienced personnel manager with good intuition is perhaps one of the most valuable assets a firm can have for selecting employees who will make a significant contribution over an extended period. Objective tests, experience, and good personal judgment are the tools a personnel manager needs to make the final selection.

**TRAINING STORE PERSONNEL**

The fifth step in the staffing process is employee training. Training programs are needed not only for new employees, but also for existing employees to update their knowledge and skills. Retail training programs vary according to the size and complexity of the retail organization, the number of employees, the type and complexity, of the job, the abilities and experience of the individual employee, and the program goals.

Regardless of the retailer's individual situation, however, every sound retail training program should address three basic questions. These elements are *what type* of training the employee should have, *where* the training should take place, and *how* the training should be done. Figure 6–3 identifies these basic elements.

### What Training to Give

Two basic kinds of training that both new and old employees need are organization orientation and functional training. **Organization orientation** is a program that either initiates new employees or updates old employees on the general organizational

| | |
|---|---|
| **WHAT** | Organizational orientation |
| | Functional training |
| **WHERE** | On the job—decentralized training |
| | Off the job—centralized training |
| **HOW** | Individual methods |
| |    "on your own" |
| |    programmed learning |
| | Sponsor method |
| | Group methods |
| |    lectures |
| |    demonstrations |
| |    case studies |
| |    role playing |
| | Executive training programs |

**FIGURE 6–3**

Elements of a retail training program

structure of the firm and its policies, rules, and regulations. It also acquaints employees with the company's history, objectives, and future expectations. Essentially, an organization orientation program makes employees aware of what the firm is trying to accomplish and how it plans to accomplish it. One aim of this program is to improve employees' morale and to make them feel they are members of the "team."

**Functional training** is a program that develops and expands the basic skills and knowledge employees need to perform their jobs successfully. Training sessions on selling techniques, customer service procedures, and inventory control are three examples of functional training directed at improving basic employee skills. Increasing employees' knowledge of the company's product lines and helping them to understand customer purchase motives are examples of knowledge-oriented, functional training.

### Where to Train

The second element of the training program concerns where training is to take place and under whose supervision. Normally, training occurs either on the job during regular working hours, off the job during scheduled training periods, or in some combination of both. **On-the-job training** is a decentralized approach that occurs on the sales floor, in the stockroom, or in some other work environment where em-

On-the-job training is the preferred method of teaching functional tasks.

ployees are performing their jobs. The trainee usually is under the direct supervision of the department manager or some other designated person responsible for handling the training program. **Off-the-job training** is conducted in centralized training classrooms away from the employees' work environment. In centralized classrooms, the trainer can use various learning aids (e.g., films, demonstrations, and role playing) under controlled conditions, allowing the employee to focus on the learning experience without interruption.

## How to Train

The third element in the retailer's training program is how each employee should be instructed; that is, which methods the retailer should use in the training process. As Figure 6–3 outlines, there are four general training methods: individual, sponsor, group, and executive. In the **individual training method**, employees "train" themselves. One individual training method is the "on your own" approach. In this training situation the employee is put on the job and expected to learn by trial and error, observation, and asking questions. In essence, this sink-or-swim approach includes no formal training. Although the retailer bears no training costs in the short run, the total costs in the long run could be substantial because of potential low employee productivity, high employee turnover, employee errors, and dissatisfied customers because of improper service.

An alternative method retailers use is programmed learning, which uses a highly structured format. First, employees study a unit of material. Second, they respond to a series of questions (true/false, multiple-choice, fill-in-the-blank, etc.) on the material they have read. Third, they receive immediate feedback on their performance in answering the questions. Fourth, they continue to repeat the first three steps until they master the material. Once employees achieve an acceptable competence level on a unit of material, they move on to the next level of instruction. Repetition is the key to **programmed learning**. These training devices are available in both written (paper-and-pencil) and machine (mechanical and computer) form.

The **sponsor method of training** uses an experienced employee to assume part or all of the responsibility for training a new employee. Most retailers believe that this one-on-one approach is the best method for teaching new employees the basic skills of selling, buying, promotion, and so forth. The sponsor's responsibilities also extend to introducing the employee to fellow workers, evaluating the employee's progress, and providing advice on the employee's problems and concerns. Successful sponsor training programs involve sponsors who volunteer for the assignment and are compensated for their efforts (e.g., with money or time off).

**Group training methods** involve the simultaneous training of several employees through lectures (or discussion, films, or slides), demonstrations (on sales or marking and stock presentations), case studies (e.g., oral and written problem-solving situations), role-playing activities (e.g., a sales or customer complaint situation),[7] computer simulations,[8] and interactive videos.[9] Large retailers use group training in centralized training facilities with specialized personnel. Group training sessions may last from five to ten minutes to update existing employees on new policies to as long as several days of classes on a wide variety of subjects. The advantage of group training is the low cost of training several employees at one time.

**Executive training programs (ETPs)** are educational sessions directed at supervisors, managers, and executives. Common among large department store and chain organizations, ETPs are designed to recruit personnel who have executive potential and to provide them with the opportunity to gain management experience. The typical ETP is a step-by-step training procedure whereby the executive trainee gains practical management experience by progressing from low- to higher-level management positions.

Figure 6–4 illustrates the ETP for Dayton Hudson department stores. As shown in Figure 6–4, Dayton Hudson creates two separate but parallel routes to senior management. By moving potential executives from one position to another, the retailer gives them complete exposure to all or most of the firm's operations, policies, and procedures.

**FIGURE 6–4**
An executive training program—Dayton Hudson department stores (source: Jules Abend, "The Fast Track," *Stores* [September 1985]: 63. Reprinted by permission of *Stores*. Copyright by National Retail Merchants Association)

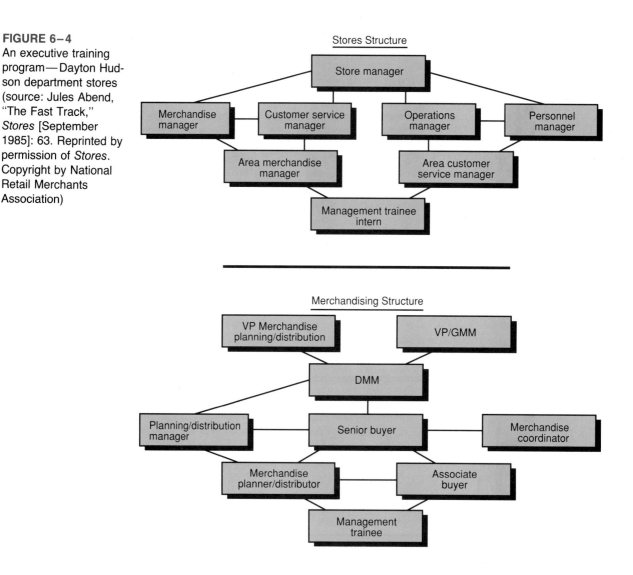

Supervision is the process of directing, coordinating, and inspecting the efforts of store employees to attain both company and individual goals. Effective supervisors can successfully satisfy the needs of the retailer (such as quality job performance, company loyalty, satisfactory profits) and the needs of the employee (such as fair treatment, a decent standard of living, a chance for advancement). The key to good supervision is knowing how to motivate employees. Motivation is the drive that moves people to act. Employees are driven to excel in a variety of ways. Some employees are motivated by money, others by praise, and still others possibly by the promise of free time to spend with their families. "There is no doubt that money can be a strong incentive for employee productivity, but it may not be a sufficient condition for it. The link between pay and performance is a bit more complex than the simple formulation that incentive pay increases motivation and performance."[10] The supervisor must discover the key that motivates each employee.

## How to Motivate

Frederick Herzberg offered one method of motivation in his theory of satisfiers and dissatisfiers.[11] Satisfiers are employment factors that produce pleasurable reactions within people's work lives. Herzberg found that the primary employment satisfiers were a challenging job, recognition of achievement, a responsible position, a chance for advancement, professional and personal growth, and an opportunity to contribute. In essence, motivation factors are conditions that enhance the employee's needs for self-esteem and self-actualization.

Dissatisfiers are employment factors that make workers unhappy with their jobs, leading to high turnover and weak performance. Oversupervision, poorly developed work rules, undesirable working conditions, restrictive company policies, and inadequate wages and fringe benefits are common examples of dissatisfiers. In general, dissatisfiers are closely associated with an individual's physiological and security needs. Given Herzberg's findings, the answer to the question "How to motivate?" is to eliminate conditions that generate dissatisfiers and initiate programs and policies that promote satisfiers.

## How to Supervise

The optimal level of employee supervision depends largely on how motivated employees are. Two opposing schools of thought on the amount of supervision that employers should exercise are the "heavy-handed" approach and the "light-handed" approach. Those who support the heavy-handed approach assume that employees are lazy, passive, self-centered, and irresponsible. With these assumptions, they maintain that employers must closely supervise and control their employees to motivate them to work toward company goals and to assume responsibilities. Retailers that subscribe to this school of thought view economic inducements as the primary means of motivation (McGregor's Theory X).[12] In particular, some retailers consider the heavy-handed approach the only way to motivate people in the lower-level positions of their stores. In modern society, however, the heavy-handed approach may not apply.

A more contemporary view of motivation and supervision is the light-handed approach. Retailers that support this view believe that providing employees with a favorable work environment can create a situation in which employees will obtain job satisfaction and their personal goals by directing their efforts toward the firm's needs (McGregor's Theory Y). Retailers that use the light-handed approach think that close supervision and control are unnecessary. Employees, they feel, will assume their responsibilities and, in part, supervise themselves if a desirable social and psychological environment is present. The previously discussed satisfiers are the keys to creating this desirable social and psychological condition. Within this kind of working environment, less supervision produces better job performance.

## EVALUATING STORE PERSONNEL

The seventh step in the store staffing process is the development of personnel evaluation procedures. Each store employee, regardless of position or level, should be periodically evaluated. The purposes of personnel evaluations are (1) to determine compensation, (2) to recommend or deny promotions and transfers, and (3) to justify demotions and terminations. Conducted constructively, personnel evaluations can be used to motivate employees, to improve store morale, to generate information for planning purposes, to encourage employee self-development, and to improve communications between the employee and employer. In developing the store's personnel evaluation methods and procedures, the retailer should decide when to evaluate, what to evaluate, and how to evaluate.

### When to Evaluate

A smart retailer evaluates personnel continuously. It would be unfair to judge an employee's contribution and performance at the end of an arbitrary time period, such as the end of the fiscal year. Instead, retailers should provide their employees with immediate feedback on their progress. This informal feedback, however, should also be accompanied by an established, formal evaluation in which employees receive a detailed account of their job performance.[13] Formal evaluations tell employees exactly what their status is. It is not unusual for new employees to be evaluated weekly or monthly. Established lower-level employees, however, are typically evaluated on a formal basis every six months, while annual evaluations for upper-level management and executive personnel are the norm.

### What to Evaluate

Retailers have learned that the most important employee factors to evaluate are performance-demonstrated skills and personal attributes. These factors appear to relate most closely to employee success. Examples of such characteristics appear in Figure 6–5. Figure 6–6 identifies those traits that executives believe are most important to employee success.

In selecting evaluation criteria and their respective measuring instruments, the retailer must consider the legal ramifications of each decision and the influence of any labor union that might be involved. It often is a good policy to seek advice regarding the legality of the employee evaluation system. In areas where unionization of labor is present, management might want to consult with appropriate union representatives before formulating evaluation methods and procedures.

| Performance characteristics | Personal attributes |
|---|---|
| Job knowledge | Enthusiasm |
| Quality of work | Loyalty |
| Quantity of work | Dependability |
| Organizing capabilities | Leadership |
| Supervision requirements | Maturity |
| Promptness | Stability |
| Peer relationships | Creativity |
| Customer relations | Honesty |
| Analytic abilities | Initiative |

**FIGURE 6−5**
Employee evaluation factors

## How to Evaluate

Retailers use a variety of methods for evaluating store personnel; the method used depends on the degree of objectivity and formality that the retailer wants. Figure 6−7 identifies several objective employee evaluation methods, which are based largely on factual and measurable criteria, and subjective methods, which are based on the evaluator's perceptions, feelings, and prejudices. Formal methods are regularly scheduled evaluations; informal methods follow no set schedule, and the criteria and procedures may or may not be known to the employee.

    **Formal objective employee evaluation procedures** include performance records and management by objectives (MBO) procedures. Performance records are quantitative measures of the employee's performance and include such varied statistics as (1) total sales dollars, (2) total number of sales transactions, (3) number of customer complaints, (4) number of merchandise returns and their dollar value, (5) number of times an employee is absent or late for work, and (6) net sales per working hour or per hourly wage. By comparing the employee's performance against the store average for any one of these criteria, the retailer can identify above-, at-, and below-average performers. These MBO procedures set measurable performance objectives for employees that should match their job descriptions. Employees are then evaluated on how well they achieved their objectives. In using MBO procedures, the

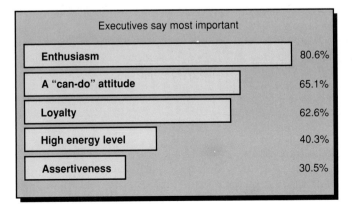

**FIGURE 6−6**
What makes workers succeed (source: Elys McLean-Ibrahim. "What Makes Workers Succeed." *USA Today* (September 25, 1987). p. B−1. Copyright © 1987 *USA Today*. Reprinted with permission.)

FIGURE 6–7
Store personnel evalu-
ation methods

| Degree of Objectivity / Degree of Formality | Objective | Subjective |
|---|---|---|
| Formal | performance records MBO (management by objectives) | rating scales checklists |
| Informal | professional shoppers | intuition |

employee is asked (1) to set objectives in specific terms, (2) to determine the method of accomplishment, (3) to set an accomplishment time frame, and (4) to determine the measure of accomplishment.

Rating scales and checklists constitute two of the more common **formal subjective employee evaluation methods**. The typical procedure is to identify and list several criteria in checklist form. The evaluator may weight the individual criteria according to their importance (see Figure 6–8). Typical scales are (1) satisfactory or unsatisfactory; (2) below average, average, or above average; and (3) poor, fair, average, good, and excellent. Given the subjective character of these ratings, many retailers prefer to have several supervisors rate each employee. The average of these ratings forms the basis for the employee's evaluation.

The most common **informal objective evaluation method** in retailing is to employ professional or mystery shoppers.[14] Professional shoppers are people who wander into a store to "shop" for merchandise in a "typical" way. Actually, they are professional investigators who attempt to learn how a retailer's employees behave toward them. This evaluation method should not be the *basis* of employee evaluation but a *supplement* to the retailer's assessment of employees' job performance.

**Informal subjective evaluation methods** have no structure and rely heavily on the supervisor's intuition. Although a supervisor's feelings and perceptions might represent a correct evaluation of an employee, the lack of objectivity and formality leaves such a method open to criticism by both employees and outside concerns (e.g., the Fair Labor Standards Law). A constant danger in using intuition as an evaluative method is the "halo effect" or the "good old boy syndrome." An employee who is a good person is not necessarily contributing effectively to the firm's efforts; in fact, such considerations often lead to other employees' accusations of favoritism.

Regardless of the method used to evaluate store personnel, employees should be made aware of the method (its criteria, measurements, and procedures), given feedback after each evaluation, and permitted to appeal the evaluation.

**COMPENSATING STORE PERSONNEL**

Equitable compensation is an integral part of the retailer's staffing process. A well-designed compensation package is not only an important factor in rewarding past performance but also an important incentive for future performance.[15] Compensation methods include the straight-salary plan, the straight-commission plan, the salary

**FIGURE 6–8**
A formal subjective employee evaluation form

Employee's name _____     Date _____

Employee's title _____     Supervisor _____

Instructions: Please review the performance of the employee whose name is listed above on each of the following items. In order to guide you in your rating, the five determinants of performance have been defined.

### Rating Points

**5 OUTSTANDING**
A truly outstanding employee whose achievements are far above acceptable. Has consistently performed far beyond established objectives and has made significant contributions beyond current position. Requires minimal direction and supervision. (Relatively few employees would be expected to achieve at this level.)

**4 SUPERIOR**
An above-average employee whose performance is clearly above acceptable. Has usually performed beyond established objectives and, at times, has made contributions beyond responsibilities of present position. Requires less than normally expected degree of direction and supervision.

**3 AVERAGE**
A fully acceptable employee who consistently meets all requirements of position. Has consistently met established objectives in a satisfactory and adequate manner. Performance requires normal degree of supervision and direction. (The majority of employees should be at this level.)

**2 BELOW AVERAGE**
A somewhat below-average employee whose performance, while not unsatisfactory, cannot be considered fully acceptable. Generally meets established objectives and expectations, but definite areas exist where achievement is substandard. Performance requires somewhat more than normal degree of direction and supervision.

**1 UNACCEPTABLE**
A far-below-average employee whose performance is barely adequate to meet the requirements of the position. Generally performs at a level below established objectives with the result that overall contribution is marginal. Performance requires an unusually high degree of supervision. (This level is considered acceptable only for employees new to the job.)

JOB CRITERIA                                                                                    POINTS

1. <u>Amount of work.</u> Consider here only the **quantity** of the employee's output.          _____
   Supervisor's comments:


2. Quality of work. Consider how well the employee does each job assigned. Include your    _____
   appraisal of such items as accuracy, thoroughness, and orderliness.
   Supervisor's comments:


3. Cooperation. How well does this employee work and interact with you and coworkers        _____
   for the accomplishment of organization goals?
   Supervisor's comments:


4. Judgment. Consider this employee's ability to reach sound and logical conclusions.        _____
   Supervisor's comments:

5. Initiative. The energy or aptitude to originate action toward organization goals. _____
   Supervisor's comments:

6. Job knowledge. How well does the employee demonstrate an understanding of the _____
   basic fundamentals, techniques, and procedures on the job?
   Supervisor's comments:

7. Interest in job. Does the employee demonstrate a real interest in the job and the orga- _____
   nization?
   Supervisor's comments:

8. Ability to communicate. How well does this employee exchange needed information _____
   with others in the work group and with supervisors?
   Supervisor's comments:

9. Dependability. Consider the employee's absences, tardiness, punctuality, timeliness in _____
   completing job assignments, and the amount of supervision required.
   Supervisor's comments:

10. Adaptability. Consider the degree to which this employee demonstrates adjustment to _____
    the varying requirements of the job.
    Supervisor's comments:

                                                                    TOTAL POINTS    _____

    Supervisor's general comments:


Instructions: After you have rated the employee and made whatever comments you feel are pertinent to each
criterion and the overall evaluation, schedule a meeting to review each item with the employee. An employee
wishing to make comments about the evaluation should be asked to do so in the following space.


Employee's comment:


Date: _____


Supervisor present (Name): _____


Employee's signature: _____    Date: _____


Notice to employee: Signing the form does not imply that you either agree or disagree with the evaluation.

Source: Norman M. Scarborough and Thomas W. Zimmerer, *Effective Small Business Management* (Columbus: Merrill Publishing Co., 1984), 521–23.

FIGURE 6–8, *continued*

plus commission plan, and the salary plus bonus plan. Long-term incentives (top-level management), annual bonuses (midlevel management) and short-term incentives (sales personnel) are all becoming more important in all retail compensation practices.[16]

### Straight-Salary Plan

The **straight-salary plan** is a fixed amount of compensation for a specified work period such as a day, week, month, or year. For example, an employee's salary might be set at $200 per week or $4 per hour. For the retailer, the straight-salary plan offers the advantages of easy administration and a high level of employer control. Under the straight-salary plan, the retailer can expect employees to engage in non-selling activities such as stocking and housekeeping. For the employee, the straight-salary plan has a known level of financial security and stability. Retailers typically use straight-salary plans when a job involves a considerable amount of customer service and nonselling time, such as stocking, receiving, clerking, and checking out.

### Straight-Commission Plan

Under a **straight-commission plan,** a store employee receives a percentage of what he or she sells. The commission percentage is either fixed (e.g., 5 percent on all sales) or variable (e.g., 6 percent on high-margin lines and 3 percent on low-margin lines). Retailers may calculate an employee's commission on the basis of *net sales* (gross sales dollars minus dollar value of returned merchandise). Retailers that use straight-commission plans are those that sell big-ticket items such as automobiles, furniture, appliances, and jewelry.

The major advantage of a straight-commission plan is the monetary incentive it creates for employees; however, this incentive often causes several problems. Salespeople on commission often become overly aggressive in trying to make a sale. High-pressure selling is also a temptation when commission sales are involved. By exerting undue pressure on the customer to buy now (as opposed to later, when a different salesperson might be serving the customer), the sale could be lost to the retailer forever. Also, commission sales tempt many salespeople to practice trading up the customer to more expensive merchandise. However, when trading up leads to a large number of returns, not only does the salesperson lose the commission, but the retailer also loses a sale and very likely the goodwill of the store's clientele.

For the commissioned salesperson, the straight-commission plan has the weaknesses of financial insecurity and instability. To overcome these limitations, many retailers have established "drawing accounts" that allow employees to draw a fixed sum of money at regular intervals against future commissions.

### Salary Plus Commission Plan

As the name implies, the **salary plus commission plan** provides employees with a salary and a commission. There are a number of variations to this plan. The *straight salary/single commission* variation uses a base salary (e.g., $200 per week) plus (1) a single commission (e.g., 1/2 percent) on all net sales up to the sales quota and a

A physical fitness center is an important benefit for both employee and employer.

larger commission (e.g., 2 percent) on all sales in excess of sales quota, *or* (2) a commission only on net sales that exceed the quota. The strengths of this plan are that it provides employees with financial security and stability while helping the retailer to control and motivate personnel. Although the combination plan is more difficult to administer, its benefits generally outweigh its costs.

### Salary Plus Bonus Plan

A popular method for compensating middle-management personnel (such as department managers, store managers, and buyers) is the **salary plus bonus plan,** which involves a straight monthly salary supplemented by either semiannual or annual bonuses for exceeding performance goals. Performance goals and related bonuses usually are set by upper management for each operating unit and usually are expressed in the form of increased sales or profits, decreased operating costs, return on equity, or return on investment.

### Fringe Benefits

The employee's total compensation package also includes fringe benefits, which vary greatly from one retail firm to another. In recent years, fringe benefits have become more important in the retailer's efforts to attract and keep qualified personnel. Fringe benefits are much more important for middle- and upper-level positions than for entry-level positions.

Among the most popular fringe benefits are (1) insurance programs covering life, health, accident, and disability; (2) sick leave; (3) personal leave time; (4) holiday leave and paid vacations; (5) pension plans; (6) profit sharing; (7) employee discounts; (8) recreation facilities; (9) coffee breaks; (10) employee parties; and (11) team sponsorships. Fringe benefits are becoming a more important form of compensation in today's leisure-oriented society, with the goal of making employees happy, content, and loyal to the store. Additional perks for company executives include club memberships, company cars, financial counseling, and spouse travel.[17]

## SUMMARY

A key ingredient in any successful retail operation is its personnel. Merchandising and operational plans are of limited value without loyal, productive employees. All retailers face the problem of finding and keeping good people.

The staffing process consists of eight steps. First, describing the job includes developing job descriptions and conducting job analyses. Second, specifying the job involves writing job classifications that not only outline the responsibilities of the position but also avoid charges of unfair employment practices. Third, recruiting store personnel includes both finding and screening potential employee candidates. The fourth step in the staffing process is selection. From the list of qualified applicants, the retailer selects individuals best suited to the job by carefully reviewing application forms, personal interviews, reference checks, testing instruments, and physical examinations.

Training store personnel is the fifth step in the staffing process. It requires the retailer to know what to train (organization orientation and functional or task training), where to train (on the job or off the job), and how to train (individual training method, programmed learning, sponsor or group training methods). Executive training programs are sessions directed at store supervisors, managers, and executives. The sixth step is supervision. An important supervising task is motivation. One method of motivating employees is to eliminate conditions that generate job dissatisfaction and to initiate programs that promote satisfaction. Supervising can be approached in a heavy-handed manner (close supervision) or in a light-handed fashion (limited supervision).

Evaluating store employees constitutes the seventh step in the staffing process. The retailer must address such issues as when to evaluate, what to evaluate, and how to evaluate personnel. Finally, the retailer must determine the type of compensation system to use. Alternatives are the straight-salary plan, straight-commission plan, salary plus commission plan, and salary plus bonus plan, all of which might involve various fringe benefits.

## STUDENT STUDY GUIDE

## KEY TERMS AND CONCEPTS

achievement tests

dissatisfier

executive training programs (ETPs)

formal objective employee evaluation

formal subjective employee evaluation

functional training

group training method

heavy-handed supervision

| | |
|---|---|
| individual training method | programmed learning |
| informal objective employee evaluation | psychological test |
| informal subjective employee evaluation | salary plus bonus plan |
| job description | salary plus commission plan |
| job specification | satisfier |
| light-handed supervision | sponsor training method |
| motivation | straight-commission plan |
| off-the job training | straight-salary plan |
| on-the-job training | supervision |
| organization orientation | |

## REVIEW QUESTIONS

1. What specific information should be obtained in a job analysis?
2. Why should a written job specification be given to a potential employee?
3. Identify the internal and external sources of prospective employees.
4. What is the most effective way to check an applicant's references?
5. List the relative advantages of a formal, highly structured interviewing process and the informal, unstructured method of interviewing.
6. What two general types of testing instruments are used to evaluate applicants? Describe each type. Which instrument is generally preferred? Why?
7. Describe the two types of training needed by both old and new employees.
8. How do on-the-job and off-the-job training differ?
9. What methods are available to the retailer for training employees? Briefly describe each method.
10. What are satisfiers and dissatisfiers? How do they affect employee motivation?
11. Compare and contrast McGregor's Theory X and Theory Y.
12. How are formal objective employee evaluations conducted? Describe the two methods.
13. Professional shoppers are used to conduct which type of employee evaluation?
14. What are the advantages of the straight-salary compensation plan? What problems result from the monetary incentive created by the straight-commission plan?
15. How does the straight salary/single commission plan differ from the straight salary/quota commission plan?

## REVIEW EXAM

True or False

_____ 1. To give the retailer the greatest degree of latitude in hiring, job descriptions should be written in the broadest terms possible.

_____ 2. Education, training, and skill requirements are considered by the federal government as unquestionable valid job criteria.

_____ 3. Telephone calls to references normally provide more complete and honest evaluations of applicants than letters.

_____ 4. Generally, retailers prefer achievement tests to psychological tests because they are easier to administer and interpret.

_____ 5. Dissatisfiers are employment factors closely related to an individual's physiological and security needs.

_____ 6. The light-handed approach to employee supervision assumes that employees will work toward the firm's goals if a desirable social and psychological work environment is present.

_____ 7. Retailers typically use straight-commission compensation plans when a job includes a considerable amount of customer service and nonselling time.

1. Obtain and analyze three retail job descriptions from your local newspaper or from the personnel director for a local retailer. Judging from the advertised job description, has the retailer made a careful determination of his personnel needs, and does the retailer provide the potential employee with the means to evaluate the job as a potential source of employment?

2. Assume you are the manager of the sporting goods department of a large department store and are responsible for conducting the initial personal interviews of the applicants for the assistant department manager's position. Develop a list of prospective questions that you would ask each applicant. Explain your reason for asking each question, as well as what answers you would view favorably for each.

3. What are the advantages and disadvantages of both on-the-job and off-the-job training?

4. Contact a major retail organization in your community and obtain the specifics of their executive training program. After reviewing their programs, explain whether or not you would seriously consider the firm as a potential employer when you graduate.

5. Under what circumstances should the retailer consider using the heavy-handed approach to employee supervision?

6. Obtain employee evaluation forms and procedures from a local retailer. Classify these forms and procedures as to their objectivity and formality. Assess the forms and procedures as to their effectiveness as employee evaluation instruments and their fairness to the employee.

## CASE 6–1
### Aubrey Creations, Inc.—Managing a Direct Marketing Sales Force*

#### BACKGROUND

Aubrey Creations, founded in 1978, sells a line of fashion jewelry (most items under $50) through the party-plan method. To attract a base of customers who are more likely to make repeat purchases, Aubrey McDonald developed an extensive line of exceptionally high-quality skin-care products. The Aubrey Beauty Collection was introduced in 1981. Prices currently range from as low as $1.95 for a single item to $111.75 for the Total Look Collection.

Total revenues for Aubrey Creations during the last year were under $10 million. Operations have been almost entirely limited to the United States, and approximately 2,000 sales consultants were involved in selling these products through the party-plan method. The company recently increased its recruitment efforts for sales consultants. Many of the leading members of this industry belong to the Direct Selling Association, a trade organization that (among other activities) enforces a strict code of ethical business conduct. Aubrey Creations, Inc. is a very active member of this organization.

#### CURRENT SITUATION

Aubrey McDonald, founder and CEO of Aubrey Creations, has "an opportunity." As for all firms in the direct-selling industry, sales revenues for Aubrey Creations tend to flatten when the economy picks up. Recent improvements in the economy have created this "opportunity" and Aubrey is searching for ways to overcome this recent decline in sales.

*This case was prepared by Jon Hawes, The University of Akron.

There is a very simple explanation for the inverse relationship between sales revenue of firms in the direct-selling industry and GNP. More than in any other field, business in the direct-selling industry depends upon the number and the intensity levels of salespeople. Few customers actively search for the products of direct-selling companies. These types of sales often require a great deal of personal selling effort to persuade people to make a purchase. Consequently, when a direct-selling organization's sales force is reduced in number and/or the existing sales force becomes less active, revenues usually decline.

During periods of reduced overall economic activity, the sales forces of direct-selling companies often grow dramatically as people attempt to supplement family income by working in this field. When the economy improves, however, people often return to full-time employment in other industries or reduce the intensity of their sales efforts in direct-selling organizations.

At Aubrey, sales consultants arrange with hosts to sponsor parties in their homes. The host receives free products for encouraging 10–15 friends to attend the party, often referred to as the "show" or "booking." Sales consultants attempt to sell either the jewelry or skin-care product lines at a particular party. The central event of a skin-care booking, for example, involves a complete makeover (at no charge) for one of the guests.

Besides selling products, sales consultants are also involved in building a sales organization. They recruit people to work in their sales organizations and receive a commission for all of the sales made by these recruits.

Sales consultants earn income based on the level of their sales and the sales of their recruits. Incomes vary widely, but a few consultants made over $100,000 in 1985. In addition, Aubrey Creations sponsors several incentive programs to reward sales consultants who reach a certain level of sales. The top prize is a new Cadillac. Many other rewards, incentives, contests, and recognition are also provided. The highlight of each year is a national conference.

### ASSIGNMENT

1. Outline a plan of action to minimize the negative effects of an improving economic climate on Aubrey Creations' sales force.
2. Develop some motivational strategies that would be appropriate regardless of the general economic conditions.
3. Suggest improvements in the compensation plan and reward structure for the sales force.

### CASE 6–2
### Braddock's Department Stores—Facing Up to the Growing Retail Labor Crunch*

As president of Braddock's Department Stores, a chain of nine stores located in central and southern California, Amy Whitmeyer's time was usually spent dealing with sales volume promotions, marketing and merchandising strategies, and long-term planning. Lately, another problem was developing that required increased attention—the increasing shortage of sales, clerical, and management personnel. In many areas of the country, particularly on the east and west coasts, the personnel shortage problem was acute; it was hampering store operations and impeding growth. Reasons for this shortage were many, but among the most prominent were (1) shrinking numbers of people in the 16–24 age group that traditionally staffed most lower-level retail positions; (2) the rapid growth of the retail sector in

*This case was prepared by Daniel Gilmore, The University of Akron.

terms of job creation; and (3) the low wages, poor working conditions, and meager benefits associated with lower-echelon positions.

Whitmeyer feared that the labor crunch would soon affect Braddock's; she was especially concerned because the turnover rate among both sales and management personnel at the company was already high. nearly 40 percent of the individuals hired for Braddock's management trainee program were not with the company after one year, a figure similar to that found by many in the industry. No detailed check of why this rate was so high had been completed by the company, but someone from Human Resources told Whitmeyer that many management trainees quit because they are unable to adjust to the hard first year of the job training (e.g., long hours, weekend hours, physical work, dealing with customers). After a year or two, things became easier, but many trainees leave before then even though company data showed that within a few years, Braddock's managers have greater opportunities and better compensation than many other firms or industries (e.g., jobs in banking and insurance).

Whitmeyer was studying a report supplied by the Human Resources Department, which outlined most of Braddock's personnel policies. As expected, the report showed that, for lower-level sales and clerical employees, Braddock's hired primarily high school and college students to work part-time; however, a few did work full-time. The firm usually relied on walk-in applicants to fill lower-level positions; newspaper want ads were used if the need was great enough. For store and corporate management positions, Braddock's hired only college graduates, who entered the firm's management training program. These trainees were chosen from unsolicited applications and also from twice-yearly recruiting trips to the two local universities.

The report also contained some of the gloomy projections about personnel shortages the company could experience in coming years. It warned that the pool of candidates from which the company now drew its applicants was contracting and that there would be increasing competition with other retailers for available candidates. The report also discussed the turnover problem within the company. Though Braddock's had not conducted any studies on the problems particular to its own employee turnover, the Human Resources department had been looking at some research that showed that, although pay and benefits were important components of an employee's decision to stay with a retail firm, other factors were influential. Specifically, the report identified five factors especially important to lower-level employees:

1. Skill variety—the number of skills and talents the job requires
2. Task identity—the degree to which an employee does a job from beginning to end with a visible outcome
3. Task significance—the impact of that job on other people
4. Autonomy—the freedom and independence an employee has to determine his/her own work procedures
5. Feedback—the direct information an employee receives about the effectiveness of his/her performance

In short, the report said these psychological aspects of the job could be as important as the monetary ones for retaining and motivating sales and clerical employees who felt their jobs were not valued by the company and that they were treated poorly by their supervisors.

The report concluded that for both management and lower-level employees, wages and benefits would probably have to be raised to attract and retain the employees the company would need in the coming years. Whitmeyer, however, felt this would not be sufficient. She realized that increasing the monetary aspects of the job would certainly be required to allow retailers to compete with other industries for employees, but everyone in the business, including many of Braddock's competitors, would be forced to do the same. The net result would be that wages, and therefore costs, would be higher than at present, but the personnel shortage would probably remain.

Whitmeyer was convinced that it would be necessary to come up with some creative techniques for attracting employees and keeping them with the company. She realized the company couldn't overhaul its personnel policies overnight, but she thought it had better start preparing now before Braddock's found it had stores full of customers—and not enough employees there to service them.

## ASSIGNMENT

Take the role of Braddock's SPO (senior personnel officer). Ms. Whitmeyer has asked you to prepare a report dealing with the following issues:

1. Evaluate Braddock's recruitment process for both management and sales employees. In light of the predicted retail labor shortage, what actions can you suggest to improve this process?

2. The employee turnover rate is high for Braddock's. Identify possible causes. What policies or practices can you recommend that might help retain both sales and management employees? Be creative.

3. Now you have come up with some solid suggestions for improving the recruiting, retaining, and motivation of employees for Braddock's. Whitmeyer will also want to know what disadvantages the company might run into if the firm adopts your suggestions. Help her out.

## ENDNOTES

1. Neil M. Ford, "Recruitment and Selection—Are There Easy Answers," *Sales Management Bulletin* 2 (Summer 1987): 3–4.
2. Jules Abend, "The Fast Track," *Stores* (September 1985): 62.
3. Jules Abend, "Taking Care of Your Own," *Stores* (November 1987): 98.
4. Robert F. Hartley, "The Weighted Application Blank," *Journal of Retailing* 46 (Spring 1970): 32–40.
5. See Richard A. Feinberg and Patricia L. Gifford, "Are Your Recruiting Efforts Doomed to Fail?" *Retail Control* (December 1985): 25–33.
6. "The Score on Psycho Testing," *Stores* (September 1985): 63.
7. See J. B. Robinson, "Role Playing as a Sales Training Tool," *Harvard Business Review* (May–June 1987): 34–35.
8. See "Trainees Build Skills in Risk-Free Contest." *Chain Store Age Executive* (June 1987): 56, 58.
9. See Robert Neff, "Videos Are Starring in More and More Training Programs," *Business Week,* 7 Sept. 1987, 108–109.
10. Richard A. Feinberg, Richard Widdows, and Amy Rummel, "Paying For Performance: What You Need to Know," *Retail Control* (April–May 1987): 40–41.
11. Frederick Herzberg, "One More Time: How Do You Motivate Employees?" *Harvard Business Review* 46 (January–February 1968): 53–62.
12. See Douglas McGregor, "The Human Side of Enterprise," in *Leadership and Motivation: Essays of Douglas McGregor,* edited by W. G. Bennis and E. Schein (Cambridge, MA: MIT Press, 1966).
13. See Charles L. Brown, "Staff Assessment and Evaluation Techniques," *Retail Control* (March 1987): 53–60.
14. See William Lundstrom and Cliff Scott, "Mystery Shoppers as a Salesperson Training Tool: Once Is Not Enough," in *Marketing: The Next Decade, Proceedings,* edited by D. M. Klein and A. E. Smith, 170–171 (Southern Marketing Association, 1985); also see "Mystery Shoppers Provide Check on Customer-Service Experience," *Marketing News,* 5 June 1987, 5; also see Art Palmer and Robert Morey, "Retail Sales Check Evaluation

Methods," *Developments in Marketing Science, Proceedings,* edited by J. M. Hawes and G. B. Glisan, 330–334 (Academy of Marketing Science, 1987).

15. James R. Terborg and Gerardo R. Ungson, "Group-Administered Bonus Pay and Retail Store Performance: A Two-Year Study of Management Compensation," *Journal of Retailing* 61 (Spring 1985): 63.

16. Jules Abend, "A Bonus Does Pay Off," *Stores* (July 1987): 69.

17. "Hewitt: Long-Term Incentives Grow, Bonuses Shrink," *Stores* (July 1987): 74.

# 7

## Objectives

☐ Appreciate the physical and psychological impact that store facilities have on customer attraction, employee morale, and store operations.

☐ Distinguish design features vital in creating a desirable store image, in targeting the appropriate consumer group, and in communicating the right impression.

☐ Understand design features necessary to create a store atmosphere conducive to buying.

☐ Identify and explain the major considerations in planning store exteriors capable of stopping and attracting customers.

☐ Specify and discuss the key features of the store's interior and their role in creating an inviting, comfortable, and convenient facility.

☐ Distinguish between various devices and techniques employed by thieves.

☐ Outline the methods used by retailers in detecting and preventing criminal activities.

# Store Layout, Design, and Security

A store and its immediate area create the environment within which a retailer must operate. The retailer must make a concentrated effort to ensure that the store's environment is conducive both to retail operations and to consumers' shopping needs. The bulk of this chapter discusses the physical aspects of the store's exterior and interior design. First, however, this chapter examines the psychological aspects of the retailer's facilities and the environment they create.

In selecting and developing a store's environment, the retailer must consider its *physical* and *psychological* impacts on customer attraction, employee morale, and store operations. Store operations and customer shopping are both enhanced by a well-planned and well-designed setting. A store's physical environment is a composite of the tangible elements of form reflected in the way land, building, equipment, and fixtures are assembled for the convenience and comfort of both customers and retailer. Equally important is the store's psychological environment—the perceived atmosphere the retailer creates. In essence, a store's psychological environment is the mental image of the store produced in customers' minds. A store's effectiveness and uniqueness lie in the retailer's ability to plan, create, and control both the store's physical and psychological setting. The psychological impressions a store makes on consumers depend on the store's image and buying atmosphere. To appeal to the fashion-conscious, upscaled shopper, Macy's upgraded its New York flagship store "by creating a theatrical environment enhanced by colorful displays and high-tech lighting and audio presentations."[1]

## Creating a Store Image

Creating a **store image** should be one of the retailer's principal concerns. The fact that it represents to the consumer a composite picture of the retailer makes image one of the most powerful tools in attracting and satisfying consumers. Creating an image, however, is a very difficult task. An image is a mental picture that forms in the human mind as a result of many different stimuli. These stimuli include the retailer's physical facilities, the store's location, product lines, service offering, pricing policies, and promotional activities.

A store's image is its personality. It is how the consumer *sees* the store as well as what the consumer *feels* about the store. It is important, therefore, that retailers know and plan what they want the consumer to see and feel.

The store's exterior and interior are key factors in the retailer's image-creating efforts. *Externally,* the position of the store on the site, its architectural design, its store front, and the placement of signs, entrances, and display windows all contribute to the store's image. *Internally,* a store's image can be created, in part, by the layout of departments and traffic aisles, the use of store displays, and the selection of store fixtures and equipment. The number of possible combinations of physical facilities and their image-creating abilities are virtually limitless.

## Creating a Buying Atmosphere

To create an atmosphere conducive to buying, a retailer should establish in the consumer a frame of mind that promotes a buying spirit. Even the economy-minded consumer wants something more than a shopping atmosphere with only the bare essentials. Today's shoppers, regardless of their principal shopping motives, are drawn to safe, attractive, and comfortable shopping environments. The store's atmosphere should be an agreeable environment for both the consumer and the retailer.

The retailer wants to influence the consumer's mood by creating an atmosphere that will positively influence buying behavior. An appealing buying atmosphere uses cues that appeal to the consumer's five senses of sight, hearing, smell, touch, and taste. These sensory cues can be strongly reinforced if they are structured around shopping themes that unify and organize the store's atmosphere. Waldenbooks, Inc., is introducing its WaldenKids stores, which sell books and educational toys and games. The WaldenKids stores mimic a playground; "kids can even crawl into the store through a carpeted tunnel. Inside, children are greeted by a video monitor playing cartoon fairy tales . . . painted primary red, yellow, and blue . . . toys from computer games to wooden railroads are just waiting for eager little hands."[2]

The following sections discuss how a retailer can use sensory appeals to effect a favorable store image and pleasant shopping environment.

*Sight Appeal.* The sense of sight provides people with more information than any other sense mode and therefore must be classified as the most important means by which retailers can appeal to consumers. **Sight appeal** can be viewed as the process of imparting stimuli, resulting in perceived visual relationships. Size, shape, and color are three primary visual stimuli a retailer can use to arouse the consumer's attention. Visual relationships are interpretations made by the "mind's eye" from visual stimuli consisting of harmony, contrast, and clash. *Harmony* is "visual agreement"; *contrast,* "visual diversity"; and *clash,* "visual conflict" that can occur among the many parts of any display, layout, or physical arrangement. In any given situation, either harmony, contrast, or clash may be the best way to create an appealing shopping atmosphere. Harmonious visual relationships are generally associated with a quieter, plusher, and more formal shopping setting, whereas contrasting and clashing visual relationships can promote an exciting, cheerful, or informal atmosphere.

The sheer physical size of a store, a display, a sign, or a department can communicate many things to many people. Size can communicate relative impor-

tance, success, strength, power, and security. Some consumers feel more secure when they buy from large stores because they believe that large stores are more capable and more willing to fix, adjust, or replace faulty merchandise. Other consumers prefer larger stores because of the prestige they associate with such operations. A smaller store, display, or department may not be perceived as being as important, successful, or powerful as its larger counterparts, but it could be viewed as more personal, intimate, or friendly.

Size is a key element in creating harmony, contrast, and clash. To achieve a harmonious atmosphere in a store department or display, the retailer should maintain a consistent size relationship among the various elements. Using *moderately* different size elements can create contrast among different departments within the store or different displays within the department. Clashing relationships can be created by using *substantially* different size elements.

Shapes arouse certain emotions within buyers. In planning store layouts and in designing store displays, the retailer should recognize that the horizontal line suggests restfulness and quiet and evokes feelings of tranquility. . . . The vertical line evokes feelings of strength, confidence and even pride. The slanted line suggests upward movement to most people . . . round curving lines connote feminity, whereas sharp, angular objects suggest masculinity. Equally important in facilities planning is the similarity or dissimilarity of shapes. "For the creation of perfect harmony in a display, shapes that correspond exactly to one another are used exclusively. Inharmonious or dissimilar shapes may be used in a display to create contrast and, in some instances, a point of emphasis."[3]

Color makes the first impression on someone looking at an object. Color is often what catches customers' eyes, keeps their attention, and stimulates them to buy. The U.S. consumer is becoming increasingly color conscious. For most customers, if the color is wrong, all is wrong.

What feelings are aroused by these various lines and shapes?

Which display represents harmony and which represents visual conflict?

The psychological impact of color is the result of the three color properties of hue, value, and intensity. *Hue* is the name of the color. *Value* is the lightness or darkness of a hue. Darker values are referred to as "shades," while lighter values are called "tints." The brightness or dullness of a hue is its *intensity.* For the retailer, color psychology is important not only in selling merchandise but also in creating the proper atmosphere for selling that merchandise.

The impact of color psychology becomes apparent as soon as we classify *hues* into "warm" and "cool" tones. The warm colors (red, yellow, and orange) and the cool colors (blue, green, and violet) symbolize different things to different consumer groups. Figure 7–1 identifies some of the associations and symbols consumers attach to colors. Warm colors give the impression of a comfortable, informal atmosphere. Cool colors, on the other hand, project a formal, aloof, icy impression.[4] When used properly, however, both warm and cool colors can create a relaxing yet stimulating atmosphere in which to shop.

*Red* is one of the most stimulating colors and should be used with considerable care. Too much red can be overpowering; it should thus be used as an accent color rather than a basic background color. To attract attention and to stimulate buyer action, red frequently appears in building signs, fixtures, and displays. Christmas and Valentine's Day are two holiday seasons when red is an appropriate display color. Shades of red are also appropriate for certain decorative themes, such as carnivals and sports.

*Yellow,* like red, is a stimulating color that must be used with caution. Yellow's principal asset is its visibility at long distances, which makes shades of yellow a logical

| Warm Colors | | | | Cool Colors | | |
|---|---|---|---|---|---|---|
| Red | Yellow | Orange | | Blue | Green | Violet |
| Love | Sunlight | Sunlight | | Coolness | Coolness | Coolness |
| Romance | Warmth | Warmth | | Aloofness | Restful | Retiring |
| Sex | Cowardice | Openness | | Fidelity | Peace | Dignity |
| Courage | Openness | Friendliness | | Calmness | Freshness | Rich |
| Danger | Friendliness | Gaiety | | Piety | Growth | |
| Fire | Gaiety | Glory | | Masculine | Softness | |
| Sinful | Glory | | | Assurance | Richness | |
| Warmth | Brightness | | | Sadness | Go | |
| Excitement | Caution | | | | | |
| Vigor | | | | | | |
| Cheerfulness | | | | | | |
| Enthusiasm | | | | | | |
| Stop | | | | | | |

**FIGURE 7–1**
Perceptions of colors

color selection for signs, walls, and poorly lit areas. The time to use yellow is in the spring, particularly around Easter. Yellow is also considered a color for children, so it is appropriate for decorating infants', children's, and toy departments.

*Orange* is used sparingly because of its high intensity and its tendency to clash with other colors. Most often thought of as a fall color (fall foliage, harvest, and Halloween), orange is used primarily for accent and not as a basic decorative color. Orange, like yellow, is a children's color and livens up a children's department by evoking warm, cheerful surroundings.

*Blues* are associated with the cool, blue sky and the calm, blue sea. As a result, retailers use blues to create a calm, relaxing shopping atmosphere. Shades of blue often appear in men's departments because this color also connotes masculinity. In addition, blue works well as a trim and as a basic background.

Like blue, *green* suggests many pleasant associations—the newness and freshness of spring and the peace and restfulness of the great outdoors. Its soft and relaxing qualities make green an ideal choice for many uses. Green is perceived as a spacious color and is therefore useful for making small areas appear larger. Its softness also helps accentuate displayed merchandise.

*Violet* is little used in retail displays, except to achieve special effects. Too-extensive use of this hue is thought to dampen shoppers' spirits.

The lightness and darkness of colors create optical illusions that retailers can use to modify the store's physical characteristics. Generally, lighter colors make a room or an object appear larger, while darker colors create an illusion of smallness. Light neutral tones (e.g., beige) are popular as fixture colors because they are perceived as warm and soft and do not detract from the displayed merchandise. On the other hand, darker colors have attention-grabbing ability; for example, by using darker colors at the back of a store, a retailer can draw consumers' attention to that area and increase the flow of customer traffic throughout the store.

The brightness and dullness of different physical facilities also affect the buying atmosphere. As with color value, color intensity can create illusions. Bright colors

Packaging relies heavily on the psychological effects of colors.

make the facilities appear larger than do duller colors. A bright color tends to create an illusion of hardness, however, whereas a dull color appears softer. As a rule, children react more favorably to brighter colors; hence, these colors' widespread use in children's departments. Adults, on the other hand, prefer softer tones, which may explain why so many retailers use pastels.

*Sound Appeal.* *Sound* can either enhance or hinder a store's buying atmosphere. In planning store facilities, it is as important to avoid undesirable sounds as it is to create desirable ones. Disturbing noises detract from a store's appeal, whereas pleasant sounds can attract customers.

Obtrusive sounds distract consumers, interrupting the buying process. Whether these sounds originate inside or outside the store, they must be either controlled or eliminated. The clicking of heels on a hard floor surface, the humming of an air conditioner, the rattling of a jackhammer in the street outside, or the blaring music of the record shop next door may represent sound "pollution" to a retailer's selling efforts. Noise avoidance is a problem tailor-made for physical facilities planning. Careful use of architectural design, construction materials, equipment, and interior decors can eliminate or at least substantially reduce most obtrusive sounds.

To create an atmosphere that encourages buying, the retailer can use **sound appeal** in a variety of ways. Sound can be a mood setter, an attention getter, and an informer. Music can relax the customer, promote a buying spirit, set the stage for a particular shopping theme (e.g., a Mexican fiesta), or remind the customer of a special season or holiday (particularly Christmas), as well as provide a generally pleasant background of familiar sounds. "If a store chooses to play music, the selection should match its image and audience—music should enhance the environment, not overwhelm it. In Ralph Lauren's Madison Avenue store the stereo plays Vivaldi and jazz in the morning and Frank Sinatra at 5 P.M."[5]

Attention-getting sound can draw customers to a particular display or department. A principal attention-getting device of stereo departments is the quality of sound emanating from the area. K Mart stores draw attention to their "specials" by loud announcements: "Attention K Mart shoppers." Finally, fast, convenient, and pleasurable shopping requires that the customer have sufficient information about the store, its merchandise, and its operations. Frequently, the retailer must inform the consumer about where to go, when to go, and how to get there.

*Scent Appeal.* The creation of **scent appeal** is a problem similar in scope to the sound-appeal problem—how to avoid unpleasant odors and how to create pleasant scents. Stale, musty, and foul odors offend everyone and are sure to create negative impressions. Inadequate ventilation, insufficient humidity control, and poorly placed and maintained sanitation facilities are frequent causes of undesirable odors. Store facilities should be designed to minimize these problems or eliminate them entirely. Pleasurable scents, on the other hand, are key ingredients in creating atmospheric conditions that induce the customer to buy. A well-placed fan in a bakery shop, candy store, or delicatessen attracts the passerby to these almost unavoidable pleasurable scents of products that are frequently bought on impulse. A store should smell like it is supposed to smell. Some stores, such as a drugstore, should smell clean and antiseptic. For others, such as an antique store, a dusty, musty smell could enhance the buying atmosphere.

How do the store atmo-
spherics differ for these
two retailers?

*Touch Appeal.* For many consumers, personal inspection—handling, squeezing, and cuddling of a product—is a prerequisite to buying. Consider the **appeal** to **touch** in the Charmin example: "It's so squeezably soft." Before buying a product, the average consumer must at least hold it, even if it cannot be removed from its package. Many consumers have become upset because supermarkets now prepackage so many of their fruits, vegetables, and meats in hopes of reducing product damage inflicted by "the squeezers." In general, however, store layouts, fixtures, equipment, and displays must encourage and facilitate the consumer's sense of touch. The chances of a sale increase substantially when the consumer handles the product. The expression "I just couldn't put it down" underscores the importance of getting the consumer to pick up a product.

*Taste Appeal.* For some food retailers, offering the consumer a taste might be a necessary condition for buying. This is often the case with specialty foods such as meats, cheeses, and bakery and dairy products. Hickory Farms and Baskin Robbins are two specialty food retailers that use **taste appeal** as part of their selling operations. In designing in-store displays, such retailers provide potential customers with a sample of the product under clean and sanitary conditions.

*Theme Appeal.* Many retailers find that a *shopping theme* helps provide a focus in planning physical facilities. **Theme appeal** is a useful vehicle around which to organize the five sensory appeals. "L. L. Bean has transformed its interior into a total environmental shopping experience, one that matches the 'outdoorsy' type of merchandise it sells. This environment includes special sound effects, live plants, waterfalls, and stocked trout ponds."[6] Any number of themes can be employed. Common themes

What are the strengths and limitations of these shopping themes? How do they appeal to your physical senses?

center around natural and holiday seasons, historical periods, current issues (energy, environment), and special events (anniversaries). Shopping themes can be organized either on a storewide, department, or product-line basis.

## THE STORE'S EXTERIOR

First impressions are so important they are often the swing factor in a consumer's decision to stop at one store or another. Frequently, a consumer's first impression about a store is produced by the exterior. The store's exterior is a key factor in stopping and attracting new customers and retaining existing customers. The major considerations in planning store exteriors are the store's position, architecture, sign, and front.

### The Store's Position

How and where the store is positioned on the site affects the retailer's ability to attract customers. In evaluating existing store facilities or planning future site layouts, the retailer should consider at least these three questions: (1) How visible is the store? (2) Is the store compatible with its surroundings? and (3) Are store facilities placed for consumer convenience?

For the physical exterior to accomplish its goals of stopping, attracting, and inviting customers to shop, customers must see it. A visible store becomes part of the consumer's mental map of where to shop for a certain product or service. Simply put, people shop more frequently at stores they are aware of, and **store visibility** is an important factor in developing that awareness. Ideally, a store should be positioned so that it is clearly visible from the major traffic arteries (foot and/or vehicle) adjacent to the site. The retailer improves the store's visibility by using the three interacting factors of setback, angle, and elevation to advantage.

Reduced visibility can result either from setting the store too far back from a traffic artery or from positioning it too close to the street. Ideally, a store should be set back far enough to give passersby a broad perspective of the entire store, but close enough to let them read major signs and see any window displays.

In positioning the store, a retailer should place the building at an angle to the traffic artery that maximizes exposure. Since the store's front is designed to stop and attract potential customers, it should face the major traffic artery.

The elevation of a site can place the retailer's store above or below the main traffic artery level. Roofs and basement walls do little to attract and inform consumers. Most consumers do not see stores that are too high or too low. These stores are also perceived as having accessibility problems.

Fitting the store to the natural lay of the land and the natural habitat can reap substantial benefits for the retailer in terms of visual impressions. In designing for **site compatibility,** the retailer should consider several issues. First, the size of the facility should be appropriate to the size of the site. Placing an oversized building on a small site produces a distorted sense of proportion that is visually disturbing to customers and noncustomers alike. Second, the type of facility should be as consistent with the surrounding area as possible. Architectural design and construction materials should demonstrate a harmonious relationship with the immediate environment. And, finally, a certain amount of open space greatly enhances the appearance of an attractive store.

In planning the store's on-site position, the retailer should consider how the position affects consumer convenience. The retailer might ask a number of questions. Does the store's position allow enough parking spaces and permit easy access to them? Can cars and trucks turn around in the parking lot? Does the position permit safe, convenient pedestrian traffic?

## The Store's Architecture

Architecture is a major factor both in making the right impression on the consumer and in developing an efficient retail operation. In most cases the store's architecture is a compromise between these two objectives.

The store's architectural motif can convey any number of different impressions as well as communicate a considerable amount of information. A certain architectural style can indicate the size and prestige of the retailer's operation, the nature of the retailer's principal product line (e.g., Taco Bell), and the retailer's affiliation (standard store designs used by chain operations). In addition, architectural design can support a central theme or focal point for the retailer's merchandising activities. For example, a *marketplace* theme can be suggested architecturally by the use of open space—open store fronts, central squares, and shopping stalls standing out in the open.

The impression-creating elements of the architecture must be balanced against the functional needs of retailer and consumer. Functional considerations that are paramount in the store's design are *costs, energy efficiency, security, operational efficiency,* and *customer convenience.*

Rapidly rising land, construction, and materials costs have made the retailer's attempt to differentiate a store from the competition increasingly difficult. Additionally, architectural freedom is limited by the costs associated with maintenance; conversely, architectural designs that reduce maintenance costs often limit customer convenience and store attractiveness.

With increased energy prices, the retailer has an overriding obligation to minimize energy costs. Energy-saving construction methods include lower ceilings, less

What impressions are projected by the architectural motif of these store facilities?

window space, proper air circulation, controlled entrances and exits, and proper insulation.

Another architectural design consideration is operational efficiency. The best allocation of store space for operational activities is where there is easy movement for customers, sales personnel, and merchandise, and where the retailer can gain maximum product exposure. Of the objectives in architectural design, maximizing selling areas and creating the highest level of product exposure are the chief concerns.

With new government regulations and public pressure, the retailer must ensure that all possible physical barriers to handicapped consumers are removed. Physical barriers can also present problems for the elderly and the consumer with small children. Eliminating physical barriers is equally important to unhindered movement of all consumers: a few steps, a narrow aisle, or a hard-to-open door, can substantially reduce consumer traffic.

Does this sign explain "who, what, where, and when"?

## The Store's Sign

A store's sign (marquee) is often the first "mark" of the retailer that a potential customer sees. Signs provide the potential customer with the "who, what, where, and when" of the retailer's offering. Signs identify *who* the retailer is by a name, logo, or some other symbol. Sears, Safeway, and Holiday Inn are immediately recognized by most consumers. Signs can also convey something more to the consumer about who the retailer is. Consider the different impressions that a sign reading "Joe's Bar and Grill" communicates as opposed to one for the "Olde English Pub." Signs also inform consumers about *what* the retailer's operation is. They transmit information concerning the type of retail operation (department store, supermarket, catalog showroom), the nature of the product line (food, hardware, clothing, gifts), the extent of the service offering (full-service bank, self-service gasoline station), and the character of the pricing strategy (discount prices, family prices). Signs inform the consumer *where* the retailer is located and in some cases how to get there (e.g., "Located at 5th and Main," or "Take the next right and follow Washington Avenue for one block"). Finally, some retailers use signs to inform the consumer *when* they are willing to provide service or when they are open (e.g., 24 hours). The store's sign should create awareness, generate interest, and invite the consumer to try the store. The size, shape, color, lighting, and materials all contribute to the sign's distinctiveness and its abilities to create awareness and interest.

## The Store's Front

A store's front is the first major impression that consumers have of a store. The three primary design elements in a facade are storefront configuration, window displays, and store entrances.

The three basic storefront configurations are the straight, angled, and arcade fronts. As illustrated in Figure 7–2, the **straight front** is a **store configuration** that runs

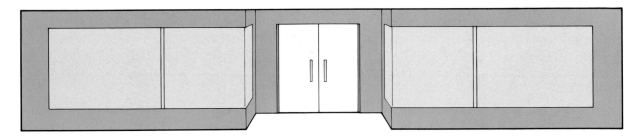

The Straight Front

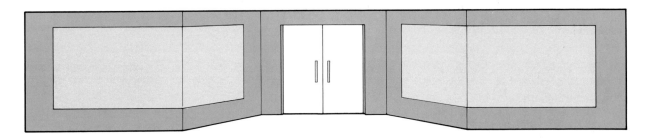

The Angled Front

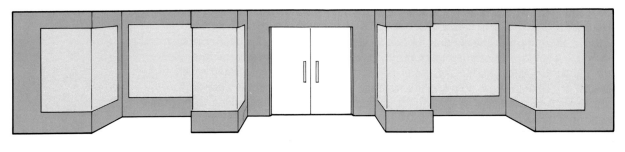

The Arcade Front

**FIGURE 7–2**
Storefront configurations

parallel to the sidewalk, street, mall, or parking lot. Usually the only break in the front is a small recess for an entrance. This storefront design is operationally efficient because it does not reduce interior selling space. It lacks consumer appeal, however, because it is monotonous and less attractive than either of the other two configurations.

Are these window displays effective? Why or why not?

The **angled-front configuration** overcomes the monotony of the straight front by positioning the store's front at a slight angle to the traffic arteries. Angled fronts also give the window shopper a better viewing angle of the merchandise in the window and reduce window glare. The entrance in an angled front is usually located at the most recessed part, to funnel and direct consumers into the store. The main limitation of the angled front is that it reduces the interior space the retailer can devote to selling.

The **arcade front** is characterized by several recessed windows and/or entrances. Its advantages are that it (1) increases the store's frontage exposure and display areas; (2) provides the shopper with several protected areas for window shopping; (3) increases the privacy under which the shopper can inspect window displays; and (4) reduces glare for a substantial part of the store front. Its disadvantage is that it considerably reduces interior space for selling and displaying merchandise.

The number, size, depth, and type of windows a store has can substantially alter its exterior appearance and the general impression it produces on consumers.

**Elevated windows** are display windows with floors of varying heights. The floor elevations range from 12 to 36 inches above sidewalk level. The choice of floor height depends on the kind of merchandise and the elevation necessary to place the display at the typical shopper's eye level. Elevated windows give consumers an excellent visual perspective of the retailer's merchandise and also protect the glass from damage that might otherwise occur at sidewalk levels. **Ramped windows** are standard display windows having a display floor higher in back than in front. The floor ramp either is a wedge or is tiered. The principal advantage of the ramped display window is the greater visual impact of merchandise displayed in the rear. **Shadow box windows** are small, box-like display windows set at eye-level heights. They are usually completely enclosed and focus the shopper's attention on a selected line of merchandise. Jewelry stores use this type of window display extensively. **Island windows** are four-sided display windows isolated from the rest of the store. Used in conjunction with the arcade storefront configuration, the island window can effectively highlight merchandise lines from all angles.

Retailers should design store entrances for the customer's *safety, comfort, and convenience,* as well as for guiding the customer into the store. Design considerations for store entrances include (1) good lighting, (2) flat entry surfaces (no steps), (3) nonskid materials, (4) easy-to-open doors (slide away or air curtains), (5) little or no entrance clutter, such as merchandise tables, and (6) doors wide enough for people carrying large parcels. In addition, store entrances must meet all access regulations for the handicapped.

## THE STORE'S INTERIOR

The store's interior must contribute to the retailer's basic objectives of minimizing operating expenses while maximizing sales and customer satisfaction. To accomplish these goals, the store's interior not only must be inviting, comfortable, and convenient for the customer, it must also permit the retailer to use interior space efficiently and effectively.

### The Store's Space

Not all of the interior space is of equal value when judged against its revenue-producing capabilities. The consumer's in-store shopping responses to different interior arrangements vary substantially. Specifically, the value of any unit of store space will vary with the floor location, with the area position within each floor, and with its location relative to various types of traffic aisles. Many retailers recognize these variations in the value of store space and allocate total store rent to sales departments according to where they are located and how valuable each space is.

The value of space in multilevel stores decreases the farther it is from the main or entry-level floor. Although experts have different opinions on exactly how to allocate rental costs to each floor, they all agree that sales areas on the main floor should be charged a higher rent than sales areas in the basement or on the second, third, and higher floors (see Figure 7–3). The additional customer exposure associated with entry-level floors justifies both the greater sales expectations (value of space) and the higher rent allocation of total store rent by floors.

The value of space also varies depending on where customers enter and how they traverse the store. In assigning value to interior store areas (and in making rent allocations), the retailer should consider the following three factors. First, the most exposed area of any floor is the immediate area surrounding the entrance. Second,

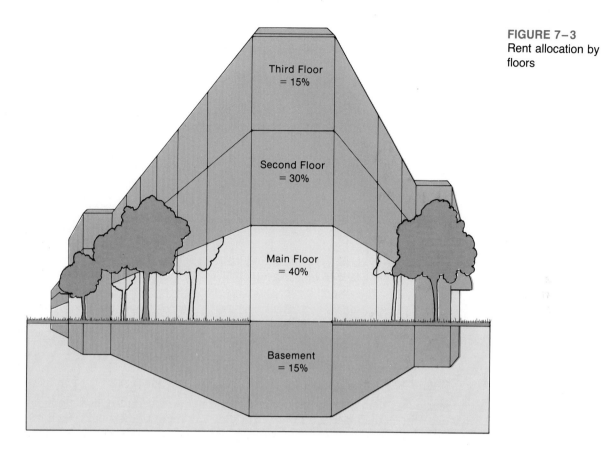

FIGURE 7–3
Rent allocation by
floors

most consumers tend to turn right when entering the store or floor. Third, a general rule of thumb is that only one-quarter of the store's customers will go more than halfway into the store. Based on these three considerations, Figure 7–4 provides one of several variations for allocating store rents to a floor area. Another rule of thumb in assigning rent allocations is the **4-3-2-1 rule** (see Figure 7–5).

Because merchandise located on primary traffic aisles greatly benefits from increased customer exposure, the retailer should assign a higher value and a higher rent to space along these aisles than to that along secondary aisles. To illustrate, Figure 7–6 classifies interior store space into high-, medium-, and low-rent areas based on position relative to primary and secondary traffic aisles. As illustrated, a high-rent area is one exposed to two primary traffic aisles, while a low-rent area is exposed only to secondary aisles. Medium-rent areas are exposed to one primary and one secondary aisle.

## The Store's Layout

A store's interior can be divided into two general areas according to usage: nonselling areas and selling areas. A **nonselling area** is space devoted to customer services, merchandise processing, and management and staff activities. Small retailers typi-

**FIGURE 7-4**
Rent allocations by
areas

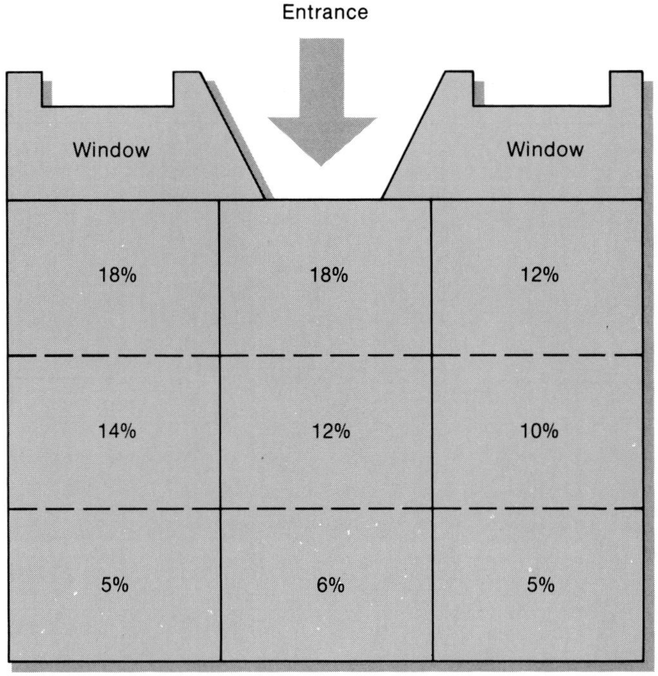

cally devote less than 10 percent of the store's interior space to nonselling areas. Large department and specialty stores usually devote more of the store's interior to nonselling areas and will designate separate areas for nonselling activities. Figure 7-7 illustrates the typical amount of space available for various types of retailers.

**FIGURE 7-5**

The 4-3-2-1 rule

> The decline in value of store space from front to back of the shop is expressed in the 4-3-2-1 rule. This rule assigns 40 percent of a store's rental cost to the front quarter of the shop, 30 percent to the second quarter, 20 percent to the third quarter, and 10 percent to the final quarter. Similarly, each quarter of the store should contribute the same percentage of sales revenue.
>
> For example, suppose that a small department store anticipates $120,000 in sales this year. Each quarter of the store should generate the following sales volume:
>
> | | | |
> |---|---|---|
> | Front quarter | $120,000 \cdot .40 =$ | $ 48,000 |
> | Second quarter | $120,000 \cdot .30 =$ | 36,000 |
> | Third quarter | $120,000 \cdot .20 =$ | 24,000 |
> | Fourth quarter | $120,000 \cdot .10 =$ | 12,000 |
> | Total | | $120,000 |

Source: Norman M. Scarborough and Thomas W. Zimmerer, *Effective Small Business Management* (Columbus: Charles E. Merrill Publishing Co., 1984), 339.

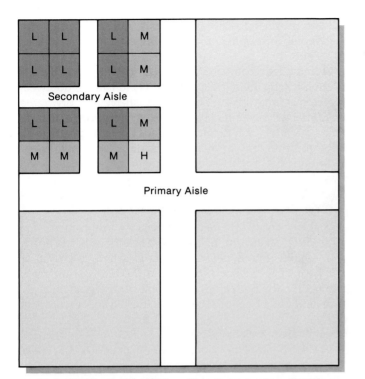

FIGURE 7–6
Rent allocations based
on traffic aisles

H = High-Rent Area   M = Medium-Rent Area   L = Low-Rent Area

**Selling space** is the area of the store devoted to the display of merchandise and the interaction between customers and store personnel. In planning the store's interior selling areas, the designer must organize merchandise into logical selling groups and allocate space, locate merchandise, and design layouts that are conducive to both the selling function and efficient overall operations.

| Type of Retail Operation | Amount of Store Space | |
|---|---|---|
| | Total Space (mean square footage) | Selling Space (mean square footage) |
| Supermarket | 48,000 | 36,209 |
| Department store | 148,000 | 119,975 |
| Discount store | 88,700 | 69,097 |
| Apparel specialty store | 21,200 | 16,536 |
| Drugstore | 14,300 | 11,440 |
| Home center | 28,300 | 22,753 |

FIGURE 7–7

Store size characteristics by type of retail organization

Source: "Annual Decision-Makers' Digest," *Chain Store Age Executive* (July 1987): pp. 36–37.

*Grouping Merchandise.* Better merchandise *planning,* greater merchandise *control,* and a more *personalized shopping atmosphere* are three important reasons for assembling merchandise into some type of natural grouping. A logical grouping of merchandise also helps customers find, compare, and select merchandise suited to their needs. The most common criteria the retailer uses are (1) functional (footwear, underwear, outerwear), (2) storage and display (racks, bins, shelves, or dry, refrigerated, frozen), and (3) target-market consumer criteria (men's, women's, children's, or economy minded, prestige oriented, convenience directed). The key points retailers must ensure in grouping merchandise are that the customer understands and appreciates the organization and that merchandise groupings are consistent with efficient operating principles.

*Allocating Space.* After a retailer has grouped merchandise according to some logical criteria, selling space must be allocated to each merchandise group. Given that each store has a limited amount of space, the retailer must select some method to allocate selling space. One method is the *model stock method,* whereby the retailer determines the amount of floor space needed to stock a desired assortment of merchandise for each grouping. For the more important merchandise groupings, the retailer allocates a sufficient amount of space to achieve the desired assortment. Merchandise groupings of lesser importance are allocated space on the basis of their assortment needs and the remaining available space.

A second method by which retailers allocate selling space is the *sales/ productivity ratio.* This method allocates selling space on the basis of sales per square foot for each merchandise group. Merchandise groups with lower sales or profit productivity are assigned space on an availability and needs basis.

*Locating Merchandise.* Where on the sales floor to put each merchandise group is the third factor in planning the sales floor. Criteria that retailers consider are rent-paying ability, consumer buying behavior, merchandise compatibility, seasonality of demand, space requirements, and display requirements. *Rent-paying ability* is the contribution that a merchandise group can generate in sales to pay the rent for the area to which it is assigned. Other things being equal, merchandise groups with the highest rent-paying ability are located in the most valuable space.

*Consumer buying behavior* criteria are based on the recognition that consumers are willing to spend different amounts of time and effort in searching for merchandise. For example, the retailer should place impulse and convenience goods in areas with high exposure (major aisles, checkout stands, etc.) because customers will not exert much effort to find them. In contrast, the retailer should locate shopping and specialty goods in less accessible areas, because consumers' purchase intents are well established and they will exert the necessary effort to find them.

The degree of relationship between various merchandise groups is termed *merchandise compatibility.* This concept states that closely related merchandise should be located together to promote complementary purchases. For example, the sale of a man's suit will increase the chances of selling men's ties and shirts if those products are located close to and are visible from the men's suit department.

Merchandise characterized by *seasonality of demand* is often accorded highly valuable, visible space during the appropriate season. In addition, merchandise groups with different seasonal selling peaks are often placed together to allow the retailer to expand or contract these lines without major changes in the store's layout. Examples are Christmas toys, lawn and garden equipment, women's coats, and women's dresses.

*Space requirements* for each merchandise group also must be considered in making in-store location decisions. For example, merchandise groups that require large amounts of floor space (e.g., a department store's furniture department) use less valuable space either at the rear of the store, on an upper floor or in the basement, or in an annex. Normally, the bulky nature of such products cannot justify their placement in higher-rent locations.

*Display requirements* also influence where the retailer places a particular group of merchandise. For example, merchandise such as clothing, which must be hung to display it properly, is located along the sides of walls or at the rear of the store, where it will not interfere with the customer's view of the store.

*Designing Layouts.* When designing sales floor layouts, the retailer must consider the arrangement of merchandise, fixtures, displays, and traffic aisles so that they accommodate the spatial and locational requirements of different merchandise groups. Selling floor layouts are extremely important because they strongly influence in-store traffic patterns, shopping atmosphere, shopping behavior, and operational efficiency. Some of the factors the retailer must consider in designing the sales floor layout include the following:

- ☐ *Type of displays* (shelves, tables, counters) and *fixtures* (stands, easels, forms, platforms)
- ☐ *Size* and *shape* of fixtures
- ☐ *Permanence* of displays and fixtures
- ☐ *Arrangement* (formal or informal balance) of displays and fixtures
- ☐ *Width* and *length* of traffic aisles
- ☐ *Positioning* of merchandise groups, customer services, and other customer attractions

Three basic layout patterns are the grid, free-form, and boutique layouts. The **grid layout** is a rectangular arrangement of displays and aisles that generally run parallel to one another. As illustrated in Figure 7–8, the grid layout represents a formal arrangement in which the size and shape of display areas and the length and width of the traffic aisles are homogeneous throughout the store. Used most frequently by supermarkets and convenience, variety, and discount stores, the grid layout offers several advantages. First, it allows the most efficient use of selling space of any of the layout patterns. Second, it simplifies shopping by creating clear, distinct traffic aisles. Third, it promotes the image of a clean, efficient shopping atmosphere. Fourth, it facilitates routine and planned shopping behavior as well as self-service and self-selection by creating a well-organized environment. And, finally, it allows more efficient operations by simplifying the stocking, marking, and housekeeping tasks, and reduces some of the problems connected with inventory and security control. The major disadvantage of the grid layout is the sterile shopping atmosphere it creates. For this reason, the grid pattern is simply inappropriate for most shopping- and specialty-goods retailers.

**FIGURE 7–8**
The grid layout

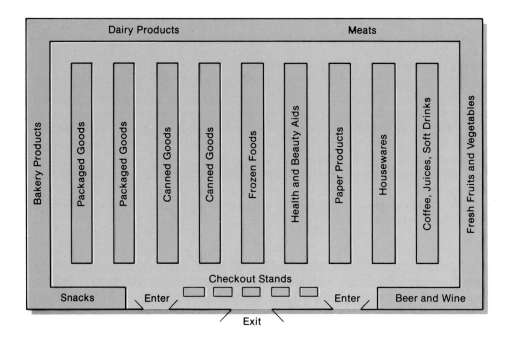

The **free-form layout,** on the other hand, arranges displays and aisles in a free-flowing pattern (see Figure 7–9). This layout employs a variety of different sizes, shapes, and styles of displays, together with fixtures positioned in an informal, un-balanced arrangement. The main benefit retailers derive from the free-form layout is the pleasant atmosphere it produces—an easy-going environment that promotes window-shopping, browsing, and exposure to more merchandise. This comfortable

**FIGURE 7–9**
The free-form layout

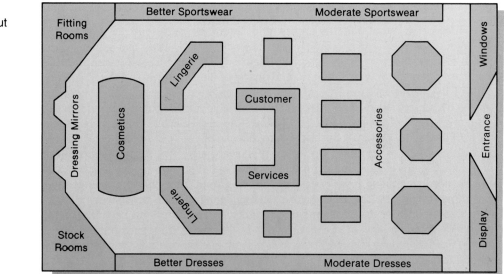

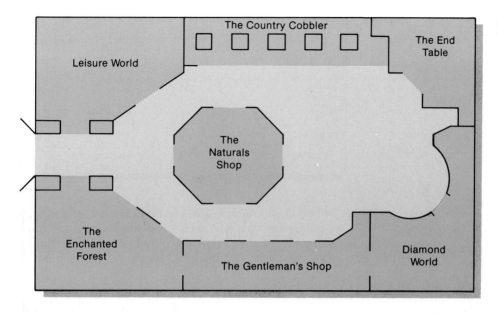

**FIGURE 7–10**
The boutique layout

environment increases the time the customer is willing to spend in the store and results in an increase in both planned and unplanned purchases. These benefits of a superior shopping atmosphere are partially offset by the increased cost of displays and fixtures, high labor requirements, additional inventory and security control problems, and the wasted selling space that normally accompany a free-form layout.

The **boutique layout** arranges the sales floor into individual, semiseparate areas, each built around a particular shopping theme. The boutique layout illustrated in Figure 7–10 shows the sales floor divided into several small specialty shops. By using displays and fixtures appropriate to a particular shopping theme and by stocking the boutique according to this theme, the retailer can create an unusual and interesting shopping experience. Carson Pirie Scott changed the second floor of its flagship store into a 60,000-square-foot mall of specialty stores called "Metropolis on 2." Each of the 26 separate stores has its own signage, display fixtures, and shopping bags—in other words, its own identity.[7] For example, the "Leisure World" boutique might include such an unconventional merchandise assortment as sporting goods, exercise equipment, home electronics (computer games, stereos, televisions), and art and music supplies. The "Naturals Shop" could feature apparel and food products along with home furnishings, all made from natural materials. To reinforce the theme, fixtures could be constructed from natural, unfinished woods. Boutique layouts have essentially the same advantages and disadvantages as free-form layouts.

Customer theft, employee pilferage, burglary, and robbery are everyday facts of life that every retailer must face and protect against. In developing a store security program, the retailer must protect not only the store and its merchandise, but also its customers and employees. This section describes how a retailer can detect and prevent many of the losses that might result from criminal activities. Although esti-

**THE STORE'S SECURITY**

**FIGURE 7–11**
Retail losses (source: National Mass Retailing Institute, *The Wall Street Journal* (May 15, 1987): 41.

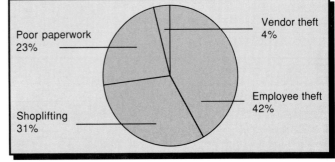

Poor paperwork 23%

Vendor theft 4%

Employee theft 42%

Shoplifting 31%

mates vary greatly, about five cents out of every dollar spent in a retail store goes to cover the losses resulting from these criminal activities and the security measures used to prevent them. As indicated in Figure 7–11, 42 percent of all losses can be attributed to employee theft, 31 percent to shoplifting, 23 percent to poor paperwork control, and 4 percent to vendors.[8]

## Customer Theft

**Shoplifting** is the act of pilfering merchandise from a store display by customers and individuals posing as customers. To *pilfer* is to commit or practice petty theft. This form of petty thievery can account for 30 to 40 percent of all stock losses the retailer suffers. Unfortunately for the store's customers, retail prices must be set high enough to cover these losses. Shoplifting occurs in three basic ways: (1) outright theft of merchandise, (2) alteration of the retailer's price tag to reflect a lower price, and (3) switching or substituting a lower price tag for the original tag.

Shoplifters fall into two general categories: the amateur who steals to satisfy physical or psychological needs and the professional who steals for a living. An **amateur shoplifter** may be anyone. Usually they neither look nor act the part. They range from juveniles to homemakers, kleptomaniacs to vagrants, and alcoholics to drug addicts. **Professional shoplifters** are in the business for the money. Professionals makes their livelihood by stealing and then reselling the merchandise. They cause serious losses for the retailer because they focus their activities on high-value merchandise that is easy to fence but difficult to trace and recover.

The amateur and the professional use a variety of devices in shoplifting. The main purpose of shoplifting devices is to conceal both the actual act of stealing and the merchandise once it has been stolen. Shoplifting devices include various types of clothing (e.g., coats, "booster" panties, wide-top boots, and other loose-fitting garments) and parcels (e.g., booster boxes, purses, umbrellas, newspapers, magazines, and shopping, school, and knitting bags). The shoplifter might also hide stolen merchandise (e.g., jewelry) in merchandise actually purchased (e.g., box of candy).

Shoplifters use a number of techniques in their pilfering activities. Shoplifters who employ these techniques can be characterized as the booster, the diverter, the blocker, the sweeper, the walker, the wearer, the carrier, the wrapper, and the price changer.

The **booster** is a shoplifter who shoves merchandise into concealed areas of parcels and/or clothing. The **diverter** is one member of a team of shoplifters who

How effective are these security devices in preventing and detecting shoplifting techniques?

attempts to divert the attention of the store's personnel while a partner shoplifts. Obstructing the vision of store personnel while they or a partner shoplift is the principal technique of **blockers.** The **sweeper** simply brushes merchandise off the counter into a shopping bag or some other type of container. The **walker** is usually a woman who has perfected the technique of walking naturally while carrying concealed merchandise between her legs. The **wearer** tries on merchandise, then wears it out of the store. The **carrier** walks in, picks up a large piece of merchandise, removes the tags, affixes a fake sales slip, and walks out. **Self-wrappers** use their own wrapping paper to wrap store merchandise before removing it from the store. And the **price changer** pays for the merchandise but only after taking a shoplifter's reduction by altering or switching the store's price tag or by removing the store tag and substituting a realistic fake.

The retailer's security program should include both shoplifting detection and shoplifting prevention measures. Detecting shoplifters is largely a matter of good observation. Successful detection involves knowing what to look for and where to look. Training store employees to be better observers not only increases the chances of detecting actual shoplifting activities but also increases the likelihood of discouraging potential shoplifters. To facilitate observation and detection, many retailers use devices such as mirrors, observation towers, closed-circuit television, and electronic bugs (see Figure 7–12). Overall, training programs, electronic devices, and guards/detectives are judged to be the most effective security measures; mirrors and locks/chains are considered less effective.[9]

### Employee Pilferage

Employee pilferage represents serious losses for many retailers. Employee theft accounts for approximately 42 to 44 percent of retail shrinkage.[10] It is not unusual for losses from employee theft to exceed those from all other forms of theft. Perhaps the single most important factor contributing to these losses is the retailer's belief that trusted employees do not and will not steal. Recognizing that the problem exists and understanding why and how employees pilfer are the first steps in developing a security program to detect and prevent losses resulting from **employee pilferers**.

Employee pilferage takes one of two forms: theft of merchandise and theft of money. Both forms of pilferage are likely to occur in a variety of ways by any or all of the retailer's employees. Opportunity and need are the two most commonly cited factors responsible for the honesty or dishonesty of employees. In the face of easy and continuous opportunities to pilfer, just about any employee could be expected to take advantage of the situation. By reducing the opportunity to pilfer, the retailer can go a long way to help keep honest employees honest. Some employees may think they need to steal to meet their basic financial obligations. Employees who are intentionally or unintentionally underpaid are prime candidates for "making up the difference" through a self-help program of pilfering. By assuring each full-time employee a "living" wage, the retailer can reduce, but not eliminate, the need factor in employee theft.

Like most thieves, the employee who pilfers money and/or merchandise develops definite patterns or modes of operation. Based on these operational modes, profiles can be developed that characterize typical methods of employee pilferage. The most common profiles include the eater, the smuggler, the discounter, the dipper, the embezzler, the partner, and the stasher.

The **eater** is the employee who samples the retailer's food and beverage lines or supplements lunch with a soft drink or dessert. The **smuggler** is the employee who takes merchandise out of the store by whatever means are available (trash cans, coats, lunch boxes, purses, and various other types of bags and packages). The **discounter** feels entitled to give unauthorized discounts to friends and relatives. The **dipper** is the store employee who steals money by dipping into the cash register or mishandles cash in some other way, such as making short rings, fraudulent refunds, or false employee discounts. The **embezzler** is most often a highly trusted employee who takes advantage of that trust to divert the retailer's funds for either permanent or temporary use. The **partner** is a store employee who does not actually pilfer the merchandise or money, but who supplies outside individuals with information (such as security procedures) or devices (such as keys) that increase the likelihood of successful theft. The **stasher** is the store employee who hides merchandise in a

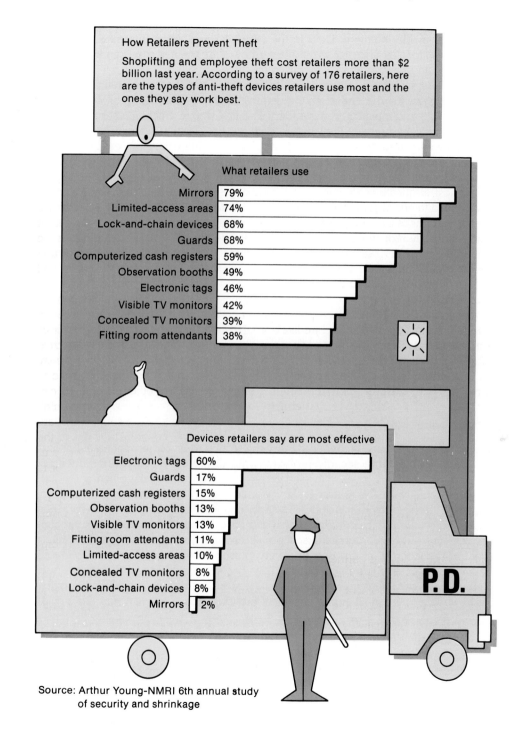

FIGURE 7–12
Observation methods
(source: adapted from
M. E. Williams, "Theft:
Stores Fight Back: For
Retailers, 'tis the Sea-
son to be Wary," Copy-
right 1984, *USA Today*.
Reprinted with permis-
sion.)

How Retailers Prevent Theft

Shoplifting and employee theft cost retailers more than $2
billion last year. According to a survey of 176 retailers, here
are the types of anti-theft devices retailers use most and the
ones they say work best.

What retailers use

| Device | Percent |
| --- | --- |
| Mirrors | 79% |
| Limited-access areas | 74% |
| Lock-and-chain devices | 68% |
| Guards | 68% |
| Computerized cash registers | 59% |
| Observation booths | 49% |
| Electronic tags | 46% |
| Visible TV monitors | 42% |
| Concealed TV monitors | 39% |
| Fitting room attendants | 38% |

Devices retailers say are most effective

| Device | Percent |
| --- | --- |
| Electronic tags | 60% |
| Guards | 17% |
| Computerized cash registers | 15% |
| Observation booths | 13% |
| Visible TV monitors | 13% |
| Fitting room attendants | 11% |
| Limited-access areas | 10% |
| Concealed TV monitors | 8% |
| Lock-and-chain devices | 8% |
| Mirrors | 2% |

P.D.

Source: Arthur Young-NMRI 6th annual study
of security and shrinkage

secure place inside the store. Later in the selling season, when the merchandise is marked down for clearance, the employee removes the stashed merchandise from its hiding place and purchases it at the discount price.

The most effective method of controlling employee theft is to create a general store atmosphere in which not even the slightest degree of dishonesty is tolerated and where honesty and integrity are rewarded. The first step in creating a security atmosphere is to stop employee theft before it starts. By carefully screening employees before they are hired and by properly training them after they are employed, the retailer can reduce the number of dishonest employees in the store. The second step in creating a security atmosphere is for management to set the example. By engaging in dishonest or questionable behavior, the manager sets the tone for an atmosphere that can lead to employee pilferage. A third step is to create a work environment that is free from unnecessary temptation. Establishing and enforcing good security policies can substantially reduce opportunities for employee theft.[11] Finally, by being aware of and interested in employees' problems, needs, and aspirations, the retailer can develop a personal relationship that encourages honesty and loyalty.

To detect, discourage, and prevent employees from pilfering, some retailers use several types of security personnel. Stationing *uniformed guards* at employee entrances/exits and requiring employees to check in and out of the store reduce opportunities for removing merchandise from the store. Retailers also use **undercover shoppers** to check on the honesty of employees. Posing as a legitimate customer, an undercover shopper can often detect the activities of the eater, the discounter, and the dipper. Additional security measures include **silent witness programs** that reward employees with cash for anonymous tips on theft activities of other employees.

### Supplier Pilferage

When developing a store security program, the retailer must remember that suppliers have some of the same security problems with dishonest employees as does the retailer. Therefore, it is prudent to take security precautions against pilfering by supplier representatives. The retailer is very vulnerable to pilfering activities of delivery personnel. These activities include (1) **short counts**—delivering fewer items than were listed on the purchase order and signed for on the invoice—and (2) **merchandise removal**—stealing merchandise from receiving, checking, stocking, and selling areas. In the latter case, dishonest delivery personnel have readily accessible concealment devices, such as empty boxes, delivery carts, and bulky work clothes. There are numerous security requirements and procedures to reduce and eliminate pilferage by supplier personnel, some of which are listed here.

1. Establish a receiving area (preferably in the rear of the store) for accepting all incoming merchandise.
2. Supervise all deliveries made directly to the sales floor and/or stockroom.
3. Limit the number of entrances to the receiving area and secure them with locks.
4. Control entry and exit to the receiving area.
5. Inform all delivery personnel that they and their equipment are subject to random inspection while they are on the store's premises.
6. Check all incoming shipments using one of the many available checking procedures.

7. Document all incoming shipments as to contents, weight, size, and condition of shipment.

## Bad Checks

Accepting checks in exchange for merchandise has become an essential part of most retailers' service offering. Accepting bad checks, however, is not part of that service. The retailer's security program must include safeguards against accepting worthless checks and appropriate procedures for recovering losses resulting from such exchanges.

Bad checks can be stolen and falsely endorsed, written on bank accounts with insufficient funds, and written on nonexistent or closed bank accounts. Also, a check can be bad if the customer stops payment on the check, or intentionally or unintentionally fills it out incorrectly, or the bank simply does not accept a particular type of check (e.g., a blank check). It is virtually impossible to avoid some bad checks. Through proper detection and prevention measures, however, the retailer can keep bad check losses at a minimum.

Clues to worthless checks are often contained on the checks themselves. By carefully examining each check not only for fraudulent information but for simple, honest mistakes in writing, the retailer can help avoid accepting checks that are intentionally or unintentionally bad. No check should be accepted without proper identification. Many retailers require at least two pieces of acceptable identification. Driver's licenses, automobile registration cards, credit cards, and employment identification cards are most accepted by retailers.

The retailer should establish a system that clearly states check-cashing policies. Employees and customers alike should be informed of the types of checks that are acceptable and the conditions under which the retailer will accept them. Some retailers use a *registration system,* whereby they request that their customers register identification information at some prior time with the store's credit or customer-service office. Once registered, the customer receives a check-cashing ID card.

## Bad Credit Cards

Sales charged to stolen, fictitious, cancelled, and expired credit cards cause substantial losses for retailers each year.[12] To reduce these costs, a good policy for retailers is to exercise as much care in accepting credit cards as in cashing checks. In accepting both third-party credit cards (bank cards, entertainment cards, etc.) and the store's own credit cards, the following procedures are recommended:

1. Check credit card against "stolen card" list.
2. Check credit card against "cancelled card" list.
3. Check credit card expiration date.
4. Compare signature on credit card with that on credit slip.
5. Obtain approval of all credit card sales above a specific amount.
6. Fill in all required information on each credit slip (date of purchase, itemized list and amounts of purchases, sales tax charges, and total amount of purchases).
7. Submit all credit card sales for immediate processing.

## Burglary and Robbery

Retail stores are prime targets for burglary and robbery because they are less secure than most other businesses.[13] This lack of security results from carelessness on the part of some retailers as well as from the general nature of the retailing business (which often requires some isolated locations, evening hours, exposed cash in registers, etc.). While retailers can do little to alter the nature of their business, they can initiate security measures to make their stores a less desirable target for burglary and robbery and reduce their harmful impact. **Burglary** is defined as "any unlawful entry to commit a felony or a theft, even though no force is used to gain entrance."[14] **Robbery** is "stealing or taking anything of value by force, or violence, or by use of fear."[15] Given the steady increase in the number of burglaries and robberies in recent times, the retailer's security program must incorporate careful measures to prevent such crimes.

Burglars usually operate under cover of darkness, after the store is closed. They gain entry by picking locks, forcing doors or windows open, using duplicate keys, or hiding in the store until it closes. Most security measures are directed at (1) preventing the burglar from gaining entry to the store and (2) securing all high-value merchandise. Most retailers use locks and lights to discourage attempts at entry, safes to secure valuables, and alarms to warn police.

Although burglary can result in substantial losses of money and merchandise, robbery is far more serious because it always holds the potential of loss of life as well as property. By definition, robbery is a violent crime in which one person uses force, or the threat of it, against another individual.

Several preventive measures might well reduce the number of robbery attempts as well as losses suffered from robberies. To reduce the risk of robbery, the retailer should heed the following guidelines:

1. Keep as little cash in each cash register as possible and remove excess cash from the register frequently.
2. Maintain a minimum level of operating cash in the store. Bank all excess cash.
3. Use armored-car service for making bank deposits. If using armored car service is impractical, vary bank trip routes and times.
4. Keep store safes locked at all times. Do not leave a safe open during operating hours.
5. Use two people to open and close the store—one for the actual opening and closing of the store and the other as an outside security lookout.
6. Exercise extreme caution when someone asks you to make an emergency opening during hours the store is closed. Before going to the store, call the police and make sure they will be there for the unscheduled opening.

These measures can help to reduce the potential loss of an employee's life and the loss of cash and merchandise.

Antirobbery defense systems are directed at discouraging and apprehending the robber. Some of the more common robbery-protection systems include panic buttons, till traps, video systems, and cash-control devices.[16]

**SUMMARY**

One of the most valuable ways the retailer can attract customers is by the appearance of the store and its immediate surroundings. The store's environment has both physical and psychological repercussions in the battle for the customer's attention and for efficient operations. By identifying the desired image, the retailer creates a store image that is right for shopping and working. Appeals to the five senses promote a favorable buying atmosphere. Sight, sound, smell, touch, and taste appeals have an obvious influence on the consumer's buying behavior.

Communication with the consumer is facilitated by the store's exterior. How and where the store is positioned on the site affect the retailer's ability to attract customers. The store should be positioned so that it is visible to the consumer, compatible with the natural environment, and convenient for on-site movement of people and vehicles. The store's architecture should incorporate features that make a good impression while remaining functionally efficient. The store's sign serves two purposes: identifying the store and attracting consumer attention. Because the store's facade often creates the consumer's first impression, the appropriate configuration, attractive window displays, and accessible store entrances are essential.

The store's interior should minimize operating expenses while maximizing sales activities and customer satisfaction. In planning store layouts, the retailer must consider that all space is not equal in sales-producing potential. Also, wise use of non-selling space helps the retailer meet consumers' service needs.

Store security calls for developing the necessary safeguards for the store and its merchandise by initiating programs for detecting and preventing losses resulting from shoplifting by customers, pilfering by employees and suppliers, passing of bad checks and credit cards, and burglary and robbery.

Shoplifting is the theft of merchandise by customers or individuals posing as customers. There are basically two types of shoplifters: those who steal from need and for psychological reasons (amateurs) and those who steal for a living (professionals). The best means of detecting shoplifters is good observation—knowing what to look for and where to look.

Store employees do steal; losses from employee pilferage exceed those from shoplifting. Opportunity and need are the two most critical causes for this type of theft. The retailer can reduce this form of theft by creating an atmosphere of honesty, by using security personnel, and by establishing strict security policies.

The retailer's security program must also extend to procedures for controlling pilferage by suppliers, for guarding against bad checks and credit cards, and for reducing opportunities for burglary and robbery.

**STUDENT STUDY GUIDE**

**KEY TERMS AND CONCEPTS**

| | |
|---|---|
| amateur shoplifter | boutique layout |
| angled-front configuration | burglary |
| arcade-front configuration | the carrier |
| the blocker | the dipper |
| the booster | the discounter |

the diverter

the eater

elevated window

the embezzler

employee pilferers

4-3-2-1 rule

free-form layout

grid layout

island window

merchandise removal

nonselling area

the partner

the price changer

professional shoplifter

ramped window

robbery

scent appeal

the self-wrapper

selling space

shadow box window

shoplifting

short count

sight appeal

silent witness program

site compatibility

the smuggler

sound appeal

the stasher

store image

store visibility

straight-front configuration

the sweeper

taste appeal

theme appeal

touch appeal

undercover shopper

the walker

the wearer

**REVIEW QUESTIONS**

1. What is store image? How is it created?
2. Describe the three types of visual relationships.
3. Describe the emotions or feelings consumers associate with horizontal lines, vertical lines, and slanted lines.
4. What determines the psychological impact of color? Explain.
5. What illusions are created by bright colors? Who prefers softer tones?
6. Discuss the three uses for sound in creating a buying atmosphere.
7. What three factors determine a store's visibility? Explain.
8. Identify the factors that the retailer considers in designing a functional facility. Explain.
9. Describe the who, what, where, and when functions of a retail store sign.
10. Compare and contrast the three basic storefront configurations.
11. What is the 4-3-2-1 rule?
12. Compare and contrast the model stock and sales productivity methods of allocating selling space.
13. How can seasonality of demand affect the in-store location of merchandise?
14. Describe the three basic layout patterns. What are the strengths and weaknesses of each pattern?
15. Identify the three basic ways by which shoplifting is accomplished.
16. Identify and describe the various types of shoplifters on the basis of their techniques.
17. Describe the major devices retailers use in observing and detecting shoplifters.
18. What are the two most commonly cited factors for explaining the dishonesty of employees?
19. What are the two most common methods of supplier pilferage?

True or False

_____ 1. The sense of sight provides people with more information than any other sense mode.

_____ 2. For the creation of perfect harmony in display, dissimilar shapes should be used.

_____ 3. A retailer using the 4-3-2-1 rule of store rent allocation would assign one percent of the store's rental cost to the back quarter of the store.

_____ 4. Using the sales-productivity ratio, the retailer allocates selling space on the basis of sales per square foot generated by a given merchandise group.

_____ 5. The walker is usually a female shoplifter who tries on merchandise, then wears it out of the store.

_____ 6. The most effective method of controlling employee theft is to create a general store atmosphere in which not even the slightest degree of dishonesty is tolerated and where honesty and integrity are rewarded.

_____ 7. Short counts involve delivering fewer items than were listed on the purchase order and signed for on the invoice.

1. Compare and contrast the image created by the physical facilities of a local Sears store with that of a local J. C. Penney store. Identify similarities and differences. How does each store communicate the right impression and the wrong impression? Provide specific examples.

2. Evaluate the sight, sound, scent, touch, taste, and theme appeals for a major franchised food retailer (e.g., McDonalds, Wendy's, Pizza Hut) in your community. Identify specific examples of both positive and negative appeals. What changes would you recommend to create a more desirable atmosphere?

3. For the retailer selected in project 2, analyze the store's position in terms of store visibility, site compatibility, and consumer convenience. Identify and explain both positive and negative aspects of the store's position.

4. Draw a comprehensive diagram of the store layout of a local discount store. Redesign the store's layout using the boutique approach. Should a discount store consider using a boutique layout? Explain your reasoning.

5. Survey your local police department and develop a statistical profile of the various types of criminal activities preying on retailers. Identify retail crime patterns (high crime areas, types of retailers and/or products that appear to be targeted by criminals, and so on). Discuss with the police the preventive measures they recommend for reducing retail security problems.

6. Should the retailer prosecute amateur shoplifters? Discuss both the positive and negative sides of this question. Develop a specific set of policies regarding when, who, and how often to prosecute. Justify your policies.

7. Identify and discuss the issues surrounding the use of polygraph (lie-detector) tests as a prerequisite for initial and continued employment. Should retailers be allowed to use such tests? Why or why not?

8. Interview a small independent retailer regarding his check-cashing policies. Determine what problems the retailer experiences in regard to cashing checks. Are the retailer's check-cashing policies adequate? Why or why not? What changes would you recommend? Justify any recommended changes.

9. Audit the burglary security system of a local retailer. Identify and explain any shortcomings in the security system. What improvements would you recommend? Why?

CASES:
PROBLEMS AND
DECISIONS

## CASE 7–1

## Fallis Foods: Investigating an Innovative Store Layout*

### BACKGROUND

Steve Fallis has a right to be proud. As the owner and manager of the largest independent supermarket in Hopkinsville, Indiana, Fallis has enjoyed remarkable success over the last 10 years. As of last year, Fallis Foods had captured a 21 percent market share. Given that there are six supermarkets in the greater Hopkinsville area, he has been quite pleased with his store's performance. Nevertheless, Fallis has no intention of resting on his laurels. For Fallis Foods to maintain its current share of the food market and have any chance of improving its market share will require considerable forward planning effort. In Fallis's mind, innovation is a major ingredient in any successful plan for the future.

In recent weeks, he has been giving a great deal of thought to making some innovative changes in the store's layout; specifically, assembling product lines into more natural groupings and locating these natural groupings within a concentrated area of the store. Bakery products, for example, are currently assembled into a number of different groupings scattered throughout the store. In the past, Fallis Foods has followed the conventional wisdom of displaying bakery products using the grouping and locating practices of competitive supermarkets. Fallis thinks, however, that regrouping bakery products into one large group and placing it at a single location could well provide the store's customers with a more convenient shopping experience; it could also provide Fallis Foods with a distinctive merchandising practice and possibly a small but significant competitive advantage.

### CURRENT SITUATION

Come Monday morning, Fallis decided to audit the store's current practices in merchandising bakery products. Armed with a blueprint of the store's layout (see Exhibit 1) and a clipboard, he proceeded to collect the following information on the in-store groupings and locations of bakery products:

1. *In-store bakery shop*—a separate in-store bakery, installed at considerable expense two years ago, that carries a full line of freshly baked breads, rolls, cakes, pies, doughnuts, pastries, cookies, and other specialty bakery items. This department has above-average markups and operating expenses. It requires several full-time employees (bakers and salesclerks). Strict supervision is necessary to avoid too many "stales" that must be sold at reduced prices or given away to charity (see location A in Exhibit 1).

2. *Commercial bakery goods*—a full gondola of commercially baked breads, rolls, and pastries delivered by national and regional vendors (bakeries) that provide the full range of services normally associated with such rack jobbers. They stock the shelves, price the merchandise, accept returns of "stales," and provide other inventory control functions. This section is a carbon copy of the commercial bakery goods section found in most supermarkets. This section is known to have a high traffic count and is located at some distance from the store's "scratch" bakery shop (see location B in Exhibit 1).

3. *Frozen bakery products*—a growing line of bakery products are those displayed in the open, chest-type frozen-food cabinets. This assortment of frozen bakery products includes mostly nationally advertised, brand-name items (e.g., Sara Lee, Morton, and Rich's). Although the assortment emphasis is on dessert items and pastries, there are several brands of frozen bread and roll dough that require baking by the consumer (see location C in Exhibit 1).

*This case was prepared by Charles R. Patton, Pan American University and Dale M. Lewison, The University of Akron.

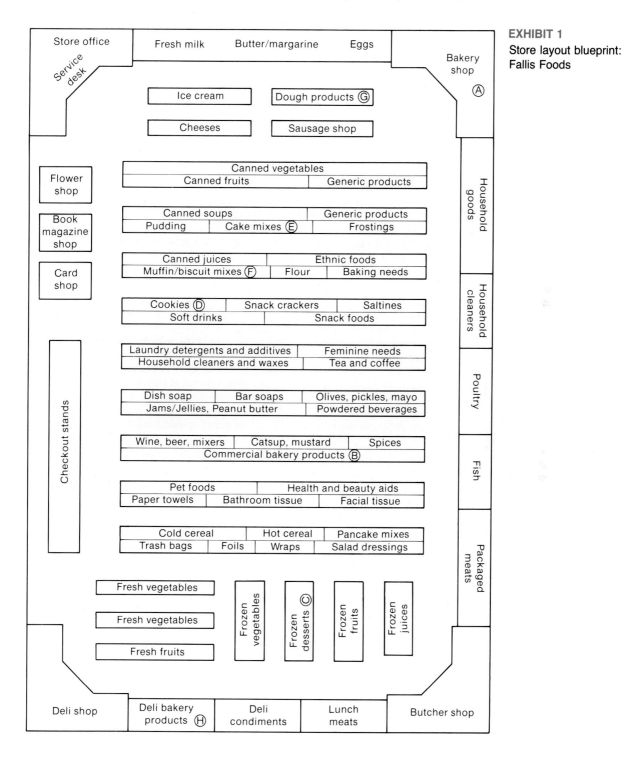

**EXHIBIT 1**

Store layout blueprint:
Fallis Foods

4. *Commercial cookies*—a large section of one gondola is devoted to packaged cookies. This product line is dominated by a few large national brands (e.g., Keebler, Nabisco, Duncan Hines, and Archway). To date, cookies baked by the store's bakery have had limited success competing against these long-established commercial products (see location D in Exhibit 1).

5. *Commercial cake mixes*—a large section of one gondola is devoted to commercial cake mixes (e.g., Duncan Hines, Betty Crocker, and Pillsbury). These are well-established product lines that offer a considerable variety of flavors. To promote complementary sales, cake frostings are located adjacent to the cake mixes (see location E in Exhibit 1).

6. *Commercial muffin, biscuit, and bread mixes*—a six-foot section of one gondola is stocked with muffin, biscuit, and homemade bread mixes. Many local competitors place all "mixes" together; however, Fallis Foods has traditionally followed customer belief that muffin, biscuit, and bread mixes are more commonly associated with flour (see location F in Exhibit 1).

7. *Refrigerated dough products*—a large, open, chest-type refrigerator is used to display a complete selection of refrigerated dough products. Items within this product line include preformed pie crusts, breakfast pastries, bread dough, refrigerated desserts, and biscuit and roll doughs (see location G in Exhibit 1).

8. *Deli bakery products*—to complement the store's complete deli department, a small wall display is devoted to deli bakery products, such as specialty breads and rolls (see location H in Exhibit 1).

Having completed the audit and a review of its findings, Fallis had arrived at several tentative conclusions. First, the store offered an extensive selection of bakery products. Until now, he never realized the extent of the variety and assortment of products currently being stocked in the various bakery departments. The total number of possible choices facing the customer is almost staggering. Fallis wondered whether this extensive selection was necessary. Did it meet customers' need for selection or did it simply confuse them? Thinking about this issue, Fallis developed a hypothetical shopping scenario that he thought might be a fairly typical experience (see Exhibit 2). The more he thought about it, the more he believed that there was a high likelihood of overkill in the selection of bakery goods currently being offered in his store.

Fallis also thought the bakery goods category appeared to have considerable duplication, perhaps too much. For example, is it necessary to stock both frozen and refrigerated pie crusts? Do customers perceive these two items to be different, and if so, is that difference important? Also, are all the various product brands and package sizes necessary? For Fallis, this issue of duplication needed close attention.

The final conclusion Fallis made centered on the issue of multiple locations for bakery products. The seven or eight current locations certainly must have some negative implications as far as customer convenience is concerned. For example, the several widely scattered locations must hinder the customer's ability to make price, brand, quality, and other relevant comparisons without considerable backtracking through the store. Multiple locations also hinder customers from finding the particular item they are looking for. In sum, it could confuse and irritate the customer.

Each of these tentative conclusions seems to support Fallis's contention that a more efficient, effective way to merchandise bakery products would be to regroup and relocate all such goods into one concentrated bakery department. The more he thought about the idea, the more he liked it. Before making any final decisions or drawing up any final plans, however, Fallis decided to contact Spatial Interactions, Inc. (SII), a consulting firm that specializes in the spatial problems associated with retailing operations (e.g., retail location and store layout and design). After discussing the idea at some length with Wayne Duff, President of SII, Fallis was convinced that an in-depth study of all the issues surrounding his

Driving home from work, Rita Thomas realized that she did not have any dessert to serve after the evening meal. Since Harold really appreciated having dessert, Rita decided to pop in at Fallis Foods to pick up something. Pie seemed like a good idea. Upon entering the store, Rita proceeded to travel around the store in her normal counter-clockwise pattern. Deciding to investigate all the possibilities, Rita made the following stops and was faced with the following choices:

*Stop 1: Frozen-food cases* (location C in Exhibit 1)
  Choice 1: Frozen 8-inch pies, six varieties, mostly nationally advertised brands, must be thawed before eating.
  Choice 2: Frozen 9-inch pies, three varieties, local and regional brands, must be baked before serving.
  Choice 3: Frozen 5-inch pies (two to three servings), four varieties, must be baked before serving.
  Choice 4: Frozen individual pie pieces, individually wrapped, three varieties, must be thawed and warmed before serving.
  Choice 5: Frozen pie crusts, individual and multiple packs, three sizes (tart 4-inch, standard 8-inch, and family 9-inch), must be thawed, filled, and baked before serving.

*Stop 2: Commercial bakery-goods section* (location B in Exhibit 1)
  Choice 1: Prepackaged pies, baked by local and regional bakeries, standard 8-inch size, one day old, seven varieties, lowest prices, ready-to-eat.
  Choice 2: Prepackaged pies, national brands, individual sizes, four varieties, ready-to-eat.
  Choice 3: 8-count box of pie-like product called Little Debbie, individual servings that are individually wrapped, one variety, ready-to-eat.

*Stop 3: Commercial cake mixes* (location E in Exhibit 1)
  Choice 1: Packaged pie crust mixes, requiring additional ingredients, must be mixed and formed into pie crust, very reasonable.
  Choice 2: Packaged pie filling mixes, requiring preparation, nine varieties.

*Stop 4: In-store bakery shop* (location A in Exhibit 1)
  Choice 1: Freshly baked pies, five varieties, baked on premises, standard 8-inch size, more expensive, ready-to-eat.
  Choice 2: Freshly baked tarts, three varieties, baked on premises, individual servings, quite expensive, ready-to-eat.

*Stop 5: Refrigerated dough products* (location G in Exhibit 1)
  Choice 1: Refrigerated pie crusts, ready-to-use, require filling, may or may not be baked, standard 8-inch size, pie dough and graham cracker base.
  Choice 2: Refrigerated pie dough, must be rolled out and shaped, requires baking.

*Stop 6: Canned goods section* (see Exhibit 1)
  Choice 1  Canned pie fillings, six varieties, ready-to-use, very inexpensive.

Having made her whirlwind tour of the store, Rita was somewhat exhausted from all the rushing about, and even more confused at all the choices. Her original intention was to simply buy a pie for tonight's dessert, but the problem is which pie in what form and flavor and at what price?

**EXHIBIT 2**
A shopping scenario

idea was essential before proceeding with any direct action. He provided Duff with a copy of the audit and the blueprint of the store's layout. He also agreed to cooperate with SII researchers assigned to the project. Fallis spent the next few hours discussing with Duff the particulars of the study. They agreed on a limited study that would do the following:

1. Identify the pros and cons of regrouping all bakery products into one concentrated location within the store. The pro and con statements should be made from two perspectives: (a) retail merchandising and operations and (b) consumer buying behavior.

2. Make a recommendation based on the pro and con statements as to what course of action would be most advisable for Fallis Foods (to be supported by a complete rationale statement).

3. Develop a store layout and design plan for remodeling the store that would incorporate a concentrated bakery-products section. The plan should also consider the regrouping and relocating of other product categories (e.g., beverages) and any recommendations related to this issue. (Note: this plan is to be developed regardless of the recommendation presented.)

## ASSIGNMENT

Assume the role of George Raymer, Project Research Director for SII. Duff has assigned the Fallis Foods project to you. A comprehensive report, complete with supporting graphics, is due within two months.

## CASE 7-2
## Hoffman-LaRoche, Inc.*

Drug abuse is one of our most serious social problems. It is also an important factor as corporations seek to increase the productivity of their employees. Experts have estimated that 10–23 percent of American workers use dangerous drugs while on the job. Employee drug abuse has been estimated to cost American industry $33 billion per year. Obviously, from social and competitive perspectives, U.S. firms are interested in reducing drug abuse among the work force.

Drug-abuse testing is seen as a viable means for screening prospective employees (nearly one-third of the Fortune 500 companies do this) and for discouraging drug use by current employees. Several pharmaceutical companies now manufacture drug-abuse tests and others are considering entry into this potentially lucrative market. In fact, a recent study indicated that the market potential for drug-abuse testing has been increasing by 10–15 percent annually and could grow to $220 million by 1991.

Hoffman-La Roche, Inc., located in Nutley, New Jersey, has already entered the market for drug-abuse testing. The company current sells about $20 million per year in various drug testing products. It recently introduced a service known as Abuscreen and has begun promoting it as 99 percent accurate in testing for the presence of marijuana, LSD, amphetamines, cocaine, morphine, barbiturates, and methaqualone.

The high reliability of Hoffman-La Roche's drug-abuse testing is of great importance in marketing these services. The company's reputation, experience, and comprehensive services to potential customers are also important factors that have enabled Hoffman-La Roche to sell its services to the 1984 Olympics, the U.S. Department of Defense, and to many other organizations. Although price is a concern, most of the prospective corporate clients place more emphasis on the quality of the drug-abuse tests.

*This case was prepared by Jon Hawes, The University of Akron.

Hoffman-La Roche recently launched a new subsidiary called Diagnostic Dimensions, which markets comprehensive services to fight drug abuse in the work force. It offers training programs, employee education, and counseling, as well as other services to help companies help their employees.

## ASSIGNMENT

Assume the role of the Director of Human Resources for the 80-unit chain of specialty apparel shops. The president of the firm believes that many of the personnel problems (e.g., employee pilferage, poor employee morale, customer complaints, and store security) are often drug-related. Although there is no firm information on what percentage of the firm's employees might be using drugs, national averages provide some guidance. As the person responsible for managing personnel problems, the president has asked you to prepare a report on the following:

1. Is drug usage a security problem?
2. Should the firm initiate a drug testing program?
3. How might a drug testing program be administered?
4. What actions should be taken if an employee is found to be using drugs?

**ENDNOTES**

1. Amy Dunkin, "Taking Macy's Out From Under the Magnifying Glass," *Business Week*, 4 Nov. 1985, 26.
2. Russell Mitchell, "Waldenbooks Tries Hooking Young Bookworms," *Business Week*, 11 May 1987, 48.
3. Kenneth H. Mills and Judith E. Paul, *Applied Visual Merchandising* (Englewood Cliffs, NJ: Prentice-Hall, 1982), 47.
4. Gail Tom, Teresa Barnett, William Lew, and Jordan Selmants, "Cueing the Consumer: The Role of Salient Cues in Consumer Perception," *The Journal of Consumer Marketing* (Spring 1987): 25.
5. Sallie Hook, "All the Retail World's a Stage," *Marketing News*, 31 July 1987, 16.
6. Ibid.
7. "Carson's Specialty," *Stores* (October 1986): 52.
8. "Retailers' Losses," *Wall Street Journal* (May 15, 1987): 41; also see Julie Abend, "Employee Theft," *Stores* (June 1986): 57–62.
9. "Spending More But Enjoying It Less," *Chain Store Age Executive* (February 1987): 71.
10. Larry Hansen, "Thwarting the In-House Thief," *USA Today*, 16 Nov. 1984, 1B.
11. See Peter D. Berlin, "A Shrinkage Success Story—Herman's World of Sporting Goods," *Retail Control* (November 1986): 37–43.
12. See "Preventing Credit Card Fraud," *Stores* (September 1985): 38, 40.
13. Discussion based on S. J. Curtis, *Preventing Burglary and Robbery Loss, Small Marketers Aids*, No. 134 (Washington, D.C.: Small Business Administration, 1968).
14. Ibid., 2.
15. Ibid.
16. See David Rowe, "Robbery," *Video Store* 5 (July 1983), 32–33.

# PART THREE
## Retail Location

# 8

## Outline

## Objectives

☐ Appreciate the considerable impact that the retail-location decision has on all other aspects of the retailer's business.

☐ Employ standardized criteria to delineate and describe regional and local market areas.

☐ Evaluate regional and local market areas by sales potential and operational suitability.

☐ Select regional and local market areas capable of meeting the sales and operational needs of a particular retailing firm.

☐ Describe the size and structural dimensions of retail trading areas.

☐ Understand and use various techniques for trading-area identification.

☐ Ascertain the gross and net adequacy of retail trading areas.

# Retail Markets and Trading Areas

The importance of location decisions cannot be overstated. A retailer that selects a poor location will always be at a competitive disadvantage. To overcome a poor location (a struggle that is not always successful), the retailer must make substantial adjustments in the product, price, and promotional mixes. These adjustments usually are expensive to implement and adversely affect the firm's profits. On the other hand, selecting a good location enhances the chances of success because it allows greater flexibility in developing the product, price, and promotional mix. This chapter discusses how regional markets, local markets, and trading areas are identified, evaluated, and selected.

Market areas come in all sizes, shapes, and descriptions. This section discusses the two general problems facing the location specialist: (1) how to identify regional markets and (2) how to identify local markets. These two problems and their particular components are illustrated in Figure 8–1.

**IDENTIFYING MARKETS**

Identifying regional markets consists of determining the "right region" of the country and the "right part of the region." The geographic extent of a regional market is not fixed and could include either one state or a multistate area. For many small, independent retailers, the regional market problem is not a concern. For the chain organization or for the retailer that intends to expand, however, the starting point in the location-decision process is to identify regional and subregional markets.

As shown in Figure 8–1, the local market problem is how to find the "right town" and the "right part of town." For our purposes, "town" refers to any size urban center that can be associated with a particular regional or subregional market.

## Regional Markets

Most business organizations have regionalized the United States in some way. Census and communication areas are two common means for identifying regional markets. Census delineations are used because of the availability of good demographic and economic data from the government. Communication media delineations are used to identify social-economic areas based on consumer media preferences.

Perhaps the most widely used regional classification system is one developed by the U.S. Census Bureau. As shown in Figure 8–2, the Census Bureau divides the

**FIGURE 8–1**
Identification of regional
and local market areas

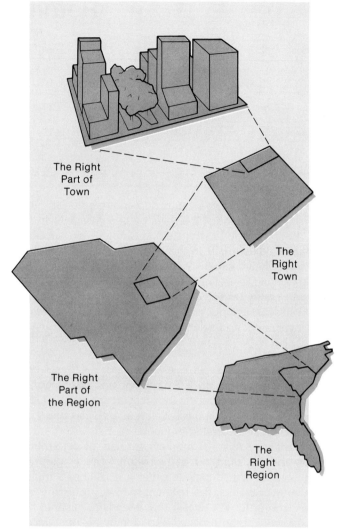

The Right
Part of
Town

The
Right
Town

The Right
Part of
the Region

The
Right
Region

United States into nine census regions. The relative importance of this **census market** classification scheme is evident from the fact that many public and private organizations use this system as the organizational framework for their information reporting and analyzing process. Two private organizations that use this classification are of particular interest to the retailer: the *Survey of Buying Power*, published annually by *Sales and Marketing Management*, and Standard Rate and Data Service's monthly rate and data publication, *Spot Television*.

Regional markets can be identified on the basis of various types of media coverage—**communication markets**. In the case of the broadcast media, a 50,000-watt radio station like WGN in Chicago is capable of providing the retailer with multistate regional coverage. On the other hand, a 5,000-watt station like KVI in Seattle/Tacoma covers only a subregional market because its output is restricted to the

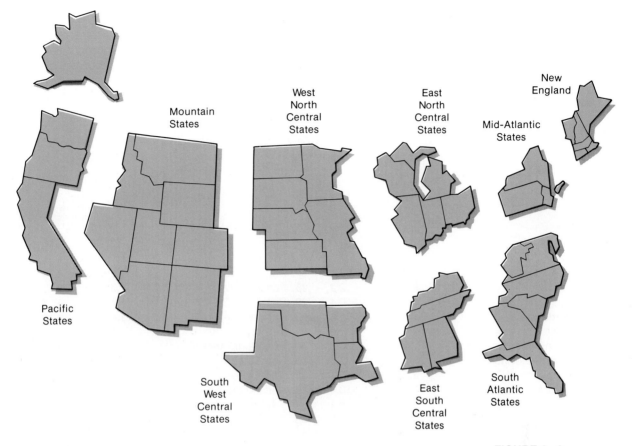

Mountain States

West North Central States

East North Central States

New England

Mid-Atlantic States

Pacific States

South West Central States

East South Central States

South Atlantic States

**FIGURE 8-2**
Census regions as defined by the Census Bureau

western portion of the state of Washington. The large-area coverage by WGN is appropriate to a multiunit retailer (such as K Mart) that has operations in each of the states WGN covers. Assuming lower advertising rates, a small retail operation finds the less extensive coverage typified by KVI more appropriate.

Print media also provide good operational definitions of regional and subregional markets. For example, the *New York News* has a multistate regional coverage. By dividing the total New York regional markets into 27 zones (a process referred to as *zoned insert marketing*), the regional market is effectively segmented into subregional markets.

Magazines also recognize the value of regional and subregional classifications. *Newsweek*, for example, has segmented the U.S. market into five regions—Western, West Central, East Central, Eastern, and Southern—and three of these regional markets are segmented further into subregional markets—Western (Pacific Northwest, Pacific Southwest, and California), Southern (Southwest, Southeast, Texas, and Florida), and Eastern (Mid-Atlantic and New England). Regional and subregional issues of magazines such as *Newsweek* provide regional and local retailers with an opportunity to advertise in prestigious publications to reach an upper-bracket audience within a selective geographic area.

## Local Markets

Finding the "right town" and the "right part of town" constitutes the local market identification problem. Faced with an array of thousands of urban centers, the retail location specialist must use some organized method to identify local markets.[1]

One method of classifying urban centers is to group them according to sales volume potential—**ABC markets.** Many retailing operations employ population and demographic analysis to determine each market's sales potential for a particular line of merchandise or a given type of retail operation. Based on their sales volume potential, urban centers can be classified in descending order as either A, B, or C markets. The exact definition of what constitutes an A, B, or C market varies from one

| 1991 Rank | Metro Market | Projected 1991 Pop. (Thous.) | Projected % Change 1986–91 | 1991 Rank | Metro Market | Projected 1991 Pop. (Thous.) | Projected % Change 1986–91 |
|---|---|---|---|---|---|---|---|
| 1. | Los Angeles-Long Beach | 8,869.6 | + 6.7% | 27. | San Francisco | 1,649.6 | + 4.2 |
| 2. | New York | 8,713.0 | + 2.2 | 28. | Kansas City | 1,582.3 | + 3.7 |
| 3. | Chicago | 6,187.9 | + 0.4 | 29. | San Jose, CA | 1,484.5 | + 5.4 |
| 4. | Philadelphia | 4,884.2 | + 1.2 | 30. | Sacramento | 1,450.9 | +11.2 |
| 5. | Detroit | 4,412.7 | + 1.2 | 31. | Cincinnati | 1,421.0 | + 0.1 |
| 6. | Boston-Lawrence-Salem-Lowell-Brockton | 3,752.9 | + 0.8 | 32. | Fort Worth-Arlington | 1,420.3 | +15.9 |
| 7. | Washington, DC | 3,744.8 | + 5.7 | 33. | New Orleans | 1,402.8 | + 4.1 |
| 8. | Houston | 3,567.9 | +10.4 | 34. | Milwaukee | 1,400.5 | + 0.4 |
| 9. | Atlanta | 2,800.3 | +10.1 | 35. | Norfolk-Virginia Beach-Newport News, VA | 1,394.9 | + 6.7 |
| 10. | Nassau-Suffolk, NY | 2,738.7 | + 2.8 | 36. | San Antonio | 1,378.6 | +10.2 |
| 11. | Dallas | 2,666.3 | +12.1 | 37. | Columbus, OH | 1,334.4 | + 2.5 |
| 12. | St. Louis | 2,498.7 | + 1.9 | 38. | Bergen-Passaic, NJ | 1,311.1 | + 0.6 |
| 13. | San Diego | 2,466.0 | +11.2 | 39. | Fort Lauderdale-Hollywood-Pompano Beach | 1,280.0 | + 9.6 |
| 14. | Minneapolis-St. Paul | 2,445.9 | + 5.3 | 40. | Indianapolis | 1,247.2 | + 2.3 |
| 15. | Baltimore | 2,374.7 | + 3.0 | 41. | Portland, OR | 1,188.3 | + 2.5 |
| 16. | Anaheim-Santa Ana | 2,341.3 | + 7.5 | 42. | Charlotte-Gastonia-Rock Hill | 1,140.3 | + 6.4 |
| 17. | Riverside-San Bernadino, CA | 2,325.2 | +15.9 | 43. | Salt Lake City-Ogden | 1,139.5 | + 8.3 |
| 18. | Phoenix | 2,221.4 | +15.9 | 44. | Hartford-New Britain-Middletown-Bristol, CT | 1,126.5 | + 2.6 |
| 19. | Tampa-St. Petersburg-Clearwater, FL | 2,133.9 | +11.4 | 45. | Oklahoma City | 1,081.0 | + 8.9 |
| 20. | Pittsburgh | 2,103.4 | − 1.7 | 46. | Monmouth-Ocean, NJ | 1,033.1 | + 7.9 |
| 21. | Oakland | 2,070.6 | + 6.2 | 47. | Orlando, FL | 1,031.4 | +14.7 |
| 22. | Newark | 1,905.4 | + 0.3 | 48. | Rochester, NY | 1,005.4 | + 1.3 |
| 23. | Miami-Hialeah | 1,901.7 | + 6.5 | 49. | Nashville, TN | 995.8 | + 6.3 |
| 24. | Seattle | 1,860.5 | + 5.8 | 50. | Middlesex-Somerset-Hunterdon, NJ | 983.6 | + 4.0 |
| 25. | Cleveland | 1,823.2 | − 1.6 | | | | |
| 26. | Denver | 1,796.3 | + 8.9 | | | | |

Source: Sales & Marketing Management's *1987 Survey of Buying Power—Part II.* © Sales & Marketing Management.

**FIGURE 8–3**
The 50 largest metro markets based on 1991 projected population

retailing organization to another because each retailing organization uses different decision variables. By identifying different-sized markets, the retailer can tailor the product, place, price, and promotional strategies to satisfy customer needs and to increase the firm's profitability.

Local markets are identified and ranked on the basis of population, retail sales, employment levels, disposable income, number of households, and a host of other factors. Figure 8–3 identifies the 50 largest metro markets based on 1991 projected population. Figure 8–4 identifies the 50 largest metro markets based on the 1991 projected household income.

| 1991 Rank | Metro Market | 1991 Average Household EBI | 1991 Rank | Metro Market | 1991 Average Household EBI |
|---|---|---|---|---|---|
| 1. | Bridgeport-Stamford-Norwalk-Danbury, CT | $73,851 | 26. | Minneapolis-St. Paul | $54,770 |
| 2. | Nassau-Suffolk, NY | 71,637 | 27. | Kenosha, WI | 53,862 |
| 3. | Lake County, IL | 68,624 | 28. | Chicago | 53,679 |
| 4. | Washington, DC | 64,031 | 29. | Santa Barbara-Santa Maria-Lompoc | 53,676 |
| 5. | Middlesex-Somerset-Hunterdon, NJ | 63,163 | 30. | Aurora-Elgin, IL | 53,529 |
| 6. | San Jose | 62,556 | 31. | Wichita, KS | 53,426 |
| 7. | Bergen-Passaic, NJ | 62,337 | 32. | Seattle | 53,416 |
| 8. | Grand Forks, ND | 61,138 | 33. | Lincoln, NE | 53,370 |
| 9. | Oxnard-Ventura, CA | 60,662 | 34. | Portsmouth-Dover-Rochester, NH | 53,264 |
| 10. | Trenton, NJ | 60,216 | 35. | Omaha | 53,216 |
| 11. | Anaheim-Santa Ana, CA | 59,777 | 36. | Richland-Kennewick-Pasco, WA | 53,086 |
| 12. | San Francisco | 58,959 | 37. | San Diego | 52,969 |
| 13. | Newark | 58,615 | 38. | Santa Cruz, CA | 52,437 |
| 14. | Midland, TX | 58,599 | 39. | Topeka | 52,392 |
| 15. | Honolulu | 58,043 | 40. | Wilmington, DE | 52,281 |
| 16. | Anchorage | 56,403 | 41. | Kalamazoo, MI | 52,108 |
| 17. | Boston-Lawrence-Salem-Lowell-Brockton | 56,325 | 42. | Rochester, MN | 52,013 |
| 18. | Hartford-New Britain-Middletown-Bristol, CT | 56,282 | 43. | Dallas | 51,877 |
| 19. | Oakland | 56,269 | 44. | Ann Arbor, MI | 51,375 |
| 20. | Monmouth-Ocean, NJ | 56,094 | 45. | Grand Rapids, MI | 51,152 |
| 21. | Poughkeepsie, NY | 55,918 | 46. | Salinas-Seaside-Monterey, CA | 51,111 |
| 22. | Brazoria, TX | 55,655 | 47. | Denver | 51,096 |
| 23. | Manchester-Nashua, NH | 55,493 | 48. | Iowa City | 51,007 |
| 24. | New London-Norwich, CT | 55,004 | 49. | Peoria, IL | 50,659 |
| 25. | New Haven-Waterbury-Meriden, CT | 54,999 | 50. | West Palm Beach-Boca Raton-Delray Beach, FL | 50,615 |
| | | | | **U.S. Average** | **$45,362** |

Source: Sales & Marketing Management's *1987 Survey of Buying Power—Part II.* © Sales & Marketing Management.

**FIGURE 8–4**
The 50 largest metro markets based on 1991 projected household income

For most retailers, there are literally "right" and "wrong" parts of town. An urban center is not simply a homogeneous mass; rather, it is a heterogeneous grouping of people and activities that can have a profound effect on a retailer's operations. The location specialist must determine the internal structure of the local market and select areas within the city that increase the retailer's chances for success.

The internal structure of urban centers is composed of many recognizable areas, including the downtown and the suburbs; shopping centers and strip shopping developments; ethnic and racial areas; residential, commercial, and industrial areas; and low-, middle-, and high-income areas. To facilitate understanding of the internal structure of cities, this chapter examines several theories of urban structure based on *land-use patterns*. Over time, these patterns emerge when certain activities (such as commercial, industrial, and residential) tend to dominate the land use of particular areas in and around the urban center. These patterns are a good indication of what type of retailing might be appropriate.

## EVALUATING MARKETS

After identifying potential market areas, the retail location specialist must evaluate each one. The identification process itself should have provided considerable insight into the various capacities of each area to support a given type of retail organization. The evaluation process involves collecting and analyzing data pertinent to a particular retailer's operation. Although we could discuss many evaluation tools, our discussion in the following sections is limited to some of the standard evaluation sources and methods.

### Standard Evaluation Sources

In evaluating retail market areas, retailing analysts primarily use two major sources: the *Survey of Buying Power* and the *Editor & Publisher Market Guide*. Both contain vast amounts of data for estimating a retail market's potential sales.

The **Survey of Buying Power** is an annual publication compiled by the editors of *Sales and Marketing Management* magazine. Three basic categories of information are of particular interest to the retail location specialist attempting to evaluate potential market areas. Those three categories are population, retail sales, and effective buying income.

The survey contains information for all census regions, states, metro areas, counties, and cities. Although the population and retail sales figures reported in the survey are self-explanatory, the expression *effective buying income* requires additional explanation. As used in the survey, effective buying income is all personal income (wages, salaries, rental income, dividends, interest, pension, welfare) less federal, state, and local personal taxes, contributions for social security insurance, and nontax payments (fines, fees, penalties). In essence, effective buying income is the rough equivalent of disposable personal income; that is, the spendable income available to the consumer.

The raw population, retail sales, and income figures provide the location specialist with a demographic overview of the *absolute* sales potential of various market areas. By comparing each identified market area to others, the location specialist can develop "relative" measures of each market's potential. In addition, the retailer can use this survey information to develop several relevant measures of a market's potential in terms of percentages, averages, ratios, and indices.

The second standard source of information for evaluating market areas is **Editor & Publisher Market Guide**. Although similar in some aspects to the *Survey of Buying Power,* the yearly editions provide additional and different information about market areas. Besides standard information on population, income, households, farm products, and retail sales for states, metro areas, counties, and cities, the guide provides specific features for each city.

## Standard Evaluation Methods

This section discusses several standard *methods* for evaluating market areas: the buying power index, the sales activity index, and the index of retail saturation.

The **buying power index,** published annually in the *Survey of Buying Power,* is "a measurement of a market's ability to buy."[2] The index is constructed using three criteria:

1. The market area's population expressed as a percentage of the total U.S. population
2. The market area's retail sales expressed as a percentage of total U.S. retail sales
3. The market area's effective buying income expressed as a percentage of the total U.S. effective buying income

The index does not equally weight each criterion as an indicator of a market area's ability to buy. Instead, each is weighted according to its perceived importance—population by 2, retail sales by 3, and effective buying income by 5. The buying power index (BPI) is calculated as follows:

$$BPI = \frac{(\text{pop.} \times 2) + (\text{retail sales} \times 3) + (\text{effect. buying inc.} \times 5)}{10 \text{ (the sum of the weights)}}$$

The higher the index value, the greater the market area's ability to buy and therefore to support retailing activities. As described by the editors of *Survey of Buying Power,* the index "is most useful in estimating the potential for mass products sold at popular prices. The further a product is removed from the mass market, the greater is the need for a BPI to be modified by more discriminating factors—income, class, age, sex, etc."[3]

The *Survey of Buying Power* also reports the standardized **sales activity index (SAI):** "a measure of the per capita retail sales of an area compared with those of the nation."[4] The SAI is calculated as follows:

$$SAI = \frac{\text{market area's \% of U.S. retail sales}}{\text{market area's \% of U.S. population}}$$

Because the numerator (retail sales) reflects all sales made in an area regardless of where the consumer is from and the denominator (population) includes only those people who live in the area, the sales activity index does not specify whether a market area's sales activity is the result of the shopping activities of area residents, nonresidents, business concerns, or some combination.

The **index of retail saturation (IRS)** is a measure of the potential sales per square foot of store space for a given product line within a particular market area.[5] As a market-area evaluation tool, it incorporates both consumer demand and competitive supply. Essentially, the index is the ratio between a market area's capacity to consume and its capacity to retail. The formulation of the index of retail saturation is expressed as

$$IRS = \frac{(C)(RE)}{RF}$$

where

$IRS$ = index of retail saturation for a given product line(s) within a particular market area

$C$ = number of customers in a particular market for a given product line

$RE$ = retail expenditures—the average dollar expenditure for a given product line(s) within a particular market area

$RF$ = retail facilities—the total square feet of selling space allocated to a given product line(s) within a particular market area

To illustrate, assume that a retail operation needs sales of $45 per square foot of selling space for a given product line to operate profitably. Also assume that the retailer is currently examining three potential market areas (see Figure 8–5). Market area A can be eliminated from further consideration because it does not meet the $45 minimum sales per square foot criterion. Both markets B and C meet the minimum sales criterion. If all other location considerations are equal, however, market B would be preferable to C because it offers the retailer more ($3.33 higher) sales potential per square foot of selling space.

The index of retail saturation allows the retailer to classify market areas on the basis of their competitive situation—understored, overstored, or saturated. **Understored market areas** are those in which the capacity to consume exceeds the capacity to retail. In other words, there are too few stores and/or too little selling space devoted

**FIGURE 8–5**
Market-area evaluation using the index of retail saturation

|  | Market Area | | |
|---|---|---|---|
|  | A | B | C |
| Number of customers (C) | 40,000 | 50,000 | 70,000 |
| Retail expenditures (RE) | $10 | $12 | $10 |
| Retail facilities (RF) | 10,000 | 12,000 | 15,000 |
| Index of retail saturation (IRS) | $40.00 | $50.00 | $46.67 |

to a product line to satisfy consumer needs. **Overstored market areas** occur when the capacity to retail exceeds the capacity to consume. In this situation, retailers have devoted too much space to a particular product line. Nevertheless, a retailer might consider this area if the store represented something unique. Finally, a **saturated market area** is one in which the capacity to retail equals the capacity of buyers to consume a product line. In this case, demand for and supply of a given product line are in equilibrium. The understored market area obviously offers the best opportunity for the retailer seeking a new location.

**SELECTING MARKETS**

On completing the market-area identification and evaluation processes, the retailer must select a regional and local market. There are no simple decision rules to aid the retailer in selection. The basis of the location decision varies with types of retailers, operational characteristics, and stated objectives. At this point, the retailer's *judgment* is the critical factor. Ultimately, the retailer should select the regional and local markets that provide sufficient levels of support (sales potential) conducive to the firm's operational needs. Generally, the market area a retailer selects represents a compromise among several promising but different market situations.

**IDENTIFYING TRADING AREAS**

A **retail trading area** is broadly defined as that area from which a store attracts its customers or obtains its business. Depending on the *kind* of retail operations, a retail trading area can be described more specifically in the following terms:

- ☐ *Drawing power*—the area from which a *shopping center* could expect to derive as much as 85 percent of its total volume
- ☐ *Per capita sales*—the area from which a *general merchandise store* can derive a minimum annual per capita sale of $1
- ☐ *Patronage probability*—the area from which potential customers come who have a probability greater than zero of purchasing a given class of products or services that either a retailer or group of retailers offers for sale
- ☐ *Retail operations*—the area from which either a marketing unit or group can operate economically, depending on volume, cost to operate, and cost to sell and/or deliver a good or service

### Trading-Area Dimensions

Trading areas range in size from a few square blocks to a radius of many miles. The size of a trading area is a function of the cumulative effects of several *operational* and *environmental* factors. The two major operational factors are *type* and *size*. *Type of retail operation* means the kind of goods and services offered. Retailers that offer specialty and shopping goods will draw consumers from a wider geographic area than retailers that offer convenience goods, because consumers are willing to exert greater effort and to travel greater distances to buy specialty and shopping goods than to buy convenience goods.

The second operational factor, *store size*, is directly related to the retailer's trading-area size. That is, the larger the retail store and the greater its selection of merchandise, the larger its trading area will be. Because of their physical size and wide range of merchandise, Bloomingdale's of New York and Rich's of Atlanta are department stores with very large trading areas.

The second set of factors that determine the size of a retailer's trading area are environmental, including (1) the number, size, and type of *neighboring stores;* (2) the nature and activity of *competing stores;* and (3) the character of the *transportation network.*

A retailer that locates near other retailers often finds that the combined trading area of all the neighboring retailers in the cluster is larger than if the store were in an isolated location. Thus, a retailer that locates in a regional shopping mall shares more potential customers from a larger area than a retailer that locates either in a small, neighborhood shopping center or in an isolated, freestanding location.

The size of a retailer's trading area also depends on the location, size, and activity of competing stores. One large department store, for example, might locate next to another large department store to facilitate consumers' comparative shopping and thus draw from a larger geographic area.

The third environmental factor, the transportation network, strongly influences a retailer's ability to attract consumers from an area. Roads with high traffic volume and faster speeds afford better site locations than those with less volume and lower speeds. Also, the number of traffic lanes, the number and nature of intersections (controlled or uncontrolled), the speed limit, and the presence or absence of barriers to uncongested movement all affect the size of the area from which a retailer can attract consumers.

Trading-area structure is the comparative ability of a retailer or a cluster of retailers to attract customers from various distances or from various customer regions. Three trading-area structures are general, composite, and proportional.

A **general trading area** provides the majority of a retailer's business. The general trading area includes any and all customers who do, or might, buy any product line the retailer carries. Thus, a customer who purchases only perfume at the store is included in the retailer's general trading area along with a customer who buys perfume, dresses, shoes, handbags, and several other products (see Figure 8–6a).

A **composite trading area** is a set of trading areas, each of which is structured according to the type of goods the retailer sells. Figure 8–6b illustrates the composite trading area for a store (or shopping center) selling convenience, shopping, and specialty goods. Because many retailers carry several lines of products, this representation is rather realistic. In this case, the retailer draws from a larger trading area for specialty goods than for shopping and convenience goods. The consumer's willingness to exert shopping effort, as described earlier, accounts for the composite-area boundary lines.

A **proportional trading area** is based on the distance customers are from the store. The farther customers are from the retail store, the less likely they are to patronize it. The closer customers are to the store, the greater the likelihood they will patronize it. As illustrated in Figure 8–6c, three distance zones—primary, secondary, and fringe—constitute the proportional trading area.

The **primary trading zone** is the area around which a retailer can expect to attract 50 to 70 percent of its business. The primary trading area is the area in which the retailer has a competitive advantage and the area from which the retailer produces the highest per capita sales. The **secondary trading zone** surrounds the primary zone

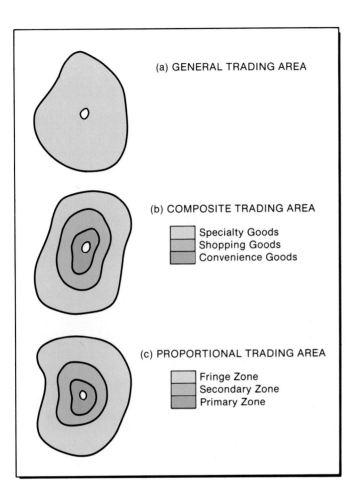

FIGURE 8–6
Trading-area structure

and generally represents 20 to 30 percent of the retailer's total sales volume. From the secondary zone, consumers usually select the store as their second or third shopping choice. The **fringe trading zone** is that area from which the retailer occasionally draws customers (5 to 10 percent of the business). Retailers generally attract customers from this zone either because "they just happened to be in the vicinity" or because they are extremely loyal to the store or its personnel.

## Trading-Area Identification

Two general research approaches for identifying trading areas are spotting techniques and retail gravity procedures. Gravity approaches are more appropriate for the new or expanding retailer, while spotting techniques are more commonly used by the existing retailer seeking to determine the extent of its present trading area.

**Spotting techniques** include several methods by which the retailer attempts to "spot" customer origins on a map. By carefully observing the magnitude and arrangement of these origins, the retailer can identify the dimensions of the trading area. Retailers normally define customer origins by home addresses, although customers' places of employment also are important. For trading-area identification, the most successful spotting techniques not only obtain the customer's address, but also provide information on the customer's buying habits. Some of the more common spotting techniques include surveys of customers' license plates, customer surveys, analyses of customer records, and studies of customer activities.

By recording the license plate numbers of automobiles in the store's parking lot, retailers can obtain customer home addresses. Sampling should include checking license plates at different times of the day, different days of the week, and different weeks of the month to ensure a representative sample. The primary advantage of this technique is that it is relatively inexpensive to administer. License plate surveys have several limitations, including the following: (1) there is no way to determine who actually drove the car to the store, or whether that car represents a regular customer or someone who just happened to be in the neighborhood; (2) a survey of license plates reveals no information on the shopping behavior of customers, such as what they bought, how much they bought, where they bought, why they bought, or if they bought anything at all; (3) the technique provides no customer demographic information, such as age, sex, occupation, and income; and (4) the number of purchasers in each car cannot be determined.

Either a personal interview, mail questionnaire, or telephone survey can provide information on who lives or works in a given area and who either current or potential customers are. Actual customers can be surveyed on the premises (within a particular store or shopping mall) by either personal interviews or take-home/mail-back questionnaires. Good surveying techniques must be employed to ensure an unbiased, representative sample. Customer surveys can provide a significant amount of information regarding demographics and shopping behavior; their limitations are cost, time, and the skill required to conduct them efficiently and effectively.

Retailers have several ways to obtain addresses of current customers as well as additional valuable information. Customer credit, service, and delivery records contain a great deal of information if properly developed and maintained. From their records, retailers can find customer addresses and places of employment, ages, sex, family status, telephone numbers, and types and amounts of purchases. Although customer credit, service, and delivery records are a fast and inexpensive means of obtaining information, they are biased because cash customers, who require no services or delivery, are omitted from the analysis.

Any method that asks or requires customers to provide their names and addresses can help identify an existing or proposed trading area. Promotional activities such as contests and sweepstakes can be effective in obtaining names and addresses. Unfortunately, they tend to be biased toward the consumer who is willing to participate (sometimes, for example, the high-income consumer would not think it worth the time).

Retailers have used several quantitative procedures to delineate retail trading areas. The one most retailers use is the **retail gravitation concept,** which provides a measure of the potential interaction between various locations by determining the relative drawing power of each location.[6] Based on the relative drawing power of a location within an area, each area can be identified as part of a trading area. Retailing analysts have developed several formulations of the gravitation concept, each of which uses a somewhat different procedure to identify trading areas. One of the more widely recognized formulations is Converse's break-even point.

Converse developed a formula that allows the retailer to calculate the break-even point in miles between competing retail centers (stores, shopping centers, or cities).[7] In essence, Converse computes the **break-even point** as the point between the competing retailing centers where the probability of a consumer patronizing each retailing center is equal. This break-even point identifies the trading-area boundary line between competing retail trade centers. By identifying the break-even point between one retail center and all competing centers, the retailer can determine the trading area. The break-even point formula is expressed as

$$BP = \frac{d}{1 + \sqrt{\dfrac{P1}{P2}}}$$

where

$BP$ = break-even point between the competing
retail centers in miles from the smaller center

$d$ = distance between the two competing retail centers

$P1$ = population of the larger retail center

$P2$ = population of the smaller retail center

Both the distance and population expressions require further explanation. Although distance is normally measured in miles, recent studies show that many people think of distance in terms of travel time. Retail analysts can use travel time to replace miles for the distance between competing retail centers. The cost of acquiring the travel-time data might impose a constraint on this approach, however.

Populations ($P1$ and $P2$) can be expressed in several different ways. The total population in each center is the most common measurement. Another approach is to use the center's total number of retailers or the total retail square footage as the population measurement. Any measurement that reflects a retail center's ability to attract customers can be used as an expression of population. Figure 8–7 illustrates the identification of shopping center trading areas using Converse's break-even point method.

---

**EVALUATING TRADING AREAS**

The basic problem of any trading-area evaluation is to answer two questions: (1) what is the total amount of business a trading area can generate now and in the future? and (2) what share of the total business can a retailer in a given location expect to attract? Although there is no standardized trading-area evaluation process, most evaluation procedures use the concepts of trading-area adequacy and trading-area potential to predict total trading-area business and the share of business a particular retailer can expect.

**Trading-area adequacy** is the ability of a trading area to support proposed and existing retail operations. This support capability may be viewed in a gross as well as net form (see Figure 8–8). **Gross adequacy** is the ability of a trading area to support a retail operation without any consideration of retail competition. That is, the gross

**FIGURE 8-7**

A problem using Converse's break-even point formula

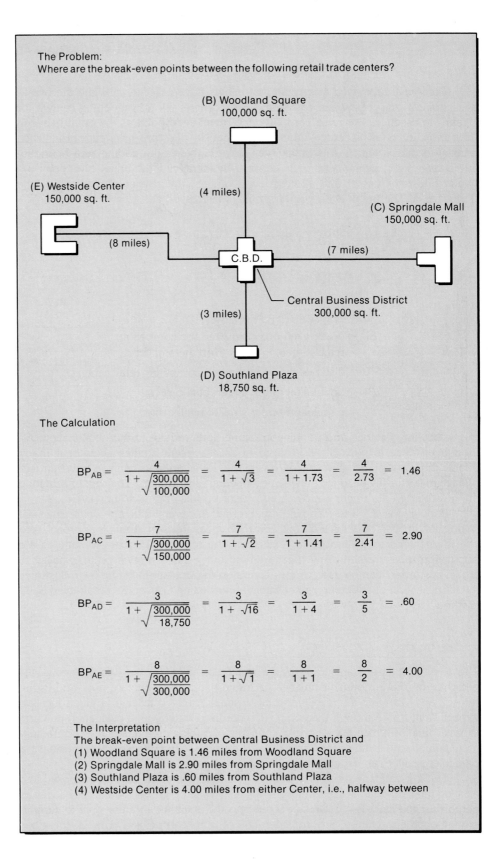

The Problem:
Where are the break-even points between the following retail trade centers?

(B) Woodland Square
100,000 sq. ft.

(E) Westside Center
150,000 sq. ft.

(4 miles)

(C) Springdale Mall
150,000 sq. ft.

(8 miles)

C.B.D.

(7 miles)

Central Business District
300,000 sq. ft.

(3 miles)

(D) Southland Plaza
18,750 sq. ft.

The Calculation

$$BP_{AB} = \frac{4}{1 + \sqrt{\dfrac{300,000}{100,000}}} = \frac{4}{1 + \sqrt{3}} = \frac{4}{1 + 1.73} = \frac{4}{2.73} = 1.46$$

$$BP_{AC} = \frac{7}{1 + \sqrt{\dfrac{300,000}{150,000}}} = \frac{7}{1 + \sqrt{2}} = \frac{7}{1 + 1.41} = \frac{7}{2.41} = 2.90$$

$$BP_{AD} = \frac{3}{1 + \sqrt{\dfrac{300,000}{18,750}}} = \frac{3}{1 + \sqrt{16}} = \frac{3}{1 + 4} = \frac{3}{5} = .60$$

$$BP_{AE} = \frac{8}{1 + \sqrt{\dfrac{300,000}{300,000}}} = \frac{8}{1 + \sqrt{1}} = \frac{8}{1 + 1} = \frac{8}{2} = 4.00$$

The Interpretation
The break-even point between Central Business District and
(1) Woodland Square is 1.46 miles from Woodland Square
(2) Springdale Mall is 2.90 miles from Springdale Mall
(3) Southland Plaza is .60 miles from Southland Plaza
(4) Westside Center is 4.00 miles from either Center, i.e., halfway between

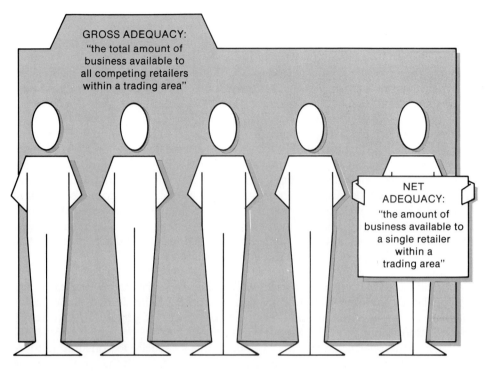

FIGURE 8-8
Elements of trading-area adequacy

adequacy measures the total amount of business available to all competing retailers within a defined trading area. On the other hand, **net adequacy** is the ability of a trading area to provide support for a retailer after competition has been taken into account.

Finally, **trading-area potential** is the predicted ability of a trading area to provide acceptable support levels for a retailer in the future.

## Gross Adequacy of Trading Areas

Measuring gross adequacy determines a trading area's total *capacity to consume*. The capacity of a retail market to consume is a function of the total *number of consumers* within a trading area at any given time and their need, willingness, and ability to purchase a particular class of goods (see Chapter 3 for detailed discussion of these four factors). To determine gross adequacy, the retailer must first consider appropriate consumption units (such as people, homes, businesses, and so forth) to count for a general class of goods. Second, the retailer must find an appropriate measure of a consumption unit's need, willingness, and ability to buy. Finally, the support capabilities of a trading area depend to some extent on sources outside the gross trading area.

After sufficiently identifying the gross trading area, a retailer needs to concentrate on the most important source of business: the area's residents. To measure a trading area's potential consumers, the retailer must analyze population/demographic and household/residential variables.

A trading area's total capacity to consume is partly a function of the total number of people who reside in that trading area. It is important to obtain an accurate population count because the total population figure plays a part in several quantitative estimates of gross and net adequacy. Although total population figures are informative, many experts think these figures need to be qualified in terms of their demographic makeup.

The actual level of support for a given line of products or services that can be expected from persons living in the trading area may come, for example, from those who have an annual income of $25,000 or more and are between the ages of twenty and thirty-five. That is, a trading area's capacity to consume may not be directly related to its total population; instead, it may be a function of the number of people who have a certain demographic makeup—such as age, sex, income, occupation, and family status. For example, measurements such as the number of children (bike store), the number of women (women's clothing store), or the number of high-income homeowners (expensive home furnishings) indicate a population count that should produce more reliable gross adequacy estimates.

Evaluating gross adequacy is a matter of identifying demographic characteristics that best indicate the consumer's need, willingness, and ability to buy and of obtaining a reliable count of the number of people who have the desired demographic makeup. At the local trading-area level, a good source of population and demographic information is the *Census of Population*.

For some retailing operations, a trading area's capacity to consume is more directly related to the *number of households* or *residential units* than to the number of people in the area. For example, a count of household or residential units is probably more indicative than a population count of a trading area's consumption capacity for hardware, furniture, and appliance goods. This relationship simply reflects the fact that the household unit purchases many goods, and the consumer's home is the prime determinant of the need for certain product lines.

A household unit count by tracts and blocks can be obtained from the *Census of Population*. A residential unit count for either census tracts or blocks is available from the *Census of Housing* and can be checked through field observation and air photographs. To reflect their consumption capacity more accurately, each residential unit can be weighted by average value, size, type of construction, and characteristics noted in housing census reports and local building permits.

Although the vast majority of a trading area's consumption capacity comes from people who live in that area, some of the consumption support does not. Consumers who reside outside a trading area contribute significantly to that area's capacity to consume.

Most trading areas are characterized by daily inward, outward, and through-migration of consumers who are attracted into the trading area for work, recreation, and other reasons, such as the need for professional services. Although these consumers might live many miles away, they do represent a significant portion of trade customers who visit the area. Some of these customers visit frequently and regularly (work trip); others visit infrequently and irregularly (recreation trip). Nevertheless, this external consumption capacity should be included in assessing a trading area's gross adequacy.

Although it is impossible to count accurately the number of consumers that make up the external consumption capacity, it *is* possible to count the number of nonresidential units likely to attract consumers to the trading area (e.g., retailers, wholesalers, manufacturers, offices, schools, churches). Since not all nonresidential units have equal consumption-generating abilities, each must be weighted according to its ability to generate traffic. Because some nonresidential units are more compatible with a retail enterprise than others, the weights a retailer assigns to each nonresidential unit should reflect the degree of consumer−retailer compatibility. Although a weighted nonresidential unit count does not fully describe or measure the impact of "outsiders" on the volume of a trading area, it does provide a reasonable estimate of this impact.

Several methods are available to estimate trading-area sales. The two most widely used techniques are the corollary data method and the per capita sales method. The **corollary data method** assumes that an identifiable relationship exists between sales for a particular class of goods and one or more trading-area characteristics (such as population, residential units, etc.). Knowledge of these relationships helps retailers estimate total sales. The **per capita sales method** estimates trading-area sales for a general product line as a function of the per capita expenditures for that product line times the total population of that trading area. As discussed earlier, retailers can obtain reliable population counts from census materials and per capita expenditure figures from consumer surveys and trade-source estimates.

## Net Adequacy of Trading Areas

To answer the question "What is my slice of the pie?" a retailer must estimate the net adequacy of the trading area. Net adequacy has been defined as the proportion of sales volume a retailer can expect to receive from the total sales in a trading area; that is, net adequacy is the percentage of gross adequacy (or market share) a retailer can expect to get. To determine net adequacy, a retailer must consider the trading area's *capacity to consume* and its *capacity to sell*.

The capacity to consume is the gross adequacy measurement. Having obtained a gross estimate of the trading area's sales volume capabilities, the retailer's problem is to find a method of allocating total sales volume to each of the trading area's existing and proposed competitors. This allocation process consists of (1) analyzing the competitive environment and (2) estimating each retailer's sales and market share.

To determine net adequacy, a retailer must first identify the competitive environment. To analyze the competitive environment, the retailer must examine the types of competition and the number and size of competitors. To gain a clearer picture of the competitive environment, a retailer can use two methods: (1) a competitive audit and (2) an outshopper analysis.

A **competitive audit** is an arbitrary, composite rating of each competitor's product, service, price, place, and promotion mixes. An audit covers a wide range of activities including eyeballing competitors' floor space, checking ad results, getting information from media people and vendors, checking competitors' prices, and evaluating the competition's merchandise mix.[8] The purpose of a competitive audit is to assess the ability of competitors to provide a marketing mix that consumers desire within the trading area. The sum of all audits is a measurement of total competition.

Retailers use a competitive audit in several ways. First, they use it to measure the total competition within the trading area (the sum of all competitors times their competitiveness rating). Second, they derive a measure of each competitor's expected share of total trading-area sales. Third, they gain a picture of an unfulfilled product position or "niche" in the trading area. The latter information can help the retailer develop a marketing strategy.

Not all consumers who live within a trading area shop exclusively in that area. A group of consumers known as "outshoppers" frequently and regularly shop outside their local trading area. These consumers spend a considerable amount of time, money, and effort making inter—trading-area shopping trips. One analyst characterizes outshoppers and their shopping behavior this way:

> Some outshoppers are looking for economic gains resulting from lower prices in larger trading centers where assortments are better and the level of competition more intense. Some outshoppers simply *seek* the diversity of unfamiliar or more stimulating surroundings . . . demographically, outshoppers are younger (25–54 year age group), are relatively well educated (had some college), and the relative income is high . . . psychographically outshoppers are active, on the "go," urban-oriented housewives who are neither time-conscious nor store-loyal shoppers. They tend to manifest a distaste for local shopping and hence a strong preference for out-of-town shopping areas.[9]

To obtain an accurate estimate of total expected sales, the retailer must perform **outshopper analysis,** subtracting outshopping sales, referred to as "sales leakage," from the trading area's gross sales to arrive at a more realistic total sales volume for the trading area. To estimate sales leakage that results from outshopping behavior, a retailer can either conduct consumer surveys or use standard adjustments. In using consumer surveys, the retailer asks trading-area consumers to estimate how much they spend locally on a particular class of goods as a percentage of their total expenditures for those goods. The retailer then can use this percentage to adjust the gross sales figure for the trading area.

A simple and less expensive method is the standard adjustment. A standard adjustment figure (e.g., 14 percent) depends on prevailing trading-area conditions. For example, if the trading area contains a large number of consumers who are similar to the demographic and psychographic profile of outshoppers, the retailer should make a standard downward adjustment (e.g., 5 percent) in gross sales. Although estimates of outshopping are not always accurate, the retailer must consider these factors in making a conservative estimate of trading-area net adequacy.

After evaluating the competitive environment, a retailer can estimate each competitor's sales. To calculate a net adequacy (i.e., the trading-area market share) figure, the retailer can use either the "total sales method" or the "sales per square foot method." Both methods use a ratio of trading-area capacity to consume (gross adequacy) to trading area capacity to sell.

With the **total sales method,** a retailer allocates an equal share of the trading area's total sales for a specific product category to each competing retailer. This calculation is shown in Figure 8–9. The advantage of this method is that it is simple and quick to calculate. A limitation, however, is the assumption that all competing retailers are equal and can generate an equal share of the trading-area sales. Because competing retailers devote different amounts of time, money, space, and effort to sales, the analyst must make adjustments to the "all are equal" assumption. The competitive audit, discussed earlier, can be used to make this adjustment.

**FIGURE 8–9**
Total sales method for estimating a retailer's sales

Another method for allocating trading-area sales to competitors is the **sales per square foot method,** whereby the retailer computes a ratio of each retailer's floor space devoted to a specific product category to the total of all retail floor space for the product category in the trading area. The calculation procedure is illustrated in Figure 8–10. This method assumes that selling space is a good predictor of a retailer's competitiveness. Variations of this method substitute amount of shelf space (linear, square, or cubic feet), sales per employee, or sales per checkout counter for sales per square foot.

## Growth Potential of Trading Areas

Before completing the trading-area evaluation process, the retailer must answer an additional question: What does the future hold for the trading area? Because the future of a trading area is an outgrowth of past and current conditions, the retailer often can learn what to expect by examining those conditions. Visual observation of an area is a simple method of looking into the future. Although lacking scientific methodology, visual inspection of current activities can produce a useful picture of the future. A retailer should consider several factors:

1. New and expanding residential areas combined with older, stable neighborhoods provide a solid base for future growth.
2. An expanding commercial or industrial base signals growth opportunities.

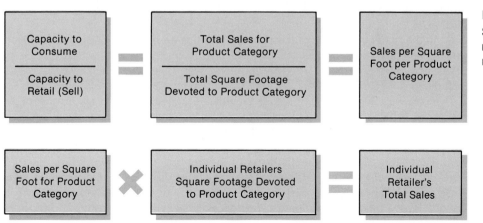

**FIGURE 8–10**
Sales per square foot method for estimating a retailer's sales

3. A good balance between items 1 and 2 reflects a stable growth rate that avoids overdependence on limited economic activity.
4. A well-developed transportation network as well as proposed future transportation networks in the trading area contribute to a trading area's growth.
5. An involved local government that takes an interest in residential and business development is a great asset.
6. A progressive social and cultural environment (theaters, museums, zoos, etc.) is a healthy climate for business.

## SELECTING TRADING AREAS

To make the final selection of a trading area, the retailer must evaluate the alternatives in accordance with each of the following criteria, referred to as a "minimum threshold":

1. A stated minimum population having the desired demographic characteristics (such as 10,000 persons)
2. A stated minimum sales volume (such as $300,000 per year)
3. A stated minimum daily traffic count (such as 5,000 vehicles per day)

If a trading area does not meet at least one or a certain combination of these minimums, the retailer excludes it from further consideration.

## SUMMARY

The retail-location problem is multidimensional. The retailer must identify, evaluate, and select a market area to support a particular operation. Market areas can be delineated as regional markets ("the right region" and the "right part of the region") and local markets (the "right town" and the "right part of town"). Based on census areas, communication areas, functional markets, *ABC* markets, and intraurban markets, the retailer can identify several regional and local market areas.

The market-area evaluation process is an attempt to ascertain a market area's relative potential. Although the retailer is free to develop original sources and methods of evaluation, several standard sources (such as the *Survey of Buying Power* and the *Editor & Publisher Market Guide*) and standard methods (such as the buying power index, quality index, sales activity index, and index of retail saturation) are readily available.

In the market-selection process, the retailer has no magical "rules of thumb" for arriving at a final decision. Instead, the retailer must use judgment and experience to select a market area from the several alternatives that have been identified and evaluated.

A retail trading area is the area from which the retailer attracts all or most of its customers. The size and internal structure of a trading area depend on several factors. Trading-area size is directly related to (1) the type and size of the retailer's operation; (2) the number, size, and type of neighboring stores; (3) the nature and actions of competing stores; and (4) the character of the transportation network. The internal structure of trading areas reflects the relative ability of either a single retailer or a cluster of retailers to attract customers from various distances or customer-source regions. Three internal trading-area structures are general, composite, and proportional.

The problem is how to identify, evaluate, and select trading-area alternatives. Retailers can identify potential trading areas through spotting techniques and retail gravity models. The retailer determines the value of each trading area by first determining its gross and then its net adequacy. To refine the net adequacy further, it then assesses the future growth potential of each area. Gross adequacy is a measure of the trading area's total capacity to consume. This consumption capacity is a function of both residential (those who live inside the trading area) and nonresidential (those who live outside the trading area) consumers. Total trading-area sales can be estimated using either the corollary data method or the per capita sales method.

Net adequacy is the level of support a given retailer can expect to attract from the trading area. A retailer's expectations must depend on the relationship between a trading area's capacity to consume and its capacity to retail. The retailer can estimate the amount of sales it can expect to derive from the trading area by dividing the trading area's capacity to consume by its capacity to retail, using either the total sales method or sales per square foot method. Before selecting which trading-area alternatives to consider further, the retailer should determine the area's future growth potential.

## STUDENT STUDY GUIDE

### KEY TERMS AND CONCEPTS

ABC market

break-even point

buying power index

census market

communication market

competitive audit

composite trading area

corollary data method

*Editor & Publisher Market Guide*

fringe trading zone

general trading area

gross adequacy

index of retail saturation (IRS)

net adequacy

outshopper analysis

overstored market area

per capita sales method

primary trading zone

proportional trading area

retail gravitation concept

retail trading area

sales activity index (SAI)

sales per square foot method

saturated market area

secondary trading zone

spotting technique

*Survey of Buying Power*

total sales method

trading-area adequacy

trading-area potential

understored market area

### REVIEW QUESTIONS

1. Describe how area coverage by various types of broadcast and print media are used in identifying market areas. Provide specific examples.
2. How are ABC markets defined?
3. Identify and describe two standard evaluation sources commonly used by retail analysts to evaluate retail market areas.

4. What do the buying power index and sales activity index measure?
5. How is the formulation of the index of retail saturation expressed? What relationship does it measure? Describe the three market-area classifications resulting from an application of the index.
6. What determines the size and structure of a retail trading area?
7. Describe the various types of composite and proportional trading area zones.
8. Compare and contrast the various types of spotting techniques.
9. How is Converse's break-even point formula expressed? Define each part of the expression.
10. What determines a trading area's capacity to consume? Describe each factor.
11. Describe the two methods for estimating trading area sales.
12. Who are outshoppers? Why are they important? Profile this consumer group.
13. How does the total sales method differ from the sales per square foot method of calculating net adequacy?

---

**REVIEW EXAM**

True or False

_____ 1. The exact definition of what constitutes an A, B, or C market varies from one retailing organization to another.

_____ 2. The *Survey of Buying Power*'s effective buying income measurement is the rough equivalent of disposable personal income.

_____ 3. Overstored market areas are those in which the capacity to consume exceeds the capacity to retail.

_____ 4. The outermost ring of a store's composite trading area is delineated by the demand for the store's convenience goods offering.

_____ 5. The primary advantage of the license plate spotting technique is that it is relatively inexpensive to administer.

_____ 6. When retailers measure gross adequacy, they measure a trading area's total capacity to consume.

_____ 7. An outshopper is a consumer who shops outside his local trading area on a frequent and regular basis.

---

## STUDENT APPLICATIONS MANUAL

---

**PROJECTS: INVESTIGATIONS AND APPLICATIONS**

1. Using the *Census of Population* for 1960, 1970, and 1980, prepare a graphic statistical profile of the population and demographic characteristics of your county (or parish or township). Calculate and illustrate the percentage changes that have occurred over the last three census periods. Identify and explain any patterns that might be of general interest to your local retailing community.

2. Select three different radio stations that are received in your community. Interview the station manager or a sales representative for each of the stations and determine the geographic and class selectivity of each station. Identify the types of retailers that would be best served by each station. Explain your selection.

3. Consult your local library for the most recent issues of the *Survey of Buying Power* and the *Editor & Publisher Market Guide*. Which of these two standard evaluation sources would you prefer to use? Why?

4. Calculate the "sales activity index" for your county.

5. Select a neighborhood within your community that has three or four convenience food stores. Using a map of the area, delineate the primary, secondary, and fringe zones for each of the store's composite trading areas. Illustrate and discuss the impact of any supermarkets within the area.

6. Gain the cooperation of a local retailer and attempt to identify his trading area using one of the spotting techniques—either a survey of license plates or customers or an examination of customer records or activities. Construct a map illustrating the retailer's trading area. Discuss the strengths and weaknesses of the technique used.

7. Using information obtained from the 1987 *Survey of Buying Power,* calculate for San Jose, California, the per capita sales for (1) food products, (2) home products (furniture, furnishings, and appliances), and (3) automotive products.

8. Develop the forms (e.g., questions, rating scales, etc.) and procedures necessary for conducting a competitive audit for a general merchandise retailer.

9. Analyze the retail growth potential of the trading area surrounding (e.g., within five blocks of) your college or university. Identify potentially positive and negative growth factors for existing and potential retailers. Provide some specific examples of retailing opportunities that might develop in the next ten years and explain the reasons you think these opportunities exist.

---

## CASE 8–1
### The Electronic Mall—Identifying and Evaluating Market Areas*

**CASES: PROBLEMS AND DECISIONS**

"I think your mall is excellent!" "I think that your mall is a wonderful place and I will be shopping here often." "I've used The Mall frequently and have found the service to be excellent, keep up the good work." "What a great idea. Now I will not have to go throughout our fair city looking for gifts for those I know little about. This is my first time on board, and I am looking forward to browsing again." "I would first like to say I'm very impressed with The Mall."

The above are but a few of the encouraging customer comments received by the mall manager. In this case, the mall is THE ELECTRONIC MALL, a shop-at-home service that enables personal computer owners to purchase goods and services via computer; this videotex shopping mall is owned and operated by CompuServe Incorporated of Columbus, Ohio. The Mall is open 24 hours a day, 365 days a year, and offers thousands of brand-name products at the touch of a keystroke.

Shoppers enter THE ELECTRONIC MALL using a personal computer and a telephone modem. Shoppers can browse The Mall by keying in "This week's Mall News"—a comprehensive product index, or a directory of all Mall merchants. Questions are promptly answered by the mall manager, an on-line representative. To make a purchase, the customer keys in the selected product together with his or her credit card number. The system reviews the selection and captures the order. Orders are then sent to a designated address via express mail or some other delivery service. Buyers receive an electronic receipt that is sent to their own on-line mailboxes. If a customer has a question about a product or a bill, he or she can send a message directly to the merchant, who will respond via electronic mail.

---

*This case was prepared by Dale Lewison and John Thanopoulos, The University of Akron, and Charles R. Patton, Pan American University. Materials for the case were obtained from promotional brochures, press releases, and advertisements supplied by CompuServe Incorporated of Columbus, Ohio.

The Mall layout and design may not look like a "bricks and mortar" facility, but it is organized into departments. A retailer can focus on one department or display merchandise in several departments. The Mall is laid out into sixteen departments:

☐ Apparel & Accessories      ☐ On-line Services

☐ Automotive      ☐ Premium Merchants

☐ Books & Periodicals      ☐ Music & Movies

☐ Gifts & Novelties      ☐ Health & Beauty

☐ Computing      ☐ Financial

☐ Gourmet & Flowers      ☐ Travel & Entertainment

☐ Hobbies & Toys      ☐ Office Supplies

☐ Merchandise & Electronics      ☐ Sports & Leisure

Electronic shopping, a phenomenon of the Information Age, is one of the ways retailers are reaching a lucrative market of busy consumers who want to shop at home. It is a direct marketing technique that takes the store to the market rather that attracting the market to the store.

### ASSIGNMENT

1. Identify and delineate the market area for THE ELECTRONIC MALL.
2. Profile and characterize the typical consumer (i.e., targeted market) who patronizes The Mall.
3. List and describe the advantages and disadvantages of this mall location for the consumer and for the retailer.
4. Describe the type of retailing format (products, prices, promotions) that is most compatible with this type of mall. Explain.

### CASE 8–2
## Jacobson's Dilemma: Location of a "Fancy" Restaurant*

### BACKGROUND

Up to now, George Jacobson had felt pretty good about all his decisions and activities in starting his own restaurant. Jacobson had been a military chef in the officers' mess at Fort Belvoir but had recently retired after 22 years in the service. Too young at 45 to simply "take it easy," Jacobson had decided to start a restaurant in Smithville, a central city in a three-county SMSA. The restaurant was positioned as a plush, moderately expensive lunch and dinner and cocktail bar type of restaurant featuring continental cuisine. Two shopping center locations were under consideration: Pinnacle Plaza and Hidden Valley Shopping Mall. Both of the intramall locations were comparable in terms of size/space, rent, and traffic, but Jacobson suspected that the shopping centers might differ considerably in terms of their trading-area characteristics.

### CURRENT SITUATION

Having spent the last three weeks collecting and organizing data on each retail center and its trading area, Jacobson believes he is ready to evaluate each center's potential as a loca-

*This case was prepared by J. B. Wilkinson, The University of Akron.

tion for a fancy restaurant. The data he has compiled concern the locational attributes of each center, the population and income characteristics of a surrounding census tracts, and the retail tenant mix found within the city and each of its major retailing centers.

## Location Characteristics

Exhibit 1 shows the location of both shopping malls in Smithville. Pinnacle Plaza (MRC 1) draws Smithville shoppers primarily from the area north of U.S. Route 72 (Census Tracts 2.01, 2.02, 3.01, 3.02, 4.01, 4.02, 5.01, 5.02, 5.03, 6.01, 6.02, 7.01, 7.02, 8, 11, and 13); Hidden Valley (MRC 3) attracts Smithville shoppers primarily from areas south of State Route 1 (Census Tracts 19.01, 19.02, 19.03, 20, 21, 22, 23, 24, 25.01, 25.02, 26, 27.01, 27.02, 28.01, 28.02, 29.01, and 29.02). In addition, Pinnacle Plaza attracts shoppers from

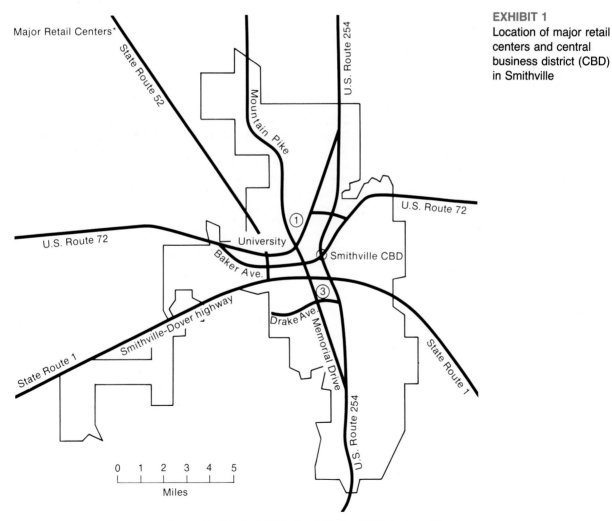

**EXHIBIT 1**

Location of major retail centers and central business district (CBD) in Smithville

*Concentration of retail stores (located inside the MSA but outside the CBD) having at least $5 million in retail sales and at least 10 retail establishments, one of which was classified as a department store (SIC 531).

northern areas outside Smithville. Mountain View (pop. 30,000) is 40 miles north of Smithville on State Route 52; Pikesville (pop. 10,000) is 20 miles north on Mountain Pike; and Jolson (pop. 15,000) is 25 miles north on U.S. Route 254. The mountainous areas to the east of Smithville are relatively unpopulated; however, Hidden Valley attracts shoppers from southern areas outside Smithville, notably Dover (pop. 30,000), which is 25 miles southwest of Smithville on State Route 1, and Marshall (pop. 25,000), which is 15 miles away on U.S. Route 254.

### Population/Income Characteristics

Exhibit 2 contains selected population and income characteristics for all census tracts that comprise each of the shopping centers' primary drawing areas.

### Major Retail Center Characteristics

The retail store mix characteristics of the major retail centers (i.e., Pinnacle Plaza and Hidden Valley), the central business district of Smithville, the City of Smithville, and the Smithville SMSA are shown in Exhibit 3, which also indicates the number of competitors.

### Additional Information

Additional information collected by George Jacobson included the following:

1. Approximately 8 percent of family median income is spent on dining out (*Expenditure Patterns of the American Family*).
2. Average sales per eating and drinking place in the United States were $172,000, with approximately 5.0 eating and drinking places per 1,000 households in the United States in 1977 (*U.S. Bureau of the Census* and *Census of Retail Trade, 1977*).
3. Pinnacle Plaza had approximately 16,000 sq. ft. of floor space allocated to eating and drinking establishments. The eating and drinking establishments in Hidden Valley occupied approximately 55,000 sq. ft. (estimated by Jacobson).
4. The number of eating and drinking establishments in the market areas of Pinnacle Plaza and Hidden Valley was 100 and 94, respectively (estimated by Jacobson).

### ASSIGNMENT

Assume the role of a consultant and advise George Jacobson. Which location do you recommend as the preferred site for his restaurant? Provide Jacobson with a complete justification for your recommendation.

| | SMSA | Smithville City | Tract 2.01 | Tract 2.02 | Tract 3.01 | Tract 3.02 |
|---|---|---|---|---|---|---|
| **AGE** | | | | | | |
| Total persons | 308,593 | 142,513 | 821 | 4,255 | 5,313 | 4,335 |
| | | | | | | |
| 3 and 4 years | 8,274 | 3,572 | 21 | 83 | 172 | 147 |
| 16 yrs and over | 230,134 | 107,383 | 624 | 3,588 | 3,741 | 2,944 |
| 18 yrs and over | 217,498 | 101,377 | 590 | 3,433 | 3,482 | 2,718 |
| 21 yrs and over | 198,327 | 92,294 | 527 | 2,242 | 3,148 | 2,478 |
| 60 yrs and over | 38,970 | 15,076 | 120 | 273 | 387 | 241 |
| 62 yrs and over | 33,840 | 12,844 | 100 | 229 | 314 | 205 |
| Median | 29.1 | 28.9 | 26.7 | 21.4 | 25.9 | 25.1 |
| **INCOME in 1979** | | | | | | |
| Households | 106,369 | 50,790 | 292 | 854 | 1,601 | 1,228 |
| Median | $15,472 | $17,843 | $11,023 | $16,741 | $16,542 | $17,476 |
| Mean | 18,678 | 21,424 | 16,716 | 17,899 | 19,419 | 18,501 |
| | | | | | | |
| Families | 84,881 | 38,746 | 238 | 743 | 1,405 | 1,101 |
| Median | $17,565 | $20,920 | $11,989 | $16,956 | $17,181 | $17,816 |
| Mean | 20,739 | 24,179 | 18,810 | 18,236 | 20,110 | 19,054 |
| | | | | | | |
| Per capita income | $6,488 | $7,661 | $6,055 | $3,921 | $5,789 | $5,284 |

| | Tract 4.01 | Tract 4.02 | Tract 5.01 | Tract 5.02 | Tract 5.03 | Tract 6.01 | Tract 6.02 |
|---|---|---|---|---|---|---|---|
| **AGE** | | | | | | | |
| Total persons | 813 | 3,970 | 2,401 | 3,291 | 2,409 | 1,917 | 2,716 |
| | | | | | | | |
| 3 and 4 years | 27 | 124 | 69 | 105 | 73 | 31 | 55 |
| 16 yrs and over | 538 | 2,724 | 1,685 | 2,263 | 1,704 | 1,438 | 2,058 |
| 18 yrs and over | 492 | 2,519 | 1,552 | 2,110 | 1,577 | 1,329 | 1,921 |
| 21 yrs and over | 453 | 2,296 | 1,401 | 1,887 | 1,437 | 1,192 | 1,749 |
| 60 yrs and over | 26 | 214 | 121 | 163 | 130 | 132 | 228 |
| 62 yrs and over | 21 | 168 | 95 | 139 | 108 | 101 | 203 |
| Median | 26.4 | 27.1 | 25.2 | 26.9 | 29.7 | 29.7 | 30.3 |
| **INCOME in 1979** | | | | | | | |
| Households | 224 | 1,167 | 698 | 970 | 737 | 591 | 928 |
| Median | $22,262 | $21,427 | $22,917 | $15,794 | $19,480 | $23,995 | $22,567 |
| Mean | 21,789 | 23,367 | 24,088 | 17,270 | 22,309 | 25,411 | 21,905 |
| | | | | | | | |
| Families | 203 | 1,053 | 665 | 843 | 649 | 534 | 825 |
| Median | $22,841 | $22,361 | $24,063 | $16,599 | $19,234 | $24,750 | $23,511 |
| Mean | 22,284 | 24,211 | 24,695 | 17,956 | 21,738 | 26,440 | 22,944 |
| | | | | | | | |
| Per capita income | $5,582 | $6,888 | $6,952 | $5,211 | $6,757 | $7,431 | $7,484 |

**EXHIBIT 2**
Population/Income characteristics for selected census tracts, Smithville SMSA, 1980

| | Tract 7.01 | Tract 7.02 | Tract 8 | Tract 11 | Tract 13 | Tract 19.01 | Tract 19.02 |
|---|---|---|---|---|---|---|---|
| **AGE** | | | | | | | |
| Total persons | 4,136 | 2,095 | 2,858 | 1,950 | 4,130 | 3,105 | 820 |
| | | | | | | | |
| 3 and 4 years | 117 | 54 | 78 | 67 | 77 | 64 | 16 |
| 16 yrs and over | 3,057 | 1,615 | 2,176 | 1,346 | 3,333 | 2,378 | 600 |
| 18 yrs and over | 2,885 | 1,540 | 2,076 | 1,260 | 3,209 | 2,213 | 543 |
| 21 yrs and over | 2,612 | 1,437 | 1,930 | 1,156 | 2,856 | 2,100 | 510 |
| 60 yrs and over | 254 | 401 | 421 | 353 | 280 | 412 | 53 |
| 62 yrs and over | 201 | 373 | 373 | 314 | 218 | 335 | 38 |
| Median | 25.8 | 31.3 | 28.9 | 26.6 | 26.7 | 37.9 | 37.2 |
| **INCOME in 1979** | | | | | | | |
| Households | 1,447 | 847 | 1,126 | 602 | 1,729 | 1,076 | 249 |
| Median | $16,865 | $11,911 | $11,458 | $6,463 | $17,899 | $31,303 | $40,510 |
| Mean | 18,333 | 14,316 | 13,347 | 8,490 | 19,003 | 38,551 | 42,356 |
| | | | | | | | |
| Families | 1,124 | 523 | 755 | 433 | 993 | 925 | 249 |
| Median | $18,289 | $17,557 | $12,392 | $7,262 | $20,040 | $35,428 | $40,510 |
| Mean | 20,079 | 18,269 | 14,744 | 9,604 | 21,617 | 42,738 | 42,356 |
| | | | | | | | |
| Per capita income | $6,332 | $5,873 | $5,245 | $2,742 | $8,067 | $13,652 | $12,573 |

| | Tract 19.03 | Tract 20 | Tract 21 | Tract 22 | Tract 23 | Tract 24 | Tract 25.01 |
|---|---|---|---|---|---|---|---|
| **AGE** | | | | | | | |
| Total persons | 2,084 | 2,555 | 5,207 | 2,961 | 5,793 | 5,011 | 2,125 |
| | | | | | | | |
| 3 and 4 years | 24 | 50 | 192 | 96 | 141 | 156 | 67 |
| 16 yrs and over | 1,630 | 2,207 | 3,896 | 2,357 | 4,451 | 3,766 | 1,679 |
| 18 yrs and over | 1,494 | 2,151 | 3,728 | 2,291 | 4,255 | 3,606 | 1,626 |
| 21 yrs and over | 1,406 | 2,051 | 3,406 | 2,103 | 3,870 | 3,143 | 1,445 |
| 60 yrs and over | 240 | 675 | 1,039 | 378 | 617 | 239 | 171 |
| 62 yrs and over | 178 | 582 | 942 | 336 | 511 | 185 | 142 |
| Median | 40.8 | 43.2 | 28.0 | 27.5 | 28.1 | 24.8 | 25.6 |
| **INCOME in 1979** | | | | | | | |
| Households | 713 | 1,197 | 2,133 | 1,182 | 2,209 | 2,014 | 1,054 |
| Median | $44,430 | $16,720 | $7,339 | $13,921 | $14,857 | $13,187 | $11,217 |
| Mean | 48,089 | 17,735 | 8,939 | 16,446 | 16,644 | 14,861 | 14,056 |
| | | | | | | | |
| Families | 665 | 825 | 1,322 | 768 | 1,593 | 1,389 | 541 |
| Median | $44,430 | $16,720 | $ 9,855 | $15,211 | $16,632 | $15,578 | $12,792 |
| Mean | 50,245 | 20,697 | 10,345 | 17,510 | 18,533 | 16,510 | 15,620 |
| | | | | | | | |
| Per capita income | $16,262 | $8,304 | $3,693 | $6,617 | $6,425 | $5,994 | $7,116 |

**EXHIBIT 2**
*continued*

| | Tract 25.02 | Tract 26 | Tract 27.01 | Tract 27.02 | Tract 28.01 | Tract 28.02 | Tract 29.01 |
|---|---|---|---|---|---|---|---|
| **AGE** | | | | | | | |
| Total persons | 1,886 | 4,513 | 2,021 | 7,111 | 3,469 | 1,953 | 7,154 |
| | | | | | | | |
| 3 and 4 years | 52 | 65 | 26 | 156 | 72 | 75 | 179 |
| 16 yrs and over | 1,490 | 3,714 | 1,633 | 5,265 | 2,606 | 1,403 | 4,993 |
| 18 yrs and over | 1,430 | 3,546 | 1,525 | 4,872 | 2,483 | 1,323 | 4,586 |
| 21 yrs and over | 1,331 | 3,338 | 1,420 | 4,552 | 2,293 | 1,221 | 4,262 |
| 60 yrs and over | 96 | 736 | 242 | 496 | 245 | 92 | 311 |
| 62 yrs and over | 69 | 641 | 184 | 391 | 192 | 69 | 241 |
| Median | 26.2 | 37.8 | 43.7 | 32.8 | 29.5 | 27.9 | 31.2 |
| **INCOME in 1979** | | | | | | | |
| Households | 882 | 1,915 | 642 | 2,442 | 1,341 | 674 | 2,140 |
| Median | $15,745 | $22,789 | $38,125 | $32,167 | $23,260 | $23,351 | $30,607 |
| Mean | 18,189 | 26,480 | 38,404 | 35,217 | 24,504 | 25,510 | 32,549 |
| | | | | | | | |
| Families | 523 | 1,294 | 599 | 2,061 | 917 | 569 | 2,006 |
| Median | $15,993 | $27,753 | $39,489 | $34,769 | $29,275 | $25,474 | $31,073 |
| Mean | 15,886 | 31,292 | 40,016 | 38,500 | 29,242 | 27,489 | 33,214 |
| | | | | | | | |
| Per capita income | $8,494 | $11,223 | $12,718 | $12,008 | $9,588 | $8,563 | $9,609 |

| | Tract 29.02 |
|---|---|
| **AGE** | |
| Total persons | 3,908 |
| | |
| 3 and 4 years | 126 |
| 16 yrs and over | 2,674 |
| 18 yrs and over | 2,505 |
| 21 yrs and over | 2,339 |
| 60 yrs and over | 125 |
| 62 yrs and over | 109 |
| Median | 28.5 |
| **INCOME in 1979** | |
| Households | 1,172 |
| Median | $26,654 |
| Mean | 27,211 |
| | |
| Familes | 1,068 |
| Median | $27,165 |
| Mean | 27,882 |
| | |
| Per capita income | $8,376 |

**EXHIBIT 2**
*continued*

| SIC Code | Kind of Business | Standard Metropolitan Statistical Area | City | Central Business District | Major Retail Centers | |
|---|---|---|---|---|---|---|
| | | | | | No. 1 | No. 3 |
| | Retail stores | | | | | |
| | Number | 2,574 | 1,208 | 158 | 48 | 77 |
| | Sales (1,000) | 941,530 | (D) | 111,086 | 43,221 | 66,452 |
| 54, 58, 591 | Convenience goods stores | | | | | |
| | Number | 810 | 379 | 35 | 10 | 20 |
| | Sales (1,000) | (D) | (D) | 8,562 | 8,269 | 10,245 |
| 53, 56, 57 594 | Shopping goods stores | | | | | |
| | Number | 726 | 375 | 73 | 33 | 40 |
| | Sales (1,000) | 239,539 | (D) | 43,066 | 34,095 | 36,511 |
| 52, 55, 59 ex. 591, 4, 6 | All other stores | | | | | |
| | Number | 1,038 | 454 | 50 | 5 | 17 |
| | Sales (1,000) | (D) | (D) | 59,458 | 857 | 19,696 |
| 58 | Eating and drinking places | | | | | |
| | Number | 332 | 214 | 20 | 4 | 13 |
| | Sales (1,000) | 69,875 | 53,303 | 5,203 | (D) | (D) |

**EXHIBIT 3**
Characteristics of major retail centers and the central business district in the Smithville SMSA, 1977

**ENDNOTES**

1. See Peter S. Carusone and Brenda J. Moscove, "Special Marketing Problems of Smaller City Retailing," *Journal of the Academy of Marketing Science* 13 (Summer 1985): 198–211.
2. 1987 *Survey of Buying Power, Sales, and Marketing Management,* 27 July 1987, C-3.
3. Ibid.
4. Ibid., C-5.
5. The following discussion is based on Bernard J. LaLonde, "New Frontiers in Store Location," *Supermarket Merchandising* (February 1963): 110.
6. See Howard L. Green, "Retail Sales Forecasting Systems," *Journal of Retailing* 62 (Fall 1986): 227–230.
7. Based on classic works of Paul D. Converse, *Retail Trade Areas in Illinois,* Business Study No. 4 (Urbana, IL: University of Illinois 1946): 30–31.
8. Lewis A. Spalding, "Strategies for Share-Boosting," *Stores* (June 1986): 11.
9. Fred D. Reynolds and William R. Darden, "International Patronage: A Psychographic Study of Consumer Outshopping," *Journal of Marketing* 36 (October 1972): 50–54.

# 9

## Objectives

☐ Classify and characterize the various types of site alternatives.

☐ Identify and use the five principles of site evaluation to assess the value of alternative sites.

☐ Describe and apply the basic method of retail site evaluation.

☐ Make a final site-selection decision through the process of elimination.

# Retail Site Location

**A** retail site is the actual physical location from which a retail business operates. Specialists in the retailing field comment that a retailer's site is one of the principal tools for obtaining and maintaining a competitive advantage through spatial monopoly. A given site is unique when its "positional qualities" serve a particular trading-area consumer in a way that no other site can match. Obviously, competing sites also are uniquely situated. The *retailer's site problem,* therefore, is how to identify, to evaluate, and to select the best available site alternative to profitably serve the needs of an identified trading-area consumer.

The first step in appraising retail site locations is to identify all potential site alternatives. The number of site alternatives in any given trading area can range from an extremely limited to a very large selection. Before attempting any formal evaluation, the retailer should screen the alternatives by asking three questions:

- ☐ **Availability**—Is the site available for rent or purchase?
- ☐ **Suitability**—Are the site and facilities of a suitable size and structure?
- ☐ **Acceptability**—Is the asking rental rate within the retailer's operating budget? Rent varies according to location, type, and size of retailing cluster, and market size and quality. While averages can be misleading, rents range from $5 to $15 per square foot for neighborhood centers, $8 to $20 for community centers, and $15 to $40 for regional centers.[1]

To be considered for further evaluation, a site alternative must meet all three screening criteria: it must be available, suitable, and acceptable.

Retail sites can be classified as either isolated or clustered. **Isolated sites** are retail locations that are geographically separated from other retailing sites. They can, however, be located next to other forms of economic and social activity. **Clustered sites** are retail locations that are either next to each other or in close proximity. From a shopping perspective, a cluster is two or more closely located retailers capable of sharing customers with minimal effort. Retail clusters are of two types: unplanned and planned. An *unplanned retail cluster* is the result of a natural evolutionary process; a *planned retail cluster* is the result of planning.

## The Isolated Site

One site alternative is to "go it alone" by selecting an absolute location isolated from other retailers. The degree of physical isolation can range from "around the corner and down the block" to "far out on the outskirts of town." In relative location terms, an isolated site is situated so that it will not normally share consumer traffic with other retailers; however, its relative location offers certain advantages in attracting customers from other sources of business. Generally, the retailer that selects an isolated site is seeking to gain either a monopolistic or an operational advantage.

**Monopolistic isolation** is a site that affords the retailer a uniquely convenient and accessible location to serve consumers. A monopolistically isolated site is isolated from competing retail sites but is uniquely situated for traffic-generating activities. Examples are a convenience-food store in a residential area, a neighborhood bar, a local service station, and a cafeteria located in an office complex. An example of monopolistic isolation familiar to students is the local campus bookstore.

Some retailers prefer to locate in isolated areas because they think it gives them greater flexibility in operating a retail business. A retailer that uses such an **operational isolation** strategy can achieve flexibility in *site geography* (site alternatives that meet the size, shape, and terrain requirements of the retailer's operation constitute site geography), *transportation network* (site alternatives that have transportation networks that generate good consumer traffic and also have good supply connections), *type of facilities* (site alternatives that permit installation of facilities that are conducive to the retailer's operations), *operating methods* (site alternatives that offer the retailer freedom of operation and avoidance of group rules that are common to shopping centers), and *operating costs* (site alternatives that give the retailer the opportunity to operate within the business's cost constraints).

## The Unplanned Clustered Site

Before widespread urban planning and zoning laws, "unplanned" retailing clusters sprang up, many of which still exist. In cities where local zoning ordinances are not strictly enforced, they continue to form. Unplanned retailing clusters are often part of larger unplanned business districts where retailers can be either clustered together or scattered with no discernible pattern. The four general types of unplanned clusters are the central business district, the secondary business district, the neighborhood business district, and the string-strip shopping cluster. A strong downtown retailing cluster is North Michigan Avenue in Chicago. In recent years this downtown area has attracted many of the nation's leading merchandisers: Bloomingdale's, Saks Fifth Avenue, Lord & Taylor, and Bonwit Teller from New York; I. Magnin from San Francisco; Neiman-Marcus from Dallas; and a host of other well-known specialty stores.[2]

The **central business district (CBD)** was, and in many cities still is, the single most important retailing cluster. Since World War II, the CBD has declined in its role as the city's principal place to shop, but despite its problems and predictions of its extinction, it and the retailing clusters within it have survived. In fact, some cities are experiencing a renaissance. Revitalized CBDs have resulted from the following efforts:

☐ Converting streets to pedestrian malls
☐ Modernizing physical facilities

What are the advantages and disadvantages of shopping in the central business district (CBD)?

- [ ] Reducing traffic congestion with one-way streets and modern traffic-control devices
- [ ] Constructing new middle- and upper-income residential complexes
- [ ] Renovating low-income residential areas
- [ ] Organizing commercial businesses to develop and promote the downtown area

Whereas some CBD revitalization projects have been extremely successful, others have failed. Successful revitalization projects include the Nicollet Mall in Minneapolis, Ghirardelli Square in San Francisco, Faneuil Hall Marketplace in Boston, and the Gallery at Market Street East in Philadelphia. The key to successful revitalization projects is not so much the development of new and existing facilities, but the creation of a safe and pleasant shopping atmosphere. "Festival marketplaces" have long been a key to reversing the flight from center cities and in developing the environment for a successful retail cluster.[3]

Most medium- and large-size cities have one or more **secondary business districts (SBDs),** located at the intersections of major traffic arteries. Some of these SBDs were originally the downtown areas of cities that were later incorporated into larger cities. Others represent the natural evolution of a retailing cluster to meet the convenience shopping needs of adjacent neighborhoods. A typical SBD generally varies from 10 to 30 stores, radiating from one or more major intersections along primary traffic arteries.

The typical store mix of an SBD includes one or two branch department stores (or some other mass merchandiser) that serve as the principal consumer attraction; several specialty, shopping, and convenience goods retailers; and various service establishments, including hair-care, dry cleaning, laundry, insurance, and real-estate services. Often one or more large, nonretailing generators (e.g., hospital, office complex, university, manufacturing plant) are in the immediate vicinity of an SBD.

The **neighborhood business district (NBD)** is a small retailing cluster that serves primarily one or two residential areas. The NBD generally contains four to five stores, usually including some combination of food and drugstores, gasoline service stations,

What are the positional strengths of this type of shopping cluster?

neighborhood bars, self-service laundries, barber shops, beauty shops, and small, general-merchandise stores. The most common structural arrangement for the NBD is the "four-corners" layout, with a retailer situated on each corner. Although the four-corners layout is generally associated with secondary and residential streets, these streets represent the major "feeder" into the adjacent residential neighborhoods.

The **string/strip cluster** develops along a major thoroughfare and depends on the consumption activity of people who travel these busy thoroughfares. The size of the string (or strip) is directly related to the average volume of traffic along a thoroughfare. Some strings stretch for miles along the heavily traveled arteries leading in and out of a CBD, whereas others are limited to one or two blocks along streets carrying a lower density of traffic. Examples of long strips are those with new and used car lots, rows of mobile home dealerships, and a strand of side-by-side fast-food restaurants.

### The Planned Clustered Site

Over the last several decades, the growth of suburban populations has given retailers the opportunity to meet the needs of the suburban shopper. The most common solution was (and still is) a one-stop shopping institution such as a planned shopping center. Through careful planning, a developer could offer a merchandise mix—products, services, prices—to meet most customer needs for convenience, shopping, and specialty goods.

A planned shopping center is "a group of commercial establishments planned, developed, owned, and managed as a unit related in location, size, and type of shops to the trade area the unit serves."[4] Shopping centers vary in nature according to their tenants and the size of the markets they serve. On the basis of type and size, shopping centers are classified as regional, community, neighborhood, and specialty centers. Figure 9–1 shows sales performance (sales per square foot) for various types of retailers at different types of malls. Occupancy costs (total charges equals

| Types of Retailers | Super Regional | Regional | Community | Neighborhood |
|---|---|---|---|---|
| Cameras | 553 | 425 | — | — |
| Jewelry | 447 | 380 | 207 | 161 |
| Key shop | 362 | — | — | — |
| Computers/calculators | 359 | — | 130 | — |
| Cookie shop | 320 | 188 | — | — |
| Leather shop | 313 | 243 | — | — |
| Film-processing store | 295 | 217 | 165 | 141 |
| Costume jewelry | 294 | 274 | — | — |
| Optometrist | 287 | 175 | 150 | — |
| Photocopy/fast printing | 285 | 163 | 132 | 92 |
| Tobacco | 281 | 258 | 114 | — |
| Candy and nuts | 282 | 239 | 176 | 7 |
| Radio/video/stereo | 280 | 230 | 150 | 143 |
| Records and tapes | 245 | 229 | 148 | — |
| Eyeglasses/optician | 246 | 220 | 150 | 119 |
| Athletic footwear | 252 | 219 | 130 | — |
| Superstore (over 30,000 sq. ft.) | — | — | 318 | 307 |
| Supermarket (over 6,000 sq. ft.) | — | — | 291 | 279 |
| Liquor and wine | 159 | — | 186 | 170 |
| Ladies' shoes | 194 | 166 | 163 | 72 |
| Drugstore | 182 | 184 | 156 | 144 |
| Fast food/carryout | 262 | 215 | 155 | 148 |
| Super drugstore | 153 | 173 | 140 | 152 |
| Ladies' specialty | 189 | 169 | 118 | 138 |

Source: *Dollars & Cents of Shopping Centers: 1987* (ULI—the Urban Land Institute, 1987, 1200 18th St. NW, Washington, DC 20036).

**FIGURE 9–1**
Sales performance for various types of retailers at different types of malls ($ sales per square foot)

rent plus common area maintenance [CAM] charges) as a percentage of sales are shown in Figure 9–2.

Regional shopping centers serve regional markets varying in size according to the type of transportation network serving the center, the location of competing centers and unplanned business districts, the willingness of consumers to travel various distances to shop, and the tenant mix. The Urban Land Institute identifies two types of regional shopping centers: a **super regional shopping center** is built around at least three and often four major department stores; a **regional shopping center** is built around one or two full-line department stores.[5] Typical sizes range from 400,000 to 600,000 square feet of gross leasable area (GLA) for the regional center to 750,000 to 1,000,000 square feet of GLA for the super regional center.

Regional and super regional centers provide consumers with an extensive assortment of convenience, shopping, and specialty goods as well as numerous personal and professional service facilities. The trend in tenant mix for shopping centers is "mixed-use developments" (MXDs). In addition to retailing establishments, these MXDs might include office buildings, recreational and entertainment facilities, residential units, hotels, government buildings, wholesaling, and light manufacturing.[6] This extensive assortment is achieved through a balanced tenancy of some 50 to 150 individual stores.

| Types of Retailers | Super Regional | Regional | Community | Neighborhood |
|---|---|---|---|---|
| Ladies' ready-to-wear | 9.91 | 9.12 | 8.04 | 7.92 |
| Jewelry | 8.08 | 7.56 | 7.06 | — |
| Fast food/carryout | 14.69 | 13.22 | 9.71 | 7.14 |
| Men's wear | 9.68 | 9.29 | — | — |
| Ladies' shoes | 11.34 | 10.77 | — | — |
| Family shoes | 10.41 | 12.03 | 8.69 | — |
| Cards and gifts | 13.09 | 12.12 | 11.36 | — |
| Ladies' specialty | 9.74 | 9.61 | 9.07 | — |
| Men's and boys' shoes | 11.12 | — | — | — |
| Unisex/jeans shop | 10.34 | 8.95 | — | — |
| Books and stationery | 9.49 | 9.06 | — | — |
| Restaurant with liquor | — | — | 7.59 | 8.50 |
| Beauty | — | — | 10.27 | 10.62 |
| Medical/dental | — | — | 9.32 | 10.39 |
| Restaurant without liquor | — | — | 7.59 | 9.23 |
| Cleaners and dyers | — | — | — | 12.57 |
| Supermarket (over 6,000 sq. ft.) | — | — | — | 1.51 |
| Drugstore | — | — | — | 3.88 |
| Videotape rentals | — | — | — | 12.61 |

Source: *Dollars & Cents of Shopping Centers: 1987.* (ULI—the Urban Land Institute, 1987, 1200 18th St. NW, Washington, DC 20036).

**FIGURE 9–2**

Facilities' cost (total charges as a percentage of sales) for various types of retailers at different types of malls (%)

Shopping centers are designed in a variety of shapes and arrangements. A given configuration must conform to the site's terrain and the tenants' space requirements, as well as provide ease of customer movement. While any number of configurations are possible, Figure 9–3 illustrates four basic shopping center configurations. The "I" plan is the simplest and most common regional shopping center configuration (Figure 9–3a). Although the "I" plan is efficient for retailer space requirements and customer movement, it does not create an interesting and exciting shopping environment.

For regional and super regional centers containing three or more major anchors, retailers can use either the "Y" plan (Figure 9–3b) or the "L" plan (Figure 9–3c). Examples of a modified "Y" plan include the TownEast Shopping Center in Mesquite, Texas, near Dallas; the Pompano Fashion Square in Pompano Beach, Florida; and the Santa Anita Fashion Park in Arcadia, California. Tysons Corner Center in Fairfax County, Virginia, and the North Park Mall in Dallas, Texas, represent modifications of the basic "L" plan.

The "X" plan serves as the basic configuration for the four-anchor, super regional center (Figure 9–3d). The best example of this configuration is Crossroads Center in Oklahoma City.

Regardless of the configuration, a key feature of most super regional and regional shopping centers is a central court. Some super regional centers also have several smaller secondary courts, each with its own character and decor. The importance of courts lies in their image-creating role. The central court is what consumers remember most often and most vividly. Hence, in recent years, more and more emphasis has been placed on court design. As one shopping center specialist writes:

. . . concentrate on excellence in the design of courts—on such various exciting
features as glass space-frame domes, special lighting fixtures, sculptural fountains,
landscaped areas, specially designed staircases, escalators, glass-enclosed elevators
(for multilevel centers) and important art work. The design of the graphics—
directional signs, banners, central symbols, and the choice of colors—also becomes
an important element in the total impact on the shopper. . . . The main court, in

**FIGURE 9–3**
Shopping center configurations

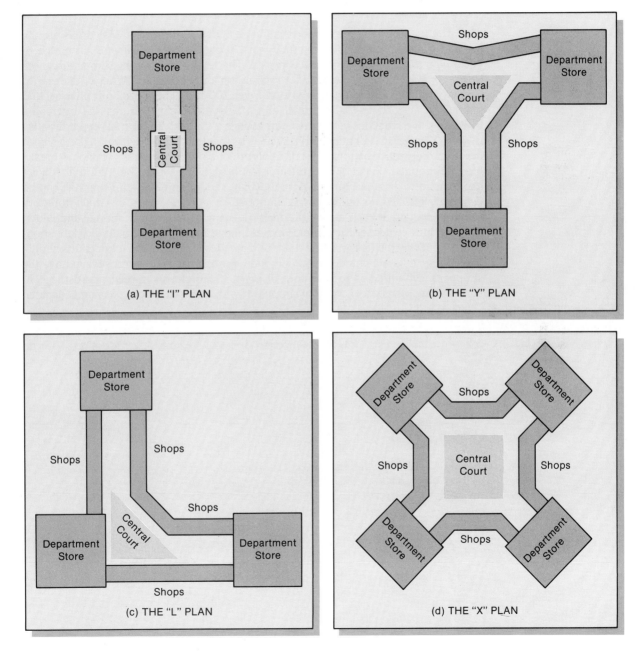

(a) THE "I" PLAN

(b) THE "Y" PLAN

(c) THE "L" PLAN

(d) THE "X" PLAN

addition to serving as an exciting place for the shopper to sit, relax, and meet friends, could also be designed for functional and profitable uses. In order to provide for this flexibility, permanent installations (i.e., fountains, plantings, artwork) should be placed so as to allow for large open areas for special events—concerts, auto and boat (as well as other large equipment) displays, art shows, and community programs. The idea of providing amphitheater-type seating in the main court adds to the possibilities of arranging festive events for both the young and the older shopper.[7]

The third design consideration is the planning of mall areas. Mall areas are the center's traffic arteries; as such, they must facilitate movement and exchange of customers throughout the entire complex. The length and width of mall areas are prime considerations in planning for movement and exchange. "Where the distance from one major store to another is long (over 700 feet), there are both physical and psychological reactions to the 'tunnel' effect."[8] Several design features help overcome these negative reactions. The most common is a "break" in the mall approximately midway between major attractions, such as the central court; however, if the distance between the central court and each department store is too long, additional breaks may be required. Secondary court areas and slight angles in the mall that require shoppers to make short turns before they can see the remainder of the mall can be extremely effective in reducing the tunnel effect. Also, a series of small storefront setbacks starting at each end of the mall makes the mall appear shorter and wider.

Besides customer movement and exchange, mall areas should facilitate shopping. "Generally the design of the malls and arcades leading to the main courts should strive for an intimate character and subdued atmosphere. The purpose is to have the shopper's eye attracted to the store displays."[9] Storefronts should afford the consumer some privacy for "window shopping" without jostling from passing pedestrian

What are the advantages of a kiosk?

A specialty mall center

traffic. On the other hand, some mall designs incorporate "kiosks" to create the happy and busy atmosphere of an open marketplace. These freestanding booths with highly specialized product lines (greeting cards, cutlery items, T-shirts, candy) and services (minibanks, snack bars, utility cashiers) add a new dimension to the mall's shopping atmosphere and contribute substantially to profitability.

Community and neighborhood shopping centers serve the market areas their names suggest. The **neighborhood shopping center** obtains its customers from one or a few neighborhoods within the immediate vicinity. Its trading area can be roughly defined as the area within a five-minute drive of the center, containing anywhere from 7,000 to 50,000 potential customers. The **community shopping center** serves a composite of many neighborhoods within a ten- to fifteen-minute drive from the center. The number of potential customers within its trading area ranges from 20,000 to 100,000. The community shopping center in a smaller city serves the entire city and often competes with the downtown area.

The size of the market areas for each of these centers is primarily a function of the center's number of stores and tenant mix. The neighborhood center usually has five to fifteen stores, with a supermarket as the principal tenant. Comprising largely convenience goods retailers, the neighborhood center sells products that meet the daily living needs of its local area. With a GLA ranging from 25,000 to 100,000 square feet, the neighborhood center frequently includes a hardware store, drugstore, and various personal-service retailers, such as beauty and barber shops.

The community center is considerably larger and more diverse in its mix of tenants than the neighborhood center. Containing from ten to thirty retail establishments with a total GLA of 75,000 to 300,000 square feet, the community center offers a wide range of shopping goods and convenience goods. It is likely to be anchored by one or more mass merchandising stores, the most common being junior department stores, discount stores, and discount department stores. Large supermarkets, food/drug combinations, and variety stores also play an important role in attracting consumers to the community center.[10] Like regional centers, atmospherics are becoming more and more important in boosting customer traffic in community shopping centers. Varying roof lines, atriums, skylights, canopies, and landscaping are currently used to enhance the shopping atmosphere.[11]

The **specialty shopping center** essentially is a miniature regional mall. Offering many of the same features as regional malls, these centers range in size from 100,000 to 300,000 square feet with fifteen to thirty specialty stores, boutiques, and service retailers. The largest store usually does not exceed 25,000 square feet. **Mini-specialty malls** range from enclosed malls with a common architectural motif and decor (e.g., Discoveries in Oklahoma City) to restored manufacturing plants, railroad stations, shipping docks, and warehouses (Quaker Square in Akron, Ohio, is a conversion of the original manufacturing plant and grain elevators of the Quaker Oats Company). Additional preservation and restoration examples include Cincinnati's West 4th Street, Denver's Tivoli Union brewery, Bullock's old downtown department store in Los Angeles, the Alabama theater in Houston, and Pioneer Square in Seattle.[12]

This section has covered several ways to describe sites. The identification process is the first step in appraising site alternatives. At this point, we turn our attention to the second step, the site-evaluation process.

## THE SITE-EVALUATION PROCESS

For any type of retailer, a number of potentially successful site alternatives exist. Unfortunately, an even greater number of unsuccessful alternatives also exist. Hence, retailers must carefully *evaluate* each alternative on the basis of several criteria.

The following sections discuss the site-evaluation process in two phases. The first section explains several principles of site evaluation and how retailers use them to assess the value of alternative sites. The second looks at several methods by which retailers evaluate alternative site locations.

### Principles of Site Evaluation

Several consumer-oriented location principles help retailers evaluate site alternatives. While there are no standard criteria by which all sites can be judged, the following location principles provide the necessary framework for developing practical solutions to the problem of retail site evaluation. These location principles are (1) interception, (2) cumulative attraction, (3) compatibility, (4) store congestion, and (5) accessibility.

The principle of **interception** covers a site's positional qualities that determine its ability to "intercept" consumers as they travel from one place to another. Interception has two distinct elements: first, a "source region" from which consumers are drawn; second, a "terminal region" or consumer destination, a region to which consumers are drawn. Examples of source and terminal regions are residential areas, office complexes, industrial plants, business districts, and shopping centers. Any point between source and terminal regions can be considered a point of interception. In considering a site's interceptor qualities, the evaluator has both an identification and an evaluation problem. The identification problem consists of determining (1) the location of source and terminal regions, (2) the lines connecting those regions, and (3) appropriate points (sites) along the connection line. The evaluation problem is one of measuring the magnitude and quality of these regions, lines, and points. Thus, the evaluator's problem is how to determine whether a site is an efficient "intervening opportunity" between known source and terminal regions.

According to the principle of **cumulative attraction,** a cluster of similar and complementary retailing activities will generally have greater drawing power than dispersed and isolated stores engaging in the same retailing activities.[13] In many large cities, certain types of retailing establishments tend to cluster in specific areas. Examples are the familiar automobile rows, mobile home cities, and restaurant alleys. The evaluator's problem in this case is how to determine whether the retail operation can benefit from the cumulative drawing power of a site's immediate environment.

Retail **compatibility** refers to the "degree to which two businesses interchange customers."[14] As a rule, the greater the compatibility between businesses located in close proximity, the greater the interchange of customers and the greater the sales volume of each compatible business. Compatibility between retailers occurs when their merchandising mixes are complementary, as in the case of an apparel shop, shoe store, and jewelry store that are located very close to one another. If there are several apparel, shoe, and jewelry stores located in the same cluster, all the better! They are not only complementary, they also provide a healthy competitive situation that satisfies the customers' need for comparison shopping and thus provide greater customer interchange for the retailers. One study found that many shopping center managers reduce cross-shopping because they spread "like establishments" (e.g., shoe stores) throughout the mall, rather than concentrating them in one area of the mall.[15] As a rule, good comparative shopping opportunities benefit all concerned.

A high degree of compatibility is more likely to occur when the pricing structures of neighboring businesses are complementary. Other things being equal, there will be greater interchange of customers between one high-margin retailer and another than between a high-margin and a low-margin retailer. Equally important in site evaluation is determining whether neighboring businesses are compatible. An exclusive dress shop would be incompatible with a pet shop, for example, because of the odor and noise produced by the pets.

At some point, the advantages of cumulative attraction and compatibility end, and the problems of site congestion begin. The principle of **store congestion** states that as locations become more saturated with stores, other business activities, and people, they become less attractive to additional shopping traffic. This phenomenon results from the limited mobility of people and cars in the area. Retailers should have learned this lesson from the original congested CBDs. While the excitement of the crowd can be a positive factor, the aggravation of a mob can be a limiting factor, discouraging customers from visiting the site. Thus, in the site-evaluation process, the retailer should estimate at what point the volume of vehicle and foot traffic would limit business, both in the present and the near future.

Perhaps the most basic of site-evaluation principles, the principle of **accessibility** states that the more easily potential consumers can approach, enter, traverse, and exit a site, the more likely they will visit the site to shop. Greater site accessibility means greater likelihood of customer visits (shopping), which means greater likelihood of higher sales volumes. Any major hindrance in any one of the four components of accessibility limits consumer traffic and sales.

Accessibility is a function of both physical and psychological dimensions. The physical dimensions of accessibility are tangible site attributes that either facilitate or hinder the actual physical movement of potential consumers into, through, or out of a site. Psychological dimensions of accessibility include how potential customers *perceive* the ease of movement toward and away from a site. If consumers believe that it is difficult, dangerous, or inconvenient to enter a site, then a psychological barrier has been created equal to any physical barrier. Retailers should consider both real and apparent barriers to accessibility. Some of the more important factors regarding accessibility are discussed in the following paragraphs.

*Number of Traffic Arteries.* The number of traffic arteries adjacent to a site has a profound effect on the consumer's ability to approach and enter the site. Other things being equal, a corner site that is approachable from two traffic arteries is more accessible than a site served by a single traffic artery. Traffic arteries are not all equal, though. Major thoroughfares provide greater accessibility to trading areas than secondary, feeder, or side streets. Side streets are only wide enough to move limited amounts of local traffic before severe congestion problems occur.

*Number of Traffic Lanes.* The more lanes in a traffic artery, the more accessible the site located on this artery. Multilane arteries are the consumer's first choice in selecting routes for most planned shopping trips. Multilanes often reduce the consumer's access to a site, however, especially with left turns. Given some drivers' hesitancy to turn left across traffic, wide roads create a psychological barrier, especially when consumers must cross two or more lanes of oncoming traffic. In essence, multilanes increase consumers' perceived risks.

*Directional Flow of Traffic Arteries.* The accessibility of any site is enhanced if the site is directly accessible from all possible directions. Any reduction in the number of directions from which the site can be approached has an adverse effect on accessibility. Usually, several traffic arteries adjacent to the site enhance accessibility. The location analyst should examine local maps to determine directional biases.

*Number of Intersections.* The number of intersections in the site's general vicinity has both positive and negative effects on accessibility. A large number of intersections offers consumers more ways to approach a site, but may also reduce accessibility because of slower speeds and the consumer's increased risk of an accident. Where intersections are plentiful, the role of traffic-control devices (such as traffic lights and stop signs) becomes critical.

*Configuration of Intersections.* Consumers generally perceive a site located on a three-corner or four-corner intersection as very accessible because these kinds of intersections are fairly standard; consumers are familiar with them and with negotiating them. When there are more than four corners at an intersection, consumers are often confused by the "unstandardized" configuration. This "zone of confusion" exists across the entire intersection and presents the potential consumer with numerous conflict situations.

*Type of Median.* The type of median associated with each of the site's adjacent traffic arteries strongly influences accessibility. Some medians are crossable, while others are not. Generally, crossable medians increase accessibility, although in varying degrees. Medians that provide a "crossover lane" are more encouraging to potential consumers attempting site entry than those without a crossover lane. Cross-

How do uncrossable medians affect a site's accessibility?

able medians that force consumers to wait in a traffic lane until crossover is possible create a perceived danger. Elevated and depressed medians serve to physically separate traffic, but they also separate traffic psychologically. Potential consumers traveling on the right side of an uncrossable median tend to feel isolated from left-side locations and become more aware of right-side locations, where access is substantially easier.

*Speed Limit on Traffic Arteries.* The speed limit on a traffic artery influences a site's accessibility, since it determines the amount of time potential customers have in which to make a decision about entering a site. Expert opinions vary over what constitutes an ideal speed limit. The limit must be high enough to encourage consumers to use the route but low enough to allow them a safe and easy approach to the site. Most experts believe a speed limit between 25 and 40 mph is best.

*Number and Type of Traffic-Control Devices.* Several different devices are used to control traffic. In terms of accessibility, *traffic lights* have enormous effect at crossovers because of the protection left-turn arrows allow. Traffic lights may be more important for their psychological value than for their physical value. "Free left turn" lights are extremely important to site accessibility. *Stop signs* are another major accessibility improvement and can increase accessibility in two ways. First, the chances of creating consumer awareness of the retailer's location and product offering are higher if traffic "stoppers" force consumers to halt and look around. Second, stop signs help to space the flow of traffic. *Traffic rule signs* also influence site accessibility. Traffic signs prohibiting U-turns and left turns can reduce accessibility. Finally, one effective way to reduce traffic confusion and to increase the actual and perceived safety and ease of entering a site is to employ *guidance lines* (turn- and through-arrows and traffic lines) to direct traffic. Any means of traffic guidance that tells the consumer how and where to go enhances accessibility.

*Size and Shape of Site.* The proposed site should be large enough to facilitate all four components of accessibility. Sufficient space should be available to allow ease of parking as well as turning and backing in and out without interfering with consumers who are entering and exiting the site. The shape of the site also can affect accessibility. The wider the site, the greater the exposure to passing traffic, thereby increasing consumer awareness of the retailer's location and activities. Finally, a site should be deep enough to allow ease of entry without interference from exiting traffic or other on-site traffic activities.

### Methods of Site Evaluation

Analysts use several methods to evaluate retail site alternatives. Some of these methods are subjective, verbal descriptions of a site's worth; others provide objective, quantitative measurements. Certain methods, however, incorporate both simplicity and objectivity without the need for specialized training or equipment. One such method is the checklist.

The **checklist method** provides the evaluator with a set of procedural steps for arriving at a subjective, yet quantitative, expression of a site's value. First, the evaluator enumerates the general factors that are usually considered in any site evaluation. A typical list of factors includes all or most of the site-evaluation principles: interception, cumulative attraction, compatibility, and accessibility. Second, for each general factor, the evaluator identifies several attribute measurements that reflect the location needs of the proposed retail operation. For example, interception, which is a key location attribute for most convenience retailers, can be divided into the volume and quality of vehicular and pedestrian traffic.

Third, each location attribute receives a subjective weight based on its relative importance to a particular type of retailer. A common weighting system assigns 3 to very important, 2 to moderately important, and 1 to slightly important attributes. The fourth step is to rate each site alternative in terms of each location attribute. Any number of rating scales can be constructed; one possible scale might range from 1 to 10, with 1 as very poor and 10 as highly superior. To illustrate, a site alternative located on a major thoroughfare with a high volume of traffic throughout the day might be rated a 9 or a 10; another site alternative located on a traffic artery characterized by high volumes of traffic only during the morning and evening rush hours could be rated either a 5 or a 6.

Step five involves calculating a weighted rating for each attribute for each site alternative. The weighted rating is obtained by multiplying each attribute rating by its weight. Sixth, the weighted ratings for all attributes are added to produce an overall rating for each site alternative. Finally, the last step is to rank all evaluated alternatives in order of their overall ratings. Figure 9–4 illustrates the checklist method for evaluating one site alternative for a fast-food restaurant. If, for example, the numerical

| Evaluation Factor | Rating | Weight | Weighted Rating |
|---|---|---|---|
| Interception | | | |
| Volume of vehicular traffic | 8 | 3 | 24 |
| Quality of vehicular traffic | 8 | 3 | 24 |
| Volume of pedestrian traffic | 3 | 3 | 9 |
| Quality of pedestrian traffic | 2 | 3 | 6 |
| Cumulative attraction | | | |
| Number of attractors | 4 | 1 | 4 |
| Degree of attraction | 5 | 1 | 5 |
| Compatibility | | | |
| Type of compatibility | 6 | 2 | 12 |
| Degree of compatibility | 7 | 1 | 7 |
| Accessibility | | | |
| Number of traffic arteries | 8 | 3 | 24 |
| Number of traffic lanes | 10 | 3 | 30 |
| Directional flow of traffic | 7 | 2 | 14 |
| Number of intersections | 7 | 2 | 14 |
| Configuration of intersections | 4 | 3 | 12 |
| Type of medians | 2 | 3 | 6 |
| Speed limits of traffic arteries | 5 | 3 | 15 |
| Number/type of traffic-control devices | 6 | 2 | 12 |
| Size and shape of site | 6 | 3 | 18 |
| Overall site rating | | | 236 |

FIGURE 9–4
The checklist method

*For definitions of evaluation factors, see the text discussion of site-evaluation criteria.

value of 236 is the highest of all evaluated alternatives, then from the standpoint of site considerations this alternative would be rated as the retailer's first choice.

Although beyond the scope of this book, several quantitative models can be used to evaluate retailer sites.[16] Two of these are analog models and regression analysis. **Analog models** are used to make sales projections for new stores based on the sales performances of existing stores. The chain retailer can approach the evaluation problem by finding the best "match" between the site characteristics of new site alternatives and those of a successful existing site. This matching process is usually quantified into a statistical model.

**Regression models** are a more rigorous approach to the problem of site location; hence, they offer certain advantages over checklist and analog approaches. First, a regression model allows "systematic consideration of both trading area factors as well as site-specific elements in a single framework. Further, regression models allow the analyst to identify the factors that are associated with various levels of revenues from stores at different sites."[17] The basic multiple regression model for analyzing determinants of retail performance is expressed as a linear function of location ($L$), store attributes ($S$), market attributes ($M$), price ($P$), and competition ($C$):

$$Y = f(L, S, M, P, C)$$

**THE SITE-SELECTION PROCESS**

The final selection of a retail site is essentially a process of elimination. By analyzing regional and local markets, assessing retail trading areas, and appraising retail site locations, the range of choices has been narrowed to site alternatives consistent with the firm's objectives, operations, and future expectations. If markets, trading areas, and sites have all been carefully evaluated, the retailer should be able to arrive at the final location decision. Normally, the retailer will not select the optimal location, but rather a compromise location that has most of the desirable attributes.

In the end, no steps, procedures, or models can totally quantify the final site-selection process. Nevertheless, with the data generated and the analysis completed in market, trading-area, and site evaluations, the retailer has sufficient information to make a good site selection.

**SUMMARY**

To appraise retail site locations, the location analyst must determine each site's ability to interact with its trading area. The retailer's problem is how to identify, evaluate, and select a good site location.

The site-identification process is the first step in appraising retail site locations. After identifying all potential site alternatives, the evaluator then can initially screen each alternative in terms of availability, suitability, and acceptability. Retail site alternatives can be classified as either isolated or clustered. Isolated sites are retail locations geographically separated from other retailer sites; they normally will not share customers with other retailers. A retailer that selects an isolated site is seeking to gain either a monopolistic or an operational advantage.

Clustered sites are retail locations that are geographically adjacent to each other or in close proximity; normally they are capable of sharing customers with minimal effort on the part of the customer. Two types of clustered sites exist. The first, an unplanned retail cluster, is one that results from the natural evolutionary process of urban growth. It includes central business districts, secondary business districts, neighborhood business districts, and string/strip clusters. The second is the planned retail cluster and includes such clusters as regional, community, neighborhood, and specialty shopping centers.

The second step in appraising retail site locations is site evaluation, based on site-evaluation principles and site-evaluation methods. Several principles used in evaluation are interception, cumulative attraction, compatibility, store congestion, and accessibility. The checklist, analog, and regression methods provide the basic framework for making both subjective and objective evaluations of retail site alternatives.

The final step in site appraisal is site selection. The process of elimination narrows the range of choices to site alternatives that are consistent with the firm's objectives, operations, and future expectations. Essentially, the task of site selection becomes one of selecting the best location from several acceptable alternatives.

# STUDENT STUDY GUIDE

**KEY TERMS**

acceptability  
accessibility  
analog model  

availability  
central business district (CBD)  
checklist method

clustered site

community shopping center

compatibility

cumulative attraction

interception

isolated site

mini-specialty mall

monopolistic isolation

neighborhood business district (NBD)

neighborhood shopping center

operational isolation

regional shopping center

regression model

retail site

secondary business district (SBD)

specialty shopping center

store congestion

string/strip cluster

suitability

super regional shopping center

**REVIEW QUESTIONS**

1. What three questions should the retailer ask in conducting an initial screening of site alternatives?
2. Why would a retailer select an isolated site?
3. What is the key to successfully revitalizing the CBD (central business district)?
4. Compare and contrast the SBDs and NBDs (secondary and neighborhood business districts).
5. What distinguishes a super regional from a regional shopping center?
6. Describe the four basic shopping center configurations.
7. How might a shopping center developer overcome the "tunnel" effect?
8. Compare and contrast a community and neighborhood shopping center.
9. What is a mini-specialty mall center?
10. Describe the site-evaluation principle of interception.
11. Why is cumulative attraction important?
12. How does the principle of compatibility affect the evaluation of a retail site?
13. Describe the role of traffic arteries and lanes in determining the accessibility of a site.
14. What role do the number and configuration of intersections play in creating an accessible site?
15. How do the number and type of traffic-control devices influence the accessibility of a retail site?
16. Describe the two quantitative methods of retail site evaluation.

**REVIEW EXAM**

True or False

_____ 1. A clustered site can be defined as two or more closely located retailers capable of sharing customers with minimal effort.

_____ 2. The key to successful revitalization projects is not so much the development of new and existing physical facilities, but the creation of a safe and pleasant shopping atmosphere.

_____ 3. A major limitation of string/strip cluster sites is that they are typically associated with higher rents than those found in central and secondary business districts.

_____ 4. The community shopping center typically offers a wide range of both convenience and shopping goods.

_____ 5. A high degree of compatibility is more likely when pricing structures of neighboring businesses complement each other.

_____ 6. Because of less traffic congestion, secondary streets generally provide a greater accessibility to trading areas than do major thoroughfares.

_____ 7. A retailer can substantially increase store accessibility by selecting a corner site where more than four corners exist at an intersection.

## STUDENT APPLICATIONS MANUAL

**PROJECTS: INVESTIGATIONS AND APPLICATIONS**

1. Investigate the business vitality of the central business district in your community. Describe the general physical, cultural, and eocnomic environment. What are the retailing strengths and weaknesses of your CBD? Characterize the types of consumers that shop there. What specific recommendations would you make to improve the shopping climate of your CBD?
2. Visit one super regional or regional shopping center and one community or neighborhood shopping center and evaluate the tenant mix of each in terms of "compatibility." Map the type and location of each retailer in the cluster, and identify and explain examples of good and poor compatibility.
3. Select the fast-food restaurant closest to your home or school. Evaluate the physical and psychological dimensions of the restaurant's site accessibility. Provide illustrations to support your evaluation.
4. Survey your local retailing community and select three similar types of specialty clothing stores in three substantially different locations. Using the "checklist method" presented in Figure 9–4 of the text, assess the site location of each store. Justify or explain your rating for each evaluation factor and make a final decision as to which store has the best site location.

**CASES: PROBLEMS AND DECISIONS**

### CASE 9–1
### The Limited, Inc.—Considering a New Location Strategy*

The Limited, Inc. has become the leading force in American retailing by offering apparel tailored to the tastes and lifestyles of fashion-conscious contemporary consumers. By positioning itself as the dominant specialist in the fashion apparel market through multiple retail formats and state-of-the-art distribution system, The Limited, Inc. has become one of the top achievers across all industries in the United States. A basic operating principle in the firm's pursuit of excellence is "to offer the absolute best customer shopping experience anywhere—the best stores—the best merchandise—the best merchandise presentation—the best customer service—the best 'everything' that a customer sees and experiences."

In the "quest for the best," The Limited is currently considering a new "cluster location strategy" that would group several or possibly all of its various retailing formats within one shopping mall. For example, within one shopping mall, The Limited, Inc. could create a store cluster comprised of (1) a Limited store, (2) Limited Express, (3) Victoria's Secret, (4) Lane Bryant, (5) Lerner Store, (6) Sizes Unlimited, and (7) Henri Bendel. Exhibit 1 profiles each of The Limited, Inc.'s retailing formats.

#### ASSIGNMENT

Evaluate the proposed cluster location strategies. As a location consultant, would you recommend it to Leslie H. Wexner, Chairman of The Limited, Inc.? Defend your recommendation. Assume Mr. Wexner wants you to develop two different cluster prototypes: (1) for an upscale shopping mall in southern California catering to upper income consumers and (2) for a typical middle-class shopping center in St. Louis. Provide supporting rationale for your prototype.

*This case was prepared by Dale Lewison and John Hawes, The University of Akron.

EXHIBIT 1
The Limited, Inc., retailing formats

☐ *Limited stores*—consists of 711 stores in every major market, with an average store size of 4,000 square feet. The Limited specializes in medium-priced fashion apparel that complements the tastes and lifestyles of contemporary women 20 to 40 years of age.

☐ *Limited Express*—offers the latest, most creative international assortment of sports-wear and accessories designed to appeal to spirited women on the cutting edge of world fashion. Store designs and merchandise displays offer fashion-forward women (15 to 25 years) an exciting place to shop. There are currently 348 stores, in most major markets, with an average size of 2,600 square feet.

☐ *Lane Bryant*—with 631 stores averaging about 4,000 square feet, Lane Bryant is the foremost retailer of women's special-size apparel—fashions for sizes 14 and up. The format's ability to supply special-size customers with attractive and fashionable sportswear, ready-to-wear, intimate apparel, and accessories has resulted in a pat-tern of continuous expansion.

☐ *Victoria's Secret*—offers an international lingerie collection that provides contempo-rary women with imaginative, high-fashion designer intimate apparel through retail and mail-order divisions. With 236 stores averaging 1,900 square feet, the goal set for this division is to bring intimate apparel out of the basement and into the van-guard of fashion.

☐ *Lerner Stores*—fashion-forward sportswear, coats, dresses, and accessories at pop-ular and budget prices. With 770 stores in every major market, with an average size in excess of 6,000 square feet, Lerner is the nation's largest specialty retailer under a single trade name.

☐ *Sizes Unlimited*—offers sportswear, dresses, and accessories, sizes 14 and up, priced below similar goods in most department and specialty stores. Sizes Unlimited offers a wide assortment of first-quality merchandise, nationally known brand labels, and private labels at prices that appeal to the value-conscious customer. The 398 stores average 3,500 square feet and can be found in most major markets.

☐ *Henri Bendel*—represents the best in international designer clothing and accessories. The store occupies a unique position at the apex of the fashion world (57th Street, Manhattan). It provides the ultrasophisticated customer with merchandise of incom-parable style and quality. Henri Bendel plans to open stores in the top forty markets in the nation.

## CASE 9–2
## Clemente Cleaners*

### BACKGROUND

Clemente Cleaners has occupied the same location on the northwest corner of Johnston Avenue and Oak Park Boulevard for the last 27 years. Bart Clemente, owner and operator of Clemente Cleaners, originally selected the site because he thought it represented a conve-nient stop for customers commuting between Walnut Valley, a large suburb, and the central business district of Omaha. Customers could drop off their cleaning on the way to work

*This case was prepared by Dale M. Lewison, The University of Akron, and Charles R. Patton, Pan American Univer-sity.

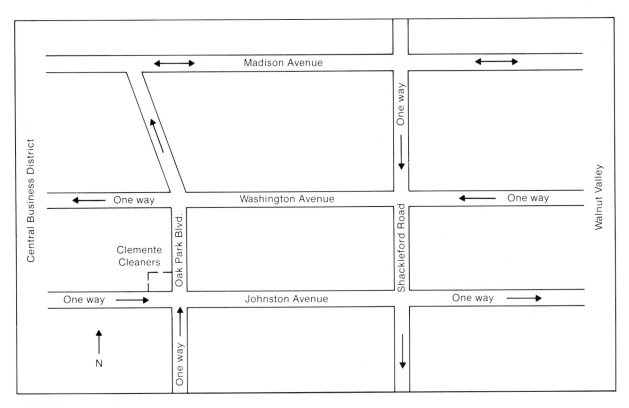

**EXHIBIT 1**

New traffic artery pattern

and pick it up on the way home. The selection of the Johnston Avenue site proved to be one of the best business decisions Clemente ever made. For 25 years, the store serviced the commuting public and Clemente enjoyed the benefits of a very successful business.

Two years ago, the Metro Traffic Engineering Department made a complete study of the numerous traffic problems that commuters were experiencing during their weekday work trips to and from the central city. After considerable deliberation, a decision was made to convert two of the major traffic arteries into one-way streets. Washington Avenue was designated a one-way westbound artery leading into the central business district, and Johnston Avenue was designated an eastbound traffic artery out of the city (Exhibit 1).

Although the realignment of traffic arteries ended numerous traffic problems, it also marked the beginning of a substantial decline in revenues for Clemente Cleaners. The present store remained reasonably profitable, but many of Clemente's long-time commuter customers found it more convenient to go elsewhere.

Many of Clemente's customers from Walnut Valley had frequently commented on how satisfied they were with Clemente Cleaners and expressed their potential support should he decide to open a second conveniently located outlet in Walnut Valley. Unfortunately, good locations are hard to find in Walnut Valley. After a 10-month search, however, Clemente has found a Madison Avenue site he thinks might be appropriate (see Exhibit 2).

From his service records, Clemente has determined that a large number of his former customers live within one mile of the site; most of these customers would have to pass the site on their shopping trips to Walnut Valley Mall and Eastland Shopping Center. Walnut Valley Mall is a large regional center anchored by Sears, J. C. Penney, and two large local de-

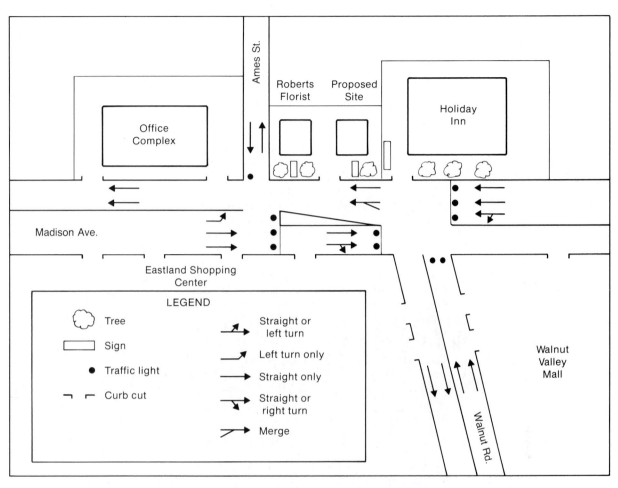

**EXHIBIT 2**
The proposed Madison
Avenue site

partment stores. A large discount store and a catalog showroom are the principal tenants of Eastland Shopping Center. In Clemente's mind, there is no question that the site's trading area contains sufficient business potential to support his proposed business venture. What troubled him was the site itself. The existing building was adequate for his needs, but he would have to share the parking lot (eight parking spaces) with Robert's Florist. In addition, Clemente was somewhat concerned with the site's accessibility.

## CURRENT SITUATION

Clemente's option on the site expires at the end of the month. Hence, he must make a decision soon. Having limited experience in site analysis, Clemente has decided to engage the services of Professor Kristopher Michael, head of the marketing department at the local state university. Michael has agreed to investigate the site accessibility issue and to make appropriate recommendations. He has also agreed to address the issue of whether Clemente should exercise the rent, lease, or buy clause of his option.

## ASSIGNMENT

Assume the role of Professor Kristopher Michael. First, prepare a written report on the pros and cons of the site's accessibility. Make whatever recommendations you think are appropriate regarding the site's accessibility. Second, prepare a report on the pros and cons of renting, leasing, or buying the location and make a recommendation to Clemente regarding this issue. Be sure to provide adequate support and rationale for all of your recommendations.

**ENDNOTES**

1. Eric C. Peterson, "Higher Rents? Downsize It," *Stores* (March 1986): 40.
2. "900 North Michigan Rises on Chicago Skyline," *Chain Store Age Executive* (April 1987): 30.
3. Joseph Weber, "Jim Rouse May Be Losing His Touch," *Business Week,* 4 April 1988, 33.
4. *Dollars and Cents of Shopping Centers* (Washington: The Urban Land Institute, 1987): 294.
5. Ibid.
6. See Eric Peterson, "MXD—Mall Excitement," *Stores* (January 1986): 144–146, 151–152, and "New Focus Emerging," *Stores* (March 1987): 36–40.
7. Louis G. Redstone, *New Dimensions in Shopping Centers and Stores* (New York: McGraw-Hill, 1973), 61, 68. Used by permission.
8. Ibid.
9. Ibid.
10. Eric C. Peterson, "What's Working Now?" *Stores* (July 1987): 50.
11. See Eric C. Peterson, "Recipes For New Sites," *Stores* (March 1985): 70–72.
12. Kurt Anderson, "Spiffing Up the Urban Heritage," *Time,* 23 Nov. 1987, 74.
13. See Richard L. Nelson, *The Selection of Retail Locations* (New York: F. W. Dodge, 1958), 58–64.
14. Ibid., 65.
15. Marvin J. Rothenberg, "Mall Marketing Principles that Affect Merchandising," *Retail Control* (October 1986): 25.
16. See Eric C. Peterson, "Site Selection," *Stores* (July 1986): 30, 34–36.
17. C. Samuel Craig, Avijit Grosh, and Sara McLafferty, "Models of the Retail Location Process: A Review," *Journal of Retailing* 60 (Spring 1984): 21.

# PART FOUR
## Retail Merchandising

# 10

**Objectives**

☐ Recognize retailers' need to market all of a product's dimensions.

☐ Understand and make the "which" and "how many" product decisions.

☐ Evaluate new and existing products and their impact on merchandising decisions.

☐ Acquire and evaluate sources of product information.

☐ Define and describe the various types of product-mix strategies.

☐ Discuss major emerging trends in the development of product mixes.

# Merchandise Assortment Planning

A s identified in Chapter 1, the retailer's problem is how to find the "right blend" of marketing ingredients that satisfy the needs of the target market. The "right blend" is the best combination of the right product, at the right time, in the right quantities, at the right price, with the right appeal. The focus of this and the next five chapters is the offering of the right product in the right quantities within the context of the right place, time, price, and appeal.

To develop product mix, the retailer must first understand what a product really is. The product is not simply some item of merchandise with certain physical and functional attributes; it is something much more complex. Before we discuss the concept of product mix, let's first examine the "total-product concept."

## Total-Product Concept

The **total-product concept** recognizes that a product is more than just the tangible object offered for sale. Retailers that sell "things" will soon discover that there is no one to sell them to. To be successful, the retailer must act on the premise that a product is more than just functional and aesthetic features; instead, it incorporates the various service features and psychological benefits conveyed by the product. In essence, the total-product concept acknowledges the need for retailers to market every one of a product's dimensions. The relationship among a product's many facets is illustrated in Figure 10–1. As shown, the total-product concept is the sum of all physical, extended, and generic products.

The **physical product** encompasses both its functional and aesthetic features. A product's functional features include the tangible elements of size, shape, and weight, together with its chemical and/or biological makeup. Functional features are extremely important because they determine to a large extent how well the product will actually perform the functions it was designed to accomplish. If a product cannot clean and polish, or brighten and freshen, or cool and heat—in short, if it can't perform the basic function it was designed to do—then all other aspects of the product are severely diminished. The aesthetic features of a product are elements that appeal to the five senses. If a product does not look, smell, feel, sound, and/or taste "right," its merchandising qualities have been substantially reduced or eliminated.

FIGURE 10–1
The total-product con-
cept

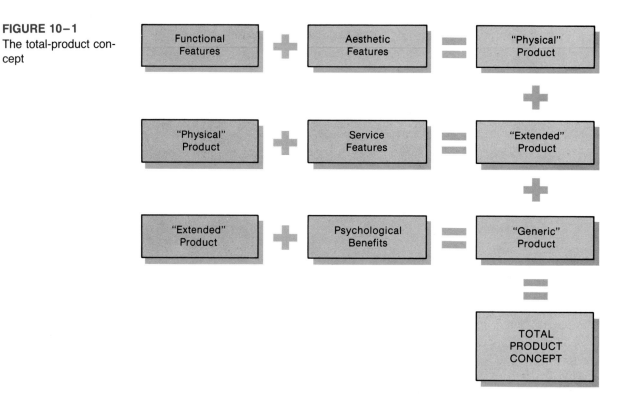

Consumers have strong preconceived ideas about how a product should look, smell, feel, sound, and taste. Wendy's "Give a little nibble" advertisement, which asks the customer to taste the meat—Is it dry and chewy? Or hot and juicy? Is it bland or is it tasty?—is directed at enhancing the perception of Wendy's hamburger as a desirable physical product.[1]

The **extended product** surrounds the physical product with the whole set of service features provided as a conditional part of the sale. Service features are "extras" that might include delivery, alterations, installation, repairs, warranties, returns, adjustments, wrapping, telephone and mail ordering, or any other service that consumers want for purchase satisfaction. A retailer must determine which service features are *required* for the purchase decision and which are simply *desired* by the customer as an added product dimension.

When consumers buy products, they seek something more than the physical and extended product: they expect to benefit in some way from the purchase. The **generic product** is defined as the extended product (functional, aesthetic, and service features) plus the expected psychological benefits that consumers derive from buying, using, and possessing the product. Consumers buy products to be beautiful, safe, thin, comfortable, and noticed, or to gain prestige, recognition, security, independence, love, or a host of other benefits. Retailers that recognize that a product's psychological endowments are as important as, if not more important than, the product itself will have considerably more to sell to their customer than just a physical product. People don't want lawn and garden tools; they want nice-looking lawns and gardens their families can play on and their neighbors can admire. To paraphrase Charles Revson of Revlon Cosmetics: We manufacture cosmetics; in the store, women seek hope and the promise of beauty.

## Product-Mix Concept

The first step in operationalizing the total-product concept is to develop the product mix. The **product-mix concept** refers to the full range or mixture of products the retailer offers to consumers. The product mix represents "appropriate combinations" of products to meet the specific needs of one or more identified target markets. If the product mix represents "appropriate combinations," the obvious question becomes "appropriate combinations of what?" The answer is "appropriate combinations of product lines and product items." A **product line** is any grouping of related products. A **product item** refers to a specific product within a product line that is unique and clearly distinguishable from other products within and outside the product line.

Based on type and degree of relationship, product lines are often subdivided to facilitate the retailer's planning of a product mix. Products can be related in terms of (1) satisfying a particular need (e.g., health or beauty aids); (2) being used together (e.g., pieces of living room furniture); or (3) being purchased or used by a similar customer group (e.g., women's, men's, or children's wearing apparel). The degree to

Is this a merchandise group, class, or category? Why is product classification important?

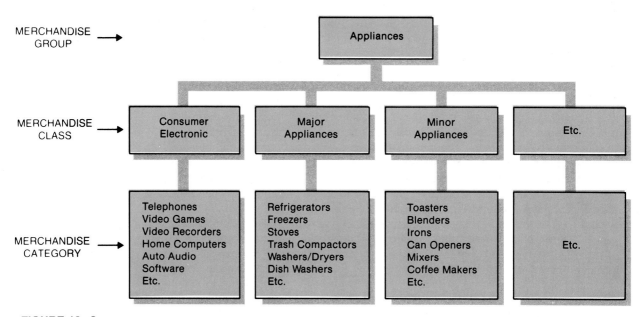

MERCHANDISE GROUP →

Appliances

MERCHANDISE CLASS →

| Consumer Electronic | Major Appliances | Minor Appliances | Etc. |

MERCHANDISE CATEGORY →

| Telephones<br>Video Games<br>Video Recorders<br>Home Computers<br>Auto Audio<br>Software<br>Etc. | Refrigerators<br>Freezers<br>Stoves<br>Trash Compactors<br>Washers/Dryers<br>Dish Washers<br>Etc. | Toasters<br>Blenders<br>Irons<br>Can Openers<br>Mixers<br>Coffee Makers<br>Etc. | Etc. |

**FIGURE 10–2**

Product-line subdivisions

which products are related also can vary greatly from a close relationship to a remote relationship. One method of classifying product lines to facilitate the retailer's development of a product mix is discussed. For illustration here, the product line is subdivided into three groupings: merchandise group, merchandise class, and merchandise category.

A **merchandise group** is a broadly related line of products that retailers and consumers associate together according to end use. Examples of merchandise groups include such wide product combinations as furniture, appliances, home furnishings, housewares, wearing apparel, sporting goods, food products, personal-care products, and automotive products.

A **merchandise class** is a closely related line of products within a merchandise group. Merchandise classes often correspond to the operating departments of a traditional department store and serve as a way to identify many specialty retailers (e.g., men's, women's, or children's wearing apparel).

A **merchandise category** is a specific line of products within a merchandise class; for example, sport and dress shirts within men's wearing apparel, lipstick and eye shadow within cosmetics, and sofas and end tables within living room furniture. It is the level within a product line at which consumer *comparison shopping* occurs.

An example of a product's three subdivisions (merchandise groups, classes, and categories) is illustrated in Figure 10–2.

Within a product line, a product item is distinguishable by its brand, style, size, color, material, price, or any combination of these factors. A *brand* is a distinctive grouping of products identified by a name, term, design, symbol, or any combination of these markings. It is used to identify the products of a particular manufacturer or seller. *Style* refers to the characteristic or distinctive form, outline, or shape of a product item. *Size* can refer to the product's actual size (e.g., 42-long or X-large) or to the size of its package (e.g., family size, 12-ounce bottle). *Colors, materials,* and *prices* are also important features in distinguishing one product item from another. The potential combinations of these features are virtually limitless in light of the large selection of brands, styles, sizes, colors, materials, and price lines available to most retailers.

## Product-Mix Decisions

In developing the product mix, the retailer faces two basic decisions: "Which product lines and items?" and "How many product lines and items?" A product is "right" only when it is "right" for all three merchandising activities of buying, stocking, and selling.

No simple criteria determine whether a product line or item should be part of the product mix. The retailer must judge each product on its own merits relative to its particular situation. In considering "which products," the retailer should ask the following questions:

1. Is the product consistent with our current and proposed product mix?
2. Is it consistent with the store image we want to portray?
3. Will the product be appropriate to existing target markets or will it require development and cultivation of new market segments?
4. What level of sales support does the product require in terms of personal selling, advertising, and sales promotions?
5. What is the existing market potential and what growth potential does the product have?
6. How susceptible is the product to demand cycles and the actions of competitors?
7. Does the product require new fixturing or specialized storage facilities, or can it be properly displayed and stored with existing fixtures and facilities?

Another basic problem for the retailer is the number of different product lines and items to include in the product mix. The retailer should ask and attempt to answer the following questions to decide "how many products."

1. Should we carry several product lines or specialize in one or a few lines?
2. How broad a selection (brands, styles, sizes) should we offer in each line?
3. How many different price lines should we offer?
4. Do we want a broad or limited market appeal?
5. Are there strong consumer preferences for certain brands and styles? If so, what are they?
6. What are the cyclical demand patterns (product, fashion, seasonal cycles) associated with the various product items?
7. What effect does an extensive or limited product offering have on inventory control and investment?

The "how many products" decision is two-dimensional, requiring decisions on both product variety and product assortment. **Product variety** is the number of different product lines the retailer stocks in the store. The retailer can engage in variety strategies ranging from a narrow variety of one or a few product lines to a wide variety encompassing a large number of product lines. **Product assortment** refers to the number of different product items the retailer stocks within a particular product line.

**FIGURE 10-3**
How many products?

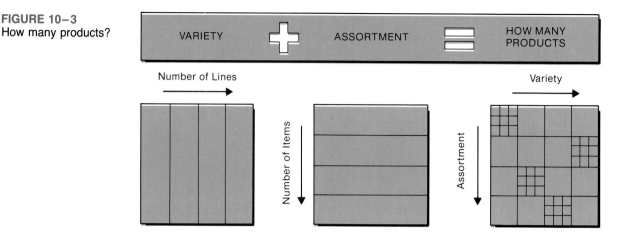

Assortment strategies vary from shallow assortments of one or a few product items within each line to deep assortments having a large selection of product items within each line. The dimensions of the "how many products" decision are illustrated in Figure 10-3. (These variety and assortment strategies are discussed more fully later in the chapter.)

## PRODUCT EVALUATION

Retailers continually are besieged with a barrage of "new" and "improved" products and must evaluate each of these products before making any product-mix decision. Some require more extensive evaluation than others. Retailers use three sets of criteria to aid them in making "which" and "how many products" decisions: product, market, and supply considerations.

### Product Considerations

Product considerations are those criteria directly concerned with the characteristics of the product itself. The three product considerations are compatibility, attributes, and profitability.

*Product Compatibility.* In developing a product mix, the retailer should consider **product compatibility**—the nature of the relationship between various product lines and between various product items within them. Based on the type of compatibility, retailers classify products as (1) substitutes, (2) complements, and (3) unrelated. The degree of product compatibility ranges from a perfect to a general relationship.

A **product substitute** is a product consumers use for the same general purpose as another product; it has the same basic functional attributes and meets the same basic consumer needs. A *perfect substitute* is a product consumers perceive as being essentially the same as another product. In this case, the consumer is totally indifferent about what product to buy and use. A *general substitute* is a product consumers perceive as being different from another product but that serves the same general purpose (e.g., Stove Top Stuffing instead of potatoes).

In deciding which products to sell, the retailer usually should avoid perfect substitutes. They divert sales from other products without adding anything in return. General substitutes represent an increase in the selection a retailer offers consumers; as such, they can increase total sales. The retailer must realize that many "new" products offered by manufacturers are often nothing more than "me-too" substitutes that add little, if anything, to the store's total sales.

A **product complement** is a product that is bought and used in conjunction with another product. A *perfect complement* is a product consumers must purchase because their original product purchase cannot function immediately or effectively without it (e.g., film is a perfect complement to a camera). *General complements* are products sold in conjunction with other products because they enhance or supplement the original purchase in some way. Apparel accessories that are color- and style-coordinated with a suit or dress are excellent examples of general complements. Both perfect and general complements are highly desirable additions to the retailer's product mix because they often represent additional, unplanned sales beyond the original, planned purchase. Also, consumers tend to be less sensitive about the price of complements; hence, retailers often sell them at above-average markups. As a rule, the depth of assortment for complements is rather extensive, and the chances for additional sales increase when consumers have a great selection.

**Unrelated products** are neither substitutes nor complements, but retailers seriously consider them for their product mix since they represent potential additional sales, theoretically at low risk and reasonable profit. Some impulse goods fit this description. Normally, unrelated products are not stocked in depth; rather, retailers often follow a strategy of "creaming," stocking and selling only the best-selling items. (The process of item additions and line combinations are discussed later in this chapter.)

*Product Attributes.* The attributes of the product itself strongly influence which and how many products retailers stock. Four **product attributes** to consider are product bulk, standardization, service requirements, and required selling method.

*Product bulk* is the weight or size of a product in relation to its value. Bulky products usually require substantial space, both on the sales floor and in the stock-

What type product is being sold—a perfect complement or a general complement?

room, and often require special handling. In addition, many bulky products typically are low in sales per square foot of floor space. In fact, some retailers have found that the space these bulky items occupy should be (and has been) turned over to more productive merchandise with higher sales per square foot.

Generally, *standardized* products fit into the retailer's routine operating procedures, whereas *nonstandardized* products often require special buying, stocking, and handling. Few products offer enough potential to the retailer to justify developing specialized merchandising skills.

Because products vary noticeably concerning *required service levels,* retailers should evaluate each product individually. If a required customer service (e.g., home delivery) is *not* part of the retailer's normal service offering, the retailer should seriously consider the product's service requirements before adding it to the product line.

*Required selling methods* are particular skills needed to sell a product. Some products call for a personal selling approach, while others can be sold on a self-service basis. Before stocking a product, a retailer should determine whether the product's required selling method is consistent with current operations.

*Product Profitability.*  In determining the merits of a product, **product profitability** is one of the most important and complex criteria retailers use, since it can be expressed and measured in so many different ways. It is sufficient to state here that each product should make some contribution to profit; the contribution can be direct in the sense of per-unit profit or indirect by creating customer traffic and additional sales on other products.

## Market Considerations

Retailers use market considerations as criteria to evaluate a product according to its compatibility with the retailer's markets and customers. In this section, products are examined relative to their life- or fashion-cycle stages, market appropriateness, life-style implications, and competitive positions.

*Product Life Cycle.*  Products pass through several stages in their lifetime, each identified by its sales performance characteristics. This series of stages is called the **product life cycle (PLC)**. Knowing what stage a product is in helps the retailer judge both its existing and future sales potential. Also, the PLC stage suggests a particular retailing strategy. The four stages of the product life cycle are *introduction, growth, maturity,* and *decline.* Figure 10–4 illustrates one basic shape of the PLC as defined by sales-performance levels.

In the *introductory stage,* products are characterized by low sales and losses, high risk, and high costs. Thus, the retailer's risks are high. Unless the manufacturer is willing to help reduce that risk (e.g., liberal return allowances), the retailer should be extremely cautious in stocking the introductory product. Nevertheless, a retailer may assume these risks to support its image as a fashion leader.

Almost without exception, the most desirable products for retailers are those in the *growth stage.* Products in the growth stage are characterized by accelerating sales, high profit levels, limited competition and lower relative costs and risk. To satisfy the growing number of customers, retailers usually stock an extensive assortment of growth products.

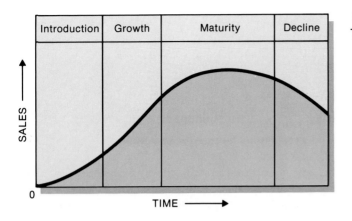

| Introduction | Growth | Maturity | Decline |
|---|---|---|---|

**FIGURE 10–4**
The product life-cycle

In the *maturity stage,* sales increase at a slower rate and finally begin to level off. Characteristics of this stage are (1) a highly competitive market, (2) falling prices and margins, (3) more intensive advertising, and (4) lower profits. Most retailers should include or continue to include mature products in their product mix because consumers expect them.

As a rule, retailers do not include *declining products* in their product mix. Normally, retailers drop these products, if they have not done so already.

*Fashion Cycle.* Like the product life cycle, the **fashion cycle** is a conceptualization of the "life of a fashion." A fashion is a product that has distinctive attributes that are currently appropriate and represent the prevailing style. Fashion is a reflection of a society's cultural, social, and economic environment at one particular point. As one fashion expert writes, "Fashion trends reflect the changes in what a culture is thinking, feeling, and doing, both in work and recreation; how an era is behaving morally; and how stable or successful a country is financially."[2]

Major fashion houses frequently distinguish between their premium-priced collections, displayed at the New York and Paris fashion shows and sold to a limited number of wealthy clients, and their classification merchandise: lower priced, with a broader appeal, and incorporating the features of last year's collections. Profits derived from classification sales subsidize the development of collections, which cast a premium halo over the classification merchandise, for which, in turn, a premium price can be charged.[3] Fashions represent great opportunities for retailers, but also substantial risks. Fashionable products include the following:

- ☐ High-margin items that can provide above-average profits
- ☐ Shopping and specialty goods that consumers will spend time, money, and effort to find
- ☐ Products that enhance the retailer's general image and help generate consumer traffic
- ☐ A means of distinguishing a retailer's operation from the competition[4]

Fashion-conscious consumers may be characterized as follows:

- ☐ Oriented toward the social world
- ☐ Gregarious and likable

□ Active participants in society
□ Self-assertive, competitive, and venturesome
□ Attention seekers and self-confident
□ Aesthetic-, power-, and status-oriented individuals[5]

The risk associated with fashion products comes from the uncertainty that surrounds both consumers' *level* of acceptance and the *duration* of their acceptance of the fashion. One management tool retailers use to reduce the risks of including fashion products in their product mix is the *fashion cycle*. During its lifetime, a fashion passes through three stages: introduction, acceptance, and decline. From its beginning in the introductory stage to its obsolescence in the decline stage, the fashion innovation struggles to obtain customer acceptance and customer adoptions. "The fashion industry thrives on the concept of psychological obsolescence. A major driving force for consumers is the continual search for newness and the discarding of the old."[6]

Customer acceptance of fashion varies significantly according to level of acceptance (as measured by sales) and the duration of that acceptance (as measured by weeks, months, years). Based on the two acceptance factors, four types of fashion cycles occur: flop, fad, ford, and classic (see Figure 10–5). A **flop** is a fashion cycle rejected by all consumer segments almost immediately. Other than for a few fashion innovators who try and then discard the fashion, a flop gains neither a significant level nor duration of acceptance. Flops are fashion items most retailers hope to avoid; they not only represent the financial loss of obsolete merchandise, they also tend to tarnish

**FIGURE 10–5**
Types of fashion cycles

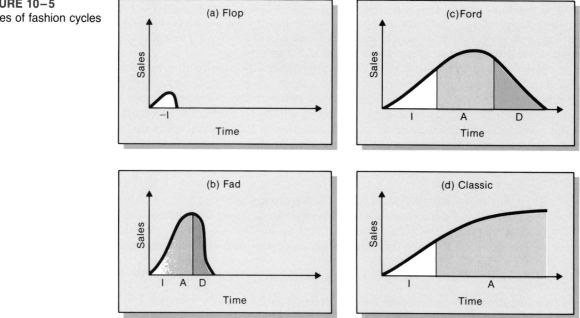

Key: I = Introductory Stage     A = Acceptance Stage     D = Decline Stage

the retailer's image as a fashion leader. Some flops are inevitable—they are the realization of the risks that go with fashion merchandising.

A **fad** is a fashion that obtains a relatively high level of customer acceptance for a short time. It is quickly accepted but rejected with the same quickness (see Figure 10–6). Typically, the lifetime of a fad ranges from a few weeks to several months. Because a relatively large number of these items can be sold at substantial markups (consumers are somewhat price insensitive regarding fads) in a short period of time, fads are extremely profitable. They are also highly risky, however, because of the short duration of the cycle. To capitalize on a fad, the retailer must stock the item at the introductory or early part of the cycle.

A best-seller in fashion merchandising is referred to as a **ford**. A ford is also referred to as a "runner" or "hot item." Fords gain wide customer acceptance over extended periods of time. Because of their wide acceptance, long-term salability, and stable demand, fords usually are produced by many different manufacturers in a

**FIGURE 10–6**
Great fads of our time

How many do you remember? How many
did you own? How long did
you keep them?

Shmoos
Rubik's Cubes
Hula Hoops
Nehru jackets
Running
Pet Rocks
Puka beads
Love beads
Indian glass beads
3-D movies
The Lindy
Skateboards
Ankle bracelets
Coonskin caps
Telephone booth packing
Flubber (from the Disney flick
    *The Absent-Minded Professor*)
Slime (mutant son of Flubber)
Nautilus
Super Balls
Dickies
Clackers
Zoot suits
E.T.
Disco

Source: Adapted from Stephen Fried, "Summer Madness," *Philadelphia* August 1983, p. 122.

Are these fashions flops, fads, fords, or classics?

variety of price lines. For the same reasons, nearly every retailer must include fords in the product mix or suffer loss of profits and loss of a fashion image.

The "classic look," the "classic cut," and the "classic shape" describe a style trend that endures for many years. The **classic** fashion has both a high level and a long duration of acceptance. Although a classic might undergo minor changes, it essentially looks the same. "The aging of the baby-boom generation has produced shifts in apparel demand. The fad orientation of the 1960s and early 1970s gave way to the 'preppie look' in the late 1970s. This look has evolved into a new approach to dressing, consisting of classically styled pieces in updated colors and traditional items combined in innovative ways. The 'layered look' and 'investment dressing' are terms fashion-conscious people use to describe these classically styled items."[7] The classic, even more than the ford, is an absolute must in the retailer's product mix. The decision relative to the classic is not whether to stock it, but rather which price line to stock from which supplier with which product features.

*Market Appropriateness.* Retailers should evaluate new-product candidates on their chances for success in the marketplace, that is, *market appropriateness*—how well the new product matches the consumption and buying needs of targeted consumers. Several characteristics that serve as good indicators of how well a product might be received by the retailer's current and potential customers are relative advantage, affinity, trialability, observability, and complexity.

**Relative advantage** is the extent to which the new product is perceived to be better than existing products. A product that offers clear-cut advantages or provides a more satisfying benefit package is more likely to attract the interest and patronage of the store's customers.

**Affinity** is the extent to which the new product is consistent with the consumer's current buying and usage behavior. Products that require noticeable behavioral modification are often viewed by consumers as being incompatible with their needs. A product that is consistent with the consumer's beliefs, values, and experiences is more likely to gain customer acceptance and a faster and higher rate of adoptions.

**Trialability** is the extent to which a new product can be tested on a trial basis. All new-product purchases involve some risk to the purchaser. Anything that substantially reduces the risk improves the chances for initial and subsequent purchases. A product that can be physically divided into small quantities and given as free samples or sold in trial sizes benefits from good trialability. If division is not possible, demonstrations and guarantees can reduce perceived risks.

**Observability** is the extent to which the consumer can see a new product's favorable attributes. If relative advantages are easily visible and can be easily described to others, the new product's probability of market success is greatly enhanced.

**Complexity** is the extent to which a new product can be easily understood or used. Products that require the consumer to invest considerable time and effort to reap any benefits will involve greater selling efforts and a slower rate of consumer adoptions.

*Life-Styles.* Life-style is a pattern of living shaped by psychological influences, social experiences, and demographic makeup. Knowing targeted consumers' activities, interests, and opinions makes retailers better able to select products that are consistent with both the consumer's life-style and the retailer's image. Developing product lines in accord with consumer living patterns is referred to as **life-style merchandising**. This method of product evaluation requires the retailer to do the following:

1. Identify target markets based on consumers' life-styles and their product, place, promotion, and price preferences.
2. Determine which life-style markets are consistent with the retailer's image and mode of doing business.
3. Evaluate which and how many products to carry based on their ability to satisfy certain life-style markets.

Many fashion retailers go to trade shows and producer markets looking for merchandise suited for their targeted consumers' life-style. One illustration of how retailers can characterize consumers' life-styles appears in Figure 10–7. Using this life-style scheme and others like it, retailers can select, purchase, and stock merchandise that matches their target consumers' life-styles.

*Competitive Conditions.* To decide which products to include in or exclude from the product mix, the retailer must consider the competitive conditions under which the

### "The Perfectionist"

- Age: 25–45
- Size: Misses 4–14
- A woman who is *first* in a fashion trend; has the most advanced taste of all customers—the "Fashion Leader."
- Active; worldly; career-oriented; involved; free-spirited; energy abounding.
- Inherently understands fashion . . . incorporates fashion into every aspect of her lifestyle.
- Uniqueness and individuality are her two main concerns—she depends on clothes as a means of self-expression.
- She is governed by her emotions. When in an adventurous mood, she seeks the most advanced fashions . . . always avant-garde, nonconforming, often impractical. When in a classic mood, her taste level is pure, clean, and sophisticated.
- She combines a mix of fashion looks to cover her variety of emotional and active lifestyle needs.
- She is extremely conscious of her body; chooses clothes to complement her figure.
- Demands and appreciates quality.
- Impressed by designers who style for her contemporary lifestyle.
- Not necessarily price conscious; buys what she desires.
- She is influenced by her surroundings when shopping.
- Does not respond well to markdowns or price promotions.
- Needs little salespeople attention.
- Expects new arrivals often.
- Buys impulsively.
- Loyal to a store wherever she feels her *mood runs free.*

### "The Updated"

- Age: 25–60
- Size: Misses 4–16
- Desires fashion after it has been modified from its pure, advanced stages. Very often *this season's updated styles were last season's perfectionist styles.*
- Demands smart-looking items; stylish, yet not extreme.
- Working girl or woman; housewife; mother.
- Desires clothes that are functional additions to her wardrobe—multipurpose.
- Desires high degree of quality, practicality, and value for the price.

- Not necessarily label conscious.
- Will buy regular stock markdowns; responds only moderately to price promotions.
- Loyal to store that separates her look, supports her type, and puts her look together for her.
- Fastest-growing misses customer type.

### "The Young Affluent"

- Age: 25–50
- Size: Misses 4–14
- Career woman, wife.
- Leads active social life; involved.
- Often attracted to designer labels.
- Ruled by current designer trends.
- Respects fine merchandise.
- Demands quality.
- Is an investment buyer; designer wardrobe builder.
- Taste level similar to updated customer, but not price conscious.

### "The Traditionalist"

- Age: 26–65
- Size: Misses 8–20
- The conformist . . . likes fashion only after it is accepted.
- Less career-oriented; more job-oriented. Oftentimes office worker, teacher, housewife.
- Does not react to, or desire, fashion extremes.
- Extremely label conscious—loyal to those she has worn and liked in the past.
- Price conscious; quality aware.
- Very practical; demands ease of care.
- Very insecure about fashion in general—must have fashion put together for her.
- Fashion influenced by peers.
- Loyal to stores and professional salespeople who service her needs.
- Responds exceptionally well to price promotions and markdowns.
- Replacement customer; conservative taste.

### "The Establishment"

- Age: 45+
- Size: Misses 8–20
- Older, refined woman—dignified.
- Active in community; holds prestigious position.
- An investment buyer; wardrobe builder.
- Loves fine workmanship, fabrics, and detail.
- Concerned with quality and value.
- Appreciates designer merchandise.
- Limitless buying ability.
- Seeks clothes that fill her needs.

Source: M. M. Cohn, Little Rock, AK.

**FIGURE 10–7**
Life-style merchandising

product is available. A **direct, or intratype, competitor** is one whose merchandising program is about the same as another retailer's. An **indirect, or intertype, competitor** is one whose merchandising program is noticeably different from that of a retailer of similar products.

A product that is available to direct competitors has no "distinctive" advantage to any retailer. In some cases, however, it might help a retailer to establish that the store's image is on par with its competitors', and therefore the retailer would want to promote comparison shopping. Adopting a product that is available to indirect competitors might either help or hurt the store's image. If upscale, indirect competitors stock the product, the retailer's image can be enhanced, but if downscale, indirect competitors stock the product, the retailer's image could be damaged.

**Competitive conditions** can be either **exclusive** (no competitors), **selective** (few competitors), or **intensive** (many competitors). The retailer's typical assortment strategy varies with competitive conditions. Retailers should carry a deep assortment of exclusive product items and a limited assortment of selective products. And, for intensively distributed products, retailers must resort to one of two strategies: (1) stock only the best-selling items to satisfy customers whose preferred item is not available and who will accept a substitute, or (2) stock a deep assortment to satisfy most customers and thereby create a store image of "complete selection."

## Supply Considerations

In evaluating what and how many products to include in the product mix, the retailer should examine not only market conditions but also supply considerations, two of which are *availability* and the *reliability* of the supplier. Before making a decision to stock a product, the retailer should study the product's **availability**.

Ideally, for the retailer to make a positive decision on a product candidate, the product should be available from normal channels, with sufficient alternative supply sources, and under terms and conditions consistent with the product's sales and profit potential. Criteria that describe a **supplier's reliability** include (1) shipping on time, (2) filling orders adequately, (3) maintaining adequate stocks (avoiding stockouts), and (4) adjusting orders to meet the retailer's changing needs.

---

There are excellent sources of information to help retailers make product-mix decisions. Internal sources include sales records, want books and slips, sales personnel, in-store testing, and customer returns. External sources are comparison shopping, consumer opinions and behavior, vendors, trade shows, trade publications, and special reporting services.

**PRODUCT INFORMATION**

## Internal Sources

The most widely used internal source of product information must be the store's past sales for various product lines and items. Past *sales records* are especially useful for deciding about staple merchandise, but may be of limited use in estimating demand for fashion merchandise, where the past may very well be the past and have little to do with what consumers want in the future.

Another method for determining what customers want is to record their inquiries about (1) products the retailer does not stock and (2) products the retailer carries but that currently are out of stock. Salespeople can systematically record inquiries in *want books* or *want slips*. *Sales personnel* are an excellent source of information. Because they have more direct contact with consumers than anyone in the firm, salespeople are in a position to observe why and how consumers buy.

Retailers frequently use **in-store testing** to judge customer wants. Products are pretested by stocking a sample order and observing customer responses.

Finally, it is as important to find out what customers do not want as it is to find out what they do want. With the abundant supply of licensed lines in recent years, many retailers like Woodward & Lothrop have adopted an in-store testing program. Unknown lines, new lines from established designers, or new collections from new companies must perform at or above certain sales expectations in test situations before total buying, stocking, and merchandising decisions are made. Store data on products customers return or require adjustment for provide valuable information on the product mix.

### External Sources

A good outside source of information on what consumers want is what other stores sell them. Through **comparison shopping** at both competing and noncompeting stores, a retailer can often discover missed product opportunities and also inspect the merchandising techniques that competitors are using to move certain products successfully. Asking consumers their opinions and observing their behavior yield first-hand information on what products consumers want and when, where, how, and why they want them. Three common methods for soliciting *consumer opinions* and observing *consumer behavior* are consumer surveys, consumer panels, and consumer counts.

What are the advantages of trade shows as sources of product information?

Being in contact daily with large numbers of retailers, *vendors* and their representatives have a wide range of experiences on which to base their product opinions. They are thus excellent sources of product information, although retailers must be somewhat wary of their reliability, and recognize their biases.

**Trade shows** are occasions when manufacturers get together to exhibit their merchandise in one place. Trade shows range from exhibitions of a particular line of products to general merchandise displays. These events allow retailers to comparison shop, to talk to various vendor representatives, and to inspect displayed merchandise.[8]

*Trade publications* are good sources of information because (1) they provide basic trade information and (2) they contain numerous advertisements of interest to the retailer. Trade publications have feature articles and special reports on topics such as new products, industry trends, merchandising tips, current developments, and legal and environmental issues.

Retailers can subscribe to numerous **specialized reporting services**. Frequently, these services offer information on certain product lines and merchandising activities (e.g., advertising, store displays, and facings). They provide retailers with information periodically (daily, weekly, monthly) in the form of newspapers, special reports, or flash reports.

---

The basic objective in planning product-mix strategies is to offer consumers an optimum number of product lines and an optimum number of product items within each line. Figure 10–8 illustrates the four basic variety/assortment combination strategies: (1) narrow variety/shallow assortment, (2) wide variety/shallow assortment,

**PRODUCT-MIX STRATEGIES**

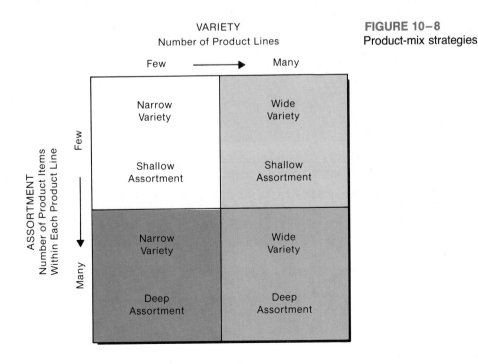

**FIGURE 10–8**
Product-mix strategies

(3) narrow variety/deep assortment, and (4) wide variety/deep assortment. These four combination strategies provide an excellent reference for retailers in crediting product-mix strategies.

### Narrow Variety/Shallow Assortment

A **narrow variety/shallow assortment strategy** offers consumers the most limited product selection (lines and items) of any of the combination strategies. Vending machines that hold only two or three choices of soft drinks, door-to-door sales representatives who sell only one product line with a limited number of product features, and the newsstand that offers only one or two newspapers are examples of retail institutions that use the narrow variety/shallow assortment strategy. The key to merchandising this limited product-mix strategy successfully is *place and time convenience*. Because it offers a limited choice, the narrow variety/shallow assortment retailer must make its offering readily available where and when consumers want it. Generally, the narrow variety/shallow assortment strategy suffers from a poor image and little, if any, customer loyalty other than that generated by convenience. A limited product mix, however, does create certain benefits. It simplifies operations, makes inventory control problems insignificant, and minimizes facility requirements. A major benefit is the retailer's small investment in inventories.

### Wide Variety/Shallow Assortment

The basic philosophy behind the **wide variety/shallow assortment strategy** is "stock a little of everything." The retailer offers a wide selection of different product lines but limits the selection of brands, styles, sizes, and so on within each line. Most variety stores (five and dime stores), general stores, and some discount houses follow this product-mix philosophy. A wide and shallow product mix offers the advantages of appealing to a broad market, satisfying the consumer in terms of product availability if not product selection, promoting one-stop shopping, and permitting reasonable control over inventories. The disadvantages of this product-mix strategy are lost sales and customer disappointment with the lack of selection within lines, low inventory turnover rate on slow-moving product lines, weak store image, and limited store loyalty.

### Narrow Variety/Deep Assortment

The "specialty" philosophy characterizes the **narrow variety/deep assortment strategy**. Some retailers try to appeal to a select group of consumers by offering only one or a few product lines with an excellent selection within each line. Specialty retailers can benefit greatly from their specialist image. By offering a specialized mix of products supported by specialized personnel, the narrow variety/deep assortment retailer can develop a distinct store image and a loyal customer following. Additional advantages to the retailer follow:

☐ Rare sales losses as a result of an inadequate selection of brands, styles, sizes, colors, and materials

- [ ] Greater likelihood of a high level of repeat shopping
- [ ] Greater specialization in the buying, managing, and selling of a limited line of products
- [ ] Good economies of scale in ordering large quantities of the same product

The principal limitation of a specialty strategy is that successful operations *depend solely on a single or limited line of products.* "Putting all the eggs in one basket" creates a high risk for the retailer that sells in a very limited market. When adverse conditions occur in the market area, the specialty retailer suffers the most.

## Wide Variety/Deep Assortment

The full-line department store best typifies the **wide variety/deep assortment strategy**. One-stop shopping is the basic philosophy of this all-inclusive product-mix strategy. A large number of product lines with supporting depth in each line allows the retailer to make a broad market appeal while satisfying most of the product needs of specific target markets. Few sales are lost as a result of an inadequate variety or assortment. Generally, satisfied customers develop store loyalty, leading to a high level of repeat shopping. Although retailers generally regard a wide variety/deep assortment strategy as the most desirable strategy from the viewpoint of selling, they also recognize the problems they must encounter in store operations. The most common problems are (1) the necessarily high level of investment in inventory to support such a diverse product mix; (2) the low stock-turnover rate associated with many marginal product lines; and (3) the large amount of space, fixtures, and equipment the retailer must have to properly merchandise such a wide range of products.

**PRODUCT-MIX TRENDS**

To survive in the contemporary world of retailing, product mixes must be adapted rapidly and creatively to the dynamics of the marketplace. Future winners in the field of retailing will be those that can best identify consumers' emerging unsatisfied needs and develop innovative product-mix strategies to satisfy them. Two emerging product-mix trends of particular interest are shotgun merchandising and rifle merchandising.

## Shotgun Merchandising

**Shotgun merchandising** is the marketing strategy of broadening the retail offering to meet consumers' expanding needs. By expanding the number of product options, retailers try to increase the size of their total market by appealing to several submarkets—attempting to satisfy the specific needs of several individual market segments. In diversifying the product mix, the shotgun merchandiser attempts to develop a general-purpose mix that will satisfy the product needs of most consumers "pretty well." A retailer can either add new product items or combine major product lines to develop a general-purpose mix.

**Item addition** involves adding to one retailer's traditional product lines the more desirable product items normally associated with another type of retailer. Book, magazine, cosmetic, and apparel racks are item additions to the supermarket's pri-

mary product offerings. In the retailing industry, item addition is often referred to as *cherry picking,* because the product item additions are those retailers consider the cream of the crop—the best of the product line. Characteristics of these product items are (1) low risk because of reasonably sure sales, (2) relatively high turnover rates, (3) adequate margins for respectable profits, (4) minimal personal selling effort, (5) routine ordering and stocking procedures, and (6) relatively low per-unit prices with high levels of impulse and unplanned purchasing.

    **Line combination** is the second shotgun strategy, in which the retailer combines two or more broad product lines into the store operation. The principle behind combining major merchandise lines is to provide consumers with a one-stop shopping opportunity for a wide range of products and therefore satisfy several needs under one roof. For example, the superstore combines many of the standard product lines of the supermarket, drugstore, variety store, and hardware store.

## Rifle Merchandising

**Rifle merchandising** is a strategy of targeting a product offering to a select group of customers. Although the number of product lines is very selective—often only one or two lines—there is a large assortment of product items within each line. In essence, the rifle merchandiser employs a penetration strategy, concentrating product options within limited lines to serve "all" the individual needs of a given market segment for a particular line of products. By concentrating on a limited line, the rifle merchandiser develops a specific-purpose mix that will satisfy very well all of the targeted consumers' specific needs for a given product. To create specific-purpose mixes, the rifle merchandiser uses one of two marketing strategies: either market positioning or multiplex distribution.

    **Market positioning** is the strategy of creating a "position" for a store and its product mix in the minds of consumers by relating it to other stores and their mixture of products. By specializing in certain product lines and by offering a choice within those lines, the rifle retailer hopes to establish a market niche and a particular market image. A long-time rifle merchandiser, The Gap, is repositioning itself to attract an older customer base. The Gap is changing its image from a teenage jeans mecca to "one of America's largest retailers of casual and active sportswear for men and women." The new target market ranges from teenagers to the dodderers in their forties.[9] Creating an image leads the rifle merchandiser to program its entire operation so that the consumer will perceive it as occupying a unique position within a particular product category (see Figure 10–9). This strategy positions the store in the minds of consumers as one that "has it all" in a particular class of merchandise.

    "No single retailing approach is likely to be sufficient in the future simply because markets are diverging more and more with respect to wants, needs, and buying power. Therefore, a single way of doing business is unlikely to appeal to all market segments."[10]

    In the last decade, rifle merchandisers have begun to operate multiple types of outlets with individual product mixes serving multiple market segments. In **multiplex distribution,** the rifle merchandiser aims at a number of different target markets.

FIGURE 10–9

The corporate level: A
market-positioning
strategy

> It used to be a dingy basement where shoppers rummaged through piles of
> bargain-priced clothes. But six months ago, Carson Pirie Scott & Co. transformed
> the 40,000-sq. ft. room into a colorful, mirrored space more befitting an exclusive
> shop in Beverly Hills than an 81-year-old department store in downtown Chicago.
> The new store-within-a-store is called Corporate Level, and it represents a bold
> attempt by Carson's to recapture the cream of the shopping masses—professional
> women who have fled department stores in search of high-quality merchandise
> and service.
>
> Targeting the Career Woman
>
> Carson's is not alone in its quest for the woman executive, who generally spends
> more on clothes than average shoppers. Many retailers provide wardrobe consultants
> for working women, and some have departments that sell "career" clothes. But Car-
> son's approach is being heralded as one of the most comprehensive. . . .
>
> Tailoring the Producer-Service Mix
>
> What makes Corporate Level different is that almost everything a customer needs
> is in one place. Designer outfits are steps away from shoes and accessories. And
> a woman not only can buy clothes but have her shoes repaired and her hair
> styled, drop off dry cleaning, make photocopies, and eat a meal. For $50 annually,
> she gets an extra package of services that allows her to cash checks, reserve a
> meeting room, and use a fashion consultant.

Source: Jo Ellen Daily, "One-Stop Shopping for the Woman on the Go," *Business Week,* 18 March 1985, 116.

Rifle merchandising is the strategy of targeting products to a select group of consumers.

Operating under the assumption that no one individual store can please all consumers, the multiplex retailer simply develops individual product mixes positioned to
meet the needs of a given market segment. J. C. Penney operates full-line department
stores, limited-line soft-goods stores, insurance centers, discount stores, catalog
desks and stores, and several foreign retail operations. The Limited also employs the
free-form concept of multiplex distribution; see Figure 10–10.

## SUMMARY

Offering the right product in the right quantities in the right place at the right time at
the right price and with the right appeal constitutes the merchandising process. To
develop a product mix, the retailer must first understand the total-product concept.
The total product is the sum of the product's functional, aesthetic, and service features
plus the psychological benefits the customer expects from buying and using the
product. Product mix refers to the full range of products a retailer offers to the
consumer; it represents "appropriate combinations" of products designed to meet the
specific needs of one or more identified target markets. It is composed of product
lines (any grouping of related products) and product items (specific products within
a product line that are clearly distinguishable). Product lines can be subclassified into
merchandise groups, classes, and categories. Product items are different brands of
products, differentiated by brand name, style, size, color, material, and price.

Product-mix decisions revolve around two separate but related decisions—
which and how many products to stock. Deciding which products requires determin-

☐ *Limited stores*—consists of 711 stores in every major market, with an average store size of 4,000 square feet. The Limited specializes in medium-priced fashion apparel that complements the tastes and lifestyles of contemporary women 20 to 40 years of age.

☐ *Limited Express*—offers the latest, most creative international assortment of sportswear and accessories designed to appeal to spirited women on the cutting edge of world fashion. Store designs and merchandise displays offer fashion-forward women (15 to 25 years) an exciting place to shop. There are currently 348 stores, in most major markets, with an average size of 2,600 square feet.

☐ *Lane Bryant*—with 631 stores averaging about 4,000 square feet, Lane Bryant is the foremost retailer of women's special-size apparel—fashions for sizes 14 and up. The format's ability to supply special-size customers with attractive and fashionable sportswear, ready-to-wear, intimate apparel, and accessories has resulted in a pattern of continuous expansion.

☐ *Victoria's Secret*—offers an international lingerie collection that provides contemporary women with imaginative, high-fashion designer intimate apparel through retail and mail-order divisions. With 236 stores averaging 1,900 square feet, the goal set for this division is to bring intimate apparel out of the basement and into the vanguard of fashion.

☐ *Lerner Stores*—fashion-forward sportswear, coats, dresses, and accessories at popular and budget prices. With 770 stores in every major market, with an average size in excess of 6,000 square feet, Lerner is the nation's largest specialty retailer under a single trade name.

☐ *Sizes Unlimited*—offers sportswear, dresses, and accessories, sizes 14 and up, priced below similar goods in most department and specialty stores. Sizes Unlimited offers a wide assortment of first-quality merchandise, nationally known brand labels, and private labels at prices that appeal to the value-conscious customer. The 398 stores average 3,500 square feet and can be found in most major markets.

☐ *Henri Bendel*—represents the best in international designer clothing and accessories. The store occupies a unique position at the apex of the fashion world (57th Street, Manhattan). It provides the ultrasophisticated customer with merchandise of incomparable style and quality. Henri Bendel plans to open stores in the top forty markets in the nation.

**FIGURE 10–10**
The Limited, Inc.: A multiple distribution retail organization

ing what product types are to be included in the product mix. Deciding how many products concerns developing product variety (number of different products to stock) and product assortment (number of different product items to stock in each product line).

Retailers use several criteria to decide which and how many products to carry: product compatibility, product attributes, product profitability, product life-cycles, fashion cycles, product appropriateness, and competitive conditions. The retailer must also consider the availability of needed products and the reliability of suppliers.

The retailer can consult several sources of information to evaluate the merits of a product. Internal sources consist of sales records, want books and slips, sales personnel, in-store testing, and customer returns. External sources of information are comparison shopping, consumer opinions and behavior, vendors, trade shows, trade publications, and special reporting services.

Regarding product mix, a retailer can use one of four variety/assortment strategies: narrow variety/shallow assortment, wide variety/shallow assortment, narrow variety/deep assortment, and wide variety/deep assortment.

Retailers are responding to the changing marketplace by employing either a shotgun or a rifle approach to merchandising. The shotgun merchandiser appeals to a combination of market segments by broadening its product lines through either product-item addition or product-line combination. The rifle merchandiser appeals to a target-market segment by using either a market-positioning strategy or a multiplex distribution system.

## STUDENT STUDY GUIDE

**KEY TERMS AND CONCEPTS**

affinity

availability of supply

classic

comparison shopping

complexity

direct and indirect competitors

exclusive, selective, and intensive competitive conditions

extended product

fad

fashion cycle

flop

ford

generic product

in-store testing

item addition

life-style merchandising

line combination

market positioning

merchandise category

merchandise class

merchandise group

multiplex distribution strategy

narrow variety/deep assortment strategy

narrow variety/shallow assortment strategy

observability

physical product

product assortment

product attribute

product compatibility

product complement

product item

product life-cycle (PLC)

product line

product-mix concept

product profitability

product substitute

product variety

relative advantage

reliability of supplier

rifle merchandising

shotgun merchandising

specialized reporting service

total-product concept

trade show

trialability

unrelated product

wide variety/deep assortment strategy

wide variety/shallow assortment strategy

**REVIEW QUESTIONS**

1. What is the total-product concept? Briefly describe each of the concept's components.
2. How do product lines differ from product items?
3. Describe the two basic decisions the retailer faces in developing the product mix.
4. Define product variety. How does it differ from product assortment?

5. Identify and describe the three basic classes of products based on product compatibility. Which of these classes of products should be included in the retailer's product mix?
6. How do the product attributes of bulk and standardization influence the retailer's decisions of which and how many products should be stocked?
7. What should the retailer's stocking strategy be for products in each of the four stages of the product life cycle?
8. Develop a profile of a fashion-conscious consumer.
9. Describe each of the four fashion cycles and discuss what the retailer's stock position should be relative to each cycle.
10. Which five product characteristics are used in evaluating new product offerings relative to their market appropriateness?
11. What is life-style merchandising?
12. What are the internal sources of product information?
13. Identify the four basic variety/assortment combination strategies used in developing a retail product mix. Briefly describe each strategy.
14. Compare and contrast the strategies of shotgun and rifle merchandising.

True or False

REVIEW EXAM

_____ 1. Aesthetic product features are extremely important because they determine to a large extent how well the product will actually perform those functions that it was designed to accomplish.
_____ 2. A product item is a specific product within a product line that is unique and clearly distinguishable from other products within and outside the product line.
_____ 3. Consumers tend to be less sensitive about the price of product complements; hence, retailers often sell complements at above-average markups.
_____ 4. Almost without exception, the most desirable products for the retailer to stock are those in the introduction stage of the product life-cycle.
_____ 5. The fashion retailer's decision relative to the classic fashion is not whether to stock it, but rather what price line to stock from what supplier with what product features.
_____ 6. Retailers are often forced to carry intensively distributed products because they are so readily available in competitive outlets and consumers expect them to be in stock.
_____ 7. The superstore is a good example of a retail organization that uses the line combination strategy.

## STUDENT APPLICATIONS MANUAL

PROJECTS:<br>INVESTIGATIONS<br>AND<br>APPLICATIONS

1. Identify and discuss the functional, aesthetic, service, and psychological features (the total product) of each of the following products: (1) a steak dinner, (2) a cologne, and (3) a 35-mm camera.
2. Survey your local supermarket and identify at least three examples of each of the following: (1) perfect substitutes, (2) general substitutes, (3) perfect complements, and (4) general complements. Explain your descriptions.
3. A fashion is a concept of what is "currently appropriate" and represents the "prevailing style" currently in vogue. Interview a local buyer of fashion apparel and identify and describe fashions that are currently appropriate for your area. Do local fashions differ from the prevailing styles that are in vogue nationally? How and why?
4. How exclusive is the Pierre Cardin name? Describe the product lines carrying the name and the distribution of those products.

5. Identify and describe some major "special reporting services" used by retailers to obtain information on products.

6. Survey retail stores in your local community and find specific examples of item addition and line combination. Do you believe these retailing strategies are being accepted by the consuming public? Why or why not?

7. Identify three limited-line stores in your community that are engaging in a "market positioning" strategy. What merchandise and operating tactics are they using to establish a market niche and a particular market image in the consumer's mind?

---

**CASES:
PROBLEMS AND
DECISIONS**

**CASE 10–1
Lockner's Department Store: The Role of a Toy Department***

### INTRODUCTION

For the last forty years, Lockner's Department Store has been recognized as one of the leading retail merchandisers in the midwestern city of Plains, Iowa (1987 population: 175,000). The area is expected to continue above-average population growth for the next twenty years. During the last four decades, Lockner's has built a reputation as an upscale retailer of quality merchandise. By carefully designing the firm's total merchandising program, Lockner's management has generally been successful in appealing to both middle- and upper-class consumers. Over the last five years, sales and profit objectives for most merchandise departments have been met or exceeded. The one exception to this is the toy department. For Bill Lockner, founder and president of the store, this situation is simply unacceptable.

### LOCKNER'S MERCHANDISING STRATEGY

#### The Product/Service Mixes

Good quality, high style, and an excellent variety of brand-name merchandise have been hallmarks of the firm's product mix. To help differentiate its product mix from competitive product offerings, Lockner's has featured a number of top-quality private labels in several different product lines. Also, a variety of specialty and imported goods not commonly found in competitive stores has been an integral part of Lockner's product strategy. To enhance its image as an upscale, full-line department store and as a one-stop shopping store, Lockner's carries a deep assortment of brands, models, styles, and colors for most product lines.

Excellent service is another key ingredient in the store's merchandising program. Lockner's offers a complete service mix with a variety of credit, delivery, and wrapping plans and alterations, repair, and layaway services. All essential and expected services are provided free of charge or at some minimal fee in a limited number of cases.

#### The Promotional/Place Mixes

Lockner's promotional strategy is directed at enhancing the store's prestige image. To do so, local newspaper advertisements focus on appeals stressing product selection and quality, service offerings, and shopping atmosphere.

Product advertisements featuring a few carefully selected items are used to inform customers of new and special merchandise. The store also runs numerous institutional ad-

---

*This case was prepared by George Prough and Dale Lewison, The University of Akron.

vertisements that attempt to communicate the message that "Lockner's is *the* place to shop." Once a customer has been attracted to the store, considerable attention is given to capitalizing on the traffic through the use of such promotional tools as attractive and accessible displays, special effects, and promotional demonstrations.

The store is located on the newly opened Hub Mall, an open-air pedestrian mall in downtown Plains. The area features many renovated or new specialty shops and more fashion-oriented shops. Lockner's was completely renovated inside and out at the same time as the mall. Both the area and the store are accessible to the area's population and offer a pleasurable and exciting shopping environment not found anywhere nearby.

## THE TOY INDUSTRY

Estimates show sales in the toy industry to be somewhere in the neighborhood of $2 billion annually. Department stores typically sell about 13 percent of all toys, games, and hobby items. However, sales in department stores indicate that they sell a higher-than-average share of dolls and educational and scientific toys.

Toys are product items with interesting life-cycles; both the level and duration of consumer acceptance can vary substantially from one toy line to another. Toys range from being very faddish product items whose life expectancy is very short (several months) to classics like Monopoly and Scrabble that remain popular for decades. Frequently, the general nature of the life-cycle for a particular new toy can be explained by the toy's origin. Currently, many new toy ideas originate in popular movies or television programs; hence, the life expectancy depends on the level and duration of popularity for these entertainment vehicles. For instance, Strawberry Shortcake products once enjoyed tremendous success, but since the demise of the television program, the popularity of these products has declined considerably. In contrast, Star Wars toys have enjoyed tremendous popularity for several years and sales are expected to continue at fairly substantial levels as a result of plans to continue sequels into the 1990s.

Technologically and socially, the toy industry has undergone considerable change during the last few decades. On the technological front, toys have evolved dramatically from the cornhusk dolls of the seventeenth century. Today, computer technology has had a major impact on toys and games in the sense that many computer games and software for home computers have broadened the appeal of such "toys" to all age groups. The old rule that toys appeal only to young children no longer applies.

In addition, today's computer and board games offer people the opportunity to exercise their analytical prowess by making key decisions that affect the outcome of the game. For all age groups, the trend appears to be away from passive games of chance to more active games of skill and decision making.

Socially, toys have evolved with the social values and moods of the country. As exemplified by the Fisher Price line of toys, educational values are often preeminent for parents shopping for toys for their younger children. Today, motives for purchasing toys include not only entertainment value but the belief that toys can play an important role in the mental, physical, and creative development of children. Contemporary social values are also reflected in the type of toys purchased for children. In past years, dolls only cried "Mama"; today dolls have more extensive vocabularies, are often anatomically correct, and are capable of a number of biological functions. Further, as the roles of men and women are becoming redefined, so too are toys and toy buying. Boys are increasingly accepting dolls (Star Wars figures, G. I. Joe figures, He-Man figures, Cabbage Patch dolls, etc.) and girls are increasingly becoming active in sports.

The toy industry is a highly competitive business. Of the estimated 125,000 toy items produced each year, approximately 12,000 achieve a high level of customer acceptance. Of the 12,000 that do gain wide acceptance, only a few will return to the same level of public acceptance the following year. Thus, knowing what is and what is not a hot item is vital to survival in the toy industry.

Product offerings are planned by toy manufacturers in April, and production levels are set at that time. Product competition takes several forms. Toy manufacturers compete for the rights to produce toy items that are expected to succeed (e.g., Star War toys), for the development of new products, and for the development of additional product features and options for existing toys. Manufacturers' representatives, printed materials, and trade shows are the major promotional vehicles used to obtain orders from wholesalers and retailers. Orders for toys are accepted from April through August, and they are filled on a first-come, first-served basis. Because the manufacturer produces a preset number of a given toy, it is essential that wholesalers and retailers place orders for "hot" items early. Advertising is vitally important on both the local and national level. To create product awareness and to promote product and brand preference, toy manufacturers advertise heavily on television during Saturday mornings and on other programs directed toward children. At the local level, manufacturers and retailers often run cooperative newspaper or other local advertising to inform customers about which stores have the product and what their prices may be.

Clearly the major target market for toys is the youth market. Children with allowances and some with baby-sitting, yardwork, and other income represent a strong economic force. In addition, children play an "influencer" role in the family. Demand for a particular toy depends heavily upon the ability of children to influence parents to purchase that item. A number of research studies show the following:

1. Children are strongly influenced by television commercials; in three out of four cases, toys preferred had recently been seen on television.
2. Peer groups are strong influences of toy preference for many children (this influence occurs in the form of the "two-step flow of communication"—television advertisements to playmates or peers who buy the product and then influence their friends to buy it, too).
3. Younger children attempt to influence parental purchasing more frequently than do older children.
4. The frequency of parents giving in to a child's requests for a particular toy increases with the age of the child.
5. Parents are preferred twice as much as peers as a source of product information, even by adolescent children.
6. Mothers are the general purchasing agents for most families; hence, they are a majority of the actual toy purchasers.

## MIKE ROGERS' SITUATION

It is February of 1988 and Mike Rogers, toy department manager for Lockner's Department Store, is contemplating the role played by the toy department in the firm's overall merchandising strategy. Currently, the toy department is used as a seasonal "leader" department; that is, its primary function is to attract consumers into the store during the Christmas season by offering an excellent selection of popular toys at very competitive prices. During the rest of the year, the toy department is largely neglected both by Lockner's management and by Lockner's customers. At these times, Lockner's stocks seasonal toys plus a variety of the most popular toys, and prices are kept competitive.

Lockner's toy stock during the nonholiday seasons consists primarily of the most popular toys and dolls. Rogers has never bought many board games, European specialty toys, specialty and collectable dolls, or the more extraordinary toys. Instead, he has chosen to stay with the basics except during the seasonal promotions.

Recently Rogers has been wondering whether a new role for the toy department might be worth considering. Rogers believes it would be appropriate to review the department's whole situation with the idea of identifying strategy alternatives and making possible recommendations for a new merchandising role for the toy department.

## ASSIGNMENT

1. What options are available for 1988–1989?
2. Identify the merchandising role you would adopt for Lockner's toy department, and justify your selection.

## CASE 10–2
## J. Rogers Department Stores Company—Evaluating A New Merchandising Program*

### BACKGROUND

Rogers' Emporium was established in 1907 by John Rogers. The foundation for the firm's present-day image as one of the leading retail merchandisers in the southwestern United States is the founder's early recognition of the potential market demand for upscale merchandise that emerged during the oil boom years. As old "J. R." used to say, "give the customers what they want, but always make a profit." This guiding principle has always served as the basic merchandising and operating policy for the firm and has given it a national reputation as a unique and profitable merchandiser of a wide variety of unusual and everyday products and services.

The firm was reorganized into J. Rogers Department Stores Company in 1952. Its success has been attributed largely to its adherence to the policy of "gross margin maintenance." It is and always has been the company's operating goal to obtain an overall 40 percent gross margin for each of its stores. The following gross margin objectives were established for each of the store's general merchandise categories: 50 percent for wearing apparel, 60 percent for accessories, 30 percent for household goods, 30 percent for household furnishings, 40 percent for consumer electronics, and 40 percent for sporting goods.

Currently, the J. Rogers Department Stores Company operates three full-line department stores at Great Plains Mall, Parkside Mall, and Southland Mall. By March of this year, the company's new store in Dixieland Mall will be open and in full operation. As with the three current stores, the new outlet will be a full-service department store appealing to the area's middle- and upper-class consumers.

As the GMM (general merchandise manager) for the last five years, Louis Stouch has been directly responsible for overseeing most of the major buying decisions for all three stores. During his tenure as GMM, Louis' track record has been outstanding as judged by the criterion of achieving the expected 40 percent overall gross margin. In each of the major merchandise categories and for most of the individual product lines, expected gross margins were realized. One of the more important exceptions has been Great Western Clothing Company's line of men's suits, The Naturals. Gross margins realized on The Naturals have varied considerably, and unsatisfactory performance levels have characterized this product line in three of the last five years. A review of Great Western's other product lines carried by J. Rogers, however, revealed a sales and gross margin performance meeting or exceeding

---

*This case was prepared by Dale M. Lewison and Jon Hawes, The University of Akron.

the firm's expectations. This latter fact would suggest the need to maintain good relationships with the Great Western Clothing Company.

## CURRENT SITUATION

With the rapidly approaching summer buying season, Stouch must make an immediate decision whether to continue to carry The Naturals line of men's suits. He has already received next year's proposed merchandising program for The Naturals (see Exhibits 1 and 2) from Sharon Neidert, national sales manager for Great Western Clothing Company. Before making any decision regarding The Naturals, a comprehensive comparative analysis between last year's merchandising program (Exhibit 3) and the proposed new program seemed in order. Having skimmed the new program, Stouch noticed a number of significant changes; perhaps these changes might be sufficient to ensure the 50 percent gross margin expectations that have not always been realized in the past. Pressed for time, he decided to ask the assistant GMM, Cheryl Nader, to conduct the comparative analysis and to recommend possible courses of action.

**EXHIBIT 1**

Mr. Louis Stouch
General Merchandise Manager
J. Rogers Department Stores
400 East Plains Ave
Dallas, Texas 78041

Dear Mr. Stouch:

    A new season is upon us and we at Great Western Clothing Company are excited about our new merchandising program for The Naturals. The new program entails numerous changes, and we believe these changes will provide you with the opportunity to realize a substantial increase in unit sales at profitable levels. With the opening of your new store and the quantity discount structure of the new merchandising program, we think it would be in your best interest to place a unit order in excess of 300 units. Our sales representative, Jeb Works, will be calling upon you shortly to finalize your order. As always, we are looking forward to working with you and your organization.

        Sincerely,

        Sharon Neidert
        National Sales Manager
        Great Western Clothing Company

| Product class | Men's apparel |
|---|---|
| Product line | "The Naturals"—mix and match suits |
| Product items | The summer "Naturals" are available as separate pieces and can be sold in any coat/slack combination (mix and match). Solid and patterned coats are available in standard sizes 30–48 and long sizes 40–48. Slacks are available in standard waist sizes. A standard length allows the slack to be altered to the customer's dimensions. |

**Merchandising program**

| List price | Coat: $90 |
|---|---|
| | Slack: $30 |
| Discount structure | |
| Trade (chain) | Coat: 30%, 15%, 10% |
| | Slack: 25%, 10%, 5% |
| Quantity (noncumulative) | Cost: 0% per unit—1–99 units |
| | 1% per unit—100–199 units |
| | 4% per unit—200–299 units |
| | 8% per unit—300 or more units |
| | Slack: 0% per unit—1–199 units |
| | 1% per unit—200–299 units |
| | 4% per unit—300 or more units |
| Cash | 2/10, n 30 |
| Promotional allowance | Coat: 0%   per unit—1–199 units |
| | 5%   per unit—200–299 units |
| | 1.5% per unit—300 or more units |
| | Slack: 0% per unit—1–299 units |
| | 1% per unit—300 or more units |
| Shipping terms | FOB origin, freight prepaid |
| Reorder delivery time | 2–3 weeks |
| Minimum reorder quantity | 1 dozen |

**EXHIBIT 2**

Year 2 merchandising program for The Naturals, Great Western Clothing Company

## ASSIGNMENT

Assume the role of Cheryl Nader and develop a comprehensive comparative analysis report for each year of The Naturals merchandising program. Having discussed the project with Louis Stouch, you have agreed to include within the report the following items:

1. A determination of the realized gross margin for the first year's program. (Sales records will show that 190 units were ordered and sold. Expense records will show that the average transportation cost per unit is 4 percent of list price, the average transit insurance cost per unit is 1 percent of list price, and the average alteration cost per unit is 1 percent of list price.)

2. A determination of the expected gross margin for the second year's program at various estimated unit sales levels (e.g., 175, 200, 250, and 300 units).

EXHIBIT 3
Year 1 merchandising
program for The Natu-
rals, Great Western
Clothing Company

| | |
|---|---|
| Product class | Men's apparel |
| Product line | "The Naturals"—two-piece suits |
| Product items | The summer "Naturals" are available in four solid colors. "The Naturals" are cut in contemporary fashion and are available in standard suit sizes of 30–48. |
| *Merchandising program* | |
| List price | Suit: $100 |
| Discount structure | |
|   Trade (chain) | Suit: 30%, 15%, 10% |
|   Quantity (cumulative) | Suit: 0% per unit—1–99 units |
| | 1% per unit—100–199 units |
| | 4% per unit—200–299 units |
| | 7% per unit—300 or more units |
| Cash (EOM) | 2/10, n 30 |
| Promotional allowances | Suit: .5% per unit |
| Shipping terms | FOB destination, freight prepaid |
| Reorder delivery time | 1–2 weeks |
| Minimum reorder quantity | 1 dozen |
| Return privilege | 5% of ordered stock |

3. A statement of the advantages and disadvantages of the first year's program as compared to the second year's program.
4. A description of the alternative courses of action that are open to the company regarding the 1989 program.
5. A recommendation and justification of which alternative the company should pursue.

**ENDNOTES**

1. Bob Garfield, "Images a Plus for Wendy's," *Advertising Age,* 13 April 1987, 30.
2. Kathryn M. Greenwood and Mary F. Murphy, *Fashion Innovation and Marketing* (New York: Macmillan, 1978), 57–58.
3. John A. Quelch, "Marketing the Premium Product," *Business Horizons* (May–June 1987): 44.
4. See Penny Gill, "European Designers," *Stores* (December 1987): 16–22.
5. Miriam Tatzel, "Skill and Motivation in Clothes Shopping: Fashion-Conscious, Independent, and Apathetic Consumers," *Journal of Retailing* 58 (Winter, 1982): 91–92.
6. Sallie Hook, "Managers Must Know Conceptual Distinctions of Fashion Marketing," *Marketing News,* 8 May 1987, 23.
7. Walter J. Salmon and Karen A. Cmar, "Private Labels Are Back in Fashion," *Harvard Business Review* (May–June 1987): 102.
8. See Robert Black, *The Trade Show Industry* (East Orleans, Mass: Trade Show Bureau, 1986): 5.
9. Jules Abend, "Widening the Gap," *Stores* (November 1985): 95.
10. Jagdish N. Sheth, "Emerging Trends for the Retailing Industry," *Journal of Retailing* 59 (Fall 1983): 14.

# 11

**Outline**

**Objectives**

☐ Comprehend the need to support the product mix with adequate customer services.

☐ Differentiate among consumer expectations for various services types and levels.

☐ Identify the principal objectives in providing customer services and discuss the factors that determine the level of services required to meet those objectives.

☐ Name the major components of the service mix and explain how each component enhances the retailer's product mix and facilitates consumers' purchase decision making.

# Customer Support Services

O ften overlooked in the retailer's merchandise mix is the service mix. Consumers buy more than a physical product; in fact, consumers expect the retailer to perform certain services before, during, and after the sale. These services often are as important as, if not more important than, the product itself. "Retailing is a 'people' business. 'People service' makes the difference—It matters not whether a company sells fashion or food, upscale or downscale, in market focus. Study the most successful self-service retailers and what you will find is that service is a key to their success."[1] This chapter describes the role of the service mix in the retailer's total merchandise mix.

The term *retail services* encompasses a wide variety of activities.[2] Retailers offer either primary services or complementary services. **Primary-service** retailers concentrate on rendering services to consumers and typically sell physical products as supplements to these services. Service is their reason for being in business. Examples of service retailers are banking, insurance, and real estate firms; firms that provide recreational and entertainment services; personal-care specialists ranging from hair stylists to health-spa owners; and establishments that provide home and auto repair and maintenance services. Retailers can obtain information on most of these service retailers from the "Selected Services" section of the *Census of Business*.

Many retailers view the services they offer as secondary or supplementary to the physical products they sell. These **complementary services** are neither their main function nor the reason these retailers are in business. Essentially, consumers and retailers consider supplementary services as "fringe benefits" that some, but not all, retailers offer in addition to their product mixes. Supplementary services enhance the retailer's merchandising program by providing "extras." Examples of supplementary services are delivery, credit, wrapping and packaging, parking, return privileges, installation, maintenance, repairs, alterations, some consulting services, and a host of other operations that only supplement the retailer's business format.

The following sections address the retailer's fundamental problem of offering supplementary services. The marketing of primary services involves most of the problems associated with marketing products; hence, many of the merchandising techniques discussed in previous chapters and those to be discussed in chapters to follow can be applied to primary-service retailing. As a matter of fact, primary-service retailers also face the problem of developing an offering of supplementary services.

**TYPES OF RETAIL SERVICES**

## THE RETAIL SERVICE PROBLEM

The basic problems retailers face in developing their service mix are essentially the same as those they encounter in developing their product mix. The service-mix decision entails determining "which services" and "how many services" they should offer consumers. Thus, retailers must decide on the level of services that will complement their product mix.

### Retail Service Types

Based on relative importance, services can be classified as essential, expected, and optional. **Essential services** are basic and necessary to a particular retail operation; without them, it is unlikely that the retailer could survive. Although essential services vary from one type of operation to another, the following services are essential to most retailers: (1) maintaining store hours, (2) providing parking facilities, (3) handling customer complaints, and (4) supplying information and assistance. **Expected services** are not essential for the retailer to operate but are expected by consumers. Delivery, credit, and alterations are three services that consumers expect from appliance, furniture, and clothing retailers, respectively. **Optional services** are neither necessary to the retailer's operation nor expected by the customers. Optional services can help a retailer develop a unique service offering and thereby distinguish itself. For example, "Rich's in Atlanta is offering automobile leasing . . . open and closed leasing contracts are available and financing is arranged. . . . Woodward & Lothrop has gone into the apartment-finding business in Washington, D.C., and environs. . . . Marshall Field has a corporate gift service."[3] McDonald's added stock repeater boards in selected restaurants where business people make up most of the morning trade.[4]

### Retail Service Levels

A **service level** is the extent to which a retailer will provide consumers with "extra" help in purchasing a product. The level of service is a function of the type and number of services the retailer provides and the terms and conditions under which they are provided. Service levels range along a continuum from a low to a high service level. A low-service–level retailer offers only services that are essential to its operation. Although these services are typically essential to the consumer's purchase of the product, some retailers even assess a separate charge for them. "Over the last 20 years, prices for services have risen about 80% more than prices for goods . . . since automation has squeezed labor out of the manufacturing process, goods have become cheap and services expensive."[5] At the other end of the continuum, high-service–level retailers offer consumers expected and optional services. At this level, retailers offer all essential and expected services free of charge; optional services may entail a separate assessment. In addition to the number, type, and conditions of services, a number of differentiating characteristics separate the service winners from the service losers (Figure 11–1).

### Retail Service Objectives

The retailer's service mix can be directed at accomplishing one or more of the following service objectives.

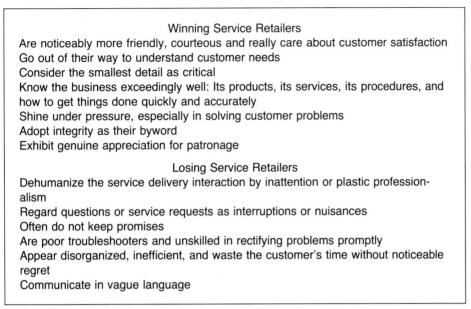

Source: George A. Rieder, " 'Show Me' : The Secret to Building a Service-Minded Culture," *Retailing Issues Letter* (Center for Retailing Studies, Texas A&M University, June 1986):1.

*Increasing Form Utility.* A few form-creating services that retailers offer include altering and tailoring for clothing products, installing appliances and home furnishings, engraving and personalizing jewelry, and assembling lawn and garden equipment.

*Facilitating Time Utility.* Consumer credit, layaway, and extended store hours are three services retailers offer to create time utility. To strengthen its time utility service mix, K Mart has introduced an automated layaway system. This computer-based system generates the layaway contract, handles customer payments, and maintains layaway records.[6]

*Enhancing Place Utility.* The best way to add place utility to a product mix is through convenient locations, delivery services, and catering services.

*Promoting Possession Utility.* To promote possession utility, retailers must provide consumers with information to facilitate the exchange of ownership process. Personal selling, fashion shows, information booths, complaint desks, bridal registries, and consultants are some of the informational services retailers offer.

*Increasing Customer Convenience.* Services that provide customer convenience and comfort include packaging, bagging, free parking, check cashing, restaurants, snack bars, restrooms, lounges, parcel checking, push carts, water fountains, and complimentary coffee. Shoppers at California-based Lucky Stores who want to pay in cash no longer have to withdraw money from their wallets or suffer through a time-consuming check-approval process. Instead, using a debit card, in just seven seconds customers can pay a retailer directly out of their checking accounts via an electronic funds transfer.[7]

*Creating a Store Image.* By offering a *full range of services,* the retailer can promote the image of being a full-service store with quality merchandise and prestige prices. Conversely, the retailer can choose to offer only services that are essential to the exchange process, thereby creating a no-frills, low-price image.

*Providing Customer and Product Security.* Restroom attendants, properly lighted stores and parking facilities, and security guards all enhance the customer's feeling of a safe and secure environment. Perhaps equally important to most customers is product security, provided by such services as warranties, return privileges, allowances, maintenance contracts, and product information. Many cosmetic companies,

What service objectives might be met by offering an on-site store cooking course?

including Elizabeth Arden and Shiseido Cosmetics, are using computer simulation to provide their customers with high-tech information about their skin and hair needs. Shiseido's makeup simulator is able to give the customer an on-screen make-over, change hair styles . . . and add henna or highlights without physical application of the product to the customer.[8]

*Improving Store Traffic.* Some stores provide (1) rooms for public and private meetings; (2) space for various types of exhibits; (3) rental services for products that might not be related to their product mix; (4) post office, utility bill collection, and entertainment ticket facilities; (5) license bureaus; and (6) various types of professional services (e.g., tax, health, and personal care). All these services tend to draw into the store customers who might not otherwise be attracted. Macy's in San Francisco created the Hospitality Room for conventioneers who are visiting the city. These traffic-building services range from offering refreshments to shopping assistance.[9]

## Retail Service Determinants

Several factors enter into the decision about what service level to offer. Guided by the previously discussed service objectives, the retailer should consider at least the following five determinants: type of merchandise, type and size of store, location of the store, service levels of competitors, and resources of the firm.

The type of merchandise a retailer carries dictates to some extent the services consumers expect and desire. The physical and psychological attributes of a product are perhaps the two most important determinants of what the retailer's service level should be. For example, consumers expect home delivery and installation when they buy furniture and appliance products; the products' bulk makes these services necessary for most consumers. Warranties, repair services, and maintenance contracts also are services most retailers offer with these types of merchandise to reduce consumers' perceived risk. In the high fashion apparel industry, consumers normally *expect* (1) sales personnel to aid in the selection and evaluation of the garment relative to the customer's needs, (2) comfortable, secure fitting rooms, (3) expert alteration and tailoring services, (4) several credit plans and check-cashing privileges for the convenience of the "cashless" consumers, and (5) quality packaging in first-class garment boxes and bags.

Consumers tend to associate certain services with specific types of retail operations. Consumers generally expect department stores to be full-service retailers, whereas they perceive the discounter as either a cash-and-carry retailer or at most a limited-service retailer. Consumers expect lawn and garden shops to provide information on when and how to care for plants, jewelry stores to repair watches and appraise jewelry, and supermarkets to provide shopping carts, check cashing, bagging, and carryout service.

A store's physical *size* also influences what service level is feasible; some services require substantial space. The type and number of services that a small retailer with limited space can offer must be restricted to those that are essential to operation or at least those that can be provided with a minimal spatial commitment.

A store's location can influence types of services. Depending on its location, the retailer should consider services that (1) overcome a locational deficiency (e.g., retailers located in the central business districts of major metropolitan areas arrange for free parking at public and private facilities), (2) *fit into a locational surrounding* (e.g., retailers located in shopping centers with quality-oriented, high-service-level retailers must offer a similar level of service), and (3) *intensify a locational advantage* (e.g., a quality lakeside restaurant provides complementary pre- or post-dinner cruises aboard a paddleboat).

Many retailers prefer to engage in *nonprice competition,* of which one form is competing with service levels. Unfortunately, this kind of competition creates a dilemma; exceeding competitors' service levels can incur additional costs that lead to higher operating margins and thus greater vulnerability to price competition. On the other hand, if the retailer offers services below that of other retailers, it is not competitive in the area of services. As a general rule, the retailer should offer a service level comparable to that of competing operations of a similar type.

Services require resources. Each service must be based on adequate facilities and equipment, trained personnel, and sufficient capital investment. In addition to having adequate resources, the retailer must decide whether a service offering is worth the resources necessary to making the service available. The key question is, "Are there better alternative uses?" For example, delivery services require storage and loading facilities, delivery trucks, stockroom clerks, and truck drivers. To justify an investment, the retailer must determine that consumers need a given service and that any resulting sales volume more than offsets the investment.

## THE RETAIL SERVICE MIX

The service mix includes all those nonproduct "extras" retailers offer consumers to enhance the merchandise mix and to facilitate purchases. The major components of the service mix include store hours, credit plans, delivery, alterations and repairs, wrapping, and customer complaints.

### Store Hours

The retailer in today's market does not work an eight-to-five job. Store hours that are convenient to the customers in its area must be provided.

**Evening hours** from Monday through Saturday have become commonplace for most supermarkets and other retailers of necessity goods. Many supermarkets are now open twenty-four hours a day; since many supermarkets are staffed all night with stocking personnel, around-the-clock openings can be accomplished within reasonable cost constraints.[10] Likewise, for many mass merchandisers operating in community and regional shopping centers, evening hours have become an expected service. The duration of hours ranges from all night to an eight, nine, or ten P.M. closing. In part, night openings are the retailer's response to changing life-styles of consumers who find it more convenient and enjoyable to shop at night.

The issue of **Sunday hours** is similar to that of night hours in all respects except for the social, religious, and legal restrictions imposed in some parts of the country. Many state and local governments have enacted laws, often referred to as "blue laws," that determine (1) whether Sunday openings are allowed, (2) what types of products can be sold on Sundays (necessities vs. nonnecessities), and (3) when and how many hours stores can be open (e.g., from one to six P.M.).

## Consumer Credit

"Charge it!" "Buy now, pay later!" "Easy terms available!" "Only $10 down and $10 a month!" "Financing is available!" "Four years to pay!" These notices proclaim that credit has become a basic way of life for many U.S. consumers. To a substantial majority, credit has become either an essential or an expected part of the retailer's service mix. The question for most retailers is not whether to offer credit, but what type of credit to offer.[11] The retailer can elect one of several different credit systems: in-house credit, third-party credit, and private-label credit.

*Credit Systems.* An **in-house credit system** is owned, operated, and managed by the retail firm. Retailers offer credit services for a variety of reasons; (1) consumers expect the service, (2) store image will be enhanced, (3) many consumers cannot afford the retailer's assortment of merchandise unless they are offered credit, (4) competitors offer credit arrangements, and (5) market and economic conditions dictate the need for credit. Offering an in-house credit plan has advantages and disadvantages for most retailers. Advantages include the following:

☐ *Customer attraction.* Stores that offer credit services tend to attract customers who are more interested in product quality, store reputation, and service offerings and less interested in prices.

☐ *Customer loyalty.* Credit-granting stores more easily build repeat business, since credit customers tend to be more loyal than cash customers.

☐ *Customer goodwill.* Credit-granting stores generally have a more personal relationship with their customers and therefore become the first place the customer shops for a particular purchase.

☐ *Increased sales.* Credit services increase total sales volume because credit customers tend to buy more goods and pay higher prices than customers who do not use credit.

☐ *Sales stabilization.* Credit sales are more evenly spread throughout the month, whereas cash sales correspond more closely with those times immediately following paydays.

☐ *Market information.* Credit applications provide considerable amounts of information (age, sex, income, occupation, etc.) on the credit consumer; credit records can reveal a history of what, when, and where (which department) the customer bought.

☐ *Promotional effort.* Because credit customers are known to be customers of the store, they are an excellent foundation on which to build a mailing or telephone list for special promotions; additionally, the monthly statement credit customers receive is an effective vehicle for promotional literature.

In addition to these advantages, retailers realize the disadvantages associated with offering credit services. The most commonly cited disadvantages are those related to increased costs:

☐ *Higher operating expenses* result from additional facilities, personnel, equipment, and communications expenses necessary to provide credit services.

☐ *Costs of fees and commissions* paid to outside credit agencies that provide part or all of the retailer's credit services.

   ☐ *Tied-up funds* diverted to accounts receivable, thereby forcing the retailer to borrow working capital.

   ☐ *Bad debts,* losses from uncollectables, are part of the risk of providing credit services.

These additional costs are acceptable if they can be covered by offsetting revenues. Some retailers realize a substantial profit from their charges for credit services; Sears, for example, makes substantial profits on its retail credit operations.

As an alternative to offering in-store credit services, many retailers use **third-party credit systems,** accepting one or more of the credit cards issued by outside institutions. Often referred to as third-party cards, the most common types are those issued by banks (MasterCard and Visa) and entertainment-card companies (American Express, Diner's Club, and Carte Blanche). Gasoline companies also issue credit cards that consumers can use at stations carrying their brands.

Major advantages to accepting third-party cards are that retailers (1) do not have the problems of establishing and maintaining a credit department; (2) are relieved of the unpleasant tasks of investigating credit applications, billing customers, and pursuing collections; (3) can offer credit to consumers who otherwise would not qualify (e.g., out-of-town consumers) and thereby make sales they might have lost; and (4) can maintain a steady cash flow, since financial institutions convert credit card sales quickly and regularly into cash minus agreed-on service charges. The retailer does, however, have certain responsibilities in accepting and processing credit card sales, including filling out sales drafts properly, cooperating with financial institutions in identifying expired and stolen cards, obtaining authorization for charges over certain purchase ceilings, and submitting sales drafts to the credit agency within an agreed-on time.

The chief disadvantages for retailers that accept credit cards are the costs of the service and the depersonalization of relationships with customers. Credit agencies charge rates varying with the retailer's potential credit sales volume and several market and competitive conditions. Since the rate is negotiable, the retailer should make every effort to obtain the best possible terms. Depersonalization comes in the form of reduced store loyalty (the customer can shop anywhere the credit card is accepted) and consumers' lost feeling of "belonging" to a store in which they have a personal account.

A **private-label credit system** is one that retailers offer under their name but that a bank operates and manages. The retail firm realizes most of the benefits associated with in-house credit systems while avoiding many of the problems associated with credit management. Typically, the cost of this type of system is comparable to that of most in-house systems, and it is an attractive option for the retailer that has had difficulty turning its credit operation into a profit center.

*Credit Plans.* Depending on the type of credit system, one or more of three different types of credit plans will be available to the consumer: the open account, the installment plan, and revolving credit. The retailer's decision about which and how many types of credit plans to offer depends on the customer's need for a particular type of credit balanced against the retailer's need for cash for operating expenses.

Often referred to as the "regular charge" or "open book credit," the **open-account credit** plan allows customers to buy merchandise and pay for it within a specific time period without finance charges or interest. Usually, the customer is expected to pay the full amount within thirty days of the billing date, although some retailers extend the due date to either sixty or ninety days to promote special occasions or to distinguish their credit services from the thirty-day services their competitors offer. This **deferred billing** is often used during the Christmas season as a sales promotion tool and as an incentive to finalize the sale of a major purchase (i.e., the appliance dealer who offers "ninety days same as cash"). Beyond the due date, if full payment is not received, the retailer can assess a finance charge. The retailer usually grants an open account without requiring the customer to make a down payment or to put up collateral to secure the purchase.

Most customers would find it impossible to purchase large-ticket items such as automobiles, furniture, and appliances if they could not make small down payments and spread the additional payments over several months or years. The **installment-credit** plan allows consumers to pay their total purchase price (less down payment) in equal installment payments over a specified time period. Usually, equal installment payments are due monthly, although weekly and quarterly payments are optional. Retailers prefer to receive a down payment on installment purchases that equals or exceeds the initial depreciation of the product. Some retailers require only a minimal down payment or no down payment to make the sale.

Retailers carry installment accounts in one of three ways: conditional sales agreements, chattel mortgages, and lease agreements. In the **conditional sales agreement**, the title of the goods passes to the consumer conditional on full payment. In a **chattel mortgage agreement**, title passes to the customer when the contract is signed, but the product is secured by a lien against it for the unpaid balance. **Lease agreements** are contracts in which the customer rents a product in the present with the option to buy in the future.

Revolving credit incorporates some of the features of both the open-account and installment plans. Of the several variations of revolving credit plans, the two most common are the fixed-term and the option-term. The **fixed-term revolving credit** plan requires the customer to pay a fixed amount on any unpaid balance at regularly scheduled intervals (usually monthly) until the amount is paid in full. Under this plan, customers have a credit limit, such as $500, and may make credit purchases up to this limit as long as they continue to pay the agreed-on fixed payment (e.g., $50) each month. People who use fixed-term revolving accounts are usually assessed a finance charge (e.g., 1.5 percent per month, or 18 percent annually) on the unpaid balance.

**Option-term revolving credit** gives customers two payment options. They can either pay the full amount of the bill within a specified number of days (typically 30) and avoid any finance charges, or they can make at least a minimum payment and be assessed finance charges on the unpaid balance. As with the fixed-term account, a credit line is established and customers are free to make purchases up to the established limit.

*Credit Management.* A retailer that decides to offer in-store credit as part of the service mix must develop a credit-management system. Although the wide range of credit-management activities is beyond the scope of this text, two activities essential to successful credit management are (1) forming sound policies for granting credit and (2) determining good procedures for collecting credit accounts.

Before granting credit to individuals, retailers should evaluate each individual on the basis of the **three C's of credit**: character, capacity, and capital.

*Character* in a credit sense refers to attributes that distinguish one individual from another in meeting obligations. Desirable traits include maturity and honesty—characteristics that indicate willingness to accept responsibility (to pay bills) regardless of the circumstances. Personal interviews, reference checks, and the applicant's credit history help the retailer evaluate this attribute.

*Capacity* is the measure of an individual's earning power and ability to pay. A credit applicant's income is important not only in deciding whether to extend credit, but also in determining how much credit to extend. The third indication of credit worthiness is *capital* (i.e., the applicant's tangible assets). Accumulation of capital suggests that the applicant is capable of managing financial affairs and gives the retailer hope of recovering losses if it becomes necessary to sue the customer for nonpayment.

A more sophisticated system for screening credit applications is a **credit-scoring system**.[12] The procedures for developing a credit-scoring system follow:

☐ *Identifying* is an examination of good and bad credit accounts to identify characteristics associated with individuals who are good or poor credit risks. Figure 11–2 is one list of general characteristics that might be used in developing a credit-scoring system.

**FIGURE 11–2**
Characteristics used in developing credit-scoring systems

| | |
|---|---|
| Telephone at home | Bank savings account |
| Own/rent living accommodations | Bank checking account |
| Age | Zip code of residence |
| Time at home address | Age of automobile |
| Industry in which employed | Make and model of automobile |
| Time with employer | Geographic area of United States |
| Time with previous employer | Finance company reference |
| Type of employment | Debt-to-income ratio |
| Number of dependents | Monthly rent/mortgage payment |
| Types of credit reference | Family size |
| Income | Telephone area code |
| Savings and loan references | Location of relatives |
| Trade-union membership | Number of children |
| Age difference between man and wife | Number of other dependents |
| Telephone at work | Ownership of life insurance |
| Length of product being purchased | Width of product being purchased |
| First letter of last name | |

Source: Noel Capon, "Credit Scoring Systems: A Critical Analysis," *Journal of Marketing* 46 (Spring, 1982): 85.

☐ *Weighting* is the weighting of each characteristic (by assigning point values) based on its ability to discriminate between good and poor credit risks.

☐ *Scoring* is the evaluation of credit applications by adding the points received on the various application characteristics to arrive at a total score.

☐ *Accepting/Rejecting* is accepting or rejecting a credit application based on minimum point score.

☐ *Limiting* is setting a credit limit based on the total points assigned to the application; the higher the score, the higher the credit limit.[13]

Most credit accounts are handled through a routine, efficient billing system without any collection problems. When credit-collection problems (such as slow payment, nonpayment, or incorrect payment) occur, the retailer must have policies and procedures to handle them. Any credit-collection procedure entails several basic steps. First, credit accounts must be *reviewed* periodically and routinely to identify delinquent accounts. Immediate identification of delinquent accounts is critical because the more overdue the account becomes, the harder it is to collect.[14] Second, the retailer should make every effort to *determine the reason* for the delinquency. If the customer faces unexpected financial problems, the retailer should strive to reach some mutually agreeable arrangement. On the other hand, if the customer has no intention of repaying the debt or is a poor manager of finances, the retailer should initiate actions to settle the account.

## Delivery Service

Delivery service is one of the most controversial aspects of a service mix. In general, delivery service is difficult to plan, execute, and control. Before including delivery service in the service mix, the retailer must have a clear understanding of when to offer it, what problems it entails, under which terms and conditions it can be offered, and what type of delivery system is most appropriate to the operation.

Many circumstances justify including delivery services in the service mix. (1) Delivery is practically indispensable in retailing such bulky products as furniture and appliances. (2) In large urban areas where customers traveling by public transportation are greatly inconvenienced by taking purchases with them, delivery is often necessary. (3) Retailers that actively solicit telephone and mail orders must provide home-delivery services. (4) Delivery services for emergency goods, such as prescription drugs, are perceived by consumers as a valuable addition to the retailer's service mix. For many elderly people and shut-ins, delivery service is an *essential* service. (5) Some retailers have a prestige image to protect and therefore must include delivery services in their merchandise mix.

Finally, delivery services can create a competitive advantage by providing extra time and place convenience. Domino's Pizza, Inc., has built a 2,000-unit chain based on the firm's unique selling proposition: "The pizza will be delivered hot in 30 minutes or it's free of charge to the consumers."[15] Quick Flix Video has gone one up on Domino's by offering home delivery for a movie/pizza combination.[16]

The problems associated with delivery service are substantial. One of the most difficult problems is immediacy. When consumers purchase a product, they want immediate possession, with delivery either the same day or within a short period. A second major problem involves "not-at-homes." Delivery personnel face a recurring problem of what to do when the customer is not at home. A third problem in offering delivery services is the variations in demand. The day-to-day, week-to-week, and month-to-month fluctuations in demand for delivery services seriously undermine management planning. During low-demand periods, personnel, equipment, and facilities are underused. During periods of high demand, the retailer has insufficient delivery capacity to handle the demand.

Retailers can elect to use either an in-store system, an independent system, or a combination of the two. **In-store delivery systems** can be either wholly owned and operated by an individual store (private store systems) or partially owned and operated with other stores (cooperative store systems). This type of delivery system gives the retailer the greatest level of control over delivery operations and the greatest flexibility in adjusting services to customer needs.

**Independent delivery systems** are owned and operated independently from the retailer. They offer their services either on a contractual basis (consolidated systems) or on an open-to-the-general-public basis (parcel post and express services). Consolidated systems are independent firms that, for a fee, will deliver a store's packages. Express services and parcel post serve the needs of the general public. Retailers can resort to these systems when the delivery destination lies outside their delivery-service area.

## Alterations and Repairs

Many retailers offer alterations and repairs both as a supplement to the sale of products and as an income-producing service. Consumers expect retailers of expensive clothing to provide alteration services, and retailers of appliances, television sets, automobiles, and other durable goods to provide repair services. Traditionally, retailers offered alteration services as part of a garment's sales price; in recent years, however, retailers have experimented with various types of alteration charges ranging from no charge for minor alterations to partial or full charge for major alterations. To facilitate product-related alterations and to justify their investment in workroom facilities, equipment, and personnel, some retailers have established income-producing tailoring operations. Retailers usually charge customers for repairs on durable goods according to the terms and conditions of product warranties and established store policies. Normally, consumers bear no charge (or at most a minimum charge) for repairs on products still under warranty or that occur within a prescribed period after the purchase date. After the warranty or policy date expires, the retailer charges the consumer for repairs on a profit-making basis. To increase their income from repair services, many chain retailers (such as Sears) offer maintenance contracts on a fixed-fee basis. In addition to creating revenues, maintenance contracts also aid retailers in fully using their repair and service departments.

The retailer that deems it necessary to provide alteration or repair services has two operation alternatives: in-store and out-of-store services. In-store alteration and repair services give the retailer all of the advantages associated with direct control of such activities; however, this alternative also presents numerous management problems and requires substantial capital investments. Out-of-store alterations are subcontracted to private-service retailers specializing in tailoring services. Retailers normally use authorized, local repair services, factory repair services, and other subcontracted private-service firms to do out-of-store repairs. Disadvantages of using out-of-store repair services are lack of control, customer inconvenience, and longer service time.

## Wrapping

The three basic types of wrapping services retailers perform are bagging or sacking, store wrap, and gift wrap. Most consumers expect retailers to place purchases in a bag even when the products are prepackaged. **Bagging** (1) facilitates handling (especially when multiple purchases are involved); (2) protects purchases from inclement weather; and (3) preserves the privacy of the customer purchase. Proper bagging takes into account the size, shape, weight, and strength of the bag and the goods that go into it. If the General Federation of Women's Clubs of Washington, D.C., has anything to say about what constitutes proper bagging, the biodegradable character of a bag will be a major determinant in bagging. This organization is wagering a campaign against the nonbiodegradable plastic bag.[17]

**Store wrap** is the wrapping of customers' purchases in a standard (color and design) wrapping paper or box. Most department and specialty stores offer this service free of charge. Store wrap not only is an additional service for many retailers but also is a way to supplement their stores' advertising programs. The retailer that

Should a retailer offer gift-wrapping services?

incorporates its prestige name with store wrap can provide additional purchase incentives for customers who either seek a prestige gift or want their gift receivers to know the present came from a prestige store.

**Gift wraps** normally incorporate additional wrapping features such as bows and ribbons to distinguish them clearly from store wraps. Because of increased costs of materials and labor, the customer normally is charged an additional fee for gift-wrapping services.

Wrapping services are handled on either a departmental or a centralized basis. **Department wrapping** is performed by either the salesperson who makes the sale or the department cashier and wrapper. The advantages of having the salesperson wrap the merchandise are convenience for the customer, the opportunity for the salesperson to make an extra sale, and enhancement of the store's image through personalized service. Disadvantages of department wrapping are that salespeople must leave their primary job of selling and that salespeople normally do not excel at gift wrapping. Many stores perform **centralized wrapping** at one central location, but many large stores centralize wrapping on each floor. Although more cost-efficient than department wrapping, this system does represent an inconvenience for customers, who must find the wrapping desk and may have to wait in line.

### Customer Complaints

In 1962, President John F. Kennedy identified four basic consumer rights: "the right to safety, the right to be informed, the right to choose, and the right to be heard." Two of these rights, the right to be heard and to be informed, are key factors in the customer-complaint process. Customers expect to be informed of all operating policies that affect their patronage, and they expect to be heard when they want to register a complaint. While customer complaints typically are viewed negatively, especially if excessive in number, they also can be viewed positively. First, a customer who complains gives the retailer a chance to identify and correct a problem. Second, customer complaints serve as a major source of information regarding the retailer's products, services, and other merchandising activities.

Most customer complaints result from one of three general causes: product-related, service-related, and customer-related difficulties. Product-related causes include the following:

1. *Poor-quality products*—inferior workmanship and materials that cause fading or bleeding colors, shrinking or stretching fabrics, and rusting or tarnishing metals
2. *Damaged products*—merchandise that is chipped, stained, soiled, ripped, spoiled, or scratched
3. *Incorrect products*—merchandise that is either mislabeled according to size and price or mismatched in terms of color and style
4. *Insufficient selection*—out-of-stock merchandise, discontinued merchandise, limited-line merchandise, and new merchandise

Service-related causes involve customer dissatisfaction with sales personnel and services such as checkout, delivery, workroom, and customer accounts. Complaints about sales personnel usually center around the salesperson's (1) *disposition* (indifferent, discourteous, unfriendly, pushy); (2) *incompetence* (lack of product knowledge, poor selling skills, lack of familiarity with store policies); (3) *dishonesty* (unfulfilled promises, false information, additional charges, incorrect change); or (4) *selling methods* (overselling customers by selling them too much of an item or by trading them up to a product they cannot afford). Complaints about delivery services include late, lost, and incorrect deliveries and untidy and unpleasant delivery personnel. Improper alterations, lengthy delays, and overcharges are the chief causes of complaints stemming from workroom services. Finally, improper handling of accounts irritates customers. Errors in billing, receipt of a bill after it has already been paid, delays in receiving account statements, and monthly literature are some of the more irksome problems.

Customers make mistakes; sometimes they are intentional, sometimes they are not. Customer mistakes are also a cause of customer-related complaints. For example, customers may purchase a product thinking it will match or fit another product they own. If it does not, they may want to return it. If the retailer does not issue a refund, then the customer surely will complain. A "change of mind" is another cause of complaint. Customers often change their minds because they later think the product is not really the style, quality, price, or color they wanted. Most consumers consider these legitimate reasons for returning goods, and they expect the retailer to make an exchange or give a refund. Questioning the customer's motives invites further customer complaints.

The retailer has several alternatives in handling consumer complaints. They include offering returns and refunds, making product adjustments, price adjustments, and service adjustments, and practicing good customer relations.

Policies on *returning merchandise* range from "no returns" or "all sales final" to "satisfaction guaranteed or your money back." A retailer that has a no-return policy should make that policy clear by posting signs, printing the policy on sales slips, verbal statements by salespeople, or a combination of these means.

Retailers can correct product-related complaints by one or more *product adjustments*. Complaints about incorrect products can easily be handled by allowing customers to exchange the incorrect product for a correct one. By offering to clean, repair, alter, or exchange products, retailers can satisfy most customers' complaints about damaged products.

One way to handle consumer complaints about poor-quality products is to substitute a higher-quality product for the poor-quality product. Finally, complaints concerning insufficient selection can be handled by either (1) agreeing to stock the product, (2) explaining why the product cannot be stocked, then offering an appropriate substitute, or (3) directing the customer to a store that stocks the desired product.

*Price adjustments* can either be given as an allowance or as a discount on the purchase price of the product. Since it is not always possible to exchange or adjust a product that has been damaged, the retailer often can satisfy customers by reducing the price of the product to compensate for the damages. Price adjustments also can include free merchandise and discount coupons.

Retailers can handle *service adjustments* in much the same way as price adjustments. For example, if a consumer says that a garment alteration is unsatisfactory, the retailer should make the additional alteration free of charge and, in many cases, should deliver the garment to the customer's home at the retailer's expense.

FIGURE 11-3

Guidelines for handling complaints

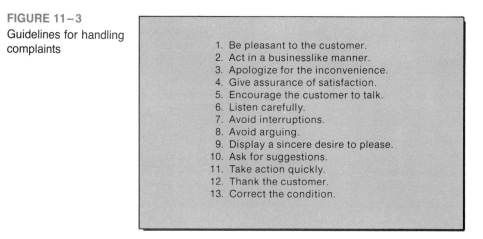

1. Be pleasant to the customer.
2. Act in a businesslike manner.
3. Apologize for the inconvenience.
4. Give assurance of satisfaction.
5. Encourage the customer to talk.
6. Listen carefully.
7. Avoid interruptions.
8. Avoid arguing.
9. Display a sincere desire to please.
10. Ask for suggestions.
11. Take action quickly.
12. Thank the customer.
13. Correct the condition.

Whether the complaint is justified or not, good *customer relations* dictate the retailer listen carefully and politely, reassure the customer, and apologize for the situation. Who knows? The individual might be a very good customer who simply had a bad day and was set off by a minor incident. By allowing the customer to register the complaint and by handling that complaint professionally, the retailer keeps a good customer.

Customer complaints in small stores usually are handled by the store owner or manager; large stores, however, must develop a system for handling complaints. Two alternatives are the centralized system and the decentralized system. All customer complaints are referred to a central office or complaint desk under a **centralized complaint system**. This arrangement allows the retailer to use personnel who are trained in the art of handling people. A **decentralized complaint system** handles customer complaints at the department level. Department salespersons usually handle minor complaints and adjustments while the department manager is responsible for major complaints. Customers generally prefer this type of system.

*How* a store handles a customer's complaint can, in many cases, be more important to the customer than the actual adjustment. Many retailers find that if they display an immediate and sincere willingness to be fair, the customer will reciprocate by being willing to accept any reasonable adjustment. There are no absolute rules or steps for handling all complaints and all customers, but the general guidelines presented in Figure 11-3 are appropriate "do's" and "don'ts" for most situations.

## SUMMARY

Retailers offer services under two sets of circumstances. Primary services are offered as part of the principal business function. Complementary services are offered in conjunction with or as a supplement to a basic product mix.

Services can be classified according to their relative importance to the consumer. Essential services are basic and necessary to a particular retail operation. Expected services are not absolutely essential for operating reasons but are necessary for customer patronage reasons: The consumer expects them to be available. Optional services are neither necessary to the retailer's operation nor expected by the retailer's customers.

The service mix can be developed to meet any number of objectives. Some of the more common service objectives are to (1) increase form utility, (2) facilitate time utility, (3) enhance place utility, (4) promote possession utility, (5) increase consumer convenience, (6) create a desirable store image, (7) provide customer and product security, and (8) increase store traffic. In deciding what level of service to offer, the retailer considers type of merchandise, type and size of the store, location of the store, service level of competitors, and the firm's resources.

The retailer's service mix can incorporate any number of services. Services basic to most retailing operations include store hours, credit, delivery, alterations and repairs, wrapping, and customer complaints.

## STUDENT STUDY GUIDE

### KEY TERMS AND CONCEPTS

bagging
centralized complaint system
centralized wrapping system
chattel mortgage agreement
complementary services
conditional sales agreement
credit-scoring system
decentralized complaint system
deferred billing
department wrapping system
essential services
evening hours
expected services
fixed-term revolving credit
gift wrap

independent delivery system
in-house credit system
installment credit
in-store delivery system
lease agreement
open-account credit
optional services
option-term revolving credit
primary services
private-label credit system
service level
Sunday hours
store wrap
third-party credit system
three C's of credit

### REVIEW QUESTIONS

1. Distinguish between a primary-service retailer and one that offers complementary services.
2. How are services classified? Describe the three classes of services and their relationship to the retailer's operation. Give examples of each type of service.
3. Identify the services the retailer should offer to increase form utility.
4. Which services might the retailer offer to promote possession utility?
5. How does store location influence the retailer's service mix?
6. Identify the two chief disadvantages for retailers that accept third-party credit cards.
7. Does a private-label credit system differ from in-store and third-party systems? How?
8. Briefly describe the three types of credit plans.
9. List the three C's of credit and describe each.
10. Outline the basic procedures for establishing a credit-scoring system.
11. Characterize the three basic types of wrapping services.
12. Identify the major product-, service-, and customer-related causes of complaints.
13. What are the alternative methods for handling customer complaints?

## REVIEW EXAM

True or False

_____ 1. A major benefit of offering optional services is that it can aid the retailer in developing a unique service offering and thereby help to distinguish his or her store from competitive store operations.

_____ 2. Expected services are basic and necessary to a particular retail operation.

_____ 3. Consumer credit, layaway, and extended store hours are all services directed at the service objective of increasing form utility.

_____ 4. Credit-granting stores more easily build repeat business because credit customers tend to be more loyal than cash customers.

_____ 5. A major disadvantage of third-party credit card sales is that they result in tied-up funds in accounts receivable, thereby forcing the retailer to borrow working capital.

_____ 6. The immediate identification of delinquent accounts is critical because the more overdue the account becomes, the harder it is to collect.

_____ 7. One acceptable alternative for handling customer complaints about insufficient selection of merchandise is to direct the customer to a store that stocks the desired product.

# STUDENT APPLICATIONS MANUAL

## PROJECTS: INVESTIGATIONS AND APPLICATIONS

1. Develop a comprehensive list of potential customer services for each of the following retailers: (1) a chain discount store, (2) a supermarket, and (3) a high-fashion boutique. For each retailer and list of services, classify each service on the basis of its importance (essential, expected, or optional) to the retailer's typical customer. Justify your classification.

2. Review the retail-service objectives; then, for each of the following retailer firms rank the objectives in order of their importance to the retailer's success: (1) a True Value hardware store, (2) a Radio Shack electronics store, (3) a 7-11 convenience store, and (4) a J. C. Penney department store. Justify your rankings.

3. In addition to the three C's of credit, what other criteria might a retailer consider for use as "signs" to indicate whether a credit applicant is a good or poor credit risk.

4. Check into the establishment of an "open account" (regular charge account) with a local retailer. What procedures (e.g., forms, requirements, restrictions, and so on) did the retailer use in establishing the account? Were the retailer's procedures adequate to ensure that you were a good credit risk and that credit collection can be handled in a routine and efficient manner? If you were asked to improve the retailer's credit management system, what would you recommend?

5. When the opportunity arises, lodge a well-prepared legitimate complaint with a local retailer. Evaluate the retailer's handling of the complaint using the guidelines presented in Figure 11–3 of the text.

## CASES: PROBLEMS AND DECISIONS

### CASE 11–1
### "Dear Manager"—Coping with Consumer Complaints*

Bill Baker was having a trying morning; the dog got into the trash (again), the bakery didn't have the muffins he wanted, and traffic was backed up all the way in. Bill tried to shake off these annoyances as he prepared to open the store.

*This case was prepared by Douglas Hausknecht, The University of Akron.

The morning at Rich's Friendly Appliances seemed to be going better when the mail came at 10:30. As manager, Bill had the responsibility of dealing with the various invoices, product announcements, payments, and the like as they came in each day. Rarely were there any real letters, except those from customers complaining about one thing or another. In his four years with the store, Bill could only remember one letter that complimented and thanked the store for its efforts. Today's mail was no exception. Mixed in with notices promising manufacturer support for another "truckload" sale and some booklets on Toast/Bake/Microwave ovens were several letters from customers (see Exhibits 1–4). These he saved for last.

After having coffee and a danish, Bill settled in to read the letters. The first was from Baltimore and came in a hand-addressed envelope (Exhibit 1). "Hey lady, we all got problems," Bill thought as he read the letter. "Forget the autobiography and tell me the problem." Bill checked the Recent Sales file for the ticket and discovered that the washer was a relatively low-price, but comparatively high-margin item. There were no notations on the delivery slip. "Well, what do you want?" Bill wondered as he finished reading the letter. "I'm certainly not going to send you a hundred bucks for this." Just then, the telephone rang and Bill set the letter aside until later.

After rescheduling a couple of deliveries, Bill returned to the mail. The next letter had been typed on obviously good-quality stationery with a civic group's letterhead (Exhibit 2). The amount of money demanded got his attention right away. "$265 rebate?" Bill fumed, "that's a pretty big chunk of this week's profit." As Bill was finishing reading the letter, one of the saleswomen came in and told him that she could close a sale if the store could "throw in" an icemaker. "No way," he exploded, "do you know how much those things cost us?" Pat was surprised at this response, but returned to the customers. She was pleased that Bill came out of the office and helped to close the sale with a half-price offer on the icemaker.

After a couple of additional telephone calls, Bill finally read the third letter (Exhibit 3). It dealt with a bottom-of-the-line microwave that sold well at a small margin. "A new glass tray will eat me up on that item," Bill thought. Checking the inventory, which showed 10 in stock, he saw that the gross markup was only $17.35.

The final letter (Exhibit 4) was another threat to sue. It seems that everyone has an underemployed lawyer these days. Having read the last letter, Bill was exhausted. He wasn't even sure how to react. He closed the office door, sat back in his chair, and spread the four letters in front of him.

Bill mused over his possible responses.

## ASSIGNMENT

1. How should Bill respond to each letter?
2. Is responding to customer calls and letters an adequate way to monitor consumer satisfaction? Suggest other methods.
3. What operational changes are indicated by these letters?

EXHIBIT 1

3900 Southwestern Blvd.
Apt. 31-C
Baltimore, MD 21227
6/13/87

Rich's Appliances
Glen Burnie, MD 21220

Dear Managers,

    I really didn't want to write this letter, but my sister-in-law said to. We really like the washer we bought, so that's not the problem.

    With three kids, my husband and myself we do a lot of cleaning. It was bad enough carrying the stuff around here in the building. The machines kept breaking down and getting dirty. Half the time only 3 washers were working and you'd have to wait for a turn.

    They finally got new machines here. But it costs like $2.00 to wash and dry a load of clothes. I guess we could use the clothesline out back, but I hate to leave my stuff out there unless I'm watching it and you know I can't do that and watch the kids too.

    We decided to get a washer and dryer cause they give us the hook-ups and the place. We saved up so we could put half down on the washer first. After we get that paid for we'll save up for the dryer.

    When we came in, the salesgirl (Trudy was her name) was so very nice. She helped us figure out what we needed and what was a good buy. The one we got wasn't on special, but it seemed like a good price. We were so pleased that delivery and hook-up were only a little bit extra.

    The people came out right on time to install the washer. (I was surprised that a woman was one of them.) They brought it in and hooked it to the water and the drain and we started a load. Everything seemed to work then and it has really worked well ever since.

    I was so proud of the new washer that I asked Mrs. Webb, our manager, to come in and see it. She said it looked like a "good, basic machine." We had some coffee and store-bought cookies.

    When she was leaving, Mrs. Webb saw a hole in the plaster wall and a tear in the staircase rug leading to the utility room. She told me that part of the lease was a damage deposit and we'd have to pay for repairs when we moved out unless we fixed it ourselves.

    I had just cleaned that staircase the day before because I knew your men (people it turns out) were coming the next day. There wasn't a hole or a tear then, I'm sure about it. They must have happened when the washer was delivered. I didn't watch too close, as I was trying to keep Nancy, our youngest, out of the way.

    When I told my sister-in-law she said to call the store. Trudy didn't know what to do about it and said you weren't in. She said to write to you because you are so busy when you are there.

    I wasn't going to bother you, but Mrs. Webb said it might cost $100 to get these things fixed right. We don't plan to move anytime soon, why else would I buy a washer and dryer, but that is a lot of money for something we didn't do. I'm sure you'll take care of this.

                Thank you for your help,

                Mrs. F. (Christine) Albenasi

Note: Letter was handwritten on loose-leaf paper and had spelling and grammar errors.

EXHIBIT 2

SUNNY HEIGHTS
NEIGHBORHOOD ASSOCIATION
Potomac, MD

June 11, 1987

Rich's Friendly Appliances
Glen Burnie Mall
Glen Burnie, MD 21220

To the manager:

As a recent purchaser of a refrigerator from your store, I must vehemently protest the quality which I received. The icemaker which is installed in the QwikChill 500 simply does not keep up with my family's needs. I am therefore requesting a credit in the amount of half of the original purchase price (i.e., $265 out of $529).

Since the refrigerator was purchased and delivered in April, we have never accumulated more than a half tub of ice cubes. While we seldom run out completely, the quantity produced forces my family to constrain its use of ice. We believe this to be completely unacceptable.

This refrigerator was needed for its ice-making ability. Because it is only able to make a half tub, I feel that it is worth only half the price. In addition, I have already invested over $400 of my own time in shopping for, helping your people install and trying to improve the performance of the refrigerator. As you can see, there is no way that I can come out even on this exchange, but I'm willing to be reasonable and settle for $265.

Please send a check, by the end of this month, to my home address:
        54 Crabcake Ln.
        Potomac, MD 21407
I have no desire to invest any additional time in shopping for a different refrigerator. I am convinced this is the best you can do.

Thank you,

James Flavin, President
JF:mtp

Note: Letter was handwritten on loose-leaf paper and had spelling and grammar errors.

**EXHIBIT 3**

William Baker, manager 295 Forest Ave.
Rich's Friendly Appliances Dorsey, MD 21076
Glen Burnie Mall June 13, 1987
Glen Burnie, MD 21220

Dear Mr. Baker:

I'm writing to request a replacement glass tray for the microwave oven (Triton #31RS) which I purchased and which was delivered on the 10th of this month. When my husband and I opened the carton, we found the tray had a crack running through about 2/3 of its length. I also did not receive the recipe book promised in the advertisement.

I hope the items are in stock, or at least available readily in the area. If so, perhaps we can have this problem cleaned up by the end of the week.

Since the oven was delivered to me, I assume that these replacement items can also be delivered. I will telephone you Friday A.M. to check on progress.

Sincerely,

Ellen Cole

Note: Letter was typed, not on stationery.

**EXHIBIT 4**

Rich's Friendly Appliance 1313 Mockingbird Ln
Glen Burnie Mall Laurel, MD 21250
Glen Burnie, MD 21220 June 13, 1987

Sir:

What's the matter with you guys? Why can't I get any decent service. I've had it with this oven and now I want it replaced.

I bought this house early in 1986, when they were building it. Since I was living alone, my friends suggested that I have a microwave oven installed instead of a regular oven. I even came down to your fine (Ha!) store and picked one out and paid extra so the contractor would substitute.

Well, let me tell you it's been nothing but trouble. No matter how many different things I try, everything is always undercooked or overcooked. Sometimes the stuff I defrost is half-cooked before I'm ready to use it.

The builder is no longer in business, but this isn't really his fault. I want you to come out and replace this piece of junk with a real, electric oven. I also want my $100 back.

If I don't have this by the end of the month, I'm going to get a lawyer and sue you. I'll also have you shut down for selling things that don't do what they are supposed to. I'll be waiting to hear from you.

(signed) Frank Martin

Note: Letter was typed on portable home computer.

## CASE 11–2
### Don't Give An Inch—Handling Returns and Adjustments*

| | |
|---|---|
| Date | Thursday, April 7, 4:35 P.M. |
| Scene: | Retail Sales Floor, Quality Auto Service Centers |
| Characters: | Mike Buckholzer, Customer; Jackie's Spouse |
| | Jackie Buckholzer, Customer; Mike's Spouse |
| | Pam Adams, Retail Sales Associate |

Action:

**Mike:** Let me get this straight—the four, all-season, steel-belted radials are on sale for $49.95 each—or a total of $200.

**Pam:** About $200 plus tax, plus balancing, and alignment.

**Mike:** What about the tire protection plan—what does it cost?

**Pam:** $79.95.

**Jackie:** According to this (pointing to sign), the protection plan includes the initial alignment and wheel balance.

**Pam:** That's right.

**Mike:** So, four tires plus the protection plan will be close to $300 with tax.

**Pam:** A few dollars less.

**Jackie:** Let's have them check and see if they can find out what is causing the rattle under the left rear side of the car.

**Pam:** Well, let's have the service people put it up on the rack and check it out.

| | |
|---|---|
| Date: | Thursday, April 7, 5:08 P.M. |
| Scene: | Auto Service Floor, Quality Auto Service Centers |
| Characters: | Mike Buckholzer, Customer; Jackie's Spouse |
| | Jackie Buckholzer, Customer; Mike's Spouse |
| | Pam Adams, Retail Sales Associate |
| | John Zee, Mechanic |

Action:

**Pam:** John, let's put this Stanza up on the rack and check it out. The Buckholzers are concerned with some noise coming from the left rear side.

**John:** (After inspecting the undercarriage of the car): Look at this exhaust system— the muffler and tail pipe are all hanging loose; the exhaust system clamps have all rusted through; two of them have already broken and another is about to. Both the muffler and the tail pipe are almost rusted through.

**Mike:** What's all that going to cost me?

**John:** Around $100, but we will have to check the price with Tri-County Nissan. Look at this (John demonstrates that the left front tire has some play in it.)

**Jackie:** What does that mean?

**John:** It means that you are going to have to replace it; sooner or later you will have trouble with it. Also, it will cause uneven wear on the new tire.

**Mike:** What about the other side? Does it need to be replaced also?

**John:** (After inspecting it.): No. It's fine, see, there's no play in this wheel.

**Mike:** How much does a new strut cost?

---

*This case was prepared by Dale Lewison and John Hawes, The University of Akron.

John: On these smaller cars, you have to replace the whole strut assembly. I will have to check the price tomorrow morning when Tri-County Nissan opens up, but with parts and labor, it shouldn't be more than $100.

Jackie: (to Mike): There goes your new golf bag.

Mike: (to Jackie): There goes your new dress.

Pam: Mr. Buckholzer, where can we contact you tomorrow morning? As soon as we check on the prices for the exhaust system and strut assembly, we will call you with a total estimate.

Mike: I have an early morning appointment but I should be back in my office from 9 A.M. to 11 A.M. My telephone number is 555-4646.

Pam: OK, we'll get hold of you then. The service manager will call you before we proceed.

Jackie: When will the car be ready?

Pam: Tomorrow afternoon.

Mike: (to Pam): We will pick it up around 4 P.M.; (to Jackie): Well, we planned on $250 and it is going to cost twice what we planned on.

Date: Friday: April 8, 9:23 A.M.

Scene: Buckholzer Residence, kitchen phone

Characters: Jackie Buckholzer, Customer
Ben Reeves, Service Manager

Action:

Jackie: Buckholzer residence.

Ben: Hello, Mrs. Buckholzer, this is Ben Reeves, Service Manager for Quality Auto Service Centers. I haven't been able to reach your husband at work. I have the estimate of the repairs that were discussed.

Jackie: Well, how much will it cost?

Ben: $490 for the exhaust system, struts, value stems, grease seals, and labor.

Jackie: That includes everything—$490 is the total bill?

Ben: That's it.

Jackie: OK, go ahead. When can we pick it up?

Ben: Late afternoon.

Date: Friday, April 8, 4:47 P.M.

Scene: Auto Service Floor, Quality Auto Service Centers

Characters: Mike Buckholzer, Customer
Jackie Buckholzer, Customer
Adam, Mechanic

Action:

Jackie: Look, there's our car, it's still up on the rack with the wheels off.

Mike: When will the Stanza be done?

Adam: In about an hour, maybe a little longer.

Jackie: We can't wait that long; we're expected for dinner.

Mike: I suppose we will have to make another trip up here tomorrow. Can we pick it up tomorrow?

Adam: Yea, that will give me plenty of time to get it done.

Date:       Saturday, April 9, 12:43 P.M.

Scene:      Retail Sales Floor, Quality Auto Service Centers

Characters:  Mike Buckholzer, Customer
             Jackie Buckholzer, Customer
             Tim Harmon, Retail Sales Associate
             Ben Reeves, Service Manager

Action:

Mike:   I am here to pick up my car.

Tim:    Your last name, please.

Mike:   Buckholzer, Mike.

Tim:    Will it be charge or cash? (Tim keys up the terminal and receives a printed invoice.) The total comes to $800.08.

Mike:   There must be some mistake. The estimate was $490.

Tim:    Let me check. (Tim agains keys up the terminal and obtains the same results.) $800.08 is the total. See here.

| | | |
|---|---|---:|
| 4 | R13 Z2 tires @ 49.30 | 197.20 |
| 1 | Tire protection plan | 79.95 |
| 4 | New Valve Stems @ 2.00 | 8.00 |
| 1 | LF Bearing FWD | 22.60 |
| 2 | Gas Strut Assemblies @ 91.00 | 182.00 |
| 1 | Repack 4 wheel bearings | 26.00 |
| 2 | Front grease seals @ 8.00 | 16.00 |
| 1 | Muffler | 200.26 |
| | Sales Tax | 36.97 |
| | TOTAL | 800.08 |

Jackie: I did not authorize this. The total cost for everything was $490, and that is all I authorized and that is all we are paying.

Tim:    Let me get the service manager.

Ben:    Is there some problem?

Mike:   Yes, there is. We had repairs completed on our car that were not authorized.

Ben:    (examining the terminal printout and the work order): Yes, Mrs. Buckholzer authorized this work. I tried to call you at your office but couldn't reach you, so I called your wife and informed her of the charges and she authorized them.

Jackie: I authorized $490, not $800. Thursday night your mechanic told us that it would be about $500 for everything.

Ben:    It is, $490 for parts and labor.

Mike:   No. The $490 includes the tires plus the protection plan plus the repairs.

Ben:    No, the $490 is only for the repairs. The tires are totally separate.

Jackie: That's not what you said. It asked you what the total bill was and you said $490, including everything.

Ben:    We operate the service business separate from tire sales. What you agreed to pay for the tires is a separate issue. I only deal with repair and installation services.

Mike: How is a customer to know that you treat these two businesses separately? Let me talk to the manager.

Ben: I am the manager on the weekend. The store manager is not in today.

Mike: Call him at home.

Ben: I can't do that.

Mike: I would like to talk to someone else, other than yourself. I don't believe you can be objective about this since you were involved.

Ben: You will have to wait until Monday.

Mike: All right. But we need the car. My daughter and granddaughter are waiting for my wife.

Ben: I can't let you have the car unless you pay the full amount.

Jackie: It's our car, and your mistake. I have people waiting for me up at the mall.

Ben: I can't help that.

Mike: I will pay the $490 agreed to and come in on Monday to talk to the manager.

Ben: No, you will have to pay the full amount.

Mike: Check your records. Less than six months ago I bought 4 new tires and a protection plan from you on my other car. I live in a new home, less than two miles from here. I am not bound to skip town over $300.

Ben: That's beside the point. I will have to have the $800 or I can't release the car.

Jackie: I need the car and I am taking it.

Ben: If you do, I will call the police and have you arrested.

Mike: It's our car. Is this the level of service you provide? Call the police right now. We'll let them decide.

Ben: No, I am not going to call the police unless you take the car.

Mike: Then call the manager or his boss or someone in charge.

Tim: Ben, I think you'd better call someone.

Ben: Keep out of this. I'll take care of it.

Mike: Okay, I find your product and service unacceptable. Your sign says my satisfaction is guaranteed. I am not satisfied. So restore my car to its original form, and I will be on my way.

Ben: I can't do that.

Mike: What the hell can you do? You can't call a manager or anyone else. You can't restore my car. You can't quote prices or provide the services you agreed to. . . .

Jackie: We have to pick the kids up.

Mike: I will be back on Monday to talk to the manager. When I do, I do not intend to accept anything except my car in its original form. I do not want your tires, struts, exhaust system, or anything else.

Date:        Monday, April 11, 9:21 A.M.

Scene:       Store Manager's Office, Quality Auto Service Centers

Characters:  Mike Buckholzer, Angry Customer
             George Wills, Store Manager

Action:

Mike:    . . . and that is basically the problem I had with your product, service, and
service manager. I want my car restored . . .

George:    . . .

## ASSIGNMENT

Assume the role of George Wills, Store Manager:

1. How would you resolve the problem with Mr. Buckholzer? Develop various scenarios for resolving the issue and identify the pros and cons for the store and for the customer. What would be your best offer to Mr. Buckholzer?
2. Who is right? Who is wrong? Why?
3. What about Ben Reeves? Any suggestions?
4. Are there any suggestions for improving the complaint-handling process?
5. Do you have other suggestions for improving the store's operations?

**ENDNOTES**

1. Leonard L. Berry, "Editors Corner," *Retailing Issues Letter,* Center for Retailing Studies, Texas A&M University (December 1986): 4.
2. See Duane L. Davis, Joseph P. Guiltinan, and Wesley H. Jones, "Service Characteristics, Consumer Search, and the Classification of Retail Services," *Journal of Retailing* 55 (Fall, 1979): 3–23.
3. "Retailers Expand Old Services, Add New Ones to Attract Customers," *Stores* (October, 1984): 52–53.
4. Peter Geiger, "Stockquotes Served with Hamburgers," *Akron Beacon Journal,* 28 Oct. 1987, F-1.
5. Joan Berger, "In the Service Sector, Nothing Is 'Free' Anymore," *Business Week,* 8 June 1987, 144.
6. "K-Mart Automates Layaway," *Chain Store Age Executive* (September 1987): 78, 80.
7. "Debit Card Systems Gain Momentum," *Chain Store Age Executive* (January 1987): 115.
8. Sandra Lee Breisch, "Cosmetic Beauty Is in the Eye of the Computer." *Advertising Age,* 2 March 1987, S-12.
9. Dinah Witchel, "The Store As Tourist Lure," *Stores* (May 1987): 112.
10. David J. Jefferson, "Southern California Supermarket Chains to Clash by Night," *Wall Street Journal,* 23 March 1988.
11. See Robert Klonoski, "Trends in Retail Payment Methods," *Retail Control* (September 1985): 46–61.
12. See Jules Abend, "Repair Job for Shoppers?" *Stores* (April 1988): 100–112; "Turmoil in Credit: What's Next?" *Stores* (April 1987): 86–90, 93; and "New Ways to Cut Risk," *Stores* (September 1987): 76.
13. See Noel Capon, "Credit Scoring Systems: A Critical Analysis," *Journal of Marketing* 46 (Spring 1982): 82–91.
14. See Peter McAllister, "'Early Warnings' on Delinquencies," *Retail Control* (March 1986): 16–27.
15. Bernie Whalen, "People-Oriented Marketing Delivers a Lot of Dough," *Marketing News* (March 1984): 4.
16. Joe Agnew, "Home Delivery Amenities Offered as Video-rental Outlets Seek Positioning," *Marketing News,* 10 April 1987, 34.
17. Kari E. Super, "Will Plastic Sack Paper Win Checkout War?" *Advertising Age* (October 1986): 5–37.

# 12

## Objectives

- [ ] Identify alternative sources of supply and channel options for procuring the product mix.
- [ ] Explain the methods and procedures for initiating and maintaining supply contacts.
- [ ] Discuss the criteria for evaluating and methods for negotiating with sources of supply.
- [ ] Discuss the strategies for deciding how many sources of supply should be used in securing merchandise.
- [ ] Describe the buying methods used in the actual purchasing of merchandise.
- [ ] Describe the necessary procedures for placing and writing a purchase order and ensuring that each order is properly processed
- [ ] Design and explain an effective in-store system for receiving, checking, marking, and stocking incoming merchandise
- [ ] Discuss the procedures for processing suppliers' invoices and returning defective merchandise

# Merchandise Buying and Handling

The merchandising buying and handling processes are a key element in the retailer's quest for securing the right products in the right quantities at the right time. In Chapter 10 we discussed knowing what merchandise the retailer wants to stock; in this chapter we discuss the methods of getting that merchandise. Figure 12–1 illustrates the sequential relationship between the buying and procuring processes, as well as the various component of each process. The merchandise *buying process* involves all the activities necessary for a successful relationship with various sources of supply and for the efficient securing of the retailer's merchandise

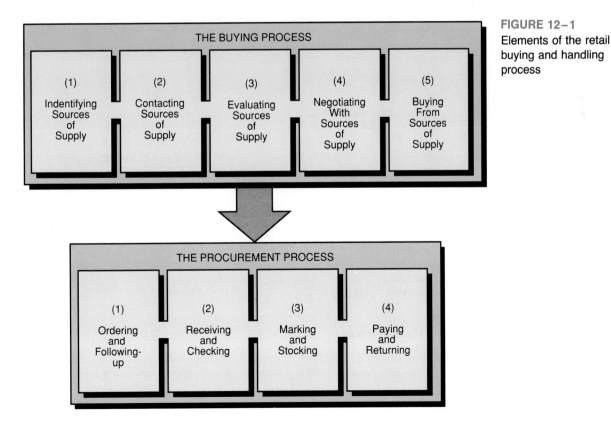

FIGURE 12–1
Elements of the retail buying and handling process

inventories. The merchandise handling *procurement process* involves all the activities of physically getting the merchandise into the store and onto the shelves. The chapter examines these two processes.

## THE MERCHANDISE BUYING PROCESS

The buying process is the retailer's first step in getting merchandise into the store. Primary concerns are determining (1) what sources of supply are available and under what terms and conditions; (2) how to contact and evaluate various suppliers; and (3) how, when, and where to negotiate with and buy from alternative supply sources. The buying process should follow, in sequence, the five steps in Figure 12–1. Retail buying can be viewed as "the decision-making process through which the retail buyer identifies, evaluates, and selects merchandise for resale to the consumer."[1]

## IDENTIFYING SOURCES OF SUPPLY

The first step in the buying process is to identify the available sources of supply. From these sources, the retailer must decide which channel to use in procuring each merchandise line. In some cases, a direct channel to the manufacturer or original producer (e.g., farmer) is preferred. In other cases, an indirect or extended supply channel using one or more intermediaries—often referred to as *middlemen*—is desired. Specifically, the retailer can select from any one or a combination of the following sources of supply:

- ☐ Raw-resource producers
- ☐ Manufacturers
- ☐ Intermediaries
- ☐ Resident buying offices

### The Raw-Resource Producer

Under certain circumstances, the retailer may elect to obtain supplies directly from the raw-resource producer. Food retailers are the most common example of retailing organizations that use this type of direct channel. Large food retailing chains (e.g., Safeway) frequently bypass traditional supply sources in their efforts to secure fresh fruits and vegetables and to obtain raw materials for their private-label brands. Buying food products directly from the raw-resource producer offers a retailer the advantages of increased speed and reduced handling, both of which are important in getting these perishables to the store fresh and with minimal damage. Other products that retailers buy directly from raw-resource producers include lumber, some construction materials, and other bulky materials that incur extra expense if handled by additional intermediaries.

### The Final Manufacturer

Large retailing organizations have the volume to consider direct purchasing from manufacturers. Where direct buying is available and feasible, several advantages can accrue to the retailer. Obtaining *fresher products* is one benefit of buying directly from the manufacturer. By avoiding wholesale storage and handling, the retailer receives the merchandise in a fresher condition. *Quicker delivery* is the second benefit; direct channels of distribution are generally faster than indirect channels in processing initial orders. Direct purchases are almost a necessity for highly perishable fashion and fad items. The third advantage of using the manufacturer as a source of supply is *lower price*. Eliminating the wholesaler and taking on the intermediary's functions enable the retailer to reduce certain costs and realize savings. Fourth, manufacturers can give retailers *more information* about their product lines than wholesalers do.

The fifth advantage of the manufacturer-to-retailer channel is *better adjustment*. Direct relationships between manufacturers and retailers lead both to more lenient adjustment policies and to quicker adjustment responses on products that the retailer's customers return. Finally, direct purchases permit the retailer to order and secure goods made to its *specifications*. Many large chain operations (e.g., J. C. Penney and Sears) have a large percentage of their goods made to their specifications and identified with their names.

### The Wholesaling Intermediary

The third alternative source of supply is wholesaling intermediaries that position themselves in the distribution channel between the manufacturer and the retailer. Their role in facilitating the transfer of goods between manufacturers and retailers varies, depending on the nature of their operations as well as the functions and services they are willing to provide. Most intermediaries do not provide the full range of wholesaling functions—buying, selling, breaking bulk, assortment creation, stocking, delivery services, credit extension, information and consultation, and title transfer. Instead, they tend to specialize in one or a limited number of these functions. Based on the number and type of functions, wholesaling intermediaries fall into several groups. Figure 12–2 identifies these groups of wholesalers. Selection of one of these types depends on the retailer's specific needs.

*Merchant Intermediaries.* **Merchant intermediaries** are wholesalers that are directly involved in the purchase and sale of goods as they move through the channel of distribution. What distinguishes merchant intermediaries from agent intermediaries is that merchants take title to the goods they deal in, while agents do not assume ownership. As illustrated in Figure 12–2, merchant intermediaries can be classified as full-function and limited-function operations. For many small and medium-sized retailers that do not have the volume of sales to buy directly from the manufacturer, merchant intermediaries represent the most important source of supply.

Full-function merchant intermediaries generally perform a full range of wholesaling functions. Based on the width of their product lines, three types of full-function merchant intermediaries can be identified. The **general merchandise wholesaler** handles a number of different and often unrelated product lines with no one product line being dominant (e.g., hardware, household durables, or personal-care products). **Single-line wholesalers** limit their activities to one general product line (e.g., either hardware, drugs, groceries, or dry goods), while **specialty-line wholesalers** restrict their activities to one specialty line within a general line of products (e.g., frozen foods).

As the name implies, limited-function merchant intermediaries limit their activities to certain wholesaling functions, in the belief that many retailers are interested only in having those functions provided and do not want to pay for services that are neither needed nor used.

Based on the functions they perform, there are several types of limited-function merchant intermediaries. The **cash-and-carry wholesaler,** for example, is the discount supermarket of the wholesaling industry because the retailer must (1) go to the

**FIGURE 12–2**
Types of wholesaling intermediaries

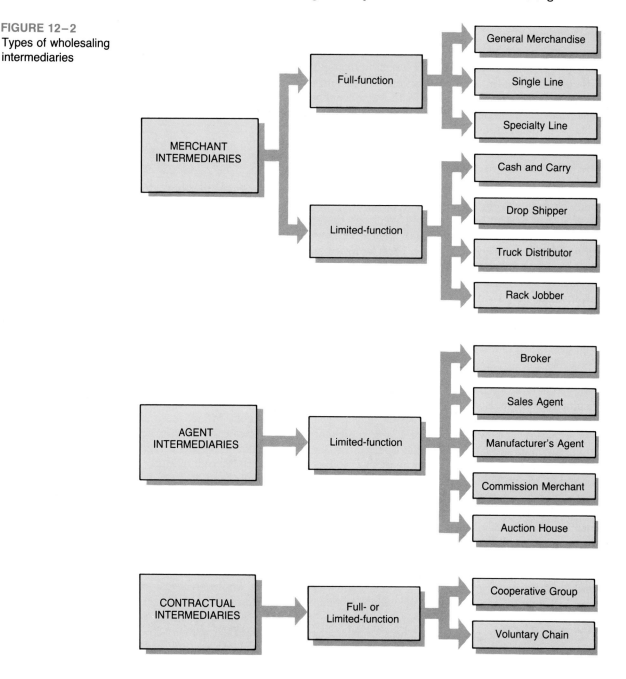

wholesaler's place of business, (2) select and assemble the order, (3) check out at a central station, (4) pay cash for the assembled order, and (5) load and transport the order.

**Drop shippers** are wholesaling operators that normally distribute bulky products, such as lumber and building materials, that are expensive to transport and handle. The drop shipper operates out of an office, takes retail orders by phone or mail, passes the orders on to the producer, and arranges to have the order shipped directly to the retailer.

The **truck distributor** essentially operates its business out of a truck. By carrying inventory on the truck, the driver/salesperson can travel an established sales route and perform the sales and delivery functions almost simultaneously.

The **rack jobber** operates in much the same way as the truck distributor, but the rack jobber usually furnishes the racks or shelves for displaying merchandise. In addition, they are responsible for stocking the racks, building attractive displays, and pricing the merchandise.

*Agent Intermediaries.* **Agent intermediaries** specialize in buying and selling merchandise for others. They facilitate the exchange process between manufacturer and retailers by bringing them together. The two distinguishing characteristics of agent intermediaries are (1) they do not take title to the goods they deal in and (2) they normally provide only a limited number of functions. Also, agent intermediaries usually work on a commission basis, may have either an intermittent or continuous working relationship with clients, and normally do not represent both buyer and seller in the same transaction.

**Brokers** are agent intermediaries whose primary function is to bring prospective buyers and sellers together to complete a transaction. **Sales agents** are agent intermediaries that assume the entire marketing function for a manufacturer.[2] The **manufacturers' agent** is essentially the sales organization for several manufacturers, within a prescribed market territory, that carry complementary product lines. **Commission merchants** take physical possession of goods, provide storage and handling, and act as the selling agent for the producer. By providing the physical facilities for producers to display their products and retailers to inspect them, the **auction house** plays an important role in the wholesaling of used cars and agricultural products.

*Contractual Intermediaries.* To combat the numerous competitive advantages of large chain organizations, many small retailers have entered into contractual arrangements with wholesalers. Typically, the retailer agrees to purchase a certain amount of merchandise from the wholesaler in return for lower prices and merchandising or promotional services. The **cooperative group** is a wholesaling organization owned by the participating retailers and from which they receive patronage refunds (therefore lower prices) based on how much each cooperative member buys from the wholesaler. The **voluntary chain** is a wholesale operation owned and operated by an independent wholesaler and that retailers may voluntarily join. Western Auto and Independent Grocers Alliance (IGA) are examples of voluntary chains.[3]

*The Resident Buying Office* **Resident buying offices** are organizations specializing in the buying function and located in major wholesaling and producing markets. Their central-market location puts the resident buyer in an excellent position to serve as the

This display is associated with which type of limited-function merchant wholesaler?

retailer's "eyes and ears" on supply conditions. The principal services resident buyers offer are information and buyer assistance. They provide information on (1) the availability of products; (2) the reliability of suppliers; (3) the present and future market and supply trends; and (4) the special deals, prices, promotions, and services that various suppliers offer. Buyer-assistance services include locating sources of supply, making initial contact with suppliers, aiding in sales negotiations by using their clout as representatives of several retailers, arranging delivery and payment schedules, and following up on orders to ensure fast and timely arrival of merchandise at the retailer's store.[4]

The two general types of buying offices are the **store-owned buying office** and the **independent buying office**. Although resident buying offices are most commonly associated with the central apparel markets of New York, Dallas, and Los Angeles, other central markets are also populated with resident buyers; for example, because High Point, North Carolina, is the capital of the U.S. furniture industry, several resident buying offices are located there.

## CONTACTING SOURCES OF SUPPLY

The second step in the buying process is to contact the potential sources of supply. Although most retailers have preferred sources, each retailer should strive to maintain as many supply-source contacts as possible. Contacts for a potential sales transaction can be initiated by either the vendor or the retailer.

### Vendor-Initiated Contacts

Vendor-initiated contacts include store visits by sales representatives and telephone and mail-order solicitations. Sales calls at the retailer's place of business represent the most common method of selling staple merchandise and offer the benefits of (1) saving time and money traveling to the market, (2) avoiding the strenuous market-search process, (3) allowing easy in-store access to inventory and sales records for reference purposes, and (4) permitting consultation with other store personnel before placing an order. For some vendors, *telephone* and *mail* are popular methods of contacting retailers. These vendors use telephone and mail contacts to prospect for customers, to make appointments for store visits, to follow up on orders, and to check on the needs of existing accounts.

### Retailer-Initiated Contacts

Like vendors, retailers make initial contacts for products they need. Visiting central markets and resident buying offices, attending merchandise shows, and making telephone and mail inquiries are the four ways retailers seek vendors' products and services.

Within central markets are concentrated the selling offices and merchandise showrooms of a large number of suppliers. In one visit the retailer can review and compare the merchandise offerings of several suppliers. Frequently, suppliers help retailers in their reviews and comparisons by setting up permanent displays in a central facility. The furniture mart in Chicago and the apparel mart in Dallas are examples of this type of facility. Associated with central markets are the resident buying offices discussed previously.

Merchandise shows or trade fairs are periodic displays of many suppliers' merchandise lines in one place at one time. Usually, a group of suppliers gets together and stages a show at a hotel or some other central facility such as a merchandise mart or convention facility.

Retailers use telephone and mail contacts to make initial inquiries on the availability of and to place last-minute orders, reorders, and orders for fill-in merchandise. When the retailer is familiar with the supplier and the merchandise, telephone and mail contacts are efficient and relatively safe.

After identifying and contacting several sources of supply, the retailer must then evaluate each supplier to determine how consistent its operating characteristics are. This third step of the buying process requires evaluation criteria and methods to rank the relative capabilities of each supply alternative to serve the retailer's needs.

**EVALUATING SOURCES OF SUPPLY**

### Evaluation Criteria

Criteria for evaluating potential suppliers are merchandise criteria, distribution criteria, price criteria, promotion criteria, and service criteria.

The first consideration in evaluating alternative sources of supply is what merchandise the supplier offers. The suitability, availability, and adaptability of the suppliers' merchandise lines are three common *merchandise criteria. Suitability* refers to how well the merchandise fits the needs of the retailer's customers and the store's image. Suitability can be judged on the basis of assortment factors such as brand, style, and price, as well as individual factors such as uniqueness, originality, durability, aesthetics, and quality. To determine *availability,* the buyer must first find out whether the supplier will accept an order. If so, will the merchandise be available in the appropriate quantities, sizes, styles, and colors? *Adaptability*—the supplier's willingness to make necessary changes in the product to meet the needs of the retailer and its customers—may involve (1) producing products to the retailer's specifications, (2) placing the retailer's private label on the product, and (3) adjusting production (color, sizes, styles) to take advantage of fast-moving items or incorporating new trends into existing merchandise lines.

An important evaluation criterion is how well suppliers perform their *distribution* functions. Past performance is usually a good indication of future performance. Also of interest to most retailers is the degree of *exclusiveness* the supplier offers in particular lines of merchandise—whether the product is offered on an exclusive (one retailer per market), selective (few retailers per market), or intensive (many retailers per market) basis. Additional distribution policies the retailer should consider for potential suppliers are (1) terms and conditions of the delivery service, (2) order size and assortment constraints, (3) initial-order processing time, (4) reorder processing time, and (5) ease and flexibility of placing an order.

*Price criteria* center around two considerations: price to the consumer and price to the retailer. Regarding the price to the consumer, the major issues the retailer should evaluate are price appropriateness and price maintenance. As discussed, the retail selling price must be appropriate to the retailer's target market. Price *appropriateness* for the prestige retailer is offering consumers top-quality merchandise at a prestige price; for the discounter, acceptable quality at the lowest price constitutes price appropriateness. Price *maintenance* is the supplier's policy of maintaining the retail selling price at or above a certain level. For a high-volume discounter that relies heavily on price appeal substantiated by price comparisons, price-maintenance policies are simply unacceptable in most cases. The second group of price considerations concerns what price the retailer must pay for the merchandise. Perhaps the most important consideration is whether the price will permit the retailer to take a sufficient markup to cover expenses, make a profit, and still be competitive in the marketplace.

The *type* and *amount* of *promotional* assistance the retailer can expect from a supplier are important evaluation criteria. Promotional assistance assumes many different forms, including advertising allowances, cooperative advertising, in-store demonstrations, free display materials, and various consumer inducements such as premiums, coupons, contests, and samples. Also, the extent to which the supplier supports the sale of merchandise through national and/or local advertising is an important factor. Some suppliers provide some or all of the following *supplementary services:*

- ☐ Financing and credit services
- ☐ Return privileges
- ☐ Warranty and repair services
- ☐ Sales force training
- ☐ Accounting services
- ☐ Inventory planning and control
- ☐ Prepackaging, prelabeling, and preticketing
- ☐ Markdown insurance
- ☐ Display units, fixtures, and signs
- ☐ Store facilities design services

Any one of these services can help the retailer reduce either operating expenses or capital investment, but it can also make the retailer more dependent on the supplier who furnishes the service.

## Evaluation Methods

To effectively evaluate alternative sources of supply, retailers must systematically assess each store using the **weighted-rating method**—a procedure for evaluating supply alternatives by assigning weighted values to each of a set of evaluation criteria. Although several weighted-rating procedures have been devised, the "decision matrix approach to vendor selection" developed by John S. Berens illustrates the method.[5]

*Step 1: Criteria Selection.* This step entails selecting criteria to evaluate sources of supply (see preceding discussion of criteria) that are most relevant to the retailer and its relationship to potential suppliers.

*Step 2: Criteria Weighting.* Predetermined weights (or levels of importance) are assigned to each evaluation criterion. Frequently, this weighting process is accomplished by simply rank-ordering all criteria from most to least important and assigning the highest value to the criterion deemed most important and subsequent lower values to those that are less important.

*Step 3: Supplier Selection.* This is a procedure for choosing which potential suppliers to include in the evaluation.

*Step 4: Supplier Rating.* In this step, each of the selected suppliers is rated on the basis of each evaluation criterion. By comparing each supplier to all other suppliers for each criterion, the retailer can assign a minimal rating to each supplier.

*Step 5: Weighted Rating.* Each supplier's rating is multiplied on each evaluation criterion (step 4) by the criterion weight (step 2) to obtain the weighted rating for each supplier. To obtain the overall weighted rating for each supplier, simply add the weighted rating of each criterion.

The retailer starts by selecting the source that received the highest weighted rating and attempts to secure the necessary commitments from that supplier. If more than one source is needed or if the highest-rated source is not available, the retailer simply proceeds down the weighted-rating list until all the needed supply sources are secured. Figure 12–3 illustrates Berens' weighted-rating method.

| | Criteria Weight (Step 2) | Supplier A | | Supplier B | | Supplier C | | Supplier D | | Supplier E | |
|---|---|---|---|---|---|---|---|---|---|---|---|
| Criterion 1: Supplier Can Fill Reorders | 6 | 3 | 18 | 2 | 12 | 4 | 24 | 1 | 6 | 0 | 0 |
| Criterion 2: Markup Is Adequate | 4 | 2 | 8 | 4 | 16 | 3 | 12 | 0 | 0 | 1 | 4 |
| Criterion 3: Customers Ask for the Line | 1 | 1 | 1 | 2 | 2 | 4 | 4 | 3 | 3 | 0 | 0 |
| Criterion 4: Supplier's Line Has Significant Changes from Season to Season | 2 | 3 | 6 | 4 | 8 | 2 | 4 | 1 | 2 | 0 | 0 |
| Criterion 5: Supplier's Line Contributes to Fashion Leadership | 5 | 2 | 10 | 1 | 5 | 0 | 0 | 3 | 15 | 4 | 20 |
| Criterion 6: Supplier's Line is Cut to Fit Customers Well | 2 | 1 | 2 | 0 | 0 | 3 | 6 | 4 | 8 | 2 | 4 |
| Criterion 7: Supplier Advertises Line in Local Media | 1 | 0 | 0 | 1 | 1 | 2 | 2 | 4 | 4 | 3 | 3 |
| Supplier TOTAL SCORES | | | 45 | | 44 | | 52 | | 38 | | 31 |

FIGURE 12–3
Decision matrix approach to supplier selection (source: John S. Berens, "A Decision Matrix Approach to Supplier Selection," *Journal of Retailing,* 47, no. 4 [Winter 1971–1972]; 52)

## NEGOTIATING WITH SOURCES OF SUPPLY

The fourth step in the buying process is active negotiation with suppliers identified in the evaluation step as potentially suitable sources. In the retailer–supplier relationship, the two most common issues subject to negotiation are *price* and *service*.

### Negotiating the Price

The price the retailer pays for the same merchandise is usually subject to negotiation. While any number of factors can conceivably influence the price the retailer pays, three factors play dominant roles: (1) list price, (2) discount and allowance terms, and (3) transportation and handling terms.

*The Starting Point: List Price.* Price negotiations usually start with the supplier's basic price list. For administrative convenience, most suppliers establish their pricing structures around basic **list prices** that they use for an extended time period. By adjusting their list prices upward or downward using various types of "add-ons" and "discounts," suppliers can avoid publishing frequently revised price lists while at the same time they can make necessary price accommodations for individual retail customers.

As the starting point for negotiation, the basic list price is a crucial element in estimating the supplier's "final" price to the retailer. Since some suppliers publish what are, in effect, inflated list prices, substantial differences in the final price can result because of large variations in discounts and allowances as well as transportation and handling terms.

*Discount and Allowance Terms.* The final selling price to the retailer is the difference between the supplier's list price and the negotiated discounts and allowances. The principal types of discounts are trade, quantity, seasonal and cash discounts, and promotional allowances.

A *trade discount* is a form of compensation that the buyer may receive for performing certain services (functions) for the supplier. Also referred to as a functional discount, the trade discount is usually used by suppliers selling merchandise through catalogs and is based on a quoted list price. The supplier offers one price to all potential buyers and makes price changes simply by adjusting the amount of the trade discount offered to any given buyer. The size of the trade discount depends on the type, quantity, and quality of the services the potential buyer is willing to provide.

Trade discounts come in single and chain forms. The **single trade discount** is expressed as a single percentage adjustment (e.g., 50 percent) to the supplier's list price. For example, a product with a list price of $200 less a 40 percent trade discount (which would amount to an $80 trade discount) costs the retailer $120 ($200 × .40 = $80; $200 − $80 = $120). Expressed as a series of percentages (e.g., 40 percent, 20 percent, 10 percent), the **chain trade discount** is applied to the list price in successive order. The first percentage discount is calculated on the original list price, the second percentage discount is calculated on the value resulting from the first calculation, and so on until each percentage discount is taken into account. The buyer that performs many services for the supplier receives the entire discount chain (40 percent, 20 percent, 10 percent), while the buyer that performs a limited number of services is offered only part of the chain (40 percent, 20 percent, or possibly only 40 percent).

Suppliers offer *quantity discounts* to retailers as an inducement to buy large quantities of merchandise. Large order quantities help reduce the supplier's selling, handling, billing, transporting, and inventory costs. Some of the cost savings are passed along to the buyer in the form of quantity discounts. At the same time, however, buying large quantities normally increases the retailer's operating expenses, ties up operating capital, and creates additional inventory-control problems. Quantity discounts are usually handled as a percentage reduction from list price or simply expressed in some form of a schedule with unit or dollar sales corresponding to a particular dollar discount amount.

Three types of quantity discounts—noncumulative, cumulative, and free merchandise—are common. A **noncumulative quantity single discount** is based on a single order or shipment. Quantity discounts that apply to several orders or shipments placed with the supplier over an extended period (usually a year) are referred to as **cumulative quantity discounts**. The "13" dozen, whereby the supplier offers one free dozen for every 12 dozen ordered, is a common way to give the retailer free merchandise instead of a price reduction or a cash payment.

**Seasonal discounts** are price reductions given to buyers who are willing to order, receive, and pay for goods during the "off season." Although the retailer can realize a savings in the cost of merchandise by taking seasonal discounts, the savings must be viewed in light of (1) additional inventory costs and problems; (2) greater risks resulting from price changes, style changes, and merchandise depreciation; and (3) restricted use of investment capital already tied up in the merchandise.

A **cash discount** is one given for making prompt payment. To encourage retailers to pay their bills before the due date, the supplier sometimes permits the retailer to deduct a certain percentage discount from the net invoice price. When negotiating cash discounts and related payment terms, the retailer needs to consider three factors: net invoice price, discount amount, and dating terms.

The first consideration in negotiating cash discounts is to establish what constitutes the net invoice price. As the base for calculating cash discounts, the net invoice price is crucial in determining the dollar amount of the discount. The **net invoice price** is the net value of the invoice or the total invoice minus all other discounts (trade, quantity, seasonal, etc.).

The second factor the retailer must consider is the **discount amount**. While a 2 percent cash discount is common in many trades, the rate ranges from no cash discounts to whatever the supplier is willing to allow. The amount of the cash discount is standardized in some industry trades; in other trades, the cash discount amount is totally negotiable.

The importance of **dating terms** is that they (1) determine the cash discount period or the amount of time the retailer has to take advantage of the cash discount and (2) provide the invoice due date or the amount of time the retailer has to pay the net invoice price in full. Ten days is the most common cash discount period, while thirty days from the dating of the invoice is a fairly standard invoice due date.

The two general classes of dating terms are immediate and future. Sometimes suppliers insist on **immediate dating,** allowing no time for the cash discount or extra time for the invoice payment. **Future dating** is the practice of allowing the retailer more time to take advantage of the cash discount or to pay the net amount of the invoice. In essence, it encourages the retailer to delay payment and helps in short-term financing of inventory. Figure 12–4 describes several types of future dating.

| FUTURE DATING TERMS | SELECTED EXAMPLES | EXPLANATION OF EXAMPLES | |
|---|---|---|---|
| | | Cash Discount Terms | Net Invoice Terms |
| Net | Net, 30 | no cash discount allowed | net amount due within 30 days of invoice date |
| Date of Invoice (DOI) | 2/10, net 30 | 2-percent discount within 10 days of invoice date | net amount due within 30 days of invoice date |
| End of Month (EOM) | 2/10, net 60, EOM | 2-percent discount within 10 days of the first day of the month following the invoice date | net amount due within 60 days of the first day of the month following the invoice date |
| Receipt of Goods (ROG) | 4/10, net 45, ROG | 4-percent discount within 10 days after receiving the goods at the retailer's place of business | net amount due within 45 days after receiving the goods at the retailer's place of business |
| Extra | 3/10-60 extra, net 90 | 3-percent discount within 70 days of invoice date | net amount due within 90 days of invoice date |

**FIGURE 12–4**

Types of future-dating terms

To gain the retailer's cooperation in promotional activities, the supplier frequently offers a promotional allowance. **Promotional allowances,** which reduce the price retailers pay suppliers for merchandise, include advertising allowances, preferred selling space, free display materials, and merchandise deals. *Advertising allowances* are discounts retailers earn by advertising the supplier's products in the local media. Retailers give vendors *preferred selling space* in return for a price reduction. A variation of this type of space consideration is the *slotting allowance—* admission fees paid by manufacturers to get their product on crowded shelves.[6] Retailers also use *free display materials* in the form of counter, window, and floor displays, signs, banners, and shelf strips, as well as various types of giveaways. Promotional allowances also can take the form of *merchandise deals* in which the supplier substitutes free merchandise for monetary allowances as compensation for performing promotional functions.

*Transportation and Handling Terms.* The retailer's actual laid-in cost of merchandise also depends on which party assumes the transportation charges and handling responsibilities. In negotiating transportation and handling terms, the retailer must consider all of these issues: Who pays transportation charges? Who bears transportation charges? Where does the title exchange hands? Who is responsible for filing claims? The payer and the bearer of transportation charges may or may not be the same person; for example, to facilitate delivery speed, the supplier may pay transportation charges when the goods are loaded at the factory but charge them back to the retailer on the invoice. In such cases the retailer ultimately bears the cost of transportation. Equally important is the point at which title to the merchandise is transferred from the supplier to the retailer. The party that has title while the goods are in transit is responsible for bearing any insurance costs that might be needed above the liability of the carrier to cover loss. The location where title exchange occurs also influences which party is responsible for filing and collecting any damage claims against the carrier. Damage claims not only can be expensive to collect in some cases but can also occupy a considerable amount of the retailer's time. Figure 12–5 illustrates the six most common expressions of transportation and handling terms. As a note of caution, however, transportation terms are characterized by a variety of expressions; therefore, retailers should not hesitate to ask for clarification of any expression they do not fully understand.

### Negotiating the Service

In addition to price, the various types and levels of services the supplier provides also are subject to negotiation. In some cases, a service is fairly standard with only minor adjustments allowed; in other cases, certain services are totally negotiable. The discussion on evaluating sources of supply identified ten different supplier services. Although services may be available, the retailer may not receive some or any of them without actively seeking them as part of the buying process. The terms and conditions for any one of these ten services must be detailed before purchase if the retailer expects the supplier to provide them.

---

The final step in the retailer's buying process is the actual purchase of the merchandise. Two issues to consider are buying strategies and buying methods.

**BUYING FROM SOURCES OF SUPPLY**

### Buying Strategies

In deciding how many different sources of supply to use in securing the store's merchandise, the retailer can elect to pursue one of two buying strategies: concentrated or dispersed.

With a **concentration strategy,** the retailer decides to use a limited number of suppliers, believing it leads to lower total costs and preferential treatment. By concentrating purchases, the retailer can lower the laid-in cost of the merchandise by taking advantage of quantity discounts and lower transportation rates. Operating expenses can be lower, since ordering, receiving, and processing of merchandise are more efficient with fewer suppliers.

Proponents of the **dispersion strategy** believe that concentrated buying is "concentrated risk," because it is dangerous to "put all your eggs in a few baskets." By spreading orders over many suppliers, these retailers believe they can (1) obtain a greater variety of merchandise, (2) be made aware of "hot" items, (3) ensure backup sources of supply, and (4) promote competitive services from different supply sources. Generally, retailers of staple merchandise tend to concentrate their purchases, whereas retailers of fashion merchandise usually elect a less-concentrated approach.

### Buying Methods

Retailers use several buying methods, depending on their circumstances. They include regular, consignment, memorandum, approval, and specification buying.

**Regular buying** involves the systematic cutting and issuing of purchase orders and reorders. The entire buying process is conducted in conjunction with the merchandise. Most staple goods and many fashion goods can be handled by this method.

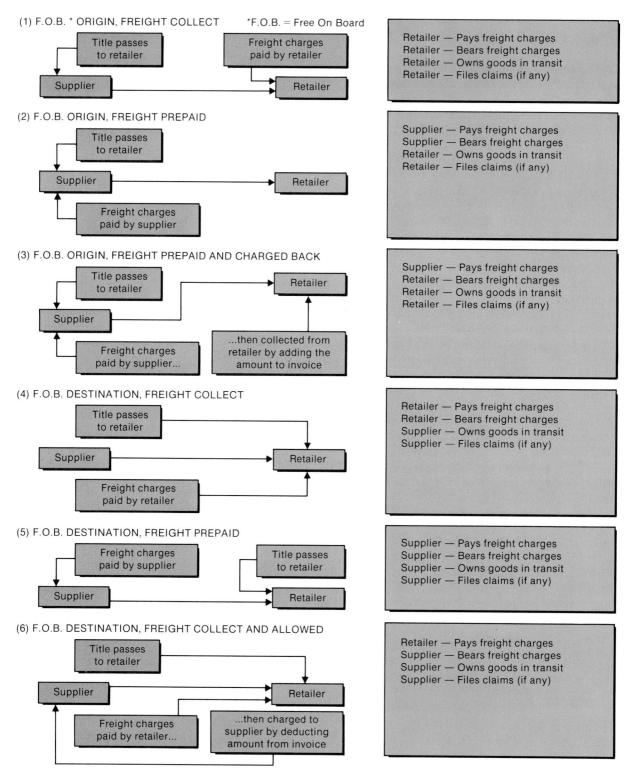

**FIGURE 12-5**

Transportation terms and conditions (source: adapted from Murray Krieger, *Practical Merchandising Math for Everyday Use* [New York: National Retail Merchants Association, 1980], 4)

Consignment buying is an arrangement whereby the supplier retains ownership of the merchandise shipped to the retailer, and the retailer (1) displays the merchandise, (2) sells it to the final consumer, (3) deducts an agreed-on percentage commission, and (4) remits the remainder to the supplier. Merchandise not sold within a prescribed time is returned to the supplier. This method of buying is usually used when the merchandise is expensive, new, or of such a high-risk nature that the extent and duration of demand are relatively unknown.

Memorandum buying is essentially a variation of consignment buying. The main difference is that the title to the merchandise exchanges hands when it is shipped to the retailer. The retailer retains the right to return to the supplier any unsold merchandise and to pay for the merchandise after it has been sold.

When merchandise is shipped to the store before the final purchase decision has been made, the retailer is buying on approval. Before the retailer can sell the merchandise it must secure ownership. Approval buying allows the retailer to inspect the merchandise before making the purchase decision and to postpone any purchase until physical possession has been secured.

Specification buying involves having merchandise made to their specifications. Specifications can range from minor changes in existing lines of merchandise to complete specifications covering raw materials, design, quality, labeling, and packaging.

---

Too many retailers focus on the buying process and fail to devote sufficient time and attention to the actual handling of the merchandise. Basically a "backroom" operation, the handling process lacks the glamour and excitement of buying. This might explain the lack of attention handling receives, but it does not justify that neglect. Close control and supervision of the handling process are as important to the retailer's profit picture as careful buying. For the buyer to secure the merchandise desired in the way intended, procedures for controlling handling must be developed and maintained. The four basic steps in the handling process are ordering and following up, receiving and checking, marking and stocking, and paying and returning.

**THE MERCHANDISE HANDLING PROCESS**

---

The first step in physically handling the retailer's merchandise is to place a purchase order and then follow up on that purchase order to ensure that it is processed properly and efficiently.

**ORDERING AND FOLLOWING UP**

## Ordering

The buyer often faces a variety of circumstances that determine which of many different types of orders must be placed. Ordering procedures might involve placing orders (1) with different suppliers at different levels in the channel of distribution; (2) at different times to accommodate past, present, and future needs; (3) for either regular or special merchandise; and (4) with complete or partial specification of terms and conditions of sale. Figure 12–6 identifies and briefly describes seven types of orders.

*Manual purchase-order systems* involve placing merchandise orders orally or in writing. Because oral agreements in some states are legally binding only up to some

**Regular orders:** Orders placed by the buyer directly with the vendor. Involves ordering regular stock items with complete specifications as to terms and conditions of sale and delivery.

**Reorders:** Orders placed with existing supplier for previously purchased goods, usually under terms and conditions specified by the original order.

**Advance orders:** Orders placed in advance of both the normal buying season and the immediate needs of the retailer. Involves ordering regular stock items in anticipation of receiving preferred treatment.

**Back orders:** Orders placed by the buyer for merchandise that was ordered but not received on time. Involves orders that the supplier intends to ship as soon as goods are available.

**Blanket orders:** Orders placed with suppliers for merchandise for all or part of a season. Involves ordering merchandise without specifying such assortment details as sizes, colors, and styles and such delivery details as when and how much to ship. Requisitions against the blanket order will be placed as the need for the merchandise arises.

**Open orders:** Orders placed with central market representatives (e.g. resident buyers) to be filled by whatever supplier the representative considers best suited to fill the order.

**Special orders:** Orders placed with suppliers for merchandise not normally carried in stock or for specially manufactured merchandise. May involve specification buying.

**FIGURE 12–6**

Types of orders

stated limit and are subject to vastly different interpretations, retailers should have them accurately transcribed into written form at the earliest possible time. When placing a written order, the buyer can use a form provided by the supplier or one provided by the retailer. It is generally recommended that retailers use their own forms whenever possible.

The **order form**, as a legally binding contract when signed by both parties, specifies the terms and conditions under which the transaction is to be conducted. These terms and conditions usually are stated on both the front and back of the order form. The front of the order form usually contains standard information on the terms and conditions of sale. The back side of the retailer's order form usually contains a standardized statement of the general conditions under which the supplier will be held legally responsible if it accepts the order.

Several technological developments for improving purchase-order management via computer linkages have emerged during the last several years; one of these is the **electronic purchase-order (EPO) system**.[7] Retail managers now have a variety of options for structuring their EPO systems. Figure 12–7 illustrates the most common structures retailers and vendors use in exchanging electronic purchase-order and invoice data. The options follow.

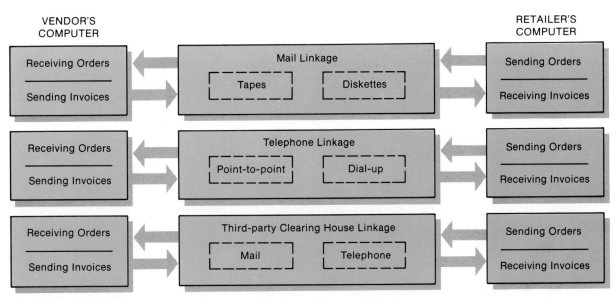

**FIGURE 12–7**
Electronic purchase-order systems

*Mail Linkages.* Purchase-order and invoice data are transcribed onto magnetic tape or diskettes and transmitted between retailers and vendors via the mail. This is a practical option for communicating a large volume of information when time is not critical.

*Telephone Linkages.* Purchase-order and invoice data are communicated between the retailer's computer and the vendor's computer via the telephone. The *point-to-point* option involves arranging transmission schedules and common protocols to allow direct computer-to-computer interchange of data. The *dial-up* option involves the storage of retailer orders and vendor invoices in on-line files and allowing each party dial-up access to these files. K Mart's dial-up system works something like this: (1) store manager electronically sends purchase orders to K Mart headquarters; (2) store order is "homogenized" in the ordering system; (3) consolidated purchase orders for each store are available each morning; and (4) each vendor has an assigned path and time slot for calling K Mart headquarters to obtain orders.[8]

*Third-party Clearing Houses.* A third-party data processing company makes arrangements to (1) receive orders and invoices, (2) sort them by addressees, (3) store them on-line, and (4) allow subsequent access by authorized addressees. This method allows use of a standardized machine language to establish a bridge for common communication, thereby eliminating the need for separate and distinct methodologies among various vendors and retailers. The May Co.-Haggar experiment with an EPO system used the clearing-house approach.[9]

To the retailer, the advantages of the EPO system include more effective inventory management, more effective open-to-buy systems, and reduction of ordering lead times, thereby improving in-stock positions and stock turnovers while reducing inventory carrying costs.

## Following Up

To be sure the right order is received in the right place at the right time, the retailer needs follow-up procedures. Following up an order is also necessary to make a purchase contract legally binding. In most cases, the original copy of the purchase order, which is sent to the supplier, constitutes a legal *offer to buy.* No purchase

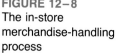

**FIGURE 12–8**
The in-store merchandise-handling process

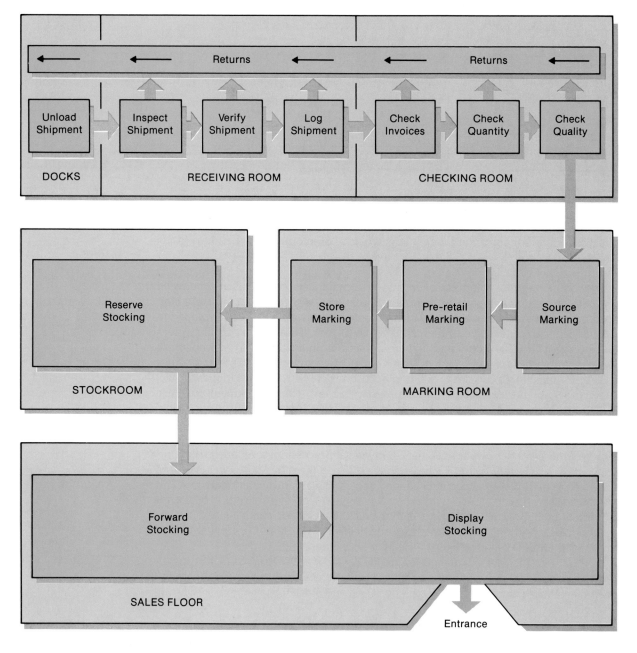

contract exists, however, until the seller *accepts* the buyer's offer. Therefore, the first step in following up an order is to determine whether the supplier has accepted the order. Suppliers usually notify the retailer of their acceptance by returning the acknowledgment copy of the order form or by using their own acceptance forms. Routine follow-up procedures are used to check for order acceptance and discrepancies between the retailer's original order and the supplier's acceptance. The buyer manually or electronically reviews the files frequently to determine which orders require additional attention. The buyer routinely sends either a postcard, a personal letter, or a telegram, or, if circumstances are urgent, makes a telephone call. There are special follow-up procedures if the importance of the order merits them. These special procedures usually involve the use of a field expediter (e.g., resident buyer) who personally visits the supplier.

Once the order has been placed and received, the retailer must efficiently process incoming shipments to ensure their timely arrival on the sales floor. Figure 12–8 illustrates in-store handling tasks for incoming merchandise shipments.

**Receiving** is the actual physical exchange of goods between the retailer and the supplier's transporting agent. It is the point at which the retailer takes physical possession of the goods. **Checking** is the process of determining whether the supplier has shipped what the retailer ordered and whether the shipment has arrived in good condition.

## RECEIVING AND CHECKING

### Receiving Process

Retailers can receive merchandise shipments through either the front door (customer entrance) or the back door. Generally, the retailer should avoid front-door receiving. The typical back-door receiving operation consists of an unloading area and a receiving area. The area devoted to unloading should permit easy maneuverability and facilitate careful handling. Usually located adjacent to the unloading area on the store's ground floor, the receiving area should be large enough to permit easy maneuverability, to allow inspection of incoming shipments, and to act as a holding area for merchandise awaiting transfer to the checking room. Proper processing normally involves inspecting, verifying, and logging incoming shipments.

Standard procedures for *inspecting* incoming merchandise involve visual inspection of the exterior of each package to determine whether the package has been damaged (crushed, punctured) or opened (broken seal). If a package has been badly damaged or opened, the receiving clerk should refuse to accept the shipment unless the carrier's employee agrees to witness the visual inspection of the contents of the package. Packages that are slightly damaged may be accepted, but before signing for the shipment, the receiving clerk should make a notation of the damage on all transportation and receiving documents.

After inspecting the shipment for visual damage, the receiving clerk should make several *verifications*. First, the clerk must verify that the shipment was ordered by consulting the file of purchase orders. Second, the completeness of the shipment must be verified. Third, the receiving clerk should verify that the actual makeup of the shipment is the same as that described on the bill of lading. The number of cartons in the shipment and the weight of each carton should also be checked. Fourth, freight charges are verified by comparing the total weight of the shipment with various rate schedules.

To facilitate and organize the processing of incoming shipments, each shipment is *logged* in a receiving record and assigned a receiving number. The **receiving record** and number follow the shipment through the checking, marking, and stocking steps of the procurement process and serve as a quick reference should problems arise. The accounting department also uses the record to verify shipment before invoices are paid.

### Checking Process

Checking involves opening each package, removing the merchandise, and examining it. The retailer can make three checks to ensure it has received what was ordered: an invoice, a quantity, and a quality check. In the **invoice check**, the retailer compares the invoice with the purchase order. The invoice is the supplier's bill and the document that itemizes particulars of the shipment in terms of merchandise assortment, quantity, and price. Checking personnel must determine whether the retailer's purchase order exactly matches the supplier's invoice.

During the **quantity check**, the checking personnel unpack and sort each package to check the actual physical contents of each package against the purchase order, the invoice, or both. Essentially, the checker sorts each package to determine whether the package contains the same number of units as listed on the invoice and purchase order. Any shortages, overages, or substitutions are noted and reported to the buyer or merchandise manager.

The third check is the **quality check**, which involves examining the merchandise for (1) any damage that is obviously the result of shipping, (2) imperfections in the merchandise, and (3) lesser-quality merchandise than the retailer ordered.

The retailer can use one of four methods to check the quantity of incoming shipments: the direct check, the blind check, the semiblind check, and the combination check. In a **direct check**, the retailer checks off from the invoice, which lists all the ordered and shipped items, each group of items as they are counted. Speed and simplicity are the principal advantages of the direct check. The **blind check** is a procedure in which the checker lists and describes each merchandise group on a blank form and then counts and records the number of items in each group. The blind method is the most accurate for checking incoming shipments, but it is also the most expensive because of the additional time and labor involved.

The **semiblind check** provides the checker with a list and description of each merchandise group in the shipment but not the quantities for each group. The checker must physically count and record the number of items in each merchandise group. The semiblind method has the advantages of being both reasonably fast and accurate. The **combination check** method is simply using the direct check method when the supplier's invoice is available and the blind or semiblind check method when the retailer does not have the supplier's invoice.

## MARKING AND STOCKING

**Marking** is affixing to merchandise the information necessary for stocking, controlling, and selling. Customers want information on the price, size, and color of merchandise before they are willing to buy, and the retailer needs to know when and from where the merchandise was secured, its cost, and where it goes to maintain proper inventory and record controls. **Stocking** includes all the activities associated with in-store and between-store distribution of merchandise. Stocking may involve moving merchandise to the sales floor for display or to the reserve or stocking rooms for storage.

## Marking Activities

The facilities, equipment, procedures, and personnel for marking merchandise should be tailored to the volume and type of merchandise. Small, hand-, and mechanically operated marking systems usually are sufficient for most small retail operations. More sophisticated mechanical and electronic systems are more appropriate for large retailing organizations with sufficient merchandise volume to justify the expense.

There are a number of ways to physically mark merchandise. The three most common marking systems are source marking, preretailing, and store marking. **Source marking** is the system by which the retailer authorizes the manufacturer or supplier to mark the merchandise before shipping it to the store. The merchandise is marked either with preprinted tickets sent to the supplier by the retailer or with tickets printed by the manufacturer based on information supplied by the retailer. Source marking reduces both in-store marking expenses and the time it takes to get the merchandise onto the sales floor.

**Preretailing** is a retail buying practice of deciding the selling price of merchandise before it is purchased and recording that price on the store's copy of the purchase order so the store's "markers" can put the selling price on the merchandise as soon as it comes through the doors. Store personnel who are responsible for marking merchandise can do so on its arrival without contacting the store buyer.

**Store marking** is the practice of having store personnel mark all merchandise after the store has received it. When using store marking, the retailer must invest in marking facilities and equipment and establish marking procedures.

Merchandise can be marked by means of hand, mechanical, and electronic equipment. *Hand marking* is done with grease pencils, ink stamps, and pens. The desired information is marked directly on either the merchandise or its package, or on a gummed label, string tag, or pin ticket attached to the merchandise.

*Mechanical marking* involves producing tags and tickets in both printed (human-readable language) and punched (machine-readable language) forms. Recent technological advancements in electronic (computer-controlled) equipment have generated a wave of new marking procedures that are compatible with various **point-of-sale (POS)** systems. *Electronic marking devices* can code prices onto tickets and tags that can be quickly and automatically read and processed by optical scanning equipment or optical character recognition (OCR) systems. *Optical scanners* usually are employed at checkout counters, where they read all the information on the ticket or tag and transmit it to the store's computer system for further processing (e.g., for inventory control and accounting records). While the checkout counter wand is the most common type of optical scanner used in general merchandise retailing, fixed-slot scanners (checkout counters with built-in laser beams that read tags as the merchandise is passed over the beam) are the predominant system in the supermarket industry. Kroger Supermarkets are currently experimenting with a checkout system that allows consumers to scan their own purchases; Figure 12–9 describes the system.

**FIGURE 12–9**

The ultimate in self-service: Self-service scanning

The Check-Robot utilizes a flat-top scanner, a touch-sensitive video display monitor, a conveyor belt, and a sensing mechanism used for security purposes.

The consumer scans each item in her shopping basket and then places it on a conveyor belt which is activated by the scanner. Overhead on the monitor, the product identification and price are displayed for the last five items scanned, scrolling upward as more items are added. The groceries move down the conveyor belt through a metal archway to a bagging area where a Kroger bagger is stationed.

After all items have been scanned, the consumer brings the receipt to a nearby payment station and tenders her bill.

At the consumer's disposal are all the functions a cashier would enjoy on a traditional POS terminal, but instead, on the touch-sensitive screen. There is a subtotal button and a button that allows the option of voicing the prices.

If a consumer comes up against a bar code that won't scan, she merely presses the numbers of the code into the video monitor, just as a cashier would do on a POS terminal. The product description and price are displayed just as if the item were scanned.

Coupons are accommodated in a rather simple way. "There's a button right beside the price [on the screen] that says 'coupon'." "When you touch that, it highlights that item on the screen and puts an asterisk next to the item on the receipt. This helps the cashier verify the product was purchased; the amount of the coupon is subtracted at the time payment is made."

Source: Reprinted by permission from "The Ultimate in Self-Service: Scan Your Own," *Chain Store Age Executive* (June 1987), p. 53. Copyright © Lebhar-Friedman Inc. 425 Park Avenue, New York, NY 10022.

With the installation of optical scanners, many retailers have elected to use a standardized marking system. These universal vendor marking (UVM) systems involve coding merchandise tags with a machine-readable code that is sponsored by one or more trade associations. The National Retail Merchants Association (NRMA) sponsored the **optical character recognition-font A (OCR-A)** code, which is equally human and machine readable. The second standardized code in common use is the **universal product code (UPC)**. Used largely within the supermarket industry, the UPC is a bar code system that identifies both the product and the manufacturer. Recently, there has been a tremendous increase in the acceptance and popularity of UPC; as a result, the NRMA endorses it as the preferred marking system for all merchandise.[10]

Many retailers have their own customized marking system. Receiving and stocking dates, for example, are coded using a transformation of the date by addition, subtraction, multiplication, or division. A receiving date of 10-12-80 could be transformed to 40-42-110 by adding 30 to the month, day, and year. Reversing their position (to 110-42-40) can further disguise the dates. **Word cost codes** use a 10-letter word or words in which no letter is repeated. Some popular word codes are MAKE PROFIT, MONEY TALKS, and REPUBLICAN. Each letter in the word code is assigned a single-digit number. For example,

MONEY        TALKS
1 2 3 4 5      6 7 8 9 0

To use such a cost code, the retailer would code EYES on the price tag for a merchandise item that costs $45.40.

Re-marking merchandise often becomes necessary because of damage, obsolescence, or an increase in the wholesale price. Some retailers manually re-mark merchandise on the sales floor by crossing out the old price and adding the new price to the ticket. While this policy permits the customer to identify the price as a reduced price, it also identifies the merchandise as being somewhat undesirable, at least at the former price. Other retailers prefer to send the merchandise back to the marking room for re-marking and to replace the old price tag with a new one. Re-marking in the marking room allows for both greater security and greater accuracy. Attaching new price tags for merchandise that has been marked down offers the retailer the opportunity to sell the merchandise at a lower price without the negative connotation of its being inferior merchandise.

Retailers frequently elect to use **bulk marking**—placing similar merchandise with the same price in a display and attaching one price card to the display. It can save time in marking and speed the delivery of merchandise to the sales floor.

## Stocking Activities

Once the merchandise has been marked, the retailer must decide where to stock the merchandise. The retailer can use an in-store or warehouse stocking plan or some combination of the two plans.

The primary goal in stocking is to move the merchandise as close as possible to its selling point. To accomplish this goal, most retailers follow the policy of **in-store stocking**, maximizing the amount of display and forward stock and minimizing the

What are the advantages of this type of in-store stocking fixture?

amount of stock in reserve. **Display stock** is stock placed on various display fixtures that customers can directly examine. **Forward stock** is backup stock that is temporarily stored on the sales floor near its selling department. Forward stock may be carried in perimeter storage areas around the department or in drawers or cupboards beneath the sales floor display fixtures. **Reserve stock** is backup stock held in reserve, usually in a central stockroom. Because reserve stocks frequently create access problems for sales personnel, most retailers prefer to limit the amount of stock in these areas. Reserve stocks usually are converted to forward or display stocks as quickly as possible.

**Warehouse stocking** is used for certain types of merchandise or under certain operating conditions. Bulky products such as furniture and appliances usually require warehouse stocking, because the retailer must limit the amount of display stock on the sales floor. Disassembled products that are sold in their cartons are usually picked up by the consumer at a warehouse delivery door or delivered to the customer's home. Seasonal products typically are held in warehouses until the appropriate selling season. For many retail organizations, the warehouse has become a distribution center responsible for receiving, checking, marking, and stocking merchandise for various outlets within the retail chain. It is more concerned with moving merchandise than storing it.[11]

## PAYING AND RETURNING

### Paying Invoices

**Paying** involves the procedures for processing and settling suppliers' invoices. Most retailers prefer to pay invoices after they have received and checked the merchandise, especially when dealing with an unknown supplier or suppliers whose return and adjustment policies on damaged merchandise and incorrect shipments are either restrictive or unknown. Sometimes invoices must be paid before receiving and checking to take full advantage of cash discounts that were negotiated.

### Returning Shipments

**Returns** occur when a retailer does not accept all or part of a shipment and sends some or all of the merchandise back to the supplier. The retailer must carefully determine whether there are legitimate reasons for the returns. Unfair returns along with unfair cancellations are two key causes of friction between suppliers and retailers. It is a good idea to contact the supplier before processing the return form and returning the merchandise. Most suppliers have their own return procedures, and retailers can save considerable time and effort by working out prior agreements on returns.

## SUMMARY

The buying process involves the five steps of identifying, contacting, evaluating, negotiating with, and buying from sources of supply.

The first step of identifying sources of supply is to establish what type of channel to use in procuring each merchandise line. The retailer has several options in selecting sources of supply, including various types of raw-resource producers, manufacturers, intermediaries, and resident buying offices.

Contacting sources of supply is the second step in the buying process. Contacts can be initiated by either the vendor or the retailer. Vendor-initiated contacts include store visits by vendor salespeople or mail and telephone solicitations. Retailers contact sources of supply by visiting central markets, using resident buying offices, attending merchandise shows, and making telephone and mail inquiries.

The third step in the buying process is evaluating various alternative suppliers. Suppliers can be evaluated on the basis of (1) the suitability, availability, and adaptability of the merchandise they offer; (2) the exclusiveness and policies associated with the supplier's distribution system; (3) the appropriateness of the supplier's price; (4) the type and amount of promotional assistance; and (5) the type and amount of supplementary services. One method for evaluating supply sources is the weighted-rating method.

Negotiating with sources of supply is the fourth step in the buying process. The two most common issues subject to negotiation are price and service. Price negotiations start with the supplier's list price and those discounts and allowances taken to adjust the list price. The most common price adjustments are trade, quantity, seasonal, and cash discounts, along with promotional allowances. Also of concern are various transportation and handling terms that affect the retailer's laid-in cost of the new merchandise.

The final step in the buying process is actual purchase of the merchandise from several suppliers, using various buying methods. The retailer can elect to concentrate purchases with a few suppliers or disperse them among many suppliers. In the actual buying process, the retailer can buy merchandise using a regular, consignment, memorandum, approval, or specification method of buying.

The merchandise handling process includes all the physical operations associated with getting merchandise into the store and onto the shelves. The four basic steps in handling are ordering and following up, receiving and checking, marking and stocking, and paying and returning.

Retailers must develop the necessary procedures for ordering merchandise—in either oral or written form—and for following up on those orders, which is necessary to make a purchase contract legally binding. Receiving is the physical exchange of goods between the retailer and the supplier's transporting agent. Retailers must plan facilities and procedures for receiving, inspecting, verifying, and logging incoming shipments. Checking is the process of determining whether the supplier has shipped what the retailer ordered and whether it has arrived in good condition. Personnel are trained to know what and how to check merchandise and when and where to report problems.

Marking is affixing to the merchandise the information necessary for stocking, controlling, and selling it. Marking systems that retailers use include source marking, preretailing, and store marking. Retailers must decide what and how much information to place on merchandise tags, where and how to attach tags to merchandise, and how to re-mark merchandise. Stocking includes the activities associated with in-store and between-store distribution of merchandise. Paying involves the procedures for processing and settling the supplier's invoice. Returning merchandise becomes necessary when there is a legitimate reason for not accepting the supplier's shipment.

## STUDENT STUDY GUIDE

**KEY TERMS AND CONCEPTS**

agent intermediary
approval buying
auction house
blind check
broker
bulk marking
cash-and-carry wholesaler
cash discount
chain trade discount
checking
combination check
commission merchant
contractual intermediary
concentration strategy
consignment buying
cooperative group
cumulative quantity discount
dating terms
direct check
discount amount
dispersion strategy
display stock
drop shipper
electronic purchase-order (EPO) systems
forward stock
future dating
general merchandise wholesaler
independent buying office
immediate dating
in-store stocking
invoice check
list price
manufacturers' agent
marking
memorandum buying
merchant intermediaries

net invoice price
noncumulative quantity single discount
optical character recognition font A (OCR-A)
order form
paying
point of sale (POS)
preretailing
promotional allowances
quality check
quantity check
rack jobber
receiving
receiving record
regular buying
reserve stock
resident buying office
returns
sales agent
seasonal discount
semiblind check
single-line wholesaler
single trade discount
source marking
specialty-line wholesaler
specification buying
stocking
store marking
store-owned buying office
truck distributor
universal product code (UPC)
voluntary chain
warehouse stocking
weighted-rating method
word cost codes

1. Why might the retailers buy directly from the manufacturer?
2. How are full-function merchant wholesalers distinguished from one another?
3. Identify and describe the four types of limited-function merchant wholesalers.
4. What types of information and buyer assistance services does the resident buying office provide?
5. How can the retailer evaluate the merchandise offered by a given supplier? Identify and discuss the evaluation criteria.
6. What distribution and delivery policies and standards should the retailer consider when evaluating a particular supplier?
7. What would be the retailer's price if a product had a list price of $40 and a trade discount structure of 30/20/5?
8. How does a cumulative quantity discount differ from a noncumulative discount?
9. What are two general classes of dating terms? Discuss each class.
10. What are promotional allowances? Describe their four common forms.
11. What issues should the retailer consider when negotiating transportation and handling terms?
12. Identify and briefly describe the five buying methods a retailer might use.
13. What options do retailers have in structuring their electronic purchase-order system?
14. The retailer makes three checks to see that it has received what was ordered. What are the three checks?
15. How might the retailer check quantities of incoming shipments?
16. Compare and contrast the three most common marking systems.
17. What are the two most common standardized marking systems for coding merchandise tags?
18. Discuss the options a retailer has for in-store stocking.

True or False

_____ 1. Merchant middlemen are wholesale sources of supply that do not take title to the goods they deal in but that are directly involved in the purchase and sale of goods as they move through the channel of distribution.

_____ 2. Central markets are periodic displays of the merchandise lines of many suppliers in one place at one time.

_____ 3. The purpose for expressing the trade discount in the form of a chain (e.g., 40, 30, 10) is to facilitate the process of offering different discounts to different buyers.

_____ 4. In memorandum buying, the retailer retains the right to return to the supplier any unsold merchandise.

_____ 5. The dial-up telephone linkage option is an electronic purchase order system that involves arranging transmission schedules and common protocols to allow direct computer-to-computer interchange of data.

_____ 6. The blind check method is generally the most accurate method for checking incoming shipments.

_____ 7. Forward stock is backup stock held in reserve, usually in a central stockroom.

## STUDENT APPLICATIONS MANUAL

**PROJECTS: INVESTIGATIONS AND APPLICATIONS**

1. Visiting central markets is a principal method used by retailers to initiate contacts with suppliers. However, many retailers are not well versed in how a central market operates, nor are they accustomed to the hectic atmosphere surrounding central markets; the net result often is "buying mistakes." Interview several retail buyers and identify the potential problems they face in making central market visits. Then, develop a set of general guidelines that the retail buyer should follow during a buying trip to a central market.

2. Developing and maintaining good supplier relationships is extremely important if the retailer expects to initiate new and keep old reliable sources of supply. Develop a list of rules that a retailer should observe in establishing and/or maintaining good relationships with vendors and suppliers.

3. Consignment buying, memorandum buying, approval buying, and specification buying are all special buying methods used by retailers under various conditions. Interview a merchandise manager for a department store or specialty store; determine under what conditions each of these special buying methods is used and why it is used.

4. Gain the cooperation of a local retailer and evaluate his/her receiving and checking system. Analyze the facilities and procedures used in receiving and checking. Determine the strengths and weaknesses of the system. What recommendations would you make for improving the system?

5. From the viewpoint of the consumer, what are the principal objections to the use of optical scanning systems that require code marking systems (e.g., universal product code)?

6. By contacting suppliers of store fixtures, obtain information (catalogs, brochures, etc.) on the types of fixtures and equipment that are available for in-store stocking of display and forward stock. Assume that you are going to be the manager of a small (20 feet wide and 50 feet deep) new exclusive men's clothing store with no separate storage room. What fixtures and equipment would you select for display and forward stock? Justify your selection.

**CASES: PROBLEMS AND DECISIONS**

### CASE 12–1
### Apex Stores—A Buy-America Campaign*

Alexander Ferris, president and chief executive officer of Apex Stores, Inc., was preparing for the 10:00 A.M. meeting he had called for the top executives in each of the corporation's four divisions. Each division represented one of the four retail store chains that were owned by Apex and which are briefly described below.

1. Fashion Works—a chain of 26 stores throughout Ohio, Michigan, Indiana, and Illinois that carry low- to medium-priced apparel for men and women.
2. Style Corner—an 18-store division featuring higher-priced women's fashions in the same Midwest market served by Fashion Works.
3. Minerva's—an upscale, fashionable chain of 21 women's clothing stores located along the West coast.
4. Cray's—a midpriced department store chain consisting of 16 units primarily operating in the Midwest, although there were plans for expansion into Pennsylvania, New York, and Maryland. Cray's carries a full line of men's and women's clothing, cosmetics, home electronics, furniture, appliances, housewares, and toys.

*This case was prepared by Daniel Gilmore, The University of Akron.

When he had them all assembled in his office at Apex's Chicago headquarters, Ferris outlined to his executives a new plan he was considering for all four of the company's divisions. He wanted to institute a policy of buying the goods sold in Apex's stores from American manufacturers whenever possible; in the past, purchases had been made without regard to a good's country or origin.

"In recent years, I've noticed a rising percentage of our overall purchases have been from foreign suppliers," Ferris said. "I think this is a trend that needs to be stopped. Concern about the U.S. trade deficit with foreign countries is growing, and I believe that we have some responsibility to do our part to reduce imports."

But Ferris then admitted that his idea was not solely driven by patriotic fervor. He thought that American consumers were increasingly sensitive to a product's country of origin and that they would react quite favorably to Apex's campaign to sell as many American-made goods as possible. Ferris was also confident that this move by Apex would take advantage of other national efforts to promote products made in America.

One, sponsored largely by the U.S. textile industry, was launched in the mid-1980s under the auspices of the Crafted with Pride in the USA Council. The council has developed an extensive ad campaign using celebrity spokespersons—working for free—proclaiming "It matters to me" and pointing to made-in-America labels on their clothing. Another independent group leads the Buy American Campaign, a nonprofit, grass-roots organization that uses its annual advertising budget of several million dollars to tout American-made goods in general. In addition, several other store chains and manufacturers had recently adopted "Buy American" promotions or policies.

"I think the time is right for us to have a Buy American policy of our own," Ferris told the executives. "I believe we should make a public promise to buy American-manufactured goods whenever we can and set some target, such as 75 percent of total purchases, to be reached in some chosen time period, such as one year. I'm open to negotiation on the specific details, but I am convinced that some step in this direction must be undertaken. Please do some research on how this will affect your divisions, and report back to me on your analysis and recommendations in two weeks."

The division presidents didn't speak as they left the office and headed down the hallway to the elevator. Once inside, however, they immediately began to discuss their boss's idea. "I was certainly not expecting that," said Erin Dietrick, head of Fashion Works. "I was just reading the other day that the National Retail Merchants Association has been lobbying Congress to keep international trade as open as possible for the benefit of consumers."

"Yes, that's true, but several large chains, such as K Mart, WalMart, and The Limited, have recently adopted Buy American campaigns of one sort or another," noted Jayne Hardin, the Style Corner's president. Responded Richard Bellows of Cray's Department Stores, "I don't care what anyone else is doing. This will certainly make my buyers' jobs a heck of a lot tougher, whatever the specifics turn out to be."

All of them agreed that whatever decision was made, it needed to be based on sound business principles, not just emotion. The question they faced is whether a Buy American campaign was really a good idea for Apex Stores, Inc.

## ASSIGNMENT

1. As mentioned in the case, several large retailers have developed Buy American purchasing policies in the past several years. What do you see as the advantages and disadvantages of these strategies?

2. From a retail buyer's point of view, how would you feel about your company decision to announce a percentage of purchases that will be made from American suppliers within a year? How might it affect your job? Your career?

3. If a Buy American policy is chosen for Apex Stores, should it be the same for all four of the divisions? What arguments can you provide in favor of employing a different strategy for each chain?

## CASE 12–2
## Showcase Gallery—Exploring Supplier Relationships*

### BACKGROUND

Frank Smith had just finalized a deal for a store facility that would become the future "Showcase Gallery." Smith had always wanted to open his own furniture store in the community and had the opportunity to do so when the previous owner of a home furnishings store retired. The investment involved a 14,000-square-foot facility located in a growing, high-income suburban area. He had been able to finance the venture through previous savings and investments by his family.

Smith has a working knowledge of the furniture trade, having been employed for 11 years as a manufacturer's representative in the industry. He brought to the venture a knowledge of case goods and upholstery and experience in interior design—a level of knowledge not commonly found among retail personnel.

The opportunity to work for himself, to be his own boss, had always been a dream. Consequently, he placed great importance upon operational autonomy. Having experienced the other half of the dealer-supplier relationship, however, Smith recognized that his autonomy might have to be tempered somewhat to achieve benefits possible only through mutual cooperation.

### CURRENT SITUATION

With the purchase of the retail facility, Smith first needed to decide which type of dealer-supplier arrangement would be most appropriate for his needs and the firm's future success. He had three alternatives: conventional arrangements, programmed merchandising, and business format franchising. As he examined each option, Smith realized that his decision not only would have significance in developing trade relations but also could have a major impact on his performance as a dealer. Before making the final decision, Frank mentally reviewed the implications of each dealer-supplier arrangement.

### Conventional Arrangement

With a conventional arrangement, Smith would typically deal with many suppliers. Because the highly fragmented furniture industry consists of many dealers and manufacturers, dependence of any one firm upon another was accordingly low. Consequently, a conventional arrangement tended to involve a relatively less enduring, loosely aligned relationship. Frank had observed that dealers were often suspicious of suppliers and did not cooperate fully for fear of being locked into a given relationship.

Despite the potential problems, some dealers thought that this arrangement gave them greater operational flexibility in serving their customers. They were not confined to particular styles or price points offered by a given manufacturer; instead, they were able to adapt quickly to the changing needs of the community by using a large number of suppliers

*This case was prepared by Jeffrey Dilts, The University of Akron.

to provide an appropriate product assortment, one that would have broad appeal to various customer groups.

## Programmed Merchandising

Programmed merchandising arrangements represent a second alternative. This type of relationship would require Smith to establish several formal or implied licensing agreements with a select number of primary suppliers. These supplier-developed arrangements are tailor-made programs designed to generate greater dealer commitment for one or more of the supplier's product lines. To encourage strong dealer commitment, the supplier offers selected retailers such customized programs as in-store merchandising assistance, advertising allowances, discount structures, and sales promotional support.

In return for the right to handle the supplier's merchandise line and to benefit from the privileges of the supplier's programs, Smith would be expected to limit his involvement with competitive products and to commit significant resources in support of each of the supplier's merchandise lines. Support requirements include maintaining a minimum level of inventory investment in each of the supplier's lines of merchandise and committing a minimum amount of floor space to permanent display of the supplier's products. Smith would also be expected to cooperate in such supplier-initiated programs as factory-authorized sales and other special sales promotions.

## Business Format Franchise

Colony House, a business format franchise, is the third alternative that Frank investigated in some depth. This option involves a tightly knit dealer-supplier arrangement in which Colony House (the franchiser) would provide Frank (the franchisee) with a patterned way of doing business. A total-store concept is provided by Colony House. This concept includes a plan for store layout and design, a complete line of merchandise, a comprehensive merchandising program, and a detailed operations manual. Colony House's total-store concept is highly coordinated to achieve a sharply focused image that appeals to a targeted group of consumers. Product assortments include early and traditional American furniture and home accessory items. In contrast to the industry's frequent style changes, Colony's continuity of established merchandise lines enables customers to purchase coordinated furniture pieces over an extended period of time.

The initial investment for a standard 12,000-square-foot operation would be approximately $250,000. Because Frank already has an existing facility, Colony House would require that he alter the exterior and interior of the building to make it consistent with the Colony House image. In return, Colony would provide architectural plans, training, and merchandising backup. Although no franchise fee was required, an annual fee (5 percent of sales) will be charged for promotional support.

Colony House believes that strong commitment is necessary for the formulated concept to succeed. Consequently, it screens retail applicants closely to determine their compatability with Colony House. Each applicant's background, personality, and business philosophy are reviewed. Franchisees, although independent businesses, are expected to adhere very closely to Colony's recommendations regarding store operations and merchandising.

## ASSIGNMENT

1. Outline the advantages and disadvantages of each supplier-dealer arrangement.
2. Recommend the most suitable supplier-dealer arrangement for Frank Smith. Provide the rationale for your recommendation.
3. Advise Smith on how your recommendation will influence his trade relations and store performance.

**ENDNOTES**

1. Richard Ettenson and Janet Wagner, "Retail Buyers' Saleability Judgments: A Comparison of Information Use Across Three Levels of Experience," *Journal of Retailing* 62 (Spring 1986): 42.
2. See Renee D. Howerton and Teresa A. Summers, "Apparel Sales Representatives: Perceptions of Their Roles and Functions," *The FIT Review* 4 (Spring 1988): 10–18.
3. See Kenneth G. Hardy and Allan J. Magrath, "Buying Groups: Clout for Small Businesses," *Harvard Business Review* (September–October 1987): 16–23.
4. See Clyde Ellison, Jr., "Auditing Imports," *Retail Control* (November 1986): 45–55.
5. John S. Berens, "A Decision Matrix Approach to Suppliers' Selection," *Journal of Retailing* 47 (Winter 1971): 52.
6. Laurie Freeman and Janet Meyers, "Grocer 'Fee' Hampers New Product Launches," *Advertising Age,* 3 Aug. 1987, 1, 60.
7. See Jules Abend, "Computer Links," *Stores* (June 1984): 75.
8. See "At K-Mart: Nearly 200 Vendors Now on a Direct Electronic Purchase Order System: How It Is Working," *Stores* (May, 1981): 50–52.
9. See Jules Abend, "Computer Links," 75.
10. See "Goal for PLG: Pre-Ticketing With UPC." *Stores* (March 1988): 30–32 and Jules Abend, "Tracking UPC Growth," *Stores* (September 1987): 52, 57–64, 70.
11. See Jules Abend, "Moving Goods Faster," *Stores* (October 1987): 60–69.

# 13

## Outline

## Objectives

☐ Plan an acceptable balance between merchandise inventories and sales.

☐ Devise and use a merchandise budget in the dollar planning of the retailer's investment in merchandise inventory.

☐ Devise and use a merchandise list in the unit planning of the retailer's merchandise assortment and support.

☐ Describe the need for merchandise control in maintaining a planned balance between the retailer's merchandise inventory and sales.

☐ Outline the method for collecting and procedures for processing merchandise data.

☐ Discuss the methods and procedures for valuing the retailer's inventories.

☐ Explain the methods and procedures for evaluating past merchandising performances.

☐ Identify the methods and procedures for making future merchandise decisions.

# Inventory Planning
# and Control

A sound policy for managing merchandise is essential to enable the retailer to offer the right product in the right place at the right time in the right quantities and at the right price. The basic ingredients of the merchandise-management process are illustrated in Figure 13–1. As portrayed, **merchandise management** focuses on planning and controlling the retailer's inventories. **Merchandise planning** consists of establishing objectives and devising plans for obtaining those objectives. The planning process normally includes both dollar planning in terms of merchandise budgets and unit planning in terms of merchandise lists. **Merchandise control** involves designing dollar and unit inventory information and analysis systems for collecting, recording, analyzing, and using merchandise data to determine whether the stated objectives have been achieved. In summary, planning is the process of establishing performance guidelines, whereas control is the process of checking on how well management is following those guidelines. This chapter is devoted to the merchandise-planning and control processes.

## MERCHANDISE PLANNING

The overall objective of merchandise planning is to satisfy both the customer's merchandise needs and the retailer's financial requirements. To accomplish that objective, the retailer must devise merchandise plans that create an acceptable balance between merchandise inventories and sales. This inventory-to-sales balance requires the retailer to plan each merchandise category carefully regarding (1) inventory investment, (2) inventory assortment, and (3) inventory support.

Inventory investment involves planning the total dollar investment in merchandise inventory so that the firm can realize its financial objectives. **Inventory assortment** is planning the number of different product items (brand, style, size, color, material, and price combinations) the retailer should stock within a particular product line and determining whether this assortment is adequate to meet the merchandise-selection needs of the firm's targeted consumers. **Inventory support** refers to planning the number of units the retailer should have on hand for each product item to meet sales estimates (e.g., stocking 100 six-packs of Coca-Cola in the 12-ounce can).

Both dollar and unit planning are essential if the retailer expects to balance inventory investment, assortment, and support. Inventory investment is the focus for dollar planning, whereas unit planning centers on the retailer's inventory assortment and support.

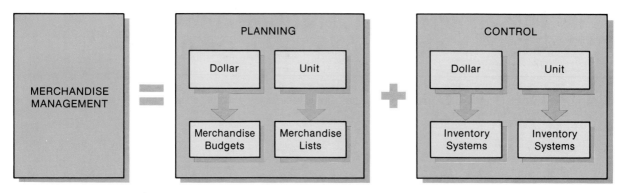

**FIGURE 13-1**
The merchandise management process

**DOLLAR PLANNING: MERCHANDISE BUDGETS**

**Dollar planning** is largely a financial-management tool that retailers use to plan the amount of total value (dollars) inventory they should carry. It answers the inventory question of how much the retailer should invest in merchandise during any specified period. Dollar planning is accomplished through a **merchandise budget**—a financial plan for managing merchandise inventory investments. The merchandise budget consists of five stages:

1. Planning sales
2. Planning stock levels
3. Planning reductions
4. Planning purchases
5. Planning profit margins

### Planning Sales

The starting point in developing the merchandise budget is sales planning. It is absolutely necessary to accurately forecast future sales; if future sales are incorrectly estimated during this initial stage, then all other aspects of the merchandise budget (stock levels, reductions, purchases, profit margins) will reflect this initial error.

Before making sales estimates, the retailer must select the control unit for which the projections will be made. The **control unit** is the merchandise grouping that serves as the basic reporting unit for various types of information (e.g., past, current, and future sales). The retailer can elect to estimate future sales for an entire store, for a merchandise division or department, or for an individual product line or item. Using merchandise categories (specific lines of products that are directly comparable and substitutable, such as toasters) as the basic control unit is recommended because it is generally much easier to aggregate information (summing merchandise categories into merchandise classes and groups) than it is to disaggregate information (breaking down merchandise groups into classes and categories).

Annual sales for each merchandise category are estimated largely by means of judgmental or qualitative methods. Two such methods are the fixed and variable adjustment procedures.

With the *fixed adjustment method,* the retailer adjusts last year's sales by some fixed percentage to estimate the coming year's sales. The direction (plus or minus) and the size (the exact percentage) of the adjustment are based on the retailer's past sales experience with each merchandise category. The fixed adjustment method usually works reasonably well in estimating future sales if a clear and stable sales trend has been established. When past sales patterns are erratic, however, a fixed percentage adjustment is inappropriate.

The second method for estimating annual sales is the *variable adjustment method.* As with the fixed adjustment method, the forecaster usually starts with an examination of the past sales history of the merchandise category. Based on the sales history, the forecaster determines a percentage change (e.g., 6 percent) that appears reasonable. The figure is then adjusted upward or downward by a degree that depends on the nature of the merchandise and its exposure and sensitivity to environmental influences. To make these adjustments, the retailer might consider the following external environmental factors: (1) the general prosperity of local and national markets; (2) rate of inflation; (3) discernible trends (growth or decline) in the size of the target market population; (4) changes in the demographic makeup of the population; (5) developing legal and/or social restrictions; (6) changing patterns of competition; and (7) changing consumer preferences and life-styles. Internal factors to consider in adjusting annual sales estimates include (1) changes in the amount and location of shelf or floor space devoted to the merchandise category; (2) changes in the amount and type of planned promotional support; and (3) changes in basic operating policies (e.g., longer store hours or higher levels of service). In summary, the **annual sales estimate** for a particular merchandise category equals the previous year's sales plus or minus a fixed or variable percentage adjustment.

Retail planning periods typically are based on one-month or several-month periods. The best operational estimate for budgetary planning purposes is **monthly sales estimates**. Estimating monthly sales involves three steps: (1) making annual sales estimates; (2) determining estimated monthly sales; and (3) adjusting monthly sales estimates using a monthly sales index.

To make monthly sales estimates, the forecaster starts with annual sales estimates, as discussed. The second step in estimating monthly sales is to allocate the annual sales estimate on a monthly basis. One way to make this allocation is to determine average estimated monthly sales by dividing the annual sales estimate by the number of months in a year (12). This figure would be a reasonably reliable estimate of monthly sales if we could assume that sales were evenly distributed over the 12 months of the year. However, monthly sales fluctuation is more the rule than the exception, hence the need to make the adjustment to the average estimated monthly sales figure.

Average estimated monthly sales are adjusted according to a *monthly sales index* based on past monthly sales records. The purpose of this adjustment is to obtain a *planned monthly sales figure,* the final estimate of each month's sales that the retailer will use throughout the budgetary process. By indexing past monthly sales, the forecaster can establish a sales norm for an "average month" by which all other monthly sales can be judged. The average month is represented by an index value of 100. Any month with an index below 100 represents monthly sales below the norm; above-average sales are represented by index values exceeding 100. For example, a monthly sales index of 76 indicates that sales for that month are 24

| Month | Actual Monthly Sales ($) | Monthly Sales Index[a] |
|---|---|---|
| January | 3,400 | 24 |
| February | 3,600 | 26 |
| March | 6,800 | 49 |
| April | 7,000 | 50 |
| May | 23,800 | 170 |
| June | 27,200 | 194 |
| July | 6,600 | 47 |
| August | 7,200 | 51 |
| September | 10,600 | 76 |
| October | 8,800 | 63 |
| November | 25,400 | 181 |
| December | 41,400 | 296 |
| Total annual sales | 168,000 | |
| Average monthly sales | 14,000 | |
| Average monthly index | | 100 |

$$^a = \frac{\text{actual monthly sales}}{\text{average monthly sales}} \times 100$$

(100 − 76) percent below the average. An index value of 181 denotes an above-average sales performance of 81 (181 − 100) percent.

The monthly sales index is obtained by dividing the actual monthly sales by average monthly sales and multiplying by 100. An example of calculating the monthly sales as seen in Figure 13–2, the actual monthly sales for men's and women's watches is highly seasonal; the sales peaks correspond to the May/June graduation and December holiday seasons. Average monthly sales are obtained by dividing the total annual sales by 12 (months in a year); in the example, $168,000 divided by 12 equals $14,000. January's monthly sales index of 24 was calculated by dividing $3,400 (actual monthly sales) by $14,000 (average monthly sales) and multiplying by 100. The remaining eleven monthly sales indexes were calculated in the same manner. Once the monthly sales index has been calculated, it can be used to adjust future (estimated) annual and average monthly sales to obtain planned monthly sales—a basic element in all the stock-planning methods.

## Planning Stock Levels

The second stage in developing a merchandise budget involves planning appropriate stock levels for a specific sales period. Ideally, the retailer's stock plan should (1) meet sales expectations, (2) avoid out-of-stock conditions, (3) guard against overstock conditions, and (4) keep inventory investment at an acceptable level. Four methods are used in planning stock requirements. They are the basic stock method, the percentage variation method, the week's supply method, and the stock/sales ratio method.

The **basic stock method** is designed to meet sales expectations and avoid out-of-stock conditions by beginning each month with stock levels that equal the estimated sales for that month plus an additional basic stock amount that serves as a "cushion" or "safety stock" in the event that actual sales exceed estimated sales. The safety stock also protects the retailer against stockouts if future shipments of merchandise are delayed or arrive damaged and must be returned to the vendor. On the negative side, safety stock means that the retailer has a larger investment in inventory and greater inventory carrying costs.

The basic stock method involves calculating the beginning-of-the-month stock (BOM stock) for each month of the sales period. The BOM stock is computed by adding a basic stock amount to each of the planned monthly sales as determined in the sales-planning stage of the budgetary process. For example, let's assume that the department manager for the jewelry department of Selmer's Department Store is in the process of planning stocks for the upcoming Christmas season (October, November, and December). Using the basic stock method, the department manager would plan the BOM stock for each of the three months (sales period) using the procedures outlined in Figure 13–3.

Figure 13–4 reconstructs the three-month Christmas sales period of October, November, and December. Based on past sales records, the retailer knows that the turnover rate (number of times the average stock on hand is sold during a given time period) for watches during this three-month sales period has averaged about two.

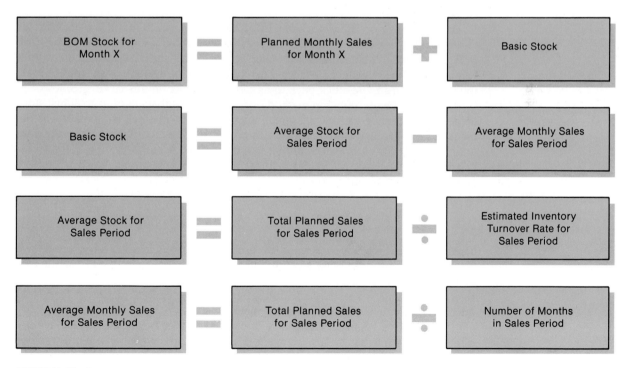

**FIGURE 13–3**
The basic stock method for determining BOM stock

FIGURE 13–4
BOM stock for men's
and women's watches
(jewelry department,
Selmer's Department
Store)

| Sales Period | Planned Monthly Sales ($)[1] | BOM Stock Using Basic Stock Method ($) | BOM Stock Using Percentage Variation Method ($) |
|---|---|---|---|
| Oct. | 9,450 | 22,950 | 27,337.50 |
| Nov. | 27,150 | 40,650 | 40,905.00 |
| Dec. | 44,400 | 57,900 | 53,460.00 |
| Total | 81,000 | — | — |

Using the information in Figure 13–4, BOM stock is determined for the month of October in the following manner:

average monthly sales for
October, November, December $= \$81,000 \div 3 = \$27,000$

average stock for October,
November, December $\quad = \$81,000 \div 2 = \$40,500$

basic stock $= \$40,500 - \$27,000 = \$13,500$

BOM stock for October $= \$9,450 + \$13,500 = \$22,950$

As shown, a basic or safety stock of $13,500 is added to each month's planned sales to arrive at the BOM stock. The BOM stocks for November and December are shown in Figure 13–4. When actual sales either exceed or fall short of planned sales for a given month, the retailer can easily adjust the amount of overage or shortfall to bring the next month's BOM stock back to its calculated level (in this case, $13,500).

The **percentage variation method** uses a procedure that attempts to adjust stock levels in accordance with actual variations in sales. BOM stock is increased or decreased from average stock for the sales period by one-half of the percentage variation in planned monthly sales for that month from the average monthly sales for the sales period. The calculating procedures for the percentage variation method are shown in Figure 13–5.

$$\text{BOM stock for October} = \$40,500 \times \frac{1}{2}\left(1 + \frac{\$9,450}{\$27,000}\right) = \$27,337.50$$

The BOM stocks for November and December have been calculated and are shown along with the October BOM stock in Figure 13–4. Retailers prefer to use the percentage variation method with merchandise categories characterized by a high turnover rate (usually exceeding six times per year) because it results in less stock fluctuation than use of the basic stock method.

The **week's supply method** is a stocking plan that determines stock levels in direct proportion to sales. As a means to plan stocks on a weekly basis, this method uses a desired annual stock turnover rate to establish the amount of stock necessary to cover a predetermined number of weeks. If the manager of Selmer's jewelry department thinks an annual stock turnover rate of eight is both desirable and fea-

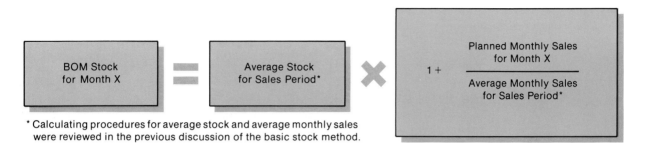

* Calculating procedures for average stock and average monthly sales
  were reviewed in the previous discussion of the basic stock method.

**FIGURE 13–5**
The percentage varia-
tion method for deter-
mining BOM stock

sible, determining stock for the start of the Christmas sales period (October) would be
done as shown in Figure 13–6. Using the data in Figure 13–4,

number of weeks to be stocked  =  52 ÷ 8 = 6.5 weeks
average weekly sales            = $180,000 ÷ 52 = $3,462
BOM stock for October          = $3,462 × 6.5 = $22,503

Having determined the number of weeks' supply to stock (6.5 weeks) and the average weekly sales ($3,462), stock levels can be replenished frequently and regularly
(e.g., weekly or biweekly) before stock shortages occur. The principal limitation of this
method is that during weeks with a slow stock turn (below annual rate), there will be
an excessive accumulation of stock. Therefore, this method is most appropriate for
retailers whose merchandise categories show stable sales and stable stock turnover
rates.

The **stock/sales ratio method** is another method retailers use to determine BOM
levels. The assumption behind this method is that the retailer should maintain a
certain ratio of goods on hand to planned monthly sales. This ratio could be 2:1, 3:1,
or any other appropriate relationship. A stock/sales ratio of 2:1 means the planned

**FIGURE 13–6**
The week's supply method of determining BOM stock

FIGURE 13–7
Stock/sales ratio
method of determining
BOM stock

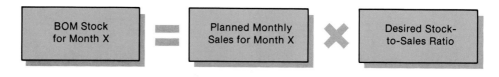

monthly sales of $5,000 would require $10,000 of stock. The key to using this method is finding a dependable stock/sales ratio, for which the best source is the retailer's own past records.

To illustrate this method, let's assume that past sales records for Selmer's jewelry department reveal that a 2:1 stock/sales ratio is desirable. Based on the planned monthly sales cited in Figure 13–4, the BOM stock for October would be calculated as shown in Figure 13–7.

$$\text{BOM stock for October} = \$9,450 \times 2 = \$18,900$$

Using the same procedures, the BOM stock for November would be $54,000, while December's BOM stock would be $88,800.

### Planning Reductions

The third stage in developing the merchandise budget is to plan reductions. **Retail reductions** can be defined as the difference between the merchandise item's original retail value and its actual final sales value. This difference is the result of three factors: markdowns, discounts, and shortages. **Markdowns** are reductions in the original retail price for the purpose of stimulating the sale of merchandise. **Discounts** are reductions in the original retail price that are granted to store employees as special fringe benefits and to special customers (e.g., clergy, senior citizens, disadvantaged consumers) in recognition of their special status. **Shortages** are reductions in the total value of the retailer's inventory as a result of shoplifting, pilfering, and merchandise being damaged and misplaced.

Planning reductions essentially involves making a percentage-of-sales (dollars) estimate for each of the three major reduction factors: markdowns, discounts, and shortages. These percentage estimates are made on the basis of past experience or obtained from trade sources. Continuing our watch example, if the retailer's past records reveal that for the month of October men's and women's watches experienced average monthly markdowns of 6 percent and discounts and shortages averaged 1.5 percent and 2.5 percent, respectively, then the total planned reductions for October would be 10 percent of planned monthly sales, or $945 (see Figure 13–4).

### Planning Purchases

Planning purchases constitutes the fourth stage in developing a merchandise budget. In this stage, the retailer plans the dollar amount of merchandise that must be purchased for a given time period (e.g., a month or a season) in view of planned sales and reductions for that period as well as the planned stock levels at the beginning of the period and the desired stock levels at the end of the period. (The ending stock usually equals the beginning stock for the next period.) The format for calculating planned purchases for a monthly planning period is as follows:

planned monthly sales
+ planned monthly reductions
+ desired end-of-the-month stock
___
= total stock needs for the month
− planned beginning-of-month stock
___
= planned monthly purchases

For illustration, let's assume that the manager of Selmer's jewelry department is planning the October purchases of men's and women's watches. From our previous discussions we have the following information concerning October: (1) planned monthly sales estimated at $9,450 (see Figure 13–4); (2) planned monthly reductions estimated at 10 percent of sales of $945; (3) desired end-of-the-month stock of $40,500 (the beginning-of-the-month stock for November—see Figure 13–4); (4) planned beginning-of-the-month stock of $22,500 (see Figure 13–4). Given this information, the planned purchases for the month of October are

| | |
|---|---|
| planned monthly sales | $ 9,450 |
| + planned monthly reductions | 945 |
| + desired end-of-the-month stock | $40,650 |
| = total stock needs for the month | $51,045 |
| − planned beginning-of-the-month stock | 22,500 |
| = planned monthly purchases | 28,545 |

The planned monthly purchases of $28,545 were computed in terms of retail prices. To find out what the manager must spend in terms of cost prices, the retailer must multiply the retail value ($28,545) by the cost equivalent (the percentage of the retail price that is the manager's cost). For example, if merchandise costs are 60 percent of the retail price, then the manager can plan to make purchases totaling $17,127 at cost prices ($28,545 × .60).

The planned monthly purchase value represents the retailer's additional merchandise needs for that month—how much merchandise must be purchased and made available during that month.

## Planning Profit Margins

An integral part of developing the merchandise budget is to allow for a reasonable profit by ensuring an adequate dollar **gross margin**—the difference between cost of goods sold and net sales. An adequate dollar gross margin must cover the operating expenses associated with buying, stocking, and selling the merchandise, as well as produce an acceptable operating profit. The procedures for determining dollar gross margin and operating profit are as follows:

net sales ($)
− cost of goods sold ($)
___
= gross margin ($)
− operating expenses ($)
___
= operating profit ($)

Retailers attempt to achieve an adequate gross margin and operating profit by planning an **initial markup percentage**—the percentage difference between the cost of the merchandise and its original retail price—that will cover expenses, profits, and reductions. The formula for calculating the initial markup percentage is

$$\frac{\text{required initial}}{\text{markup percentage}} = \frac{\text{expenses} + \text{profits} + \text{reductions}}{\text{sales} + \text{reductions}}$$

Sales and reduction estimates are obtained from the sales and reduction planning stages of the merchandise budget. Expense estimates are based on past experience as revealed by expense records. After making sales, reduction, and expense estimates, the retailer can then establish a realistic profit objective. To facilitate easy planning, reductions, expenses, and profits are estimated as a *percentage of sales*. For example, in planning the required initial markup percentage on men's and women's watches for the coming year (1990), the manager of Selmer's jewelry department has estimated total annual sales of $180,000, reductions at 10 percent of sales or $18,000, and anticipated expenses at 20 percent of sales or $36,000. Further, assuming that the manager desires a profit objective of 12 percent of sales or $21,600, which is considered both feasible and acceptable, the manager calculates the required initial markup on watches:

$$\frac{\text{required initial}}{\text{markup percentage}} = \frac{\$36,000 + \$21,600 + \$18,000}{\$180,000 + \$18,000} = 38.2\%$$

The same formula can be used when expenses, profits, reductions, and sales are expressed in percentage terms (sales equals 100 percent). For example,

$$\frac{\text{required initial}}{\text{markup percentage}} = \frac{20\% + 12\% + 10\%}{100\% + 10\%} = 38.2\%$$

This required initial markup percentage represents an overall average for a merchandise category (e.g., watches). As long as this category average is maintained, the actual initial markup on any individual merchandise item (a watch of a particular brand, style, and price) can vary from the average to adjust to different demand conditions, competitive circumstances, and other external and internal merchandising factors.

## UNIT PLANNING: MERCHANDISE LISTS

Unit planning is an operational management tool to plan the merchandise assortment and support. It is directed at determining the amount of inventory the retailer should carry by item and by units and answers the inventory questions of how many product items (assortment) and how many units of each item (support) to stock. Unit planning involves the use of several *merchandise lists*—a set of operational plans for managing total selection of merchandise. Based on the type of merchandise the retailer carries, one or more of the following three merchandise lists will apply.

1. Basic stock list—for planning staple merchandise
2. Model stock list—for planning fashion merchandise
3. Never-out list—for planning key items and best-sellers

Merchandise lists essentially represent the "ideal" stock for meeting the consumer's merchandise needs in terms of assortment and support.

## Basic Stock List

The **basic stock list** is a planning instrument retailers use to determine the assortment and support for staple merchandise. **Staples** are product items for which sales are either very stable or highly variable but very predictable. In either case, estimates of the required assortment of merchandise items and the number of support units for each item can be made with a relatively high degree of accuracy. Thus, in planning for staple merchandise, the retailer can develop a very specific stocking plan. The basic stock list is a schedule or listing of "stock-keeping units" (SKU) for staple merchandise. A **stock-keeping unit** is a merchandise category for which separate records (sales and stock) are maintained; an SKU can consist of a single merchandise item or a group of items. The basic stock list usually identifies each SKU in precise terms. A retailer can use the following product characteristics to distinguish clearly an SKU of staple merchandise: (1) brand name, (2) style or model number, (3) product or package size, (4) product color or material, (5) retail and/or cost price of the product, and (6) manufacturer's name and identification number. In addition to a complete listing of SKUs, the basic stock list also contains a detailed description of the stock position for each SKU by stock levels (merchandise support, or total number of units). Also, this description of stock support normally identifies (1) a minimum stock level to be on hand, (2) actual stock on hand, (3) amount of stock on order, (4) planned sales, and (5) actual sales. Figure 13–8 illustrates one of several possible forms for recording the information contained in a basic stock list.

Given the "essential" character of staple merchandise in the consumer's buying behavior patterns, close supervision over the stock position of staples is absolutely necessary. The simple fact that consumers expect an adequate supply of staple merchandise makes it all the more important to have an adequate supply. A stockout of a particular staple forces consumers to look elsewhere for the item; in the process of looking elsewhere, they may decide to switch to a competitor whose stock of staples is well maintained.

## Model Stock List

Stock planning for fashion merchandise is accomplished through use of the **model stock list**—a schedule or listing of SKUs for fashion merchandise. The model stock list differs from the basic stock list because it defines each SKU in general rather than precise terms. Common criteria in identifying a model SKU are *general price lines* ("better dresses" at $100, $150, and $200 or "moderate dresses" at $40, $60, and $80); *distribution of sizes* (misses 8, 10, 12, 14, and 16); *certain basic colors* (black cocktail dresses or navy-blue blazers); *general style features* (long and short sleeve dresses or crew neck, v-neck, and turtleneck sweaters); and *product materials* (wool, cotton, and polyester dresses). The more general character of each SKU in a model stock plan reflects the transience of fashion merchandise, which represents only the currently prevailing style. The likelihood of style changes within a short period and the high probability that market demand (sales) will fluctuate considerably within any selling season require a more general approach to stock planning. If the model stock

| Stock Keeping Unit | | Vendor Description | | | Merchandise Description | | | | | | Stock Description | | | | |
|---|---|---|---|---|---|---|---|---|---|---|---|---|---|---|---|
| Number | Name | Manuf. Name | Manuf. I.D. | Brand | Style/ Model | Material | Color | Size | Price R  C | | | Quarters | | | |
| | | | | | | | | | | | | 1 | 2 | 3 | 4 |
| | | | | | | | | | | | MS | | | | |
| | | | | | | | | | | | PS | | | | |
| | | | | | | | | | | | AS | | | | |
| | | | | | | | | | | | OH | | | | |
| | | | | | | | | | | | OO | | | | |
| | | | | | | | | | | | MS | | | | |
| | | | | | | | | | | | PS | | | | |
| | | | | | | | | | | | AS | | | | |
| | | | | | | | | | | | OH | | | | |
| | | | | | | | | | | | OO | | | | |
| | | | | | | | | | | | MS | | | | |
| | | | | | | | | | | | PS | | | | |
| | | | | | | | | | | | AS | | | | |
| | | | | | | | | | | | OH | | | | |
| | | | | | | | | | | | OO | | | | |
| | | | | | | | | | | | MS | | | | |
| | | | | | | | | | | | PS | | | | |
| | | | | | | | | | | | AS | | | | |
| | | | | | | | | | | | OH | | | | |
| | | | | | | | | | | | OO | | | | |

Key: R = Retail Price    PS = Planned Sales    OH = Stock on Hand
      C = Cost Price        AS = Actual Sales     OO = Stock on Order
      MS = Minimum Stock

**FIGURE 13–8**
A basic stock list form

list calls for 300 "better dresses" equally distributed among the $100, $150, and $200 price lines, the retailer is still free to adapt to specific fashion trends that are currently stylish. In the initial planning of model stock lists, desired support quantities for each SKU are established on the basis of past sales experience. The exact distribution of those quantities among the various assortment features (e.g., colors, styles, and materials) is left to the buyer's judgment about what is and will be appropriate for the store's customers. In essence, the model stock list provides general guidelines on the size and composition of an ideal stock of fashion merchandise, without specifying the exact nature of the merchandise assortment or support.

The form used to plan the model stock list differs somewhat from the basic stock list form. First, the vendor description is usually absent or abbreviated. Second, the merchandise description is more generalized. Finally, the stock description is frequently more detailed, breaking down each season (quarter) into desired stock levels at various times within the season: beginning of the season, seasonal peak, and end of the season.

## Never-Out List

The **never-out list** is a specially created list of merchandise items that are identified as key items or best-sellers for which the retailer wants extra protection against the possibility of a stockout. As a result of the high level of demand for these items, many retailers establish rigid stock requirements. For example, a retailer might specify that 99 percent of all items on the never-out list must be on hand and on display at all times. Stockouts of these key items result in permanent loss of sales. Typically, the consumer simply will not wait to purchase best-sellers. Never-out lists can include fast-selling staples, key seasonal items, and best-selling fashion merchandise. The integrity of the never-out list is preserved through regular and frequent revision. The importance of the never-out list is underscored by the fact that many chain organizations expect individual store managers to have a near-perfect record in maintaining the stock levels for merchandise on the list. Even a moderate number of stockouts of merchandise on the list is considered an indication of poor management.

**Merchandise control** is the process of designing and maintaining inventory systems for controlling the planned balance between inventory and sales. "Inventory control provides the necessary parameters to the planning process."[1] Merchandise control can be viewed as the sum of two types of inventory systems: an inventory-information system and an inventory-analysis system. The **inventory-information system** is the set of methods and procedures for collecting and processing merchandise data pertinent to the planning and control of merchandise inventories. The **inventory-analysis system** includes methods for evaluating the retailer's past merchandising performance and decision-making tools for controlling future merchandising activities. As with merchandise planning, merchandise control relies on the retailer's inventory information and analysis systems to control inventory investment as well as inventory assortment and support.

 The retailer's merchandise controls must be able to supplement the basic merchandising decisions of buying, stocking, and selling. Our discussion of merchandise control starts with how merchandise data are collected and processed. It then examines the methods and tools for evaluating and using merchandise data.

**MERCHANDISE CONTROL**

To control their inventories effectively, retailers must have an efficient means of obtaining information on the inventories' past and current status. An adequate inventory-information system is a prerequisite to planning and controlling future merchandising activities. Before examining the major types of inventory-information systems, let's consider the kinds of information retailers need for controlling inventories and sources for that information.

**INVENTORY-INFORMATION SYSTEMS**

## Inventory Information

Merchandise investment and merchandise assortment and support are the principal elements the retailer wants to control. To complement merchandise planning, the retailer's inventory-information system must be capable of providing both dollar control and unit control. **Dollar control** considers the "value" of merchandise and attempts to identify the dollar amount of investment in merchandise. Dollar control requires the retailer to collect, record, and analyze merchandise data in terms of dollars. **Unit control** deals not with dollars but with the number of different product items (assortment) and the number of units stocked within each item (support). It is the number of physical units (sales, purchases, and stock levels) recorded and analyzed.

The retailer's source of inventory information is the inventory system. Inventory systems differ depending on when (perpetually or periodically) inventory is taken and how (book or physical) it is taken. Based on these two factors, inventory procedures can be classified as either perpetual book inventory systems or periodic physical inventory systems.

A **perpetual book inventory** refers to a system of inventory taking and information gathering on a continuous or ongoing basis using various accounting records to compute stock on hand at any given time. The purchase, sales, and markdown figures needed to calculate stock on hand are derived from internal accounting records that must be kept current if the computed book inventory is to correctly reflect the retailer's true stock position. In summary, a perpetual book inventory represents an up-to-the-minute, -day, or -week accounting system in which all transactions that affect inventory are considered as they occur or shortly thereafter. Its major advantage is that the retailer can determine stock on hand as required by operating conditions and the need for inventory information.

A **periodic physical inventory** refers to a system of gathering stock information intermittently (usually once or twice a year) using an actual physical count and inspection of the merchandise items to compute sales for the period since the last physical inventory. Limitations of a periodic physical inventory system are the time-consuming process of making an actual, physical count of each merchandise item and the fact that most retailers have faster, easier, and more time-saving methods for obtaining sales information. Nevertheless, a physical inventory must be taken at least once a year for income tax reporting purposes. A physical count of the retailer's inventory also is necessary to determine stock shortages (book inventory minus physical inventory).

### Inventory Systems

The major types of inventory-information systems used in merchandise control are (1) dollar/perpetual/book, (2) dollar/periodic/physical, (3) unit/perpetual/book, and (4) unit/periodic/physical. Let's examine these systems.

Dollar control using a **dollar/perpetual/book inventory** system provides the retailer with continuous information on the amount of inventory (dollars) that should be on hand at any given time as determined by internal accounting records. The basic procedures for calculating a perpetual book inventory in dollars are as follows:

$$
\begin{aligned}
&\quad\text{beginning stock on hand}\\
+\ &\underline{\text{purchases}}\\
=\ &\text{total stock handled}\\
-\ &\text{sales}\\
+\ &\underline{\text{markdowns}}\\
=\ &\text{ending stock on hand}
\end{aligned}
$$

Dollar control systems express values either in terms of retail prices or cost prices.

In the preceding formulation, the beginning stock-on-hand value is the ending stock-on-hand value from the preceding accounting period. Merchandise data concerning purchases, sales, and markdowns are obtained from the appropriate internal accounting records. The computed ending stock on hand is the dollar value of the retailer's inventory, provided no shortages have occurred. To determine actual stock shortages, the retailer would have to check the book inventory by taking a physical inventory. Many retailers use an estimated shortage percentage (e.g., 2 percent) based on past experience to adjust the ending stock-on-hand value perpetually. A complete up-to-the-minute information system capable of reporting all relevant transactions (purchases, sales, and markdowns) as they occur is necessary.

A **dollar/periodic/physical inventory** system for dollar control provides the retailer with periodic information on the amount of inventory (dollars) actually on hand at a given time as determined by a physical count and valuation of the merchandise. It permits the retailer to compute the dollar amount of sales since the last physical count. A periodic physical inventory usually is computed at designated intervals (monthly, quarterly, or semiannually) using the following basic procedure:

$$
\begin{array}{ll}
  & \text{beginning stock on hand} \\
+ & \text{purchases} \\
\hline
= & \text{total stock handled} \\
- & \text{ending stock on hand} \\
\hline
= & \text{sales and markdowns} \\
- & \text{markdowns} \\
\hline
= & \text{sales}
\end{array}
$$

The beginning stock on hand is the value of the ending stock on hand brought forward from the previous accounting period. Internal purchases and markdown records are used to determine the dollar amount of purchases and markdowns since the last accounting. The ending stock-on-hand figure is derived from a physical count and valuation of the merchandise inventory. The sales figure is computed as shown and incorporates the value of whatever shortages have occurred. Most retailers have easier and more timely means to obtain sales information.

A perpetual book inventory system for unit control—a **unit/perpetual/book inventory** system—involves continuous recording of all transactions (e.g., number of units sold or purchased), which changes the unit status of the retailer's merchandise inventory. Each unit transaction is posted as it occurs or shortly thereafter (e.g., on a daily basis). Perpetual unit control provides a running total of the number of units of a given type that are flowing into and out of the store or department and helps the retailer continuously control the balance between units on hand and unit sales.

Perpetual unit control systems are maintained manually or through the use of various automatic recording systems. A *manual system* of perpetual unit control is maintained by the retailer's accounting personnel, who continuously record merchandise data on standard forms. To determine stock on hand, the accountant simply adds the number of units received during the accounting period and subtracts the number of units sold. The beginning stock on hand is the ending stock on hand for the previous accounting period. The number of units received into stock is obtained from records furnished by the receiving department or clerk. Information on the number of units sold can be gathered by means of a number of manual systems, such as (1) *point-of-sale-tallies* (sales personnel keep track of the number of units sold by making a tally mark on a merchandise list after each sale); (2) *price-ticket stubs* (sales personnel remove information stubs from price tickets when the merchandise is sold and collect, sort, and tally the number of units sold); and (3) *cash-register stubs* (sales personnel remove information stubs from receipts before giving them to customers; these stubs are then used to determine the number of units sold).

*Automatic systems* of perpetual unit control accomplish the same tasks as manual systems except they are a faster, more timely, and more accurate means of obtaining inventory information. Several automatic systems are available, including tag and point-of-sale systems. A *tag system* uses prepunched merchandise tags containing basic assortment information that are attached to each merchandise item. These tags are collected when the item is sold and sent to a data processing facility where the information is fed into the computer. *Point-of-sale (POS) systems* use cash registers or terminals capable of transmitting assortment information (e.g., style, price, color, material) directly to the central data processing facility as the sale is being recorded. A number of different methods can be used to record sales and assortment information in a point-of-sale system. Two common methods are (1) *optical scanners,* which read codes (e.g., Universal Product Code) that have been premarked or imprinted on the merchandise item or package, and (2) *terminal keys,* which transmit data directly to the computer when sales personnel depress them. Point-of-sale systems are becoming the dominant form of gathering merchandise information.[2]

Unit control also can be achieved by making a periodic physical check on the status of the retailer's inventory—**unit/periodic/physical inventory**. For example, the department manager may be assigned to monitor stock levels for all merchandise items within the department at regular intervals. Stock levels are monitored by a visual inspection or a physical count.

For a visual inspection, stock-control personnel visually examine the stock of each item to determine whether sales have depleted the stock to the point of reordering. Several methods can determine at a glance the general condition of the stock; for example, merchandise (e.g., hardware items) can be placed on a sequentially numbered pegboard (e.g., 1 to 25). When the stock reaches a certain level, say 10, then 15 units are reordered. Visual inspection is a reasonably appropriate inventory-information system for staple merchandise of low unit value that the retailer can quickly obtain from suppliers.

The second method of monitoring stock levels and determining unit sales is a *physical count*—actually counting and recording the number of units on hand at regular intervals. The retailer attempts to determine the number of units sold since the last physical count by adding purchases during the intervening period to the beginning stock on hand and then subtracting the ending stock on hand obtained from the current physical count. For example, to determine monthly unit sales for a merchandise item for which the retailer began the month with 300 units on hand, purchased 80 units during the month, and ended the month with 190 units (as determined by physical count), the following computations are necessary:

|   | | |
|---|---|---|
| | beginning monthly stock on hand | 300 units |
| + | monthly purchases | + 80 units |
| = | total stock handled during the month | = 380 units |
| − | ending monthly stock on hand | − 190 units |
| = | monthly sales (including shortages) | = 190 units |

A physical counting system is considerably more time-consuming and expensive than the visual inspection method.

## Inventory Valuation

A major financial concern of every retailer is determining the actual worth of the inventory on hand. How the retailer establishes the value of the inventory can have a profound effect on the outcome of various financial statements (e.g., the income statement and the balance sheet). Retailers can value their inventories at cost (what they paid for the merchandise) or at retail (what they can sell the merchandise for).

*The Cost Method.* Small retailers generally prefer the **cost method of inventory valuation** because it is easy to understand, easy to implement, and requires a limited amount of record keeping. The retailer simply values merchandise inventory at the original cost to the store each time a physical inventory is taken. One of two procedures typically is used in computing the cost value of merchandise items. First, the original cost can be coded on the price tag or merchandise container. The second procedure is to imprint a serialized reference number on each price tag corresponding to an itemized merchandise stock-control list containing the per-unit cost of each item.

A major problem of the cost method occurs when the retailer procures various shipments at different times during inflationary periods. If the wholesale price of an inventory item remained constant, the retailer's costs for various shipments of the same product would be identical. Unfortunately, fluctuating wholesale prices are usually the rule. The mere fact that inflation exists creates a problem—different shipments of identical products are purchased at different wholesale prices (cost to retailer). The retailer then must decide which cost value to use. FIFO (first-in, first-out) and LIFO (last-in, first-out) are two inventory costing methods used to resolve this dilemma.

The **FIFO (first-in, first-out) method** assumes that merchandise items are sold in the order in which they are purchased; that is, older stock is sold before newer stock that was purchased at a later date. The cost of the oldest units in stock determines the retailer's cost of goods sold.

"Under **LIFO—the last-in, first-out method**—recent acquisition costs are used to price inventory (even though in actuality, the inventory bought last is not sold first)."[3] The cost of the newest units in stock determines the retailer's cost of goods sold. During a rising market (increasing wholesale prices), the LIFO method results in tax savings as a result of lower gross profits.

Although the cost method is simple, it does have several disadvantages. First, a cost valuation of inventory requires a physical count of the merchandise, and the need to count and decode prices is both time-consuming and costly. Second, the cost method does not provide a book inventory of what merchandise ought to be on hand. Therefore, the retailer has no means to determine shortages. Finally, the cost method is often untimely because physical inventory is usually taken only once or twice a year. As a result, the retailer cannot prepare weekly, monthly, and quarterly financial statements. The disadvantages of the cost method can be largely overcome if the retailer elects to employ the retail method of inventory valuation.

*The Retail Method.* The **retail method of inventory valuation** allows the retailer to estimate the cost value of an ending inventory for a particular accounting period without taking a physical inventory. Essentially, the retail method is a book inventory system whereby the cost value for each group of related merchandise (e.g., a department) is based on its retail value (selling price). By determining the percentage relationship between the total cost and the total retail value of the merchandise available for sale during an accounting period, the retailer can obtain a reliable estimate of the ending inventory value at cost. To use the retail method, the retailer must make the following calculations: (1) the total merchandise available for sale, (2) the cost complement, (3) the total retail deductions, and (4) the ending inventory at retail and cost values.

The *total merchandise available for sale* is illustrated in the following example:

|  | Cost ($) | Retail ($) |
|---|---|---|
| beginning inventory | 120,000 | 200,000 |
| + net purchases | 80,000 | 140,000 |
| + additional markons | — | 2,000 |
| + freight charges | 4,000 | — |
| = total merchandise available | 204,000 | 342,000 |

As shown, beginning inventory and purchase figures are kept both at cost and at retail values. The beginning inventory is the ending inventory brought forward from the previous accounting period, obtained from the stock ledger that the accounting department maintains. Net purchases represent all purchases the retailer made during the accounting period minus any returns to the vendor. A purchase journal is used to record all purchase transactions. Any additional markons taken since setting the original retail price are added to the retail value of the inventory to reflect the market value of the merchandise. A price-change journal is maintained to keep track of additional markons as well as markdowns and other changes in the original retail selling price. Finally, freight charges, obtained from the purchase journal, are added to portray the true cost of the merchandise correctly. These charges are obtained from the purchases journal.

The *cost complement* is the average relationship of cost to retail value for all merchandise available for sale during an accounting period. In essence, it is the complement of the cumulative markup percentage. The cost complement is computed as follows:

$$\text{cost complement} = \frac{\text{cost value of inventory}}{\text{retail value of inventory}}$$

Using the previous example in which the value of the total merchandise available for sale equaled $204,000 at cost and $342,000 at retail, then

$$\text{cost complement} = \frac{\$204,000}{\$342,000} = .5965$$

In this example, the retailer's merchandise cost is, on the average, equal to 59.65 percent of the retail value of the merchandise.

The third step in the retail method of inventory valuation is to determine the total merchandise available for sale. *Retail deductions* include merchandise that has been sold, marked down, discounted, stolen, and lost. Total retail deductions are obtained by adding all the deductions, reducing the retail value of the merchandise that was available for sale. To continue our illustration,

| | |
|---|---|
| sales for period | $160,000 |
| + markdowns | $ 30,000 |
| + discounts | $ 10,000 |
| + shortages (estimated) | $ 2,000 |
| = total retail deductions | $202,000 |

The sales figure for the accounting period represents both cash and credit sales and is obtained from the retailer's sales journal. The amount of markdowns taken during the accounting period and the amount of the discounts granted to employees and special customers can be secured from the price-change journal. Because shortages resulting from shoplifting, employee pilfering, and lost merchandise cannot be determined without a physical inventory, the retailer usually estimates the shortage figure based on past experience.

The final step in implementing the retail method is to determine the value of *ending inventory at retail and at cost.* The retail value of ending inventory is computed by subtracting total retail deductions from total merchandise available for sale at retail. In our example,

| | |
|---|---|
| total merchandise available at retail | $342,000 |
| − total retail deductions | $202,000 |
| = ending inventory at retail | $140,000 |

The cost value of ending inventory is calculated by multiplying the ending inventory at retail by the cost complement in the following manner:

$$\frac{\text{ending inventory}}{\text{at cost}} = \frac{\text{ending inventory}}{\text{at retail}} \times \frac{\text{cost}}{\text{complement}}$$

$$\frac{\text{ending inventory}}{\text{at cost}} = \$140,000 \times .5965 = \$83,510$$

While the figure $83,510 is only an estimate of the true cost value of the ending inventory, it is sufficiently reliable to allow the retailer to estimate both the cost of goods sold and gross margin for the accounting period. To complete our example:

| | |
|---|---|
| total merchandise available at retail | $204,000 |
| − ending inventory at retail | $83,510 |
| = cost of goods sold | $120,490 |

| | |
|---|---|
| sales for the period | $160,000 |
| − cost of goods sold | $120,490 |
| = gross margin | $39,510 |

Although the retail method has the disadvantages of requiring the retailer to keep more records (stock ledger and sales, purchases, and price-change journals) and use averages to estimate cost values, its advantages are numerous. The retail method forces the retailer to "think retail" in that it highlights both retail and cost figures. Second, frequent and regular calculations of various financial and operating statements are possible as a result of the availability of cost and retail information. Third, when the retail method is used, physical inventories are taken in retail prices, thereby eliminating the costly, time-consuming job of decoding cost prices. Fourth, the retail method facilitates planning and control on a departmental basis. Sales, purchases, inventories, and price-change information are recorded by department and can be used to evaluate each department's performance. Fifth, by providing a book figure on what inventory should be on hand, the retail method allows the retailer to determine shortages each time a physical inventory is taken. Sixth, the retail method facilitates planning for insurance coverage and collecting insurance claims by providing an up-to-date valuation of inventory.

## INVENTORY-ANALYSIS SYSTEM

Inventory information is useful only when it provides the retailer with insights into past mistakes and with foresight for future planning. Merchandise data collected and processed by the inventory-information system can be used to evaluate past performances and to plan future actions. A determination of stock turnover and return on inventory investment are the principal methods for evaluating the retailer's past performance in controlling merchandise inventories. The dollar and unit open-to-buy methods are two of the more important tools for controlling future merchandising activities.

### Stock Turnover

**Stock turnover** is the rate at which the retailer depletes and replenishes stock. Specifically, stock turnover is defined as the number of times during a specific period (usually annual) that the average stock on hand is sold, generally on an annual basis.

Stock turnover rates can be calculated in both dollars (at retail or at cost) and units. The formulas for figuring stock turnover rates are shown in Figure 13–9. (Data

**FIGURE 13–9**
Computing stock turnover rates

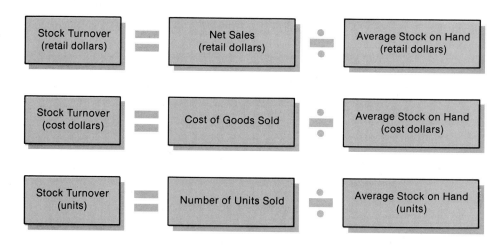

| Stock Turnover (retail dollars) | = | Net Sales (retail dollars) | ÷ | Average Stock on Hand (retail dollars) |

| Stock Turnover (cost dollars) | = | Cost of Goods Sold | ÷ | Average Stock on Hand (cost dollars) |

| Stock Turnover (units) | = | Number of Units Sold | ÷ | Average Stock on Hand (units) |

on net sales, cost of goods sold, and number of units sold are obtained from the inventory-information system, discussed in a preceding section.) **Average stock** on hand for any time period is defined as the sum of the stock on hand at the beginning of the period, at each intervening period, and at the end of the period divided by the number of stock listings. For example, the average stock at retail for the summer season of June, July, and August would be calculated as follows:

| June 1 | $60,000 |
|--------|---------|
| July 1 | $40,000 |
| August 1 | $50,000 |
| August 31 | $35,000 |
| total inventory: | $185,000 |

$$\text{average stock} = \frac{\text{total inventory}}{\text{number of listings}}$$

$$\text{average stock (June–August)} = \frac{\$185,000}{4} = \$46,250$$

If the net sales (retail dollars) for the three-month summer season were $220,000, then the stock turnover rate at retail would be

$$\text{stock turnover at retail} = \frac{\text{net sales}}{\text{average stock on hand}}$$

$$\text{stock turnover at retail (June–August)} = \frac{\$220,000}{\$46,250} = 4.76$$

High stock turnover rates generally reflect good merchandise planning and control. Several benefits accrue to retailers with a high rate of stock turnover. They include the following: (1) *Fresher merchandise:* With a rapid stock turnover there is more frequent replacement of merchandise and, therefore, a continuous flow of new and fresh merchandise into the store. (2) *Fewer markdowns and less depreciation:* A fast stock turnover is associated with a faster rate of sales and, therefore, reduced losses resulting from style or fashion obsolescence and soiled or damaged merchandise. (3) *Lower expense:* A quick stock turnover helps to reduce inventories and, therefore, reduce such inventory expenses as interest and insurance payments, storage costs, and taxes on inventory; it also helps to reduce promotional costs, since a new and fresh selection of merchandise tends to more easily sell itself. (4) *Greater sales:* A rapid stock turnover allows the retailer to adjust the merchandise assortment according to the changing needs of the target market and, therefore, to generate more customer interest and a greater sales volume. (5) *Higher returns:* A rapid stock turnover resulting in an increase in sales and a corresponding decrease in stocks will generate a higher return on inventory investment, hence, a more productive and efficient use of the retailer's capital.

Increasing the rate of stock turnover requires the retailer to control the size and content of its inventory. Strategies for increasing stock turnover include (1) limiting merchandise assortment to the most popular brands, styles, sizes, colors, and price lines; (2) reducing merchandise support by maintaining a minimum reserve or safety stock; (3) clearing out slow-moving stock through price reductions; and (4) increasing the promotional effort in an attempt to increase sales.

A high rate of stock turnover is not without its problems. Excessively high stock turns can mean the retailer is buying in too-small quantities. If so, then the retailer is (1) not taking full advantage of available quantity discounts; (2) adding to the costs of transportation and handling; and (3) increasing accounting costs by processing too many orders. Another potential problem with high stock turnover is the danger of losing sales because of stockouts.

### Return on Inventory Investment

The second method for evaluating past performance in controlling merchandise inventories is **return on inventory investment**—the ratio of gross margin dollars to the average stock on hand. This ratio tells the retailer the dollar investment in inventory needed to achieve a desired gross profit (gross margin dollars). Specifically, return on inventory investment can be expressed as shown in Figure 13–10. Essentially, return on inventory investment concerns the relationship between stock turnover and profitability. The importance of this ratio is that it allows the retailer to evaluate past and future effects of turnover on a store's (or department's) profitability. Before initiating plans to increase the stock turnover rate, the retailer should first determine how a higher stock turnover rate might affect profitability.

### Open-to-Buy

Open-to-buy is one of the retailer's most important tools for controlling future merchandise inventories. This tool helps the retailer decide how much to buy. **Open-to-buy** is the amount of new merchandise the retailer can buy during a specific time period without exceeding the planned purchases for that period. Open-to-buy represents the difference between what the retailer plans to buy and what it has already bought—planned purchases minus purchase commitments. Open-to-buy applies to both dollar and unit control. Dollar open-to-buy sets a financial constraint on the retailer's buying activities, whereas unit open-to-buy controls assortment and support in the buying process.

**FIGURE 13–10**
Computing return on inventory investment

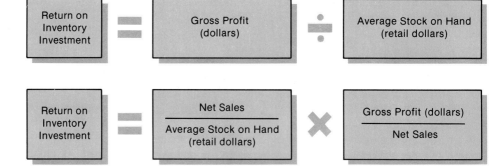

Open-to-buy is a versatile control tool. The retailer can use it to control purchase activities on a daily, weekly, or monthly basis. Also, open-to-buy can help control purchases of any classification or subclassification of merchandise. As a control tool, it allows the retailer to allocate purchases so stocks are maintained at predetermined levels by either the merchandise budget (dollar planning and control) or a merchandise list (unit planning and control).

*Dollar Open-to-Buy.* Dollar open-to-buy is used to determine the amount of money the retailer has to spend for new merchandise at any given time. It can be calculated and recorded at both retail and cost prices. To calculate **dollar open-to-buy at retail** prices for any day of a monthly period, the buyer starts with planned monthly purchases and subtracts purchase commitments already made during the month. To obtain **dollar open-to-buy at cost,** the buyer simply multiplies open-to-buy at retail by the complement of the initial markup percentage. Figure 13–11 shows the formula for determining open-to-buy at cost.

To illustrate, a buyer for a women's apparel department is planning a trip to the market on April 15 and wants to know how much she can buy without exceeding the budget. Examination of the merchandise budget for April reveals that planned sales for the month were $70,000, while reductions (shortages, markdowns, and discounts) were $4,000. Inventory records reveal that the store started the month with $60,000 worth of inventory and plans call for an ending inventory of $50,000. A review of purchase orders indicates that the department has made purchase commitments of $14,000 since the beginning of the month. Given an initial markup percentage of 50 percent on retail, the buyer calculates the dollar open-to-buy to be $50,000 at retail and $25,000 at cost. These figures were obtained by first calculating planned purchases for April ($70,000 + $4,000 + $50,000 − $60,000 = $64,000),

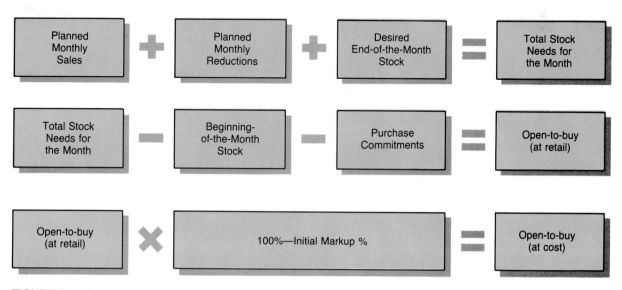

FIGURE 13–11

Computing dollar open-to-buy at retail (top) and open-to-buy at cost (bottom)

then subtracting all purchase commitments ($14,000) made through the 15th of the month.

*Unit Open-to-Buy.* For the retailer engaged in unit control, unit open-to-buy is a successful and necessary tool in preventing stockouts and overstocking. Unit open-to-buy is most frequently used to control inventories of staple merchandise. This method lends itself to formal and systematic procedures for reordering merchandise that has well-established and predictable sales trends. **Unit open-to-buy** calculations involve two steps: (1) determining maximum inventory and (2) computing the unit open-to-buy quantity.

*Step 1: Determine maximum inventory.* **Maximum inventory** is the number of merchandise units the retailer needs to cover expected sales during the reorder and delivery periods plus a safety stock for either unexpected sales or problems in securing the merchandise. The formula for determining maximum inventory is shown in Figure 13–12.

As an illustration, a hardware retailer reorders a staple item of merchandise every six weeks, expecting that delivery will take three weeks. Based on past experience, the hardware retailer expects to sell approximately 40 units a week and considers a two-week safety stock necessary. The maximum inventory (MI) for the merchandise is 440 units. It is calculated as follows:

$$
\begin{aligned}
MI &= (6 \text{ weeks} + 3 \text{ weeks}) \times 40 \text{ units} + 80 \text{ units} \\
&= (9 \text{ weeks}) \times 40 \text{ units} + 80 \text{ units} \\
&= 360 \text{ units} + 80 \text{ units} \\
&= 440 \text{ units}
\end{aligned}
$$

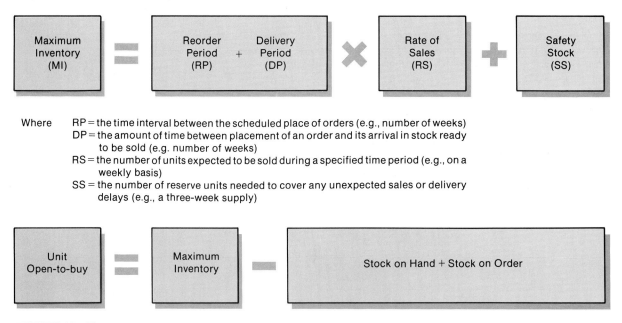

Where    RP = the time interval between the scheduled place of orders (e.g., number of weeks)
DP = the amount of time between placement of an order and its arrival in stock ready to be sold (e.g. number of weeks)
RS = the number of units expected to be sold during a specified time period (e.g., on a weekly basis)
SS = the number of reserve units needed to cover any unexpected sales or delivery delays (e.g., a three-week supply)

**FIGURE 13–12**
Computing unit open-to-buy

The hardware retailer therefore must stock 440 units to cover the reorder period and delivery period and to ensure a safety stock capable of covering two weeks' sales if the reorder is delayed or sales are higher than expected.

*Step 2: Compute unit open-to-buy.* Maximum inventory represents the number of merchandise units the retailer is open-to-buy if there is no stock on hand (SOH) or stock on order (SOO). Unit open-to-buy is defined as maximum inventory minus stock on hand and stock on order. The computation formula is shown in Figure 13–12. Suppose our hardware dealer determines that it had 210 units on hand (obtained from the inventory-information system) and 90 units on order (obtained from purchase orders). Then,

$$\text{open-to-buy} = 440 - (210 + 90) \text{ (or 140 units)}$$

**SUMMARY**

Establishing merchandise objectives and devising tactics for obtaining the objectives make up the focal point for the merchandise-planning process. The planning process normally includes both dollar planning, in terms of merchandise budgets, and unit planning, as accomplished through merchandise lists. The retailer must carefully plan inventory investment (the total dollar amount invested in merchandise), inventory assortment (the number of different products stocked within a particular product line), and inventory support (the number of units to be stocked for each product item).

Dollar planning is accomplished by means of a merchandise budget—a financial plan for managing merchandise inventory investments—that requires the retailer to consider (1) sales, (2) stock levels, (3) reductions, (4) purchases, and (5) profit margins. The retailer uses unit planning to determine the amount of inventory to carry in terms of items (assortment) and units (support). A merchandise list—a set of operational plans for managing the retailer's total selection of merchandise—is used in unit planning. Based on the type of merchandise the retailer carries, one or more of the following lists are appropriate: basic stock list (for planning staple merchandise), model stock list (for planning fashion merchandise), and never-out list (for planning key items and best-sellers).

Merchandise control involves designing dollar- and unit-inventory-information and -analysis systems for collecting, recording, analyzing, and using merchandise data to control the planned balance between the retailer's merchandise inventory and sales. Merchandise control is the necessary complement to merchandise planning.

An inventory-information system is a set of methods and procedures for collecting and processing merchandise data that are pertinent to planning and controlling merchandise inventories. Depending on the kind of information needed and the available sources of that information, the retailer can elect to use (1) a dollar/perpetual/book system, (2) a dollar/periodic/physical system, (3) a unit/perpetual/book system, or (4) a unit/periodic/physical system. An essential element in dollar control is knowing the true value of inventories. The two methods of inventory valuation are the cost method and the retail method. The cost method is simpler, whereas the retail method provides more timely and useful information.

The inventory-analysis system includes methods for evaluating the retailer's past merchandising performance as well as the decision-making tools available for controlling future merchandising activities. Stock turnover analysis and return on inventory investment ratios are used to evaluate the retailer's past performance.

## STUDENT STUDY GUIDE

**KEY TERMS AND CONCEPTS**

annual sales estimates

average stock

basic stock list

basic stock method

control unit

cost method of inventory valuation

discounts

dollar control

dollar open-to-buy at cost

dollar open-to-buy at retail

dollar/periodic/physical inventory

dollar/perpetual/book inventory

dollar planning

first-in, first out (FIFO) method of costing inventories

gross margin

initial markup percentage

inventory-analysis system

inventory assortment

inventory-information system

inventory investment

inventory support

last-in, first-out (LIFO) method of costing inventories

markdowns

maximum inventory

merchandise budget

merchandise control

merchandise management

merchandise planning

model stock list

monthly sales estimates

never-out list

open-to-buy

percentage variation method

periodic physical inventory

perpetual book inventory

retail method of inventory valuation

retail reductions

return on inventory investment

shortages

staples

stock-keeping unit (SKU)

stock/sales ratio method

stock turnover

unit control

unit open-to-buy

unit/periodic/physical inventory

unit/perpetual/book inventory

week's supply method

**REVIEW QUESTIONS**

1. Distinguish among the three concepts of inventory investment, assortment, and support.
2. What is a merchandise budget? Identify the five stages in developing a merchandise budget.
3. How does the variable adjustment method differ from the fixed adjustment method of estimating annual sales?
4. Gina Lewis is the department manager of the "better dresses" department. Having estimated planned monthly sales for the upcoming year, Gina must now plan the appropriate stock levels for the fall season. To obtain a better idea of the stock that will be needed, Gina has decided to calculate BOM stock for each month using both basic stock and percentage

variation methods. Using an estimated inventory turnover rate of two, calculate the BOM stock for each month using both methods.

*Planned Monthly Sales*

| | |
|---|---|
| August | $32,000 |
| Sept. | $18,000 |
| Oct. | $10,000 |

5. A hardware retailer estimates its total annual sales for plumbing equipment to be $72,000 and hopes to achieve an annual stock turnover rate of six. Using the week's supply method, calculate the BOM stock for January.
6. What are retail reductions? Identify and describe the cause of retail reductions.
7. How are planned monthly purchases determined?
8. Given the following information, calculate the required initial markup percentage:

   1. Sales                     $240,000
   2. Expenses          22 percent of sales
   3. Reductions         8 percent of sales
   4. Desired profit     14 percent of sales

9. What is an SKU? How are SKUs distinguished from one another?
10. Basic stock lists are used as a planning instrument for what type of merchandise?
11. What is a model stock list? What criteria are used in identifying a model stock-keeping unit?
12. What are never-out lists used for?
13. What distinguishes perpetual book inventory from periodic physical inventory?
14. What types of manual and automatic systems are used to gather information on the number of units sold?
15. How are stock levels monitored in a unit/periodic/physical inventory system? Briefly describe each method.
16. Describe the FIFO and LIFO methods of costing inventories.
17. List the advantages of the retail method of inventory valuation.
18. What are the benefits and limitations of high stock turnover rates?
19. Why is the return on inventory investment ratio important?
20. What are the procedural steps for determining dollar open-to-buy?
21. What is maximum inventory? How is it computed? What role does it have in determining unit open-to-buy?

---

True or False

**REVIEW EXAM**

_____  1. Inventory assortment and support is the focus for dollar planning.
_____  2. The fixed adjustment method usually works reasonably well in estimating future sales if a clear and stable sales trend has been established.
_____  3. The stock-to-sales ratio method of planning inventory levels requires the retailer use a 2 stock units to 1 sales unit ratio.
_____  4. The model stock list is used for planning inventory assortment and support for staple merchandise.
_____  5. For most retailers, a periodic physical inventory is the fastest, easiest, and most time-saving method they have for obtaining sales information.

_____ 6. When the LIFO method of inventory costing is used, the cost of the oldest unit in stock determines the retailer's cost of goods sold.

_____ 7. Excessively high stock turnover rates could mean that the retailer is buying in too small quantities.

# STUDENT APPLICATIONS MANUAL

**PROJECTS: INVESTIGATIONS AND APPLICATIONS**

1. A number of general approaches and methods can be used to makes sales estimates. The fixed and variable adjustment method of forecasting was discussed in this chapter. Identify and discuss two additional sales estimating techniques. From the viewpoint of the retailer, what are the advantages and disadvantages of each? Under what circumstances is each method appropriate for estimating retail sales?

2. Gain the cooperation of a local independent retailer and develop a complete merchandising budget for a given product line utilizing the format discussed in the text. What difficulties did you encounter in developing the budget? How did you overcome these difficulties? What format changes would you recommend for improving the budgetary process as outlined in the text?

3. Secure an interview with a local department or specialty store buyer. Determine what product lines or items are included on the store's never-out list and why those products are on the list. Using the information gathered in the interview, develop a set of criteria and guidelines for determining what products should be included on the never-out list.

4. By making a visual survey of several hardware, variety, and sporting goods stores, identify and describe several examples of the "visual inspection" method used in a unit/periodic/physical inventory information system.

5. Retailers can calculate stock turnover in retail dollars, cost dollars, and units. Describe the circumstances and reasons why a retailer would employ each of these methods for calculating stock turnover.

6. Identify and explain several causes for low stock turnover rate.

7. What is the June dollar open-to-buy at retail for the sporting goods department, given the following information as of June 1:

| | |
|---|---|
| Planned sales for June | $42,000 |
| Planned reductions for June | $ 1,000 |
| Planned stock for June 30 | $50,000 |
| Actual stock on June 1 | $30,000 |
| Existing purchase commitments | $ 4,000 |

What is the June dollar open-to-buy at cost, assuming a 44 percent initial markup on retail?

8. From past experience, John Rogers knows that sales for men's underwear are characterized by a well-established pattern. Therefore, he expects to sell approximately 180 units per week. To guard against unexpected sales of delivery delays, John plans to maintain a four-week safety stock. Normally, John places reorders every eight weeks and allows four weeks for delivery. By checking the stock and purchase records, John determines that he has 600 units on hand and 200 units on order. What is John's unit open-to-buy?

CASE 13–1
## Value Shoes—Planning Monthly Sales and Stock Levels*

Value Shoes is a price-oriented family shoe store located in a community shopping center. Catering to the lower-income shopper, Value Shoes is a low-margin operation that requires careful attention to planning and controlling inventory. As owner and operator of Value Shoes, Tom Nelson strives to incorporate all the objective inventory control procedures he learned from attending several Small Business Administration seminars.

Today's task is to develop sales and stock plans for the children's shoe department. Given the sales seasonality of children's shoes, developing sales estimates and monthly stock plans can be challenging. Using the variable adjustment method, Tom arrived at an annual sales estimate of $9,000 for 1989. Tom now faces the tasks of calculating the planned monthly sales for each month and the beginning-of-the-month (BOM) stock for each month of the first quarter. If the annual turnover rate of four turns and the monthly sales pattern (see Exhibit 1) hold true for 1989, then the task should not be too difficult.

### ASSIGNMENT

Assume the role of Tom Nelson and complete the tasks of calculating the planned monthly sales and the BOM stock for January, February, and March.

|         | 1984 | 1985 | 1986 | 1987 | 1988 |
|---------|------|------|------|------|------|
| Jan.    | 400  | 400  | 500  | 600  | 600  |
| Feb.    | 300  | 400  | 400  | 500  | 700  |
| March   | 300  | 400  | 500  | 600  | 800  |
| April   | 800  | 800  | 900  | 1000 | 1200 |
| May     | 700  | 700  | 800  | 800  | 900  |
| June    | 400  | 500  | 600  | 500  | 700  |
| July    | 200  | 300  | 300  | 500  | 700  |
| Aug.    | 600  | 600  | 600  | 700  | 800  |
| Sept.   | 900  | 1100 | 1400 | 1500 | 1800 |
| Oct.    | 500  | 700  | 600  | 700  | 800  |
| Nov.    | 400  | 500  | 500  | 600  | 700  |
| Dec.    | 700  | 800  | 900  | 1000 | 1200 |

**EXHIBIT 1**
Value Shoes, monthly sales record[a] children's shoes

[a]Rounded to the nearest hundred.

*This case was prepared by Dale Lewison and John Thanopoulos, The University of Akron.

## CASE 13-2

## Itty-Bitty Baby Boutique—Selecting An Inventory Valuation System*

### BACKGROUND

Recent changes in the federal tax law authorized by the Economic Recovery Act of 1981 prompted many trade journals to publish articles about the new regulations that simplify the last-in, first-out (LIFO) method of inventory valuation used by retailers. Consequently, Millie Marie Baker, owner of Itty-Bitty Baby Boutique, was rethinking her use of the "traditional" retail method of inventory valuation that estimates ending inventory at the lower of cost or market (LCM).

### CURRENT SITUATION

Early in June of 1982, Baker consulted Bill Truly, senior auditor for B. S. Cheatum & Co., for an opinion. His response is shown in Exhibit 2.

**EXHIBIT 2**

---

B. S. Cheatum & Co.
MEMORANDUM

Date:   July 5, 1982
TO:    Ms. Millie Marie Baker, Owner
         Itty-Bitty Baby Boutique
FROM: Bill Truly, Senior Auditor
         B. S. Cheatum & Co.
RE:    Possible LIFO Election

    Your request for a formal comparison of current inventory valuation procedures to an appropriate dollar-value LIFO method for Itty-Bitty Baby Boutique has received careful consideration. Because Itty-Bitty is a specialty store that carries a full line of infant apparel and some baby furniture and equipment, we believe that use of the Department Store Inventory Price Index for "Infants' Wear" will be acceptable to the IRS. The comparison shown below is premised on this assumption.

    To demonstrate the value of dollar-value LIFO to your business, we reconstructed your 1981 income statement as it would have been if dollar-value LIFO had been elected for that year. Schedule 1 (Exhibit 3) is a simplified version of your 1981 income statement. Schedule 2 (Exhibit 4) explains determination of 1981 ending inventory under the retail method, lower of cost or market inventory valuation model. Schedule 3 (Exhibit 5) illustrates the calculations necessary to estimate ending inventory under dollar-value LIFO using 1981 data. Notice that the cost ratio used to reduce the inventory increment to cost is based on purchases and is the complement of the net markon percentage—cumulative markon less markdowns expressed as a percentage of retail. The relevant BLS Department Store Inventory Price Indexes for Infants' Wear are shown below.

*Infants' Wear*

|  | Price Index (Jan. 1941 = 100) | Percent Change from Jan. 19xx to Jan. 19xx + 1 |
|---|---|---|
| Jan. 1980 | 378.8 | |
| Jan. 1981 | 420.7 | 11.1 |
| Jan. 1982 | 444.7 | 5.7 |

---

*This case was prepared by J. B. Wilkinson, The University of Akron.

EXHIBIT 2
*continued*

In this illustration, your base year would begin Jan. 1, 1981. Consequently, the Jan. 1981 price index represents 100.0, and the adjusted price index for any year ended December 31, 19xx, is found by dividing the following January index by the Jan. 1981, index. The adjusted price index for the year ended December 31, 1981, is 105.7 (444.7/420.7) and is used to determine the 1981 ending inventory in base-year retail dollars.

Notice that the retail value of ending inventory that was found for the LCM model is reduced to base-year cost (at retail) by dividing by the adjusted LIFO price index (105.7/100). An incremental inventory layer occurs if ending inventory at base-year cost exceeds the previous year's ending inventory at base-year cost. A decrement occurs if ending inventory at base-year cost is less than the previous year's ending inventory at base-year cost. When a decrement occurs, previous inventory layers must be liquidated in reverse order. Increments or decrements are first determined with base-year retail dollars and then converted to relevant current-year retail dollars by the appropriate LIFO price index and adjusted to cost, using the cost ratio. Ending inventory is the sum of base-year inventory at base-year cost and the increments, if any, at current relevant year costs.

For the year ended December 31, 1981, ending inventory under the "traditional" retail method, LCM, was $370,000. Ending inventory at LIFO cost would have been $351,328. It follows that cost of sales is $1,080,000 under the LCM model and $1,098,672 under dollar-value LIFO. However, LIFO is a cost method. If you had elected LIFO for the year ended December 31, 1981, the beginning inventory would have had to be restated to cost. The $350,000 beginning inventory is stated at lower of cost or market. We estimate that a positive adjustment of $68,800 would have been required. This adjustment would reduce the LIFO cost of sales to $1,029,872. Thus, gross margin would have been $770,128 under LIFO. At a marginal tax rate of 50%, your tax bill would have been $25,063 more under dollar-value LIFO.

It is difficult to project what your 1982 dollar-value LIFO experience might be. We do estimate that you would have to restate 1982 beginning inventory to cost. That adjustment is likely to be around $74,000. Also, we are concerned about your expected markdowns as a percent of sales. The LCM model allows you to reduce ending inventory to lower of cost or market. Dollar-value LIFO only removes the efects of inflation. Which is best for you? Do you expect high markdowns as a percent of sales in the future? Another consideration is your ability to correctly predict sales and plans for inventory leveles sufficient to prevent decrements. Inventory decrements under LIFO cause older costs (lower costs in periods of inflation) to enter the calculation of cost of sales. As a result, most businesses control inventory levels carefully to prevent liquidation of previous inventory layers.

We advise you to consider this decision carefully. Expected price-level changes, inventory levels, and markdowns are important factors in estimating the financial advantage of electing dollar-value LIFO.

Please let us know your decision as soon as possible.

EXHIBIT 3

Schedule 1: 1981 Income Data for Itty-Bitty Baby Boutique

| | |
|---|---:|
| Net sales | $1,800,000 |
| less cost of sales[a] | 1,080,000 |
| Gross profit | 720,000 |
| less operating expense | 666,000 |
| Operating profit | $    54,000 |

Note:
[a]Cost of sales is computed as follows: Beginning inventory (at cost) + Purchases (at cost) − Ending inventory (at cost). Ending inventory for Itty-Bitty was valued at lower of cost or market using the retail method. These computations are shown in Schedule 2.

EXHIBIT 4

Schedule 2: Determination of 1981 Ending Inventory Using Retail Method, LCM Model

| | At Cost | At Retail | Cost Ratio |
|---|---|---|---|
| Inventory, Jan. 1, 1981 | $  350,000 | $  698,000 | |
| Purchases | 1,100,000 | 2,200,000 | |
| Net additional markups | _____ | 2,000 | |
| Total (incl. beginning inv.) | $1,450,000 | $2,900,000 | .50 |
| Deduct: | | | |
| Sales | | (1,800,000) | |
| Net markdowns | | (360,000) | |
| Ending inventory at LCM | $  370,000[a] | $  740,000 | |

Note:
[a]Ending inventory at LCM was found by reducing ending inventory at retail to cost through application of the cost ratio. The cost ratio for the LCM model is computed by dividing total merchandise available for sale at cost by total merchandise available for sale at retail before markdowns.

ASSIGNMENT

Advise Baker on the basis of Truly's comments. Should she switch to dollar-value LIFO? Why? Why not?

EXHIBIT 5

Schedule 3: Determination of 1981 Ending Inventory Using the Dollar-Value LIFO Method

Steps:

**1.** Price index for the year ended December 31, 1981 (Jan. 1, 1981 = 100) is 105.7.

**2.** Computation of cost ratio and ending inventory at retail.

|  | At Cost | At Retail | Cost Ratio |
|---|---|---|---|
| Inventory, Jan. 1, 1981 | $ 350,000 | $ 698,000 | |
| Purchases | 1,100,000 | 2,200,000 | |
| Net additional markups | | 2,000 | |
| Net markdowns | _____ | (360,000) | |
| Total (excl. beginning inv.) | 1,100,000 | 1,842,000 | .60 |
| Total (incl. beginning inv.) | $1,450,000 | $2,540,000 | |
| Deduct: | | | |
| Sales | | (1,800,000) | |
| Ending inv. at retail | | $ 740,000 | |
| Ending inv. at cost | $ 440,000 | | |

**3.** Computation of ending inventory at LIFO cost.

|  | At Cost | At Retail |
|---|---|---|
| Ending inv. at retail deflated to base year retail $ | | $ 700,095[a] |
| Base layer: at base-yr. cost | $ 350,000 | |
| at base-yr. retail | | (698,000) |
| Increment (or decrement) at base-year retail | | 2,095 |
| Increment (or decrement) at current-year retail | | 2,214[b] |
| Increment (or decrement) at current-year cost | 1,328[c] | |
| Total ending inventory at LIFO cost | $ 351,328 | |

Notes:
[a]$740,000/1.057
[b]$2,095 × 1.057
[c]$2,214 × .60

---

1. William L. Clarke, "Integrating the Logistics of Merchandise Management," *Retail Control* (June/July 1987): 26.
2. See "NRMA's New POS Study," *Stores* (April 1987): 67–74 and "Point-of-Sale '86: A New Study," *Stores* (November 1986): 88–90.
3. "LIFO Survey Shows It's Here to Stay," *Chain Store Age Executive* (January, 1984): 32.

# PART FIVE
# Retail Prices and Promotions

# 14

## Objectives

☐ Set specific, measurable price objectives consistent with the needs of both the consumer and the retailer.

☐ Assess the impact of demand, competition, cost, product, and legal considerations on the retailer's price-setting activities.

☐ Describe the methods by which retailers set their prices.

☐ Differentiate the numerous policies supplementing and modifying retail price-setting methods.

☐ Explain the need to adapt prices to the changing external and internal environmental conditions of the retail firm.

☐ Differentiate among the three basic types of price adjustments.

☐ Identify the necessities of price markdowns and explain the factors that determine when and how great a price markdown should be taken.

# Price Setting and Adjusting

T he right price is one that consumers are willing and able to pay and retailers are willing to accept in exchange for merchandise and services. The right price allows the retailer to make a fair profit while providing the consumer with value satisfaction before, during, and after the sale. For the retailer, "effective pricing can be achieved with neither a rule of thumb nor a mathematical formula. It is, like advertising, a creative process. It requires both insight to identify buyer segments and imagination to design pricing strategies that distinguish among them."[1] From the consumer's viewpoint, price can act as a forceful attraction or as an absolute repellent in the consumer's store-selection process. It can also serve as either an incentive or a deterrent in the decision to buy. Some consumers consider price the most important criterion in selecting stores and products; others are far less sensitive to price.

This chapter examines price-setting objectives, determinants, methods, and policies as well as the various means of adjusting retail prices: discounts, markons, and markdowns.

## Price-Setting Objectives

In any decision-making process, the decision maker should establish objectives. Price setting is no exception. Before the retailer can effectively establish prices consistent both with the firm's requirements and the consumer's expectations, it should set specific, measurable objectives based on well-thought-out pricing guidelines. Retail price objectives are generally categorized in three groups: sales objectives, profit objectives, and competitive objectives.

*Sales Objectives.* Retailers usually state sales objectives in terms of either sales volume or market share. The primary reason for setting **sales-volume objectives** is to achieve future sales growth or to maintain current sales levels. Sales growth in the form of "beating last year's sales" by some percentage is a common objective for many retailers. **Market-share objectives** are price-setting goals that retailers set to increase or maintain their share of the total market. Many retailers prefer market-share objectives to sales objectives because the former represent a relative measure of how well they are performing in the market compared to competitors. As a pricing objective, *market-share growth* may be a preferred goal for a new and expanding product market rather than for an older one because many competitors in the former situation are more interested in increasing their sales as opposed to their market share. In mature and stable product markets, however, *market-share maintenance* is generally the more accepted pricing objective. Price-cutting activities in mature markets force competitors to meet the new price, lowering profit margins for all concerned.

*Profit Objectives.* Profit maximization and target return on investment and on net sales are retailers' three most-cited profit objectives for guiding price-setting decisions. **Profit-maximization objectives** seek the highest possible profit through pricing and other merchandising activities. In practice, a profit-maximization objective is at the expense of other wholesalers, manufacturers, and customers. Such activities will lead to conflict, thereby jeopardizing the retailer's source of supply and damaging the retailer's image.

**Target return objectives** are profit objectives for guiding price-setting decisions. Target returns are usually expressed as a certain percentage return on either capital investment or net sales. *Return on investment* (ROI) is a ratio of profits to capital investments (facilities, fixtures, equipment, inventory, etc.).

*Return on net sales* (ROS) is the percentage value derived by dividing dollar profit by net sales. To achieve this targeted return, retailers set prices by using markup percentages large enough to cover all appropriate operating expenses (payroll, rent, utilities, professional services, etc.), plus the desired dollar profit per unit needed to generate the targeted percentage return on net sales.

*Competitive Objectives.* **Competitive price objectives** also take several forms, including (1) meeting competition, (2) preventing competition, and (3) nonprice competition. Some retailers simply follow the leader in their price-setting activities; their price objectives can best be described as meeting their major competitor's price.[2] Certain retailers within a given trade area act as price leaders for some product lines. The price followers simply adjust their prices accordingly. Other retailers take preventing competition as their pricing objective and set their prices low enough to discourage additional competitors from entering the market. Finally, some retailers prefer to avoid price competition; they would rather compete on the basis of better product or service offerings, better locations and facilities, greater promotional efforts, or any other merchandising activities except price.

## Price-Setting Determinants

Each retailer faces several considerations in trying to establish a selling price that will both sell the merchandise and offer a profitable return. The retailer should examine demand, competitive, cost, product, and legal factors.

*Demand Considerations.* Consumers' perceptions of and reactions to different prices must be taken into account before making price-setting decisions. By studying their target market's consuming behavior, retailers often can find circumstances in which they can use price to communicate status, quality, value, or economy. Other consumers, or even the same consumers under different purchase conditions, more closely reflect the **law of demand**—consumers will buy more products at lower prices than at higher prices. The retailer must consider the effects of different price levels on consumer demand. This effect is called **price elasticity of demand**—a measure of the effect a price change has on consumer demand (i.e., the number of units sold). Demand elasticity describes the relationship between a percentage change in price and a percentage change in quantity sold. *Elastic demand* is a condition in which a change in price strongly influences consumer demand. For example, consumer demand is more elastic for stock-up items (nonperishable goods like soap, toothpaste, canned foods, etc.) than for non–stock-up items (perishables and low usage rate goods).[3] *Inelastic demand* occurs when a change in price has little or no influence on consumer demand. A good way to remember the difference between elastic demand and inelastic demand is to consider the consumer's degree of *sensitivity* to a price change. Inelastic demand means that consumers are relatively insensitive to a change in price, whereas under elastic demand conditions, they are sensitive to price changes.

In some cases, changing the price of a merchandise item will change the demand for not only that item but also a different item. *Cross-elasticity of demand* occurs when a change in the price of one product results in a change in demand for another product. For example, the demand for a complementary product (e.g., film) may decrease as a result of increased prices and reduced demand for the product it complements (e.g., cameras).

*Competitive Considerations.* It is imperative to consider competitors' pricing actions in setting prices. Although prices need not equal those of competitors, the retailer should provide consumers with a price difference within an acceptable range. In their minds, consumers will accept and justify some price differential among competitive retail stores because of differences in service, location, and product-mix factors. In setting prices, retailers must realize that price competition is one of the least distinctive forms of competition. Price cuts by the retailer can be instantaneously offset by competitors that easily match the lower price. Retailers should consider the alternative forms of competition (product or service) before engaging in aggressive price-setting activities that could have a serious negative impact on their profitability.[4]

The freedom a retailer enjoys in setting prices depends on estimates of its competitive position. A retailer that judges its competitive position as strong because of a distinctive retail mix, highly loyal consumers, or a unique store image has greater freedom in price-setting decisions. On the other hand, "me-too" retailers that lack distinctiveness in the nonprice areas of their operations are restricted to a me-too pricing strategy.

Finally, the retailer must recognize that the competitor's price is more important for some merchandise items than for others. First, the retailer must closely consider products that consumers purchase frequently and the supplier distributes intensively because consumers can easily make price comparisons. Second, for products with high unit value—big-ticket items—retailers need to seriously consider competitors' prices because consumers perceive it worth their while to compare prices for these expensive items.

*Cost Considerations.* A major determinant in any price-setting decision is the cost the retailer must pay for merchandise. In defining merchandise cost, it is important to include not only the actual cost of the merchandise but also all costs incurred in getting the merchandise into the store and preparing it for sale. Retailers determine merchandise costs by following the procedure outlined in Figure 14–1. Calculating merchandise cost this way gives the retailer a more accurate picture of the true cost. For many retailers, merchandise cost is both a reference and starting point for price-setting decisions. Their approach to the pricing problem is cost-oriented; they set the retail selling price of a product at a level high enough to cover not only the cost of the merchandise but also the fixed and variable expenses associated with merchandising the product plus an additional profit margin.

*Product Considerations.* Retailers should not make price-setting decisions without considering the product's characteristics. Different products can command different prices at different times and in different locations.

Retailers must first consider *product perishability* and its associated risks. Perishable products often require higher initial prices to cover markdowns that become necessary as the product loses its marketability. It is also worth noting that a retailer might decide to set a lower initial price on some highly perishable products to move them out before a loss in marketability occurs. Product perishability takes several forms:

☐ *Physical perishability*—loss of marketability resulting from physical damage or deterioration of the product
☐ *Style or fashion perishability*—a loss of marketability as a result of style, fashion, or model obsolescence (as in being "out of style" or "the old model")
☐ *Seasonal perishability*—loss of marketability because the product is out of season

*Product quality*, whether perceived or real, is another major product determinant the retailer should examine before setting a price. Depending on the price/quality image the retailer wants to project, one of several possible pricing strategies can be used. Figure 14–2 illustrates nine possible pricing strategies based on product quality. From this figure, we see that the retailer can assume quite a number of roles in offering a particular product-quality level at various price levels.

*Product uniqueness* is a characteristic that retailers can exploit to realize a premium price. Consumers who seek something different tend to be insensitive to price and therefore willing to pay higher prices for products that exhibit originality.[5]

**FIGURE 14–1**

Determining merchandise cost

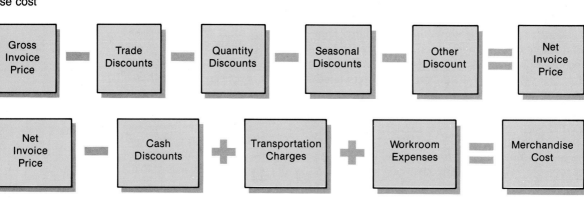

PRODUCT PRICE

|  | High | Medium | Low |
|---|---|---|---|
| High | Premium Strategy | Penetration Strategy | Superbargain Strategy |
| Medium | Overpricing Strategy | Average-Quality Strategy | Bargain Strategy |
| Low | Hit-and-run Strategy | Shoddy-Goods Strategy | Cheap-Goods Strategy |

PRODUCT QUALITY

**FIGURE 14-2**
Product-quality considerations in price-setting decisions (source: Phillip Kotler, *Principles of Marketing* [Englewood Cliffs, NJ: Prentice-Hall, 1980], 402)

*Legal Considerations.* Price-setting decisions are subject to numerous legal constraints. According to law, any pricing activity that any governmental agency considers to be a present or probable restraint on trade or an unfair trade practice can be illegal. Price setting is perhaps the most regulated aspect of the retailer's business.

## Price-Setting Methods

Price-setting decisions are both an art and a science. A policy of setting low prices might well produce high sales volumes but inadequate profit margins. High prices usually allow for excellent profit margins; however, the merchandise must be sold before those profits can be realized. Knowing when a price is too high or too low is an art that comes with the experience of being in the business. Nevertheless, certain price-setting methods blend the art of experience with the science of retail mathematics.

*Markup Method of Pricing.* Markup is the difference between the cost of the merchandise and its retail price. Although markup appears to be a relatively simple concept, it incorporates several complex relationships expressed in a variety of ways.

    **Dollar markup** is a cost-oriented approach to setting prices wherein the retailer adds to the cost of the merchandise a dollar amount large enough to cover related operating expenses and to provide a given dollar profit. Dollar markup is used most frequently for big-ticket items (i.e., jewelry) because dollar values simply appear more real. However, dollar markup can be deceptive when one compares different lines of merchandise.

    **Percentage markups** usually are calculated to facilitate the process of setting prices and to permit comparisons between merchandise lines and departments. In calculating percentage markups, the retailer must first determine the markup base. Markups can be calculated on the cost of the merchandise or on the retail selling price. Formulas for calculating percentage markups are illustrated in Figure 14-3. Suppose, for example, that a hardware retailer pays $80 for a power lawnmower that

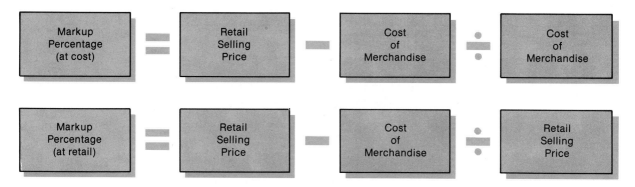

**FIGURE 14–3**
Determining markup percentage (at cost or at retail)

sells at retail for $150. The retailer's percentage markup on cost would be 87.5 percent, whereas on retail it is 46.7 percent. The calculations are as follows:

$$\text{markup percentage at cost} = \frac{\$150 - \$80}{\$80} = 87.5\%$$

$$\text{markup percentage at retail} = \frac{\$150 - \$80}{\$150} = 46.7\%$$

In practice, retailers prefer to compute markups on the retail base. Given its popularity, we will focus on retail-based markups for the remainder of our discussion.

Retailers find a cumulative markup on a group of merchandise items (e.g., a product line) useful in daily operations. The retailer must calculate **cumulative markup** based on the weight each item contributes to the total markup of all the items in the merchandise group. To illustrate, the buyer for the men's department of a large specialty store wants to determine the cumulative markup on a stock of men's summer suits. A check of inventory and purchase records for the month of June reveals that the month started with an inventory costing $20,000 that retails for $40,000. Additional purchases costing $16,000 and retailing for $30,000 have been added since the beginning of the month. The total cost and retail value of the merchandise follows:

|  | Cost | Retail |
|---|---|---|
| beginning stock | $20,000 | $40,000 |
| additional purchases | +$16,000 | +$30,000 |
| total stock | $36,000 | $70,000 |

The cumulative markup percentage at retail is computed as

$$\text{markup percentage at retail} = \frac{\text{retail (\$)} - \text{cost (\$)}}{\text{retail}}$$

$$= \frac{\$70,000 - \$36,000}{\$70,000} = 48.6\%$$

Using the cumulative markup percentage, the retailer can adjust markup plans throughout the merchandising season.

We must now distinguish among three kinds of markup: the initial markup, the maintained markup, and the gross margin. **Initial markup** refers to the difference between merchandise cost and the original retail price. Stated differently, it represents the first markup placed on a merchandise item. Rarely, however, does the retailer receive the initial markup for each item within a merchandise line because of the retail reductions that decrease the original retail price set for the item. Retail reductions take the form of shortages, discounts granted to employees and special customers, and markdowns.

A **maintained markup** is the difference between gross merchandise cost and actual selling price. Stated differently, maintained markup equals initial markup minus all retail reductions; that is, initial markup is what the retailer originally hoped to receive, and maintained markup is what the retailer actually received.

The **initial markup percentage** is the key element in guiding the retailer's price-setting decisions. Essentially, this pricing strategy establishes the initial markup percentage—and therefore the retail price—to achieve a specified target profit. The basic formula for calculating the initial markup percentage is shown in Figure 14-4. As shown, the initial markup percentage equals the sum of the operating expenses, operating profit, alterations cost, and retail reduction, divided by the sum of the net sales and retail reduction. The initial markup must be large enough to cover store operating expenses and retail reductions as well as to provide a profit and to cover any alteration costs.

As a brief illustration of the initial markup percentage formula, consider the following problem. A sporting goods retailer wants to know the appropriate initial markup percentage on a new line of tennis rackets. Planning records reveal these figures: (1) estimated operating expenses of 28 percent, (2) planned operating profit of 12 percent, (3) estimated alteration cost (e.g., stringing rackets) of 4 percent, (4) expected shortages of 2 percent, (5) planned markdowns of 4 percent, and (6) estimated employee discounts of 1 percent. Using the preceding formula, the initial markup percentage should be as follows:

$$\text{initial markup \%} = \frac{28\% + 12\% + 4\% + 7\%}{100\% + 7\%}$$

$$= \frac{51}{107} = 47.7\%$$

To determine the actual percentage markup realized after the foregoing computations have been completed, the retailer can use the maintained markup percentage formula expressed in Figure 14-4. For example, if the retailer had originally planned for an initial markup of 40 percent, and retail reductions amounting to 8 percent actually occurred, then

$$\text{maintained markup \%} = .40 - [.08(1.00 - .40)]$$

$$= .352 \text{ or } 35.2\%$$

The retail reduction percentage is adjusted because it was based on net sales, while the initial markup percentage was based on the original retail price.

**Gross margin** refers to the difference between net sales and total merchandise costs. As such, it is closely related to maintained markup (net sales minus gross

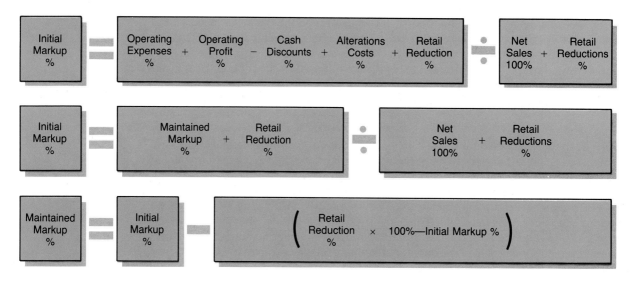

**FIGURE 14–4**
Computing the initial and maintained markup percentage

merchandise costs). The differences between gross margin and maintained markup or between total merchandise cost and gross merchandise costs are adjustments for cash discounts and alteration costs. This difference can be illustrated as follows:

$$\text{gross margin} = \text{maintained markup} + \text{cash discounts} - \text{alteration costs}$$

$$\text{maintained markup} = \text{gross margin} - \text{cash discounts} + \text{alteration costs}$$

If there were no cash discounts or alteration costs, then gross margin would equal maintained markup.

*Competitive Pricing Method.* A competitive pricing method means the retailer sets prices in relation to competitors' prices. It is largely a judgmental price-setting method whereby the retailer uses competitive prices as reference points for price-setting decisions. Competitive price setting is popular among some retailers because it is simple to administer: the basic decision rules are to price either below, at, or above competitors' price levels. In most cases, it is not a question of being a high- or a low-price retailer; rather, the decision is to select higher or lower prices than those of competitors.

One price-setting alternative is **pricing below the competition**. Mass merchandisers, such as discounters, attempt to undersell competitors. Pricing below competition is a price-setting policy aimed at generating large dollar revenues to achieve a desired dollar target return. In other words, these retailers practice a low-price, high-volume, high-turnover pricing strategy.

To successfully sell merchandise at low prices and still generate sufficient profit margins calls for certain merchandising strategies. To price below competition, the retailer not only must secure merchandise at a lower cost, but must also keep operating expenses as low as possible. The lower-price retailer usually stocks and sells "presold" or "self-sold" merchandise, thereby reducing advertising and personal selling expenses. Additionally, these retailers keep their service offerings at the minimum levels necessary to sell the merchandise. Their physical facilities are spartan and project an austere image. In addition, the structure of the store's management organization is generally flat (the number and specialization of managers are minimal and general). Pricing below competition is not without its risks. This aggressive price-setting strategy often leads to pricing wars that put considerable strain on the profitability of all competing retailers within the trading area.

The second alternative method of competitive price setting open to the retailer is selling a merchandise item at the "going" or traditional price within the store's general trading area. **Pricing with the competition** implies that the retailer has, in general, elected to de-emphasize the price factor as a major merchandising tool and instead decided to compete on a location, product, service, and promotion basis.

Some retailers attempt to differentiate themselves by setting prices above the going trading-area price. Although the higher-priced stores do not expect to achieve the turnover rates of their lower-priced competitors, they do expect their products to make a fair contribution to the store's fixed operating expenses. At the same time, the higher-priced retailer expects its products to make a substantially *greater per-unit profit* than the lower-priced retailer's products.

Strategically, if the retailer chooses **pricing above the competition,** then it must include several of these consumer benefits: (1) many free services, (2) higher-quality merchandise, (3) exclusive merchandise, (4) personalized sales attention, (5) plusher shopping atmosphere, (6) full staffing in all functional areas of store operations, (7) prestige image, (8) superconvenient locations, and (9) longer store hours. Many exclusive specialty shops and some department stores engage in price-setting strategies that establish prices above those of less-prestigious competitors.

*Vendor Pricing Method.* A third price-setting alternative is to let the manufacturer or wholesaler determine the retail price. This type of price setting assumes the form of a "suggested retail price." Vendors suggest retail prices by supplying the retailer with a price list, printing the price on the package, or affixing a price tag to the merchandise. While they are not legally required to use the suggested retail price, many retailers think it represents a fair estimate of the going market price for certain products. As guidelines for retailers, the vendor's suggested price is not appropriate when (1) it fails to provide a sufficient margin to cover merchandise costs, store operating expenses, and an adequate profit; (2) it fails to stimulate sufficient sales; (3) it simply is not competitive with merchandise of a similar quality; or (4) it fails to provide the retailer's customers with the value they deserve.

## Price-Setting Policies

Retailers are also guided by a number of price-setting policies that supplement and modify price-setting methods. For example, a retailer may set prices by using the markup method. The established retail price (e.g., $40) is then modified to accommodate an odd-pricing policy (e.g., $39.95). This section discusses several price-setting policies: the one-price policy, the variable-price policy, the multiple-price policy, odd-pricing, unit pricing, and price lining.

Most U.S. retailers follow a **one-price policy,** charging *all* customers the same price for the same product under similar circumstances. In contrast to many foreign

How might the retailer misuse this type of price-setting policy?

consumers, most U.S. consumers are accustomed to paying the established price marked on the merchandise. Price "haggling" or "bargaining" is usually limited to big-ticket items, such as automobiles and appliances, and to used merchandise for which the price is subject to negotiation. A one-price policy greatly facilitates the speed at which each transaction can be made, helps simplify the retailer's various accounting records, and makes a self-service strategy possible.

A **variable-price policy** allows the customer to negotiate the final selling price. The best bargainers receive the lowest prices. Retailers that use variable pricing deal in merchandise with one or more of the following characteristics: (1) high initial markups, (2) need for personal selling, (3) unstandardized or specialized product features, (4) service requirements, and (5) infrequent purchase rates. Variable pricing gives the retailer price flexibility and increases its ability to adjust to the consumer's purchase motivations, but it can increase the retailer's labor costs, selling time, and dissatisfaction among any customers who were unable to negotiate the same low price as some other customers.

A **multiple-price policy** attempts to increase both unit and dollar sales volume. This pricing strategy gives customers a discount for making quantity purchases; that is, the retailer offers a reduced price if consumers are willing to purchase several units at the multiple-unit price. For example, the retailer can price a can of peas at $.50 each or three for $1.37. Retailers commonly use multiple-unit pricing with products purchased regularly and frequently and characterized by a low per-unit price (e.g., basic staples).

**Odd pricing** is the strategy of setting prices that end in odd numbers (e.g., $.49, $1.99, $9.95, and $29.50). By setting prices below even-dollar amounts, the retailer is relying on the psychological ploy that consumers perceive odd prices as substantially below even prices (e.g., $2.95 is perceived to be considerably less than $3.00). The theory is that consumers will think of a $2.95 price in terms of $2.00 rather than $3.00.

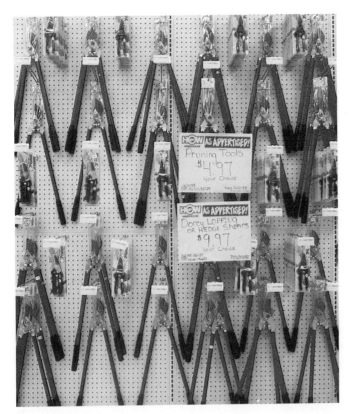

What is the psychology
involved with odd
pricing?

The strategy of odd pricing varies with the general price level of the product.[6]
Products with low per-unit prices (under $5) are odd priced at one or two cents below
an even price (e.g., $.49, $1.99, and $3.98). As the per-unit price increases, products
are priced at odd values that represent a greater reduction from even prices. For
example, products ranging in price from $10 to $20 tend to be odd priced at $9.95
or $19.95—a five-cent differential. Nine- and five-dollar odd endings are common
among big-ticket items (e.g., $199 and $495). While nine and five are the most
common odd-price endings, retailers also use three and seven to project a bargain-
price image.

Given the multiplicity of package sizes and shapes together with the diversity of
price tags and product labels, many consumers cannot determine which purchase is
the best value for the money. As a result, some retailers have initiated a unit-pricing
system to eliminate this uncertainty. **Unit pricing** is the retailing practice of posting
prices on a per-unit-measurement basis. By stating the price per ounce, pound, quart,
or yard for each brand, the retailer helps the consumer compare prices among
products of different sizes, shapes, and quantities. Per-unit price tags are usually
posted on shelf facings directly above or below the product. Maintaining a unit price
system usually means that the retailer will incur additional time, labor, equipment,
and material expenses.

The objective of a **price-lining** policy is to direct retail prices at a targeted
consumer group. To accomplish this objective, the retailer must perform two tasks.

First, the retailer must identify the appropriate pricing zone for each targeted consumer group. A **pricing zone** is a range of prices that appeals to a particular group of consumers either for *demographic reasons* (e.g., income or occupation); *psychographic reasons* (e.g., life-style or personality); *product usage reasons* (e.g., heavy or light users); or *product benefit reasons* (e.g., economy, function, or sociability). Usually, retailers identify price zones in broad terms; for example, economy price range, intermediate or family price range, and prestige or luxury price range. Although most retailers tend to focus on one broadly defined price range, some retailers try to cover more than one range (e.g., middle-to-high) but rarely try to appeal to all three ranges. Attempting to cover the entire price range would defeat the target-marketing objective of a price-lining strategy.

**Pricing lines** are *specific pricing points established within pricing zones.* Assume, for example, that a specialty store retailer has identified three pricing zones for men's suits: (1) the low-range suit (under $100), (2) the middle-range suit ($100 to $200), and (3) the high-range suit (above $200). Also suppose the retailer has targeted the middle-price-range consumer as the one to whom it wishes to appeal. Then, the retailer might establish price lines at $119.95, $159.95, and $189.95. The use of price lines is commonly associated with shopping goods and in particular with wearing apparel.

A price-lining policy has several advantages for both consumer and retailer. Advantages for the consumer are that (1) it facilitates comparison among merchandise items and (2) it reduces shopping confusion and frustration and helps the consumer make purchase decisions. For the retailer, price lining (1) simplifies the personal selling effort, (2) makes advertising and sales promotion more effective, (3) increases the chances of trading up the customer to the next price, (4) creates an image of good merchandise depth and support, and (5) simplifies the buying process, because the buyer secures only merchandise that can be profitably priced at a given pricing point.

A price-lining policy also creates some difficulties. If the retailer does not carefully establish pricing points, it is likely to project to consumers an image of inadequate merchandise assortment and consequently eliminate customers who are either above or below the price lines they seek. A second potential problem is that retailers find it extremely difficult to reduce one line without reducing all lines. To do so destroys the carefully planned spread between all price lines. Price lining also makes it easier for competitors to develop successful competitive-pricing strategies.

## ADJUSTING THE RETAIL PRICE

Price adjustments are one means for the retailer to adapt to changing external and internal environmental conditions. Retailers often find it necessary to adjust prices either upward or downward. The three basic types of adjustment are discounts, markons, and markdowns.

### Discount Adjustments

In the previous discussion on developing the merchandise budget we examined the role of markdowns, discounts, and shortages in planning retail reductions. **Discounts** were defined as reductions in the original retail price, granted to store employees as special fringe benefits and to special customers (e.g., clergy, senior citizens, and some disadvantaged consumers) in recognition of their special circumstances. Regardless of the reason for granting the discount, each discount given represents a downward adjustment in price and as such has a direct impact on profit margins. Employee discounts represent a supplementary means of compensating employees and are frequently used as a motivational tool. Customer discounts are granted to special consumer segments for a number of reasons. Drugstores frequently give "golden-agers" discounts to customers over the age of 65.

## Markon Adjustments

Retailers use the term *markon* in a variety of ways. Here, however, **markon** refers to markups taken after the initial selling price has been established. In essence, a markon represents an additional markup and an upward adjustment in the initial selling price. Upward adjustments are needed to cover increases in wholesale prices and operating expenses as well as to correct consumers' quality perceptions of merchandise. When consumers believe the quality of a product is questionable because of its low price, retailers sometimes can correct this misconception by increasing the price, thereby taking advantage of the perceived price–quality relationship. Retailers also take additional markons when the demand for an item is high and consumer price sensitivity for the item is low.

## Markdown Adjustments

A **markdown** is a downward adjustment in the original selling price of a merchandise item. A markdown represents the difference between what the merchandise was originally valued at and what it actually sells for. Markdowns, together with shortages and employee and customer discounts, are the three major factors retailers consider in planning retail reductions. Retailers use both dollars and percentages to express markdowns. "All men's slacks reduced $5!" is a typical dollar markdown expression. Per-unit **markdown percentages** are computed as a percentage of the reduced selling price or as a percentage of the original selling price. The latter expression is generally referred to as the off-retail markdown percentage.

The formula for computing per-unit markdowns as a percentage of the reduced price is shown in Figure 14–5. For example, a dress originally priced at $30 is reduced to $20; the markdown as a percentage of the reduced price would be ($30 − $10)/$20 or 50 percent. This procedure is generally preferred for expressing reduced prices.

The **off-retail markdown percentage** formula is also shown in Figure 14–5. The off-retail markdown percentage on the same dress would be 33.33 percent or ($30 − $20)/$30.

*Causes of Markdowns.* Retailers must take markdowns for a number of reasons, some of which are beyond the retailer's control (generally, unforeseen shifts in consumer expectations and unexpected changes in the retail market environment). In other cases, markdowns are caused by errors in the retailer's judgment. Markdown causes can be categorized as buying-, selling-, and operational-related.

*Buying-related causes* are retailers' errors in buying or procuring merchandise. Price reductions are often necessary to adjust for errors in the assortment, support,

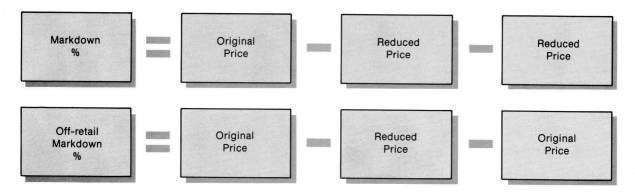

**FIGURE 14-5**

Determining markdown percentage

and quality of merchandise the retailer purchased, as well as for mistakes in timing of purchases.

*Assortment errors* occur when the retailer buys brands, styles, models, sizes, colors, and materials that do not match what consumers want to buy. *Support errors* are quantity errors that result when the retailer buys too much merchandise. *Timing errors* occur when retailers secure merchandise at the wrong time; they fail to match retail inventories with what their consumers want when they want it. *Misjudging the quality* of merchandise consumers expect is another reason retailers take markdowns. To move merchandise with unacceptable materials or workmanship, retailers must reduce prices.

*Selling-related causes* of markdowns include errors in pricing, attempts to stimulate sales or to gain competitive price parity, and various policies and practices relating to the sale of merchandise.

A *pricing error* is any set price that does not create customer interest in the merchandise. Initial prices can be set too high or too low. High prices result in lost sales because consumers' perceptions of value are not satisfied. Low prices result in customer concern over quality.

Retailers frequently use markdowns to *stimulate sales*. Sales-stimulation markdowns can take the form of loss or low-price leaders, special or promotional prices, a multiunit pricing scheme, or the use of coupons and premiums.

Sometimes retailers use markdowns to achieve *competitive parity*. Direct and indirect competitors that sell the same (or similar) merchandise at lower prices have a comparative shopping advantage over other retailers in their trading areas. Retailers take markdowns to achieve competitive price parity when they cannot justify the price differential.

*Selling policies* also can create conditions that lead to markdowns. First, a policy of "aggressive selling" (e.g., trading the customer up to higher-priced merchandise) can lead to an above-average rate of merchandise returns. It may be late in the selling season by the time the merchandise makes it back to the sales floor, and the retailer must reduce prices to clear the merchandise out by the end of the season. Second, a policy of "assortment maintenance"—the image-building policy of carrying a complete selection until late into the selling season—will require markdowns in the form of clearance sales. Finally, a selling policy that encourages customers to take home merchandise and is supported by a liberal return policy increases the likelihood of taking markdowns.

*Operationally related causes* involve both internal and external circumstances that create the need for some type of corrective action in the form of a price reduction. Two such circumstances are market shifts and distressed merchandise.

*Market shifts* are changes in demand levels for a particular merchandise line. Faddish and fashion merchandise often have fast and sometimes unexpected changes in both level and duration of customer acceptance. Introduction of a new product or a new brand can have unsettling effects on the demand for existing products already in stock.

By its very nature, *distressed merchandise* requires price reductions. Merchandise that becomes damaged, dirty, or shopworn must be marked down to compensate the purchaser for the obvious reduction in value. Odd lots (e.g., a set with one or more pieces missing) also require markdowns.

*Timing of Markdowns.* An important issue for every retailer is *when* to take markdowns.[7] Opinions differ; some retailers prefer to take early markdowns, but others feel that a policy of late markdowns is the more profitable strategy.

**Early markdowns** reduce the selling price of a merchandise item when either of two conditions is present: (1) there is a notable slack in the rate of sales for that item or (2) the item has been in stock for a specific time period (e.g., six weeks). Proponents of early markdowns cite a number of advantages. (1) *Fresher stock:* Early markdowns help make room for new merchandise by weeding out slow movers, thereby freeing investment capital and selling and storage space. (2) *Smaller markdowns:* Early markdowns reduce the size of the markdown required to sell the merchandise because some demand for the item still remains, and because the chances of the item's becoming shopworn are substantially reduced. (3) *Reduced selling expenses:* Early markdowns promote rapid clearance of merchandise without the additional advertising and personal selling expenses normally associated with major sale promotion campaigns. (4) *Increased customer traffic:* Early markdowns encourage customers to take advantage of reduced prices (both advertised and unadvertised specials) because of the continuous availability of marked-down merchandise. (5) *Reduced selling risks:* Early markdowns permit sufficient time to take a second and possibly a third price reduction in one selling season if they become necessary to move the merchandise. (6) *Heightened market appropriateness:* Early markdowns prevent repetitive showing of dated merchandise at regular prices. Market appropriateness is extremely important in selling fashion merchandise. Many fashion-oriented consumers are willing to buy only new arrivals at full prices, and they expect a continuous influx of new merchandise. Other fashion-oriented consumers are willing to buy fashion merchandise that is well along in the fashion cycle only if the price has been reduced.

Some retailers have an early-markdown policy that takes markdowns on a routine basis. **Automatic markdown** policies reduce prices by a fixed percentage at regular intervals. Automatic markdowns are generally taken without regard to how well the merchandise is selling.

**Late markdowns** maintain the original selling price until late in the selling season, at which time a major clearance sale is held. A policy of taking late markdowns is most common with smaller specialty retailers and the more prestige- or status-oriented stores. Late-markdown advocates stress these advantages: (1) *They preserve exclusive image.* Late markdowns help prestige retailers preserve a store image of high quality and exclusiveness by not mixing sale-priced goods with regular-priced merchandise and by not mixing regular, prestige-oriented customers with bargain-seekers during the normal course of the selling season. (2) *They encourage creative selling.* Late markdowns allow sufficient time for the retailer to experiment with different selling approaches. By displaying the merchandise in different places and ways, the retailer can often influence the demand for that item. (3) *They allow "late bloomers."* Late markdowns allow each merchandise line a trial sales period of sufficient duration to realize the line's full potential. (4) *They reduce purchase postponement.* Late markdowns discourage customers from waiting until the merchandise item is placed on sale before making a purchase. (5) *They create the "big event."* Late markdowns allow the retailer to accumulate large quantities of regularly stocked merchandise for a major clearance sale.

*Size of Markdowns.* The purpose of a markdown is to increase the customer's incentive to buy the merchandise. Each markdown, therefore, should be large enough to attract customers' attention and induce them to buy. At the same time,

Does this sales promotion device represent a markdown for the retailer?

unnecessarily deep markdowns will adversely affect the retailer's profit margins. Some retailers believe in making the first "bath" count; that is, they take deep initial markdowns, thereby reducing the need for later, more drastic markdowns. Other retailers think taking several shallow markdowns is the best approach to clearing merchandise with the least-negative impact on profit margins. Some retailers are making more extensive use of the "straw man" policy schemes—"a phony regular price which is quickly lowered, the sale price which is what the retailer actually expects to sell at, and deeper markdowns, as necessary, to clear the merchandise out."[8]

Highly perishable merchandise (e.g., a particular fashion near the end of its fashion cycle) typically requires substantial markdowns as part of the clearance effort. Fashionable and seasonal items often require initial markdowns of 25 to 50 percent, whereas 10- to 15-percent markdowns on staple merchandise usually are sufficient to create customer interest.

The original retail selling price of the merchandise influences the size of the markdown needed to generate customer interest. On average, the retailer must reduce the price at least 15 percent to create customer attention. In some cases, a much larger markdown is needed to induce the customer to buy.

The amount of markdown the retailer takes also depends on the time in the selling season. Early in the selling season the retailer can take smaller markdowns knowing that, if the merchandise fails to sell at the reduced price, there is still time to take additional markdowns. Late markdowns must usually be deeper to stimulate sales. Several additional factors determine the size of the markdown. For example, the need for substantial markdowns often depends on the number of units in stock that require clearance, the need for space (storage and selling), and the need for investment capital.

## Markdown Strategies

Retailers use many pricing strategies that incorporate markdowns either directly or indirectly. Clearance sales are examples of direct markdowns. Indirect price reductions are best exemplified by the retailer's use of coupons, premiums, and trading stamps.

*Promotional Pricing Strategies.* All promotional pricing strategies have at least one thing in common: They are designed to draw consumers into the store where, it is hoped, they will purchase not only reduced merchandise but also regularly priced merchandise. To this end, retailers use a variety of promotional pricing strategies. Typical are sale prices, prices with coupons and premiums, leader prices, and special-purchase prices.

*Sales* are an everyday occurrence in most retail markets. Retailers cite a variety of reasons for holding sales, such as clearances, liquidations, and closeouts. Retailers also use several different occasions for conducting a sale: seasonal sales (spring, summer, fall, winter), anniversary sales, and before-, during-, and after-holiday sales. The actual markdown or price reduction is expressed in a variety of ways. Reduced sale prices are expressed as (1) a certain dollar or percentage value "off" the original selling price, (2) as a multiple-unit price (e.g., three for $9.97), or (3) as a fraction of the original selling price.

*Coupons* are sales promotion devices in the form of redeemable cards (e.g., direct mail) or cut-outs (e.g., newspapers) that allow the customer to purchase specific merchandise at a reduced price. Although coupons issued by the manufacturer represent a reduced price for the consumer, they do not represent a markdown for the retailer, because the manufacturer reimburses the retailer for any payments made to customers. Coupons issued by the retailer *do* represent markdowns, however, because the retailer bears the cost of the difference between the original and reduced selling price.

*Premiums* include free merchandise or merchandise that has been drastically reduced. Retailers normally offer premiums to consumers after they have completed some requirement (such as test driving an automobile, filling out a form, or buying a certain dollar amount of merchandise). In a general sense, the cost to the retailer of premiums represents an indirect markdown.

**Leader pricing** is the strategy of selling key merchandise items below their normal markup or, in some cases, even below the retailer's merchandise costs (negative markup). The main objective of leader pricing is to attract consumers to the store in the hope that they also will purchase other merchandise that has normal markups.[9] To be effective, leader merchandise should include well-known (frequently national brands), widely used items priced low enough to attract most income groups and to be easily recognized as a bargain.[10]

Leader pricing strategies differ depending on the extent of the markdown and the retailer's purpose in attracting the potential customer. The three types of leader pricing strategies are low-leaders, loss-leaders, and bait-leaders. **Low-leaders** are prices set below the customary selling price but above the retailer's actual cost of the merchandise. Customer attraction is the principal objective of the low-leader strategy. **Loss-leaders** are prices reduced to or below the retailer's cost of the merchandise. Such drastic price cuts aim to improve substantially the store's customer traffic. To make loss-leaders profitable, sales of regular-priced merchandise must be great enough to more than offset the losses generated by the sale of loss-leaders.

A **bait-leader** is an extremely attractive advertised price on merchandise that the retailer does not intend to sell; the attractive advertised price is "bait" to get the customer into the store. Having accomplished this, the retailer attempts to switch the customer from the merchandise featured in the advertisement to merchandise priced at full markup—hence the common description for this pricing strategy as "bait and switch." The legal nature of "bait and switch" is somewhat fuzzy. It is usually considered an unfair trade practice (deceptive pricing), however, if the retailer absolutely refuses to sell the advertised merchandise.

A **special-purchase price** is a low advertised price on merchandise the retailer has purchased at reduced prices. Because these promotional prices are initially set below the retailer's customary price for such merchandise, indirectly they represent a markdown pricing strategy. The purpose for special-purchase pricing is the same as for most promotional pricing: to generate customer traffic. The legalities of *first* establishing a going market price is the most commonly cited reason for not directly advertising special purchases as reduced in price. Special-purchase pricing is most often associated with large chain-store retailers that enjoy buying economies of scale.

*Price-Line Adjustment Strategies.* For the retailer whose original price-setting strategies included pricing zones (a range of prices) and pricing lines (at specific pricing points), markdown adjustments create a slightly different price-reduction problem. Essentially, two general problems exist. First, the retailer must determine the *amount of the markdown;* then the *public nature of the markdown.*

Shallow markdowns usually involve reducing the price of an item from one pricing point within a pricing zone to a lower pricing point within the same zone and may be adequate for small clearance sales to dispose of a limited number of units. Deep markdowns are taken by moving a merchandise line from a pricing point in one zone to a pricing point in a lower pricing zone. Deep markdowns become necessary when the retailer considers the merchandise inappropriate for the targeted customer within the original pricing zone but possibly suited to the value expectations of targeted customers within a lower pricing zone.

The second issue in making price-line adjustments is whether to inform the customer that a markdown adjustment has been made. The retailer may decide to drop a merchandise item from one price point to a lower pricing point without informing customers of the item's markdown condition simply by replacing the old price tag with a new price. On the other hand, the retailer may choose to inform the public of the reduced price when only a few merchandise units are involved or when the negative impact (e.g., reduced quality perception) created by the markdown is thought to be outweighed by the positive aspects of the reduction (e.g., its promotion value). If the retailer believes it is beneficial for the customer to know about the price reduction, there are two ways to communicate the information: re-mark the old price tag so that the reduction is shown on the original tag or mark the merchandise down to an "off" pricing point.

### Markdown Control

Some markdowns are inevitable, the natural result of the risks retailers assume in going into business. An extremely low markdown percentage could indicate that the retailer is not assuming sufficient risks to take advantage of emerging market opportunities. On the other hand, excessive markdowns are often indicative of poor planning and control procedures. By carefully planning sales, stock levels, purchases, and profit margins, the retailer can control to a reasonable extent both the amount and the timing of markdowns. To facilitate **markdown control** many retailers require their buyers to maintain records on the causes or reasons for taking markdowns on a particular merchandise item. Careful analysis of these records allows the retailer to take corrective action when necessary and detect excessive markdowns.

---

**SUMMARY**

Retailers view prices in terms of their ability to generate profits, sales, and consumer traffic, as well as how they affect the store's image. In setting retail prices, the retailer can elect to be guided by profit, sales, or competitive objectives. A number of factors influence the retailer's price-setting decisions, including demand, competitive, cost, product, and legal considerations.

Retail price-setting methods include those that are cost-oriented (markups), competition-oriented, and vendor-oriented. Retailers often use numerous different pricing policies in refining their price-setting tactics. For example, retailers can use a one-price policy, a variable-price policy, a multiple-unit policy, odd pricing, unit pricing, and price lining as guidelines for their stores' prices.

Retailers use price adjustments as adaptive mechanisms to accommodate changing market conditions and operating requirements. Both upward and downward adjustments are needed from time to time to adapt to the dynamic retailing environment. Three common types of price adjustments are discounts, markons, and markdowns.

Markdowns represent a downward movement in prices and are often necesary to clear certain merchandise items from inventory. The three general causes for markdowns are buying-related (e.g., assortment, support, and timing errors as well as misjudgment of merchandise quality and problems associated with suppliers); selling-related (e.g., attempts to stimulate sales, to achieve competitive parity, and to correct improper selling policies); and operational-related (e.g., market shifts and distressed merchandise). Some retailers prefer to take early markdowns, whereas others believe late markdowns are more profitable. The size of the markdown depends on the type of merchandise, the price of the item, and the time in the selling season. Markdown pricing strategies include promotional strategies (sales, coupons, premiums, price leaders, and special-purchase prices) and price-line adjustment tactics. To avoid excessive and unnecessary markdowns, the retailer must establish markdown control policies.

## STUDENT STUDY GUIDE

**KEY TERMS AND CONCEPTS**

automatic markdown
bait-leader
competitive price objectives
cumulative markup
discount
dollar markup
early markdown
gross margin
initial markup
initial markup percentage
late markdown
law of demand
leader pricing
loss-leader
low-leader
maintained markup
markdown
markdown control
markdown percentage
market-share objectives

markon
multiple-price policy
odd pricing
off-retail markdown percentage
one-price policy
percentage markup
price elasticity of demand
price lining
pricing above the competition
pricing below the competition
pricing line
pricing with the competition
pricing zone
profit-maximization objectives
sales-volume objectives
special-purchase pricing
target return objectives
unit pricing
variable-price policy

1. When might the retailer prefer a market-share maintenance objective over a market-share growth objective?
2. How are two target return-pricing objectives expressed? Explain each expression.
3. What does price elasticity of demand measure?
4. From a product perspective, when are competitive price levels a more important pricing consideration?
5. Discuss how merchandising costs are determined.
6. Identify and discuss the several forms of product perishability.
7. Identify the formulas for calculating percentage markup at retail and at cost.
8. Compare and contrast the initial and maintained markups.
9. Which merchandising strategies are essential to a successful below-competition pricing strategy?
10. When is the vendor's suggested selling price not appropriate?
11. Distinguish pricing zones and pricing lines. Discuss each.
12. What are the advantages to the consumer and to the retailer of a price-lining policy?
13. What is a markon? When are markons applied?
14. Describe the two methods for computing markdowns.
15. Briefly describe the four selling-related causes of markdowns.
16. What are the advantages of early markdowns?
17. What size markdown should the retailer take?
18. Describe typical promotional pricing strategies used by the retailer.
19. Differentiate among low-, loss-, and bait-leaders.

True or False

_____ 1. Market-share growth is an appropriate pricing objective in expanding product markets.
_____ 2. Price competition is one of the least distinctive forms of competition.
_____ 3. Maintained markup equals initial markup minus all retail reductions.
_____ 4. Pricing lining makes it easier for competitors to develop successful competitive pricing strategies.
_____ 5. A liberal return policy is one method a retailer should use to help reduce the need for taking price markdowns.
_____ 6. A policy of late markdowns usually means the retailer must take deep markdowns to stimulate sales.
_____ 7. Loss-leaders are prices set below the retailer's customary selling price but above the retailer's actual merchandise cost.

## STUDENT APPLICATIONS MANUAL

1. Are retailers "free" to set whatever prices they feel are necessary to make a profit? Explain your answer.
2. If a retailer elects to use sales volume objectives in setting retail prices, how will it affect merchandising decisions regarding location, store facilities, product mix, and promotional strategies?
3. Some retailers prefer to avoid price competition; they prefer to engage in nonprice competition. Why?

**4.** Under what market conditions should a retailer consider "meeting competition" as a pricing objective?

**5.** Why do many small retailers prefer to compute percentage markups at cost rather than at retail?

**6.** Visit the following types of retailers and observe what price-setting policies are employed: (1) a major chain department store (e.g., Sears), (2) a major discount chain (e.g., K Mart), (3) a franchised fast-food restaurant chain (e.g., Pizza Hut), and (4) a major shoe chain (e.g., Kinney). Provide specific examples.

**7.** "'An automatic markdown policy is generally a good policy for all apparel retailers." Do you agree or disagree with the preceding statement? Justify and explain your answer. From the retailer's viewpoint, discuss the pros and cons of increasing the price (markons) of existing stock as soon as increases in wholesale prices are announced.

**8.** Develop a set of guidelines that all retailers should adhere to when advertising reduced prices, regardless of what markdown strategy is used.

---

## CASES: PROBLEMS AND DECISIONS

### CASE 14–1
### Free Bacon or Only $1.49—Testing Price Offerings*

The fast-food industry is typically confronted with a sales slump during the first quarter of each year. During this period, when the frequency of customer visits declines, competitors in the hamburger segment of the industry attempt to booster total sales, to improve customer counts, and to increase average sales by offering reduced prices on their smaller-size, lower-price hamburgers.

In planning for this predictable downturn in sales, Wendy's International, the fourth largest hamburger chain, decided one year to try a different competitive product strategy by offering a "quality sale," that is, a create-a-meal deal that involves a more upscaled product item—the bacon cheeseburger. The intended target market was adult males, 18 to 25 years of age, known to be heavy fast-food users. The problem was how to express and portray the sales terms to the consumer. Should the meal deal be expressed as a value-enhancement offer or a price-reduction offer. Wendy's management wants to test the two price expressions in the following manner. The value-enhancement offer was to be expressed as follows:

"FREE BACON"—Order a bacon cheeseburger
and get the bacon free

The rationale behind this offer was that *free* would enhance readership of Wendy's ads and would be perceived in a more favorable light because the total value of the offer would appear to be worth more than the actual savings because of the consumer belief of getting something for nothing.

The price reduction offer was to be expressed as

ONLY $1.49—Get Our Bacon Cheeseburger
Special for Only $1.49

The belief the customers would find a concrete dollar amount easier to retail to than a free offer provided the basic premise for this type of offer.

---

*This case was prepared by Dale M. Lewison and Douglas Hausknecht, The University of Akron, and was based on an article by Marty Abbott, "Cut-price message vs. 'free' offer," *Advertising Age* (Feburary 22, 1987): 44.

## ASSIGNMENT

Assume the role of an account manager for Wendy's sales-promotion agency:

1. Develop a hypothesis as to which of the two price offers will be most effective in achieving a favorable customer response. Support your hypothesis with a complete rationale for your beliefs.
2. Develop and conduct a market test of the two sales-promotion offers suggested by Wendy's management to determine which is the most effective. Report your findings and analysis.
3. Identify two variations for each of the price expressions—value enhancement and price reductions. Conduct a market test on your suggestions and report your results.

**ENDNOTES**

1. Thomas Nagle, "Pricing as Creative Marketing," *Business Horizons* (July/August 1983): 15.
2. See Lynn L. Judd and Barry T. Lewis, "Do Retailer Pricing Strategies and the Perceived Competitive Situation Influence Retailing Success," in *Developments in Marketing Science, Proceedings,* eds. J. M. Hawes and G. B. Glisan (Academy of Marketing Science, 1987): 296–300.
3. David S. Lituack, Rogert J. Calantone, and Paul R. Warshaw, "An Examination of Short-term Retail Grocery Price Effects," *Journal of Retailing* 61 (Fall 1985): 10.
4. See Robin T. Peterson, "Price Cutting Can't Be Sole Strategy," *Marketing News,* 23 Oct. 1987, 10, 12.
5. Thomas T. Nagle, *The Strategy of Tactics of Pricing* (Englewood Cliffs, NJ: Prentice-Hall, 1987): 59.
6. "Penny Pricing Facing Pinch From Nickel Discounts: Restaurant Study," *Marketing News,* 11 April 1986, 14.
7. See Michael Levy, "How to Determine When to Take Markdowns and How Much They Should Be," *Retail Control* (January 1987): 35–48.
8. Leonard L. Berry, "Multidimensional Strategies Can Combat Price Wars," *Marketing News,* 31 Jan. 1986, 10.
9. See Rockney G. Walters and Heikki J. Rinne, "An Empirical Investigation into the Impact of Price Promotions on Retail Store Performance," *Journal of Retailing* 62 (Fall 1986): 237–66.
10. See Gerard J. Tellis, "Beyond the Many Faces of Price: An Integration of Pricing Strategies," *Journal of Marketing* 50 (October 1986): 146–60.

# 15

## Objectives

☐ Describe the communication process and discuss its impact on retail promotions.

☐ Identify and define the five major components of the retailer's promotion mix.

☐ Discern the role of retail advertising in attracting, informing, and motivating consumers.

☐ Specify and analyze the components necessary for planning a successful retail advertising program.

☐ Delineate the organizational structures and the advertising functions necessary for accomplishing an effective advertising program.

☐ Discuss the instruments and methodologies for evaluating advertising effectiveness.

# Retail Advertising

U nlike most other businesses, retailers do not generally take their product to market. Instead, they rely on consumers to take the initiative of visiting their stores or placing an order by phone or mail. Most consumers will not take this initiative unless they are in some way motivated to do so. Before consumers will visit a particular store, however, they must be aware of its existence, know its location, and have some idea of what is available inside. They also may want information about prices they must pay, the terms of sale they can expect, services available, store hours and so forth. In addition, consumers need to be persuaded that a particular retailer's offering is most suited to their needs. Effective retailers supply this information and persuasion, generally through their retail promotional efforts.

**Promotion** involves providing the consumer information regarding the retailer's store and its product–service offering as well as influencing consumer perceptions, attitudes, and behavior toward the store and what it has to offer. As implied in the definition, promotion is both an informative and persuasive communication process; therefore, it is useful to view the retailer's promotional efforts from the standpoint of the communication process. For example, Consolidated Stores Corp., operator of Odd Lots and Big Lots closeout stores, uses newspaper ads that stress its good prices (persuasive communications) "but instead of just listing merchandise and prices, the ads tell exactly why the manufacturer closed out the goods. That way, customers won't suspect that the products are irregular, damaged, or counterfeit" (informative communications).[1]

## The Communication Process

The **communication process** involves transmitting meaningful messages between senders (i.e., retailers) and receivers (i.e., target consumers). Figure 15–1 illustrates the communication process and its participants (senders and receivers), processes (encoding and decoding), and acts (transmission and feedback). Let's review the workings of this basic communication model.

The *source* of the communication process is the **sender**—a retailer that wants to inform or persuade a select group of consumers (**receivers**) about the benefits of an idea (e.g., lower prices, quality merchandise, high fashion, fast service, or con-

**FIGURE 15–1**

The communication process

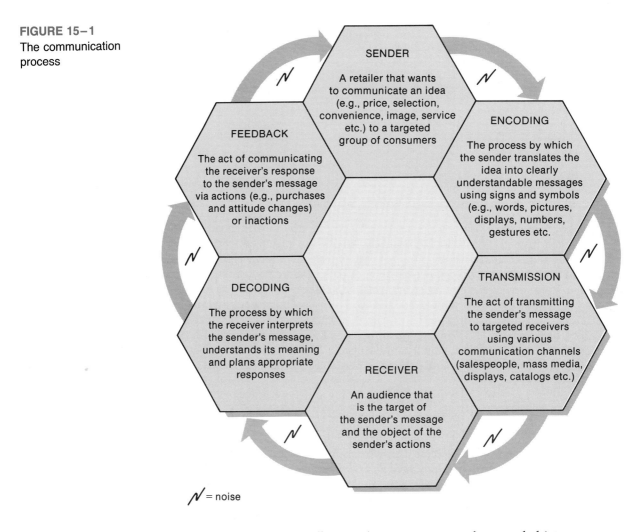

$\mathcal{N}$ = noise

temporary image). To be effective, the message must be **encoded** into messages using signs and symbols (e.g., words, displays, pictures, or gestures) that (1) promote understanding of the idea, (2) attract attention of the intended audiences, (3) stimulate needs felt by the intended audiences, and (4) suggest a course of action for need satisfaction. Having developed an effective message, the sender must then select the most appropriate communication channel or *medium* (e.g., salespeople, newspapers, magazines, radio, television, direct mail, in-store displays, and sales promotions) for **transmitting** the message to consumers targeted as the most suitable **receivers** of the message. The receiver or target audience is the intended *destination* of the sender's message and the *object* of the sender's promotional efforts (e.g., creating awareness, generating interest, and initiating behavioral change).

Upon reception of the message, the receiver **decodes** it and interprets its meaning either correctly or incorrectly, depending on how well the message was encoded and the decoder's experience and skill with the communication process. After the decoding process has been completed, the receiver may or may not react (e.g., visit the store, phone in an order, or do nothing). The nature of the receiver's *response* or lack of it is then communicated back to the sender as **feedback**. The information gained through the feedback mechanism is vital in developing and encoding new ideas for future promotions. A final element in the communication process is **noise**—anything that occurs during the communication process that distracts senders or receivers, interferes with the encoding and decoding activity, or interrupts the transmission or feedback process (see Figure 15–1).

## The Promotion Mix

The retailer's promotion mix comprises various combinations of the five basic promotional elements: advertising, personal selling, store displays, sales promotions, and publicity. The remainder of this chapter is devoted to an in-depth look at the advertising function. Chapter 16 discusses personal selling, and Chapter 17 examines the issues surrounding store displays, sales promotions, and publicity.

Retailers inform consumers about their stores, merchandise, services, or ideas and persuade consumers to accept their point of view or direct them toward desirable courses of action. To develop and implement the promotion mix, retailers use some combination of these elements:

- ☐ **Advertising**—indirect, impersonal communication carried by a mass medium and paid for by an identified retailer
- ☐ **Personal selling**—direct, face-to-face communication between a retail salesperson and a retail consumer
- ☐ **Store displays**—direct, impersonal in-store presentations and exhibitions of merchandise together with related information
- ☐ **Sales promotions**—direct and indirect impersonal inducements that offer an extra value to consumers
- ☐ **Publicity**—indirect, impersonal communication (positive or negative) carried by a mass medium that is neither paid for nor credited to an identified sponsor

Figure 15–2 compares the general characteristics of each type of promotion.

Retail advertising includes all paid forms of impersonal communications about stores, merchandise, service, or ideas by an identified retailer. Its purpose is to favorably influence consumers' attitudes and perceptions about the store, its merchandise, and its activities and to induce sales directly or indirectly. To distinguish it from publicity, advertising is described as a *paid* form of communication. Advertising is impersonal because the message is delivered through the public medium to many consumers simultaneously; this distinguishes it from personal selling (see Figure 15–2).

**RETAIL ADVERTISING**

### Understanding How Advertising Works

Consumers go through a series of steps, at varying rates, before they are motivated to accept something such as a store or a product and to take the action to patronize the business or buy the product they have accepted. Communications theorists have

| PROMOTION TYPE / CHARACTERISTIC | ADVERTISING | PERSONAL SELLING | STORE DISPLAY | SALES PROMOTION | PUBLICITY |
|---|---|---|---|---|---|
| MODE OF COMMUNICATION | Indirect Nonpersonal | Direct Face-to-face | Direct Nonpersonal | Indirect Nonpersonal | Indirect Nonpersonal |
| REGULARITY OF ACTIVITY | Regular | Regular | Regular | Irregular | Irregular |
| FLEXIBILITY OF MESSAGE | Unvarying Uniform | Personalized Tailored | Unvarying Uniform | Unvarying Uniform | Beyond Retailer's Control |
| DIRECTNESS OF FEEDBACK | Indirect Feedback | Direct Feedback | Indirect Feedback | Indirect Feedback | Indirect Feedback |
| CONTROL OF MESSAGE CONTENT | Controllable | Controllable | Controllable | Controllable | Uncontrollable |
| IDENTITY OF SPONSOR | Identified | Identified | Identified | Identified | Unidentified |
| COST PER CONTACT | Low to Moderate | High | Varies | Varies | No Cost |

**FIGURE 15–2**

Characteristic profile of types of promotion (source: adapted from William Zikmund and Michael d'Amico, *Marketing* [New York: John Wiley & Sons, 1984], 494)

proposed several models of this personal "adoption" process, most of which are similar. The model presented here is known as **DAGMAR (defining advertising goals for measured advertising results)**. Developed by Russell Colley, the model describes a sequence of steps through which prospective customers move from total unawareness of a store and its offering to store patronage and purchase (action).

As Figure 15–3 illustrates, several steps intervene between unawareness and action (or store selection). Through advertising, the retailer can help consumers move to *awareness* of the store and its offerings; to *comprehension* or understanding of the store and its image, price structure, services, and so on; to *conviction* or favorable attitudes toward the store. To build awareness and comprehension, each time Wal-Mart enters a new market, they precede the opening with a "pre-awareness campaign" using TV and print advertisements one month before the doors open. When an outlet opens, Wal-Mart does monthly direct mailings and weekly newspaper inserts to obtain continuing favorable consumer response.[2] Although advertising cannot accomplish this process alone (other aspects of the retailer's marketing mix also play important roles in moving customers through this behavioral sequence), it plays a major role, particularly in the awareness and comprehension steps.

Advertising affects a large number of people simultaneously with a single message because of the mass media it uses. Although it is itself a mass form of com-

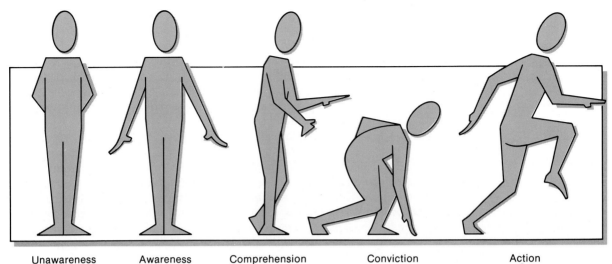

| Unawareness | Awareness | Comprehension | Conviction | Action |

**FIGURE 15–3**
The DAGMAR consumer-adoption model (source: adapted from Russell H. Colley, *Defining Advertising Goals for Measured Advertising Results* [New York: Association for National Advertisers, Inc., 1961], 46–69)

munication (and therefore impersonal), the ultimate effects of advertising are often magnified by personal communications among consumers. This phenomenon, known as the **two-step flow of communications,** is illustrated in Figure 15–4.

The first step in the process is the communications flow from media to opinion leaders. (**Opinion leaders** are persons whose attitudes, opinions, preferences, and actions affect others.) The second step is word-of-mouth communications from opinion leaders to others (followers). This communication may occur through personal conversations (a "fashionable" woman tells her friends where she bought her new coat) or through nonverbal personal communications (the friends notice the label in her coat). Regardless of how the second step takes place, it is crucial to the influence advertising has on consumers.

**FIGURE 15–4**
Two-step flow model of communications

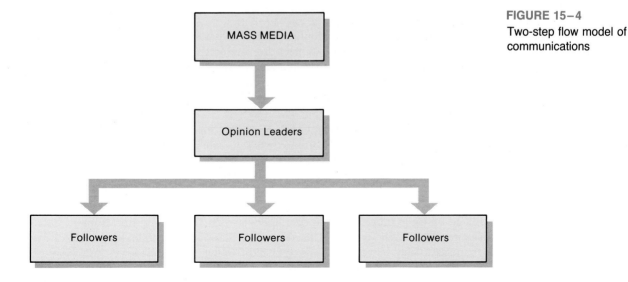

### Identifying Types of Advertising

Retail advertising has two basic purposes: to get customers into the store and to contribute to the store's image. The first purpose is immediate: Today's advertising brings buyers into the store tomorrow. Retailers also want long-run, or delayed, results from advertising. They want customers to know "who" the store is in relation to competitors and the community as a whole. Accordingly, retailers undertake two kinds of advertising: product and institutional.

**Product advertising** presents specific merchandise for sale and urges customers to come to the store immediately to buy. This indirect form of advertising helps to create and maintain the store's reputation through its merchandise. Product advertising themes center around promoting merchandise that is new, exclusive, and of superior quality and design as well as around themes relating to complete assortments and merchandise events. Announcements of sales, special promotions, or other immediate-purpose advertising are other types of product advertising.

**Institutional advertising** sells the store generally as an enjoyable place to shop. Through institutional advertising, the store helps to establish its image as a fashion leader, price leader, leader in offering wide merchandise selection, superior service, or quality, or whatever image the store chooses to cultivate. To "neutralize" the junk food misconception about its food, McDonald's ran a series of magazine ads stressing the nutritional value of its food.[3] In reality, practically all of a store's product advertising should communicate its institutional image as well. The art, copy, typography, and logotype of product advertising all help to convey store image.

Another way a retailer might undertake product advertising economically is to take advantage of **cooperative advertising**. Manufacturers prepare print and broadcast advertising material of their own products and allow the retailer to insert its store name and address in the ad, then manufacturer and retailer split the cost of media space or time to run the ad. Usually the cost split is 50:50, although the percentages vary. Some manufacturers also make direct-mail advertising of their products available to retailers to distribute to their customers.

---

**PLANNING THE ADVERTISING FUNCTION**

Planning the advertising function involves (1) a statement of objectives (the specific results the retailer expects to achieve from advertising), and (2) development of a budget (the determination and allocation of money to accomplish the objectives).

### Determining Advertising Objectives

Some of the more common types of advertising objectives used by retailers to direct their advertising effort include (1) store image, (2) store positioning, (3) traffic generation, and (4) special events advertising. Each of these objectives assumes that the retailer has a clear idea of what consumers are being targeted by the store.

To acquire and keep regular customers, every store needs to be thought of as unique in some way by its target market. The retailer may wish to establish a *store image* by size (large), merchandise specialization (Early American furniture store), clientele ("designer" lines for "discriminating" shoppers), fashion leadership or merchandise quality (always presenting fashion "news"), or price levels (not being undersold on products with well-known prices).

# Save $60 And A Trip To Guangzhou.

Cheung Settee, 45″ in width, has plenty of room for two. And snugly seats three.
Regular Price $159.99, Sale **$129.88.**

Cheung Armchair is perfect for catnaps.
Regular Price $79.99, Sale **$59.88.**

Cheung Table. 20″W x 40″L x 17″H. Regular Price $69.99, Sale **$59.88.**

Cushions sold separately. Selection may vary by store.

The Cheung Group pictured above was handmade in the town of Guangzhou, China. A very nice place to visit, but geographically inconvenient for wicker furniture shopping. Pier 1, on the other hand, is close by and has The Cheung Group on sale this week. Stop by and see its honey-colored finish and its long-lasting lacquer coating. Feel its sturdy, tightly woven construction. And choose from dozens of colorful seat cushions. By doing so, you'll save yourself $60. And a very long, tiring trek to Guangzhou.

**Pier 1 imports®**
A Place To Discover.™

This product advertisement offers specific merchandise (wicker furniture) and urges customers to buy immediately so as to save $60. (Courtesy of The Richards Group)

*Walt Frazier, 1955*

Even as a kid I had an eye for colors and style. Even my cool demeanor was evident. But things are not always the way they seem, and it was many years later before I felt cool and confident in front of a camera.

*Walt Frazier*

This advertisement promotes the store's image as a long-established business that remains up-to-date ("serving cool customers for 100 years"). (Courtesy of Fallon McElligott)

# A GERMAN FORTNIGHT

OCTOBER 17-NOVEMBER 5. CELEBRATING 300 YEARS OF GERMAN IMMIGRATION IN NORTH AMERICA.

Succumb to the outrageous luxury of Baden-Baden. ■ Where Napoleon III and the Kaiser along with their courts summered and "took the cure" — the legendary waters of the river Oos. ■ ■ We've recaptured the famous spa in Cosmetics. ■ With its own Lancaster Beauty Farm with lotions, scrubs, masques and massage creams to cleanse and purify body and facial skin. ■ And Ralph Lauren makeup artists to make a healthy glow more glowing. ■ ■ Ah, what wonders these waters work. ■ Complimentary makeovers by Ralph Lauren and Lancaster teams, daily. ■ ■ ■ Lancaster facials, 30.00. Make your appointment: 741-6911, ext. 2101, First Floor, Downtown.

*Neiman-Marcus*

A special-event advertisement

*Store positioning* is a term advertisers use in reference to attempts to get the market to think of the store in a certain way in relation to its competition. Wendy's now-famous television ad, "Where's the beef?" was an extremely successful commercial that positioned Wendy's as the restaurant with the large burger, one with more beef than the competitive products offered by McDonald's (Big Mac) or Burger King (The Whopper).[4]

*Traffic generation* refers to the number of people who visit the store and the frequency with which they visit. In general, the more consumers who visit the store, the greater the store's sales. Retailers can generate traffic in many ways. One of the surest methods is to provide customers with a special purpose for visiting, which can be achieved through sales, "theme" promotions (such as bridal seminars), special-merchandise showings, or demonstrations.

*Special events* give customers particular reasons for visiting the store. Sales-promotional events are planned in advance, oriented around some theme, and co-ordinated through merchandising, store decoration, and advertising. One of retailing's most famous special events is Dallas's Nieman-Marcus annual "Fortnight," a two-week fall happening featuring a unique theme. For example, the store may create an exotic atmosphere of some foreign country complete with displays and sales of rare and exclusive merchandise. The event induces many customers to visit the store out of curiosity, many of whom make purchases totally unrelated to the special advertised event.

## Developing Advertising Budgets

Executing the advertising campaign requires spending money. Therefore, determining the advertising appropriation is the next step in developing a comprehensive advertising plan. Although many retailers use the terms *appropriation* and *budget* synonymously, *appropriation* refers to the total expenditure for advertising undertaken in a time period, whereas *budget* refers to the allocation of the total expenditure across departments, merchandise lines, advertising media, and planning periods such as weeks, months, and seasons.

Most retailers consider the following as advertising expenses: (1) space and time costs in print and broadcast media; (2) advertising-department salaries and travel and entertainment expenses; (3) cost of advertising consultants; (4) advertising research services; (5) media costs for contests, premiums, and sampling promotions; and (6) direct-mail advertising to consumers. Other expenditures that some retailers include as advertising expenses are catalogs, point-of-sale materials, window display installation services, consumer contest awards, product tags, and signs on company-owned vehicles.

*Budgeting* refers to the process of dividing the total advertising appropriation into its various components; in other words, splitting up the advertising "pie." **Advertising budget** allocations are made on the basis of departments, merchandise lines, media, and time periods. At different times, the store will want to feature different items in its product line and de-emphasize promotion of others items. Some stores choose to promote high-markup, low-turnover items heavily and de-emphasize lower-markup, higher-turnover items. Others may elect either to introduce a new line or to achieve a higher market penetration in a given line.

Retailers can select from among several different advertising media. Some media give retailers discounts for signing long-term contracts; it is therefore important to determine how much of the total advertising appropriation to devote to each of the media to make those expenditures more efficient.

Finally, most retailers advertise more at certain times and less at others. Some advertise extensively before and during heavy buying periods, while others attempt to offset slack periods with heavier advertising. Most retailers develop quarterly and monthly advertising budgets, but others develop extremely short-run budgets such as two-week intervals.

Retailers use many methods to determine their advertising budgets. These range in sophistication from little more than guesswork to highly sophisticated techniques.

The **educated-guess method** depends on intuition and practical experience to develop an advertising budget. The retailer simply looks at last year's sales and advertising expenditures, determines what it hopes to accomplish this year, considers other necessary expenditures, and chooses an amount to spend on advertising next year.

To develop a budget with the **percentage-of-sales method** method, the retailer takes a predetermined percentage of either the previous year's sales or the estimated sales for the coming year to calculate how much to spend on advertising. The percentage figure is based on either the "traditional" figure the company has taken in the past, personal "insight," or an industry average. The method is popular among retailers because it is simple; unfortunately, it has no logical tie-in with achieving advertising objectives.

The **competitive parity method** sets advertising appropriation at the amount equal to that of retailer's competitors. This method has drawbacks that, under most conditions, make it undesirable to use.

One of the most logical methods of advertising appropriation and budgeting is the **objective and task method,** by which retailers follow a four-step process:

1. Establish the objectives for advertising.
2. Determine the type and amounts of advertising necessary to accomplish these objectives.
3. Determine the overall cost of the advertisement.
4. Schedule the advertisements day by day.

The last step allows for budgeting the total appropriation across media, product lines, and time periods. The objective and task budgeting method offers several strengths. First, advertising expenditures are based on specifically stated objectives, not on "guesstimates" or competitors' advertising expenditures. Second, this method forces the retailer into *planning* an advertising strategy and becoming a part of it. Third, it helps the retailer create criteria against which to measure performance.

---

Day-to-day advertising functions include deciding which products to promote, developing copy and artwork, and scheduling and placing ads in the media. How the store is organized to execute these functions depends on its size and the funds available for specialized personnel to perform the functions.

**ORGANIZING THE ADVERTISING FUNCTION**

### Establishing Advertising Departments

The owner-manager or one of the partners in small sole proprietorships and partnerships must handle the advertising function. With so many other store duties to perform, the main function is to establish advertising objectives, appropriations, and budgets and to work with outside advertising specialists—usually freelancers, media representatives, and advertising agencies.

Large stores have small advertising departments with an advertising manager who supervises artists, copywriters, and production specialists. The manager usually is responsible for establishing objectives, appropriations, budgets, and scheduling and for working with store merchandise managers and other managers to determine what will be promoted and how. This is usually the person who interacts with outside specialists in agencies and the media. Because most retailers advertise primarily in newspapers, the artists and copywriters spend most of their time developing newspaper copy. Broadcast advertising usually is produced with the help of agencies or personnel from the television and radio stations.

### Using Outside Advertising Specialists

Freelancers, advertising agencies, and media representatives are the three principal advertising specialists available to the retailer. An **advertising freelancer** might be an artist, copywriter, or photographer who produces advertising on a part-time basis. Freelancers usually operate alone, but sometimes have a small staff, charge a fee or an hourly rate for work, and work on their own premises or at the retailer's store. **Media representatives** are the employees of newspapers and radio or television stations whose principal job is to sell advertising space and time. These specialists also can arrange to produce the retailer's advertisements. Usually, newspapers do not charge for production and take compensation only for the space they sell. Radio stations normally do not charge for production, only for time, but charge a production fee for the tapes they make if they are broadcast on other stations. Television stations generally charge a fee for producing commercials in addition to the air time. Although **advertising agencies** produce the majority of national advertising, most retailers do not use them because of costs.

**EXECUTING THE ADVERTISING FUNCTION**

Few retailers become directly involved in creating advertising. Nonetheless, all must be able to distinguish good, effective advertising from poor, ineffective advertising. "Creating" advertising is the responsibility of "creative" advertising personnel: artists, copywriters, and others who work for the store, agency, or media. This section introduces the basic process of creating newspaper advertising and selecting advertising media.

### Creating Retail Advertisements

There are as many processes for creating ads as there are creators of ads. In general, though, the creator of an advertisement must take into account the following steps for developing an effective ad:

1. Determine the purpose of the advertisement.
2. Decide on the basic message.

3. Select the communications approach.
4. Develop the total advertisement, part by part.

*The Purpose of the Advertisement.* An individual advertisement can have one or more purposes, such as promoting the store as a whole, making customers aware of a special event, focusing on a single product, or highlighting several products. Regardless of the purpose for a single advertisement, all advertising has some degree of "institutional" content as well. To achieve the double benefit of special-purpose advertising and institutional advertising, the retailer should select a special theme, product, or combination of products to feature but should always maintain the same style in advertisements. Other purposes also must be considered: Is the advertising intended to elicit an immediate response? If so, perhaps direct action ("Come in today") should be suggested.

*The Basic Message.* Two basic elements in persuasive communications such as advertising are *what is said* and *how it is said*—substance and style. Too many advertisers concentrate on style and forget about substance, but the substance must be clear before advertising can be effective. Stipulating the basic **advertisement message** is determining what to say. Most retail advertising messages are quite simple: "Ours is a high-fashion store"; "Our women's coats are of highest quality"; "Our meat selection is the best in town." But the message should not be pulled out of thin air. Instead, it should be based on the target customer's wants and needs and the ability of the advertised product to *satisfy* those wants and needs. The combination of these two is the advertising *appeal.* If, for example, the advertiser thinks its target customers are concerned not with the quality of a coat but with its social acceptability, then the basic appeal of the message should be "Fashionable women wear this coat," not "This coat will last for five years." Note that both messages stress the *benefit* consumers derive from buying and not the *features* of the coat from which they derive the benefit. Although the retailer's advertisement can point out that a coat has a double-stitched lining (a product feature), the resulting benefit (the lining is unlikely to separate from the coat) is the basic message the retailer should stress.

*The Communications Approach.* In determining the **communications approach,** the advertiser turns attention from *what* to say to *how* to say it. Most messages can be effectively communicated by either a rational or an emotional approach. The *rational* approach uses facts, narrative, and logical reasoning to persuade the consumer. The *emotional* approach appeals to the consumer's sense of aesthetics, ego, or feelings. For example, a tire dealer may effectively use a rational approach to promote snow tires ("You can get there on time—even if you wake up to snow") or it may arouse a husband's fear and protective instincts by depicting a solemn wife and two wide-eyed children under the headline, "Are you sure they'll get home tonight?" Although both approaches can be effective, advertising practitioners believe the emotional approach is more effective.

*The Total Advertisement.* The **total advertisement** consists of several components: headline, illustration, copy, logotype or "signature," and layout (the visual arrangement). Although each component has a specific purpose, they work together to accomplish the ad's basic purpose: *to motivate the consumer to action.* It is worthwhile here to reiterate the phases of the consumer's mental adoption process outlined earlier in this chapter: moving from nonawareness through awareness, comprehension, conviction, and motivation.

The principal purpose of an ad's **layout** is to capture attention and guide consumers through all parts of the advertisement. Several other layout considerations merit attention. For example, one old advertising rule of thumb is that the principal focal point of the layout should fall five-eighths from the top. Sparse illustrations with lots of white space suggest quality and prestige, whereas cluttered ads suggest discounting and a price appeal.

An ad's **headline** performs several functions besides getting attention. It should motivate the reader to review the remainder of the ad by *providing news* ("Blatt's Biggest Sale Ever!"), *selecting readers* ("Now You Can Get Organized"), and *arousing curiosity* ("Color TV for a Dollar a Day? Want to Know More?"). In general, the more original or unique the headline, the better. The headline condenses the basic advertising message, telling the reader essentially what is to come.

**Illustrations** help build consumer comprehension. The most common illustration is a drawing or a photograph of the product. The illustration can depict the product alone, isolate certain product features or details, show the product in context (such as illustrating a sofa in a completely furnished living room), depict the product in use, or illustrate how a consumer can derive a benefit from the product.

The **copy**—what is actually said in the advertisement—helps develop consumer comprehension, conviction, and action. In brief, good advertising copy should be simple and readable, yet vivid in word selection; it should be conversational in tone, interesting, enthusiastic, informative, point out benefits, and suggest action. Effective copy can be brief or lengthy; however, the chance that anyone will read long copy is remote.

The **logotype**, or *logo* in common usage, is the store's distinctive "signature" that appears in all advertising. It usually is coordinated with the store's sign, with its point-of-purchase advertising, labels, shopping bags, and so forth. Done in a distinctive style, script, or type, the logo identifies the store in the consumer's mind in much the same way that a trademark identifies a product or company. A logo is effective when it suggests the store's "character" or the nature of the retailer's merchandise. A good logo communicates the store's personality and product offerings.

### Selecting Advertising Media

The retailer's advertising message must be carried to the market by some communications vehicle, called advertising *media*. The retailer can select from among *print media*, such as newspapers, shopping publications, and magazines; *broadcast media*, such as radio and television; *sign media*, such as outdoor and transit; and *miscellaneous media*, including point-of-purchase media and advertising specialties, such as calendars or ashtrays. The retailer also can choose to become its own medium and use direct advertising to the consumer through mailed or hand-delivered letters, circulars, and catalogs.

*Media Characteristics.* There are many characteristics to consider in choosing advertising media. Some media are costly, some are inexpensive; some communicate a given message well, others poorly; some present the message continuously, others are instantaneous.

## MY, MY. THE CLIENT'S REALLY LOOKING FORWARD TO YOUR PRESENTATION.

Maybe this time, just once, he'll have an open mind. But then again, well, he's always been one to make snap judgements.

To sell that proposal, your staff is going to need every slight advantage, every bit of confidence. Who knows? Maybe they need Juster's.

We offer an unique Corporate Clothing Program that can make their business wardrobes work harder. You know, give them that little extra edge. Help them wrestle with those unnerving corporate situations. And come out on top.

When your company participates, your employees receive a seminar on proper business dressing, personal consultation, special tailoring services, plus other valuable incentives. Call us at 333-1431, and ask how this exclusive program can work for you.

Juster's. We can give your employees' clothing the right kind of bite.

**SURVIVAL OF THE FITTEST** Juster's

Nicollet Mall, Southdale, Brookdale, Ridgedale, Rosedale, Highland Village.

Does this headline arouse your curiosity? Do you think the illustration is effective?
(Courtesty of Miller Meester/DBK&0)

**Communication effectiveness** refers to a medium's ability to deliver the desired impact to the target market. Print media show consumers pictures and words they can see and read. With radio, consumers can only listen to the message, whereas television allows them to both see and hear the retailer's communication. The print media are generally thought to be effective with an intelligent audience, whereas the broadcast media are more effective with a less intelligent audience.

**Geographic selectivity** is a medium's ability to "home in" on a specific geographic area such as a city and its surrounding area. This is an important media characteristic to a retailer because most customers live in the local area. A medium that delivers the message to many people outside the retailer's market has a high degree of "wasted" circulation, viewership, or listenership since these people are unlikely to buy from that retailer. Of the major media, local newspapers and local radio and television stations offer the retailer reasonably good geographic selectivity.

**Audience selectivity** refers to the medium's ability to present the message to a certain target audience within a population. Most magazines appeal to people with special interests, such as antique collectors, golfers, and electronics hobbyists. Radio stations also have a high degree of audience selectivity because their programming formats (e.g., country and western music, classical music, rock) appeal to distinct groups of consumers. Television also can be highly selective when individual programs are considered. On the whole, people who watch "Monday Night Football" have different interests from those who watch "Days of Our Lives." Audience selectivity can be increased by placing ads in strategic locations *within* a newspaper (for example, an ad for a sporting goods store in the sports section).

**Flexibility** refers to the number of different "things" the advertiser can do in the medium. Direct mail, for example, allows the advertiser to enclose money, coupons, pencils, postage-paid envelopes—in fact, practically anything, limited only by the advertiser's ingenuity. Radio, on the other hand, can provide words, music, and sound, but nothing more.

**Impact** refers to how well a medium stimulates particular behavioral responses within the target market. Television and magazines are better than other media in building store images, for example, whereas newspapers and the yellow pages of a telephone directory are better at generating immediate purchase behavior.

**Prestige** is the amount of status consumers attach to a medium. In general, consumers attribute more prestige to advertising in print media than in broadcast media. Naturally, the prestige of print media varies with the individual publication (e.g., the *New Yorker* versus *Mad* magazine).

**Immediacy** is the medium's ability to present a timely or newsworthy message. Radio announcements, for example, can be prepared today and aired tomorrow, whereas magazines require one to three months' notice in advance of the issue date. Newspapers also need very little lead time (usually 24 hours) to place a retailer's ad.

**Life** means the length of time the announcement continues to "sell." Broadcast announcements are gone in an instant and must be repeated to be effective, but a newspaper ad may "live" for several hours while people read the paper. Ads in magazines, which people read leisurely, may continue to "live" for several weeks since consumers leave them in their homes and re-expose themselves to them over a long period of time.

**Coverage** refers to the percentage of a given market that a medium reaches. A newspaper might be read by 70 to 90 percent of adults in a certain city, whereas only a fraction of the same market may be reached by a "hard rock" FM radio station.

Although coverage is often an important criterion in reaching a market, it must be considered in light of audience selectivity.

**Cost** should be viewed in both absolute and relative terms. Absolute cost is the amount of money a retailer must pay to run an advertisement in a medium; for example, the cost of a full-page ad in a newspaper might be $2,000 for one day. *Relative cost* is the number of dollars the retailer spends to reach a specific number of people; for example, if the full-page newspaper ad reaches 300,000 people, then the relative cost is $6.67 per 1,000 readers. If, on the other hand, the retailer spends $250 on a radio ad, much less money is spent in absolute terms, but if the message is heard by only 25,000 people, then the relative cost would be $10.00 per 1,000 listeners.

**Frequency** refers to the number of times the same viewer or reader may be exposed to the same advertisement. A consumer might pass an outdoor poster twice daily for 90 days, whereas a radio spot might be broadcast a dozen times before a person hears it once. Similarly, consumers are likely to read newspapers only once per day but see a magazine ad in one issue several times.

*Newspaper Advertising.* Newspapers have always made up the bulk of retail advertising, probably because their local nature fits the retailer's desire for geographic coverage, prestige, and immediacy. In addition, newspapers are a "participative" medium that people read partly for the advertising; in fact, many consumers use newspapers as a shopping guide. As mentioned, retailers gain some measure of audience selectivity by advertising in specific sections of the paper, such as the sports, society, and financial sections. The cost of **newspaper advertising** is neither the highest nor the lowest of the available media.

By size and format, newspapers are classified as either standard or tabloid. Most large newspapers are standard; that is, they are about 23.5 inches deep and eight columns wide, with each column about 2 inches wide. Tabloid newspapers are smaller "booklet" papers, five columns wide by about 14 inches deep, or about half the size of standard newspapers. The *New York Daily News* is an example of a tabloid newspaper.

Newspapers also are classified as dailies and weeklies, although some "dailies" are published only four to six days a week, and some "weeklies" are published two or three times per week. Newspapers may be metropolitan, community, or shopping newspapers. Metropolitan newspapers are circulated over an entire metropolitan area (e.g., the *New York Times*), whereas community newspapers are published for a portion of a city or a suburb (e.g., *Newsday*, the Long Island newspaper). Shopping newspapers are comprised mostly of retail and classified advertising.

Newspapers sell two kinds of advertising space: *classified* and *display*. Classified advertising is carried in a special section and used only by certain kinds of retailers, such as automobile dealers. Most retailers, however, use display advertising, which is spread throughout the newspaper. The basic unit of space the retailer buys from the newspaper is *agate line* (or "line" in common use). An agate line is one column wide and 1/14 of an inch deep. Fourteen lines of space thus equals one *column inch*, the basic space unit for smaller papers. (The width of a column is not a factor in calculating newspaper space.) One full page of advertising equals about 2,400 lines or approximately 172 column inches, depending on the size of the paper.

Newspapers publish their rates on *rate cards* that they make available to customers. A retailer that buys newspaper space one time with no stipulations would pay the paper's *open rate*. Few retailers, however, actually pay the open rate since the cost of newspaper space generally decreases with the quantity bought and increases as the retailer improves the "quality" of its advertising by specifying a particular position in the paper or by using color. Most retailers that advertise regularly make *space contracts* with the newspaper, by which the retailer agrees to use a certain amount of space over the year and to pay a certain amount per line that is lower than the paper's open rate for the same space.

Unless otherwise specified, newspaper rates are "ROP" (run of the paper), meaning the paper will put the ad wherever it sees fit in composing the paper. This is not necessarily undesirable, because newspapers do the best they can to make up an attractive paper and place advertising where it fits best. A retailer who is willing to pay a premium called a *position charge* can, however, specify a position in the paper. The retailer can then specify the first three pages, the sports, society, or financial section, or even a specific page. Some retailers even rent a certain space permanently.

Most newspapers can print in color, and color advertising is becoming more common. Needless to say, the retailer pays more for color, and the more color used, the more the retailer pays. Many newspapers also can insert preprinted color advertisements.

Newspaper rate structures are determined by circulation: The greater the circulation, the higher the rates, and vice versa. A paper's paid and unpaid circulation is audited by the Audit Bureau of Circulations, which publishes a report of circulations throughout the paper's city and its retail trading zone, the area beyond the city proper for which the city is a trade center. To compare newspapers' advertising rates, which vary widely, advertisers commonly use a calculation called the *milline rate,* which is the paper's cost of getting a line of advertising to a million people.

*Magazine Advertising.* Few retailers advertise in consumer magazines. Although magazines do offer a high degree of prestige, audience selectivity, and impact (when used correctly), they generally lack geographic selectivity, which is what the vast majority of retailers require. Because magazines' advertising rates, like newspapers', are based on total circulation, a retailer that places an ad must pay for wasted circulation outside its trading area. Thus, a Kansas City retailer that advertises in a nationally circulated magazine pays to advertise not only to Kansas City residents but also to readers in Maine and Louisiana. To offset this disadvantage, many magazines publish regional editions (same editorial matter, different advertising) for certain geographic areas (e.g., Southwest) and major cities (e.g., New York). City and regional magazines have grown in both number and circulation, and the greater geographic selection of these magazines makes them a more feasible advertising medium for some retailers.

Magazines also require a considerable period of time between publication date and the date advertising materials must be available. Magazines therefore do not accommodate the immediate-response advertising that makes up the majority of retail business. Most retailers that use magazines are either nationwide chains or stores with branches in several cities in a limited area.

**Magazine advertising** space usually is bought in pages and fractions, such as half page, one-third page, or two-thirds page. Generally, the only premium positions are inside the front cover, the inside and outside of the back cover, opposite the table of contents, and the center spread. Magazine rates, like newspaper rates, are based on circulations, and the rate structures, circulations, facts of publication, and publication requirements are published in *Standard Rate and Data Service*.

*Radio Advertising.* Americans own about five radio receivers per household, and American retailers have used radio extensively almost since its inception. Among its advantages are low cost and a high degree of geographic and audience selectivity. Although radio broadcasters claim otherwise, sound alone is not a very good communications medium. Therefore, advertisers should stick with a simple message, make it easy to remember (hence the radio "jingle"), and repeat the message frequently.

Like other media advertising rates, radio rates are based on audience sizes. *Coverage* is the geographic area over which the station's signal can be heard; *audience* refers to the number of people who actually listen.

Some 50,000-watt "clear-channel" radio stations broadcast over a large geographic area, including many areas outside the retailer's market area. *Regional* stations cover smaller geographic areas that are much larger than a typical city. *Local* stations (1,000 watts or less) broadcast a signal that usually does not carry further than about 25 miles, and most listeners are clearly in the retailer's market area.

Radio stations appeal to highly specialized audiences because of their programming: rock and roll stations, easy-listening stations, classical music stations, all-news stations, or talk-show stations. Moreover, radio listeners are much more station-loyal than television viewers, who switch freely from one channel to another. Radio is particularly important to drivers, who have their radios tuned in about 62 percent of their "drive time"; peak drive times are 7 to 9 A.M. and 4 to 6 P.M.

**Radio advertising** is sold as either *network* radio (buying from several stations that air joint programming) or *spot* radio (bought from individual stations). Because most retailers want to advertise in one city only, most buy spot radio announcements. Stations divide their total air time into classes, usually labeled AAA, AA, A, B, and C, with the best times being early morning (6 to 10 A.M.) and late afternoon (3 to 7 P.M.). Generally, the fewest people listen at night, so this time is the cheapest. Spot announcements usually are sold in one-minute, thirty-second, and ten-second periods for a certain number of repetitions (e.g., 15, 50, or 150 times). Retailers often buy weekly "package plans" for a number of repetitions of a message of a certain duration over a certain time class; for example, retailers can select 20 thirty-second announcements in class AA time for a week. They also can buy joint sponsorship of certain programs, such as the daily stock market report. *Standard Rate and Data Service* lists radio stations' packages and rates and describes their programming.

Radio rates are based on audience size. Estimates of the number and characteristics of listeners at certain times of the day are made by companies like The Pulse, Inc., and American Research Bureau. These statistics are sold to radio stations, which in turn make them available to potential advertisers. The retailer, as an advertiser, can write its own radio copy and have the station "produce" it—provide the announcer and develop a musical background and whatever sound effects are needed. Normally, the station does not charge for this service if the retailer runs the message on the producing station.

*Television Advertising.* Television is the most glamorous and conspicuous advertising medium in this country. Reaching about 99 percent of all U.S. homes, **television advertising** garners a large amount of advertising dollars but not from retailers.

Although television is an excellent communications medium, its high cost constraints also eliminate all but the largest retailers from using it regularly. Moreover, preparing of television commercials requires expertise that store advertising departments do not usually have, so most retailers depend on advertising agencies to produce and place their television commercials. Television stations also will produce commercials for a fee.

Like radio time, television time is sold as network or spot time. Unlike radio, the majority of television programming originates from the major networks. Since most retailers' markets are localized, again only the largest nationwide chains can buy network television time. Most retailers buy spot announcements from local stations. In contrast to the number of radio stations, only a few television stations operate in most cities.

Television time rate structures and measurements of audience size on which rates are based are quite complex. A complete discussion is beyond the scope of this book; the reader is referred to any standard advertising text. In general, television stations divide their time into classes based on size of audience at a given time. The larger the audience, the higher the cost of advertising time. *Prime time,* when most people watch television, is 7:30 to 11 P.M. on the East and West coasts and 6:30 to 10 P.M. in the Midwest. *Fringe time* comprises the hours immediately preceding and following prime time. *Daytime* and *late nighttime,* the least expensive times, are when the fewest people watch television. Advertising rates, therefore, are lowest during the times with few viewers and highest during prime time, which normally attacts the most viewers.

Local stations sell spot announcements in and around programming at certain times, as well as packages of announcements much like radio packages. As in almost all media, television stations allow advertisers a quantity discount; the greater the number of repetitions, the lower the cost per repetition. The retailer can buy one-minute, thirty-second, and ten-second spots (or combinations of these), or it may buy partial sponsorship of the station's local programming.

The sizes of local stations' television audiences are measured by firms such as the A. C. Nielsen Company and the American Research Bureau. By means of diaries, electronic recording devices, and interviews, these companies estimate the number of people in the station's market area watching various television programs.

*Sign Advertising.* Retailers use outdoor advertising media extensively, especially posters, bulletins, and spectaculars. **Sign advertising** gives retailers impact, coverage, frequency, geographic selectivity, and a long life for a relatively low cost per thousand. Outdoor signs, however, are good for presenting only a short reminder message, perhaps the store name, an illustration, and a few words of copy.

Outdoor signs are owned or leased by local "plant operators" that install the advertisers' messages and are responsible for maintaining the signs and the surrounding areas. The three basic outdoor signs are the thirty-sheet, 12- by 25-foot *poster* that most people call a "billboard," *painted bulletins,* and outdoor *spectaculars.* Painted bulletins are signs approximately 14 by 48 feet on which the advertising message is actually painted in sections by an artist working from a miniature. When the advertisement is painted in sections, the advertiser can move the message to another location. Outdoor spectaculars are nonstandardized, custom-made signs that use elaborate lighting, falling water, rising steam, billowing smoke, and other tech-

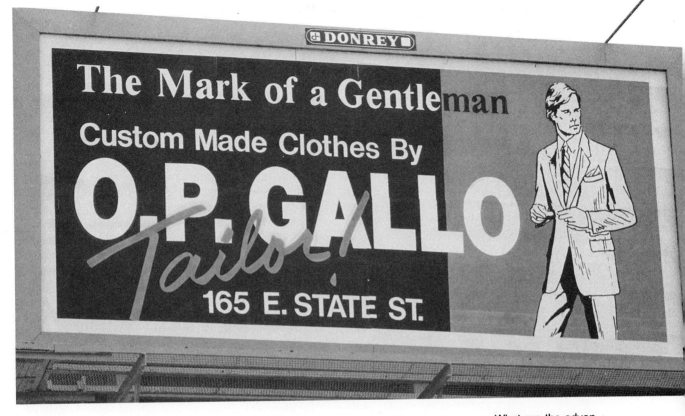

What are the advantages and disadvantages of this type of advertising?

niques to attract consumers' attention. Although these signs have higher attention value, they are quite costly to produce.

Outdoor signs usually are bought in "showings" for periods of time of ninety days and up. A number 100 showing is a number of signs sufficient for a daily exposure of the message to a population equal to that of the market area. Other showing sizes are number 75, 50, 25, and 150; a showing size of 75, for example, means that the number of signs will expose the advertiser's message to 75 percent of the market area. The number of signs in a showing is not fixed. Fewer signs are necessary if they are exposed to heavy traffic, whereas more signs are needed if they are exposed to light-traffic areas. The Traffic Audit Bureau, Inc., audits, by markets, the "circulation" of posters and bulletins (the amount of traffic passing by) and publishes the results in *The Audited Circulation Values of Outdoor Advertising*. The medium's prices are based on these circulation figures.

*Transit advertising* includes car cards, exterior displays, and station posters. *Car cards* are the posters (usually 11 by 28 inches) displayed on interior wall racks in buses, subway trains, and the cars of rapid transit systems. *Exterior displays,* which vary in size, are the advertisements shown on the outside of buses, cars, and taxis. *Station posters* are signs displayed in the interiors of subway, railroad, and rapid-transit stations.

Advertisers buy transit advertising from transit-advertising companies, also known as *operators,* which function much the same as outdoor plant operators. Car cards normally are sold in *runs.* A full run is two cards in every bus, car, and so forth in the market. Half runs and quarter runs are also possible. The rate structure in transit advertising is similar to that of outdoor advertising because it is based on the volume of traffic passing through bus and train routes. The rates for exterior or traveling displays and station posters are not standardized but, as for outdoor showings, are based on the number of people who view them. The cost per thousand for transit advertising is calculated in the same way as for outdoor media. Like outdoor advertising, transit advertising is relatively inexpensive.

*Direct Advertising.* **Direct advertising** is a medium that retailers use extensively to communicate their product offerings to a select group of consumers. The retailer creates an advertisement and distributes it directly to consumers through the mail or through personal distribution of circulars, handbills, and other printed matter. Although direct advertising is expensive in terms of cost per thousand, it is the most selective medium, since the ads are read only by people the retailer selects. It also is a personal form of advertising and extremely flexible. Direct advertising can include pictures, letters, records, pencils, coins, coupons, premiums, samples, and any other gifts the retailer chooses to include.

Retailers may choose to distribute direct advertising to their charge customers or other known or potential customers, or they may buy a mailing list from "mailing-list houses," which sell lists for a certain charge per thousand names. The variety of these lists is astonishing, ranging from magazine subscribers to professional groups to hobbyists to owners of certain products. The retailer never sees these lists; instead, advertising pieces are sent to the mailing-list house, which addresses and mails them. Some retailers prepare their own direct advertising, whereas others choose agencies to prepare it and arrange for distribution.

Unlike most other advertising media, the effectiveness of direct advertising can be directly measured if the advertisement calls for a response or an order. By dividing the total sales resulting from customer responses by the total cost of preparing and distributing the direct-advertising materials, the retailer can establish a measure of the cost per sale or response for this promotion.

---

**CONTROLLING THE ADVERTISING FUNCTION**

To establish some measure of control over its advertising effort, the retailer must evaluate the effects of advertising. The retailer must first establish specific, measurable advertising objectives (discussed at the beginning of this chapter), then acquire or develop instruments and methodologies to determine whether those objectives were met. As mentioned, advertising objectives can be stated in terms of either sales or communications levels. Because sales are affected by factors both internal and external to the retailer's operations, meaningful measurements of **advertising effectiveness** are difficult to make, especially in the long run. Short-run advertising objectives can be measured broadly, however, if we assume very few changes occur in the short run (one day to a week).[5] If noticeable changes do occur in this short run, then the retailer must temper its evaluation of advertising effectiveness in light of this information or consider the evaluation a failure. Given that external and internal factors remain relatively stable, the retailer can make a gross measurement of its advertising's sales effectiveness in two ways. (1) For all advertising messages designed to stimulate immediate sales (such as coupons, half-price sales, etc.), the retailer can measure dollar sales increases, increases in number of purchases, increases in store traffic, and so on against those for a comparable period (e.g., last year at the same time or last week). (2) For any direct-advertising campaign, the retailer can measure in-store and out-of-store inquiries, sales increases, or traffic increases. Increases in sales, consumer traffic, and number of purchases are all important success measurements for advertising. An even more appropriate measure of success of a retail promotion, though, is to compare the gross profits from additional sales generated by the promotion to the cost of the promotion.[6] One method for obtaining this measurement is shown in Figure 15–5.

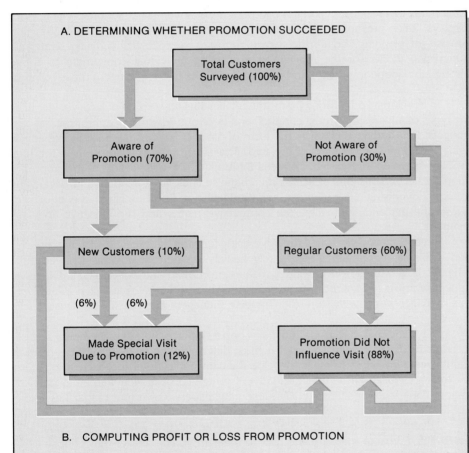

**FIGURE 15–5**
The effectiveness of advertising (source: Irwin Broh, "Measure Success of Promotions with In-Store Customer Surveys," *Marketing News,* 13 May 1983, 17)

A. DETERMINING WHETHER PROMOTION SUCCEEDED

Total Customers Surveyed (100%)

Aware of Promotion (70%)

Not Aware of Promotion (30%)

New Customers (10%)

Regular Customers (60%)

(6%)   (6%)

Made Special Visit Due to Promotion (12%)

Promotion Did Not Influence Visit (88%)

B. COMPUTING PROFIT OR LOSS FROM PROMOTION

| | |
|---|---|
| Made special visit due to promotion | 12% |
| × Number of transactions during promotions | 1,000 |
| = Number of special visits | 120 |
| × Average purchase by customer making a special visit | $20 |
| = Additional sales due to promotion | $2,400 |
| × Gross profit percentage | 40% |
| − Additional gross profit from promotion | $960 |
| − Cost of promotion | $2,000 |
| − Net profit (loss) on promotion | ($1,040) |

Advertising designed to achieve communications objectives should be measured over the long run. Changes in customer awareness, attitudes, perceptions, and behavioral intentions toward the store should be measured either by personal interviews or mail surveys. In this case, the retailer must use both pretest and posttest measurement to establish possible changes in consumers' opinions of the store.

## SUMMARY

Promotion is the fourth element in the retail mix. It involves providing consumers with information about the retailer's store and its offering and influencing their perceptions, attitudes, and behavior. Promotion is also closely related to the communication process because transmitting meaningful messages through the retailer's promotion mix involves the five major components of advertising, personal selling, store displays, sales promotion, and publicity. Managing the retail advertising function consists of planning, organizing, executing, and controlling advertising strategies. Advertising works for the retailer by prompting individual consumers to move through the adoption process and by stimulating the two-step flow of mass communications.

In developing advertising plans, the retailer sets advertising objectives, identifies the types of advertising it must conduct, and develops advertising appropriations and budgets. Retail advertising takes the form of product advertising, institutional advertising, or some combination of the two. The advertising appropriation is the total amount spent on advertising, whereas the budget is the allocation of this appropriation across departments or across merchandise lines, time periods, and advertising media. Advertising appropriation and budgeting methods include the educated-guess, the percentage-of-sales, the competitive parity, and the objective and task methods.

Organizing and executing the advertising function depends heavily on store size and available funds. Small stores rely heavily on outside advertising specialists, whereas large stores normally have a sales promotion and advertising manager to supervise artists, copywriters, publicity directors, and display managers. In addition, this manager works with store merchandise managers and outside advertising specialists.

Executing the advertising function consists of creating advertisements and selecting advertising media. The retailer must determine the purpose of the advertisement, create the basic message, develop the communications approach, and finalize the total advertisement. A total print advertisement consists of layout, headline, illustration, copy, and logotype. Retailers use newspapers, consumer magazines, radio, television, sign media, direct advertising, and numerous other miscellaneous media.

Advertising control, the job of evaluating advertising effectiveness, consists of determining what to measure and how to measure it. The retailer may choose either sales or communications measures and from among numerous methods of measuring advertising effectiveness.

## STUDENT STUDY GUIDE

### KEY TERMS AND CONCEPTS

advertising

advertisement message

advertising agency

advertising budget

advertising effectiveness

advertising freelancer

audience selectivity

communication effectiveness

communication process

communications approach

competitive parity method

cooperative advertising

copy

cost

coverage

DAGMAR

decoding

direct advertising

educated-guess method

encoding

feedback

flexibility

frequency

geographic selectivity

headline

illustration

immediacy

impact

institutional advertising

layout

life

logotype

magazine advertising

media representative

newspaper advertising

noise

objective and task method

opinion leaders

percentage-of-sales method

personal selling

prestige

product advertising

promotion

publicity

radio advertising

receivers

sales promotion

senders

sign advertising

store displays

television advertising

total advertisement

transmission

two-step flow of communications

---

**REVIEW QUESTIONS**

1. Identify and briefly describe the various participants, processes, and acts of the communication process.
2. List the five elements of the promotion mix. Define each element.
3. How is product advertising different from institutional advertising?
4. What is the purpose of an advertising objective aimed at store positioning?
5. What considerations should the retailer take into account when allocating advertising budgets?
6. Describe the four-step objective and task method of determining the retailer's advertising budget.
7. Do retailers make extensive use of advertising agencies? Why or why not?
8. In developing the basic advertising message, the retailer is concerned with which two issues?
9. Which two general communication approaches are used to convey the retailer's message?
10. List the five components of a total advertisement and define each component.
11. Which media characteristics do retailers consider when selecting the most appropriate types of media for communicating with their consumers?
12. Newspapers sell two kinds of advertising space. What are they? How is newspaper space measured?
13. Explain the following newspaper advertising concepts: open rate, space contract, ROP, and position charge.
14. How are newspaper rate structures determined?

15. Identify the positive and negative aspects of magazine advertising from the retailer's viewpoint.
16. How is radio advertising sold?
17. From the retailer's perspective, what are the positive and negative characteristics of television advertising?
18. What are the three types of outdoor advertising? Describe each type.

## REVIEW EXAM

True or False

_____ 1. The difference beween advertising and publicity is that advertising refers to television media and publicity refers to print media.
_____ 2. In cooperative advertising, the retailer and the manufacturer split the cost of media space.
_____ 3. The "percentage of sale" method of setting advertising expenditures is generally accepted as the best means to determine an advertising budget.
_____ 4. Copy is the store's distinct signature, which appears in all advertising.
_____ 5. Radio advertising is characterized by greater immediacy than magazine advertising.
_____ 6. Television advertising is the most important advertising medium for retailers as defined by total advertising expenditures.
_____ 7. Direct advertising is one of the least expensive methods of advertising.

## STUDENT APPLICATIONS MANUAL

## PROJECTS: INVESTIGATIONS AND APPLICATIONS

1. To benefit from the "two-step flow of communication process," the retailer must identify, reach, and work with opinion leaders. For specific products and/or stores in your community, identify potential opinion leaders, describe how the retailer might secure their cooperation, and discuss some specific examples of how retailers and opinion leaders might work together to create greater consumer awareness of the retailer, to enhance store image, and to promote store traffic.
2. By surveying your local newspaper, identify advertisements directed toward the objectives of (1) building store image, (2) positioning the store in the market, (3) generating store traffic, and(4) creating special events. Which of your advertisements is most effective in accomplishing its objective? Why?
3. Discuss the pros and cons of participating in "cooperative advertising." Under what circumstances should a retailer agree to cooperative advertising?
4. Discuss why a retailer might elect to heavily promote high-markup, low-turnover products and to de-emphasize or eliminate the promotion of low-markup, high-turnover products.
5. Assume the following retailers have budgeted 3 percent of their estimated $600,000 sales volume for advertising: (1) a record and tape store, (3) a campus book store, and (3) a children's shoe store. Identify and describe the major media and time considerations they need to bear in mind in allocating their advertising budgets. Develop a media and time allocating their advertising budgets. Develop a media and time allocation plan for each store and justify each plan.
6. Identify two retailers in your community that currently do not have a "logo." For each retailer, develop a distinctive logo that they could use with their advertising. Be creative!
7. List four major radio stations that serve your community. Interview each station manager and determine the audience selectivity of each station. Identify the types of retailers that would best be served by each station. Explain.

## CASE 15-1
### Barbara's Florist—Planning Advertising Appropriation*

Barbara's Florist, owned and operated by Greg and Barbara Berry, is a full-service florist shop which had operated in Austin, Texas, for nearly twenty years. Barbara's primarily sold cut flowers, arrangements, and plants. The store offered home delivery and was a member of the FTD national network of florists.

Barbara's stressed its ability to handle large weddings, religious celebrations, and funerals. The store employed three designers of floral arrangements (including Barbara Berry) and all of the designers plus Greg Berry and a part-time cashier performed sales duties. All of the full-time employees had considerable expertise with respect to the plants they handled.

Currently, Barbara's imports most of its fresh-cut flowers and all of its roses from California, Florida, or outside the United States. Last year Barbara's instituted a unique pricing policy of undercutting other florists. In fact, almost two-thirds of Barbara's stock sold for less than a dollar per stem. Lower prices were believed to have increased the volume of sales and helped to differentiate Barbara's from other florists.

Despite lower prices, Barbara's marketed only high-quality floral items. Because consumers perceived a strong, direct correlation between the price of flowers and their quality, Barbara's management believed it as important to stress quality as price in promotional efforts.

## FLORIST INDUSTRY TRENDS

The fact that nationally most florists were small businesses was not an indication that they were struggling financially. On the contrary, the industry was in good health despite a reasonably prolonged period of tight money, inflation, and cost-consciousness by consumers.

As an industry, florists had experienced steady growth over the last five years, and sales were projected to increase in the neighborhood of 15 percent during the coming year. Florists had done particularly well in the growing market for fresh-cut roses and other flowers. Twenty percent of total industry sales were roses, and the growth of this segment was expected to continue to be very strong.

However, a threat of some concern to the florist industry's growth was the entrance of supermarkets, nurseries, and discount stores into the fresh-cut flower market. These new entries had in the past concentrated their efforts in the green plants market and had met relatively little success because of the overall weakness of this market. However, many of these larger retailers had begun carrying fresh-cut flowers at lower prices than florists could match. Although at the present time approximately 88 percent of the purchasers of such flowers buy from a florist, the new entries into this market introduced some uncertainty with respect to the long-run structure of the fresh-cut flower market.

Historically, florists had higher sales in the months of April, May, and December (see Exhibit 1). Further, roughly 80 percent of all purchases of floral items were for use as gifts and 20 percent were bought for personal use. Flowers and plants were generally considered a "safe" gift in that they were emotionally appealing and the vast majority of people appreciated receiving them.

National FTD data indicated that the times or reasons for flower purchases as gifts were as follows: get well, 15 percent; funeral, 14 percent; anniversary, 13 percent; Mother's Day, 11 percent; surprise, 10 percent; birthday, 9 percent; holiday, 8 percent, and others, 20 percent. (Note that inclusion of non-FTD sales by local FTD members would change these estimates somewhat.) Further, most flower purchases were singular in nature. That is, they were bought on a cash-and-carry basis exclusive of other flower purchases. The

Source: Charles Patti and John Murphy, *Cases In Advertising and Promotion Management* (New York: John Wiley & Sons, 1983): 123–128.

**EXHIBIT 1**
Percentage of Retail
Sales by Month

|  | Jan. | Feb. | Mar. | Apr. | May | June | July | Aug. | Sept. | Oct. | Nov. | Dec. |
|---|---|---|---|---|---|---|---|---|---|---|---|---|
| All retail stores | 7.0 | 6.9 | 8.2 | 8.0 | 8.4 | 8.5 | 8.2 | 8.8 | 8.2 | 8.6 | 8.9 | 10.3 |
| Florists | 6.7 | 8.2 | 7.5 | 10.0 | 13.7 | 6.3 | 6.2 | 5.8 | 6.4 | 6.7 | 7.0 | 15.5 |

Source: U.S. Department of Commerce and Florists' Transworld Delivery Assn.

most frequently purchased items were arrangements, which accounted for slightly less than 50 percent of all flower purchases nationwide from florists.

## TARGET MARKETS

In organizing the firm's marketing efforts, Barbara's management identified two distinct target markets. The firm's primary market consisted of students attending the University of Texas. The secondary market consisted of individuals who lived or worked in close geographic proximity (within one mile) to Barbara's location. This geographic market area included downtown Austin, student neighborhoods, and some very affluent residential areas west of downtown and the university.

The University of Texas student body was a transitory market that experienced considerable turnover each year. The enrollment figures for the most recent academic year were as follows: fall, 48,000; spring, 44,000; and summer, 20,000. These students were primarily aged 18 to 22, were 50 percent female, came from middle- and upper-middle-income families, and had considerable discretionary income.

The individuals in the secondary target were primarily upscale adults who lived near Barbara's. Past expeience indicated that these adults tended to be either young professionals, age 25 to 35, evenly split between men and women, or older adults, age 50+, primarily females. These adult prospects were almost all upscale demographically in terms of income, value of home, education, employment classification, and so on.

## COMPETITION

Barbara's competed in a market that was highly fragmented, with no truly dominant florist competitor. Most of the 93 local firms listed in the Yellow Pages under "Florists—Retail" could be classified as reasonably small businesses grossing under $100,000 per year. Eighty-nine percent of Austin's florists had only one location. Freytag's had the most locations with five, and another larger florists—Connely-Hillen—had three locations. The bulk of the other multiple outlet florists had two locations.

Five of Barbara's competitors appeared to cater to some extent to the university market. Significantly, all five were located in close proximity to the university campus. Barbara's location, approximately a half mile from the campus, put the firm at a disadvantage. To help compensate for this disadvantage, Barbara's prices were set somewhat lower than these direct competitors. In addition, Barbara's had initiated a much larger advertising effort directed toward university students than any of the other florists.

## CURRENT SALES AND ADVERTISING

During the current year, Barbara's had total projected sales of $151,000 (see Exhibit 2 for a breakdown of sales by month). It is important to note, however, that the current year was unusual in that a flood in late May had almost completely destroyed the shop and necessitated a move to a new location across the street. As a result, Barbara's had no sales in

|  | Sales | Ad Expenditures |
|---|---|---|
| January | $ 10,000 | $ 220 |
| February | 16,000 | 360 |
| March | 10,000 | 220 |
| April | 16,000 | 220 |
| May | 17,000 | 420 |
| June | 0 | 0 |
| July | 11,000 | 700 |
| August | 11,000 | 800 |
| September | 8,000 | 850 |
| October | 14,000[a] | 1,050[a] |
| November | 18,000[a] | 700[a] |
| December | 20,000[a] | 700[a] |
|  | $151,000[a] | $6,240[a] |

[a]Estimated.
Source: Company records and management forecasts.

June. Sales of flowers and plants this year were projected to break down roughly as follows: individual cut flowers, 10 percent; arrangements, 75 percent; and plants, 15 percent.

Barbara's was projected to invest approximately $6,240 in advertising during the current year. This total was broken down by media vehicles as follows: *Daily Texan* (student newspaper), $1,200; *Austin American Statesman,* $1,000; radio, $2,400; television, $0; magazines, $0; circulars, $680; and Yellow Pages (quarter page), $960. A complete summary of ad spending projections by month for the current year is presented in Exhibit 2.

## NEXT YEAR'S ADVERTISING BUDGET

In developing an advertising plan for next year, Barbara's management wanted to make greater use of advertising to help achieve a $60,000 increase in sales over the current year. Management was convinced that this was a realistic goal based on the assumption of an effective and expanded advertising commitment. They were willing to invest a percentage of forecasted sales well beyond the florist industry-wide average percentage of advertising-to-sales ratio to achieve this growth and to build their consumer franchise for the future.

As a part of an increased emphasis on advertising, management had approved a new series of print ads for next year. Management felt these ads were appropriate and would do much to build Barbara's image and, at the same time, help to increase sales. The new campaign's ads were viewed as appropriate for both target markets.

Management's task now was to determine an appropriate advertising appropriation for the coming year and to develop a reasonable rationale supporting the recommended amount. In addition, after identifying an appropriate total amount to invest in advertising, management would develop a budget allocation and supporting rationale.

The proposed budget, to cover January 1 through December 31, was to be allocated across each of the following categories: by media types and vehicles, by target markets, by product lines, and by months of the year. Further, the budget was to include a contingency fund to ensure some flexibility in the conduct of Barbara's advertising program.

Finally, management was convinced that next year's media schedule should include monthly ads in *Third Coast* magazine. It was believed that this tabloid-sized magazine publication would represent a "good buy" in reaching both the primary and secondary target markets. At this point, it had become clear that decisions related to both budgeting and media planning were interrelated. Representative media costs are presented in Exhibits 3–5.

**EXHIBIT 3**
Newspaper(s): Monthly
Earned Rate (per column inch—columns
wide × inches deep)

| | Austin American-Stateman[a] | | Daily Texan[b] | |
| Inches | Daily | Sunday | Inches | Daily |
|---|---|---|---|---|
| Open | $14.25 | $15.25 | Open | $5.69 |
| 1–24 | 11.83 | 12.76 | 20 | 5.13 |
| 25 | 10.66 | 11.50 | 50 | 4.40 |
| 50 | 9.85 | 10.63 | 100 | 4.22 |
| 100 | 9.52 | 10.27 | 200 | 4.01 |
| 500 | 9.32 | 10.05 | 300 | 3.82 |
| 1,000 | 9.20 | 9.93 | 400 | 3.70 |
| 2,000 | 9.07 | 9.78 | 500 | 3.58 |
| 5,000 | 8.93 | 9.63 | 750 | 3.51 |
| 7,000 | 8.49 | 9.15 | 1,000 | 3.45 |

[a]Additional charge for color daily or Sunday: 1 color = $390; 2 color = $528; 3 color = $624. Minimum ad size = 70 inches.

[b]Additional charge for color: 1 color = $130; 2 color = $170; 3 color = $205. Minimum ad size = 50 inches.

**EXHIBIT 4**
Magazine: *Third Coast*
(published monthly,
black and white only)

| Ad Size | 1x | 3x | 6x | 12x |
|---|---|---|---|---|
| Full Page | $625 | $570 | $535 | $495 |
| 2/3 | 460 | 420 | 405 | 390 |
| 1/2 | 395 | 360 | 340 | 315 |
| 1/3 | 290 | 265 | 240 | 215 |
| 1/4 | 230 | 205 | 185 | 170 |
| 1/6 | 170 | 150 | 135 | 120 |

**EXHIBIT 5**
Broadcast (30-second spots):
*KLBJ FM*
Mornings (6–10) and
evenings (3–10)
Thursday, Friday,
Saturday   $44
Monday, Tuesday,
Wednesday   $39

| KTBC Channel 7 (CBS) | | KTVV Channel 36 (NBC) | |
|---|---|---|---|
| 7–9 A.M. | $40 | 7–9 A.M. | $25 |
| 9–11:30 A.M. | 50 | 9–12 A.M. | 20 |
| 11:30–3:30 P.M. | 125 | 12–12:30 P.M. | 25 |
| 3:30–4:00 P.M. | 70 | 12:30–1 A.M. | 20 |
| 4–5 P.M. | 50 | 1–3 P.M. | 25 |
| 5–5:30 P.M. | 150 | 3–5 P.M. | 45 |
| 5:30–6 P.M. | 350 | 5–5:30 P.M. | 65 |
| 6–6:30 P.M. | 400 | 6–7 P.M. | 105 |
| 6:30–7 P.M. | 300 | 10:30–11:30 P.M. | 105 |
| 10–10:30 P.M. | 450 | | |
| 10:30–11 P.M. | 400 | | |

**ASSIGNMENT**

1. In planning the advertising appropriation for the coming year, how large a role is the level of investment during the current year likely to play? What impact might the new advertising campaign (see Exhibit 2) have on deciding how much to invest in advertising?

2. How realistic is the sales increase forecasted for the coming year? How should this forecast be related to the level of advertising investment?

3. What are the major considerations that should be evaluated in establishing an amount to invest in advertising? What factors are most important in allocating the advertising investment across budget categories, such as target markets and months of the year?

## CASE 15–2
## Campbell Clothiers—Assessing an Advertising Opportunity*

### BACKGROUND

Campbell Clothiers is a local chain of specialty stores that offers an extensive selection of men's and women's sporting and casual apparel and accessories. By appealing to the up-scale tastes of middle- and upper-class consumers for fashionable casual and sporting apparel, Gabe and Sandy Campbell have successfully expanded their operation to include nine stores in northeastern Ohio. The success of Campbell Clothiers can be attributed to a number of merchandising factors. Campbell's is known for its unique offering of high-quality product lines, plush yet exciting store atmospherics, friendly and competent salespeople, and image-building promotions.

Campbell's tends to limit its product selection to middle and upper pricing lines and points; however, the store's January and July clearance sales have almost become a legend in the local area as a value-packed sales promotion. Although each of these factors has been an important ingredient in Campbell's successful merchandising blend, the store's management team believes the most important overall success ingredient is the organization's commitment to maintaining and cultivating its image of exclusivity. At Campbell Clothiers, exclusive means being unique, selective, different, tasteful, and distinctive in all of its merchandising activities.

### CURRENT SITUATION

The morning had started peacefully for Jacqueline Theiss, sales promotion manager for Campbell Clothiers. As usual it did not stay that way. Campbell's new sportswear buyer, Kris Kovach, burst into Theiss' office:

*Kris:* Jacqueline, I just heard that Michizuki cancelled its sponsorship of the Super Bowl of Golf. This is a great opportunity to promote our new line of men's and women's sportswear by Outdoor World! A 20-percent-off sale would really draw in customer traffic.

*Jacqueline:* What makes you think that?

*Kris:* Surely, WWTV is going to have to unload a lot of local air time in a hurry. If we act fast I know we can get some prime time slots at bargain rates. A sale this early in the season would really attract some attention.

*Jacqueline:* Where do you propose we get the money for this unexpected blessing? Not to mention the fact that two weeks is hardly enough time to plan, schedule, shoot, and edit a commercial.

*Kris:* You must have some money stuck away somewhere. And, I have already checked with Outdoor World and they have several canned commercials avail-

---

*This case was prepared by Kenneth Mast and Dale Lewison, The University of Akron.

able for a small fee. All we would have to do is add our sales promotional message and store identification to the end of the film.

*Jacqueline:* Assuming we can find the money—which is a big assumption—and these canned commercials are available and acceptable, is it worthwhile to spend this type of money on this particular product line?

*Kris:* You bet it is! Outdoor World is a well known national brand, it offers something for both men and women, and we have sufficient stock in all of our stores to support this type of sales promotion effort.

*Jacqueline:* Well Kris, I have a meeting in five minutes. Let me think about it and I will get back to you with a decision by tomorrow afternoon.

*Kris:* OK, but we need to act quickly or we will lose this opportunity. I would really appreciate your support on this; it can be a successful campaign.

After her 10 o'clock meeting and lunch, Theiss contacted her account representative at WWTV and learned that Michizuki had in fact cancelled its sponsorship of the Super Bowl of Golf; Theiss was offered a 30-percent discount off the rate book price for local spots during the tournament. The minimum number of 30-second spots was six: four spots on Saturday and two spots on Sunday. In a quick mental calculation, Theiss determined the total minimum cost would be approximately $30,000 for air time. She indicated her interest in the spots and informed the account representative that she would make a decision within 24 hours.

The considerable time constraints surrounding the decision and numerous other pressing business matters led Theiss to seek help from Tyler Smith, the advertising manager for Campbell Clothiers. In the lengthy discussion that ensued, Theiss identified several key issues.

1. The $30,000 minimum price tag for air time would consume about 40 percent of Campbell's reserve advertising budget set aside each year for unexpected situations. It would leave a $45,000 reserve for the remainder of the year. This assumes that the expected $5,000 needed for producing the commercial and paying the fees asked by Outdoor World could be found elsewhere.

2. Kris Kovach has already spent most of her promotional budget and an examination of her promotional expenditures revealed inadequate support of the Outdoor World line of sportswear. Through luncheon and grapevine conversations, Theiss discovered that the line was not selling as well as had been expected and that Kovach was feeling a great deal of heat from the general merchandise manager.

3. Although the Super Bowl of Golf is the single most important local sporting event during the year, its appeal is still limited to a rather select group of customers.

4. WWTV is a satellite station affiliate of the national network that has broadcasting rights to the Super Bowl of Golf. WWTV is a UHF station whose broadcast signal provides only partial coverage of the company's nine-store trading areas. Specifically, WWTV provides 100 percent coverage of five store trading areas, 50 percent coverage of two store trading areas, and little or no coverage for two trading areas.

With the key issues of concern being identified, Tyler agreed to drop everything and to study the entire situation. He thought that by noon tomorrow he could recommend possible alternative courses of action.

## ASSIGNMENT

Assume Tyler Smith's role. Write a report outlining the various alternative courses of action. Recommend which alternative action the company should pursue and provide a complete justification for your recommendation.

**ENDNOTES**

1. Stephen Phillips, "Can the Closeout King Unload Its Woes?" *Business Week,* 7 Dec. 1987, 94.
2. Laurie Freeman, "Wal-Mart Blankets Wisconsin," *Advertising Age,* 17 Aug. 1987, 26MW.
3. Scott Hume, "McDonald's Heavy in Print for Nutrition," *Advertising Age,* 19 Jan. 1987, 2.
4. David Kettlewell, "Positioning, Not Sales, Is Real Value of Wendy's Ad," *Format* (June 1984): 1.
5. See "Ad Effectiveness: Can It Be Calculated?" *Chain Store Age Executive* (September 1987): 64–68.
6. Irwin Broh, "Measure Success of Promotions with In-Store Customer Surveys," *Marketing News,* 13 May 1983, 17.

# 16

**Outline**

**Objectives**

- ☐ Explain why the basis for personal selling is good communications.
- ☐ Identify the traits and skills of a good salesperson.
- ☐ Name and discuss the seven steps of the retail selling process.
- ☐ Describe procedures for training, motivating, and evaluating salespeople.

# Personal Selling

"In a product's long journey from the producer to the customer, the last two feet are the most important. That 'last two feet' is the distance across the sales counter."[1] Retail selling is a special kind of selling whereby the customer comes to the store with a general or specific need in mind. The retail salesperson must close the sale while the customer is still in the store; otherwise, the sale might be lost forever.[2]

**Personal selling** is, perhaps, the most important element in the store image-creating process. Salespeople are usually the first people in the store to interact with customers on a face-to-face basis; thus, they have tremendous influence on how consumers perceive a store. In sum, salespeople are a significant factor in enhancing or detracting from the consumer's total impressions of a retail store. This chapter covers personal selling as a communication process, the characteristics of a good salesperson, and the steps in the retail selling process.

**PERSONAL COMMUNICATIONS**

The basis for *all* personal selling is personal communications. Communication is *not* something you do *to* someone, but something you do *with* someone. **Personal communication** is the process of exchanging ideas and meanings with other people. Although one person is listening, even that person is active, not passive, in every communications situation. Figure 16–1 shows the basic elements of the communications interaction between a customer and a salesperson.

The model also illustrates that both customer and salesperson are simultaneously sending and receiving information. The transmission and reception of information come in many forms, such as words, objects, fragrances, colors, gestures, appearances, music, and voice qualities (e.g., emotionally irritated, elated), to name but a few modes. With all of these communications channels occurring at the same time, a good salesperson must be a good listener and observer and adapt quickly to each moment in the selling situation.

**THE EFFECTIVE SALESPERSON**

Whether a salesperson is an "order getter" or an "order taker," certain qualities or characteristics are needed to be effective. **Order getters** must be aggressive to obtain sales. They must persuade customers that what they are selling is best for them. Order getters use creative selling approaches to sell the product, the store, and themselves. These people are responsible for creating sales through persuasive com-

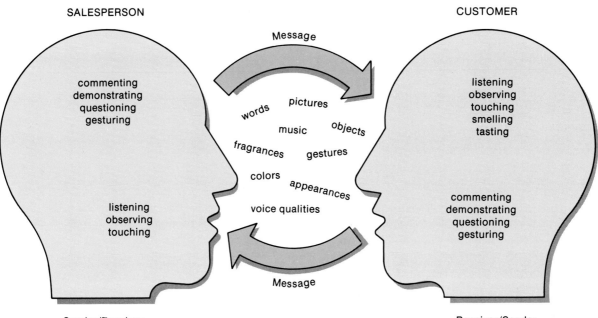

SALESPERSON

Message

commenting
demonstrating
questioning
gesturing

words   pictures
music   objects
fragrances   gestures
colors   appearances
voice qualities

listening
observing
touching

Sender/Receiver

CUSTOMER

listening
observing
touching
smelling
tasting

commenting
demonstrating
questioning
gesturing

Message

Receiver/Sender

**FIGURE 16–1**

A communications model of the customer–salesperson interaction (a partial adaptation from Robert F. Spohn and Robert Y. Allen, *Retailing* [Reston, VA: Reston Publishing, 1977], 236)

munications. Examples of order getters are salespeople in jewelry stores, clothing stores, and appliance stores and encyclopedia and insurance salespeople. **Order takers** simply comply with customers' requests for certain types of merchandise. Examples of order takers are gasoline attendants and counter persons at fast-food restaurants. Although they have little room for creative selling, order takers can increase sales through minimal suggestive selling, such as "Would you like french fries with your order?" The more difficult job (and more rewarding) is order getting. Although most of the characteristics described in this section apply more to the order getter, they are traits that can also help order takers to be successful. Characteristics of an effective salesperson fall into four categories: physical traits, personality traits, individual skills, and message-presentation skills.

### Physical Traits

Although there may be a fine line between **physical traits,** such as personal grooming and hygiene, and personality traits, they are sufficiently different to discuss separately. Clean clothing, shined shoes, clean, well-groomed hair, clean teeth and fresh breath, a well-shaven, clean-smelling body, and a pleasant smile are essential. Of course, these physical features can quickly be negated by an unpleasant personality. These traits will not be elaborated upon; every person is aware of them. Obviously, personal grooming and hygiene are extremely important ingredients in good personal selling.

### Personality Traits

**Personality traits** are individual characteristics people acquire over a lifetime. These traits become an inherent part of a person through prior learning. Good salespeople have developed personality traits of sociability, curiosity, imagination, creativity, enthusiasm, sincerity, ambition, and reliability. Good salespeople get along with people, want to know, want to try new ways, want to do something different, have great interest in their work, are honest about their work and dealings with others, want to achieve certain self-imposed objectives, and state the truth about the product they sell.

## Individual Skills

One can develop **individual selling skills** if one is willing to work on them. (It can, however, be difficult to separate individual skills from personality traits over time.) Based on research, several skills an individual can acquire are (1) perceived expertise, (2) perceived credibility, (3) positive attitude, (4) good listenership, (5) salesperson–customer similarity, and (6) adaptability.

*Expertise.* Salespeople whom customers **perceive as expert** have a much greater chance of making a sale than salespeople whom customers perceive as having less expertise. People who are high in expertise are those who are more qualified than others to speak on a particular topic. Salespeople with special education or training, information, and knowledge to talk about the product they sell have the expertise to be effective at their job. The key word in this discussion, however, is *perceived.* No matter how expert the salesperson, selling effectiveness depends on whether the customer *perceives* the person as an expert.

*Credibility.* Similarly, how effective a salesperson will be in making a sale depends partly on how **credible the customer perceives** the person to be. The more credible a salesperson is perceived to be, the more sales are likely to be made. A credible salesperson is believable, trustworthy, and honest in dealing with customers. Research in this area shows strong evidence of the persuasive powers of people who are perceived as credible.

*Attitude.* A salesperson is more effective with a positive rather than a negative attitude toward himself or herself, the message (and product), and the customer. A **positive attitude** means self-confidence, not arrogance. Successful salespeople have confidence in their abilities to do their job. A salesperson also must have a positive attitude toward the product and what is said about it. If the salesperson does not believe in the product, why should the customer? Finally, a salesperson must have a positive attitude toward customers, demonstrated by paying careful attention to what the customer says, showing respect for the customer, and not "talking down" to the customer. Customers quickly notice a salesperson's positive attitude toward them and react favorably to it.

*Listening Skills.* Salespeople too often overlook **listening skills**. Some sales clerks are so busy talking and listening to themselves that they fail to listen to their customers. Failure to be a good listener can lead to lost sales. If they do not listen carefully, salespeople cannot determine customers' needs, wants, or preferences. Good listening skills not only improve the salesperson's chances of making a sale but also can provide feedback through the salesperson to top management about

**FIGURE 16–2**
Guidelines for developing good listening skills

1. Do not only listen to the words themselves, but also watch carefully for nonverbal cues to the real intentions of the customer.
2. Practice being interested in what customers have to say. Remember you are not always the most interesting person around.
3. Be sensitive to the customer's personal pronouns, such as "I", "we", "you", "us" and "our". These are cues to things that really interest the customer.
4. Do not be distracted by peculiarities in the speech of the customer.
5. Establish eye contact with customer.
6. Ask clarifying questions to test your understanding of a message.
7. Shut up and listen when the customer wants to talk.
8. Relax. Try not to give the customer the impression that you are just waiting to jump in and start talking.
9. Do not assume you understand the customer's problem or need. Keep listening while they keep talking.
10. Listen for ideas, not just words.

Source: Ronald B. Marks, *Personal Selling,* 2d ed. (Boston: Allyn and Bacon, Inc., 1985), 130–31.

changes that might be made in store policies, merchandise lines, and a variety of other aspects of store operations. Figure 16–2 presents some guidelines for developing good listening skills.

*Similarity.* People are persuaded more by a communicator they perceive to be similar to themselves. Salespersons who can quickly discover a **salesperson–customer**

Describe the perceived salesperson–customer similarity in this selling situation.

**similarity** can capitalize on this common characteristic to enhance their chances of making the sale. A salesperson can detect similarities by asking questions, listening, and observing. For example, if the customer is accompanied by children and the salesperson is a parent, the subject can be brought up in conversation. The more specific the similarities, the better. *Perceived similarity* can be based on personality, dress, race, skin color, religion, politics, interests, group affiliations, and many more attributes. Clever salespersons quickly determine similarities between themselves and their customers and use them in casual talk. The simple rule here is to either show or express some similarity between salespersons and their customers.

*Adaptability.* **Good salespeople demonstrate adaptability** to differences in customer types. Figure 16–3 shows the types of customers that salespeople will encounter and suggests how they should react to each type. Salespeople must learn to identify customer types and adapt accordingly, without losing their own identity.

## Message-Presentation Skills

Through training, salespeople can develop **skills in message presentation** that will help them become more persuasive and increase sales.

*Message Strategy.* Salespeople can present merchandise to customers either by explaining only the product's strengths and benefits (one-sided message) or by describing the product's weaknesses as well as strengths (two-sided message). Although it might sound strange to mention a product's weaknesses to customers (or the strength of competitors' products), this strategy works under certain circumstances. When consumers are not knowledgeable about a product, however, the general rule is to present a one-sided message; that is, to be more persuasive and produce more sales, it is better to tell them only about benefits, advantages, and strengths. When customers lack product knowledge, they are unable to comprehend product weaknesses and will become confused if the salesperson tries to explain them. Therefore, to this audience, sell *only the strong points of the product.*

On the other hand, if the salesperson is presenting a product to a customer who is very knowledgeable about the product, the best strategy is to explain the product's strengths as well as its weaknesses or to describe both the product's strengths and the competing products' strengths. Since the customer is knowledgeable about the product, he or she will have already recognized the weakness in the merchandise or the strengths of other retailers' products. Do not, therefore, insult the customer's product knowledge or intelligence. Instead, salespeople should admit to *minor* weaknesses in a brand or *minor* strengths in those of competitors. Customers will respect the salesperson's honesty and he or she will be more credible to them. When using the two-sided message, one's own merchandise "wins"—there are fewer weaknesses in one's merchandise or fewer strengths in competitors' brands. Determining a customer's knowledge level can produce good results.

*Message Positioning.* Salespeople should place their strongest selling points at the beginning (opening) and the end (closing) of the message, *never* in the middle. Psychologists tell us that people remember the beginning and ending of a message better than the middle. Salespeople, therefore, should always capture the customer's

| Basic Types of Customer | Basic Characteristic | Secondary Characteristic | Other Characteristics | What Salesperson Should Say or Do |
|---|---|---|---|---|
| Arguer | Takes issue with each statement of salesperson | Disbelieves claims, tries to catch salesperson in error | Cautious, slow to decide | Demonstrate; show product knowledge; use "Yes, but . . ." |
| Chip on shoulder | Definitely in a bad mood | Indignation; angry at slight provocation | Acts as if being deliberately baited | Avoid argument; stick to basic facts; show good assortment |
| Decisive | Knows what is wanted | Customer confident choice is right | Not interested in another opinion—respects sales person's brevity | Win sale—not argument; sell self; tactfully inject opinion |
| Doubting Thomas | Doesn't trust sales talk | Hates to be managed | Arrives at decision cautiously | Back up merchandise statements by manufacturers' tags, labels; demonstrate merchandise; let customer handle merchandise |
| Fact-finder | Interested in factual information—detailed | Alert to sales person's errors in description | Looks for actual tags and labels | Emphasize label and manufacturer's facts; volunteer care information |
| Hesitant | Ill at ease—sensitive | Shopping at unaccustomed price range | Unsure of own judgment | Make customer comfortable; use friendliness and respect |
| Impulsive | Quick to decide or select | Impatience | Liable to break off sale abruptly | Close rapidly; avoid oversell, overtalk; note key points |
| Look around | Little ability to make own decisions | Anxious—fearful of making a mistake | Wants sales person's aid in decision—wants adviser—wants to do "right thing" | Emphasize merits of product and service, "zeroing" in on customer-expressed needs and doubts |
| Procrastinator | I'll wait 'til tomorrow | Lacks confidence in own judgment | Insecure | Reinforce customers' judgments |
| Silent | Not talking—but thinking! | Appears indifferent but truly listening | Appears nonchalant | Ask direct questions—straightforward approach |
| Think it over | Refers to need to consult someone | Looking for another adviser | Not sure of own uncertainty | Get agreement on small points; draw out opinions; use points agreed upon for close |

Source: C. Winston Borgen, *Learning Experiences in Retailing* (Santa Monica, CA: Goodyear Publishing), 293.

**FIGURE 16–3**

Customer types and what salespersons should say or do

attention with strong points of the merchandise at the beginning of the sales presentation and summarize those points in the closing.

*Customer Conclusions.* The general selling rule is to draw a conclusion in the sales presentation, summarizing reasons the product is right for the customer. Unfortunately, many customers cannot add together the logical statements they hear as to why they should purchase the merchandise. Therefore, the salesperson should do it for them by quickly summarizing major points and telling them (in conclusion) why they should buy. The exception to this rule is when one encounters highly intelligent people who can easily draw conclusions for themselves and drawing a conclusion insults the intelligence of the prospective buyer.

*Customer Participation.* Salespeople are more likely to sell a product when they can get the prospective buyer to try it as they explain its benefits. Psychologists tell us that *active participation* not only helps consumers learn the benefits of a product but also helps persuade them to purchase it. The rule in retail selling is to let customers touch, feel, smell, taste, and hear the product. Get them to take a test drive, taste the sausage, smell the ham, feel the power as they maneuver the dials, play the video game, see how the diamond ring looks on the hand. Customers' active involvement and participation with the product in the store is a powerful selling technique— perhaps the most effective way to present the "message."

*Message Appeals.* All people have emotions, and the "heart" often rules the mind. Salespeople must recognize and use their customers' emotions to good advantage. We all would like to believe we make buying decisions rationally and logically, but usually we do not. Instead, we purchase most products largely on an emotional basis. To ourselves we say, "Doesn't this dress look nice on me!" "This car is sexy (therefore it makes me sexy)," "Won't my husband think I'm a good cook if I use this brand of product!" Given these emotional aspects of purchase behavior, salespeople should acquire the skill of describing their merchandise in emotional terms.

---

Several basic steps occur in every selling situation. The length of time that a salesperson takes in each step depends on the product, the customer, and the selling situation. The seven steps of the retail selling process appear in Figure 16–4.

**THE RETAIL SELLING PROCESS**

### Preparing for Customers

Preparing for the customer is the first step in the selling process. In this stage, the salesperson does the *preliminary* work necessary for effective interaction with the customer. This stage can be subdivided into long-run preparation and short-run preparation.

In long-run preparation, the salesperson learns store policies and procedures and gains knowledge about the merchandise. These learning activities include becoming familiar with store operating procedures, return policies, and guarantees; learning to operate merchandise that the store (or department) sells; and knowing manufacturer warranties—to name but a few. Short-term preparations are daily and weekly activities, including learning what merchandise is currently in stock; which

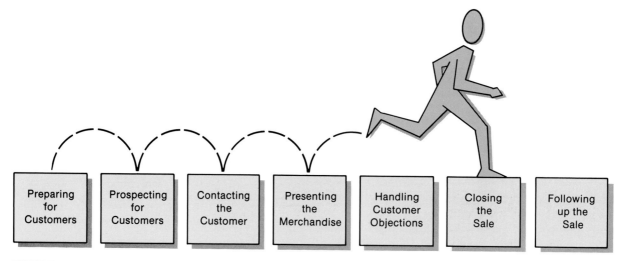

**FIGURE 16–4**

The seven steps of the
retail selling process

items are on sale; recent changes in store policies and operating procedures; changes that have occurred in new styles, fashions, and models of merchandise; and dozens of other day-to-day store happenings.

In both the short and long run, store management and the salesperson share in the responsibility for preparing to meet customers. Management must continually inform salespeople in a prompt, clear way about store operating policies and procedures. Salespeople must constantly update themselves on changes in merchandise, manufacturers' policies relating to the merchandise, and the store's literature and sales aids. For either party to fail in these responsibilities could mean lost sales.

### Prospecting for Customers

Prospecting is the process of finding people who are *willing* to buy the merchandise a store has to offer and are *able* to pay for that merchandise. Salespeople learn through experience how to spot good prospects. Good prospects generally display more interest in the merchandise than poor prospects who are "just browsing." A variety of behavioral cues set good prospects apart from the poor prospects; for example, carrying several bags of merchandise from other stores is often a clue to a shopper's interest in making additional purchases.

Prospecting is particularly important when the store is full of customers. An alert salesperson can single out prime prospects and not waste time with browsers. When the store is not busy, salespeople should attend to everyone, including weak prospects, to build possible future business and enhance the store's image of concern for its customers.

### Contacting the Customer

*Initial impressions* are important determinants in successfully making a sale. A warm smile and an appearance of genuine interest in customers and their needs are parts of a good initial impression. At the beginning of the contact, the salesperson should make an opening comment that quickly captures the buyer's attention and arouses interest. Further, the first words should be positive and should stimulate any needs the customer might be displaying. If a woman is holding up a blouse to examine, the salesperson might open by saying, "That blouse certainly would look nice on you. Would you like to try it on?" This opening compliments the woman's taste in clothing, stimulates her need to "look nice," and requests her to take an *action* (try it on). A simple "May I help you?" is a routine, worn-out phrase that almost invites the customer to turn down the request.

Openings should be original and appropriate to the situation. Consider the following examples of customer situations and potential salesperson responses.

*Situation 1:* Customer looking at a home video game.

☐ *Preferred opening* Salesperson: "Press this button like this [salesperson turns game on], and the game's all set to go. Why don't you try your luck?"

☐ *Nonpreferred opening* Salesperson: "Do you need some help in how to operate this thing?" Customer: "[Gads, he thinks I'm stupid or something.] No, I was just looking."

*Situation 2:* Woman looking at a coat in an exclusive, high-fashion women's clothing store.

☐ *Preferred opening* "That's 100-percent mink. Please let me help you on with it to see how it looks and feels."

☐ *Nonpreferred opening* "Want some help?" Customer: "[She thinks I don't know how to put on a coat!] No, thank you."

*Situation 3:* Shopper looking at a telephone in a phone center store.

☐ *Preferred opening* "That phone will make a call for you if simply one button is pressed. Look how easy it is to operate."

☐ *Nonpreferred opening* "Are you interested in a phone?"

In summary, a salesperson's opening statement at the point of initial contact can determine whether conversation will continue and, therefore, whether the sale can be made. A good opening should attract the customer's attention, arouse interest, stimulate a customer need, and be original to the situation. A poor opening is generally one the customer can answer with a yes or a no. In a selling situation, a good beginning is usually necessary for a happy ending (the sale).

## Presenting the Merchandise

After making initial contact, the salesperson is in a position to present the merchandise and the sales message. How the salesperson should present the merchandise depends on the customer. Because customers are not identical, the salesperson's presentations should not be identical; instead, they should be tailored to the individual and the circumstances. Some basic guidelines can help the salesperson make a good presentation. Remember, however, that salespeople must continually exercise their creativity to adapt to particular customers and circumstances.

*Learn the Customer's Needs and Wants.* To know what merchandise to show, the salesperson must learn what the customer needs and wants. Asking key questions and listening attentively help the salesperson to determine what merchandise the store has that might meet those needs and wants. "The pay in selling is far greater for asking the right questions than for knowing the right answer—a closed mouth gathers no foot."[3] At this point, the salesperson must closely observe the customer's reactions to each piece of merchandise shown to determine the level of product interest; that is, whether the product is a "must have," "should have," or "would be nice to have" item. The salesperson can also, in this initial presentation, determine whether to try **trading up**—attempting to sell higher-quality, higher-priced merchandise or to sell a larger quantity than the customer originally intended to buy. The salesperson may believe the customer would be better satisfied with more durable, stronger, lighter, heavier, bigger, or softer materials or may think the customer needs a larger quantity to complete the job or to save money.

*Reduce Customers' Perceived Risk.* Customers run the risk that the product they buy might not perform correctly, might fall apart or break down, might embarrass them in a social setting (a "gold" necklace chain turns the neck green), or might be unsafe (it might injure their children or blow up in their faces). These concerns are particularly strong for high-cost items; refrigerators, washers, cars, sets of tires, houses, and television sets represent substantial outlays of money and therefore risk. Perceived risk takes the form of financial, physical, or social risk. Therefore, products with high perceived risk must be accompanied by assurances of satisfactory performance. The salesperson should stress the manufacturer's warranty, the retailer's money-back guarantee, the retailer's in-house repair facilities, the dependable brand name, and so on. This selling situation might also be an opportunity for the salesperson to trade up the customer to higher-quality merchandise to reduce perceived risk and thus make the sale.

*Demonstrate the Product.* Some products lend themselves to demonstration better than others, but virtually all products can be demonstrated somehow. Demonstrating the merchandise means the customer sees the product in action—its features, benefits, and possible advantages. While demonstrating the product, the salesperson

Successful retail sales representatives demonstrate the product and actively involve the customer.

should point out the unique features and benefits to reinforce what the customer is seeing. A product can often sell itself, particularly if the salesperson helps a little. Demonstrations can also help reduce some customers' perceived risk in purchasing the product.

*Actively Involve the Customer.* Get customers actively involved with the product! Have them touch, smell, taste, hear, and feel it. "Push the accelerator and feel the power, *experience* its smooth ride, *listen* to the quiet of the engine and the outside air, *touch* the soft velour seats," a car salesperson might say while the customer is actually using, controlling, and experiencing the product.

Chances of persuading customers to buy a product improve greatly when they actively interact with it. A good salesperson points out how the product affects the customer's five senses ("Smell the manly scent of this cologne." "Taste the rich flavor of this coffee." "Feel the softness of this sweater.") The more of the customer's senses a salesperson can stimulate, the greater the chance of a sale.

*Sell Product Benefits.* This guideline has been alluded to in the last several pages, but not specifically stated. It is deserving of separate attention. "In the factory we produce cosmetics; in the store we sell the promise and hope of beauty!" "We don't sell the steak, we sell the sizzle." What all manufacturers, retailers, and salespeople must realize is that they don't sell physical products, but the physical, social, and psychological *benefits* they provide consumers. People don't buy lawn mowers, they buy trim lawns. Customers buy, in effect, the end result (the benefit), not the product for the product's sake. Therefore, salespeople should sell benefits.

*Make the Message Simple.* Too often salespeople present merchandise in *technical* terms and phrases that the average customer does not understand. As a result, many customers are frightened off or confused and a sale is lost. Good salespeople present the product message in words that are clear and understandable to the customer. The salesperson must be ready to adapt quickly to each consumer's level of understanding and sophistication. Sometimes the salesperson must use analogies and speak simply; for other customers, the salesperson might engage in technical conversation. The sales-message level should be geared to the customer's product-knowledge level. Thus a "golden rule" is to *communicate the message at the customer's level of understanding and knowledge.* Salespeople should not talk "over their customers' heads" or insult their intelligence by speaking too simply.

## Handling Objections

Consumers who do not purchase a product immediately after the merchandise presentation are likely to have perceived "stumbling blocks," objections to buying the product. A salesperson must anticipate objections and know how to handle each type. Figure 16–5 summarizes techniques of handling customer objections. Customer objections are of five kinds: product, price, place (store), timing, and salesperson.

Some consumers think the *product* is just not right for them. It is too big, too small, too heavy, too light, does not look right on them, is too simple, too complex, or one of a host of other objections. If the consumer has talked to the salesperson up

| Method | When to Use | How to Use |
|---|---|---|
| Head-on | With objections arising from incorrect information | Salespeople directly, but politely, deny the truth of the objection; to avoid alienating prospects, it is helpful to offer proof |
| Indirect denial | With objections arising from incorrect information | Salespeople never directly tell prospects that they are wrong, but still manage to correct the mistaken impression |
| Compensation | With valid objections, but where compensating factors are present | Salespeople agree with prospects initially, but then proceed to point out factors that outweigh or compensate for the objection (for this reason, it is often called the "yes, but" technique) |
| "Feel, felt, found" | With emotional objections, especially when prospects have retreated from their adult ego states, and when the prospect fails to see the value of a particular feature and benefit | Salespeople express their understanding for how prospects feel, indicate that they are okay since others have also felt that way, but have found their fears to be without substance |
| Boomerang | When the objection can be turned into a positive factor | Salespeople take the objection and turn it into a reason for buying |
| Forestalling | With any type of objection | From prior experience, salespeople anticipate an objection and incorporate an answer into the presentation itself, hoping to forestall the objection from ever coming up |

Source: Ronald B. Marks, *Personal Selling* (Boston: Allyn and Bacon, Inc., 1985), 326.

**FIGURE 16–5**
Summary of objection-handling techniques

to this point, there is generally some interest in the merchandise. Therefore, the customer can still be sold by overcoming the objections. The salesperson must be creative and adaptable in handling objections. If the customer says "This doesn't look right on me," it probably means "My friends (family, co-workers, boss, etc.) wouldn't like it." A creative salesperson counters with reasons the customer's reference groups might well approve of this merchandise. This approach reinforces the customer's self-image and gives supporting approval from others for making the purchase. In other cases, customers may object to the product by saying they are not sure it will perform as it should, to which the salesperson should reiterate the proven record of the product, its warranties, and store guarantees. The customer must be reassured that the product's benefits are genuine and that it will perform as stated.

Price is a common customer objection that takes two forms. First, the customer really wants the product but doesn't have the cash to pay for it. In this case, the salesperson can emphasize the store's easy credit terms. In other cases, the customer does not consider the product worth the price; for these customers, the salesperson must emphasize product value, perhaps by mentioning that competitors' prices are about the same even though their products do not have comparable features, warranties, or guarantees.

Customers may not like the store itself. An advertisement or a display caught their eye, they came into the store and saw something they liked, but they usually don't shop in this store or "a store like this" and therefore feel uncomfortable buying here. To meet this kind of objection, the salesperson must assure customers of the integrity of the store, its management, and its merchandise.

Putting the purchase off (timing) is another objection salespeople frequently encounter. Customers might not know exactly why they don't want to buy now; they just don't. Customers usually use the "timing" objection to conceal their real objections. Thus, this type of objection is difficult for salespeople to handle, since they do not understand its underlying motives. Handling this objection is "groping in the dark." Nevertheless, the salesperson can emphasize the need to buy immediately ("The sale ends today at this extraordinarily low price" or "There are only a few left in stock").

One last possible customer objection can be to the salesperson. Shifty eyes, long hair, short hair, conservative dress, wild dress, garlic on the breath, or any number of other "faults" may turn away a customer. The customer simply says "I don't like dealing with this 'character'." Whatever the reason, the salesperson is often unlikely to detect it. If the salesperson guesses that this is the objection, he or she should direct the customer's attention to the product—its benefits, its advantages, or its need-fulfilling capacities—or turn the sale over to another salesperson.

### Closing the Sale

Closing the sale is the "natural" conclusion to the selling process. The salesperson has prepared to meet the customer, has greeted the customer, has presented the merchandise, and has handled customer objections (if any). Now the salesperson is at the point of suggesting that the customer make the purchase. Timing in the closing stage, however, is critical. Customers often provide verbal or physical (body language) cues that suggest they might be ready to make a purchase. Figure 16–6 identifies several physical and verbal cues for potential closing opportunities. In timing the closing, the salesperson must adapt to the individual customer and circumstances. Some customers do not want to be rushed into making a final decision; others don't want to wait too long to have the sales person begin to close. Still other customers do not know how to make the decision or won't make the decision without help. In this latter situation, the salesperson must tell them to make the purchase. These people need someone to make decisions for them. In some in-

---

### Physical cues provided by customers

1. The customer closely reexamines the merchandise under consideration.
2. The customer reaches for his billfold or opens her purse.
3. The customer samples the product for the second or third time.
4. The customer is nodding in agreement as the terms and conditions of sale are explained.
5. The customer is smiling and appears excited as he or she admires the merchandise.
6. The customer intensely studies the service contract.

### Verbal cues provided by customers

1. The customer asks "Do you offer free home delivery?"
2. The customer remarks "I always wanted a pair of Porsche sunglasses."
3. The customer inquires "Do you have this item in red?"
4. The customer states "This ring is a real bargain."
5. The customer exclaims "I feel like a million bucks in this outfit!"
6. The customer requests "Can you complete the installation by Friday?"

---

**FIGURE 16–6**
Spotting closing cues

stances, customers have a friend or relative with them. A salesperson who detects that the customer's companion likes the product might ask how the companion likes the product ("How do you think the dress looks on Ms. Jones?"). In other cases, customers definitely make up their own minds and don't want to be pushed. In dealing with customers like these, the salesperson can remind them of their need and how the merchandise meets that need, restate the advantages and benefits of the merchandise, and explain why they must buy now and not put off the decision.

Skilled salespeople have developed several closing techniques that move the customer toward the purchase decision. After the customer has examined several pieces of merchandise, for example, the salesperson usually can determine which one or two merchandise items the customer prefers. To avoid confusing the customer and to aid in the final decision, the salesperson should put away the less-preferred items. If the customer has tried on seven rings, the five or six least-preferred rings should be put back in their cases. "I can tell this is the one you really like the most," the salesperson might say. "May I wrap this for you? Will this be cash or charge?" Figure 16–7 identifies seven of the more common closing techniques.

Another aspect of closing a sale is to show customers other merchandise that complements the item they are going to buy. This technique is called **suggestive selling**. If the customer is buying a sport coat, the salesperson can suggest a shirt and tie that are a "perfect" match for the coat. Suggestive selling is a service to customers who might not have thought of purchasing complementary items to enhance the appearance or use of their intended purchase. Also, the store and the salesperson can make additional sales. Both customers and salespeople benefit from suggestive selling when the additional items represent true benefits for the customer.

Next, the salesperson must perform several *administrative* tasks in closing the sale, such as ringing up the sale on the cash register, checking the accuracy of the

| Technique | Definition | Example |
|---|---|---|
| Direct close | The salesperson asks the customer directly for the order | "Can I write this order up for you?" |
| Assumptive close | The salesperson assumes the customer is going to buy and proceeds with completing the sales transaction | "Would you like to have this gift wrapped?" |
| Alternative close | The salesperson asks the customer to make a choice in which either alternative is favorable to the retailer | "Will this be cash or charge?" |
| Summary/agreement close | The salesperson closes by summarizing the major features, benefits, and advantages of the product and obtains an affirmative agreement from the customer on each point | "This dishwasher has the features you were looking for"—YES "You want free home delivery"—YES "It is in your price range"—YES "Let's write up the sale." |
| Balance-sheet close | The salesperson starts by listing the advantages and disadvantages of making the purchase and closes by pointing out how the advantages outweigh the disadvantages | "This dishwasher is on sale; it has all the features you asked for, you have 90 days to pay for it without any financial charges, and we will deliver it free. Even though we can not deliver it until next week, now is the time to buy." |
| Emotional close | The salesperson attempts to close the sale by appealing to the customer's emotions (love, fear, acceptance, recognition) | "The safety of your children could well depend on this smoke alarm. Now is the time to get it installed." |
| Standing-room-only close | The salesperson tries to get the customer to act immediately by stressing that the offer is limited | "The sale ends today." "This is the last one we have in stock." |

**FIGURE 16–7**
Types of closing techniques

address and other parts of the check the customer may present, verifying the customer's credit card, and boxing, bagging, or wrapping the merchandise. Finally, closing the sale is not complete until the salesperson has said thank you, asked the customer to come back, and has said good-bye. These comments appear to be, and perhaps are, routine; however, most customers expect and appreciate them.

### Following up the Sale

A good salesperson continues to sell the customer *after* the sale. The sale is not over once the customer has walked out the door. Many customers are happy about their purchases at the time they buy them, but later begin to doubt the wisdom of their buying decision. The "doubt" phase usually affects consumers who have made a substantial investment of time, effort, and money. Examples of substantial investments are purchases of furniture, major appliances, cars, expensive jewelry, houses, and some clothing. During this phase, customers might have regrets, might not be wholly satisfied with the purchase, and might never return to the store (lost future business). Therefore, a salesperson should follow up the sale by assuring customers they have made the right decision, the merchandise is of good quality, their friends and relatives will approve, and the store and manufacturer back the merchandise. Salespeople have three ways to follow up a sale: (1) writing a letter to the customer, (2) telephoning the customer, and (3) personally visiting the customer. Telephone calls or letters are the best options for following up a sale, with the latter preferred over the former. Sometimes telephone calls are viewed negatively because (1) customers were suspicious about the salesperson's motives for the call ("That salesman is trying to get me to buy something else"); (2) customers had had unpleasant experiences with previous salespeople who called on the telephone to sell them something they didn't want in the first place; and (3) the telephone caught the customer at a bad time (in the shower). Letters, on the other hand, can be taken from the mailbox and read at a time convenient to the customer. Therefore, the rule on sales follow-up is to send the customer a letter.

Jordan Marsh, the Boston area department store, has a unique sales—follow-up procedure called "I Guarantee It." It works this way:

> All sales associates are supplied with business cards with their name and department telephone number and reply cards for suggestions, which they hand to every customer with whom they come in contact. Imprinted on the card is the "I Guarantee It!" pledge which states: "It has been a pleasure assisting you today. I hope I was able to make your visit to Jordan Marsh a pleasant experience. If you are dissatisfied with your purchase in any way, please bring it to my attention. I guarantee your personal satisfaction in our merchandise and service. Thank You."[4]

## SUMMARY

Personal selling is a communication process between salesperson and customer. Communication is a two-way process in which both members actively exchange ideas and meanings. The characteristics of a good salesperson generally can be divided into physical traits, personality traits, individual skills, and message-presentation skills.

Steps in the retail selling process are (1) preparing for the customer, (2) prospecting for customers, (3) contacting the customer, (4) presenting the merchandise, (5) handling objections, (6) closing the sale, and (7) following up the sale. A good salesperson prepares well for the sale even before greeting the customer, then adapts throughout the sale to each customer and set of store circumstances as they arise at the time.

In all, salespeople are perhaps the retailer's most valuable asset. They interact face-to-face with customers to make the sale and to project the kind of image the retailer desires. Thus, an investment in salespeople is a wise decision.

**KEY TERMS AND CONCEPTS**

adaptability of salesperson

individual selling skills

listening skills

message-presentation skills

order getter

order taker

perceived credibility

perceived expertise

personal communication

personal selling

personality traits

physical traits

positive attitude

salesperson – customer similarity

suggestive selling

trading up

**REVIEW QUESTIONS**

1. How are personal selling and personal communications related?
2. What are some of the personality traits of a good salesperson?
3. Describe the role of salesperson expertise and credibility in the selling process.
4. How can a salesperson improve listening skills?
5. Does salesperson – customer similarity affect the selling process? How?
6. When should a salesperson use a one-sided sales message? When is a two-sided sales message appropriate?
7. Where should the strongest selling points be positioned within a sales message?
8. Should the salesperson draw conclusions for the customer? Are there any exceptions?
9. How can salespeople integrate emotional terms into a sales presentation?
10. What should the salesperson determine in prospecting for customers?
11. Describe the sales practice of trading-up the customer.
12. Which three forms of perceived risk are part of each customer purchase? How can a retail salesperson reduce perceived risks?
13. What should the retail salesperson sell?
14. What are the most common methods for handling customer objections? Give an original (nontextbook) example of each technique.
15. When should a salesperson attempt to close a sale?
16. Describe the various types of closing techniques available to the salesperson. Give an original example of each technique.
17. What is the best option for following up a sale? Why?

**REVIEW EXAM**

True or False

_____ 1. Order getters are sales personnel who simply comply with customers' requests for merchandise.

_____ 2. Customers are persuaded more by a salesperson they perceive to be similar to themselves.

_____ 3. When consumers are not knowledgeable about the product, the general rule is to present them with a two-sided message.

_____ 4. "May I help you" is a well-established opening that any retail salesperson can use successfully in contacting the potential customer.

_____ 5. The forestalling method of handling objections can be used with any type of objection.

_____ 6. "The sale ends today" is a good example of the standing-room-only close.

_____ 7. Telephone calls are an extremely effective tool in following up sales and reducing customer doubt about their purchases.

## STUDENT APPLICATIONS MANUAL

**PROJECTS: INVESTIGATIONS AND APPLICATIONS**

1. One of the most effective ways to obtain information about any aspect of the retailer's operation is to ask consumers what they think. Review the characteristics of a good salesperson; then, develop a form that can be used by consumers to evaluate the performance of store salespeople.
2. Salespeople can make a sales presentation using either a one- or two-sided message. Select a specific product (i.e., a specific brand, style, model, and size), and develop a sales presentation using a two-sided message.
3. Customers often have hidden objections and are reluctant to express their concerns. In other cases, customers often state a false objection because they do not want to tell the true reasons (e.g., cannot afford the product) for their lack of willingness to make a purchase commitment. Nevertheless, the hidden and false objection can kill the sale. Conduct a literature search or interview experienced salespeople to ascertain methods for discovering and overcoming these hidden or false objections.
4. Discuss the statement "Retail selling is essentially a problem-solving situation; that is, customers are looking for solutions to problems, not products." If this problem-solving theory of retail selling is true, how should a retail salesperson approach the selling situation?

**CASES: PROBLEMS AND DECISIONS**

### CASE 16–1
### Is It Bait and Switch—or Is It Trading Up?*

**BACKGROUND**

The morning edition of the *Cleveland Gazette* carried two sales advertisements featuring special promotions on color television sets. Prough Home Centers, a chain of home appliance stores with eighty-four outlets in fourteen states, ran an advetisement featuring repossessed color televisions (See Exhibit 1). The second advertisement (see Exhibit 2) was placed by The World of Entertainment, a specialty electronics store chain with outlets in eight states; it featured deep discounting of new, brand-name color televisions.

**EXHIBIT 1**

```
PROUGH HOME CENTERS

"The Professionals in Home Appliances"
Saturday Only
Repossessed, Repaired, Resold
COLOR TELEVISIONS
At Rock Bottom Prices
Starting at $99.95
LIKE NEW
```

**EXHIBIT 2**

```
THE WORLD OF ENTERTAINMENT
Proudly Presents
NEW, NAME BRAND, FAMILY SIZE
COLOR TELEVISIONS
$279.95
"We Buy Straight From the Factory"
DON'T MISS THIS DEAL
SALE ENDS SOON
```

*This case was prepared by Joseph McCafferty, The University of Akron.

## CURRENT SITUATION

### The Johnsons' Experience

Dave and Carol Johnson, a newly wed couple, had been holding off purchasing a new color television until the right sale came along. The Prough Home Center ad caught Dave's attention. The price of $99.95 seemed almost too good to be true. The Johnsons lived only six blocks from the nearest outlet, so they decided to check out what specific items were available. Carol reminded Dave that the advetisement did specify "repossessed" color televisions, but Dave dismissed Carol's comment, saying "At $99.95, who cares! So long as we can get a couple of good years of trouble-free service out of it, I'll be happy."

Upon entering the store, the Johnsons were met by Kathy O'Brian, a top performer in the store's sales department. Dave told O'Brian they had seen Prough's newspaper advertisement and expressed an interest in seeing which sets were available. Kathy informed the Johnsons that although the used sets were in good working order, many of the models had nicks and scratches and the lower-priced sets were generally smaller portable models with even more wear and tear. To support her statement, Kathy explained that the set advertised for $99.95 was a 12-inch, two-year-old model. Dave replied that he expected as much but would still like to see the selection of used sets.

As they started to the back of the store where the used sets were on display, O'Brian stopped them at a 14-inch Sony with remote control. "You know," she said, "this is the best set in the store. It's also the best value. This color portable comes complete with remote control and automatic tuning. The regular price on this Sony is $499 but it is currently on sale for $399, terms are 90 days same as cash. In addition, Sony has a great limited warranty, so you would not have to worry about any major repair bills. I really think this set offers excellent value. You really should consider taking advantage of this offer." As a commissioned salesperson, Kathy stood to benefit financially from the sale of a more expensive set.

"We really would like to look at the used sets if we could," Dave said.

"Sure," O'Brian replied. "I just wanted to show you an opportunity to make a real value purchase. Personally, I feel the smart buy is a new set because there is very little risk with such a purchase."

"What risk?" Carol asked.

"Well, as you would expect, the manufacturer's warranties are no longer in force on the used sets," O'Brian replied. "And the store's guarantee is limited to 30 days." Seeing that this final clincher had sold the Johnsons, O'Brian hurriedly started writing up the sales contract on the new Sony.

### The Criss' Experience

The same day across town, Betty Criss was skimming the *Cleveland Gazette.* The sales promotion advertisement by The World of Entertainment caught Betty's eye. Betty and her husband, Dick, had been watching television on a portable set for a long time and she thought the time had come to get a big 24-inch console television. When Betty saw The World's offer of "family size" color televisions for $279.95, she knew that the time to buy a new color television had come. Dick Criss expressed some concern about this "almost too good to be true deal" but agreed to accompany Betty to the local outlet in Leipply Square.

Betty walked confidently into The World of Entertainment that night and expressed her interest in the color television console she had seen advertised. Bob Sproat, department manager, led Betty and Dick to a 19-inch color portable. "This is it! This is as family size as you can get," Sproat said. "We've been having trouble with the picture on this one all day, so let's see if I can get one in for you now."

Much to Sproat's delight, Betty's face shriveled at the sight of this family size portable. The truth was that The World of Entertainment had none of these sets in stock at the moment and the earliest Sproat could get one with an immediate order was 60 days, if he was lucky. He sensed an excellent opportunity to unload one of the many big console sets in stock. "This portable set has a very limited manufacturer's warranty and the store's guarantee is limited to 30 days. You've already seen the tough time I've had getting a clear picture. This particular model has already given us nothing but trouble. I doubt that it would last more than a couple of years, if that long."

Sproat stepped around the set on sale to a big color console on display in an adjacent setting. Betty's face lit up. Bob kicked his sales pitch into high gear. "Look at this beautiful console. It's got a great finish and would complement the decor of any home. The manufacturer's warranty is excellent and we have a full-service department to support the warranty. It's a bit more in price than the one on sale, but look at how much more you're getting. At this price, I think we can even throw in a remote control. Personally, I would hate to see you get stuck with that other trouble maker when I can let you walk out of here today with this set." After extolling all of the big console's virtues, Sproat tried once again to get a clear picture on the portable, but without success.

As Betty and Dick stared at the fuzzy picture, Bob whipped out a sales contract and started filling in the necessary information. Within 20 miinutes, Betty and Dick were driving home with a new 24-inch console in the back of the station wagon. "I thought he said he would deliver this thing," Dick said. "For $625.95 you would think he would at least have it delivered."

"He would have," Betty replied, "but they wouldn't be able to deliver it until the end of next week."

## ASSIGNMENT

1. Discuss the legal implications concerning the two sales experiences. What remedies might each family attempt, if any?
2. Discuss the moral and ethical implications of the advertising and selling techniques employed by each retailer. Look at the transaction from both sides. Do retailers and consumers really deal at arm's length (with equal knowledge of the product and its value)?

## CASE 16–2
### The Case of Mary Adams*

Mary Adams had just celebrated her youngest child's eighth birthday. She was bored with "just being a housewife" and wanted to work part-time. Her husband, Carl, an electrician, thought it would be nice to have the extra money, especially during the slack periods of the year for electricians.

Trecaso's Jewelry is a small but elegant jewelry store. Traditionally, the store has been operated by family members. Robert Trecaso and his son Tony had continued to operate the business since Robert's father died over ten years ago. The Trecasos now realized that the jewelry store was growing rapidly and that other employees were needed. They had known Mary for many years from church activities and asked her is she would like to work for them. Mary accepted the job eagerly and began the next week.

*This case was prepared by Scott Cevasco and Jon Hawes, The University of Akron.

Mary loved jewelry and this enthusiasm showed when she interacted with customers. As she continued to learn more and more about the business, her sales levels continued to increase. Robert, Tony, and Laura (Robert's wife and also a part-time sales employee at Trecaso's Jewelry) were delighted with the progress Mary was making. The business ran smoothly—sales increased each quarter.

After about a year and a half, Mary's attitude began to change. She thought she should receive fringe benefits other than health insurance and a two-week vacation. She also wanted an increase in her salary beyond minimum wage. The Trecasos said they would like to start a retirement plan, among other possible fringe benefits, but sales for the last half of the year had not met expectations and they consequently stated that they could not afford to meet Mary's demands.

Mary yelled back. "That's not fair, you promised me!" Neither Robert nor Tony remembered promising anything. They had only said that they wanted to offer these benefits if they would afford to do so.

After this incident, Mary's sales began to decline. She lost interest in customers and moped about the store. She also made mistakes on almost everything she was asked to do. She did not record bank deposits correctly. She sent checks for the wrong amounts to the wrong wholesalers. She also set up the display counters in disarray. The Trecasos were afraid to let her do anything because she was constantly doing it wrong. They could not understand this because they were the same tasks she had previously been doing so effectively.

The Trecasos knew that they had to do something. They tried to talk to her about these mistakes, but Mary only said, "I'll be more careful the next time." They were afraid to threaten her with losing her job because she was very sensitive to criticism. Also, they really needed the extra person with the Christmas season starting in a month. They also knew it was very hard to hire someone they could trust. The Trecasos scheduled a meeting to discuss how to deal with Mary Adams.

## ASSIGNMENT

1. How important is personal selling in the promotion mix for a store such as Trecaso's Jewelry?
2. What basic person selling tasks does Mary Adams perform?
3. Is following up the sale likely to be an important step in the personal selling process as far as Mary Adams is concerned?
4. What do you think of Robert and Tony Trecaso's efforts to train and develop, compensate, and motivate Mary Adams?
5. What should the Trecasos do to help Mary Adams?

---

**ENDNOTES**

1. David L. Kurtz, H. Robert Dodge, and Jay E. Klopmaker, *Professional Selling*, 4th ed. (Plano, TX: Business Publications, 1985): 365.
2. Frederic A. Russell, Frank H. Beach, Richard H. Buskirk, *Selling: Principles and Practices*, 12th ed. (New York: McGraw-Hill Book Company, 1988): 373.
3. Hank Trisler, "Stop Telling—Start Selling," *Personal Selling Power* 7 (September 1987): 20.
4. "How Jordan Marsh People 'Guarantee It'," *Stores* (September 1985): 68.

# 17

## Outline

## Objectives

- Discuss the unique contribution of visual merchandising, sales incentives, and publicity to communicating the retailer's merchandising messages to consumers.

- Plan and construct an effective in-store display.

- List many innovative sales-incentive tools and describe how they attract customers and stimulate purchases.

- Explain how to plan favorable publicity and manage unplanned publicity.

# Visual Merchandising, Sales Incentives, and Publicity

To supplement the advertising program, the retailer must offer in-store promotional support, provide special purchase inducements, and capitalize on public events that affect the store and its personnel. This chapter examines the role of visual merchandising, sales incentives, and publicity as part of the retailer's total promotional effort.

Advertising may attract consumers to the store, but it is primarily the retailer's visual displays that make the sale after the consumer is in the store. Retail displays are nonpersonal, in-store presentations and exhibitions of merchandise together with related information. In practice, retail displays are used (1) to maximize product exposure, (2) to enhance product appearance, (3) to stimulate product interest, (4) to exhibit product information, (5) to facilitate sales transactions, (6) to ensure product security, (7) to provide product storage, (8) to remind customers of planned purchases, and (9) to generate additional sales of impulse items.

"Merchandise displays must gain the attention of consumers, provide proper balance, be constructed in proper proportion, be hard-hitting, and convey their message quickly. The consumer only spends an average of 11 seconds observing a display."[1] In addition, retail displays are essential ingredients in creating the store's shopping atmospherics because the sight, sound, touch, taste, and scent appeals are largely the result of in-store displays. Every business has a personality, and each display should contribute to expressing the store's personality: be it black and white Art Deco or soft and earthy Mom and Pop.[2] (Refer to the section on creating store image and buying atmosphere in Chapter 7.) Here we will discuss types of interior displays and their content and arrangements.

## Types of Displays

Store interiors are the sums of all the displays designed to sell the retailer's merchandise. While retail displays can be classified in various ways, we shall identify four general types of displays: selection, special, point-of-purchase, and audiovisual.

*Selection Displays.* Nearly all the merchandise for which retailers rely on self-service and self-selection selling is presented to the consumer in the form of **selection displays**. These mass displays typically occupy rows of stationary aisle and wall units

521

A selection display

(shelves, counters, tables, racks, and bins) designed to expose the complete assortment of merchandise to the consumer. Selection display units are generally "open" to promote merchandise inspection. Their primary functions are to provide customer access to the store's merchandise and to facilitate self-service sales transactions. As a rule, retailers use selection displays to exhibit their normal, everyday assortments of convenience and shopping goods. Effective selection displays should present the merchandise in (1) logical selling or usage groupings; (2) a simple, well-organized arrangement; (3) a clean, neat condition; (4) an attractive, informative setting; and (5) a safe, secure state. Customer convenience and operational efficiency are the watchwords for good selection displays.

*Special Displays.* A **special display** is a notable presentation of merchandise designed to attract special attention and make a lasting impression on the consumer. Special displays use highly desirable in-store locations, special display equipment or fixtures, and distinctive merchandise.

Placing special displays in highly desirable locations ensures maximum exposure for the display and its merchandise, thereby significantly affecting the number of units sold.[3] End-of-aisles, counter tops, checkout stands, store entrances and exits, and freestanding units in high-traffic areas are all preferred locations for attracting special attention from shoppers. Unique combinations of display equipment (counters, tables, racks, shelves, bins, mobiles) and display fixtures (stands, easels, millinery heads, forms, set pieces) help create a dramatic setting that will attract consumer attention and build shopper interest. The choice of display equipment and fixtures depends on the merchandise, the amount of space available, and the effect sought.

A special display

Although store location and display equipment and fixtures are extremely important in constructing a special display, the key to successful display merchandising is the merchandise itself. Special displays highlight merchandise that can attract customers into the store, build the store's image, improve sales volume, or increase net profits. Special displays therefore are reserved for advertised, best-selling, high-margin, and high-fashion merchandise, together with product items suitable to impulse and complementary buying behavior. Merchandise selected for special displays should also lend itself to good display techniques, which create a favorable sight, sound, taste, touch, or scent appeal.

*Point-of-Purchase Displays.* A **point-of-purchase (POP) display** is a particular type of special display. Retailers make heavy use of POP materials to stimulate immediate purchase behavior. The POPs are often the first and last chance retailers and manufacturers have to tell customers about merchandise. The importance of POP displays is suggested by the fact that "80.7% of supermarket and drugstore shoppers make their final purchasing decisions in the store. Shoppers also say 60.4% of their super-

A point-of-purchase display

market purchases aren't planned."[4] Point-of-purchase displays include items such as counter displays, window displays, shelf extenders, grocery-cart ads, floor-stand displays, dumpbins, end-aisle stands, banners, shelf talkers, clocks, counter cards, sniff teasers, and video-screen displays. Point-of-purchase displays are designed to attract customer attention and interest, reinforce the store's creative theme, and fit in with the store's interior decoration.

In recent years, retailers have begun to "program" their on-site promotions. The idea is to stage a sequence of steps that lead the prospective customer from some point outside the store to the ultimate point of making a purchase decision. Grocers have been particularly active in using POP materials to increase their sales. Promotional materials such as handbills, bag stuffers, and window signs remind shoppers of what they saw advertised in the local newspapers. Counter decorations include hanging dummy products, manufacturers' signs, and price signs. To draw attention to special sales, some retailers use in-store microphones; K Mart, for example, announces its "blue light specials" over a public-address system. Each K Mart department is supposed to announce a "special sale" on an item for fifteen minutes each day. The purpose of this kind of promotion is to keep customers in the store to "shop around." K Mart's experience has been that people will "hang around all day" to get a "blue light special." Thus, such POP promotion not only increases store traffic but maintains it for longer periods of time. Finally, POP displays make the store a more exciting and fun place to shop. This latter benefit can well mean the difference between a loyal customer or one that shops around.[5]

An audiovisual display

*Audiovisual Displays.* The trend in fashion retailing is to make a video statement by applying current technology to stimulate consumer purchases. Retailers now use **visual merchandising, audio merchandising,** and/or **audiovisual merchandising** to sell products. Three key applications of audiovisual merchandising are (1) to display the depth and breadth of product lines (e.g., Florsheim Express Shops can show all shoe sizes and styles); (2) to use kiosks to explain the benefits of different products (e.g., Best Products, a catalog showroom, uses kiosks to help merchandise electronic products); and (3) to provide customers with basic price information (e.g., customers at Zale's jewelers can view video displays to determine price and quality ranges before seeing a salesperson).[6] These display approaches use technology to "speak" to and to "show" the consumer available merchandise. Devices include *shelf talkers* (tape recordings describing the merchandise audibly); rear-screen projections (slide projectors that present wide-screen, color pictures of the merchandise and its use); and audiovisual displays (a combination of sound and videotape or slides to present the product's story). As technology changes, so will sales promotions.

## Display Elements

To communicate the desired message effectively, the retailer must carefully consider and plan each element of a display. Display elements include the merchandise, shelf display areas or window display, props, colors, background materials, lighting, and signs.[7] The retailer must consider the contrast, repetition, motion, harmony, balance, rhythm, and proportion of each display to draw attention to it (see Figure 17–1).

## Display Content

Display content is the type and amount of merchandise to be set off. Cluttered displays of unrelated merchandise attract little attention and are ineffective in stimulating customer interest. To ensure good display content, many retailers confine their efforts to one of three groupings.

Display elements must be evaluated to determine how well and if they attract and hold the attention of passersby.

*Contrast is one way to attract attention.* Contrast is achieved by using different colors, lighting, form (size and shape), lettering, or textures.

*Repetition attracts consumer attention by duplicating an object to reinforce and strengthen the impression.* By displaying 20 tennis rackets, the image is created of a store with a wide assortment of merchandise in that category.

*Physical motion is a powerful attention getter, as is dominance.* If an item is much larger than other items in a display, it will be the dominant item and will draw attention to the entire display.

Once attention has been harnessed, the next step is to direct that attention to the intended message. Harmony and graduation frequently are used to accomplish this.

Harmony refers to the unification of merchandise, lighting, props, shelf space, and showcards to create a pleasing effect. Balance, emphasis, rhythm, and proportion work to focus attention on the central point.

Formal balanced displays in which one side is duplicated by the other tend to produce feelings of dignity, neatness, and order. Informally balanced displays in which one side does not exactly match the other tend to generate excitement and are less stuffy.

Rhythm refers to the eye's path after initial contact with the display. The objective is to hold the eye until the entire display is seen.

Design specialists use vertical lines to create the image of height, strength, and dignity. Horizontal lines connote calmness, width, and sophistication; diagonal lines create action, and curved lines suggest continuity and femininity.

Proportion concerns the relative sizes of the display's various objects. Attention can be directed to the desired focal point by arranging items in a graduated pattern from the small to the large.

The proportion concept also involves the positioning of objects in patterns. Popular display patterns include pyramids, steps, zigzags, repetition, and mass.

The image of height and formality is created with pyramids, while the zigzag is a popular method of displaying clothing to create an aura of excitement.

Repetition arrangements are used primarily in shelf merchandising situations. Merchandise items are placed equidistant from one another in a straight, horizontal line.

The mass arrangement is the placement of a large quantity of merchandise in either neatly stacked lines or in jumbled dump bins to convey the image of a sale item.

Source: Ray Marquardt, "Merchandise Displays Are Most Effective When Marketing, Artistic Factors Combine," *Marketing News*, 16 August 1983, 3.

**FIGURE 17–1**
Developing an attractive display

Unit groupings of merchandise highlight a separate category of product items (e.g., shoes, shirts, cocktail dresses, or handbags). Unit groupings contain merchandise that is almost identical (e.g., five black leather handbags of different sizes) or closely related (e.g., three red leather handbags and five brown suede bags). **Related groupings** of merchandise are ensemble displays that present accessory items along with the featured merchandise; for example, a mannequin may be dressed in a matching sportswear outfit with sporting accessories (e.g., tennis racket and bag). The principal idea behind the inclusion of accessory items is to remind the customer of a need for more than the featured item; in other words, the retailer is using suggestive selling. A display of either unit or related groupings should contain an odd number of product items. Consumers perceive an odd number of items as more intriguing; hence, the items attract more attention and create a more dramatic setting.

A unit grouping display

When displaying an even number of merchandise items (e.g., a set of eight stemmed glasses), it is recommended that one item be set apart from the rest or differentiated in some other way (e.g., elevated).

**Theme groupings** display merchandise according to a central theme or setting. Themes provide a focus in planning displays and are useful vehicles around which the five sensory appeals can be employed. The number of possible display themes is unlimited. For example, there are product themes ("Shoes complete the appearance"), seasonal themes ("Swing into spring"), patronage themes ("Cheaper by the dozen"), usage themes ("Mealtime magic"), occasion themes ("Along the bridal path"), color themes ("Pastel softness"), life-style themes ("The swinging singles set"), holiday themes ("Santa approved"), as well as themes based on historical, current, and special events.

A related grouping
(ensemble) display

## Display Arrangements

Display arrangement is organizing display merchandise into interesting, pleasing, and stimulating patterns. Haphazard arrangement of merchandise items can substantially reduce a display's effectiveness. Selection displays are simply arranged in some well-organized fashion, but special-display merchandise frequently is presented in one of four definite arrangement patterns: the pyramid, zig-zag, step, or fan arrangement. Figure 17-2 illustrates these patterns.

   **Pyramid arrangements** are triangular displays of merchandise in vertical (stacked) or horizontal (unstacked) form. "The pyramid begins at a large or broad base and progresses up to an apex, or point, at the highest level."[8] The vertical pyramid can be two or three dimensional and is well suited to displaying boxed and canned merchandise; it also represents efficient use of space. The base of a horizontal pyramid is placed in the rear of the display to achieve the proper visual perspective. When displaying different-sized merchandise items, larger items are positioned at the base and the smallest item occupies the apex. Figure 17-2(a) illustrates the use of

A theme display

pedestal displayers arranged in a pyramid fashion—an effective arrangement pattern for window, counter, and table displays.

**Zig-zag arrangements** are modified pyramids that zig and zag their way to the apex of the display. No two display levels are at the same height. This arrangement is less monotonous than the pyramid; it is perceived to be more fluid and graceful, and perhaps more feminine. A zig-zag pattern of pedestal displayers (such as the one shown in Figure 17–2[b]) is especially appropriate for displaying women's jewelry, cosmetics, small apparel items, and shoes.

**Step arrangements** are essentially that: a series of steps. "Step arrangements lead the eye in a direct line; they begin at a low point on one side of a display area and progress directly to a higher point on the opposite side of that area."[9] Typically, step displays are constructed so that the base of each step increases in area (see Figure 17–2[c]); the larger base area is used to display accessory items, while the steps are used for the featured merchandise. The step arrangement is well suited to displaying a wide variety of merchandise.

**Fan arrangements** spread up and out from a small base, thereby directing the viewer's eyes upward and outward. Figure 17–2(d) illustrates this inverted-pyramid arrangement. The fan pattern is appropriate for displaying merchandise ranging from clothing goods to sporting goods.

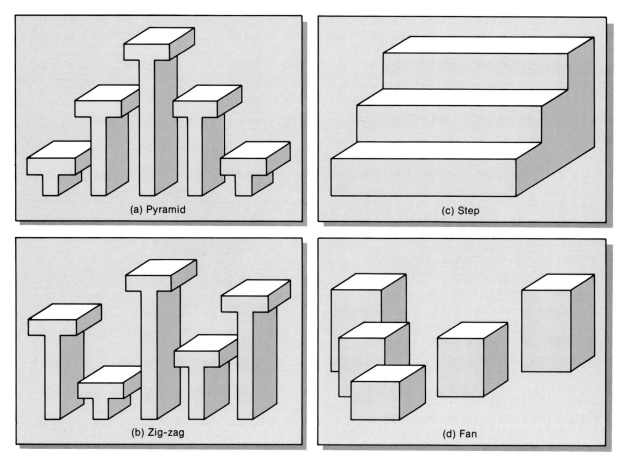

**FIGURE 17-2**
A gallery of display arrangements

## SALES INCENTIVES

Retailers use the term *sales incentive* in many different ways. A common usage includes all promotional activities other than advertising, personal selling, and publicity as sales incentives or sales promotions. This text defines **sales incentive** as any direct or indirect nonpersonal inducement that offers extra value to the consumers. Retailers use these "extras" to supplement advertising, personal selling, and other merchandising activities. Typically, sales incentives are temporary offers extended to the customer to stimulate an immediate response—the purchase of a good or service. Sales incentives are targeting activities in that they are directed at triggering particular customer actions.

### Coupons

Coupons are manufacturer or retailer certificates that give consumers a price reduction on specific kinds of merchandise. Consumers obtain coupons from newspapers, magazines, mail, on and in packages, door-to-door, and in-store advertising supplements. **Couponing** attracts customers to the store. Shoppers come into the store to purchase the "bargain" but usually end up buying other merchandise as well.

Couponing is popular with consumers and is a relatively low-cost sales incentive program; however, it also has its problems. First, everyone is into the act. With billions of coupons distributed each year, it becomes more difficult to gain customer attention and to get "one up" on competitors. A second problem is in coupon distribution. In-pack coupons, for example, only create repurchases by current users, not new users, which is a major objective in couponing.[10] One study shows that 47 percent of frequent coupon redeemers use coupons for brands they would have bought anyway.[11] Third, misredemption (illegal redemption) is a major problem. Fourth, complex coupons (e.g., self-destruct, sticky, multiple purchase, and size-specification coupons) add significantly to handling time at checkout counters, and often consumers misunderstand these coupons.[12]

## Sampling

**Sampling** involves giving the customer a free trial or sample of the product; it gets the customer involved with the product through hands-on experience. Trial use invites active participation, which can quickly lead to a customer purchase decision; however, only some products should be sampled. The kinds of products retailers can sample have low unit cost, are small in size, and are subject to high repeat sales. Supermarkets hand out samples of sausage; bakeries provide sample pastries; Hickory Farms places cheese and crackers at convenient points throughout its stores so customers can sample them. Sampling is generally quite expensive, but because it gives customers direct experience and involvement with the product, it is thus a powerful tool to induce purchases.

## Premiums

A **premium** is a merchandise item given to the consumer free of charge or at a substantial price reduction as an inducement to purchase another product or to participate in an activity, or both. Essentially, a premium is a bonus or gift given to a qualified customer. A customer purchase is the most common way to qualify for a premium; however, premiums are sometimes given for visiting the store or participating in an activity (e.g., taste-testing a new product). Store visits and participation events are often referred to as "traffic-building premiums." Several types of premiums involve retailers with manufacturers in this kind of effort to create sales incentives: self-liquidating, direct or value pack, mail-in, and continuing premiums.

**Self-liquidating premiums** require the consumer to pay something for the premium; typically, the consumer must pay an amount sufficient to cover the costs associated with the premium. Successful self-liquidating premiums are merchandise items that usually cannot be obtained elsewhere, and their uniqueness makes them valued gifts that consumers perceive to be worth considerably more than what they have to pay for them. The cosmetic industry in concert with many department and specialty store retailers provides an excellent example of self-liquidating premium offers. These offers take the form of purchase with purchase (PWP) and gift with purchase (GWP) premiums, which account for a large percentage of cosmetic and fragrance sales.[13] These PWP and GWP premiums might consist of garment bags, overnight totes, sunglasses, billfolds, ties, and other apparel items complete with the insignias of the company or designer (e.g., Calvin Klein, Ralph Lauren, and others). Creating and maintaining customer sales and return trade was the goal of McDonald's offer of "Garfield" coffee cups for $.99 each time a customer purchased a breakfast item. The customer had to make several trips to McDonald's to get a full set of cups because a different cup was available each week for four weeks.

**Direct premiums** or value packs are free gifts given to the customer at the time of purchase. The gift can be (1) attached to the product package, "on packs"; (2) contained in the product package, "in packs"; (3) found adjacent to the product package, "near packs"; or (4) provided in special decorator packages with the product, "container-packs." To the extent that these direct premiums generate store traffic and ensure rapid product turnover, they are desirable additions to both the retailers' and manufacturers' sales incentive program. When direct premiums require additional shelf space, however (e.g., near-packs), special handling (e.g., on-packs), or result in other cost-generating activities, the retailer must closely evaluate the cost–benefit aspects.

**Mail-in premiums** require the customer to send in a proof-of-purchase to receive a free gift. This type of premium encourages first-time or repeat purchases; however, given the extra effort required of the customer, it has limited acceptance on the part of the general consuming public. But if the retailer does not have to get involved with processing and handling the mail-in offer, this type of premium is still another weapon in a successful sales incentive arsenal.

**Continuity premiums** require the customer to make repeat purchases of products and services to benefit from the premium offer. This kind of premium is offered as part of a continuous, on-going sales incentive program. The customer's length and degree of involvement usually determines the value of the gift; longer and greater involvement results in bigger and better gifts. The most common type of continuity premiums are trading stamps. Sperry and Hutchinson (S&H) Green stamps and Quality Stamp Company are two organizations that are working to revive this once important sales incentive tool that enjoyed peak popularity in the 1960s.[14] Pressure-sensitive stamps, more convenient stamp collection books, and better gift selection catalogs are some of the improvements for enhancing the image of this kind of inducement and convincing both retailers and consumers to return to trading stamps as a buyer reward system.

Competing with trading stamps is a new type of continuity premium—the frequent buyer program. This format gives customers bonus points for each purchase, with the number of points corresponding to the amount of purchase. Zayre's, the discount store, has its "Frequent Z" program:

> Customers get 3,000 bonus points for joining the program, then 100 points for each dollar they spend in Zayre discount department stores. The points may be redeemed for gifts in the Frequent Z catalog. "There's just no points in shopping anywhere else" is the theme of TV spots. . . . The gift catalog, which is handled by a separate fulfillment house, includes such items as an Anne Klein quartz watch and a Simmons hide-a-bed. Consumers would have to rack up 7.8 million points for a trip to Hawaii.[15]

Sears is also experimenting with its version of a frequent buyer program; Bonus Club shoppers can get incentives ranging from $5 gift certificates to automobiles.[16]

## Contests and Sweepstakes

**Contests** and **sweepstakes** are theme-based sales incentive programs designed to create a special event that generates customer involvement with the store and its merchandise. Contests are promotional activities in which participants compete for rewards; successful participants are selected on the basis of their skill in completing a particular task (e.g., designing a store advertisement or completing a puzzle).

Sweepstakes are promotions in which customers win prizes based on chance. For the sweepstakes to be legal, however, the customer cannot be required to risk money for a chance; the major requirement is that the customer fill out an entry form to have a chance to win. Sweepstakes involve pure chance and minimal effort for entrants. Because of relaxation in "games of chance" laws, more retailers are turning to sweepstakes in their sales promotion programs.

> The growth and variety of sweepstakes are endless. There is the "straight" sweepstakes, where the winning entry blank is pulled out of a crowded drum of hopefuls. And the "matching" sweepstakes, where numbers or symbols are matched to a pre-selected number or symbol.
>
> Then there is the "instant win" (rub-off or wash-off) variety of sweepstakes —the hottest item right now. And let us not forget the "programmed learning" type of sweepstakes, where the entrant is required to give back some information from a label, package or advertisement, with winners chosen from the "correct" entries.[17]

## Specialty Advertising

The Specialty Advertising Association defines **specialty** advertising as a useful article of merchandise that is imprinted with an advertisement and given to the customer without obligation. Specialty items can range from inexpensive key chains to expensive travel bags. To be successful, a specialty should be useful, fashionable, and appropriate for the targeted consumer. A good rule for the retailer to remember about a specialty item is that the store's name will be on the item; hence, the item should be consistent with the store's image.

## Tie-ins

Sales incentive **tie-ins** are another approach to attracting attention to a store's offerings. McDonald's, for example, tied in with Paramount Pictures to offer Star Trek meals: "children's meals in boxes with Star Trek designs on the outside and space-age plastic toys inside."[18] Such tie-ins can benefit both parties; in this case, McDonald's was "hitchhiking" on the potential success of the movie *Star Trek*. Sears used a national television campaign to promote "its exclusive collection of children's clothing, bedding, watches, and plush animals tied to and coinciding with the opening of 'An American Tail,' Steven Spielberg's first animated film."[19] Successful tie-ins can generate excitement, enthusiasm, and sales, but if the tie-in (such as a movie) bombs, the retailer can suffer.

Tie-ins assume a variety of forms. Besides a tie-in with an entertainment event, tie-ins can occur in conjunction with national holidays, special occasions, sporting events, local celebrations, annual conventions, unusual events, and other products, to name but a few ways. The purpose of tie-ins is to capitalize on the excitement generated by momentary trends or events. They are by definition transient—how many people today would buy a coffee mug with a bicentennial decal (1776–1976) on it?

Tie-ins of complementary merchandise have several advantages:

- ☐ *Increased awareness.* By promoting two or more compatible pieces of merchandise, the retailer can attract more attention than by promoting a single piece of merchandise.
- ☐ *Increased readership.* Readership of advertising sales promotion literature will increase, particularly if there is a logical tie-in between the merchandise.
- ☐ *Reinforced image.* Where there are natural "go-togethers," the image of the store's merchandise can be reinforced because of the combined benefits the consumer will derive from using both pieces of merchandise together.
- ☐ *Cross-brand trial.* If customers are loyal to one brand of a store's merchandise, they are likely to try the complementary merchandise because of the "promotional marriage."
- ☐ *Cost-efficiency.* Retailers can save money by promoting tie-ins; that is, two or more pieces of merchandise can be promoted together, achieving a synergistic effect.

## PUBLICITY

**Publicity** is one of the tools of public relations. It can be defined as positive or negative communication that is indirect and nonpersonal, is carried by a mass medium, and is neither paid for nor credited to an identified sponsor. A key concern to the retailer regarding publicity is that the firm has no control over *what* is said (the message), *how* it is said (the presentation), *to whom* it is said (the audience), and *how often* it is said (the message frequency). Nevertheless, publicity plays an important supportive role in enhancing and augmenting product and store advertising. "Publicity's nonpaid source lends a level of credibility unavailable to advertiser sponsored messages, producing a heightened potential for informative and persuasive impact."[20] Hence, it behooves the retailer to appreciate both the positive and negative results of good and bad publicity. A positive story can greatly enhance the retailer's image; on the other hand, that positive image can be negated by one incidence of negative publicity. Although retailers cannot control publicity, they can take steps to gain favorable publicity and to lessen the impact of negative publicity.

### Kinds of Publicity

Publicity can be either planned or unplanned. **Planned publicity** means the retailer exercises some control over the news item. Regarding **unplanned publicity,** the retailer simply responds to the uncontrollable events as they occur. Planned publicity includes press releases, press conferences, photographs, letters to the editor, editorials, and special events (see Figure 17–3). Large retailers typically send out dozens of news releases about their stores and activities. Further, they use press conferences to describe major new events that might be of interest to the public. Pictures and drawings are useful for showing store-expansion plans, new equipment to better serve customers, and so forth; these are generally newsworthy items that bring attention to the retailer. These approaches to gaining favorable publicity are subject to

FIGURE 17–3
What makes an event "special"?

Special events don't necessarily equal participating in an auto show or sponsoring a rock tour—not all sponsorships are special events. As might be expected, the line between special events and other promotion techniques can be fuzzy. But, there are distinct characteristics common to all promotions that fall under the classification of special events:

■ A special event is in most cases a leisure pursuit, either sports or something that fits within the broad definition of the arts.

■ It involves some form of public participation on the part of the audience—attending a fest, competing in a triathlon—as opposed to seeing an ad or reading about a product.

■ Unlike ad campaigns, which may run as long as they are effective, special events occur within a prescribed time frame and have a definite opening and closing.

■ An event is independently legitimate; it can stand on its own merits apart from any sponsor. Furthermore, the event does not form part of the primary commercial function of the sponsoring body (but there is usually some link between the sponsoring organization and the event). In other words, horse races are not special events because they are the chief business of their sponsor, the track authority. So too, for sweepstakes, coupons and premiums. While they may be nifty promotions, they are created exclusively to step up direct sales of their sponsor's product and can not stand alone.

On the other hand, the New York City Marathon is a special event because it is an entity apart from sponsor Manufacturers Hanover Trust, and running is not the chief function of the bank.

■ The sponsoring body of a special event expects a return on its investment. While foundations often support charitable and civic ventures, they rarely sponsor a special event.

■ The bulk of publicity derived from a special event happens spontaneously, usually within an editorial, not an advertising, context. This is quite different from advertising where mentions are specifically placed and paid for.

Source: Reprinted with permission of *Advertising Age,* 18 April 1983. Copyright Crain Communications Inc.

the whims of the news media because they select what they consider newsworthy. The media, however, do have space or time to fill, and persistence and continually disseminated media releases increase the likelihood of favorable coverage.

## Developing a Publicity Story

To develop a publicity story, the retailer first must identify the *kinds* of stories the media accepts and the *criteria* they use to make decisions. This step gives retailers basic ideas on which to develop stories.

Stories that depict new and unusual events, store innovations, improvements in working conditions, new store openings, and stories that are currently important to the public often attract the interest of the news media. Publicity must also be newsworthy, somewhat unusual, appeal to a broad cross section of the public, and must

FIGURE 17–4
Guidelines for obtaining
successful placement
of publicity stories

1. **Know deadlines**. Time governs every newspaper. News events should be scheduled, whenever possible, to accommodate deadlines.
2. **Generally write, don't call.** Reporters are barraged by deadlines. They are busiest right around deadline time, late afternoon for morning newspapers and morning for afternoon papers. Thus, it's preferable to mail or messenger news releases rather than trying to explain them over the telephone. Also, follow-up calls to reporters to "make sure you got our release" should be avoided. If reporters are unclear on a certain point, they'll call to check.
3. **Direct the release to a specific person or editor.** Newspapers are divided into departments—business, sports, style, entertainment, and the like. The release directed to a specific person or editor has a greater chance of being read than one addressed simply to "editor."
4. **Make personal contact.** Knowing a reporter may not result in an immediate story, but it can pay residual dividends. Those who know the local weekly editor or the daily, city editor have an advantage over colleagues who don't. Also, when a reporter uses your story idea, follow up with a note of commendation—particularly on the story's accuracy.
5. **Don't badger.** Newspapers are generally fiercely independent about the copy they use. Even a major advertiser will usually fail in getting a piece of puffery published. Badgering an editor about a certain story is bad form. So is complaining excessively about the treatment given a certain story. Worst of all, it achieves little to act outraged when a newspaper chooses not to run a story.
6. **Use "exclusives" sparingly.** Sometimes public relations people promise "exclusive" stories to particular newspapers. The exclusive promises one newspaper a "scoop" over its competitors. For example, practitioners will frequently arrange to have a visiting executive interviewed by only one local newspaper. While the chances of securing a story are heightened by the promise of an exclusive, there is a risk of alienating the other papers. Thus, the exclusive should be used sparingly.
7. **When you call, do your own calling**. Reporters and editors generally don't have assistants. Most do not like to be kept waiting by a secretary calling for the boss. Public relations professionals should make their own initial and follow-up calls. Letting a secretary "handle" a journalist can alienate a good news contact.

Source: Fraser P. Seitel, *The Practice of Public Relations,* 2nd ed. (Columbus, OH: Merrill, 1984), 340–42.

be truthful. Publicity stories are more effective if they are dramatic or emotional and if they show action or human interest through photographs and illustrations.

Retailers increase the chance of successfully placing news releases and other publicity items if they adapt to the operational methods and personal references of the targeted media. Figure 17–4 lists guidelines for successfully placing news stories with newspapers. Most of the guidelines are equally important when dealing with magazines, radio, and television personnel.

**SUMMARY**

Visual merchandising, sales incentives, and publicity are effective retail promotional tools. They stimulate quick customer action to purchase, and they influence customer attitudes toward and images of the store and its merchandise.

As in-store visual presentations of the merchandise, retail displays assume a key role in creating a shopping atmosphere and enhancing the consumer's buying mood. Depending on their objectives, retailers use a variety of methods to present merchandise, including selection, special, point-of-purchase, and audiovisual displays. To ensure effective displays, retailers plan merchandise exhibits by controlling content (unit, related, and theme groupings) and arrangements (pyramid, zig-zag, step, and fan patterns).

Coupons, sampling, premiums, contests, sweepstakes, specialties, and tie-ins are among the many devices retailers use to communicate with customers about their store and their merchandise. Sales incentive approaches are limited only by the retailer's imagination. With ongoing technological innovations, businesses are creating growing numbers of sales incentive tools to stimulate customer interest in their merchandise.

Publicity is another important part of a retailer's promotion program. Good publicity can bring attention to a retailer and its merchandise and help build a good store reputation and sales. Bad publicity can ruin a retailer. A retailer therefore must learn how to manage its publicity.

## STUDENT STUDY GUIDE

**KEY TERMS AND CONCEPTS**

audio merchandising

audiovisual merchandising

contests

continuity premiums

couponing

direct premiums

fan arrangements

mail-in premiums

planned publicity

point-of-purchase (POP) display

premiums

publicity

pyramid arrangements

related groupings

sales incentives

sampling

selection display

self-liquidating premiums

special display

specialties

step arrangements

sweepstakes

theme groupings

tie-ins

unit groupings

unplanned publicity

visual merchandising

zig-zag arrangements

**REVIEW QUESTIONS**

1. What merchandising objectives might a retailer achieve through in-store displays?
2. What is the primary function of a selection display?
3. Special displays should be reserved for what type of merchandise?
4. Identify the types of items that are appropriate for a point-of-purchase display.

5. What display elements should the retailer consider in creating attention-getting displays? Briefly explain each element.
6. Describe the three types of display content and give an example of each type.
7. Which four arrangement patterns are used in store displays? Describe each arrangement.
8. What is a sales incentive?
9. What is the primary purpose of sampling?
10. Compare and contrast the various types of premiums.
11. What is the difference between a contest and a sweepstakes? Describe the four types of sweepstakes retailers use.
12. Identify the advantages of tie-in promotions.
13. What doesn't the retailer control in publicity-related stories?

## REVIEW EXAM

True or False

_____ 1. Selection display units are generally "open displays" to promote merchandise inspection.

_____ 2. An even number of items within a display is perceived by shoppers as being more intriguing and capable of attracting more attention.

_____ 3. A major goal of using ensemble displays is to facilitiate suggestive selling.

_____ 4. The zig-zag display arrangement is perceived by customers to be less monotonous than the pyramid arrangement.

_____ 5. McDonald's "Garfield" coffee cups are a good example of direct premiums.

_____ 6. Sweepstakes are sales incentives that involve pure chance and a minimal effort on the part of the customer.

_____ 7. One advantage of publicity is that the public perceives news stories as having higher credibility than advertising.

# STUDENT APPLICATIONS MANUAL

## PROJECTS: INVESTIGATIONS AND APPLICATIONS

1. Evaluate the retail displays of a local specialty retailer. Consider the location, equipment, fixtures, merchandise, content, and arrangement used in each display. Are they effective? What changes would you recommend? Why?
2. "Strangely enough, coupons work best with older, more affluent, better educated, urban consumers and married consumers than with consumers who need the savings more— the less affluent, young, single, and less educated." Explain why.
3. Sampling is generally used in association with products characterized by low per-unit cost. What actions might the retailer take to allow the consumer to sample high per-unit-cost products.
4. The effectiveness of any sales incentive tool varies according to the operational and merchandising characteristics of a given type of retailer. Identify the most and least effective sales incentive tools for each of the following retailers: (1) a small gift shop; (2) a hardware store; (3) a fast food restaurant; and (4) a cosmetic department. Explain your selections.
5. Assume you are the owner/operator of a sporting goods store. What might you do gain favorable publicity for your store? Detail how you would go about achieving this feat.

## CASE 17–1
### Photo Imaging Centers—Promoting a New Product/Service through Visual Merchandising*

Historically, the success of the specialty camera store business was dependent on several factors: (1) a highly technical product that was at the leading edge of technolgy, (2) a knowledgeable sales force who could educate, train, and service the customer, (3) the limited or exclusive distribution of branded merchandise, and (4) pricing points that allowed sufficient margins to support a high level of customer service. in the 1970s, the retail camera market changed drastically; automatic cameras requiring low user-skill levels eliminated much of the need for highly trained salespeople and specialized camera equipment service mixes. The 1970s also saw the mass distribution of all types of cameras and associated accessories; this in turn encouraged price reduction as a major competitive merchandising strategy. With declining sales volume and reduced profit margins, specialty camera stores were forced to change their marketing approach. The strategic choices were two: (1) become a discount specialty camera store emphasizing price or (2) develop a unique specialty product/service mix to appeal to the more service-oriented customer.

Photo Imaging Centers (PIC), a full-line specialty camera and photo supplier retailer, operates three retail mall outlets within the greater metro area. Faced with the destructive competitive dynamics of the local market, PIC's management team elected to pursue a strategic course of action that would incorporate a unique combination of products with a complete mix of photographic and imaging services. A particular tactic within the total strategy was to develop the product/service concept of the "Home Decorating Studio."

PIC's Home Decorating Studio is a product-service concept based on the idea that individuals can decorate their home using their own personal photographic art. Both skilled and unskilled photographers can take photographs that could be turned into decorative art with the proper professional guidance and enhancement from PIC. This type of product/ service line would be substituted for the now-popular poster and pop-art types of decor. The Home Decorating Studio offers a combination of products and services that represent a complete cycle of potential sales. The cycle starts with the sale of various types of films, proceeds to film processing and finishing, and finishes with photographic enlargements that can be professionally matted and framed.

It is PIC's belief that once customers get involved with this entire system, they would become dependent upon PIC for the entire process. Equally important is the fact that individuals would have personal involvement and pride in home decor that they had done themselves. If PIC's professional touch could enhance the customers' art decor, a considerable potential for return trade exists. Additional benefits of the particular concept is that it represents a component of the business with high margins, thereby making PIC less dependent on camera equipment sales at narrower margins. This new offering will also attract new customers, who can be enticed to make purchases of complementary product and service lines.

To enhance the image of PIC as a leader in quality photographic imagery, a new department was added to each store—PIC's Photographic Art Gallery. The department displays and sells the photographic art of professional, well-known local and state photographers. The works of good amateur photographers are also displayed and sold. The monthly "showing of the featured artist" has gained PIC favorable publicity and has been an excellent vehicle for drawing new customers into the stores.

*This case was prepared by Dale Lewison and Jon Hawes, The University of Akron.

| PHASE I<br>Customer Attraction | PHASE II<br>Customer Information | PHASE III<br>Customer Decision |
|---|---|---|
| The use of the *advertising* and *publicity* elements of the promotional mix to create an *awareness of* and an *interest in* the Home Decorating Studio and complementary components of PIC's products/services mix. | The use of the *visual merchandising* and *store display* elements of the promotional mix to promote consumer *comprehension* and *understanding* of the Home Decorating Studio and complementary components of PIC's products/services mix. | The use of *personal selling* and *sales promotion* elements of the promotion mix to ensure consumer *conviction* and *partonage* of the Home Decorating Studio and complementary components of PIC's products services mix. |

The arrows (→) appear between PHASE I and PHASE II, and between PHASE II and PHASE III.

**EXHIBIT 1**
PIC's merchandising system

To launch the Home Decorating Studio concept, PIC developed a three-phase merchandising system (see Exhibit 1) supported by a general statement of goals (see Exhibit 2). The standardized store layout for each of PIC's outlets is shown in Exhibit 3.

The problem facing the management team today is to plan Phase II of PIC's merchandising system. More specifically, the team is concerned with Part 1 of Phase II—designing the in-store visual exhibition of the various types of products and services that comprise the integrated merchandising system. The visual exhibition (see Exhibit 4) is to be a wall display 50 feet long and 10 feet high (floor to ceiling).

**EXHIBIT 2**
PIC's merchandising objectives

> PHASE I: Customer Attraction
> 1. To develop a print (newspaper) and broadcast (radio) advertising campaign that will create general consumer awareness of and interest in PIC's Home Decorating Studio—a new product/service offering.
> 2. To develop a publicity campaign that will promote and increase public traffic for PIC's Photographic Art Gallery—an image-building cultural center.
>
> PHASE II: Customer Information
> 1. To plan an in-store visual exhibition of PIC's Home Decorating Studio to illustrate the various types of products and services that comprise this integrated merchandising system.
> 2. To plan in-store displays of complementary products that can be merchandised in conjunction with or as supplements to the products and services that comprise the Home Decorating Studio.
>
> PHASE III: Customer Decision
> 1. To devise a personal selling process that will assist store sales personnel in securing customer involvement with the Home Decorating Studio by developing techniques for customer prospecting, customer contact, merchandise presentation, handing objections, and sales closure.
> 2. To devise sales promotion incentives that will help induce potential customers to make a positive decision regarding their involvement with the Home Decorating Studio.

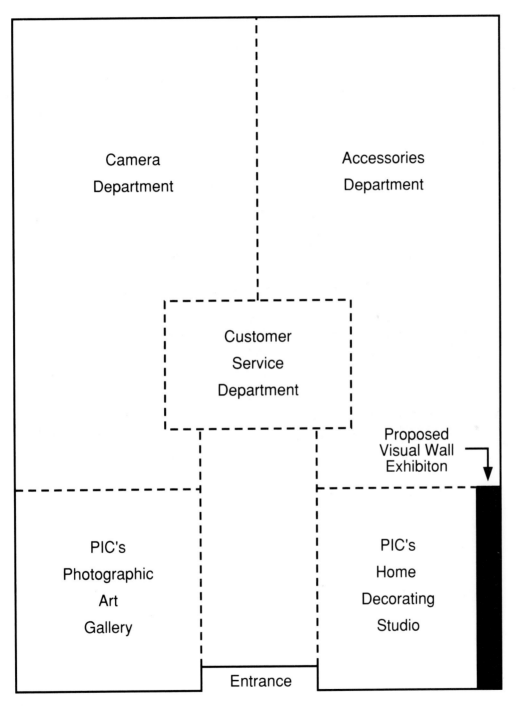

**EXHIBIT 3**
PIC's store layout

**EXHIBIT 4**

PIC's proposed visual merchandising wall display

```
┌─────────────────────────────────────────────────────────────────┐  ┊
│                                                                   │  ┊
│              Processing                                           │  ┊
│     Film →    and      → Enlarging → Matting → Framing → Displaying│ 10 feet
│              Finishing                                             │  ┊
│                                                                   │  ┊
└─────────────────────────────────────────────────────────────────┘  ┊
|----------------------------------- 50 feet -----------------------------------|
```

## ASSIGNMENT

Assume the role of an outside consultant who specializes in visual merchandising and retail displays. PIC'smanagement team has asked you to develop two alternative wall-display layouts that would meet the information objectives identified in Phase II—Customer Information. Each alternative display should provide both the visual and verbal information needed by the customer to fully appreciate and understand the entire home decorating concept. The complete line of products (e.g., film or frames) and services (e.g., finishing or enlarging) (see Exhibit 4) must be incorporated into each alternative display. As part of the final report, PIC expects a scale diagram of each alternative display and a complete verbal description of the display and its strengths and weaknesses.

## CASE 17–2
## Audiomobile, Inc.—Developing a Sales Incentive Program*

Audiomobile, Inc. specialized in the sale, installation, and service of car stereos, phones, and burglar alarm systems. The firm's president, Brett Barta, was always interested in finding new products or services that might help in expanding the business or improving the productivity of the firm's facilities, equipment, and labor force. The auto aftermarket could be a bit seasonal at times; hence, the right complementary product or service line could help fill in the slow periods. Last year, Brett added a complementary service that he felt was ideally suited to his operation: auto detailing—the process of making cars look like new by using advanced cleaning and polishing techniques. It's called "detailing" because you get all the details normal car cleaning misses, from the roof to the tires; inside and out.

    To introduce and to inform potential customers of the new service, Brett (1) added the service to the list of services identified in his half-page yellow pages ad, (2) ran one four-column-inch advertisement for four weeks in the sports section of the local newspaper, (3) installed a new outdoor sign, and (4) hung two point-of-sale placards. In addition, sales and service people attempted suggestive selling on all customers who visited the store for one of the other services. To assist in this suggestive selling effort, Brett had a brochure printed that identified the specific detailing services that were performed on each car.

    Although the auto detailing service generated a respectable trade, Brett was still somewhat disappointed. There always seemed to be some hesitancy on the part of potential customers to buy the service. In discussing the situation with his father-in-law, Professor Mike Lewis, it was suggested that perhaps some sort of sales incentive might be needed to overcome the observed hesitancy and to move the potential customer toward a favorable decision. Coupons, premiums, contests, and sweepstakes were just a few of the sales incentives that were discussed. Mike agreed to use the problem as a project in the fall semester of his retailing class; it would be the least he could do for the two complementary detailings Brett had done for the 'ol boy.

*This case was prepared by Dale Lewison and Douglas Hausknecht, The University of Akron.

## ASSIGNMENT

You are part of a student group in Dr. Lewis's Retailing course. Develop three sales incentive programs that would assist Brett in overcoming sales resistance. Each program should be complete with respect to objectives, operating procedures, artwork, and so on.

**ENDNOTES**

1. Ray Marquardt, "Merchandise Displays Are Most Effective When Marketing, Artistic Factors Are Combined," *Marketing News,* 19 Aug. 1983, 3.
2. Dinah Witchel, "NRMA Honors Joe Cicio," *Stores* (June 1986): 52.
3. Jean Paul Gagnon and Jane T. Osterhaus, "Research Note: Effectiveness of Floor Displays on the Sales of Retail Products," *Journal of Retailing* 61 (Spring 1985): 115.
4. Lisa Phillips, "POP Enriched by Impulse Food Buying," *Advertising Age,* 17 Nov. 1986, S-25.
5. Joe Agnew, "POP Displays Are Becoming a Matter of Consumer Convenience," *Marketing News,* 9 Oct. 1987, 14.
6. Cyndee Miller, "Trend in Fashion Retailing Is to Make a Video Statement," *Marketing News,* 4 Dec. 1987, 14.
7. Marquardt, "Merchandise Displays," 3.
8. See Kenneth Mills and Judith Paul, *Visual Merchandising* (Englewood Cliffs, NJ: Prentice-Hall, 1983): 37.
9. Ibid.
10. Kevin Higgins, "Couponing's Growth Is Easy to Understand," *Advertising Age,* 8 Sept. 1984, 12.
11. Marji Simon, "Survey Probes Strengths, Weaknesses of Promotions," *Marketing News* (June 1984): 4.
12. P. Rajan Varadarajan, "Issue of Efficient Coupon Handling and Processing Pits Manufacturers Against Retailers, Coupon Clearinghouses," *Marketing News* (September 1984): 13.
13. See Dottie Enrico, "GWP and PWP: Pros and Cons," *Stores* (September 1986): 63–68.
14. Diane Schneidman, "Trading Stamps Face Redemption as Viable Marketing Tool," *Marketing News,* 13 Feb. 1987, 1, 28.
15. Janet Meyers, "Zayre Will Target Frequent Buyers in Bonus Program," *Advertising Age,* 14 Oct. 1987, 7.
16. Francine Schwadel, "Sears Plans to Offer Promotional Prizes to Frequent Buyers," *Wall Street Journal,* 1 March 1988.
17. Eileen Norris, "Everyone Will Grab at a Chance to Win," *Advertising Age,* 22 Aug. 1983, 10.
18. "McDonald's Plans Next Film Tie," *Advertising Age,* 11 Feb. 1980, 44.
19. Sara E. Stern, "Sears Line Tails New Spielberg Film," *Advertising Age,* 3 Nov. 1986, 33.
20. Daniel L. Sherrell and R. Eric Reidanback, "A Consumer Response Framework for Negative Publicity: Suggestions for Response Strategies," *Akron Business and Economic Review* 17 (Summer 1986): 37.

# PART SIX
# Retail Opportunities

# 18

## Outline

## Objectives

☐ Distinguish personal attributes and personality traits essential to the successful retailer.

☐ Judge the opportunities associated with a retailing career.

☐ Assess one's own personal strengths and weaknesses as applicable to the retailing field.

☐ Plan a successful employment-search process.

☐ Decide whether one is the kind of person who can successfully start and run an independent retail business.

# Careers in Retailing

So you want to consider being a retailer? Or at least you might want to consider entering the retailing field. This chapter provides a glimpse of what it is like to be in retailing. You will discover some of the joys and, yes, also some of the frustrations involved in the retailing field. You will learn that people must have special characteristics to be successful retailers. You will read about employment opportunities, ownership opportunities, employment features in a retailing career, and the personal attributes of retailers. After you have read this chapter, you can decide—is retailing for you?

Whether a neophyte or a veteran, an independent entrepreneur or a chain store employee, the individual engaged in retailing must have certain personality traits and attributes to succeed in the marketplace. Some of the more successful retailer personality types include the people pleaser, the risk taker, the problem solver, the decision maker, and the retail entrepreneur. Although these personalities are not mutually exclusive, they are discussed individually to facilitate understanding.

## RETAILER ATTRIBUTES AND PERSONALITIES

### The People Pleaser

The retailer is in the people business. No other type of business deals so directly with so many people in such a variety of ways. Successful retailers have a genuine interest in and general liking for *people*. "People-pleasing" retailers can "read" their customers' minds, guess their wants and needs, anticipate their likes and dislikes, understand their hopes and fears, and adapt to their customers' viewpoints. As **people pleasers**, retailers can talk with their customers in a common language. Successful merchandising is largely a matter of good communications. Finally, people-pleasing retailers can appreciate their customers, empathize with them, and recognize their motives.

### The Risk Taker

*Risks* are an inherent part of any business, and retailing is no exception. There are risks in deciding where to locate, how many and which markets to serve, how extensive a product line to offer, and which and how many services to provide.

Because no retailer can precisely determine what every customer wants or provide everything that all competitors are doing better, risks are simply unavoidable in retailing. The **risk taker** not only is willing to assume the inherent chances of going into business but is able to tell a good merchandising risk from a bad one. A successful risk taker can reduce risk by gathering and analyzing pertinent information.

### The Problem Solver

The retailer not only understands retailing problem situations but enjoys solving them—is an active **problem solver**. As discussed in Chapter 1, retailing can be described as a problem of how to satisfy customers at a profit. Therefore, the retailer must have the capacity, determination, and stamina to overcome all the barriers associated with any problem-solving situation. A typical retail operation faces a wide diversity of problems, ranging from the physical problems of getting the merchandise into the store and onto the shelves to the mental and emotional problems of handling dissatisfied and vocal customers. Regardless of the situation, the retailer must be prepared to solve not only routine problems but also unusual ones. What's more, the retailer should enjoy it!

### The Decision Maker

The number of managerial decisions a retailer faces can be large, and the range of possible choices in each decision can be equally broad. Retailers must make daily decisions about locations, facilities, merchandise, prices, promotions, and service, and they must make periodic decisions about staff, suppliers, and investors. Not everyone is willing or able to make these decisions under pressure of time and with limited knowledge of the marketplace. To the **decision maker**, making choices under adverse and uncertain conditions is natural. The decision maker must understand and adapt daily to a changing marketplace. Such a person's strength lies in the ability and desire to make moment-by-moment and year-by-year decisions on a continual basis.

### The Retail Entrepreneur

A retail **entrepreneur** organizes, manages, and assumes the responsibilities of running a retail business. Although the term entrepreneur generally refers to an individual, the concept of entrepreneurship is actually appropriate to all retail organizations, since entrepreneurial skills are needed in all successful retailing careers. Like most skills, entrepreneurship exists in degrees. The following list of ten entrepreneurial attributes are important in creating an organizational culture that enhances the retailer's chances for success:

☐ Take risks but always be careful to minimize exposure. Take reasonable risks based on a clear evaluation of the expected and unexpected.
☐ Focus on opportunities rather than on problems, and make the primary focus customer needs rather than internal interests or limitations.
☐ Constantly seek improvement. It is the keystone of productivity, profitability, and customer satisfaction.

☐ Keep a clear head when it comes to your perception of reality. Be impressed with productivity and not appearances.

☐ Emphasize personal contact. Stay in touch with employees at all levels. Recognize the importance of your own example, emphasizing an open-door policy and personal contact as a leadership style.

☐ Keep things simple. Complex solutions in themselves don't necessarily produce incremental profits but often reduce opportunities.

☐ Allow for some level of ambiguity. Everything need not be tightly wrapped in a neat package or carefully explained in a manual.

☐ Court both change and flexibility to find improved service opportunities and increased efficiencies. Understand that every opportunity has an elusive life and is a moving target.

☐ Discourage focus on the negative, which will tend to produce a fear of failure and squelch the entrepreneurial spirit.

☐ Be purposeful and communicate the vision. The entrepreneurial spirit feeds off purposeful pursuit. There is a driving passion to make each opportunity work when everyone understands the corporate direction and the focus on consumers.[1]

No single measurement is appropriate for all individuals, and no one test measures all the attributes a retailer needs to be successful in retailing. Two psychologists, however, have developed what they deem indicators of what makes a successful retailing entrepreneur. A summary of this test of entrepreneurial mental skills and attitudes is shown in Figure 18–1.

The entrepreneurial skills of people-pleasing, decision-making, problem-solving, and risk-taking people, together with the abilities for organizing and managing, can be acquired to a degree in a formal learning situation, such as a college classroom, or in an informal learning situation, such as a work setting. Most people learn entrepreneurial skills in both ways.

The ideas in this book have built on and expanded whatever entrepreneurial skills you have and given you new insights into the world of retailing and the entrepreneurial spirit that people need to launch prosperous retailing careers.

To judge career opportunities in different fields, one should investigate the employment features for each career path. We will discuss several key aspects of a retailing career: employment security, employee compensation, working conditions, career advancement, and job satisfaction.

## EMPLOYMENT ASPECTS OF A RETAILING CAREER

### Employment Security

Employment in the retail sector offers the capable individual a high level of job security. Several factors account for this security. First, although all economic sectors suffer during a recession, the decline in retail employment is notably less than employment losses in either the manufacturing or wholesaling sectors. Even during recessionary periods, consumers continue to buy. They do, however, become more selective in making purchases. Second, the large number of employment opportu-

Your psychological makeup can play a strong role in making your business a success or a failure. Here are some questions based on ideas supplied by Richard Boyatzis and David Winter, two psychologists who have studied the entrepreneurial character. The questions are designed to reveal whether you have entrepreneurial attitudes. Even if no answer fits your feelings precisely, choose the one that comes closest. (The answers to these questions are provided in the chapter summary.)

1. If you have a free evening, would you most likely (a) watch TV, (b) visit a friend, (c) work on a hobby?
2. In your daydreams, would you most likely appear as (a) a millionaire floating on a yacht, (b) a detective who has solved a difficult case, (c) a politician giving an election night victory speech?
3. To exercise, would you rather (a) join an athletic club, (b) join a neighborhood team, (c) do some jogging at your own pace?
4. When asked to work with others on a team, which would you anticipate with most pleasure? (a) Other people coming up with good ideas, (b) cooperating with others, (c) getting other people to do what you want.
5. Which game would you rather play? (a) Monopoly, (b) roulette, (c) bingo.
6. Your employer asks you to take over a company project that is failing. Would you tell him that you will (a) take it, (b) won't take it because you're up to your gills in work, (c) give him an answer in a couple of days when you have more information?
7. In school, were you more likely to choose courses emphasizing (a) fieldwork, (b) papers, (c) exams?
8. In buying a refrigerator, would you (a) stay with an established, well-known brand, (b) ask your friends what they bought, (c) compare thoroughly the advantages of different brands?
9. While on a business trip in Europe, you are late for an appointment with a client in a neighboring town. Your train has been delayed indefinitely. Would you (a) rent a car to get there, (b) wait for the next scheduled train, (c) reschedule the appointment?
10. Do you believe people you know who have succeeded in business (a) have connections, (b) are more clever than you are, (c) are about the same as you but maybe work a little harder?
11. An employee who is your friend is not doing his job. Would you (a) take him out for a drink, hint broadly that things are not going right and hope he gets the message, (b) leave him alone and hope he straightens out, (c) give him a strong warning and fire him if he doesn't shape up?
12. You come home to spend a relaxing evening and find that your toilet has just overflowed. Would you (a) study your home repair book to see if you can fix it yourself, (b) persuade a handy friend to fix it for you, (c) call a plumber?
13. Do you enjoy playing cards most when you (a) play with good friends, (b) play with people who challenge you, (c) play for high stakes?
14. You operate a small office-cleaning business. A close friend and competitor suddenly dies of a heart attack. Would you (a) reassure his wife that you will never try to take away any customers, (b) propose a merger, (c) go to your former competitor's customers and offer them a better deal?

Source: Marlys Harris, "The Entrepreneur—Do You Have What It Takes?" *Money* 7 (March, 1978), 52.

**FIGURE 18–1**

Testing the entrepreneurial you

nities in retailing creates a high level of job mobility, and increased mobility generally results in increased job security. The third factor accounting for the high level of job security in retailing is "transferability of skills." Good merchandising skills can easily be transferred from one department to another within a firm, from one type of retailer to a different retailing operation, and even from retailing firms to wholesaling and manufacturing companies.

## Employee Compensation

Retail salaries vary considerably, ranging from minimum wage for lower-echelon, part-time employees to competitive salaries for upper-echelon managers. Where starting retail salaries are somewhat lower than those in other industries, the multitude of managerial levels within most retailing organizations provide opportunities for rapid advancement and can often result in a higher salary for the retail manager in just a few years.

## Working Conditions

Retail working conditions have their pluses and minuses. On the plus side, the retail employee enjoys the benefits of a variety of work assignments, a number of pleasant work environments, and a host of people-oriented work relationships. If "variety is the spice of life," then the prospective employee should find a retailing career attractive. The variety of work assignments stems from two factors. First, continuously changing economic conditions, regular changes in merchandising seasons, and the attraction of new and old customers make the retail business highly dynamic. These conditions foster new and interesting challenges for the retail employee. Second, the natural progression in training retail management personnel requires that the employee gain experience with all aspects of business. Typical retail training programs involve experiences with merchandising (e.g., buying and selling responsibilities); operations management (e.g., inventory planning and control responsibilities); sales promotion (e.g., advertising and retail display responsibilities); and personnel management (e.g., recruiting and training store personnel). Figure 18–2 illustrates these programs.

The pleasant work environment is the result of the retailer's efforts to create a *buying atmosphere*. Contrasted with the sterile atmosphere of most offices, the opportunity to work in an exciting and stimulating store environment is a definite plus of retail employment. Many individuals find that "action is where the people are." Given the people-oriented nature of the retailing business, individuals who crave action should find a retailing career very rewarding.

The most commonly cited minuses of a retailing career concern working hours. Of particular concern are the questions of how long and when employees work. While lower-echelon positions have a "normal" work week of 40 hours, the aspiring management trainee should expect to work considerably longer. Compared to the hours expected at lower-level managerial positions in other businesses, however, the retail manager's work week is reasonable. The longer retail store hours of recent years have resulted in more supervision during nonstandard working times. Because of these extended hours, both management and nonmanagement personnel are expected to work off-hours (such as evenings), off-days (such as weekends), and some off-times (such as holidays).

## Career Advancement

The opportunities for rapid advancement in retailing result from several interacting factors: the number of retail establishments, the diversity of retailing positions, and the number of managerial levels. The number of retail establishments is large and

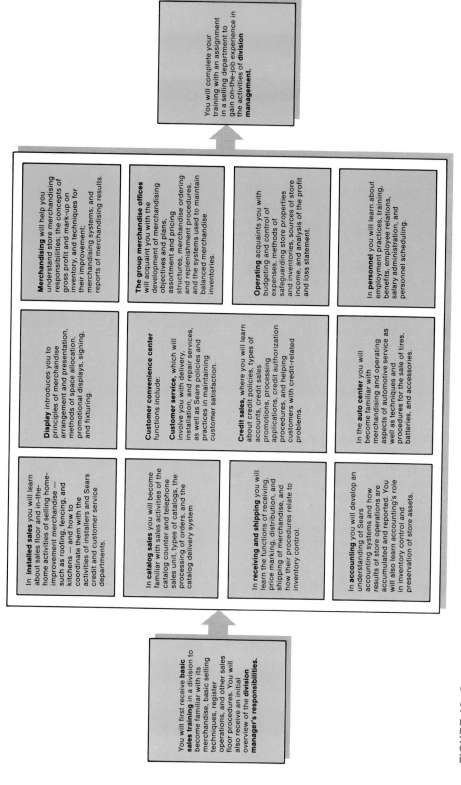

**FIGURE 18–2**

Retail training programs: A variety of work experiences—the Sears model (source: *Retail Management Careers*, Sears Merchandise Group, company brochure, 9)

expanding. As a result, managerial positions abound. For the ambitious and talented, finding potential positions for career advancement is not difficult. Equally important in finding a career environment where rapid advancement is possible is a job market characterized by a diversity of positions. Retailing has enough diversity to allow all individuals to seek and to foster a career niche best suited to their talents (see Figure 18–3). Additionally, upward mobility need not be hampered by an individual's getting locked into a particular type of job that suits neither the talents nor the aspirations of the individual.

The third factor contributing to an accelerated rate of advancement is the typical retail organization's large number of managerial levels. Consider, for example, the managerial levels one might find in a department store chain: assistant department manager, department manager, assistant merchandise and/or promotions manager, assistant store manager, store manager—and upward into the various district, regional, and national managerial positions. The aspiring retail manager does not have to wait for a chance at the one big career break. Making small yet steady career advancements gives the retail manager greater control over future opportunities and greater satisfaction from current job responsibilities.

Consider a final note: retailing offers women some of the best opportunities for professional advancement in the business world. These opportunities arise in part from women's power as the majority of customers at many stores. The belief that women managers have both greater understanding of women shoppers' needs and greater ability for developing meaningful relationships with this group of customers has created a career path for women in retailing that can definitely be characterized by rapid advancement.

## Job Satisfaction

Many aspects of a retailing career can provide job satisfaction. Some of the aspects already mentioned are the diversity of job responsibilities, potential for rapid advancement, opportunities to work with people, challenges of a continually changing environment, and competitive levels of compensation. Others are the freedom to use one's initiative, quick recognition of one's abilities, and continuous opportunities to demonstrate leadership.

The nature of a retail store's operating and merchandising activities gives employees and managers a considerable degree of independence. The opportunity for motivated individuals to use their initiative in assuming responsibilities and making meaningful decisions is rewarding and tends to promote considerable job satisfaction. Retailing careers provide many opportunities for people who want the freedom to "do their thing."

Retailing offers ample opportunities to demonstrate one's talents and abilities and have those talents and abilities recognized. Most people need feedback before they can judge how satisfied they are with their performance. Where else can one get a daily rating of job performance? Large retailing organizations compute sales, expense, and profit figures daily, by means of electronic data processing systems, for each operating unit. The opportunity to assume a leadership role is a key factor to job satisfaction for some individuals. The people-intensive nature of retailing offers unlimited occasions for leadership-minded people to "stand out" rather than "fit in."

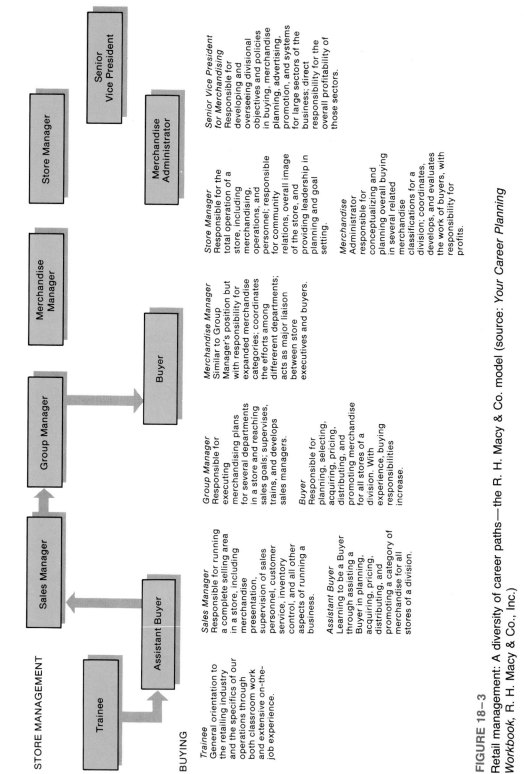

**STORE MANAGEMENT**

Trainee → Assistant Buyer → Sales Manager → Group Manager → Merchandise Manager → Store Manager → Senior Vice President

Group Manager → Buyer

Merchandise Administrator

**BUYING**

*Trainee*
General orientation to the retailing industry and the specifics of our operations through both classroom work and extensive on-the-job experience.

*Assistant Buyer*
Learning to be a Buyer through assisting a Buyer in planning, acquiring, pricing, distributing, and promoting a category of merchandise for all stores of a division.

*Sales Manager*
Responsible for running a complete selling area in a store, including merchandise presentation, supervision of sales personnel, customer service, inventory control, and all other aspects of running a business.

*Group Manager*
Responsible for executing merchandising plans for several departments in a store and reaching sales goals; supervises, trains, and develops sales managers.

*Buyer*
Responsible for planning, selecting, acquiring, pricing, distributing, and promoting merchandise for all stores of a division. With experience, buying responsibilities increase.

*Merchandise Manager*
Similar to Group Manager's position but with responsibility for expanded merchandise categories; coordinates the efforts among differerent departments; acts as major liaison between store executives and buyers.

*Store Manager*
Responsible for the total operation of a store, including merchandising, operations, and personnel; responsible for community relations, overall image of the store, and providing leadership in planning and goal setting.

*Merchandise Administrator*
responsible for conceptualizing and planning overall buying in several related merchandise classifications for a division; coordinates, develops, and evaluates the work of buyers, with responsibility for profits.

*Senior Vice President for Merchandising*
Responsible for developing and overseeing divisional objectives and policies in buying, merchandise planning, advertising, promotion, and systems for large sectors of the business; direct responsibility for the overall profitability of those sectors.

**FIGURE 18–3**

Retail management: A diversity of career paths—the R. H. Macy & Co. model (source: *Your Career Planning Workbook*, R. H. Macy & Co., Inc.)

Finally, many people relate job satisfaction at least in some degree to the status or image of their field of endeavor within the general business community. In recent years, as retailers have become a dominant force in the marketing and distribution of goods, their status has reached parity with other business careers.

Employment choices are among the most important decisions people make and represent long-term commitments with profound effects on professional, personal, and family lives as well as general life-styles. Therefore, it behooves anyone to approach an employment choice with the utmost preparation. The first step in planning for employment is to assess one's personal strengths and weaknesses, hopes and aspirations, and career goals and objectives.

## Making a Personal Assessment

*The Life Audit.* For understandable reasons, no one has your best interest at heart as much as you do. No one can know and understand you or your abilities, interests, and aspirations as well as you. Unfortunately, many individuals do not really know themselves well because they have never taken the time to assess what they want and expect out of life. A **life audit** is an attempt to seek insight into one's true feelings about one's abilities and aspirations. A form of self-analysis, a life audit involves simply answering truthfully a series of questions about one's expectations. No prescribed set of questions is appropriate for every life audit; however, the audit should include questions regarding family issues, personal values, general attitudes, basic beliefs, and personal goals and objectives.

*The Career Audit.* To start and maintain a successful career, you need a career plan that includes necessary strategies and tactics for success. To develop a career plan, you should first conduct a **career audit**. Figure 18–4 illustrates a career audit, a set of twenty questions that many executive recruiters believe will help you discover yourself and your career aspirations. These questions not only are useful in developing initial career plans, but also can serve as guidelines to continually evaluate career assets and liabilities. One of the most difficult aspects of a job search, especially for recent college graduates, is determining what job function is most interesting to them.[2]

After making both a life and a career audit, the final step in a personal assessment is to identify life and career goals. For clarity and future reference, you should write down these goals and file them in a secure place. Although your goals will undergo many modifications during your life and career, specifying goals in writing forces you to assess what you want from your life and your career.

## Securing a Retail Position

After you have completed a personal assessment, you are then ready to secure a retail position—the **employment-search process**. This discussion covers how to identify prospective employers, obtain a personal interview, prepare for an interview, and participate in the interview.

FIGURE 18–4
Twenty questions to
ask in making a career
audit

1. Do I work better in a large or small corporation?
2. How important is geographic location to me? To my family?
3. Am I a loner, or do I work better as a member of a group?
4. Am I more comfortable following than leading?
5. Do I analyze better than I execute?
6. Am I an innovator?
7. Do I work more successfully under pressure?
8. Am I a good planner?
9. Am I a good listener?
10. Do I think well on my feet?
11. Do I express myself well orally? In writing?
12. What characteristics do I admire in others?
13. Which function of my job do I perform most effectively?
14. Which do I perform least effectively?
15. What do I enjoy doing most?
16. In the past six months, what accomplishment has most satisfied me? Which has been the most difficult?
17. What have I done to correct my shortcomings?
18. What level of responsibility do I aspire to in five years?
19. What should I be earning then?
20. How will I achieve these levels?

Source: Robert Ankerson, "Marketing a New Product," *MBA: Master In Business Administration* (October, 1975), 28.

*Identifying Prospective Employers.* Prospective employer identification is a process of organizing opportunities. The four steps include listing employment criteria, ranking employment criteria, scaling employment preferences, and matching job preferences with prospective employers.

*Step 1: Listing employment criteria.* In the initial stages of an employment search, you must determine the general conditions under which you are willing to accept a job; that is, your **employment criteria**. Although the particulars of any job (e.g., salary) are determined during actual employment negotiation, you may have certain preconditions regarding employment. Common preconditions involve location (local or regional preference), organization (type of retailer), and position (type of job).

*Step 2: Ranking employment criteria.* Not all the criteria identified in Step 1 will necessarily be equally important to you. Step 2 of the prospective employer-identification process therefore requires that you rank each of the employment criteria according to importance. You may judge some criteria extremely important or essential; others might be preferences but not absolutely essential.

*Step 3: Scaling employment preferences.* The third step in identifying prospective employers is to develop a **preference scale of employment opportunities.** This step requires developing general job descriptions for first, second, and third preference levels. For example, your most-preferred job description might be an assistant manager of a women's apparel department in a major Chicago metro-area department store, preferably somewhere in the northwest part of the city. On the other end of the scale, your least-preferred job description might be the same type of job in some other metro areas.

*Step 4: Matching job preferences with prospective employers.* Now that you have listed, ranked, and scaled your preferences, the final step in the employer-identification process is to match those preferences with prospective employers. The matching process consists of compiling a list of jobs and screening that list of prospective employers according to your scaled preferences.

It will be to your benefit to explore all possible sources in compiling a **jobs list**. The campus placement office is a logical starting point, as it represents one of the most fruitful sources for good leads for potential employment. It also provides a number of services (e.g., setting up personal interviews) that can greatly facilitate your employment-search process. You also need to systematically check the employment sections of local and national newspapers as well as trade and professional journals, magazines, and newspapers. Commercial employment agencies are still another source. Before making any commitments to one of these agencies, however, be sure you fully understand what services they provide and under what conditions and terms. You can obtain additional job leads by sending inquiries to the personnel departments of retail firms you believe have the potential to offer the kind of employment you desire. Finally, some of the best leads to employment opportunities come through personal contacts. Professors, friends, relatives, and social and professional acquaintances often provide an inside track to opportunities.

Screening a jobs list is a fairly routine procedure if you have carefully completed the previous step in the employment- search process—scaling employment preferences. Jobs-list screening involves (1) reducing your jobs list to employment opportunities that meet your minimum requirements for employment and then (2) rank ordering the remaining jobs on the list according to your preferences. This screening results in a list of available and acceptable employment opportunities rank ordered from most to least desirable.

*Obtaining a Personal Interview.* Personal interviews are a way for retailers to question and observe job applicants in a face-to-face situation. Most retailers consider interviews essential to hiring. By contacting the personnel department and completing an application form, qualified applicants normally will be granted a personal interview.

The **personal interview process** for most managerial positions is much more involved. Typically, it involves a series of personal interviews with various managers at different levels. Obtaining the initial interview can be quite simple or extremely difficult. There are several methods for obtaining the initial interview with retailing firms. They include (1) obtaining an on-campus interview schedule from the school placement office and scheduling an interview through that office; (2) contacting the store's personnel office and making arrangements for the initial interview; (3) asking personal contacts to set up a personal interview; and (4) writing brief letters and making telephone calls and personal visits to one or more of the firm's managers to discuss possible employment opportunities. If you choose to use the last method, you should expect some difficulty in getting to the right person. Your persistence can also help you to land the job you want.

*Preparing for a Personal Interview.* Lack of preparation is perhaps the most common error applicants make in the personal-interview process. Preparing for a personal interview involves getting to know something about the firm interviewing you and helping the firm in its efforts to get to know you.

Before the interview, you should do some research on the firm. Your ability to talk knowledgeably about the firm and its activities will pay substantial dividends during the actual interview. Preparation not only will make a favorable impression on the interviewer, but will also allow you to answer and to ask meaningful questions. Your information search on the firm should help you to discuss the firm's organizational structure, market positions, merchandising strategies, financial positions, and future prospects. Examining various trade magazines, industrial directories, and other reference books can provide a good general picture of the firm and its operations.

To help the firm get to know you, you will need to prepare a résumé, which should include (1) a brief statement of personal data (e.g., name, address, telephone number, marital status, date of birth, health status, and physical condition); (2) a brief outline of educational experience (i.e., type of degree, name of school, date of graduation, major and minor fields of study, class ranking, scholarships, honors, awards, and extracurricular activities); (3) a short history of work experience (i.e., a list of jobs, position and responsibilities, names of employers, and dates of employment); and (4) a summary of other activities, interests, and skills that support your professional credentials. Also, you might wish to include a list of references and a short statement of your career objectives. In preparing a résumé, the following guidelines are helpful:

1. *Be concise.* The purpose of a résumé is to stimulate the interviewer's interest and not to tell your life story. A one-page résumé is sufficient to create this interest.
2. *Be factual.* Experienced interviewers will recognize résumé "puffery" and generally take a dim view of it. A statement of a few real accomplishments is received much more favorably than a list of artificial ones.
3. *Be professional.* A well-organized, neatly produced résumé is an excellent "scene setter" for your personal interview.

*Taking a Personal Interview.* The interview situation varies according to the interviewer's personal preferences. Some interview situations are conducted formally in a structured question-and-answer format. Other interview situations are informal, conducted without any apparent structure. Whether the interview is formal or informal, your ability to read the interview situation and to react accordingly will determine your success. All interviews, formal or informal, usually have four parts: (1) rapport building—a few minutes of chit-chat to open the interview; (2) questions and answers—information exchange; (3) the sell—applicant outlines what he or she can do for the retailer while the retailer explains the opportunities available with the organization; and (4) the close—each party, if favorably impressed, tries to end the interview on a positive note.[3] No absolute rules apply in taking a personal interview, but the guidelines that follow are useful in most situations.

□ Dress appropriately. The job or position for which you are interviewing will provide you with cues on how to dress. Do not overdress or underdress for the occasion.

□ Be prepared for openers. Many interviewers like to open their interviews with broad questions such as "What do you expect out of life?" "Why do you want to work for our firm?" "Where do you want to be in your career 10 years from now?" or "What do you think you can do for our company?"

□ Be relaxed. Interviewers expect a reasonable amount of nervousness; however, excessive nervousness may well suggest to the interviewer that you are unable to handle pressure situations. Avoid nervous gestures.

□ Listen carefully. Let the interviewer guide the interview, at least during the initial stages. Interviewers provide cues as to how they want to conduct the interview and what they want to talk about. Good listening skills are noticed by an interviewer. Also, by listening carefully, you will be able to fully understand the nature of the questions and thus give better responses.

□ Ask questions. If you want a job with the interviewer's company, you should be able to show your interest by asking intelligent questions about the firm.

□ Be informative. You should answer the interviewer's questions fully and quickly but avoid talking too much or too fast. Most of the interviewer's questions will require more than a yes or no answer; however, you should avoid telling your life story, boasting about your accomplishments, and complaining about your problems.

□ Be somewhat aggressive. It is better to be perceived as a little too aggressive rather than too passive. Interviewers usually view a reasonable amount of aggressiveness favorably. The right impression to portray might be that you are a "mover" but not a "shaker."

□ Be honest. Answer questions as truthfully as you can. Interviewers recognize that everyone has strengths and weaknesses. Frankly admitting a weakness adds credibility to the statements you make about your strengths.

## OWNERSHIP OPPORTUNITIES

Regardless of their income, many people who work for others feel they are living a hand-to-mouth, paycheck-to-paycheck existence. According to one old adage, the only way to get ahead is to get other people to work for you or to get money working for you—the idea is that income and perhaps job satisfaction are limited when you work for someone else. Many people find that self-employment is the answer to a better income, greater independence, a more rewarding career, and an improved life-style. Many people think that going into business for themselves is the only way they can fully realize their hopes and aspirations. To have a chance at realizing their personal, career, and life goals, these individuals are willing to assume the considerable burdens and risks of owning and operating their own businesses. "Armed with a good, marketable idea or product and a lot of high-energy talent, you, too, can probably raise the cost to start your own company. In fact, unless your product is a real dud, you will probably do fine for anywhere from six months to two years. At that point, though, chances are pretty good that you will end up the way most new business startups do. You will either run out of money or, if business is booming, out of the capacity to grow fast enough to keep up with your sales."[4]

Are you the kind of person who could succeed as an independent retailer? To help answer this question, we offer a self-evaluation test that should provide you with some insight into whether you have the personal attributes to become an independent retailer (see Figure 18–5).

If, after taking the self-evaluation test, you decide that you do have what it takes to be an independent retailer, three options are open to you: (1) starting a new business; (2) buying an existing business; or (3) securing a franchise. Each option has advantages and disadvantages that you should fully explore. Figure 18–6 compares issues surrounding the decision to start a new business or buy an existing one. The principal concerns associated with securing a franchise are outlined in Figure 18–7.

**FIGURE 18–5**
Do you have what it takes to be an independent retailer?

Under each question, check the answer that says what you feel or comes closest to it. Be honest with yourself.

*Are you a self-starter?*
☐ I do things on my own. Nobody has to tell me to get going.
☐ If someone gets me started, I keep going all right.
☐ Easy does it, man. I don't put myself out until I have to.

*How do you feel about other people?*
☐ I like people. I can get along with just about anybody.
☐ I have plenty of friends—I don't need anyone else.
☐ Most people bug me.

*Can you lead others?*
☐ I can get most people to go along when I start something.
☐ I can give the orders if someone tells me what we should do.
☐ I let someone else get things moving. Then I go along if I feel like it.

*Can you take responsibility?*
☐ I like to take charge of things and see them through.
☐ I'll take over if I have to, but I'd rather let someone else be responsible.
☐ There's always some eager beaver around wanting to show how smart he is. I say let him.

*How good an organizer are you?*
☐ I like to have a plan before I start. I'm usually the one to get things lined up when the gang wants to do something.
☐ I do all right unless things get too goofed up. Then I cop out.
☐ You get all set and then something comes along and blows the whole bag. So I just take things as they come.

*How good a worker are you?*
☐ I can keep going as long as I need to. I don't mind working hard for something I want.
☐ I'll work hard for a while, but when I've had enough, that's it, man!
☐ I can't see that hard work gets you anywhere.

*Can you make decisions?*
☐ I can make up my mind in a hurry if I have to. It usually turns out O.K., too.
☐ I can if I have plenty of time. If I have to make up my mind fast, I think later I should have decided the other way.
☐ I don't like to be the one who has to decide things. I'd probably blow it.

*Can people trust what you say?*
☐ You bet they can. I don't say things I don't mean.
☐ I try to be on the level most of the time, but sometimes I just say what's easiest.
☐ What's the sweat if the other fellow doesn't know the difference?

*Can you stick with it?*
☐ If I make up my mind to do something, I don't let *anything* stop me.
☐ I usually finish what I start—if it doesn't get fouled up.
☐ If it doesn't go right away, I turn off. Why beat your brains out?

*How good is your health?*
☐ Man, I *never* run down!
☐ I have enough energy for most things I want to do.
☐ I run out of juice sooner than most of my friends seem to.

*Now count the checks you made.*
How many checks are there beside the *first* answer to each question? ———————
How many checks are there beside the *second* answer to each question? ———————
How many checks are there beside the *third* answer to each question? ———————

  If most of your checks are beside the first answer, you probably have what it takes to run a business. If not, you're likely to have more trouble than you can handle by yourself. Better find a partner who is strong on the points you're weak on. If many checks are beside the third answer, not even a good partner will be able to shore you up.

Source: *Checklist for Going into Business,* Small Marketers Aids No. 71, Small Business Administration (October, 1976), 4–5.

**FIGURE 18–5**
*continued*

**FIGURE 18–6**
To start or buy?

  Should I start my own business from scratch or should I purchase an existing business? These are the two alternatives facing the potential small business manager. If the business is started fresh, there are these advantages:

1. You can create a business in your own image. The business is not a made-over version of someone else's place, but it is formed the way you think it should be.
2. You do not run the risk of purchasing a business with a poor reputation that you would inherit.
3. The concept you have for the business is so unusual that only a new business is possible.

  The creation of a new business also has some substantial drawbacks. Some of the disadvantages include:

1. Too small a market for your product or service.
2. High cost of new equipment.
3. Lack of a source of advice on how things are done and who can be trusted.
4. Lack of name recognition. It may take a long time to persuade customers to give your business a try.

  Buying an existing business also has advantages and disadvantages. The major advantages are:

1. A successful business may provide the buyer with an immediate source of income.
2. An existing business may already be in the best location.
3. An existing business already has employees who are trained and suppliers who have established ties to the business.

**FIGURE 18–6**
*continued*

4. Equipment is already installed and the productive capacity of the business is known.
5. Inventories are in place, and suppliers have extended trade credit which can be continued.
6. There is no loss of momentum. The business is already operating.
7. You have the opportunity to obtain advice and counsel from the previous owner.
8. Often, you can purchase the business you want at a price much lower than the cost of starting the same business from scratch.

Purchasing an existing business can have some real drawbacks, such as the following:

1. You can be misled, and end up with a business that is a "dog."
2. The business could have been so poorly managed by the previous owner that you inherit a great deal of ill will.
3. A poorly managed business may have employees who are unsuited to the business or poorly trained.
4. The location of the business may have become, or is becoming, unsuitable.
5. The equipment may have been poorly maintained or even be obsolete.
6. Change can be difficult to introduce in an established business.
7. Inventory may be out of date, damaged, or obsolete.
8. You can pay too much for the business.

To avoid buying a business that cannot be made profitable, investigate six critical areas:

1. Why does the owner wish to sell? Look for the real reason and do not simply accept what you are told.
2. Determine the physical condition of the business. Consider the building and its location.
3. Conduct a thorough analysis of the market for your products or services. Who are your present and potential customers? You cannot know too much about your customers. Conduct an equally thorough analysis of your competitors, both direct and indirect. How do they operate and why do customers prefer them?
4. Consider all of the legal factors which might constrain the expansion and growth of the business. Become familiar with zoning restrictions.
5. Identify the actual owner of the business and all liens that might exist.
6. Using the material covered in previous chapters, analyze the financial condition of the business.

The business can be evaluated on the basis of its assets, its future earnings, or a combination of both. Don't confuse the value of a business with its price. Price is determined through negotiation. The bargaining zone represents that area within which agreement can be reached.

Source: Norman M. Scarborough and Thomas W. Zimmerer, *Effective Small Business Management* (Columbus: Merrill Publishing Co., 1984), 130–31.

**FIGURE 18–7**
A retail franchise: Is it for you?

**The Franchisor and the Franchise**

1. Is the potential market for the product or service adequate to support your franchise? Will the prices you charge be in line with the market?
2. Is the market's population growing, remaining static, or shrinking? Is the demand for your product or service growing, remaining static, or shrinking?
3. Is the product or service safe and reputable?
4. What will the competition, direct or indirect, be in your sales territory? Do any other franchisees operate in this general area?

5. Is the franchise international, national, regional, or local in scope? Does it involve full- or part-time involvement?

6. How many years has the franchisor been in operation? Does it have a sound reputation for honest dealings with franchisees?

7. How many franchise outlets now exist? How many will there be a year from now? How many outlets are company-owned?

8. How many franchisees have failed? Why?

9. What services and assistance will the franchisor provide? Training programs? Advertising assistance? Financial aid? Are these one-time programs or are they continuous in nature?

10. Will the firm perform a location analysis to help you find a suitable site?

11. Will the franchisor offer you exclusive distribution rights for the length of the agreement, or may it sell to other franchises in this area?

12. What facilities and equipment are required for the franchise? Who pays for construction? Is there a lease agreement?

13. What is the total cost of the franchise? What are the initial capital requirements? Will the franchisor provide financial assistance? Of what nature? What is the interest rate? Is the franchisor financially sound enough to fulfill all its promises?

14. How much is the franchise fee? **Exactly** what does it cover? Are there any continuing fees? What additional fees are there?

15. Does the franchisor provide an estimate of expenses and income? Are they reasonable for your particular area? Are they sufficiently documented?

16. Does the franchisor offer a written contract which covers all the details of the agreement? Have your attorney and your accountant studied its terms and approved it? Do **you** understand the implications of the contract?

17. What is the length of the franchise agreement? Under what circumstances can it be terminated? If you terminate the contract, what are the costs to you? What are the terms and costs of renewal?

18. Are you allowed to sell the franchise to a third party? If so, will you receive the proceeds?

19. Is there a national advertising program? How is it financed? What media are used? What help is provided for local advertising?

**The Franchisee—You**

20. Are you qualified to operate a franchise successfully? Do you have adequate drive, skills, experience, education, patience, and financial capacity? Are you prepared to work hard?

21. Are you willing to sacrifice some autonomy in operating a business to own a franchise?

22. Can you tolerate the financial risk?

23. Are you genuinely interested in the product or service you will be selling?

24. Has the franchisor investigated your background thoroughly enough to decide you are qualified to operate the franchise?

25. What can this franchisor do for you that you cannot do for yourself?

Source: Norman M. Scarborough and Thomas W. Zimmerer, *Effective Small Business Management* (Columbus: Merrill Publishing Co., 1984), 101–2.

**FIGURE 18–7**
*continued*

**SUMMARY**

Successful retailers like people and enjoy working with them. They understand the risks associated with any business enterprise and are willing to assume those risks. They are challenged by problems and enjoy solving them. And, they are willing to make decisions and to accept the responsibility that goes with making them. These people-pleasing, risk-taking, problem-solving, and decision-making personality traits are best summed up in the skills of the retail entrepreneur.

Figure 18–1 showed some of the indicators of entrepreneurial attitudes. (Note: The best answers to these questions are [1] c, [2] b, [3] c, [4] a, [5] a, [6] c, [7] a, [8] c, [9] a, [10] c, [11] c, [12] a, [13] b, and [14] c. Score one point for each correct answer. Questions 1, 2, 3, 7, 9, and 12 suggest whether you are a realistic problem solver who can run a business without constant help from others. Questions 5, 6, and 8 probe whether you take calculated risks and seek information before you act. Questions 4, 10, 13, and 14 show whether you, like the classic entrepreneur, find other people satisfying when they help fulfill your need to win. Question 11 reveals whether you take responsibility for your destiny—and your business. If you score between 11 and 14 points, you could have a good chance to succeed. If you score from 7 to 10 points, you'd better have a superb business idea or a lot of money to help you out. If you score 7 or less, stay where you are.)

The employment aspects of a retailing career involve (1) above-average employment security; (2) competitive compensation in managerial positions and below-average compensation in lower-echelon positions; (3) a variety of work assignments; (4) pleasant work environment; (5) opportunities for rapid advancement; (6) the satisfaction of using one's initiative, (7) the quick recognition of one's abilities, and (8) the opportunity to demonstrate leadership.

Employment opportunities in retailing are numerous and diverse. Finding a retail position, however, requires preparation and planning. Before starting the employment-search process, one must make a personal assessment consisting of life and career audits. These audits help identify personal and professional strengths and weaknesses as well as clarify one's hopes and aspirations. The audits also provide direction for developing personal and professional goals and objectives.

The employment-search process consists of identifying prospective employers and obtaining, preparing for, and taking personal interviews. To identify possible employers, prospective employees should list and then rank their employment criteria, scale their employment preferences, and match their job preferences with prospective employers.

Methods for getting a personal interview include contacting the school placement office or the store's personnel office, using personal contacts to set up interviews, and writing letters and making phone calls or personal visits to the appropriate store managers. Before an interview, the applicant should prepare a résumé and conduct research on the firm.

Finally, common sense is the best rule for taking a personal interview. Other helpful guidelines are to dress appropriately, be prepared for openers, be relaxed, listen carefully, ask questions, be informative, be somewhat aggressive, and be honest.

Each year, thousands of people start retail businesses, hoping to realize personal and professional goals they cannot achieve by working for someone else. Some people have what it takes to own and operate a business successfully, whereas others probably do not. The self-evaluation test in Figure 18–5 provides some insight into whether an individual has what it takes. (If you have not already taken the test, do so now.) Your instructor can guide discussion on the answers you give and provide insights into your probable success at operating a business of your own.

## STUDENT STUDY GUIDE

**KEY TERMS AND CONCEPTS**

career audit

decision maker

employment criteria

employment preference scale

employment-search process

entrepreneur

jobs list

life audit

people pleaser

personal interview process

problem solver

risk taker

**REVIEW QUESTIONS**

1. Identify the characteristics of a people pleaser.
2. Describe the factors that account for the relatively high level of job security in the retail-management field.
3. How do retail salaries stack up against salaries in other businesses?
4. Why might a retailing career be described in terms of the old adage "variety is the spice of life"?
5. Why are there numerous opportunities for rapid career advancement in the field of retailing?
6. What is a life audit? What is a career audit?
7. Describe briefly the four steps in identifying prospective employers.
8. What are the various options open to the prospective employee in obtaining an initial interview with a retail firm?
9. What information should be included on your resume?
10. Cite the eight guidelines for taking a personal interview.
11. What are the advantages and disadvantages of starting your own business from scratch?

**REVIEW EXAM**

True or False

_____ 1. Risks can be eliminated if the retailer plans carefully.
_____ 2. Emloyment in the retail sector offers the individual a relatively low level of job security.
_____ 3. Job advancement in retailing is retarded somewhat by the limited number of managerial levels in most retail organizations.
_____ 4. The career audit is an attmept by individuals to seek insight into their true feelings about their own abilities and aspirations.
_____ 5. A well-developed résumé of four to five pages is an appropriate vehicle for introducing the applicant during the initial interview.
_____ 6. Aggressive behavior is totally inappropriate behavior during any interview situation.

# STUDENT APPLICATIONS MANUAL

**PROJECTS: INVESTIGATIONS AND APPLICATIONS**

1. Take the entrepreneurial test in the text. Using the answers and explanations in the chapter summary, evaluate your entrepreneurial skills. What are your strengths and weaknesses?
2. Review the employment aspects of a retailing career? Are you interested in pursuing a retailing career? Why or why not?
3. Develop a set of questions for conducting a life audit. Then conduct the audit by answering the questions you developed.
4. Conduct a career audit by answering the questions posed in Figure 18—4.
5. Using the four-step process discussed in the text, identify several prospective retail employers that would meet your employment expectations. Describe the criteria you used in selecting these prospective employers.
6. Prepare a current résumé. Then, evalute its strengths and weaknesses. Next, develop a plan for improving it.
7. Using the self-evaluation test in Figure 18—5, do you have what it takes to be an independent retailer? Why or why not? Explain.

**ENDNOTES**

1. Donald Zale, "The Need to Rekindle the Entrepreneurial Spirit," *Retailing Issues Letter* (Center for Retailing Studies, Texas A&M University, September 1986): 2.
2. Susan Bernard, "Your Job Search Countdown," *Business Week's Careers* 3 (October/ Winter Preview 1985): 96.
3. Marilyn M. Kennedy, "How To Win the Interview Game," *Business Week's Careers* 5 (September 1987): 17.
4. Rita Stollman, "Should You Take The Plunge?" *Business Week's Careers* 3 (October/ Winter Preview 1985): 51.

# NAME INDEX

# SUBJECT INDEX